What they're saying about

The Complete Guide to Bed & Breakfasts, Inns & Guesthouses...

...all necessary information about facilities, prices, pets, children, amenities, credit cards and the like. Like France's Michelin...
—New York Times

Definitive and worth the room in your reference library.
—Los Angeles Times

...innovative and useful...
—Washington Post

A must for the adventurous...who still like the Hobbity creature comforts.
—St. Louis Post-Dispatch

What has long been overdue: a list of the basic information of where, how much and what facilities are offered at the inns and guesthouses.
—San Francisco Examiner

Standing out from the crowd for its thoroughness and helpful cross-indexing...
—Chicago Sun Times

A quaint, charming and economical way to travel—all in one book.
—Waldenbooks (as seen in USA Today)

Little descriptions provide all the essentials: romance, historical landmarks, golf/fishing, gourmet food, or, just as important, low prices. Take your pick!
—National Motorist

For those travelling by car, lodging is always a main concern...The Complete Guide to Bed & Breakfasts, Inns & Guesthouses provides listings and descriptions of more than 1,200 inns.
—Minneapolis Star & Tribune

THE COMPLETE GUIDE

BED & BREAKFAST INNS & GUESTHOUSES

IN THE UNITED STATES AND CANADA

PAMELA LANIER

Other B

22 Days
Bed & B
All-Suit
Elegant
Condo
Golf Re
Golf Re

The infor
without n
before ma
is absolut
may som
author to

For fur
The
In
P.O.
Oak

John

© 199
All rig
Printe

1990-

ISSN
ISBN

Distr
W.W.
New

Cov
Des
Typ

For J.C. Dolphin Valdes

Acknowledgments

Corrine Rednour and George Lanier for your help, love, and support—thank you.

For Jane Foster, Project Coordinator, who gave her all to this update, many many thanks.

To my friends who were so generous with their time and skills:

Venetia Young, Carol McBride, Marianne Barth, Vincent Yu, Madelyn Furze, Rus Quon, Terry Lacey, John Garrett, Lucy Rush, Chris Manley, Mary Kreuger, Mr. Wiley, Adele Novelli, Ruth Young, Mrs. Gieselman (the best English teacher ever), Mary Institute, Ingrid Head, Sumi Timberlake, Asha Goldberg, Marvin Downey, Marguerite Tafoya, Peggy Dennis, Judy Jacobs, Derek Ng, Katherine Bertolucci, Leslie Chan, Margaret Callahan, Mary Ellen Callahan, and Glenna Goulet.

Special thanks to Richard Paoli.

To the great folks in the Chambers of Commerce, State and Regional Departments of Tourism, I am most grateful.

To the innkeepers themselves who are so busy, yet found the time to fill out our forms and provide us with all sorts of information, I wish you all great success.

To the staff at John Muir Publications who have given so much to make this book possible, thank you.

Special thanks to Mort and Martha Liebman of Copygraphics, Inc. in Santa Fe, New Mexico, for their dedication and care in bringing this book to type. You helped make it fun.

CONTENTS

VOTE

FOR YOUR CHOICE OF
INN OF THE YEAR

Did you find your stay at a Bed & Breakfast, Inn or Guesthouse listed in this Guide particularly enjoyable? Use the form in the back of the book or just drop us a note and we'll add your vote for the "Inn of the Year."

The winning entry will be featured in the next edition of **The Complete Guide to Bed & Breakfasts, Inns and Guesthouses in the U.S. and Canada**.

Please base your decision on:
- Helpfulness of Innkeeper   • Quality of Service
- Cleanliness   • Amenities   • Decor   • Food

Look for the winning Inn in the next Updated & Revised edition of **The Complete Guide to Bed & Breakfasts, Inns and Guesthouses in the U.S. and Canada.**

1990 INN OF THE YEAR

THE VERANDA
SENOIA, GEORGIA

Built in 1906-07 by C.F. Hollberg and called the Hollberg Hotel, it was placed on the National Register of Historic Places in the 1970s and renamed The Veranda. Jan and Bobby Boal purchased the building in 1985 and opened as a bed and breakfast inn in 1986.

Guests rave about an original Veranda recipe, Breakfast Mushrooms, which can be spooned over poached or scrambled eggs, served as a spread on toast points, or added to hot dishes for a brunch buffet. Dinners include mouth-watering appetizers such as baked pastries of ham and cheese with apricot mustard, salads served with original Veranda dressing, a main course of Veal Ione with pasta and cherry tomatoes, and irresistible homemade desserts.

Before becoming innkeepers, Jan and Bobby operated a small business selling to museum shops. Jan continues to teach full-time at Georgia Tech but will retire in June 1990. Innkeeping involves long hours and hard work, but for the Boals, the most rewarding aspect of it is getting to know their guests, whom they find a wonderful group of people.

INNS OF THE YEAR
HONOR ROLL

1985   Joshua Grindle Inn, Mendocino, CA
1986   Carter House, Eureka, CA
1987   Governor's Inn, Ludlow, VT
1988   Seacrest Manor, Rockport, MA
1989   Wedgewood Inn, New Hope, PA

Introduction

There was a time, and it wasn't that long ago, when bed and breakfast inns were a rarity in the United States. Travelers made do at a hotel or motel; there was no alternative. The few bed and breakfast inns were scattered across the rural areas of New England and California. They were little known to most travelers; often their only advertisement was by word of mouth.

But in a few short years that has changed, and changed in a way that could only be called dramatic. There has been an explosion in the number of bed and breakfast inns. Today, inns can be found in every state, and often in cities; they have become true alternatives to a chain motel room or the city hotel with its hundreds of cubicles.

This sudden increase in bed and breakfast inns started less than a decade ago when Americans, faced with higher costs for foreign travel, began to explore the backroads and hidden comunities of their own country.

Other factors have influenced the growth and popularity of bed and breakfast inns. Among them, the desire to get away from the daily routine and sameness of city life; the desire to be pampered; for a few days; and also the desire to stay in a place with time to make new friends among the other guests.

The restored older homes that have become bed and breakfast inns answer those desires. The setting most often is rural; the innkeepers provide the service—not a staff with name tags—and the parlor is a gathering place for the handful of guests. They are a home away from home.

The proliferation of these inns as an alternative lodging has created some confusion. It's been difficult to find—in one place—up-to-date and thorough information about the great variety of inns.

Some books published in the past five or six years have tried to provide this information. But those books focused on one region of the country or named too few inns. While some earlier books gave detailed descriptions of the inns, few bothered to provide information about the type of breakfast served, whether there are rooms for non-smokers, and such things as whether the inn offered free use of bicycles or whether it had a hot tub.

An effort to collect as much information about as many inns as possible in one book has been overdue. Now that has been remedied. You hold a copy of the result in your hands.

Richard Paoli,
Travel Editor
San Francisco Examiner

How to Use this Guide

Organization

This book is organized alphabetically by state and, within a state, alphabetically by city or town. The inns appear first. At the back of the guide are listings of the reservation service organizations serving each state and inns with special characteristics.

Three Types of Accommodations

Inn: Webster's defines an inn as a "house built for the lodging and entertainment of travelers." All the inns in this book fulfill this description. Many also provide meals, at least breakfast, although a few do not. Most of these inns have under 30 guest rooms.

Bed and Breakfast: Can be anything from a home with three or more rooms to, more typically, a large house or mansion with eight or nine guest accommodations which serves breakfast in the morning.

Guest House: Private homes welcoming travelers, some of which may be contacted directly but most of which are reserved through a reservation service organization. A comprehensive list of RSOs appears toward the back of this guide.

Breakfasts

We define a **full breakfast** as one being along English lines, including eggs and/or meat as well as the usual breads, toast, juice and coffee.

Continental breakfast means coffee, juice, bread or pastry.

Continental plus is a breakfast of coffee, juice, and choice of several breads and pastry and possibly more.

Meals

Bear in mind that inns that do not serve meals are usually located near a variety of restaurants.

Can We Get a Drink?

Those inns without a license will generally chill your bottles and provide you with set-ups upon request.

Prices

We include a price code to give you an idea of each inn's rates. Generally, the coded prices indicate a given lodging's lowest priced double room, double occupancy rate as follows:

$—under $50 $$—$50-$75 $$$—$75 plus

Appearing to the right of the price code is a code indicating the type of food services available:

B&B: Breakfast included in quoted rate

EP (European Plan): No meals

MAP (Modified American Plan): Includes breakfast and dinner

AP (American Plan): Includes all three meals

All prices are subject to change. Please be sure to confirm rates and services when you make your reservations.

Credit Cards and Checks

If an establishment accepts credit cards, it will be listed as VISA, MC or AMEX. Most inns will accept your personal check with proper identification, but be sure to confirm when you book.

Reservations

Reservations are essential at most inns, particularly during busy seasons, and are appreciated at other times. Be sure to reserve, even if only a few hours in advance, to avoid disappointment. When you book, feel free to discuss your requirements and confirm prices, services and other details. We have found innkeepers to be delightfully helpful.

Most inns will hold your reservation until 6 p.m. If you plan to arrive later, please phone ahead to let them know.

A deposit or advance payment is required at some inns.

Children, Pets and Smoking

Children, pets and smoking present special difficulties for many inns. Whether they are allowed, limited, or not permitted is generally noted as follows:

	Yes	Limited	No
Children	C-yes	C-ltd	C-no
Pets	P-yes	P-ltd	P-no
Smoking	S-yes	S-ltd	S-no
Handicapped	H-yes	H-ltd	H-no

Accessibility for the Handicapped

Because many inns are housed in old buildings, access for handicapped persons in many cases is limited. Where this information is available, we have noted it in the same line as limitations on children, pets and smoking. Be sure to confirm your exact requirements when you book.

Big Cities

In many big cities there are very few small, intimate accommodations. We have searched out as many as possible. We strongly advise you to investigate the guest house alternative, which can provide you with anything from a penthouse in New York to your own quiet quarters with a private entrance in the suburbs. See our RSO listings at the back of the book.

Farms

Many B&Bs are located in a rural environment, some on working farms. We have provided a partial list of farm vacation experiences. What a restorative for the city-weary. They can make a great family vacation—just be sure to keep a close eye on the kids around farm equipment.

Bathrooms

Though shared baths are the norm in Europe, this is sometimes a touchy subject in the U.S.A. We list the number of private baths available directly next to the number of rooms. Bear in mind that those inns with shared baths generally have more than one.

Manners

Please keep in mind when you go to an inn that innkeeping is a very hard job. It is amazing that innkeepers manage to maintain such a thoroughly cheerful and delightful presence despite the long hours. Do feel free to ask your innkeeper for help or suggestions, but please don't expect him to be your personal servant. You may have to carry your own bags.

When in accommodations with shared baths, be sure to straighten the bathroom as a courtesy to your fellow guests. If you come in late, please do so on tiptoe, mindful of the many other patrons visiting the inn for a little R&R.

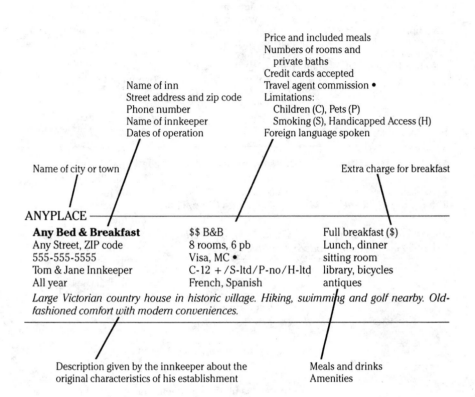

Price and included meals
Numbers of rooms and
    private baths
Credit cards accepted
Name of inn   Travel agent commission •
Street address and zip code   Limitations:
Phone number   Children (C), Pets (P)
Name of innkeeper   Smoking (S), Handicapped Access (H)
Dates of operation   Foreign language spoken

Name of city or town   Extra charge for breakfast

ANYPLACE
Any Bed & Breakfast $$ B&B   Full breakfast ($)
Any Street, ZIP code   8 rooms, 6 pb   Lunch, dinner
555-555-5555   Visa, MC •   sitting room
Tom & Jane Innkeeper   C-12 + / S-ltd / P-no / H-ltd   library, bicycles
All year   French, Spanish   antiques
Large Victorian country house in historic village. Hiking, swimming and golf nearby. Old-fashioned comfort with modern conveniences.

Description given by the innkeeper about the   Meals and drinks
original characteristics of his establishment   Amenities

Sample Bed & Breakfast Listing

6   How to Use this Guide

Ejemplo de una entrada para las posadas con cama & desayuno

Ciudad o pueblo nombre

Nombre de la posada
Dirección
Teléfono
Fechas de temporada

Precio del alojamiento
Qué comidas van incluídas
Número de cuartos y número
    de cuartos con baño privado
Tarjetas de crédito aceptables
Limitaciones:
    niños (C); animales domésticos (P); prohibido
    fumar (S); entradas para minusválidos (H)
Se habla idiomas extranjeros

Comidas y bebidas
Entretenimientos

ANYPLACE

Any Bed & Breakfast
Any Street, ZIP code
555-555-5555
Tom & Jane Innkeeper
All year

$$ B&B
8 rooms, 6 pb
Visa, MC •
C-12+/S-ltd/P-no/H-ltd
French, Spanish

Full breakfast
Lunch, dinner
sitting room
library, bicycles
antiques

Large Victorian country house in historic village. Hiking, swimming and golf nearby. Old fashioned comfort with modern conveniences.

Descripción proporcionada por el dueño de la posada
sobre las características especiales y originales del
establecimiento

Mode d'emploi

Nom de ville

Prix des chambres Repas inclus ou non
Nombre de chambres et
chambres avec salle de
bain privés
Cartes de crédit acceptées

Repas, boissons possibles

Commodités

ANYPLACE

Any Bed & Breakfast
Any Street, ZIP code
555-555-5555
Tom & Jane Innkeeper
All year

$$ B&B
8 rooms, 6 pb
Visa, MC •
C-12+/S-ltd/P-no/H-ltd
French, Spanish

Full breakfast
Lunch, dinner
sitting room
library, bicycles
antiques

Large Victorian country house in historic village. Hiking, swimming and golf nearby. Old fashioned comfort with modern conveniences.

Nom de l'auberge
Addresse
Téléphone
Dates d'ouverture s'il n'y a
pas de dates ouvert toute
l'année

Restrictions
Enfants—Animaux
Fumeurs—Handicappés
On parle les langues etrangéres

L'aubergiste décrit ce qui rend son auberge unique

Erläuterung der Eintragungen der Unterkunfsstätte

Name der Stadt oder
Ortschaft

Name der Unterkunft
Adresse
Telefon-Nummer
Zu welcher Jahreszeit offen?

Preis für die Unterkunft, und
welche Mahlzeiten im Preis
einbegriffen sind
Anzahl der Zimmer, und
wieviel mit eigenem
Badezimmer (=pb)
Beschränkungen in Bezug auf
Kinder, Haustiere, Rauchen,
oder für Behinderte geeignet
(yes=ja; ltd=beschränkt;
no=nicht zugelassen)
Man sprecht fremdsprachen

Was für ein Frühstück?
Andere Mahlzeiten und Bars

Was gibt's sonst noch?

ANYPLACE

Any Bed & Breakfast
Any Street, ZIP code
555-555-5555
Tom & Jane Innkeeper
All year

$$ B&B
8 rooms, 6 pb
Visa, MC •
C-12+/S-ltd/P-no/H-ltd
French, Spanish

Full breakfast
Lunch, dinner,
sitting room
library, bicycles
antiques

Large Victorian country house in historic village. Hiking, swimming and golf nearby. Old fashioned comfort with modern conveniences.

Beschreibung des Gastwirts,
was an diesem Gästehaus ein-
malig oder besonders
bemerkenswert ist

旅館名
住所
電話番号
利用期間。

朝食のタイプ
その他の設備
昼食、夕食、アルコールのサービス

都市又は町の名

ANYPLACE

Any Bed & Breakfast
Any Street, ZIP code
555-555-5555
Tom & Jane Innkeeper
All year

$$ B&B
8 rooms, 6 pb
Visa, MC •
C-12+/S-ltd/P-no/H-ltd
French, Spanish

Full breakfast
Lunch, dinner
sitting room
library, bicycles
antiques

Large Victorian country house in historic village. Hiking, swimming and golf nearby. Old fashioned comfort with modern conveniences.

Alabama

Mentone Inn	$$ B&B	Full breakfast
P.O. Box 284, 35984	15 rooms, 15 pb	Afternoon tea
Hwy 117	•	Catering
205-634-4836	C-ltd/S-no/P-no/H-no	Sitting room
Betsy, Alice & Si		video, spa, sun deck
End April—end October		

Country mountain hideaway, antiques. Relax. Near shops, restaurants, golfing, hiking, trail rides. Fly into Ft. Payne airport. On Alabama Historical Register.

More Inns...

Victoria   1604 Quintard Ave., Anniston 36201   205-236-0503
Dancy-Polk House   901 Railroad St. N.W., Decatur 35601   205-353-3579
Rutherford Johnson House   P.O. Box 202, Main St., Franklin 36444   205-282-4423
Blue Shadows   Box 432, Rural Rt. 2, Greensboro   205-624-3637
Bed & Breakfast Montgomery   P.O. Box 886, Millbrook 36054   205-285-5421
Krafts' Korner   90 Carlile Dr., Mobile 36619   205-666-6819
Malaga Inn   359 Church St., Mobile 36602   205-438-4701
Vincent-Doan Home   1664 Springhill Avenue, Mobile 33604   205-433-7121
Brunton House   112 College Ave., Scottsboro 35768   205-259-1298

Alaska

42nd Avenue Annex

410 W. 42nd Ave., 99503

907-561-8895

Margaret F. Watts

June—October

$ EP

2 rooms

French

Continental breakfast $

Sitting room

European-style B&B including homemade quilts, shared bath, complete breakfast, within one block radius of Scottdale, Cattle Company and Sea Galley. Antiques and homey styling.

Darbyshire House B&B

528 "N" St., 99501

907-279-0703/907-345-4761

Ralph & Irene Darbyshire

All year

$$ B&B

1 rooms, 1 pb

•

C-10+/S-ltd/P-no/H-no

Spanish

Continental plus

Sitting room with TV

Sun room

outdoor decks

boat charters

Downtown Anchorage! Walk to restaurants, shopping. Seventeen-room architect-designed waterfront home provides spectacular views of inlet, mountains.

Green Bough Inn

3832 Young St., 99508

907-562-4636

Phyllis & Jerry Jost

All year

$ B&B

3 rooms

•

C-yes/S-no/P-ltd/H-no

Continental plus

Sitting room

TV, radio, piano

outdoor deck

Anchorage's oldest independent B&B, located midtown—close to everything. Comfortable, relaxed living. Mountain view. Your hosts are 20-year Alaskans.

Pilot's Row B&B

217 East 11th Ave., 99501

907-274-3305

Jim Murphy

All year

$$ B&B

2 rooms

•

C-yes

Full breakfast

Comp. tea & coffee

Sitting room w/fireplace

Historic home within walking distance of downtown. Our intriguing home highlights a beautiful array of stained glass and natural wood.

Glacier Bay Country Inn

Box 5, Dub-Al-U Ranch, 99826

907-697-2288

Al & Annie Unrein

All year

$$$ AP

8 rooms, 7 pb

•

C-yes/S-no/P-no/H-no

Full breakfast

All meals included

Library, sitting room

bicycles, hiking

Glacier Bay yacht tours

Idyllic homestead blends comfortable country living with the Alaskan wilderness. Yacht tours of Glacier Bay. A fisherman's dream, traveler's paradise, professional's retreat.

10   Alaska

GUSTAVUS ───────────────────────────────

Gustavus Inn	$$$ AP	Full breakfast
P.O. Box 60, 99826	12 rooms, 3 pb	Lunch & dinner included
1 Mi. Gustavus Rd.	•	Bar, tea
907-697-2254	C-yes/S-ltd/P-ltd/H-ltd	Bicycles, fishing poles
JoAnn & David Lesh	French, Spanish	airport pickup
All year		

Your home in Glacier Bay features garden fresh produce and local seafood in a family-style homestead atmosphere.

Puffin's Bed & Breakfast	$ B&B	Full breakfast
P.O. Box 3, 99826	3 rooms, 3 pb	Dinner, coffee, tea
907-697-2260/907-289-9787	Visa, MC, AmEx •	Separate lodge
Sandy & Chuck Schroth	C-yes/S-yes/P-yes	bicycles
Mid-April—September		

Modern cabins with Alaskan art, quiet country atmosphere, hearty homestead breakfast; fishing, wildlife; photography-charters, Glacier Bay tours, travel service.

HAINES ───────────────────────────────

Summer Inn Bed & Breakfast	$$ B&B	Full breakfast
P.O. Box 1198, 99827	5 rooms	Afternoon tea
247 Second Ave.	Visa, MC •	Snacks
907-766-2970	C-yes/S-no/P-no/H-no	Sitting room
Mary Ellen, Bob Summer	Some Spanish	library
All year		

Historical house in beautiful coastal town; walking distance to downtown; near Eagle Preserve; full homemade breakfast. Be our guest in this unique Alaskan community.

HOMER ───────────────────────────────

Homer B&B/Seekins	$$ B&B	Full breakfast
Box 1264, 99603	9 rooms, 7 pb	Kitchen facilities
2 Mi. E. Hill on Race Rd.	Visa, MC •	Snacks, sitting room
907-235-8996/907-235-8998	C-ltd/S-ltd/P-no/H-ltd	outdoor sauna, TV
Floyd & Gert Seekins		tours arranged
All year		

Fantastic view of bay, mountains and glaciers. Clean, quiet Alaskan hospitality. Cabin and guest houses. Moose wander into the yard. Referrals for B&Bs. Salmon and halibut fishing.

JUNEAU ───────────────────────────────

Alaskan Hotel	$ EP	Coffee
167 S. Franklin, 99801	40 rooms, 10 pb	Bar service
800-327-9347	Visa, MC, AmEx, DC •	Hot tubs, sauna
Betty Adams	C-yes/S-yes/P-no/H-no	some kitchenettes
All year		TVs, phones

On National Register of historic sites. We have over 50 pieces of stained glass; rooms are refurnished in bordello style with red or blue velvet drapes, oak antique furniture.

Dawson's Bed & Breakfast	$ B&B	Full breakfast
1941 Glacier Hwy, 99801	5 rooms, 3 pb	Airport pickup
907-586-9708	Visa, MC •	
Dave & Velma Dawson	S-yes/P-no/H-no	
All year		

Courtesy car pickup from airport/ferry. Two miles from downtown on bus route. Clean modern home with laundry facilities, parking.

LAKE LOUISE

Evergreen Lodge
HC 1 Box 1709 GennAllen, 99588
Mile 16.5, Lake Louise Rd
907-822-3250
Ed & Shelley Peck
All year

$$ EP
11 rooms, 3 pb
•
C-yes/S-yes/P-yes/H-no

Lunch, dinner, snacks
Comp. wine with dinner
Bar service
Sitting room, sauna
canoe, motorboats, dock

Comfortable, rustic lodge overlooking lake. Cabins and rooms. Summer fishing, winter skiing, ice-fishing. Watch moose and caribou from the lodge!

NOME

Aurora House B&B
P.O. Box 1318-IG, 99762
562 E. 3rd
907-443-2700
All year

$$ B&B
2 rooms
Visa, MC, AmEx, DC •
C-yes

Full breakfast
Library

When traveling to Nome, treat yourself to clean, homey accommodations. Information available at rural village tours and B&Bs.

PETERSBURG

Scandia House
P.O. Box 689, 99833
110 Nordic Dr. N.
907-772-4281
Mike & Helen Dean
All year

$ B&B
24 rooms, 17 pb
Visa, MC, AmEx, DC •
C-yes/S-yes/P-no/H-no

Continental breakfast
Sack lunch
Sitting room
hot tubs
sauna

Let us introduce you to our small Norwegian fishing community. We offer fishing charters, sightseeing, hiking, and walking tours.

SEWARD

Swiss Chalet B&B
P.O. Box 1734, Eagle Ln, 99664
907-224-3939
Charlotte L. Freeman
Memorial Day—Labor Day

$$ B&B
3 rooms, 1 pb
Visa, MC •
C-no/S-no/P-no/H-no

Full breakfast
Comp. coffee or tea
Sitting room

Located a block off the Seward Highway by Exit Glacier Road. A ten-minute ride to the Boat Harbor.

TALKEETNA

River Beauty B&B
P.O. Box 525, 99676
Main St. & River Park
907-733-2741
All year

$$ B&B
5 rooms, 2 pb
Visa •
C-yes/S-yes/H-yes

Full breakfast
Restaurant nearby
Full kitchen use avail.
Outdoor barbecues

Enjoy the splendor of Mt. McKinley and year-round wilderness recreation in rustic Talkeetna; accessible by automobile, railroad or aircraft.

WASILLA

Yukon Don's B&B Inn
HC 31 5086, 99687
2221 Macabon
907-376-7472
Don Tanner
All year

$ B&B
6 rooms
•
C-yes/S-no/P-yes/H-no

Continental breakfast
Restaurant nearby
Sitting room
library
exercise room

Extraordinary view; 30-year Alaskan resident; great collection of Alaskana; each room has unique Alaskan decor.

More Inns...

A Log Home B&B   2440 Sprucewood St., Anchorage 99508   907-276-8527
Adams House B&B   700 W. 21st, Anchorage 99508   907-274-1944
All The Comforts of Home   12531 Turk's Turn St., Anchorage 99516   907-345-4279
Anchorage Eagle Nest Hotel   4110 Spenard Rd. (BB), Anchorage 99503   907-243-3433
Chugach View B&B   1639 Sunrise Drive, Anchorage 99508   907-279-8824
Fay's Bed & Breakfast   P.O. Box 2378, Anchorage 99510   907-243-0139
Grandview Gardens B&B   1579 Sunrise Drive, Anchorage 99508   907-277-7378
Hillcrest Haven   1455 Hillcrest Drive, Anchorage 99503   907-274-3086
Favorite Bay Inn   Box 101, Angoon 99820   907-788-3123
Whaler's Cove Lodge   Box 101-VP, Angoon 99820   907-788-3123
Wilson's Hotel   P.O. Box 969, Bethel 99559   907-543-3841
Adventures Unlimited Lodge   Box 89-RD, Cantwell 99729
Arctic Circle Hot Springs   P.O. Box 69, Central 99730   907-520-5113
Reluctant Fisherman Inn   Box 150, Cordova 99574   907-424-Box 80090, Fairbanks 99708
907-455-6550
Iniakeek Lake Lodge   Box 80424, Fairbanks 99701   907-479-6354
Sophie Station Hotel   1717 University Ave., Fairbanks 99701   907-479-3650
Summit Lake Lodge   P.O. Box 1955, Fairbanks 99707   907-822-3969
Tolovan B&B   4538 Tolovan, Fairbanks 99701   907-479-6004
Chistochina Trading Post   Mile 32, Tok/Slann Hwy., Gakona 99586   907-822-3366
Bear Creek Camp/Youth Hstl   Box 1158, Haines 99827   907-766-2259
Cache Inn Lodge   Box 441-VP, Haines 99827   907-766-2910
Fort Seward B&B   House 1, Box 5, Haines 99827   907-766-2856
Jotel Halsingland   P.O. Box 1589, Haines 99827   907-766-2000
Quiet Place Lodge   Box 6474, Halibut Cove 99603   907-296-2212
Driftwood Inn   135 W. Bunnell Ave., Homer 99603   907-235-8019
Halibut Cove Cabins   P.O. Box 1990, Homer 99603   907-296-2214
JP Bed & Breakfast   Box 2256, Homer 99603
Kachemak Bay Wilderness   Box 956-VP, Homer 99603   907-235-8910
Lakewood Inn   984 Ocean Drive, #1, Homer 99608   907-235-6144
Magic Canyon Ranch   40015 Waterman Rd., Homer 99603   907-235-6077
Sadie Cove Wilderness Ldge   Box 2265-VP, Homer 99603   907-235-7766
Tutka Bay Lodge   Box 960 F, Homer 99603   907-235-3905
Wild Rose Bed & Breakfast   Box 665, Homer 99603   907-235-8780
Willard's Moose Lodge   SRA Box 28, Homer 99603   907-235-8830
Admiralty Inn   9040 Glacier Hwy., Juneau 99801   907-789-3263
Juneau Hostel   614 Harris St., Juneau 99801   907-586-9559
Louie's Place-Elfin Cove   P.O. Box 020704, Juneau 99802   907-586-2032
Mullins House   526 Seward St., Juneau 99801   907-586-2959
Silver Bow Inn   120 BW Second St., Juneau 99801   907-586-4146
Tenakee Inn   167 S. Franklin, Juneau 99801   907-586-1000
Daniels Lake Lodge B&B   Box 2939-BW, Kenali 99611   907-776-5578
Hidden Inlet Lodge   Box 3047-VP, Ketchikan 99901   907-225-4656
Waterfall Resort   P.O. Box 6440, Ketchikan 99901   800-544-5125
Fireweed Lodge   Box 116-VP, Klawock 99925   907-755-2930
Kalsin Inn Ranch   Box 1696 VP, Kodiak 99615

Manley Lodge 100 Landing Road-VP, Manley Hot Springs 99756 907-672-3161
Oceanview Manor B&B Box 65, 490 Front St., Nome 99762 907-443-2133
Hatcher Pass Lodge Box 2655-BB, Palmer 99645 907-745-5897
Sheep Mountain Lodge Star Route C, Box 4890, Palmer 99645 907-745-5121
Weathervane House SRD 9589x, Palmer 99645 907-745-5168
Paxson Lodge 1185 TD Richardson Hwy, Paxson 99737 907-822-3330
Beachcomber Inn Box 1027, Petersburg 99833 907-772-3888
Heger Haus B&B P.O. Box 485, Petersburg 99833 907-772-4877
Little Norway Inn B&B Box 192-BW, Petersburg 99833
Afognak Wilderness Lodge Seal Bay 99697 907-486-6442
High Tide Originals Main Street, Seldonia 99663 907-234-7850
Seldonia Rowing Club Box 41, Seldonia 99663 907-234-7614
Annie McKenzie's Boardwalk P.O. Box 72, Seldovia 99663 907-234-7816
Karras Bed and Breakfast 230 Akogwanton St., Sitka 99835 907-747-3978
Sitka Youth Hostel P.O. Box 2645, Sitka 99835 907-747-6332
Golden North Hotel P.O. Box 431, Skagway 99840 907-983-2294
Irene's Inn Box 538-VP, Skagway 99840 907-983-2520
Skagway Inn Box 13, Skagway 99840 907-983-2289
Wind Valley Lodge Box 354-VP, Skagway 99840 907-983-2236
Skwentna Roadhouse 100 Happiness Lane, Skwentna 99667
Bunk House Inn Box 3100-VP, Soldotna 99669 907-262-4584
Internat'l Riverside Inn Box 910-VP, Soldotna 99669 907-262-4451
Fairview Inn P.O. Box 379-VP, Talkeetna 99676 907-733-2423
Twister Creek Union Talkeetan Span, Talkeetna 99676 907-258-1717
Tok Bed & Breakfast P.O. Box 515, Tok 99780 907-883-5621
Reflection Pond B&B Mile 11 Petersville Rd., Trapper Creek 99683 907-733-2457
Trapper Creek B&B P.O. Box 13068, Trapper Creek 99683 907-733-2220
Bed & Breakfast—Valdez Box 442, Valdez 99686 907-835-4211
Lake House P.O. Box 1499, Valdez 99686 907-835-4752
Rainbow Lodge Mile 4, Richardson Hwy., Valdez 99686
Totem Inn P.O. Box 648 BB, Valdez 99686 907-835-4443
1260 Inn Mile 1260 AK Hwy., Via Tok 99780 907-778-2205
Mat-Su Resort Bogard Road-Mile 1.3, Wasilla 99687 907-376-3228
Sportman's Inn Box 698-VP, Whittier 99693
Clarke Bed & Breakfast Box 1020, Wrangell 99686 907-874-2125
Yes Bay Lodge Yes Bay 99950 907-247-1575

Arizona

AJO

Managers House Inn B&B
One Greenway Dr., 85321
602-387-6505
Martin & Faith Jeffries
September—June

$$ B&B
5 rooms, 5 pb
Visa, MC •
C-no/S-no/P-no/H-yes

Full breakfast
Comp. brandy, ice cream
Sitting room, library
tennic courts, hot tubs
coin laundry, gift shop

Copper Mine Manager's Hilltop Mansion, circa 1919, overlooks town and Open Pit Mine. Near Organ Pipe National Monument. Generous southwestern hospitality.

BISBEE

Greenway House
401 Cole Ave., 85603
602-432-7170
Joy O'Clock, Dr. George Knox
All year

$$$ B&B
8 rooms, 8 pb
Visa, MC
S-ltd/H-yes

Continental plus
Comp. wine
Snacks
Sitting room, library
billiard game room, BBQs

Picturesque copper mining town in mile-high setting. Luxury accommodations in 1906 mansion. Craftsman architecture, furnished with antiques.

Inn at Castle Rock
P.O. Box 161, 85603
112 Tombstone Canyon Rd.
602-432-7195
James Babcock
All year

$ B&B
12 rooms, 10 pb
•
C-yes/S-yes/P-yes/H-no
Spanish

Continental plus
Full breakfast (wkdays)
2 sitting rooms
piano, library
fireplaces

Turn-of-the-century hotel with antique and 1920s furnishings, lovely gardens. Friendly atmosphere provides unique introduction to town.

CHANDLER

Cone's Tourist Home
2804 W. Warner Rd., 85224
602-839-0369
Howard & Beverly Cone
September—May

$ B&B
1 rooms, 1 pb
C-yes/S-yes/P-yes/H-no

Continental breakfast
Sitting room, piano
TV, telephones

Lovely contemporary home on 2 country acres, 18 mi. SE of downtown Phoenix. Offering kitchen, barbecue facilities, large parlor, Arizona Room.

FLAGSTAFF

Arizona Mountain Inn
685 Lake Mary Rd., 86001
602-774-8959
Mr. & Mrs. Ray Wanek & Family
All year

$$ EP
5 rooms, 1 pb
Visa, MC
C-no/S-no/P-no/H-no

Continental plus
Comp. wine
Sitting room, hot tub
playground
volley & basketball

Old-English-style inn and furnished chalets amidst 13 acres of Ponderosa pines. A peaceful paradise for year-round activities; near fishing, hiking, and skiing.

Bayview Hotel B&B Inn, Aptos, CA

FLAGSTAFF

Dierker House B&B
423 W. Cherry, 86001
602-774-3249
Dorothea Dierker
All year

$ B&B
3 rooms
C-12+/S-yes/P-ltd/H-no

Full breakfast 8 a.m.
Cont. plus early or late
Comp. wine
Garden room
pool table, bicycles

Guest area has private entrance, sitting room and pleasant kitchen. Spacious, airy bedrooms with king beds and down comforters.

PEARCE

Grapevine Canyon Ranch
P.O. Box 302, 85625
Highland Rd.
602-826-3185
All year

$$$ AP
8 rooms, 8 pb
Visa, MC, Discover •
C-no/S-yes/P-no/H-no
Chek, some Spanish

All meals included
Sitting room, library
swimming pool
horseback riding $

An intimate guest ranch providing first-class accommodations with emphasis on horseback riding on 64,000 acres of spectacular mountain country.

PHOENIX

Westways "Private" Resort
P.O. Box 41624, 85080
602-582-3868
Darrell Trapp & Brian Curran
All year

$$$ B&B
6 rooms, 6 pb
Visa, MC, Disc •
C-yes/S-yes/P-no/H-ltd
French, Spanish

Full breakfast
Snacks, lunch on request
Library, sitting room
hot tub, tennis courts
swimming pool, bicycles

Deluxe small oasis resort with Southwest contemporary decor. Golf, tennis, swimming, bicycling and exercise equipment available. Beautiful desert landscape.

16   Arizona

Lynx Creek Farm B&B	$$$ B&B	Full breakfast
P.O. Box 4301, 86302	2 rooms, 2 pb	Comp. wine, snacks
555 Onyx Dr.	Visa, MC •	Bicycles, pool
602-778-9573	C-yes/S-no/P-ltd/H-no	hot tubs
Greg & Catherine Temple	Spanish	recreation near
All year		

Charming retreat on 25-acre apple farm. Spacious, antique-filled suites. Beautiful views and climate. Huge gourmet breakfasts include our own fruits and vegetables.

Marks House Inn	$$ B&B	Full breakfast
203 E. Union, 86303	5 rooms, 5 pb	Afternoon tea
602-778-4632		Comp. wine
Gregory & Bonnie Miller		
All year		

Queen Anne featuring hand-painted murals, antiques and city views. One room has a copper tub! 1 block to famous Whiskey Row.

Prescott Pines Inn B&B	$ EP	Full breakfast $3
901 White Spar Rd., 86303	13 rooms, 13 pb	Kitchenettes
Hwy. 89 S.	Visa, MC, Disc •	Sitting room, library
602-445-7270/800-541-5374	C-yes/S-ltd/P-no/H-ltd	porches, ceiling fans
Jean Wu, Michael Acton	some French & German	games, patio w/BBQ
All year		

Ponderosa pines embrace this restored 1902 country Victorian inn. Delicious breakfasts, romantic fireplaces, fragrant gardens and soothing fountain. Memories are made here.

Briar Patch Inn	$$$ B&B	Continental plus
Star Route 3, Box 1002, 86336	15 rooms, 15 pb	Sitting room
Hwy. 89A N.	Visa, MC •	library
602-282-2342	C-yes/S-ltd/P-no/H-ltd	creek swimming
Jo Ann & Ike Olson	German	
All year		

Delightful inn on 8 acres of Oak Creek Canyon spendor. Caring staff, bird watcher's paradise, chamber music events, hiking. Relaxing, therapeutic ambience!

Garland's Oak Creek Lodge	$$$ MAP	Full breakfast
P.O. Box 152, Hwy 89A, 86336	15 rooms, 15 pb	Dinner, bar
602-282-3343	Visa, MC	Sitting room
Mary & Gary Garland	C-yes/S-ltd/P-no/H-ltd	piano
End March—mid-November	German	clay tennis court (fee)

Lovely historic lodge nestled in gorgeous red rock setting of Oak Creek Canyon. Rustic log cabins, excellent gourmet meals, friendly staff.

Graham's B&B Inn	$$$ B&B	Full breakfast
P.O. Box 912, 86336	5 rooms, 5 pb	Comp. wine/appetizers
150 Canyon Circle Dr.	Visa, MC	Sitting room, games
602-284-1425	C-12+/S-no/P-no/H-no	golf nearby
Bill & Marni Graham		hot tub, swimming pool
Closed last 3 wks Jan.		

Comfortable elegance amidst Arizona's spectacular red rock country. Choose early American, antique, art deco, contemporary or Southwest-style room decor. Mobile Four-Star.

SEDONA

L'Auberge de Sedona Resort
P.O. Box B, 86336
301 Little Lane
602-282-7131
Eric Umstattd
All year

$$$ EP
Visa, MC, AmEx, Diners •
C-yes/S-yes/P-no/H-yes
French, Spanish

Comp. coffee
Restaurant, bar service
Breakfast, lunch, dinner
Sitting room, library
sauna, swimming pool

A private paradise surrounded by a stunning display of natural beauty. Creekside cabins & orchard-view rooms. Creekside French Gourmet restaurant and Orchards Seafood Grill.

Rose Tree Inn
376 Cedar St., 86336
602-282-2065
Rachel M. Gillespie
All year

$ EP
4 rooms, 4 pb
Visa, MC •
C-yes/S-yes/P-no/H-no

Bar service
Comp. coffee & tea
Kitchenettes, patios
library, bicycles
jacuzzi, courtyard

Sedona's "best kept secret"! Quaint, quiet accommodations nestled in a gorgeous English garden environment within walking distance of "Old Town."

Sipapu Lodge
P.O. Box 552, 86336
65 Piki Dr.
602-282-2833
Lea Pace, Vicent Mollan
All year

$$ B&B
5 rooms, 3 pb
C-yes/S-no/P-yes/H-no

Full breakfast
Comp. wine
Sitting room
library
massage technician

Spacious rooms surround guests with influences of Northern Arizona's Native Americans. Enjoy a full Southwest breakfast in our country setting.

Slide Rock Lodge & Cabins
Star Route 3, Box 1141, 86336
Hwy 89A, Oak Creek Canyon
602-282-3531
Bogomir & Milena Pfeifer
All year

$$ B&B
24 rooms, 24 pb
Visa, MC
C-yes/S-ltd/P-no/H-no
Slovenian (Yugoslavia)

Continental breakfast
Full equipped kitchens
Picnic area, BBQ grills
fireplaces
4 cabins with jacuzzis

Scenic location in wonderful Oak Creek Canyon. Quiet getaway in friendly environment. Unique and rustic cabins, some couples only.

TUCSON

Arizona Inn
2200 E. Elm St., 85719
602-325-1541/800-421-1093
Mrs. John Doar
All year

$$ EP/B&B
80 rooms, 80 pb
Visa, MC, AmEx •
C-yes/S-yes/P-yes/H-yes
Spanish, French, German

Full breakfast
Restaurant, bar
Lunch, dinner, snacks
Sitting room, library
tennis courts, pool

Historic landmark, family owned and operated since 1930. Spanish Colonial cottages with individually decorated guest rooms. Romantic oasis located in exclusive neighborhood.

Hacienda del Sol Ranch
5601 N Hacienda del Sol, 85718
602-299-1501
Kathy Davenport, Greg Rhodes
All year

$ EP
29 rooms, 21 pb
Visa, MC, AmEx, DC, Dis •
C-yes/S-yes/P-yes/H-no
Spanish

Breakfast $
Restaurant, bar service
Afternoon tea, hot tubs
horseback riding, tennis
putting green, pool

Catalina foothills getaway with gorgeous landscaping and fountains. Many activities available, including weekly authentic western barbecue. Extended-stay packages available.

18   Arizona

June's Bed & Breakfast	$ B&B	Continental plus
3212 W. Holladay St., 85746	2 rooms	Comp. wine
602-578-0857	•	Sitting room, piano
June Henderson	C-no/S-no/P-no/H-no	swimming pool
All year		art studio

Mountainside home with pool. Majestic towering mountains. Hiking in the desert. Sparkling city lights. Beautiful backyard & patio. Owner's artwork for sale in her art studio.

La Posada del Valle Inn	$$$ B&B	Continental plus (wkdys)
1640 N. Campbell Ave., 85719	5 rooms, 5 pb	Full breakfast (wkends)
602-795-3840	Visa, MC •	Comp. wine, tea
Charles & Debbi Bryant	C-17+/S-no/P-no/H-no	Library, sitting room
All year	Spanish	courtyard, patios

Elegant 1920s inn nestled in the heart of the city, offering gourmet breakfast, afternoon tea; catering available for special functions.

Peppertrees B&B Inn	$$ B&B	Full breakfast
724 E. University Rd., 85719	4 rooms	Picnic lunch to go
602-622-7167	•	Comp. wine, tea, snacks
Marjorie G. Martin	C-ltd/S-ltd/P-no/H-no	Library, walk to many
All year		fine restaurants

A warm and friendly territorial home furnished with antiques, serving memorable gourmet breakfasts. Easy walk to Univ. of Ariz., downtown, shopping. On the old trolley line.

More Inns...

Bisbee Inn   45 OK Street P.O. Box 18, Bisbee 85603   602-432-5131
Adobe Inn-Carefree   Box 1081, Carefree 85377   602-488-4444
Cochise Hotel   Box 27, Cochise 85606   602-384-3156
Cedar B&B   425 W. Cedar, Flagstaff 86001   602-774-1636
Walking L Ranch   RR 4, Box 721B, Flagstaff 86001   602-779-2219
Villa Galleria B&B   16650 E. Hawk Drive, Fountain Hills 85268   602-837-1400
Valley 'O the Sun B&B   P.O. Box 2214, Scottsdale 85252   602-941-1281
Moore's Music Museum B&B   3085 W. Hwy 89A, Sedona 86336   602-282-3419
Casa Suecia B&B   Suite 181, P.O. Box 36883, Tucson 86704
El Presidio Inn   297 North Main, Tucson 85701   602-623-6151
La Madera Ranch & Resort   9061 E. Woodland Road, Tucson 85749   602-749-2773
Myer's Blue Corn House   4215 E. Kilmer, Tucson 85711   602-327-4663
Kay El Bar Ranch   Box 2480, Wickenburg 85358   602-684-7593
Rancho De Los Caballeros   Box 1148, Wickenburg 85358   602-684-5484

Arkansas

Great Southern Hotel	$ B&B	Full breakfast
127 W. Cedar, 72021	4 rooms, 4 pb	Lunch & dinner (Mon-Sat)
501-734-4955	AmEx, Visa, MC	Victorian tearoom
Stanley & Dorcas Prince	C-no/S-yes/P-no/H-yes	Banquet & meeting rooms
All year		exercise room, sauna

Restored in true Victorian elegance, featuring serene dining and rooms that reflect a quaint homey atmosphere reminiscent of bygone days.

The 5-B's	$ B&B	Full breakfast
P.O. Box 364, 72040	4 rooms, 2 pb	Comp. wine, snacks
210 S. 2nd St.	C-yes/S-no/P-no/H-no	Sitting room
501-256-4789		library
Ann & Roy Hille		
All year		

Restored colonial revival home on National Register of Historic Places; tastefully furnished with antiques and collectibles; in small town located in rural setting.

Brownstone Inn	$$ B&B	Full breakfast
P.O. Box 409, 72632	4 rooms, 4 pb	Afternoon tea on request
75 Hillside	Visa, MC	Sitting room
501-253-7505	C-ltd/S-ltd/P-no/H-yes	
Virginia Rush, John Rakes		
March—December		

The original facade of the Ozarka Water Company currently houses nostalgic antique filled guest rooms overlooking a well-kept yard.

Carriage House	$$$ EP	Coffee, tea
75 Lookout Lane, 72632	2 rooms, 2 pb	Soft drinks, juice
501-253-8310	Visa, MC, AmEx	Fireplace, pool table
Suzie Bell	C-yes/S-yes	hot tubs, patio
All year	Spanish	

100-year-old renovated carriage house with original horse stalls & troughs. Pool table, fireplace, private patio, hot tub. Located in a historic district. Secluded.

Crescent Cottage Inn	$$ B&B	Full breakfast
211 Spring St., 72632	3 rooms, 3 pb	Coffee before breakfast
501-253-6022	Visa, MC	Sitting room
Ron & Brenda Bell	C-no/S-no/P-no/H-no	2 rooms with color TV
All year		telephones

Crescent Cottage Inn is nestled in the historic part of Eureka Springs overlooking East Mountain. Close to quaint shops and fine restaurants.

20 Arkansas

EUREKA SPRINGS ――――――――――――――――――――――――

Crescent Moon Townhouse $$$ B&B Continental plus
P.O. Box 429, 72632 1 rooms, 1 pb Comp. wine (on request)
28 Spring St. Visa, MC, AmEx Sitting room
501-253-9463 C-yes/S-yes/P-ltd/H-no hot tubs, decks
Nedra Forrest color TV, VCR, stereo
All year

Entire floor of an 1898 limestone building. Antiques, stained glass and polished wood. Two bedrooms, kitchen, bath and living room sleeps up to 4. Private deck with hot tub.

Dairy Hollow House $$$ B&B Full breakfast
515 Spring St., 72632 7 rooms, 7 pb Dinners by reservation
501-253-7444 Visa, MC, AmEx • Thursday-Sunday
N. Shank, C. Dragonwagon C-ltd/S-ltd/P-no/H-no Sitting room, hot tub
All year fireplaces in rooms

Restored Ozark farmhouse in historic district. Antiques, flowers, great breakfasts. "Nouveau 'Zarks" dinners by reservation for guests. The Ozarks' first B&B.

Flatiron Flats $$$ B&B "Breakfast checks"
25 Spring St., 72632 2 rooms, 2 pb Comp. rose or chablis
501-253-9434/800-421-9615 Visa, MC, AmEx, Disc • Fruit basket with fruit,
Jimmy & Candy Adair C-no/S-ltd/P-no/H-no nuts, mints, cheese
All year Sitting room, hot tubs

The Flatiron Building is the focal point of historic downtown, featuring two elegant suites in the heart of Eureka Springs.

Four Winds Bed & Breakfast $ B&B Continental breakfast
3 Echols St., 72632 2 rooms, 1 pb Gourmet breakfast $5
501-253-9169 • Comp. wine, snacks
Laura Menees C-ltd/S-yes/P-ltd/H-no Porch, deck, hammock
All year French, Spanish Kitchen privileges

Furnished in English Country antiques with original art and whimsical collections. Charming upper suite with a deck suspended in the trees offers a magnificent view.

Heart of the Hills Inn $$ B&B Full gourmet breakfast
5 Summit, 72632 5 rooms, 5 pb Comp. cold drink
62 Business Visa, MC Sitting room
501-253-7468 C-yes/S-no/P-no/H-no porches, antiques
Jan Jacobs Weber cottage, crib
All year

Victorian charm in Victorian town; great breakfasts on deck or sun room; Southern hospitality; TV and bath in each suite.

Heartstone Inn & Cottages $$ B&B Full gourmet breakfast
35 Kingshighway, 72632 9 rooms, 9 pb Comp. tea
501-253-8916 Visa, MC Sitting room
Iris & Bill Simantel C-yes/S-yes/P-no/H-no breakfast room with deck
February—mid-December color cable TV in rooms

Award-winning inn. Antique furnishings, private baths and entrances. Some queen beds. Historic district. Near all attractions. "Best breakfast in the Ozarks"—NY Times 1989.

EUREKA SPRINGS

The Old Homestead	$$ B&B	Full breakfast
82 Armstrong, 72632	4 rooms, 4 pb	Comp. wine
501-253-7501	Visa, MC	Sitting room
Pat Kile	C-no/S-yes/P-no/H-no	gift shop of area work
All year		

Lovely 1890 stone building in historic downtown area, ½ block to trolley depot, restaurants and shops. Rooms individually decorated with antiques.

Piedmont House	$$ B&B	Full breakfast
165 Spring St., 72632	8 rooms, 8 pb	Comp. coffee,
501-253-9258	Visa	Lemonade, cake, muffins
Rose & Larry Olivet	C-12+/S-ltd/H-yes	Sitting room, library
All year		wraparound porch

Over 100 years old with original guest book also over 100 years old. "Homey" atmosphere; comfortable rooms and beautiful views of the mountain and Christ of the Ozark Statue.

Singleton House B&B	$ B&B	Full breakfast
11 Singleton, 72632	5 rooms, 3 pb	Dinner on train (RSVP)
501-253-9111	Visa, MC, Discover •	Passion play (RSVP)
Barbara Gavron	C-yes/S-ltd/P-no/H-no	honeymoon cottage
All year		Sunday hiking club

Circa 1894 antiques, folk art; breakfast balcony overlooks magical garden & pond; in historic district. Walk to shops & cafes. Passion play—RSVP, dinner on train.

Sweet Seasons Cottages	$$ EP	Full kitchen
P.O. Box 642, 72632	10 rooms, 10 pb	Coffeemakers
77 Spring St.	Visa, MC, AmEx •	Sitting rooms
501-253-7603	C-yes/S-yes/P-yes/H-ask	cable color TV
Marcia Yearsley		jacuzzis for two
All year		

Restored Victorian cottages near downtown village. Each with full kitchen, fireplace and enchanting decor, antiques, handmade crafts. Spectacular views, private settings.

HELENA

Edwardian Inn	$$ B&B	Continental plus
317 S. Biscoe, 72342	12 rooms, 12 pb	Wine & cheese sometimes
501-338-9155	Visa, MC, AmEx	Sitting room
Jerri Steed	C-yes/S-yes/P-yes/H-yes	color TVs, phones
All year		conference room

The Edwardian Inn offers twelve antique guest rooms, private bath and continental breakfast. Elegance and romance from the turn of the century.

HOT SPRINGS

Vintage Comfort B&B Inn	$$ B&B	Full breakfast
303 Quapaw Ave., 71901	4 rooms, 4 pb	Comp. wine & cheese
501-623-3258	Visa, MC •	Sitting room
Helen R. Bartlett	C-6+/S-no/P-no/H-no	antique reed organ
All year		

1903 Queen Anne home decorated with antiques, soft, light colors; featuring Southern hospitality. Romantic atmosphere ideal for weddings and honeymoons.

HOT SPRINGS NAT'L PARK

Williams House B&B Inn	$$ B&B	Full breakfast
420 Quapaw St., 71901	6 rooms, 4 pb	Afternoon tea
501-624-4275	Visa, MC •	Sitting rooms, fireplace
Mary & Gary Riley	C-4+/S-ltd/P-ask/H-no	piano, picnic tables
All year		BBQ, hiking trail maps

Williams House shows Victorian flair for convenience and elegance. Your home away from home, nestled in Oachita Mountains. Romantic atmosphere. Mystery weekends.

LITTLE ROCK

Quapaw Inn	$ B&B	Continental plus
1868 S. Gaines, 72206	4 rooms, 1 pb	Snacks
501-376-6873	Visa, MC •	airport pickup
Dottie Woodwind	C-ltd	sitting room, library
All year		exercycle, BYOB happy hr

Little Rock's only B&B inn offers line-dried linens, privacy and antiques. Four minutes from downtown; ten minutes from airport.

MOUNTAIN VIEW

Commercial Hotel—A Vintage Guest House	$ EP	Breakfast available ($)
P.O. Box 72, 72560	8 rooms, 3 pb	Bakery on premises
Peabody at Washington St.	AmEx	Sitting room
501-269-4383	C-yes/S-no/P-no/H-no	porch
Todd & Andrea Budy		entertainment
All year Nov-Mar by res.		

Restored country inn on historic Courthouse Square; gourmet bakery on premises; close to Ozark Folk Center and Blanchard Springs Caverns. Old-time music on our porch.

PINE BLUFF

Margland 11 B&B Inn	$$$ B&B	Full breakfast
P.O. Box 8594, 71611	6 rooms, 6 pb	Comp. wine, tea
703 W. 2nd	Visa, MC, AmEx •	Snacks
501-536-6000	C-yes/S-yes/P-no/H-yes	Sitting room, jacuzzi
Wanda Bateman		cable TV
All year		

Elegant curves and soothing colors on the outside and luxurious furnishings inside. Each suite upstairs has its own character.

WASHINGTON

Old Washington Jail	$ B&B	Full breakfast
P.O. Box 157, 71862	4 rooms, 4 pb	Afternoon tea, snacks
501-983-2790	C-yes	Sitting room
Wendy & Kay McCorkle		
All year		

Building served as country jail 1872-1939. Located in historic state park. Victorian antiques. Full breakfast. Quiet friendly atmosphere.

More Inns. . .

May House　101 Railroad Avenue, Clarksville 72830　501-754-6851
Bridgeford Cottage　263 Spring St., Eureka Springs 72632　501-253-7853
Coach House Inn　140 South Main, Eureka Springs 72632　501-253-8099
Elmwood House　110 Spring, Eureka Springs 72632　501-253-7227
Eureka Springs & N. Arkans　P.O. Box 310, Eureka Springs 72632　501-253-9623
Johnson's Hilltop Cabin　Rt. 1, Box 503, Eureka Springs 72632　501-253-9537
Lake Lucerne Resort　P.O. Box 441, Eureka Springs 72632　501-253-8085
Lookout Cottage　12 Lookout Circle, Eureka Springs 72632　501-253-9545

Magnolia Guest Cottage   180 Spring St., Eureka Springs 72632   501-253-9463
Maplewood B&B   4 Armstrong St., Eureka Springs 72632   501-253-8053
New Orleans Hotel   63 Spring St., Eureka Springs 72632   501-253-8630
Oak Crest Cottages   Rt. 2, Box 26, Eureka Springs 72632   501-253-9493
Palace Hotel & Bathhouse   135 Spring, Eureka Springs 72632   501-253-7474
Red Bud Valley Resort   RR 1, Box 500, Eureka Springs 72632   501-253-9028
Redbud Manor   7 Kingshighway, Eureka Springs 72632   501-253-9649
Riverview Resort   RR 2 Box 475, Eureka Springs 72632   501-253-8367
Scandia Inn B&B Cottages   33 Avo, Hwy 62 West, Eureka Springs 72632   501-253-8922
School House Inn   15 Kansas St., Eureka Springs 72632   501-253-7854
Tatman-Garret House   P.O. Box 171, Eureka Springs 72632   501-253-7617
White Flower Cottage   62 Kingshighway, Eureka Springs 72632   501-253-9636
Corn Cob Inn   Rt. 1, Box 183, Everton 72633   501-429-6545
Eton House   1485 Eton, Fayetteville 72703   501-521-6344
Mount Kessler Inn   P.O. Box 3033, Fayetteville 72701
McCartney House   500 S. 19th St., Fort Smith 72901   501-782-9057
Merry Go Round Cottage   412 North 8th, Fort Smith 72901   501-783-3472
Thomas Quinn Guest House   815 North B St., Fort Smith 72901   501-782-0499
Dogwood Inn B&B   U.S. 62, Garfield 72732   604-287-4213
Anna's House   P.O. Box 58, Gilbert 72636   501-439-2888
Oak Tree Inn   Vinegar Hill, 110 W., Heber Springs 72543   501-362-6111
Stillmeadow Farm   Rt. 1, Box 434-D, Hot Springs 71913   501-525-9994
Dogwood Manor   906 Malvern Ave., Hot Springs Nat'l Park 71901   501-624-0896
Cliff House Inn   Scenic Ark., Highway 7, Jasper 72641   501-446-2292
Tanyard Springs   Route 3, Box 335, Morrilton 72110   501-727-5200
Inn at Mountain View   Courthouse Square, Mountain View 72560   501-269-4200
Hammons Chapel Farm   1 mile of Ark. 5, Romance 72136   501-849-2819
Red Raven Inn   P.O. Box 1217, Yellville 72687   501-449-5168

California

ALAMEDA

Garratt Mansion	$$ B&B	Full breakfast
900 Union St., 94501	5 rooms, 2 pb	Comp. beverages & tea
415-521-4779	•	Bicycles
Royce & Betty Gladden	C-yes/S-no/P-no/H-no	sitting room
All year		

An elegant Victorian in a quiet island community just 20 min. from downtown San Francisco, offering personalized attention.

Webster House	$$ B&B	Continental plus
1238 Versailles Ave., 94501	4 rooms	Comp. wine, champagne
415-523-9697	Visa, MC •	snacks, and coffees
Andrew & Susan McCormack	C-ltd/S-ltd	Outside deck, waterfall
All year		sun porch, library, games

22nd City Historical Monument. Quaint, enchanting Gothic Revival Cottage is the oldest house in Alameda. Walk to beach, windsurfing, shops, golf. San Francisco 30 min. away.

24 California

ALBION

Fensalden Inn
P.O. Box 99, 95410
33810 Navarro Ridge Rd.
707-937-4042
Scott & Frances Brazil
All year

$$$ B&B
7 rooms, 7 pb
Visa, MC
C-ltd/S-ltd/P-ltd/H-ltd

Full breakfast
Comp. wine
Sitting room
parlor
library

Historic country inn with spectacular ocean views—and only ten minutes from the village of Mendocino.

AMADOR CITY

Mine House Inn
P.O. Box 245, S. Hwy 49, 95601
209-267-5900
Peter Daubenspeck
All year

$ B&B
7 rooms, 7 pb
•
C-yes/to-yes/P-no/H-no
Portuguese

Continental breakfast
Art gallery/sitting room
swimming pool
gift shop

Former Keystone Gold Mining Company office building, all rooms furnished in Victorian antiques. Relive a night from the gold rush days.

ANAHEIM

Anaheim Bed & Breakfast
1327 S. Hickory, 92805
714-533-1884
Margot & Lars Palmgren
All year

$ B&B
3 rooms
C-yes/S-no
Ger, Swed, Nor, Dan, Fr

Full breakfast
Sitting room

Comfortable home in residential section near Disneyland and convention centers. View of Disneyland fireworks nightly during summer from backyard. Long-time European hosts.

Anaheim Country Inn
856 S. Walnut St., 92802
714-778-0150
Lois Ramont, Marilyn Watson
All year

$$ B&B
8 rooms, 4 pb
Visa, MC •
C-12+/S-ltd/P-no/H-no

Full breakfast
Comp. tea, wine
Hot tub
sitting room
organ

Large historic house near Disneyland. Garden & trees, off-street parking, antiques, warm homey atmosphere. Complimentary appetizers before dinner.

ANGWIN

Big Yellow Sunflower B&B
235 Sky Oaks, 94508
707-965-3885
Dale & Betty Clement
All year

$$ B&B
2 rooms, 1 pb
•
C-yes/S-ltd/P-no/H-no

Full breakfast
Light supper
Piano, fireplace
comp. videotape rental
queen beds, bicycles

Secluded, spacious suite above Napa Valley. Private entrance, deck, bath, fireplace and kitchenette. Country cooking, charm and hospitality; in hills away from crowds.

ANGWIN (NAPA VALLEY)

Forest Manor
415 Cold Springs Rd., 94508
707-965-3538
Harold & Corlene Lambeth
All year

$$$ B&B
3 rooms, 3 pb
Visa,MC •
C-12+/S-ltd/P-no/H-no
Thai, French

Continental plus
Tea, fruit basket
Jacuzzi, refrig., limo
sitting room, piano
organ, 53' pool & spa

Beautiful secluded 20-acre English Tudor forested estate in Napa Wine Country. Massive carved beams, fireplaces, decks, air-conditioning, game rooms.

APTOS

Apple Lane Inn
6265 Soquel Dr., 95003
408-475-6868
Ann Farley
All year

$$ B&B
5 rooms, 3 pb
Visa, MC •
C-no/S-ltd/P-no/H-no

Full breakfast
Comp. beverages
Sitting room
player piano
library

Victorian farmhouse furnished with beautiful antiques offers country charm. Quiet, yet close to everything, including fine restaurants.

Bayview Hotel B&B Inn
8041 Soquel Dr., 95003
408-688-8654
Freda Sprietsma
All year

$$$ B&B
8 rooms, 8 pb
Visa, MC •
C-5+/S-no/P-no/H-no
French, Italian

Continental plus
Lunch, dinner
Restaurant
Sitting room

1878 California Victorian furnished with lovely antiques; near beaches, hiking trails, bicycle routes, golf, tennis, fishing, antique shops and restaurants.

Mangels House
P.O. Box 302, 95001
570 Aptos Creek Rd.
408-688-7982
Jacqueline Fisher
All year exc. Xmas 3 dys

$$$ B&B
5 rooms, 2 pb
Visa, MC •
C-12+/S-ltd/P-no/H-no
French, Spanish

Full breakfast
Comp. wine
Sitting room, fireplace
piano; table tennis and
darts on back porch

Casual elegance in country setting, only 5 min. drive to Hwy. 1. Acres of private gardens on edge of Redwood State park. Two-thirds of a mile from beach; golf.

ARCATA

Plough and the Stars Inn
1800 27th St., 95521
707-822-8236
Melissa & Bill Hans
February—mid-Dec.

$$$ B&B
5 rooms, 2 pb
C-12+/S-yes/P-ltd/H-ltd

Full breakfast
Comp. wine
Three common rooms

1860's farmhouse on two acres of pastoral grounds; casual, country atmosphere; first-class hospitality. Redwoods, seashore, wildlife marsh minutes away.

ARROYO GRANDE

Rose Victorian Inn
789 Valley Rd., 93420
805-481-5566
Ross & Diana Cox
All year

$$$ MAP
5 rooms
Visa, MC •
C-16+/S-ltd/P-no/H-ltd

Full breakfast
Dinner, Restaurant, bar
Sitting room, piano

Majestic 98-year-old mansion; Pacific Ocean, sand dune views; gourmet dinners; breakfast of Eggs Benedict in dining room with crystal chandeliers.

AUBURN

Lincoln House B&B
191 Lincoln Way, 95603
916-885-8880
Howard & Ginny Leal
All year

$$ B&B
3 rooms, 3 pb
•
C-yes/S-ltd

Full breakfast
Afternoon tea
Swimming pool

Our storybook inn amplifies the charm of the Gold Country. Enjoy a full breakfast in our dining room with a majestic view of the Sierras.

Cain House, Bridgeport, CA

AUBURN

Power's Mansion Inn
164 Cleveland Ave., 95603
916-885-1166
Judith & Rene Vincent
All year

$$$ B&B
13 rooms, 13 pb
Visa, MC, AmEx •
C-yes/S-no/P-no/H-no
French, Spanish

Continental plus
Other meals by Request
Comp. wine, terry robes
Deluxe amenities
fireplaces, patios/decks

1885 mansion, ten thousand sq. ft., built from gold-mining fortune. Has elegance of detailed restoration and antique furnishings with queen beds and central air and heat.

AVALON

Gull House B&B Home
P.O. Box 1381, 90704
344 Whittley Ave.
213-510-2547/800-442-4884
Bob & Hattie Michalis
April 1—October 31

$$$ B&B
2 rooms, 2 pb
•
C-no/S-yes/P-no/H-no

Continental plus
Comp. fruit basket
Refrigerator
pool, whirlpool, BBQ
taxi to boat terminal

Deluxe suites in quiet residential area. Breakfast on patio. Beach, sights & activities on this beautiful island. Perfect for couples. Make reservations well in advance.

BEN LOMOND

Chateau Des Fleurs
7995 Hwy 9, 95005
408-336-8943
Lee & Laura Jonas
All year

$$$ B&B
3 rooms, 3 pb
Visa, MC
C-no/S-no/P-no/H-no

Full breakfast
Comp. champagne
Library, sitting room
organ, antique piano
swimming, tennis nearby

A Victorian mansion once owned by the Bartlett (pear) family, this inn is spacious, special, sensational, historic, quiet, unforgettable, surrounded by evergreens & wineries.

BENICIA

Captain Dillingham's Inn	$$ B&B	Full buffet breakfast
145 East D St., 94510	10 rooms, 9 pb	Comp. wine, snacks
707-746-7164/800-544-2278	Visa, MC, AmEx, DC, CB •	Sitting room
Roger & Denny Steck	C-yes/S-yes/P-no/H-yes	library
All year		jacuzzis in 8 rooms

Dillingham's, centered in Benicia's historic waterfront district, offers jacuzzi-equipped accommodations in a lush garden atmosphere.

BERKELEY

B&B Accomm. in Berkeley	$$ B&B	Full breakfast
2235 Carleton St., 94704	3 rooms, 3 pb	Comp. tea, wine
415-548-7556	C-ask/S-no/P-no/H-yes	Library
John & Helen Muller	Spanish, German	indoor exercise equip.
All year		

Private and spacious accommodations near University of California, the Marina, famous Gourmet Ghetto and BART.

BIG BEAR LAKE

Switzerland Haus	$$$ B&B	Continental plus
P.O. Box 256, 92315	5 rooms, 5 pb	Snacks
41829 Switzerland	C-no/S-no/P-no/H-no	
714-866-3729		
Lorri & Warner Clarke		
All year		

Warm, inviting Swiss chalet, only steps to Snow Summit Ski Slopes. Custom-designed rooms with private baths and patios.

BISHOP

Matlick House	$$ B&B	Full breakfast
1313 Rowan Lane, 93514	5 rooms, 5 pb	Lunch/dinner with notice
619-873-3133	•	comp. wine, snacks
Nanette Robidart	C-no/S-ltd/P-no	Sitting room
All year		

1906 ranch house; antiques throughout; picturesque views of the eastern Sierras. Minutes from skiing, fishing, hiking & other outdoor sports.

BOONVILLE

Bear Wallow Resort	$$ EP	Restaurant
P.O. Box 533, 95415	8 rooms, 8 pb	Steak House Fri. & Sat.
2300 Mountain View Rd.	Visa, MC •	Full bar & kitchens
707-895-3335	C-yes/S-yes/P-yes/H-no	Library, lodge
Bob & Roxanne Hedges		hot tub, swimming pool
All year		

Romantic secluded cottages on 40 acres of redwoods; fireplace, kitchen, queen bed, beamed ceiling, deck, view, private, quiet.

Toll House Inn	$$$ B&B	Full breakfast
P.O. Box 268, 95415	5 rooms, 3 pb	Dinner by reservation
15301 Hwy. 253	•	Complimentary wine
707-895-3630	C-ltd/S-no/P-no/H-yes	Sitting room, library
Beverly E. Nesbitt		hot tub, piano
All year		

Mendocino wine country. Flocks of sheep, deer & wild pigs—540 acres of pastures. Built in 1912 in the Bell Valley. The folk language Boonthing began here.

BRIDGEPORT ────────────────────────────────

Cain House	$$$ B&B	Full breakfast
11 Main St., 93517	6 rooms, 6 pb	Comp. wine, snacks
P.O. Box 454	Visa, MC, AmEx •	Sitting room
619-932-7040	S-no/P-no/H-no	tennis courts
Marachal L. Myers		
All year		

The grandeur of the eastern Sierras is the perfect setting for evening wine and cheese. Complimentary full breakfast included.

CALISTOGA ────────────────────────────────

Brannan Cottage Inn	$$$ B&B	Full breakfast
109 Wapoo Ave., 94515	6 rooms, 6 pb	Comp. wine
707-942-4200	Visa, MC •	Sitting room
Jay & Dottie Richolson	C-yes/S-yes/P-yes/H-yes	
All year	French, Spanish	

Charming 1860 National Register cottage-style Victorian, original wildflower stencils, country furnishings, lovely grounds, close to famous spas, wineries.

Calistoga Inn	$ B&B	Continental breakfast
1250 Lincoln Av., 94515	17 rooms	Dinner, bar
707-942-4101	Visa, MC	pub-brewery
Sue Dunsford	C-yes/S-yes/P-no/H-no	beer & wine garden
All year	Spanish, French	

Small, affordable country hotel. Nationally recognized restaurant and publike bar in the heart of California's premium wine country. Redecorated with new, firm beds.

Culver's, A Country Inn	$$$ B&B	Full breakfast
1805 Foothill Blvd, 94515	7 rooms	Comp. sherry
707-942-4535	Visa, MC •	Living room w/fireplace
Meg & Tony Wheatley	C-12+/S-ltd/P-no/H-yes	hot tub, sauna, pool
All year		piano

Comfortable, elegant Victorian home circa 1875, restored historical landmark in Napa Valley. Easy access to wineries, spas, gliding, ballooning, restaurants.

Foothill House	$$$ B&B	Continental plus
3037 Foothill Blvd, 94515	3 rooms, 3 pb	Comp. wine & cheese
707-942-6933	Visa, MC	Whirlpool bath in suite
Susan & Michael Clow	C-no/S-no/P-no/H-no	air-conditioning
All year		sitting room

In a country setting, Foothill House offers 3 spacious rooms individually decorated with antiques, each with private bath, entrance and fireplace.

Mount View Hotel	$$ B&B	Continental b'fast (M-F)
1457 Lincoln Ave., 94515	34 rooms, 34 pb	Lunch, dinner, bar
707-942-6877	Major credit cards	Jacuzzi, swimming pool
Scott Ulrich	C-yes/S-yes/P-no/H-yes	mesquite BBQ, golf
All year		tennis, entertainment

An Art Deco dream in all its European elegance. The only full-service hotel in Calistoga.

CALISTOGA

Pine Street Inn
1202 Pine St., 94515
707-942-6829
Tom & Jean Lunney
All year

$$ B&B
16 rooms, 16 pb
Visa, MC
C-no/S-yes/P-no/H-no

Continental plus
Afternoon tea
Sitting room
pool, hot tubs, bicycles
garden patio for dining

A country French-style inn with floral gardens. Theme rooms, antiques. Pool and whirlpool overlook vineyards. Secluded yet close to shops and restaurants.

Pink Mansion
1415 Foothill Blvd., 94515
707-942-0558
Jeff Seyfried
All year

$$$ B&B
5 rooms, 5 pb
Visa, MC •
C-12+/S-no/P-no/H-yes
Spanish

Full breakfast
Lunch, dinner
Comp. wine with cheese
Library, A/C, parlor
indoor pool, bicycles

Restored 1875 home combines turn-of-the-century elegance with modern amenities to provide our wine country travelers with old-fashioned comfort.

Quail Mountain B&B
4455 N. St. Helena Hwy, 94515
707-942-0316
Don & Alma Swiers
All year

$$$ B&B
3 rooms, 3 pb
Visa, MC •
C-no/S-no/P-no/H-no

Full breakfast
Comp. wine
Sitting room, library
hot tubs, pool, gardens
vineyards, private decks

Secluded, wooded, luxury country estate close to wineries, restaurants, spas, gliding, ballooning. Rooms individually decorated with art works and antiques.

Scarlett's Country Inn
3918 Silverado Tr., 94515
707-942-6669
Scarlett Dwyer, Kim Stevenson
All year

$$$ B&B
3 rooms, 3 pb
•
C-yes/S-yes/P-no/H-no
Spanish

Continental plus
Comp. wine
Swimming pool
sitting room

Secluded French country farmhouse overlooking vineyards in famed Napa Valley. Breakfast served by woodland swimming pool. Close to spas and wineries.

Trailside Inn
4201 Silverado Tr., 94515
707-942-4106
Randy & Lani Gray
All year

$$$ B&B
3 rooms, 3 pb
•
C-yes/S-yes/P-no/H-no

Continental breakfast
Comp. wine
Fireplace, kitchens
library, A/C
private decks

1930s farmhouse comfortably decorated with quilts and antiques. Each suite has private entrance, 3 rooms plus bath, fireplace, a/c, Each suite sleeps up to four people.

Wine Way Inn
1019 Foothill Blvd., 94515
707-942-0680
Allen & Dede Good
All year

$$ B&B
6 rooms, 6 pb
Visa, MC •
C-10+/S-ltd/P-no/H-no

Full breakfast
Comp. wine
Living room, fireplace
mineral baths nearby
air-conditioning, gazebo

Country charm in town; hillside borders spacious multilevel deck; central location to explore renowned vineyards of Napa/Sonoma.

CALISTOGA

Wishing Well Inn	$$$ B&B	Full country breakfast
2653 Foothill Blvd., 94515	3 rooms, 3 pb	Tea, lemonade, snacks
Hwy. 128	Visa, MC •	Comp. wine, sitting room
707-942-5534	C-yes/S-no/P-no/H-yes	Fireplace, hot tubs
Marina & Keith Dinsmoor	Russian	swimming pool, bikes, TV
All year		

Elegant country farmhouse on four historical areas. Full breakfast served on deck overlooking orchard or poolside with view of Mount Saint Helen.

Zinfandel House	$$ B&B	Continental plus
1253 Summit Dr., 94515	3 rooms, 2 pb	Comp. wine
707-942-0733	C-no/S-no/P-no/H-no	Library
Bette & George Starke		sitting room
All year		hot tub

Beautiful home situated on wooded hillside overlooking vineyards and mountains. Lovely breakfast served on outside deck or in dining room.

CAMBRIA

Beach House	$$$ B&B	Continental plus
6360 Moonstone Beach Dr, 93428	7 rooms, 7 pb	Afternoon tea
805-927-3136	Visa, MC •	Sitting room
Penny Hitch, Tigg Morales	C-ltd/S-no/P-no/H-no	bicycles
All year		patios & decks

Oceanfront home with fireplaces, patios, decks and bicycles. Five miles to Hearst Castle. Rural atmosphere, gorgeous sunsets. Peace and relaxation.

Olallieberry Inn	$$$ B&B	Continental plus
2476 Main St., 93428	6 rooms, 6 pb	Comp. wine & appetizers
805-927-3222	•	Sitting room, parlor
L. Byers, V. Kilpatrick	C-13+/S-no/P-no/H-yes	gathering room
All year		tennis & swimming priv.

The Olallieberry Inn is a completely restored 110-year-old Greek Revival home registered with the Historic House Association of America.

Pickford House B&B	$$ B&B	Full breakfast
2555 MacLeod Way, 93428	8 rooms, 8 pb	Afternoon wine/beer
805-927-8619	Visa, MC •	Hors d'oeuvres, cookies
Anna Larsen	C-12+/S-ltd/P-no/H-yes	Piano, sitting room
All year		hot tub

All rooms named after silent-film-era stars and furnished with genuine antiques. Full breakfast included. All rooms have showers and tubs. Homemade fruit breads and cakes.

CARMEL

Cobblestone Inn	$$$ B&B	Full breakfast
P.O. Box 3185, 93921	24 rooms, 24 pb	Comp. tea, wine
Junipero & 8th Sts	AmEx, Visa, MC •	Sitting room
408-625-5222	C-yes/S-ltd/P-no/H-no	terrace, bicycles
Shelley Post Claudel		picnics avail.
All year		

Charming country inn nestled in English garden. Each room has a fireplace and country decor, turndown service, beverages and morning paper. Member of Four Sisters' Inns.

CARMEL

Green Lantern Inn
P.O. Box 2619, 93921
7th & Casanova
408-624-4392
Lisse Telfler
All year

$$ B&B
19 rooms, 19 pb
Visa, MC, AmEx, Disc •
C-yes/S-yes/P-no/H-no

Continental plus
Sitting room

Quaint cottages sprinkled in flowering gardens. Each room is different and so close to the ocean, you can hear the waves. Part of Four Sisters' Inns.

Holiday House
P.O. Box 782, 93921
Camino Real at 7th Ave.
408-624-6267
Dieter & Ruth Back
All year

$$$ B&B
6 rooms, 4 pb
C-14+/S-ltd/P-no/H-no
German

Full breakfast
Comp. wine
Garden
sitting room, library

Lovely inn personifying Carmel charm, in quiet residential area, walking distance to town and beach. Ocean views, beautiful garden.

The Homestead
P.O. Box 1285, 93921
8th & Lincoln Sts.
408-624-4119
Betty Colletto
All year

$$ EP
12 rooms, 12 pb
C-yes/S-yes

Comp. coffee in rooms
4 cottages w/kitchens
2 cottages w/fireplaces

A unique inn nestled in the heart of Carmel. Rooms and cottages with private baths, some kitchens & fireplaces. Reasonably priced and close to town.

Lincoln Green Inn
P.O. Box 2747, 93921
Carmelo btwn 15th & 16th
408-624-1880/800-262-1262
Honey Jones, Dennis Levett
All year

$$$ B&B
4 rooms, 4 pb
Visa, MC, AmEx •
C-yes/S-yes/P-yes/H-yes

Continental plus
Comp. tea, wine
English garden

Four charming English country-style cottages set in a formal English garden behind a white picket fence; nestled in a quaint residential area near ocean.

Monte Verde Inn
P.O. Box 3373, 93921
Ocean Ave. & Monte Verde
408-624-6046/800-328-7707
John J. Nahas
All year

$$$ B&B
10 rooms, 10 pb
Visa, MC, AmEx
C-yes/P-ltd/H-yes
French, some Spanish

Continental plus
Several decks
lovely private garden

A lovely country inn surrounded by beautiful gardens and patios in the perfect Carmel location. Some fireplaces; ocean views; all private baths; parking available.

CARMEL

Stonehouse Inn
P.O. Box 2517, 93921
8th below Monte Verde
408-624-4569
Virginia Carey
All year

$$$ B&B
6 rooms
Visa, MC •
C-14+/S-no/P-no/H-no

Full breakfast
Wine, appetizers, sherry
Sitting room
fireplace
bicycles

Historic Carmel house built in 1906, traditional Bed & Breakfast. Within walking distance of shopping, restaurants, beach.

Sunset House
P.O. Box 1925, 93921
Camino Real @ Ocean & 7th
408-624-4884
Gee Gee & De Emory
All year

$$$ B&B
3 rooms, 3 pb
Visa, MC
C-no/S-yes/P-no/H-no

Continental plus
Living room

An elegant small inn. Woodburning fireplaces, ocean views. Romantic, quiet homelike surroundings. Breakfast served in your room. A magnificent garden.

Tally Ho Inn
P.O. Box 3726, 93921
Monte Verde at 6th St.
408-624-2232
Barbara Torell
All year

$$$ B&B
14 rooms, 14 pb
Visa, MC, AmEx •
C-yes/S-yes/P-no/H-no
some French

Continental plus
Afternoon tea
Floral garden, sun deck
fireplaces, ocean views
close to beach

This English country inn has bountiful gardens with sweeping ocean views from individually appointed rooms and sun decks. Former home of cartoonist Jimmy Hatlo.

CARMEL VALLEY

Los Laureles Lodge
Carmel Valley Rd., 93924
408-659-2233
Robert C. Tschupp
All year

$$ B&B
30 rooms, 30 pb
Visa, MC •
C-yes/S-yes/P-no/H-yes
German, Spanish, French

Continental plus
Restaurant, bar
Lunch, dinner
Library, hot tubs
swimming pool, sauna

Historic American country inn nestled in sunny Carmel Valley; outstanding golf packages; restaurant serves 3 meals daily, specializing in fresh California cuisine.

Robles del Rio Lodge
200 Punta Del Monte, 93924
408-659-3705
The Gurries Family
All year

$$ B&B
31 rooms, 31 pb
Visa, MC •
C-yes/S-yes/P-no/H-yes
Spanish, French

Continental plus
French restaurant
Sitting room, hot tub
sauna, swimming pool
tennis courts

A charming country hideaway high atop a mountain. Breathtaking view of the beautiful Carmel Valley. Newly renovated.

Valley Lodge
P.O. Box 93, 93924
Carmel Valley & Ford Rds.
408-659-2261/800-641-4646
Peter & Sherry Coakley
All year

$$$ B&B
35 rooms, 35 pb
Visa, AmEx, MC, Disc. •
C-yes/S-yes/P-yes/H-yes
French, Spanish

Continental plus
Comp. newspaper
library, hot tub
sauna, swimming pool
fitness ctr., conf. ctr.

Quiet location, lovely grounds. A romantic setting for lovers of privacy, nature, hiking, golf, tennis, swimming, riding—and just plain lovers. Cozy fireplace cottages.

California 33

CARMEL-BY-THE-SEA

Vagabond's House Inn
P.O. Box 2747, 93921
4th & Dolores
408-624-7738/800-262-1262
Honey Jones, Dennis Levett
All year

$$$ B&B
11 rooms, 11 pb
Visa, MC •
C-12+/S-yes/P-yes/H-no
French

Continental plus to room
Sitting room w/fireplace
Tennis, golf, library
off-street parking
2 blocks to downtown

Antique clocks and pictures, quilted bedspreads, fresh flowers, plants, shelves filled with old books. Sherry by the fireplace; breakfast served in your room.

CHICO

Bullard House B&B Inn
256 E. 1st Ave., 95926
916-342-5912
Patrick & Patricia Macarthy
All year

$$ B&B
4 rooms
C-no/S-no/P-no/H-no

Continental breakfast
Bicycles
sitting room
piano

Restored country Victorian in small college town, near Bidwell Park and Mansion. Quiet, restful and secure.

CLOVERDALE

Ye Olde Shelford House
29955 River Rd., 95425
707-894-5956
Ina & Al Sauder
All year

$$$ B&B
6 rooms, 6 pb
Visa, MC •
C-10+/S-ltd/P-no/H-no

Full breakfast
Comp. tea, wine
Hot tub, sitting room
pool, bicycles
entertainment

Stately 1880s Victorian, genuine antiques, wraparound porch overlooking vineyards. Delicious breakfast in formal dining room or porch. "Surry & Sip" ride to wineries.

COLOMA

Vineyard House
P.O. Box 176, 95613
Cold Springs Rd. off H.49
916-622-2217
The Herreras & David Buskirk
Exc. Mon/Tues Oct—May

$$ B&B
7 rooms, 1 pb
Visa, MC, BA •
C-16+/S-yes/P-no/H-no

Continental breakfast
Dinner, saloon
Sitting room, piano

Country charm in the middle of Coloma's picturesque river valley, featuring antique-filled rooms and full dining room service.

COLUMBIA

City Hotel
Main St., P.O. Box 1870, 95310
209-532-1479
Tom Bender
All year

$$ B&B
9 rooms, 9 pb
Visa, MC, AmEx •
C-yes/S-ltd/P-no/H-no

Continental plus
French restaurant
Sitting room, piano
Anchor Steam beer on
draft in saloon

Historical location in a state-preserved Gold Rush town; 9 antique-appointed rooms; small elegant dining room and authentic saloon.

Fallon Hotel
P.O. Box 1870, 95310
Washington St.
209-532-1470
Tom Bender
All year

$$ B&B
14 rooms, 14 pb
Visa, MC •
C-no/S-ltd/P-no/H-yes

Continental plus
Comp. wine
Sitting room
rose garden
avail. for receptions

Restored Victorian hotel, full of antiques in state-preserved Gold Rush town. Elegant and intimate. Near Yosemite.

34   California

CORONADO

1894 Victorian—Bonni Mari	$$$ B&B	Continental plus
1000 Eight St., 92118	4 rooms, 4 pb	Ethnic & health foods
619-435-2200	•	Sitting room, bicycles
Bonnie Marie Kinosian	C-yes/S-ltd/P-no/H-yes	bilevel outdoor patio
All year		sun deck, dance studio

Vacation, exercise, dance package! Owner, host, dance teacher, Bonni Marie Kinosian. Three-story Victorian. Pre-Civil War sleigh beds, brass beds, warm personal atmosphere.

DAVENPORT

New Davenport B&B Inn	$$ B&B	Full breakfast
31 Davenport Ave., 95017	12 rooms, 12 pb	Restaurant, gift shop
Box J	Visa, MC, AmEx	Comp. champagne
408-425-1818	C-ltd/S-no/P-no/H-yes	Sitting room, gallery
Bruce & Marcia McDougal		
All year		

Charming ocean-view rooms decorated with antiques, handcrafts and ethnic treasures. Complimentary champagne. Artist/owners. Beach access.

DAVIS

University Inn	$ B&B	Full breakfast
340 "A" St., 95616	4 rooms, 4 pb	Comp. tea
916-756-8648	Visa, MC, AmEx •	2 sitting rooms
Lynda & Ross Yancher	C-yes/S-no/P-no/H-yes	bicycles
All year		refrigerators in rooms

A great taste of Davis, ten steps from the University. Design your own breakfast. Private parking, quiet location. Rooms with private bath, private phone, TV & refrigerator.

DEL MAR

Rock Haus Inn	$$$ B&B	Continental plus
410 15th St., 92014	10 rooms, 4 pb	Comp. wine
619-481-3764	Visa, MC, Dscvr. •	Sitting room, piano
Doris Holmes	C-16+/S-no/P-no/H-no	player piano, veranda
All year		

Romantic getaway to quaint seaside village. Most rooms have ocean views in this historic landmark. Goose-down comforters, Amtrak pickup.

ELK

Elk Cove Inn	$$$ B&B	Full breakfast
P.O. Box 367, 95432	9 rooms, 7 pb	Dinner included Saturday
6300 S. Hwy. 1	C-12+/S-no/P-no/H-ltd	Sitting room, piano, bar
707-877-3321	Ger., Span., Fr., Ital.	library, stereo
Hildrun-Uta Triebess		
All year		

1883 Victorian—original old-fashioned country inn, outstanding dramatic ocean views; specializing in German and French cuisine and personal service.

Greenwood Pier Inn	$$ B&B	Continental breakfast
Box 36, 95432	10 rooms, 10 pb	Dinner available
5940 S. Hwy. 1	Visa, MC	Sitting room
707-877-9997	C-yes/S-yes/P-ltd/H-ltd	piano, entertainment
Kendrick & Isabel Petty	Spanish	On the Ocean!
All year		

Spectacular views from ocean bluff on the Mendocino coast. All rooms have fireplaces and private baths. Artist hosts have designed for your comfort.

ELK

Harbor House Inn by the Sea
Box 369, 95432
5600 S. Hwy 1
707-877-3203
Dean & Helen Turner
All year

$$$ MAP
10 rooms, 10 pb
C-16+/S-ltd/P-no/H-no
French, Spanish

Full breakfast
Full dinner, wine list
Sitting room, piano
fireplaces, parlor stove
gardens, private beach

Spectacular north coast vistas of the sea. Renowned country gourmet cuisine. Wine lover's paradise. Rooms include original artwork, fireplaces or parlor stoves, and decks.

EUREKA

Carter House
1033 Third St., 95501
707-445-1390
Mark & Christi Carter
All year

$$$ B&B
7 rooms, 4 pb
Visa, MC, AmEx •
C-10+/S-ltd/P-no/H-no
Spanish, French

Full breakfast
Dinner (by reservation)
comp. wine & snacks
Sitting rooms, gardens
corporate rates

New Victorian. Enjoy wines & appetizers before dinner, cordials or teas & cookies at bedtime. Warm hospitality; a breakfast you'll never forget. OUR 1986 INN OF THE YEAR.

Chalet de France
SR Box 20A, Kneeland PO, 95549
17687 Kneeland Rd.
707-443-6512/707-444-3144
Doug & Lili Vieyra
All year

$$$ AP
2 rooms
•
C-no/S-no/P-no/H-no
French, Flemish, Dutch

French gourmet breakfast
Lunch, dinner, snacks
Library, games, records
darts, croquet, bicycles
fishing, swimming, hiking

Swiss-Bavarian mountain chalet at 1,000 feet, offering three gourmet meals and 40-mile views; surrounded by 30 square miles of wilderness; 20 miles east of Eureka.

Hotel Carter
301 "L" St., 95501
707-444-8062/707-445-1390
Mark & Christi Carter
All year

$$ B&B
20 rooms, 20 pb
Visa, MC, AmEx •
C-yes/S-yes/P-no/H-yes

Continental breakfast
Dinner (by reservation)
comp. wine, beer,
hors d'oeuvres
Sitting room

Luxury full-service small hotel, attentive staff, antiques and art, in-room phones. Intimate hotel of quality.

Old Town B&B Inn
1521 Third St., 95501
707-445-3951
Leigh & Diane Benson
All year

$$ B&B
5 rooms, 3 pb
Visa, MC, AmEx •
C-10+/S-no/P-no/H-no

Full country breakfast
Comp. wine
Evening social hour
sitting room w/fireplace
therapeutic massage $

Historic 1871 home, graciously decorated with antiques. Historical landmark. Original home of the Williams Carson family. Close to Old Town.

FERNDALE

Ferndale Inn
P.O. Box 887, 95536
619 Main St.
707-786-4307
Danielle & Jim McManamom
All year

$$ B&B
5 rooms, 2 pb
Visa, MC, AmEx
C-8+/S-no/P-no/H-yes

Full breakfast
Comp. wine, snacks
afternoon tea
honeymoon cottage avail.
bicycles

Built in 1859, a truly relaxing Victorian setting. Great breakfast. Our antique music room includes pump organ and piano among others.

FERNDALE

Gingerbread Mansion
400 Berding St., 95536
707-786-4000
Wendy Hatfield, Ken Torbert
All year

$$$ B&B
8 rooms, 8 pb
Visa, MC •
C-10+/S-no/P-no/H-no
Port., Span., Fr., Jap.

Continental plus
Afternoon tea & cake
4 guest parlors
library w/fireplace
English gardens, bikes

Northern California's most photographed inn! Large, elegant rooms, Victorian splendor, twin clawfoot tubs ("his & her bubble baths"). Fairy tale village. Turndown w/chocolate.

Shaw House Inn
P.O. Box 1125, 95536
703 Main St.
707-786-9958
Norma & Ken Bessingpas
All year

$$ B&B
5 rooms, 2 pb
•
C-15+/S-ltd/P-no/H-no

Continental plus
Comp. wine
Sitting room
library
organ

Ferndale's elegant inn—first house built in Ferndale (1854). Antiques, fresh flowers, wine; join other guests in library, parlor, enclosed deck.

FORT BRAGG

Grey Whale Inn
615 N. Main St., 95437
707-964-0640/800-382-7244
John & Colette Bailey
All year

$$ B&B
14 rooms, 14 pb
Visa, MC, AmEx •
C-12+/S-yes/P-no/H-yes

Full buffet breakfast
Mendocino County wines
Sitting room, conf. room
TV theater room w/VCR
lounge, pool table

Historic north coast landmark. Comfortably furnished, some antiques. Ocean view suites/rooms, wheelchair suite, three kitchens. Extensive art collection.

FREESTONE

Green Apple Inn
520 Bohemian Hwy., 95472
707-874-2526
Rogers & Rosemary Hoffman
All year

$$ B&B
4 rooms, 1 pb
Visa, MC •
C-6+/H-yes
Spanish

Full breakfast
Comp. wine
Sitting room w/fireplace
bicycles

1860 farmhouse in a sunny meadow backed by redwoods. Located in a designated historic village near coast and wine country.

FREMONT

Lord Bradley's Inn
43344 Mission Blvd., 94539
Mission San Jose
415-490-0520
Keith & Anne Medeiros
All year

$$ B&B
8 rooms, 8 pb
Visa, MC
C-no/S-ltd/P-ltd/H-yes
Spanish

Continental plus
Comp. wine
Sitting room

Adjacent to historic Mission San Jose de Guadalupe; nestled below Mission Peak. Kite fliers' paradise; Victorian-decorated, gourmet breakfasts.

GEORGETOWN

American River Hotel
P.O. Box 43, 95634
Main at Orleans St.
916-333-4499
M.& W. Collin, C.& N. LaMorte
All year

$$ B&B
20 rooms, 11 pb
Visa, MC, AmEx
P-no/H-yes

Full breakfast
Evening refreshments
Barbecue, games
player piano, bicycles
hot tubs, swimming pool

An enchanting setting for weddings, honeymoons, anniversaries or retreat, corporate getaways, or just a weekend away from the world.

California 37

GEYSERVILLE

Campbell Ranch Inn
1475 Canyon Rd., 95441
707-857-3476
Mary Jane & Jerry Campbell
All year

$$$ B&B
5 rooms, 5 pb
Visa, MC •
C-10+/S-no/P-no/H-no

Full breakfast from menu
Evening bedtime snack
Sitting room, piano
tennis court, bicycles
pool, hot tub spa

35-acre rural setting in heart of Sonoma County's wine country with tennis court, swimming pool & spa. Private cottage unit. Fresh flowers, evening dessert, and homemade pie.

Hope-Merrill/
Hope-Bosworth
P.O. Box 42, 95441
21253 Geyserville Ave.
707-857-3356
Robert & Rosalie Hope
All year

$$ B&B
12 rooms, 7 pb
Visa, MC, AmEx •
C-ask/H-ltd

Full country breakfast
Comp. wine
Sitting room
library
swimming pool

Victorians in the heart of Sonoma County's wine country. Old-fashioned hospitality; delicious food. Unique Stage-A-Picnic in the vineyards.

GILROY

Country Rose Inn-A B&B
P.O. Box 1804, 95021
455 Fitzgerald Ave.
408-842-0441
Rose M. Hernandez
All year

$$ B&B
5 rooms, 5 pb
Visa, MC •
C-no/S-no/P-no/H-no
Spanish

Continental plus
Afternoon tea
Sitting room, library
grand piano, porch
horseshoes, shuffle brd

Rural, secluded B&B featuring serenity, antiques. Near Gilroy Garlic Festival, county airport, ballooning, hiking, bicycling. Pivotal to Yosemite, San Francisco, Monterey.

Valley Lodge, Carmel Valley, CA

GLEN ELLEN

Glenelly Inn	$$$ B&B	Full breakfast
5131 Warm Springs Rd., 95442	8 rooms, 8 pb	Comp. wine & cheese
707-996-6720	Visa, MC •	Sitting room
Gray & Addie Mattox	S-ltd	fireplace
All year	some French	reading material

Serene setting in the heart of Sonoma wine country. Old oaks and spacious lawns. Close to Jack London State Park. 1½ hours from San Francisco.

GRASS VALLEY

Swan-Levine House	$$ B&B	Full breakfast
328 S. Church St., 95945	4 rooms, 1 pb	Sitting rooms, piano
916-272-1873	Visa, MC	swimming pool
Howard & Margaret Levine	C-yes/S-no/P-ask/H-no	badminton, art gallery
All year		printmaking

1880 Queen Anne Victorian. Guests may observe and participate in the process of printmaking. Surrounded by park and museum sites.

GUALALA

Gualala Hotel	$ B&B	Continental breakfast
P.O. Box 675, 95445	19 rooms, 5 pb	Dinner
39301 S. Hwy. 1	Visa, MC	Complimentary wine
707-884-3441	C-yes/S-no/P-no/H-no	Sitting room, piano
Howard E. Curtis		
All year		

Historic 1903 hotel, overlooking the ocean, furnished with original antiques. Extensive wine shop, family-style meals.

North Coast Country Inn	$$$ B&B	Full breakfast
34591 S. Highway 1, 95445	4 rooms, 4 pb	Wet bar in all rooms
707-884-4537	Visa, MC •	Hot tub, library, gazebo
Loren & Nancy Flanagan	C-12+/S-no/P-no/H-no	antique shop, fireplaces
All year		beach access

A cluster of weathered redwood buildings on a forested hillside overlooking the Pacific Ocean. Close to golf, tennis and riding facilities. Antique shop at inn.

Whale Watch Inn by the Sea	$$$ B&B	Full breakfast
35100 Hwy. 1, 95445	18 rooms, 18 pb	Comp. wine
707-884-3667	Visa, MC, AmEx	Lounge w/fireplace
All year	C-no/S-no/P-no/H-no	

Intimate, private contemporary hideaway on Anchor Bay bluff. Sweeping ocean views. Fireplaces, individual spas, private decks. Breakfast delivered to guests' rooms.

GUERNEVILLE

Ridenhour Ranch House Inn	$$ B&B	Full gourmet breakfast
12850 River Rd., 95446	8 rooms, 5 pb	Dinner $ weekends
707-887-1033	Visa, MC •	comp. wine
Rick Jewell	C-10+/S-ltd/P-no/H-yes	Picnic lunches, hot tub
All year exc. Jan & Feb		sitting room, fireplace

Country inn on the Russian River in the heart of the lush and lovely Sonoma wine country. Adjacent to historic Korbel Champagne Cellars. Fresh flowers.

GUERNEVILLE

Santanella House	$$$ B&B	Full breakfast
12130 Hwy. 116, 95446	4 rooms, 4 pb	Comp. wine, snacks
707-869-9488	C-no/S-no/P-no/H-yes	Hot tub
Alan & Joyce Ferrington		sitting room, library
All year		2 rooms w/fireplaces

Redwood-surrounded winemaster's home across from Chardonnay vineyard. Covered veranda, woodstove heat, wine cellar. Near Russian River and Korbel Cellars.

HALF MOON BAY

Mill Rose Inn	$$$ B&B	Full breakfast
615 Mill St., 94019	6 rooms, 6 pb	Comp. tea, wine
415-726-9794	major credit cards •	Sitting room, cable TV
Eve & Terry Baldwin	C-12+/S-no/P-no/H-no	fireplaces & spas in rms
All year	French, Spanish	bicycles, phones

Exquisitely appointed flower-filled rooms and suites with private bath, entrance. English country rose garden by the sea. Perfect for weddings, business meetings.

Old Thyme Inn	$$ B&B	Full breakfast
779 Main St., 94019	6 rooms, 4 pb	Comp. wine
415-726-1616	Visa, MC •	Library
Simon & Anne Lowings	C-ltd/S-ltd/P-no/H-no	sitting room
All year	French	herb garden

1890 Victorian with herb garden on historic Main Street. Some private baths with large whirlpool tubs, fireplaces. Great breakfasts.

San Benito House	$$ B&B	Continental plus
356 Main St., 94019	12 rooms, 9 pb	Lunch, dinner, bar
415-726-3425	credit cards ok •	Sauna, sun deck
Carol Mickelsen	C-no/S-yes/P-no/H-no	croquet, gardens
All year	Portuguese	

A romantic bed and breakfast just south of San Francisco. Historic inn, gourmet restaurant, western-style saloon and garden-deli cafe.

HEALDSBURG

Calderwood	$$$ B&B	Full breakfast
25 W. Grant St., 95448	5 rooms, 5 pb	Comp. wine
P.O. Box 967	ask when making res. •	Afternoon tea, snacks
707-431-1110	S-no/P-no/H-no	Sitting room
Bob & Chris Maxwell		
All year		

Gracious Queen Anne Victorian furnished with antiques; gardens; gourmet breakfast, afternoon tea. Close to the Russian River and numerous wineries.

Camellia Inn	$$ B&B	Full breakfast
211 North St., 95448	9 rooms, 7 pb	Comp. wine & cheese
707-433-8182	Visa, MC •	Sitting room
Del & Ray Lewand	C-ltd/S-yes/P-no/H-ltd	swimming pool, 2 rooms
All year		w/fireplace & jacuzzi

Elegant Italianate Victorian built 1869, near Sonoma's finest wineries—beautifully restored and furnished with antiques, oriental rugs.

40 California

Frampton House
489 Powell Ave., 95448
707-433-5084
Paula S. Bogle
All year

$$ B&B
3 rooms, 3 pb
Visa, MC •
C-yes/S-no/P-no/H-no
Spanish

Full breakfast
Snacks, comp. wine
Library, sitting room
hot tub, sauna, pool
bicycles, entertainment

An escape from the ordinary. Emphasis on privacy and service. Centrally located for wine country and Sonoma coast. Lavish breakfast.

The Haydon House
321 Haydon St., 95448
707-433-5228
Richard & Joanne Claus
January—mid-December

$$ B&B
8 rooms, 4 pb
Visa, MC •
C-12+/S-ltd/P-no/H-no
French

Full breakfast
Two parlors
organ
Victorian cottage

Intimate, beautifully restored & furnished Queen Anne in heart of wine country. Well-known for abundant country-style breakfast. Attention to detail is our hallmark.

Healdsburg Inn
P.O. Box 1196, 95448
116 Matheson St.
707-433-6991
Dyanne Celi, Genny Jenkins
All year

$$$ B&B
9 rooms, 9 pb
Visa, MC, AmEx •
C-7+/S-ltd/P-no/H-no

Full breakfast
Wine tasting (Fri. eve.)
Champagne brunch (wkend)
Rooftop garden, gift shop
gallery, fireplaces

Individually appointed Victorian rooms. Centrally located overlooking old town plaza. Breakfast served on airy roof garden.

Madrona Manor-Country Inn
1001 Westside Rd., 95448
P.O. Box 818
707-433-4231
John & Carol Muir
All year

$$$ B&B
20 rooms, 20 pb
Visa, MC, AmEx, DC, CB •
C-yes/S-yes/P-ltd/H-yes
Spanish

Full breakfast
Gourmet restaurant
Music room, robes
antique rosewood piano
swimming pool, billiards

Circa 1881, furnished with antiques. All rooms with private baths. Carriage house. Wine country, canoeing, bicycling, historical points of interest. February "daffodil" month.

Raford House
10630 Wohler Rd., 95448
707-887-9573
Alan Baitinger & Beth Foster
All year

$$ B&B
7 rooms, 5 pb
Visa, MC •
C-ltd/S-ltd/P-no/H-ltd

Continental plus
Bicycles

Victorian farmhouse overlooks the vineyards of Sonoma County. Country setting just ½ hour away from San Francisco. County historical landmark.

Strawberry Creek Inn
P.O. Box 1818, 92349
26370 State Hwy 243
714-659-3202
Diana Dugan, Jim Goff
All year

$$ B&B
9 rooms, 7 pb
Visa, MC
C-no/S-no/P-no/H-ltd

Full breakfast
Comp. wine in afternoon
Library, fireplaces
sitting room
refrigerators

Country inn located in the pines where comfort mixes with nostalgia in a uniquely decorated home. Many hiking trails, quiet walks along the creek.

INVERNESS

Blackthorne Inn
P.O. Box 712, 94937
266 Vallejo Ave.
415-663-8621
Susan Hemphill Wigert
All year

$$$ B&B
5 rooms, 5 pb
Visa, MC •
C-no/S-ltd/P-no/H-no

Full breakfast buffet
Comp. tea, sherry
wet bar sink area
Sitting room w/fireplace
hot tub

Sunset Magazine (April 1983) describes the Blackthorne Inn as "a carpenter's fantasy, with decks, hot tub, fireman's pole, and spiral staircase."

Dancing Coyote Beach
P.O. Box 98, 94937
12794 Sir Francis Drake
415-669-7200
Kay Ramsey
All year

$$$ B&B
3 rooms, 3 pb
Visa, MC •
C-yes/P-no/H-no

Full breakfast
Coffee & tea
Popcorn poppers
fireplace, kitchen, deck
living room, library

The best of both worlds... Privacy while being catered to. Three lovely, fully equipped cottages nestled among pines on secluded beach. A unique bed & breakfast.

Fairwinds Farm B&B
82 Drake's Summit, 94937
P.O. Box 581
415-663-9454
Joyce H. Goldfield
All year

$$$ B&B
1 rooms, 1 pb
•
C-yes/S-no/P-no/H-no
Sign language

Full breakfast
Afternoon tea, snacks
Full kitchen, library
TV, stereo, fireplace
hot tubs, garden w/pond

One large cottage sleeps 6. Ridge-top cottage adjoins 68,000-acre National Seashore. Ocean view from hot tub. Fireplace, garden with ponds and swing. Barnyard animals.

Holly Tree Inn
3 Silverhills Rd., 94956
Box 642, Pt. Reyes Sta.
415-663-1554
Diane & Tom Balogh
All year

$$$ B&B
5 rooms, 5 pb
Visa, MC •
C-ltd/S-ltd/P-no/H-no

Hearty country breakfast
Comp. sherry, tea
Sitting room
fireplaces

Romantic country inn on 19 acres in a coastal valley near San Francisco. Breakfast by the curved hearth. Herb gardens.

Rosemary Cottage
Box 619, 94937
75 Balboa Ave.
415-663-9338
Suzanne Storch
All year

$$$ B&B
1 rooms, 1 pb
C-yes/S-yes/P-no/H-no

Full breakfast
Comp. tea, coffee
Kitchen
Decks, fireplace
garden

Charming, romantic French country cottage nestled in secluded garden with dramatic forest views. Close to beaches; families welcome.

Ten Inverness Way
P.O. Box 63, 94937
10 Inverness Way
415-669-1648
Mary E. Davies
All year

$$$ B&B
4 rooms, 4 pb
•
C-ltd/S-ltd/P-no/H-no
French, Spanish

Full breakfast
Comp. sherry
Sitting room
library, piano
hot tub (by appointment)

A classic bed and breakfast inn for lovers of handmade quilts, hearty breakfasts, great hikes and good books.

IONE

The Heirloom	$$ B&B	Full breakfast
P.O. Box 322, 95640	6 rooms, 4 pb	Complimentary tea, wine
214 Shakeley Ln.	•	Sitting room, piano
209-274-4468	C-12+/S-yes/P-no/H-yes	bicycles, croquet
Pat Cross, Melisande Hubbs		fireplaces, balconies
All year		

Petite 1863 colonial mansion—private garden setting, verandas, fireplaces, heirloom antiques, French country breakfast, comfort, gracious hospitality. Private dinners.

JACKSON

Gate House Inn	$$ B&B	Continental plus
1330 Jackson Gate Rd., 95642	5 rooms, 5 pb	Screened BBQ room
209-223-3500	Visa, MC •	Sitting room
Stan & Bev Smith	C-ltd/S-no/P-no/H-ltd	swimming pool
All year		greenhouse, gardens

Stately 1900 Victorian in original prime condition with one acre of beautiful landscaped gardens. The only one of its kind in county.

Wedgewood Inn	$$$ B&B	Full gourmet breakfast
11941 Narcissus Rd., 95642	6 rooms, 6 pb	Snacks, comp. wine
209-296-4300	Visa, MC, Discover •	Sitting room
Vic & Jeannine Beltz	C-no/S-no/P-no/H-no	porch
All year		

Charming replica Victorian tucked away on wooded acreage. Antique decor, afternoon refreshments, porch swing, wood burning stoves. Full gourmet breakfast.

JAMESTOWN

National Hotel/Restaurant	$ B&B	Continental
P.O. Box 502, 95327	11 rooms, 5 pb	Full restaurant, bar
Main St.	Visa, MC •	
209-984-3446	C-8+/S-yes/P-no/H-no	
S. Willey, P. Peterson	Spanish	
All year		

Ambience and nostalgia of Gold Rush Days blended with 20th-century comfort. Restaurant recognized in Bon Appetit.

JULIAN

Butterfield B&B	$$ B&B	Full breakfast
P.O. Box 1115, 92036	5 rooms, 1 pb	Afternoon tea, snacks
2284 Sunset Dr.	C-no/S-no/P-no/H-yes	Lunch & dinner for
619-765-2179		weddings
Raymond Trimmins		Victorian wedding gazebo
All year		

Gourmet breakfast, weddings in Victorian Wedding Gazebo with patio receptions. Christmas every day in Santa's Cottage. Wooded mountain setting; walking, hiking, biking.

Julian Gold Rush Hotel	$$ B&B	Full breakfast
P.O. Box 1856, 92036	18 rooms, 5 pb	Dining room
2032 Main St.	•	Sitting room, piano
619-765-0201	C-ltd/S-yes/P-no/H-no	cottage
Steve & Gig Ballinger		
All year		

Sole surviving hotel in the southern mother lode of California, restored to its full glory in genuine American antiques. All original guest rooms are now open.

KELSEY

Mountainside B&B
P.O. Box 165, 95643
5821 Spanish Flat Rd.
916-626-0983
Paul & Mary Mello
All year

$$ B&B
4 rooms, 3 pb
•
C-10+/S-ltd/P-no/H-no

Full breakfast
Comp. beverage
Sitting room
library
hot tubs

1929 country home, 80-acre wooded retreat. 180-degree view of Sacramento Valley. Dorm for groups available. River rafting, ballooning, gold country.

KLAMATH

Requa Inn
451 Requa Rd., 95548
707-482-8205
Paul Homby
March—October

$ B&B
15 rooms, 15 pb
Visa, MC, AmEx
C-no/S-yes/P-no/H-no

Full breakfast
Restaurant, dinner
Afternoon tea
beer & wine available
Sitting room

Located on majestic Klamath River in Redwood National Park. A relaxing, romantic retreat. Stroll through woods, swim, boat, or fish. Wonderful dining.

LA JOLLA

Irish Cottage
5623 Taft Ave., 92037
619-454-6075.
Mary Kaye Miller
All year ex. Thnks, Xmas

$$ B&B
2 rooms, 2 pb
•
C-no/S-no/P-no/H-no
Irish

Full breakfast
Comp. wine

Charming antique-filled cottage within walking distance of ocean. Close to restaurants. French doors open onto flower-filled patio. Quiet neighborhood. Half-hour to Old Mexico.

Prospect Park Inn
1110 Prospect St., 92037
619-454-0133
Brigitte Schmidt
All year

$$$ B&B
25 rooms, 25 pb
Visa, MC, AmEx •
C-yes/S-yes/P-no/H-no
Ger., Sp,. Fr., Flem.

Continental breakfast
Afternoon tea
Sitting room
AC in all rooms & suites

In the heart of La Jolla, this small hotel recaptures an era of charm and graciousness. Most rooms offer spectacular ocean views.

LAGUNA BEACH

Carriage House
1322 Catalina St., 92651
714-494-8945
Dee, Vernon & Tom Taylor
All year

$$$ B&B
10 rooms, 10 pb
•
C-yes/S-yes/P-ltd/H-no

Continental plus
Comp. wine
Ocean swimming

Colonial New Orleans-style carriage house with central brick courtyard, tropical landscaping. Six suites each with sitting room, bedroom, bath.

Casa Laguna Inn
2510 South Coast Hwy, 92651
714-494-2996
Jerry & Luanne Siegel
All year

$$$ B&B
20 rooms, 20 pb
Visa, MC, AmEx, DC •
C-yes/S-yes/P-no/H-no

Continental plus
Aftn tea/wine/appetizers
Sitting room
library, entertainment
heated swimming pool

Panoramic ocean views and Spanish architecture. Gardens, heated pool, landmark "Bell Tower." Continental plus breakfast, tea/wine, light snacks, live music.

44   California

LAGUNA BEACH ————————————————————————————————

Eiler's Inn
741 South Coast Hwy, 92651
714-494-3004
Henk & Annette Wirtz
All year

$$$ B&B
12 rooms, 12 pb
Visa, MC, AmEx •
C-ltd/S-yes/P-no/H-no
German, French, Dutch

Continental plus
Comp. wine
Sitting room

Romantic country inn, ocean ½ block, walking distance to village. Courtyard and fountain where breakfast, wine and cheese are served.

Spray Cliff
P.O. Box 403, 92677
714-499-4022
Loreli Iske
All year

$$$ B&B
2 rooms, 2 pb
•
C-yes/S-no/P-no/H-no

Full breakfast
Sitting room
private balconies

Romantic oceanfront. View pelicans, dolphins, Catalina sunsets from canopy bed. Private balcony for candlelit dining or sunbathing. Secluded sandy beach, lapping waves.

LAKE ARROWHEAD ————————————————————————————

Chateau Du Lac
911 Hospital Rd., 92352
P.O. Box 1098
714-337-6488
Jody & Oscar Wilson
All year

$$$ B&B
6 rooms, 4 pb
Visa, MC, AmEx •
C-no/S-no/P-no/H-no

Full breakfast
Comp. wine, tea, snacks
Dinner by appointment
Sitting room, library
hot tubs in room

The Chateau du Lac overlooks a beautiful view of Lake Arrowhead. It's a warm and friendly place to stay. We do weddings, showers, and birthday parties, too.

Eagles Landing
P.O. Box 1510, Blue Jay, 92317
27406 Cedarwood
714-336-2642
Dorothy & Jack Stone
All year

$$ B&B
4 rooms, 4 pb
•
C-16+/S-no/P-no/H-no

Continental plus
Comp. wine
Picnic lunches
Catered dinner in suite
Sitting room

Enjoy home-style hospitality in an atmosphere reminiscent of a cozy European mountain inn. Decks overlook beautiful Lake Arrowhead. Year-round fun.

Romantique Lakeview Lodge
P.O. Box 128, 92352
28051 Hwy 189
714-337-6633
All year

$$$ B&B
8 rooms, 8 pb
Visa, MC, AmEx
C-10+/S-no/P-no/H-yes
Spanish

Continental plus
Snacks, comp. wine
Afternoon tea
Sitting room, library
TV, VCR & movies in room

Furnished with original antiques, crystal, lace, luxurious baths. Nestled in mountains at beautiful Lake Arrowhead. Breathtaking panoramic view. Walk to restaurants and shops.

LEMON COVE ——————————————————————————————————

Lemon Cove B&B Inn
33038 Sierra Hwy., 93244
209-597-2555
Pat & Kay Bonette
All year

$ B&B
6 rooms, 3 pb
Visa, MC •
C-no/S-no/P-no/H-no
Spanish

Large country breakfast
Comp. wine, snacks
Sitting room
pool
whirlpool

Country home nestled in fragrant orange groves. Conveniently located by Sequoia Parks. Delicious surprise breakfast served in elegant dinning room.

LITTLE RIVER

Victorian Farmhouse
P.O. Box 357, 95456
7001 N. Hwy 1
707-937-0697
George & Carol Molnar
All year

$$$ B&B
10 rooms, 7 pb
•
C-10+ /S-ltd/P-no/H-no
Hungarian

Continental plus
Comp. wine & sherry
Sitting room
7 rooms w/fireplace

Built in 1877; short walk to the ocean. Enjoy deer, flower gardens, creek, or sitting in our small orchard. Quiet atmosphere.

LONG BEACH

Crane's Nest
319 W. 12th St., 90813
213-435-4084/213-436-4499
Ione Washburn
All year

$$ B&B
3 rooms, 1 pb
Visa, MC
C-12+ /S-ltd/P-no/H-no

Continental plus
Restaurant nearby
Afternoon tea on request
Sitting room
Japanese garden

Turn-of-the-century setting with Oriental flavor. In historic district near downtown Long Beach. Relax in Japanese garden by waterfall.

LOS ALMOS

1880 Union Hotel
P.O. Box 616, 93440
362 Bell St.
805-344-2744
Dick
All year

$$$ B&B
22 rooms, 9 pb
•
C-no/S-yes/H-no

Full breakfast
Restaurant, dinner, bar
Sitting room, library
hot tubs, pool, billards
tours in 1918 tour car

Step back in time. . .choose your own world, either the ambience of the old hotel or the house of make-believe. Then experience it.

LOS ANGELES

Channel Road Inn
219 W. Channel Rd., 90402
Santa Monica
213-459-1920
Susan Zolla
All year

$$$ B&B
14 rooms, 14 pb
Visa, MC •
C-yes/S-yes/P-no/H-yes
Spanish, French, German

Continental plus (wkdys)
Full breakfast (Sunday)
Aftn. tea, comp. wine
Sitting room, library
bicycles, hot tubs

Elegant historic home converted to luxury inn. Located one block from the sea and furnished in period antiques.

Eastlake Victorian Inn
1442 Kellam Ave., 90026
213-250-1620
Murray Burns, Planaria Price
All year

$$ B&B
8 rooms, 3 pb
•
C-12+ /S-ltd/P-no/H-no
French

Full breakfast
Comp. tea/wine/sherry
Sitting room, garden
occas. chamber concerts
Greek revival gazebo

1887 elegant Victorian, authentic antiques, hilltop historic residential district three min. from downtown L.A. Best central location; hot air balloon flights.

Salisbury House
2273 W. 20th St., 90018
213-737-7817
Sue & Jay German
All year

$$ B&B
5 rooms, 3 pb
Visa, MC, AmEx •
C-10+ /S-ltd/P-no/H-no

Full gourmet breakfast
Comp. wine
Sitting room

Experience the ultimate in bed and breakfast luxury and turn-of-the-century charm. Has been used as location for movies and commercials.

46 California

LOS ANGELES

Terrace Manor
1353 Alvarado Terrace, 90006
213-381-1478
Sandy & Shirley Spillman
All year

$$ B&B
5 rooms, 5 pb
•
C-8+/S-ltd/P-no/H-no

Full breakfast
Comp. wine
Sitting room w/TV
magic shows, passes to
private Hollywood club

Listed on National Register of Historic Places. Furnished with antiques. Original 1902 stained glass. Guests may visit Hollywood private club.

West Adams B&B Inn
1650 Westmoreland Blvd., 90006
213-737-5041
Jon Rake, Jeffrey Stvrtecky
All year

$$$ B&B
3 rooms, 1 pb
Visa, MC, AmEx •
C-yes/S-ltd/P-no/H-no
Spanish, French

Full gourmet breakfast
Afternoon tea, snacks
Sitting room
library, historic tours
off-street parking

Elegance and charm in splendid 1913 Craftsman home near downtown, convention center. Themed rooms, antiques, spectacular fireplace, extraordinary original beds.

MAMMOTH LAKES

Snow Goose B&B Inn
P.O. Box 946, 93546
57 Forest Trail
619-934-2660/800-874-7368
Wes & Laurie Johnson
All year

$$ B&B
20 rooms, 20 pb
Visa, MC, AmEx •
C-yes/S-yes/P-yes/H-no

Full breakfast
Comp. wine
Sitting room
bicycles
hot tubs

Winter ski resort/Sierra's summer getaway—European-style deluxe mountain bed and breakfast. Offering special ski packages midweek.

Tamarack Lodge Retreat
P.O. Box 69, 93546
Twin Lakes Rd.
619-934-2442
Carol & David Watson
All year

$$ EP
37 rooms, 31 pb
Visa, MC •
C-yes/S-ltd/P-no/H-ltd

Full breakfast $
Restaurant, lunch/dinner
Afternoon tea, snacks
Sitting room
boats (summ), ski (wint)

Historic High Sierra lakeside lodge; regionally acclaimed Lakefront Restaurant. Major cross-country ski resort in winter; four-season fishing, hiking, biking.

MARIPOSA

Granny's Garden B&B
7333 Hwy. 49 N., 95338
209-377-8342
Dave & Dixie Trabucco
May—October

$$$ B&B
3 rooms, 1 pb
Visa, MC •
C-12+/S-yes/P-no/H-no
Spanish

Continental plus
Comp. coffee/tea/wine
Sitting room/sun porch
gazebo, antiques, spa
flower-filled garden

Yosemite National Park is one hour's drive from this 1896 Victorian farmhouse. Spa, gazebo, sun porch, flower-filled gardens, antiques. Very romantic.

Meadow Creek Ranch Inn
2669 Triangle & Hwy 49S, 95338
209-966-3843
Bob & Carol Shockley
All year

$$ B&B
4 rooms, 1 pb
Visa, MC, AmEx, •
C-ltd/S-ltd/P-no/H-no
Spanish

Full breakfast
Comp. appetizers
Sitting room
airport pickup
antiques

Originally an 1858 stagecoach stop on the Golden Chain Highway. Front door to Yosemite National Park. Furnished with European and country antiques.

MARIPOSA ─────────────────────────────

Oak Meadows, II B&B $$ B&B   Continental plus
5263 Hwy 140 N., 95338   6 rooms, 6 pb   Sitting room
P.O. Box 619   Visa, MC •
209-742-6161   C-yes/S-no/P-no/H-no
Don & Francie Starchman
All year

Relax in luxury. Located in town. Near Yosemite. Rooms decorated with brass beds and handmade quilts. All private baths.

Pelennor B&B $ B&B   Full breakfast
3871 Hwy. 49 S., 95338   4 rooms   Kitchen
209-966-2832   •   Sitting room
Dick & Gwendolyn Foster   C-yes/S-ltd/P-ltd/H-ltd   spa & lap pool
All year

Quiet country accommodations at economical rates. Enjoy the stars while listening to a tune on the bagpipes.

MCCLOUD ─────────────────────────────

McCloud Guest House $$ B&B   Continental plus
P.O. Box 1510, 96057   5 rooms, 5 pb   Restaurant, dinner
606 W. Colombero Dr.   Visa, MC   Comp. sherry
916-964-3160   C-no/S-ltd/P-no/H-no   Antique pool table
The Leighs & The Abreus   library, bicycles
All year

Completely restored 1907 country inn & restaurant near Mt. Shasta. Former guests include: President Hoover, Jean Harlow and the Hearst Family.

MENDOCINO ─────────────────────────────

Agate Cove Inn B&B $$ B&B   Full country breakfast
P.O. Box 1150, 95460   10 rooms, 10 pb   Comp. wine
11201 Lansing St.   Visa, MC, AmEx   Common room w/antiques
707-937-0551   C-12+ /S-ltd/P-ltd/H-no   spectacular ocean views
Jake/Sallie McConnell Zahavi
All year

Private cottages with fireplaces & ocean views. Near Mendocino-North Coast arts center. Whale watching November-March. Winter mid-week discounts November 1-April 30.

Brewery Gulch Inn $$ B&B   Full country breakfast
9350 Highway One, 95460   5 rooms, 4 pb   Sitting room
707-937-4752   Visa, MC, AmEx •   fireplaces
Leo & Gen Pallanck   C-no/S-no/P-no/H-no   down pillows
All year   gardens

Brewery Gulch is unhurried. Authentic pre-Victorian farm surrounded by two acres of flowers and tree gardens. Full country breakfast served when you want it.

Cypress House $$$ B&B   Full breakfast
P.O. Box 303, 95460   1 rooms, 1 pb   Comp. brandy
45250 Chapman Dr.   German, French, Spanish   Basket of fruit
707-937-1456   Sitting room
Pamela Lopresto   library, stereo
All year

A private garden cottage just for two overlooking Mendocino Bay and Village. Fireplace; hot tub; down comforter; fresh flowers and much more!

Gingerbread Mansion, Ferndale, CA

MENDOCINO

Headlands Inn	$$$ B&B	Full breakfast to room
P.O. Box 132, 95460	5 rooms, 5 pb	Comp. wine, min. water
Howard St. at Albion	C-16+/S-no/P-no/H-ltd	2 guest parlors
707-937-4431	Limited Spanish	antique piano, organ
Pat & Rod Stofle		English-style garden
All year		

Restored 1868 Victorian home with unusual period antiques in picturesque Mendocino Village. All rooms have private baths, fireplaces, and Q/K beds. Many have ocean views.

Joshua Grindle Inn	$$ B&B	Full breakfast
P.O. Box 647, 95460	10 rooms, 10 pb	Comp. wine
44800 Little Lake Rd.	C-no/S-no/P-no/H-yes	Sitting room
707-937-4143		piano
James & Arlene Moorehead		
All year		

Historic country charm in coastal village of Mendocino. Antiques, fireplaces, private baths. Near shops, galleries, restaurants. OUR 1985 INN OF THE YEAR!

MENDOCINO

MacCallum House Inn	$ B&B	Continental breakfast
P.O. Box 206, 95460	20 rooms, 8 pb	Restaurant, bar
45020 Albion St.	Visa, MC •	Sitting room
707-937-0289	C-yes/S-yes/P-no/H-no	
Melanie & Joe Reding		
All year		

The MacCallum House provides friendly, personal attention to guests in handsome, authentically restored Victorian home in the village of Mendocino.

Mendocino Village Inn	$$ B&B	Full breakfast
P.O. Box 626, 95460	12 rooms, 10 pb	Comp. wine
44860 Main St.	Visa, MC	Sitting room
707-937-0246	C-10+/S-no/P-no/H-no	library
Sue & Tom Allen	Spanish, Japanese	
All year		

Hummingbirds, Picassos, Navajo rugs, fireplaces, French roast coffee, Vivaldi, four-poster beds, migrating whales, scones, fuchsias, 12-ft. ceilings. Newly restored.

Stanford Inn by the Sea	$$$ B&B	Continental plus
P.O. Box 487, 95460	25 rooms, 25 pb	Comp. wine
Hwy 1, Comptche-Ukiah Rd.	Visa, MC, AmEx, CB, DC	Sitting room, telephones
707-937-5615	C-yes/S-yes/P-yes/H-yes	nurseries, llamas
Joan & Jeff Stanford	French, Spanish	bicycles, canoes
All year		

A truly elegant country inn in a pastoral setting. All accommodations with ocean views, fireplaces, decks, antiques, four-posters and TVs.

Whitegate Inn	$$ B&B	Full breakfast
P.O. Box 150, 95460	5 rooms, 5 pb	Comp. wine
499 Howard St.	C-13+/S-no/P-no/H-no	Deck with gazebo
707-937-4892		sitting room
Patricia Patton		old organ
All year		

Located in historic Mendocino, one of the town's more elegant homes, all rooms furnished with antiques.

MILL VALLEY

Mountain Home Inn	$$$ B&B	Continental plus
810 Panoramic Hwy., 94941	10 rooms, 10 pb	Lunch, dinner, wine/beer
415-381-9000	Visa, MC •	Jacuzzis
Ed & Susan Cunningham	C-ltd/S-yes/P-no/H-yes	hiking trails
All year		

Two-and-a-half-million-dollar restored classic California luxury inn. Adjacent to parklands, Muir Woods. Panoramic S.F. Bay views; jacuzzis, fireplaces, terraces.

MIRAMAR

Cypress Inn	$$$ B&B	Full breakfast
407 Mirada Rd., 94019	8 rooms, 8 pb	Afternoon tea
415-726-6002	Visa, MC, AmEx •	Comp. wine, snacks
Victoria Platt, Michael Fogli	C-yes/S-ltd/P-no/H-yes	Sitting room
All year		hot tubs

Beachfront luxury—spectacular views from each room. Deck, fireplaces, gourmet breakfast. 5 miles of sandy beach. Fine dining, shopping, golf and jazz nearby.

50   California

MONTARA

Goose & Turrets
P.O. Box 370937, 94037
835 George St.
415-728-5451
Raymond & Emily Hoche-Mong
All year

$$$ B&B
5 rooms, 2 pb
Visa, MC, AmEx •
C-yes/P-no
French

Full breakfast
Afternoon tea, snacks
Sitting room w/woodstove
gardens
airport pickup

Solitude. Bonhomie. Cozy down comforters, towel warmers, and fantastic breakfasts. 30 minutes from San Francisco; ½ mile from Pacific Ocean.

MONTEREY

Charlaine's Bay View B&B
44 Sierra Vista Dr., 93940
408-655-0177
Charles & Charlaine Carter
All year

$$$ B&B
2 rooms, 1 pb
C-13+/S-ltd/P-yes/H-yes
Spanish

Continental plus
Comp. wine
Sitting room
access to clubs, tennis,
and golf

In the heart of Monterey, Carmel, Pebble Beach and Big Sur. Panoramic bay view! Golf, tennis, whale watching, hiking, aquarium, fishing all year.

The Jabberwock
598 Laine St., 93940
408-372-4777
Jim & Barbara Allen
All year

$$$ B&B
7 rooms, 3 pb
C-no/S-ltd/P-no/H-no
Spanish, French, Danish

Full breakfast
Sherry & hors d'oeuvres
Sitting room

Once a convent, this Victorian home is above Cannery Row. Sherry on the sun porch overlooking Monterey Bay, gardens & waterfalls. Near Monterey Bay Aquarium.

Old Monterey Inn
500 Martin St., 93940
408-375-8284
Ann & Gene Swett
All year

$$$ B&B
10 rooms, 10 pb
C-16+/S-no/P-no/H-no

Full breakfast
Comp. beverages anytime
Sitting room

An architectural gem in a forestlike setting, the inn is a charming English country house with a unique sense of history and romance.

MUIR BEACH

Pelican Inn
10 Pacific Way, 94965
415-383-6000
Charles Felix
All year

$$$ B&B
6 rooms, 6 pb
Visa, MC
C-ltd/S-yes/P-no/H-ltd

Full English breakfast
Comp. sherry
Sitting room
piano
entertainment

Romantic English inn, between ocean and redwoods, capturing the spirit of the 16th century. Only 20 minutes from Golden Gate Bridge.

MURPHYS

Dunbar House, 1880
P.O. Box 1375, 95247
271 Jones St.
209-728-2897
Barbara & Bob Costa
All year

$$$ B&B
5 rooms, 5 pb
Visa, MC •
C-10+/S-no/P-no/H-no

Full country breakfast
Comp. wine & snacks
Sitting room
wood-burning stoves
clawfoot tubs

Restored 1880 home with historical designation located in Murphys, Queen of the Sierra. Walking distance to Main Street. A place to be pampered.

NAPA

Coombs Residence Inn	$$$ B&B	Continental breakfast
720 Seminary St., 94559	4 rooms, 1 pb	Comp. beverages, cheese
707-257-0789	Visa, MC •	Sitting rooms, fireplace
Pearl & Dave Campbell	C-no/S-no/P-no/H-no	piano, bicycles, TV
All year	Spanish	swimming pool, hot tub

Victorian splendor. A home with a personality of its own. European style with down comforters and pillows, terry robes and lots of TLC.

Country Garden Inn	$$$ B&B	Full breakfast
1815 Silverado Trail, 94558	10 rooms, 6 pb	Comp. wine, tea
707-255-1197	Visa, MC, AmEx •	Snacks, jacuzzi, decks
Lisa & George Smith	C-no/S-no/P-no/H-yes	Sitting room
All year		private hot tubs

The Country Garden, on 1½ acres of woodland riverside property is decorated in a very English style with antiques and heirlooms, and of course, true English hospitality.

Crossroads Inn	$$$ B&B	Continental plus
6380 Silverado Trail, 94558	3 rooms, 3 pb	Comp. wine, snacks
707-944-0646	Visa, MC	Afternoon tea
N.& S. Scott, R.& G. Maxwells	C-14+/S-no/P-no/H-no	Sitting room, library
All year		bicycles, hot tubs

Sweeping Napa Valley views; custom 2-person spas; complete privacy; king-sized beds, wine bars and full baths complement each suite.

Napa Inn	$$$ B&B	Full breakfast
1137 Warren St., 94559	4 rooms, 4 pb	Afternoon refreshments
707-257-1444	C-16+/S-no/P-no/H-no	Homebaked breads & cakes
Doug & Carol Morales		Sitting room w/fireplace
All year		antiques, gardens

Beautiful, old Queen Anne Victorian furnished with antiques. Located on quiet street in the old historical area of Napa. Conveniently located to wineries and restaurants.

NEVADA CITY

Downey House B&B	$$ B&B	Full breakfast
517 W. Broad St., 95959	6 rooms, 6 pb	Afternoon tea
916-265-2815	Visa, MC •	Snacks
Miriam Wright	C-12+	Sitting room
All year		library

Light, comfortable view rooms. Lovely garden and terrace. Very near fine restaurants, shops, theaters, galleries, museums and outdoor recreational facilities.

Grandmere's Inn	$$$ B&B	Full breakfast
449 Broad St., 95959	6 rooms, 6 pb	Dinner by arrangement
916-265-4660	Visa, MC	Sitting room
Annette Meade	C-ltd/S-no/P-no/H-ltd	
All year		

Historic landmark with country French decor in the heart of Nevada City. Lovely grounds suitable for weddings and private parties.

NEVADA CITY

Piety Hill Inn
523 Sacramento St., 95959
916-265-2245
Barbara & Trieve Tanner
All year

$$ B&B
7 rooms, 7 pb
Visa, MC •
C-12+/S-yes/P-no/H-yes
French, German

Full breakfast
Comp. wine & sherry
Flowers, candy
garden, barbecue
gazebo shaded spa

Quaint, uniquely decorated cottages offer quiet seclusion in a grassy garden setting. Breakfast brought to you! Historic Nevada City a short walk.

Red Castle Inn
109 Prospect St., 95959
916-265-5135
Conley & Mary Louise Weaver
All year

$$ B&B
8 rooms, 6 pb
•
C-ltd/S-ltd/P-no/H-no

Full buffet breakfast
Formal Xmas day dinner
Complimentary sherry
Victorian high tea
Parlor, antique organ

Gothic revival, elegant, homey, lush grounds, on the edge of a nature lover's dream, in a sophisticated mountain town. Vegetarian breakfasts and horse & buggy rides available.

NEWPORT BEACH

Little Inn on the Bay
617 Lido Park Dr., 92663
714-673-8800
Herrick & Jan Hanson
All year

$$$ B&B
30 rooms, 30 pb
Visa, MC, AmEx, DC •
C-yes/S-yes/P-no/H-no
Spanish

Continental breakfast
Comp. wine, hors d'oeuvres
Library, pool
comp. bay cruise
comp. bicycles

All the warmth & charm of an 1800s New England country inn. Complimentary bay cruise and bicycles. Walk to beach & quaint shops. Continental breakfast, wine & hors d'oeuvres.

Portofino Beach Hotel
2306 W. Oceanfront, 92663
714-673-7030
Christine Luetto
All year

$$$ B&B
12 rooms, 12 pb
Visa, MC, AmEx, DC, CB •
C-no/S-ltd/P-no/H-no
Italian, French, Spanish

Continental plus
Comp. wine & cheese
Antique beer & wine bar
Catalina Isl. day trips
sightseeing, boating

Nestled in the sand in beautiful Newport Beach. Enjoy our European hideaway, furnished in antiques. Complimentary wine and cheese included.

NIPTON

Hotel Nipton
HCR #1, Box 357, 92364
72 Nipton Rd.
619-856-2335
Roxanne & Gerald Freeman
All year

$ B&B
5 rooms
Visa, MC •
C-yes/S-yes/P-no/H-no
Spanish

Continental breakfast
Lunch, dinner, snacks
Sitting room
hot tub
horse trails

19th-century desert hideaway with antiques; home cooked breakfast served in our cafe next door; in east Mojave desert national scenic area; horses stay for free.

NORTH HOLLYWOOD

La Maida House
11154 La Maida St., 91601
818-769-3857
Megan & Helen Timothy
All year

$$ B&B
6 rooms, 4 pb
C-16+/S-no/P-no/H-no

Continental plus
Lunch, dinner, wine
Sitting room, den
solarium
1881 grand piano

An elegant city hideaway in the midst of Los Angeles' many diversified cultural and recreational attractions.

OCCIDENTAL

Heart's Desire Inn
P.O. Box 857, 95465
3657 Church St.
707-874-1311
Howard E. Selinger
All year

$$$ B&B
8 rooms, 8 pb
Visa, MC, AmEx •
C-no/S-no/P-no/H-yes
German

Continental plus
Comp. wine
Restaurant nearby
Sitting room, library
bicycles, tennis nearby

Completely renovated 1867 Victorian with European ambience. Rooms feature antique furnishings, goose down comforters, elegant appointments, private baths. Sumptuous breakfasts.

OJAI

Ojai Manor Hotel
210 E. Matilija, 93023
P.O. Box 608
805-646-0961
Mary Nelson
All year

$$$ B&B
6 rooms
Visa, MC •
C-12+/S-ltd/P-no/H-no
Spanish

Continental plus
Comp. wine
Sitting room
bicycles
health club nearby

1874 schoolhouse, now a B&B in the heart of town. Walk to shops, restaurants, golf and tennis. Minutes drive to Los Padres National Forest and hot springs.

OLEMA

Bear Valley Inn
P.O. Box 33, 94950
88 Bear Valley Rd,
415-663-1777
Ron & Joanne Nowell
All year

$$ B&B
3 rooms
C-no/S-no/P-no/H-no

Full breakfast
Comp. sherry
Sitting room w/fireplace
bicycles for rent

1899 Victorian ranch house just a half-mile from Point Reyes National Park Visitors Center and main trailhead. Bicycle and horse rentals nearby.

Roundstone Farm
P.O. Box 217, 94950
9940 Sir Francis Drake
415-663-1020
Inger Fisher
All year

$$$ B&B
4 rooms, 4 pb
Visa, MC •
C-no/S-ltd/P-no/H-no

Full breakfast
Afternoon tea
4 fireplaces
sitting room
10-acre horse ranch

Located at Point Reyes National Seashore Visitor Center. 65,000 acres of mountains, forests, meadows & beaches. We provide an escape for all seasons. 30 mi. from S.F.

ORLAND

Inn at Shallow Creek Farm
Rt. 3, Box 3176, 95963
916-865-4093
Kurt & Mary Glaeseman
All year

$ B&B
4 rooms, 2 pb
•
C-no/S-ltd/P-no/H-no
French, German, Spanish

Continental plus
Sitting room, library
near recreational lake,
hiking & bird watching

Known for its gracious country hospitality, the inn offers peaceful surroundings, antique furnishings, gourmet breakfasts and farm-fresh produce.

OROSI

Valley View Citrus Ranch
14801 Ave. 428, 93647
209-528-2275
Tom & Ruth Flippen
All year

$$ B&B
4 rooms, 2 pb
•
C-yes/S-ltd/P-ask/H-yes

Full breakfast
Comp. wine
Sitting room
organ
tennis courts

Colorful garden, clay tennis court, breakfast in gazebo, air-conditioning, fireplace, antiques, sunsets, serenity. 45 min. to Sequoia National Park.

54   California

OROVILLE

Jean Pratt's Riverside B&B · $ B&B · Full breakfast
P.O. Box 2334, 95965 · 7 rooms, 7 pb · Comp. wine
1124 Middlehoft Lane · Visa, MC · River waterfront
916-533-1413 · C-ask/S-ltd/P-ltd/H-yes · deck overlooking river
Jean Pratt
All year

Waterfront hideaway (canoes available). Near I-5, Sacramento, Feather River Canyon, Gold Era historical sites, Oroville Dam, golfing, fishing. Gold panning on premises.

PACIFIC GROVE

The Centrella Hotel · $$$ B&B · Full breakfast
P.O. Box 51157, 93950 · 26 rooms, 25 pb · Tea/wine/hors d'oeuvres
612 Central Ave. · Visa, MC, AmEx • · Parlor
408-372-3372 · C-ltd/S-ltd/P-no/H-yes · dining room
Diana Vandergrift · Italian · cribs avail. free
All year

Restored Victorian award winner for interior design. Ocean, lovers' point and many attractions of the Monterey Peninsula. Fireplaces in suites.

Gosby House Inn · $$$ B&B · Full breakfast
643 Lighthouse Ave., 93950 · 22 rooms, 20 pb · Comp. tea, wine
408-375-1287 · AmEx, Visa, MC • · Sitting room
Kelly Short · C-yes/S-ltd/P-no/H-no · bicycles
All year

Romantic Victorian mansion. Antique furniture, cheerful pastel fabrics and fireplaces abound. Enjoy turndown service and morning paper. Part of Four Sisters' Inns.

Green Gables Inn · $$$ B&B · Full breakfast
104 Fifth St., 93950 · 11 rooms, 7 pb · Comp. tea, wine
408-375-2095 · AmEx, Visa, MC • · Sitting room, bathrobes
Claudia Long · C-ltd/S-ltd/P-no/H-no · bicycles, newspapers
All year · coffee/breakfast in room

Spectacular Victorian mansion with views of Monterey Bay. Individually decorated rooms with antiques and beautiful fabrics. The most romantic inn around.

Martine Inn · $$$ B&B · Full breakfast
255 Ocean View Blvd., 93950 · 19 rooms, 19 pb · Picnic basket lunches
408-373-3388 · Visa, MC, AmEx • · Comp. wine, snacks
Marion & Don Martine · C-yes/S-yes/P-no/H-yes · Sitting room, game room
All year · Italian, Russian, Span. · bicycles, conf. room

12,000 sq. ft. mansion on Monterey Bay. Elegant museum quality American antiques. Breakfast served on old Sheffield silver, crystal, Victorian china, and lace.

Roserox Country Inn · $$$ B&B · Continental plus
557 Ocean View Blvd., 93950 · 8 rooms, 4 pb · Comp. bar, wine & cheese
408-373-ROSE · • · Tea, bicycles, horseshoes
Dawn Browncroft · C-ltd/S-ltd/P-no/H-no · Croquet, sitting room w/
All year · fireplaces, library

Intimate historic Victorian on shores of the Pacific. Honeymoon Suite, antique brass beds, feather quilts, clawfoot tubs. Breakfast in bed. Spectacular ocean views.

PACIFIC GROVE

Seven Gables Inn — $$$ B&B — Continental plus
555 Ocean View Blvd., 93950 — 14 rooms, 14 pb — High tea
408-372-4341 — • — grand Victorian parlor
The Flatley Family — C-12+/S-no/P-no/H-no — aquarium tickets
All year — French, Spanish — ocean views—every room

Family-run, grand Victorian mansion at the very edge of Monterey Bay. Fine antique furnishings throughout. Incomparable ocean views from all rooms. Gardens.

PALM SPRINGS

Casa Cody — $ B&B — Continental plus
175 S. Cahuilla, 92262 — 17 rooms, 18 pb — Comp. wine (Saturday)
619-320-9346 — Visa, MC, AmEx • — Library, bicycles
Frank Tysen, Therese Mayes — C-ask/S-ask/P-ask/H-yes — hot tubs, swimming pools
All year — French, Dutch, German — hiking, horseback riding

Romantic, historic hideaway in the heart of Palm Springs Village. Rooms, one or two bedrooms with kitchens and wood-burning fireplace. Beautifully restored in Santa Fe style.

Villa Royale Inn — $$$ B&B — Continental plus
1620 S. Indian Trail, 92264 — 31 rooms, 31 pb — Lunch, dinner
619-327-2314 — Visa, MC, AmEx • — Restaurant, bar service
C. Murawski, R. Lee — C-no/S-yes/P-no/H-yes — Comp. wine, aftn. tea
All year — Tennis courts, 2 pools

Rooms & villas decorated as different European countries on 3½ acres of flowering gardens. Private patios, spas, fireplaces, poolside gourmet dinners. Villas, hotel rooms.

PALO ALTO

Victorian on Lytton — $$$ B&B — Continental plus
555 Lytton Ave., 94301 — 10 rooms, 10 pb — Comp. appetizers,
415-322-8555 — Visa, MC • — port & sherry
Maxwell & Susan Hall — C-15+/S-no/P-no/H-yes — Occasional entertainment
All year

A lovely Victorian built in 1895 offering a combination of forgotten elegance with a touch of European grace.

PHILO

Philo Pottery Inn — $$ B&B — Full New England breakf.
P.O. Box 166, 95466 — 5 rooms, 3 pb — Comp. wine
8550 Hwy 128 — C-8+/S-ltd/P-no/H-ltd — Evening tea
707-895-3069 — Library
Judy & Bill Hardardt — piano
February—New Year

1888 redwood stagecoach stop—country antiques and English garden—near Anderson Valley Wineries and restaurants. Philo Pottery Gallery.

PLACERVILLE

River Rock Inn — $$ B&B — Full breakfast
1756 Georgetown Dr., 95667 — 4 rooms, 2 pb — Comp. sherry
916-622-7640 — • — Sitting room
Dorothy Irvin — C-yes/S-ltd/P-no/H-ltd — hot tub
All year

Relax on the 110' deck overlooking the American River, fish and pan for gold in the front yard. Quiet and beautiful.

POINT REYES

Jasmine Cottage	$$$ B&B	Full breakfast
P.O. Box 56, 94956	1 rooms, 1 pb	Comp. teas & coffee
11561 Coast Rt. 1	•	Large naturalist library
415-663-1166	C-yes/S-no/P-yes/H-no	picnic area, patio
Karen Gray		surrounded by gardens
All year		

Secluded country cottage sleeps four. Completely furnished, fully equipped kitchen, writing desk, library, woodburning stove, queen-sized bed, sun room, patio, garden.

Marsh Cottage	$$$ B&B	Full breakfast
P.O. Box 1121, 94956	1 rooms, 1 pb	Comp. coffee/tea/wine
415-669-7168	C-yes/S-no/P-no/H-no	Sitting area
Wendy Schwartz		fireplace
All year		

Cheerful, carefully appointed private cottage along bay. Kitchen, fireplace, antiques; extraordinary setting for romantics and naturalists.

Thirty-Nine Cypress	$$$ B&B	Full breakfast
P.O. Box 176, 94956	3 rooms, 1 pb	Comp. wine
39 Cypress Way	•	Sitting room
415-663-1709	C-no/S-no/P-no/H-yes	bicycle
Julia Bartlett	French	hot tub
All year		

Antiques, original art, oriental rugs, spectacular view! Close to beaches, 140 miles of hiking trails. Horseback riding arrangements available.

POINT REYES STATION

Cricket Cottage	$$$ B&B	Full breakfast
P.O. Box 627, 94956	1 rooms, 1 pb	Comp. wine, fruit
18 Cypress Rd.	C-yes/P-ltd/H-yes	Library, hot tubs
415-663-9139		private garden
Penelope Livingston		Franklin fireplace
All year		

A garden cottage with private hot tub. Cozy, romantic furnishings; original art. Located near Point Reyes National Seashore and Tomales Bay Headlands.

Horseshore Farm Cottage	$$$ B&B	Continental plus
P.O. Box 332, 94956	1 rooms, 1 pb	Kitchen facilities
39 Drake's Summit	C-yes/S-yes/H-yes	stocked refrigerator
415-663-9401		Hiking trails
Paki Stedwell-Wright		
All year		

A single-unit cottage in the evergreen woods of Inverness Ridge. Private, woodsy. Walk to trails of the Point Reyes National Seashore.

POINT RICHMOND

East Brother Light Station	$$$ MAP	Continental plus
117 Park Place, 94801	4 rooms, 2 pb	Dinner, wine
415-233-2385	C-ltd/S-ltd/P-no/H-no	Parlor
Linda/Leigh Hurley		
All year		

Escape to an island within sight of the San Francisco skyline. Share the history of a 110-year-old lighthouse.

PRINCETON BY-THE-SEA

Pillar Point Inn
380 Capristrano Rd., 94018
P.O. Box 388, El Granada
415-728-7377
Dick Anderton
All year

$$$ B&B
11 rooms, 11 pb
Visa, MC, AmEx •
C-12+/S-ltd/P-no/H-yes
Span., Port., Ital.

Full breakfast
Comp. wine, snacks, tea
Sitting room, library
meeting & conf. room
near beach, tennis

Elegant European-style seaside lodging. Every luxurious fireplace room has panoramic ocean views. Harbor, beach and coastal mountain setting. VCRs in rooms.

QUINCY

Feather Bed
P.O. Box 3200, 95971
542 Jackson St.
916-283-0102
Chuck & Dianna Goubert
All year

$$ B&B
6 rooms, 6 pb
Visa, MC, AmEx •
C-13+/S-no/P-no/H-no

Full breakfast
Comp. wine
Sitting room
bicycles

Country Victorian in forested surroundings, relaxing our specialty, antiques in individually decorated rooms, located on Heritage Walk. Recreation area.

RANCHO CUCAMONGA

Christmas House B&B Inn
9240 Archibald Ave., 91730
714-980-6450
Janice Ilsley
All year

$$ B&B
5 rooms, 2 pb
Visa, MC •
C-yes/S-ltd/P-no/H-no

Continental plus (wkdy)
Full breakfast (wkends)
Catered dinner by resv.
aftn. tea, one hot tub
Library, 2 rm fireplaces

1904 Victorian mansion with 7 fireplaces, intricate woodwork, gracious hospitality. Located minutes from Ontario International Airport, 40 miles east of Los Angeles.

RED BLUFF

Faulkner House
1029 Jefferson St., 96080
916-529-0520
Harvey & Mary Klingler
All year

$ B&B
4 rooms, 1 pb
•
C-no/S-ltd/P-no/H-no

Full breakfast
Comp. wine
Sitting room
bicycles

1890s Queen Anne Victorian furnished in antiques. Screened porch on quiet street, hiking and skiing nearby. Visit Ide Adobe or Victorian Museum, Sacramento River.

REDDING

Palisades Paradise B&B
1200 Palisades Ave., 96003
916-223-5305
Gail Goetz
All year

$$ B&B
2 rooms
Visa, MC •
C-yes/S-ltd/P-no/H-ask

Full breakfast
Comp. wine
Snacks
Sitting room
hot tubs

Breathtaking view of Sacramento River, mountains, and city from a secluded contemporary home in Redding. Gateway to the Shasta-Cascade Wonderland.

REDLANDS

Morey Mansion B&B Inn
190 Terracina Blvd., 92373
714-793-7970
All year

$$ B&B
7 rooms, 3 pb
Visa, MC, AmEx
C-14+/S-ltd/P-no/H-no

Full breakfast
Comp. tea, wine
Sitting room, library
2 pianos, 2 organs
bicycles

Historic landmark Victorian home. Onion dome, beveled and leaded windows, interior abounds with antiques. Near mountain, lake and ski resorts.

58 California

REDONDO BEACH ────────────────────────────────────

Ocean Breeze Inn	$ B&B	Continental breakfast
122 S. Juanita Ave., 90277	2 rooms, 2 pb	Comp. fruit, flowers
213-316-5123	C-yes/S-yes/P-ltd/H-ltd	Bicycles, whirlpool
Norris & Betty Binding		TV, airport pickup
All year		senior discounts

Large, luxurious rooms. Quiet neighborhood. Private entrance, bath with 6-foot spa. Near beach, L.A. Airport, Disneyland and all attractions; good restaurants, shopping.

RUTHERFORD ────────────────────────────────────

Rancho Caymus Inn	$$$ B&B	Continental breakfast
P.O. Box 78, 94573	26 rooms, 26 pb	Comp. wine
1140 Rutherford Rd.	Visa, MC •	Sitting room, piano
707-963-1777	C-12+/S-yes/P-no/H-yes	Jacuzzi
Therese Varney		
All year		

Located in the "Heart of the Napa Valley," this Spanish-style inn, with 26 suites encircling private gardens, captures the rustic spirit of early California.

SACRAMENTO ────────────────────────────────────

Amber House B&B Inn	$$ B&B	Full gourmet breakfast
1315 22nd St., 95816	5 rooms, 5 pb	Comp. wine, tea
916-444-8085	Visa, MC, AmEx •	Sitting room, library
Michael & Jane Richardson	C-no/S-ltd/P-no/H-no	tandem bicycle, private
All year		phones, airport pickup

"Tailored elegance" framed by towering old elm trees—beautifully appointed bedrooms, wine presented in gracious living room.

Aunt Abigail's B&B Inn	$$ B&B	Full breakfast
2120 "G" St., 95816	5 rooms, 5 pb	Comp. evening tea/coffee
916-441-5007	credit cards accepted •	Secluded garden, piano
Susanne Ventura	C-ltd/S-no/P-no/H-no	sitting rooms, fireplace
All year		hot tub, games

Grand old mansion in the heart of the State Capitol. Large and comfortable, delicious breakfasts, a/c. Ideal for business travelers and romantic escapes.

Bear Flag Inn	$ B&B	Full breakfast
2814 "I" St., 95816	5 rooms, 5 pb	Comp. wine
916-448-5417	Visa, MC •	Sitting room, fireplace
Dean & Lisa Wofford	C-ask/S-ltd/P-no/H-no	shaded garden
All year		deck w/hammock

Antiques, wine, books, fireplace & conversation await guests in restored downtown Arts & Crafts home. Walk to restaurants & tourist spots.

Hartley House Inn	$$ B&B	Full gourmet breakfast
700 22nd St., 95816	5 rooms, 5 pb	Comp. tea, wine
916-447-7829	•	Sitting room, piano
Randall V. Hartley	C-ask/S-ltd/P-no/H-no	private telephones
All year	French	fully air-conditioned

Turn-of-the-century colonial revival finely appointed with antique furniture, oriental carpets, lace curtains, patchwork quilts, vintage magazines and items of nostalgia.

Old Thyme Inn, Half Moon Bay, CA

SAINT HELENA ――――――――――――――――――――――――――

Bartels Ranch/Country Inn	$$$ B&B	Hearty continental plus
1200 Conn Valley Rd., 94574	3 rooms, 3 pb	Catered lunch & dinner
707-963-4001	Visa, MC, AmEx, Disc ●	Aftn. tea, comp. wine
Jayme Bartels	C-ask/S-yes/P-no/H-yes	Library, sauna, jacuzzi
All year	Spanish, German	darts, horseshoes, golf

Elegant, secluded romantic wine country estate. Award-winning accommodations. 10,000-acre views; entertainment room, fireplace, billiards, bicycles. Champagne under the stars.

Bylund House B&B Inn	$$$ B&B	Continental plus
2000 Howell Mtn. Rd., 94574	2 rooms, 2 pb	Comp. wine
707-963-9073	●	Sitting room
Bill & Diane Bylund	C-no/S-ltd/P-no/H-no	swimming pool
All year		bicycles

Elegant wine country villa designed by owner-architect, located in secluded valley with sweeping views. Two very private rooms with views, balconies and European feather beds!

Chalet Bernensis	$ B&B	Continental plus
225 St. Helena Hwy, 94574	9 rooms, 4 pb	Comp. wine
707-963-4423	Visa, MC	Sitting room
Jack & Essie Doty	C-no/S-no/P-no/H-no	
All year		

Century-old Victorian—handmade quilts, Victorian or turn-of-the-century oak furniture, iron & brass beds (queen size). Center of wine country.

60   California

SAINT HELENA ──────────────────────────────────────

Cinnamon Bear B&B
1407 Kearney St., 94574
707-963-4653
Genny Jenkins, Brenda
All year

$$$ B&B
3 rooms, 3 pb
Visa, MC, AmEx
C-10+ /S-ltd/P-no/H-no

Full breakfast
Comp. wine
Sitting room, piano
fireplace
classical music or swing

Homesick for a visit to your favorite aunt's house? Bring your teddy and come to the Napa Valley wine country.

Cornerstone B&B Inn
1308 Main St., 94574
707-963-1891
Margie Hinton
All year

$$ B&B
12 rooms
Visa, MC, AmEx •
C-yes/S-yes/P-no/H-no
Spanish

Continental plus
Comp. wine
Sitting room
antiques

Victorian charm. 1891 reminiscent of the unique hotels of Europe. Complimentary wine close to shops, wineries & fine restaurants.

Creekside Inn
945 Main St., 94574
707-963-7244
J. Nicholson, V. Toogood
All year

$$$ B&B
3 rooms
C-no/S-no/P-no/H-no

Continental plus
Sitting room

Country French atmosphere in the very heart of St. Helena, yet peacefully sheltered. White Sulphur Creek ripples past secluded rear patio garden.

Elsie's Conn Valley Inn
726 Rossi Rd., 94574
707-963-4614
Elsie Asplund Hudak
All year

$$ B&B
3 rooms, 1 pb
•
C-ltd/S-ltd/P-no/H-no
Finnish

Continental plus
Comp. beverage, cheese
& crackers, library
Sitting room, fireplace
extensive gardens & yard

Peaceful country hideaway, vineyards, lake trails. Genuine antiques. Continental plus breakfast served indoors or in the garden.

Erika's-Hillside
285 Fawn Park, 94574
707-963-2887
Erika Cunningham
All year

$$ B&B
3 rooms, 2 pb
•
C-ltd/S-ltd/P-no/H-no
German

Continental breakfast
Comp. wine
Sitting room

Romantic hillside chalet with European influence. Overlooking the heart of the Napa Valley wine country.

Hotel St. Helena
1309 Main St., 94574
707-963-4388
Athena & Mary Martin
All year

$$$ B&B
17 rooms, 13 pb
Visa, MC •
C-no/S-yes/P-no/H-no

Continental breakfast
Wine & beer bar
Sitting room
weddings, reunions, etc.

Restored Victorian located in downtown St. Helena in the heart of the Napa Valley. Specialty shops in courtyard. Facilities available for weddings, reunions, etc.

SAINT HELENA ─────────────────────────────────

Ink House Bed & Breakfast	$$$ B&B	Continental breakfast
1575 St. Helena Hwy., 94574	4 rooms, 4 pb	Comp. wine
707-963-3890	•	Parlor
Lois Clark	C-no/S-no/P-no/H-no	antique pump organ
All year		

Private, in beautiful St. Helena, antiques, parlor, continental with homemade pastries. Rooftop observatory with views of vineyards and valley hills.

Oliver House Country Inn	$$$ B&B	Continental plus
2970 Silverado Tr., 94574	4 rooms, 4 pb	Sitting room
707-963-4089	Visa •	walk to wineries
Richard & Clara Oliver	C-ltd/S-ltd/P-no/H-no	
All year	German	

Warm intimate country atmosphere. Picturesque Swiss chalet overlooking acres of vineyard. Fireplaces, private baths, queen-sized beds, balconies with view.

Shady Oaks Country Inn	$$ B&B	Full gourmet breakfast
399 Zinfandel Lane, 94574	4 rooms, 4 pb	Comp. wine/hors d'oeuvre
707-963-1190	AmEx, Visa, MC •	Sitting room, fireplace
Lisa & John Wild-Runnells	C-6+/S-yes/P-no/H-yes	library, croquet, bikes
All year		hot tub, sauna nearby

Romantic and secluded on two acres among the finest wineries in Napa Valley. Elegant ambience; country comfort. Full champagne breakfast.

Villa St. Helena	$$$ B&B	Continental breakfast
2727 Sulphur Springs Av, 94574	3 rooms, 3 pb	Comp. wine
707-963-2514	Visa, MC, AmEx •	Swimming pool
Ralph & Carolyn Cotton	C-ltd/S-ltd/P-no/H-no	library
All year		hiking, walking trails

Secluded hilltop Mediterranean villa overlooking Napa Valley. Romantic antique-filled rooms, fireplaces, private entrances; elaborate breakfast. Country elegance.

Wine Country Cottage	$$$ B&B	Continental plus
400 Meadowood Ln., 94574	3 rooms, 3 pb	
P.O. Box 295	C-yes/S-yes/P-no/H-no	
709-963-0852		
Jan Strong		
All year		

Relax in this cozy cottage secluded in a private woodland setting of several acres. Victorian charm and beauty surround you.

Wine Country Inn	$$$ B&B	Continental plus buffet
1152 Lodi Lane, 94574	25 rooms, 25 pb	Patios, balconies
707-963-7077	Visa, MC •	swimming pool
James Smith	C-12+/S-yes/P-no/H-yes	whirlpool
All year exc. Dec. 12-26		

Beautiful country inn furnished with antiques and nestled in the heart of the wine country.

62 California

SAN ANDREAS

Robin's Nest
P.O. Box 1408, 95249
247 W. St. Charles-Hwy 49
209-754-1076
Robin Brooks
All year

$$ B&B
9 rooms, 7 pb
•
C-12+/S-yes/P-no/H-no
some Spanish

Full breakfast
Coffee/tea/wine/brandy
Library, entertainment
tennis, swimming pool
musical instruments

Romantic Victorian mansion on Historical Register. Rural quiet and elegance. Central heat and a/c. Gourmet breakfast. Guest use of private tennis/swim club.

SAN DIEGO

Britt House
406 Maple St., 92103
619-234-2926
D. Martin, K. Cordua, E. Lord
All year

$$$ B&B
10 rooms, 1 pb
Visa, MC, AmEx •
C-ltd/S-ltd/P-no/H-ltd

Full breakfast
Formal afternoon tea
Sitting room, piano
sauna

Queen Anne Victorian home with 2-story stained glass windows. Homemade breakfast and afternoon tea. Two blocks from Balboa Park. Available for small parties & weddings.

Carole's B&B Inn
3227 Grim Ave., 92104
619-280-5258
C. Dugdale, M. O'Brien
All year

$$ B&B
8 rooms, 3 pb
•
C-no/S-yes/P-no/H-no

Continental plus
Comp. wine, cheese
Sitting room
swimming pool
player piano, cable TV

Historical site, antiques, large pool. Close to zoo, Balboa Park. Centrally located. Friendly, congenial atmosphere. House built in 1904 and tastefully redecorated.

The Cottage
P.O. Box 3292, 92103
3829 Albatross St.
619-299-1564
Carol & Robert Emerick
All year

$ B&B
2 rooms, 2 pb
Visa, MC •
C-yes/S-no/P-no/H-no

Continental plus

Relaxation in a garden setting with turn-of-the-century ambience is offered in a residential downtown San Diego neighborhood.

Harbor Hill Guest House
2330 Albatross St., 92101
619-233-0638
Dorothy A. Milbourn
All year

$$ B&B
6 rooms, 6 pb
•
C-yes/S-yes/P-no/H-no

Continental breakfast
Large sun deck & garden
barbecue
Rooms with harbor views

Private entrances, guest kitchens, continental breakfast. Close to Balboa Park, zoo, museums, Sea World, Old Town, harbor, shopping, theater. Ideal for families and reunions.

Heritage Park B&B Inn
2470 Heritage Park Row, 92110
619-295-7088
Lori Chandler
All year

$$$ B&B
9 rooms, 5 pb
Visa, MC •
C-14+/S-no/P-no/H-yes
Spanish

Full breakfast
Picnics, dinners, wine
Sitting room, library
bicycles
vintage films

Beautifully restored 1889 Queen Anne mansion in historic Old Town. Tantalizing breakfasts. Film classics shown nightly, antiques, romantic candlelight dinners.

SAN DIEGO ——————

Surf Manor and Cottages $$ B&B Self-catered full brkfst
P.O. Box 7695, 92107 7 rooms, 7 pb Kitchens
619-225-9765 • Stocked refrigerator
Jerri Grady C-yes/S-yes/P-no/H-no Living rooms
All year

Charming one-and two-bedroom suites. Oceanfront apartments and quaint beach cottages. Antiques and country prints. Near all of San Diego's attractions.

Westbourne Windansea B&B 3 rooms, 2 pb Full breakfast
P.O. Box 91223, 92109 • Snacks
619-456-9634 C-13+/S-no/P-no/H-no Sitting room, library
Sherry & Joey Cash tennis courts 1 block
All year ocean & beaches 1 block

Walk to ocean, beaches, shopping and restaurants. Magazine quality guest rooms. Quiet. So much to see and do. Continental and full breakfast each morning.

SAN FRANCISCO ——————

Alamo Square Inn $$$ B&B Full breakfast
719 Scott St., 94117 5 rooms Comp. tea, wine
415-922-2055 Visa, MC, AmEx • Sitting room
Wayne M. Corn C-ltd/S-ltd/P-no/H-no bicycles
All year German, French entertainment (harpist)

Fine restoration of a magnificent mansion. Graced by European furnishings and Oriental rugs, flowers from the garden and host committed to excellence.

Albion House Inn $$ B&B Full breakfast
135 Gough St., 94102 8 rooms, 8 pb Comp. wine
415-621-0896 Visa, MC, AmEx • Sitting room
Jan Robert de Gier C-yes/S-yes/P-no/H-no
All year Soanish

An elegant city hideaway conveniently located near the Opera House, just moments away from Union Square and other tourist attractions.

Amsterdam Hotel $$ B&B Continental breakfast
749 Taylor St., 94108 30 rooms, 22 pb Sitting room
415-673-3277/800-637-3444 Visa, MC, AmEx • library
Mel & Barbara Thomas C-yes/S-yes/P-no/H-no
All year

Located on Nob Hill. Enjoy our continental breakfast in our dining room or in our garden setting patio.

Archbishop's Mansion Inn $$$ B&B Continental plus
1000 Fulton St., 94117 15 rooms, 15 pb Wine, tea, bar
800-543-5820 Visa, MC, AmEx • Sitting room, piano
J. Shannon, R. Woellmer C-ltd/S-no/P-no/H-no reception & conference
All year facilities

Historic French chateau on the park—luxurious lodging in the "Belle Epoque" style. Beautiful conference and reception rooms. VIP service.

64 California

SAN FRANCISCO ————————————————————————————————————

Art Center Wamsley Gallery
1902 Filbert & Laguna, 94123
415-567-1526
Helvi & George Wamsley
All year

$$ B&B
4 rooms, 4 pb
Visa, MC •
C-ltd/S-no/P-no/H-no
Finnish

Continental plus
Picnic lunch, kitchens
Studio room, art gallery
art supplies available
enclosed patio

Art shows, classes, garden art, upstairs workroom & art materials. We offer an Art Package that includes 3 days lodging, museum tour, buffet. Corner of Laguna & Filbert.

Bed & Breakfast Inn
4 Charlton Ct., 94123
415-921-9784
Marily & Bob Kavanaugh
All year

$$ B&B
10 rooms, 7 pb
C-no/S-yes/P-no/H-no
French, Italian

Continental breakfast
Comp. wine
Sitting room, library
garden

San Francisco's first "country inn." Ten unique accommodations are romantic hideaways. You're a very special person to the owners and staff.

Casa Arguello
225 Arguello Blvd., 94118
415-752-9482
Emma Baires
All year

$ B&B
5 rooms, 5 pb
C-7+/S-no/P-no/H-no
Spanish

Continental plus
Sitting room, TV

An elegant townhouse near Golden Gate Park, the Presidio, Golden Gate Bridge, 10 min. to Union Square.

Casita Blanca
330 Edgehill Way, 94127
415-564-9339
Joan Bard
All year

$$$ B&B
1 rooms, 1 pb
•
C-ltd/S-yes/P-no/H-no
Spanish

Continental breakfast
Two night minimum
Furnished homes avail.in
Carmel, Tahoe, Maui, Palm
Desert. Request brochure

Casita Blanca is a detached cottage in a secluded forest area. View of Golden Gate. Fireplace, patio, completely furnished. Other homes in California & Hawaii available.

The Garden Studio
1387 Sixth Ave., 94122
415-753-3574
Alice & John Micklewright
All year

$$ EP
1 rooms, 1 pb
C-yes/S-no/P-no/H-no
French

Coffee
Garden, private entrance
full kitchen
TV, radio

On lower level of charming Edwardian home; 2 blocks from Golden Gate Park. Studio opens to garden, has private entrance, private bath, fully equipped kitchen, queen-sized bed.

Golden Gate Hotel
775 Bush St., 94108
415-392-3702
John & Renate Kenaston
All year

$$ B&B
23 rooms, 14 pb
Visa, MC, AmEx, DC •
C-yes/S-yes/P-ltd/H-no
German, French

Continental breakfast
Afternoon tea
Sitting room
sightseeing tours

Charming turn-of-the-century hotel. Friendly atmosphere. Antique furnishings, fresh flowers. Ideal Nob Hill location. Corner cable car stop.

SAN FRANCISCO

Grove Inn
890 Grove St., 94117	$ B&B	Continental breakfast
415-929-0780	16 rooms, 9 pb	Sitting room
Klaus & Roselta Zimmermann	Visa, MC, AmEx •	bicycles
All year	C-yes/S-ltd/P-no/H-no	laundry
	Italian, German	

Turn-of-the-century Victorian, fully restored, simply furnished. Community kitchen, refrigerator. Part of Alamo Square Historic district.

Inn San Francisco
943 S. Van Ness Ave., 94110	$$ B&B	Continental plus
415-641-0188	15 rooms, 13 pb	2 sitting rooms, library
Joel & Deborah Daily	Visa, MC, AmEx •	sun deck, gazebo
All year	C-12+/S-yes/P-no/H-no	hot tub, phones, TV's
		garden, off-street prkng

A grand 27-room 1872 Victorian mansion furnished in 19th-century antiques. Garden room, hot tub, fresh flowers in rooms. Newly opened garden cottage suite has 4 rooms.

Inn on Castro
321 Castro St., 94114	$$$ B&B	Continental plus
415-861-0321	5 rooms, 5 pb	Comp. tea, wine
Joel M. Roman	Visa, MC, AmEx	Sitting room
All year	C-no/S-ltd/P-no/H-no	bicycles
	Spanish, Italian, French	

Restored Victorian, lush contemporary interiors, filled with an abundance of art, accessories, plants, flowers, and especially friendliness.

Marina Inn
3110 Octavia St., 94123	$$ B&B	Continental
415-928-1000	Visa, MC, AmEx, Disc •	Afternoon tea
Ms. Suzie Baum	C-yes/S-yes/P-no/H-yes	comp. sherry
All year	Filipino	Sitting room
		coffee

Victorian hotel, fine furnishings, private bath, color TV, telephone, turndown service. Near Fisherman's Wharf, Ghirardelli Square & Marina Green.

Moffatt House
431 Hugo St., 94122	$ B&B	Continental plus
415-661-6210	4 rooms	Hot beverages, kitchen
Ruth Moffatt	•	Tennis, bicycles nearby
All year	C-yes/S-yes/P-yes/H-no	Jap. Tea Garden tickets
	Spanish, French, Italian	runner's discount

Walk to Golden Gate Park's major attractions from our Edwardian home. Safe location for active, independent guests. Excellent public transportation.

The Monte Cristo
600 Presidio Ave., 94115	$$ B&B	Continental plus
415-931-1875	14 rooms, 12 pb	Comp. tea, wine
Frances G. Allan	Visa, MC, AmEx •	Parlor w/fireplace
All year	C-no/S-yes/P-no/H-yes	phones, TV
	French, Spanish	

1875 hotel-saloon-bordello, furnished with antiques. Each room uniquely decorated—Georgian four-poster, Chinese wedding bed, spindle bed, etc.

SAN FRANCISCO ───

Nolan House	$$$ B&B	Full breakfast
1071 Page St., 94117	6 rooms, 4 pb	Comp. wine at check-in
415-863-0384	Visa, MC •	Cordials & mints
Timothy W. Beaver	C-yes/S-ltd/P-no/H-no	Sitting room, hot tubs
All year		feather beds, parking

Classic Victorian hospitality in tastefully restored "Painted Lady." Antique furnishings. Walking distance to Golden Gate Park and Haight-Ashbury District.

Obrero Hotel & Restaurant	$ B&B	Full European breakfast
1208 Stockton St., 94133	12 rooms	Basque dinners
415-989-3960	C-ltd/S-no/P-no/H-no	
Bambi McDonald	Fr., Ger., It., Canton.	
All year		

Friendly slice of life in bustling Chinatown adjacent to North Beach, within walking distance of Union Square and Fisherman's Wharf.

Petite Auberge	$$$ B&B	Full breakfast
863 Bush St., 94108	26 rooms, 26 pb	Comp. wine, tea
415-928-6000	AmEx, Visa, MC •	Sitting room
Carolyn Vaughan	C-yes/S-ltd/P-no/H-no	near Cable Car line
All year		

Romantic French country inn near Union Square in San Francisco. Turndown service, robes, afternoon wine and hors d'oeuvres. Honeymoon packages. One of the Four Sisters' Inns.

Red Victorian B&B Inn	$$ B&B	Continental plus
1665 Haight St., 94117	15 rooms, 4 pb	Afternoon tea
415-864-1978	Visa, MC, AmEx •	Meditation room
Jeffrey Hirsch, Barbara Cooke	C-ltd/S-no/P-no/H-no	peace gallery
All year	Spanish, German	Transformational art

Near Golden Gate Park in colorful Haight-Ashbury, our "New Age" hotel welcomes creative thinkers, friendly people. 35 restaurants nearby.

Sherman House	$$$ EP	Continental plus $
2160 Green Street, 94123	15 rooms, 15 pb	Lunch, dinner, beer/wine
415-563-3600	Major credit cards	Sitting room, piano
All year	C-ltd/S-yes/P-no/H-yes	
	Fr, Sp, It, Ger, Portug.	

Luxury, full-service hotel. Superb appointments, formal gardens, garage, full concierge and valet services, 24-hour room service, view of bay.

Spreckels Mansion	$$$ B&B	Continental plus
737 Buena Vista West, 94117	10 rooms, 8 pb	Comp. wine
415-861-3008	Visa, MC, AmEx •	Sitting room
Kathleen Austin	C-yes/S-yes/P-no/H-no	library
All year	German, French, Spanish	private phone

The magic of the Victorian era with all the modern comforts. Spacious rooms are individually decorated with fine antiques. Breakfast brought to room. Unsurpassed hospitality.

SAN FRANCISCO

Union Street Inn	$$$ B&B	Continental plus
2229 Union St., 94123	6 rooms, 4 pb	Comp. wine
415-346-0424	Visa, MC, AmEx •	Sitting room
Helen Stewart, Charlene Brown	C-yes/S-ltd/P-no/H-no	jacuzzi
All year		

Charming, elegant inn located in lively shopping/entertainment area of San Francisco; romantic old-fashioned garden, private carriage house with jacuzzi.

Victorian Inn on the Park	$$$ B&B	Continental plus
301 Lyon St., 94117	12 rooms, 12 pb	Comp. wine
415-931-1830	Visa, MC, AmEx •	homemade breads, cheeses
William & Lisa Benau	C-ltd/S-yes/P-no/H-no	Parlor, library
All year		phone, TV on request

1897 Queen Anne Victorian—near Golden Gate Park, downtown. Antiques and private baths. A registered historic landmark.

White Swan Inn	$$$ B&B	Full breakfast
845 Bush Street, 94108	26 rooms, 26 pb	Comp. tea, wine, cookies
415-775-1755	Visa, MC, AmEx •	library, sitting room
Carolyn Vaughan	C-yes/S-ltd/P-no/H-no	garden
All year	Fr., Cantonese, Tagalog	near Cable Car line

English garden inn, in cosmopolitan San Francisco; built in 1908. Business conference facilities; country breakfast; afternoon appetizers. Special services.

Willows B&B Inn	$$ B&B	Continental plus
710-14th St., 94114	11 rooms	Comp. tea, wine
415-431-4770	Visa, MC, AmEx, DC, CB	Sitting room
Tim Farquhar, Brad Goessler	C-no/S-yes/P-no/H-no	
All year		

A distinctive country inn within the city. Willow furnishing, Laura Ashley decor, lush plants, breakfast in bed, robes. Telephones and parking. Attentive, personal service.

SAN GREGORIO

Rancho San Gregorio	$$ B&B	Full country breakfast
Route 1, Box 54, 94074	5 rooms, 4 pb	Comp. wine & beverages
5086 La Honda Rd.	•	snacks
415-747-0810	C-yes/S-ltd	Sitting room
Bud & Lee Raynor		library
All year		

California Mission-style coastal retreat; serene; spectacular views of wooded hills; friendly hospitality; hearty breakfast; 40 miles south of San Francisco.

SAN JOSE

Briar Rose	$$ B&B	Full breakfast
897 E. Jackson St., 95112	5 rooms, 3 pb	Afternoon tea
408-279-5999	Visa, MC, AmEx •	Comp. wine, snacks
James & Cheryl Fuhring	C-yes/S-ltd/P-no/H-no	Sitting room, library
All year		porch, gardens

An 1875 Victorian once a flourishing walnut orchard restored to its former grandeur. Period furnishings grace rooms, fabulously wallpapered with Bradbury & Bradbury papers.

68 California

SAN LUIS OBISPO

Apple Farm Inn
2015 Monterey St., 93401
805-544-2040/800-255-2040
Bob Davis
All year

$$$ EP
67 rooms, 67 pb
Visa, MC, AmEx •
C-yes/S-yes/P-no/H-yes

Restaurant
All meals served
Swimming pool, hot tubs
gift shop, mill house
working water wheel

Memorable lodging experience; uniquely appointed rooms—canopy beds, fireplaces, turrets, cozy window seats. Working water wheel. Mill house. Rated four diamond.

SAN MIGUEL

Darken Downs Equestre-Inn
Star Route Box 4562, 93451
Hog Canyon
805-467-3589
Darlene & Kenneth Ramey
All year

$$ B&B
2 rooms, 2 pb
C-no/S-no/P-no/H-no
some Spanish

Continental plus
Afternoon tea
bedtime snacks
Living room w/library
facilities for horses

Spanish-style ranch house on 9 acres. Guests welcomed with or without horses. Arena. Breakfast in dining room or on terrace overlooking facility. No rental available.

SAN PEDRO

Grand Cottages
809 S. Grand Ave., 90731
213-548-1240
B. Clayton, M. Ginsburg
All year

$$$ B&B
4 rooms, 4 pb
Visa, MC, AmEx, DC •
French, Ger, Ital, Span

Full breakfast
Lunch & dinner Tue-Fri
Restaurant
comp. champagne, snacks
Private porch, garden

Beautifully restored California bungalow suites, adjoining award-winning gourmet Grand House Restaurant. Romantic hideaway near ocean, shopping, and sightseeing.

SAN RAFAEL

Casa Soldavini
531 "C" St., 94901
415-454-3140
Linda Soldavini, Dan Cassidy
All year

$$ B&B
3 rooms, 2 pb
•
C-no/S-no/P-no/H-no

Continental plus
Afternoon tea, snacks
Picnic baskets
Sitting room
bicycles

1932 winemaker's home, nestled in a quaint Italian neighborhood near Mission San Rafael. Close to everything. Enjoy 1930s movies & melodies or just relax on our front porch.

Panama Hotel & Restaurant
4 Bayview St., 94901
415-457-3993
Daniel T. Mill
All year

$ B&B
16 rooms, 8 pb
Major credit cards
C-yes/S-yes/P-no/H-s

Continental plus
Dinner
Beer, wine

A landmark inn and restaunt for 60 years, between San Francisco and wine country. The Panama is celebrated for its eccentric charm.

SANTA BARBARA

Bath Street Inn
1720 Bath St., 93101
805-682-9680
Susan Brown, Nancy Stover
All year

$$ B&B
7 rooms, 7 pb
Visa, MC, AmEx •
C-12+/S-yes/P-no/H-no

Continental plus
Comp. wine
Sitting & dining rooms
TV room, library
bicycles

Luxurious 3-story Victorian, panoramic views, balconies, brick courtyards. Lovely gardens create country inn environment; blocks from downtown.

SANTA BARBARA

Bayberry Inn
111 W. Valerio St., 93101
805-682-3199
Keith Pomeroy, Carlton Wagner
All year

$$$ B&B
8 rooms, 8 pb
Visa, MC •
C-no/S-no/P-no/H-yes

Full breakfast
Comp. wine
Sitting room, piano
bicycles
jacuzzi

A gracious in-town bed & breakfast inn within walking distance to shops, fine restaurants and entertainment, only 1 ½ mi. to beach. Fireplaces.

Blue Quail Inn & Cottages
1908 Bath St., 93101
805-687-2300
Jeanise Suding Eaton
All year exc. Dec 24-25

$$ B&B
9 rooms, 5 pb
Visa, MC •
C-12+/S-ltd/P-no/H-no

Full breakfast
Picnic lunches, cider
Sitting room
bicycles

Charming country atmosphere in a quiet residential area of Santa Barbara. Guest rooms, suites and private cottages filled with antiques.

Cheshire Cat Inn
36 W. Valerio St., 93101
805-569-1610
George Mari & Jane Shillan
All year

$$$ B&B
11 rooms, 11 pb
•
C-14+/S-no/P-no/H-no

Continental plus
Comp. wine
Library, sitting room
bicycles, hot tub
cooking school

Victorian elegance, uniquely decorated in Laura Ashley and English antiques; private baths, jacuzzis, balconies, fireplaces, gardens; convenient location, parking.

Glenborough Inn B&B
1327 Bath St., 93101
805-966-0589
David/Judy Groan, Laurel Fard
All year

$$ B&B
9 rooms, 5 pb
Visa, MC, AmEx •
C-12+/S-ltd/P-no/H-no

Full gourmet breakfast
Exotic juices/coffee/tea
Bedtime snacks, jacuzzi
Parlor w/fireplace
refrigerator available

Lovely grounds, elegant antique-filled rooms and suites, breakfast in bed, enclosed jacuzzi create a relaxing romantic holiday or business trip.

Long's Seaview B&B
317 Piedmont Rd., 93105
805-687-2947
Bob & LaVerne Long
All year

$$ B&B
1 rooms, 1 pb
C-12+/S-no/P-no/H-no

Full breakfast until 9am
Cont. breakfast after 9
comp. wine
Hot tub, gardens, patio

Home with a lovely view, furnished with antiques. Quiet neighborhood. Full breakfast served on the patio. Homemade jams and fresh fruits.

Ocean View House
P.O. Box 20065, 93102
805-966-6659
Carolyn & Bill Canfield
All year

$$ B&B
2 rooms, 1 pb
C-yes/S-ltd/P-ltd/H-no

Continental plus
Comp. wine
Beach towels & chairs

Breakfast on the patio while viewing sailboats and the Channel Islands. Private home in a quiet neighborhood. $10 extra for single night stay.

SANTA BARBARA ────────────────────────────────────

Old Yacht Club Inn | $$ B&B | Full breakfast
431 Corona Del Mar Dr., 93103 | 9 rooms, 5 pb | Dinner, beer & wine
805-962-1277 | Visa, MC, AmEx • | Bicycles
N.Donaldson, S.Hunt, L.Caruso | C-13+/S-ltd/P-no/H-no | towels
All year | Spanish | beach chairs

A 1912 California classic. Beautifully decorated antique-filled rooms. Gourmet breakfast. Dinner on weekends. Half block to beautiful beach.

────────────────────────────────────

Olive House | $$ B&B | Continental plus
1604 Olive St., 93101 | 5 rooms, 5 pb | Afternoon refreshments
805-962-4902 | Visa, MC • | Sitting room, library
Lois & Bob Poire | C-14+ | bicycles, fireplace
All year | | studio grand piano

Quiet comfort in lovingly restored California Craftsman pattern home. Bay windows, ocean views. Large sunny dining room setting for lively breakfast conversation.

────────────────────────────────────

The Parsonage | $$$ B&B | Full breakfast
1600 Olive St., 93101 | 6 rooms, 6 pb | Comp. wine
805-962-9336 | • | Sitting room
Hilde Michelmore | C-no/S-ltd/P-no/H-no |
All year | German |

A beautifully restored Queen Anne Victorian. An oasis of elegance with ocean and mountain views. Close to everything. German spoken.

Fairwinds Farm B&B, Inverness, CA

SANTA BARBARA

Sandman at the Beach	$$ B&B	Continental plus
18 Bath St., 93101	20 rooms, 22 pb	Afternoon tea
805-963-4418	Visa, MC, AmEx, Dis, En •	Comp. wine
Marie Johnsen	C-yes/S-yes/P-ask/H-yes	Sitting room
All year	French, Spanish, Arabic	hot tubs

Spanish-style villa, quiet, charming. One block from beach. Courtyard jacuzzi. Several units with fireplaces and kitchens.

Simpson House Inn	$$ B&B	Full breakfast
121 E. Arrellaga, 93101	6 rooms, 5 pb	Comp. wine
805-963-7067	Visa, MC •	Sitting room
Gillean Wilson, Linda Davies	C-no/S-ltd/P-no/H-yes	verandas, library
All year	Spanish, French, Danish	bicycles

1874 Victorian estate secluded in English gardens. Elegant antiques, art. Delicious leisurely breakfast on verandas. Walk to historic downtown.

Valli's View	$$ B&B	Full breakfast
340 N. Sierra Vista, 93108	2 rooms, 2 pb	Comp. wine
805-969-1272	•	Train/airport pickup
Valli & Larry Stevens	C-yes/P-ltd/H-yes	garden swing, patios
All year		deck, mountain views

A secluded home nestled in Montecito foothills provides peace and tranquillity, yet near city. Gourmet breakfast on patio or by fireplace.

SANTA CLARA

Madison Street Inn	$$ B&B	Full breakfast
1390 Madison St., 95050	5 rooms, 3 pb	Lunch, dinner by arr.
408-249-5541	Visa, MC, AmEx •	Complimentary wine
Ralph & Theresa Wigginton	C-yes/S-ltd/P-no/H-no	Library, sitting room
All year	French	hot tub, bicycles, pool

Santa Clara's only inn! A beautiful Victorian; landscaped gardens. Eggs Benedict is a breakfast favorite. Close to Winchester Mystery House. Weekend dinner package.

SANTA CRUZ

Babbling Brook Inn	$$$ B&B	Full buffet breakfast
1025 Laurel St., 95060	12 rooms, 12 pb	Afternoon wine & cheese
408-427-2437	Visa, MC, AmEx, Disc •	Picnic baskets
Tom & Helen King	C-no/S-ltd/P-no/H-ltd	phone & TV in rooms
All year		fireplaces

Secluded inn among waterfalls, gardens, gazebo, Laurel Creek, pines and redwoods. Complimentary wine, fireplaces. 12 rooms in country French decor; private bathrooms, decks.

Chateau Victorian, B&B Inn	$$$ B&B	Continental plus
118 First St., 95060	7 rooms, 7 pb	Comp. wine
408-458-9458	Visa, MC, AmEx	Sitting room, carpeting
Franz & Alice-June Benjamin	C-no/S-no/P-no/H-no	2 decks, patio
All year	German	fireplaces in rooms

One block from the beach and the boardwalk, in the heart of the Santa Cruz fun area.

72   California

SANTA CRUZ

Darling House
314 W. Cliff Dr., 95060
408-458-1958
Darrell & Karen Darling
All year

$$$ B&B
8 rooms, 2 pb
Visa, MC, AmEx •
C-ltd/S-ltd/P-no/H-ltd

Continental plus
Comp. beverage
Sitting room,
library. hot tub spa
double size bathtubs

1910 ocean-side mansion with beveled glass, Tiffany lamps, Chippendale antiques, open hearths and hardwood interiors. Walk to beach.

SANTA ROSA

Cooper's Grove Ranch
5763 Sonoma Mountain Rd, 95404
707-571-1928
All year

$$$ EP
5 rooms, 2 pb
C-yes/S-yes/P-yes/H-ltd
Spanish

Private full kitchen
Fireplaces, hiking
Horseback riding
flower gardens
private decks, BBQs

Two private cottages on country land in California's wine country. Kitchens, beautiful views, red-wood grove, picnic area, swimming, fishing, riding.

The Gables
4257 Petaluma Hill Rd., 95404
707-585-7777
Michael & Judith Ogne
All year

$$$ B&B
5 rooms, 5 pb
Visa, MC, AmEx •
C-ltd/S-yes/P-ltd/H-yes

Continental plus
Lunch, dinner, beer/wine
Sitting room, piano
entertainment, parking
conferences, weddings

Built in 1877, National Register of Historic Places; museum-quality restoration; European-Victorian decor. Gateway to wine country; elegant, rural location.

Gee-Gee's B&B Home
7810 Sonoma Hwy. 12, 95409
707-833-6667
Gerda Heaton-Weisz
All year

$$ B&B
4 rooms, 1 pb
•
C-no/S-no/P-no/H-no
French, German

Full breakfast
Sitting room
fireplace, TV
decks, RV parking
bicycles, swimming pool

Comfortable home on one acre in the Valley of the Moon—enchanting country setting. One mile to renowned wineries, golf course, horseback riding, jogging/hiking trails.

Hilltop House B&B
9550 St. Helena Rd., 95404
707-944-0880
Annette & Bill Gevarter
All year

$$$ B&B
2 rooms, 2 pb
•
C-12+/S-no/P-no/H-yes

Full breakfast
Comp. wine, snacks
Guest refrigerator
Sitting room, hot tub
hiking trails

A secluded mountain hideaway in a romantic setting on 135 acres of unspoiled wilderness, offers a hang glider's view of the Mayacamas Mountains.

Pygmalion House B&B
331 Orange St., 95407
707-526-3407
Lola L. Wright
All year

$$ B&B
5 rooms, 5 pb
•
C-10+/S-ltd/P-no/H-no

Full breakfast
Comp. tea
Sitting room, fireplace
television
central A/C & heat

Delightfully restored Queen Anne cottage central to Northern California wine country, San Francisco Bay area and North Coast resort areas.

SAUSALITO

Butterfly Tree
P.O. Box 790, 94966
415-383-8447
Karla Andersdatter
All year

$$$ B&B
4 rooms, 3 pb
C-ask/S-no/P-no/H-no
Spanish

Full breakfast
Comp. wine
Sitting room, library
nature walk to ocean
herb garden, butterflies

Secluded retreat for special occasions. Within recreational area and Muir Woods. Ocean view. Walk to beach, 30 min. from San Francisco. Monarch butterflies are winter guests.

Casa Madrona Hotel
801 Bridgeway, 94965
415-332-0502/800-288-0502
Lisa Winn, John Mays
All year

$$$ B&B
34 rooms, 34 pb
Visa, MC, AmEx
C-yes/S-yes/P-no/H-ltd
German, French, Spanish

Continental breakfast
Restaurant
Wine & cheese hour
Outdoor dining
Spa

Casa Madrona offers the privacy and coziness of a European country inn with individually decorated rooms, spectacular views of S.F. Bay & yacht harbor.

Sausalito Hotel
16 El Portal, 94965
415-332-4155
Liz MacDonald, Gene Hiller
All year

$$$ B&B
15 rooms, 9 pb
Visa, MC, AmEx •
C-ltd/S-yes/P-ltd/H-no

Continental plus

European-style hotel furnished in Victorian antiques. Located in heart of Sausalito and adjacent to San Francisco ferry.

SEAL BEACH

Seal Beach Inn & Gardens
212 5th St., 90740
213-493-2416
Marjorie Bettenhausen
All year

$$$ B&B
23 rooms, 23 pb
Visa, MC, AmEx •
C-ltd/S-ltd/P-no/H-no

Lavish full breakfast
Swimming pool
sitting rooms
guest library

Charming French Mediterranean inn, antique street lights, ornate fences, brick courtyard, private pool, exquisite gardens, near Disneyland & Long Beach.

SKYFOREST

Storybrook Inn
P.O. Box 362, 92385
28717 Hwy 18
714-336-1483
Kathleen & John Wooley
All year

$$$ B&B
10 rooms, 10 pb
Visa, MC, AmEx •
H-yes
some French, Italian

Full breakfast
Elaborate social hour
Aftn. tea, snacks
Picnic lunch, dinner
Library, hot tubs

Great escape to an elegant mountain inn by Lake Arrowhead. Nine charmingly decorated rooms with antiques and private baths. Separate rustic 1930s cabin also available.

SOMERSET

Fitzpatrick Winery Lodge
7740 Fairplay Rd., 95684
209-245-3248
Brian & Diana Fitzpatrick
All year

$$ B&B
5 rooms, 5 pb
Visa, MC •
C-yes/S-no/P-no/H-ltd

Full breakfast
Plowman's lunch
Comp. wine, bar service
Sitting room, hot tub
therapeutic massage

Handmade log lodge atop a hill at 2500-foot elevation with spectacular views overlooking El Dorado's wine country. Country charm and Irish hospitality.

SONOMA

Chalet B&B
18935 5th St. W., 95476
707-938-3129
Joe Leese, Bill Faulkner
All year exc. Xmas

$$$ B&B
6 rooms, 3 pb
Visa, MC
C-ltd/S-ltd/P-ltd/H-no

Continental plus
Comp. wine, tea
Deck, hot tub, bicycles
sitting room

Swiss-style chalet & cottages. 3-acre wine country farm setting. Located in the "Heart of Sonoma Valley" near historic plaza. Antiques, feather beds. Beautiful deck & garden.

Sonoma Hotel
110 W. Spain St., 95476
707-996-2996
Dorene & John Musilli
All year

$$ B&B
17 rooms, 5 pb
Visa, MC, AmEx •
C-yes/S-yes

Continental breakfast
Comp. wine, snacks
Restaurant, lunch/dinner
Bar service
Garden patio

Vintage hotel nationally acclaimed; bed & breakfast ambience, exceptional dining amidst antiques or on the garden patio.

Victorian Garden Inn
316 E. Napa St., 95476
707-996-5339
Donna Lewis
All year

$$ B&B
4 rooms, 3 pb
Visa, MC, AmEx •
C-ltd/S-ltd/P-no/H-no
Spanish

Continental plus
Comp. wine
Sitting room
piano
swimming pool

Secluded, large 1870 Greek revival farmhouse. Antiques, private entrances, fireplaces, Victorian rose gardens, winding paths, near plaza. Gracious hospitality.

SONORA

Barretta Gardens Inn
700 S. Barretta St., 95370
209-532-6039
Bob & Betty & Martin
All year

$$$ B&B
4 rooms, 1 pb
Visa, MC •
C-ask/S-ltd/P-no/H-ltd

Full breakfast
Comp. tea, wine
Three parlors
sun porch

Our inn provides comfort and serenity in a lovely garden setting. Close to town, summer and winter activities close by.

La Casa Inglesa B&B
18047 Lime Kiln Rd., 95370
209-532-5822
Mary & John Monser
All year exc. Xmas week

$$ B&B
5 rooms, 5 pb
C-no/S-no/P-no/H-no
Spanish

Full breakfast
Comp. coffee, tea,
soft drinks
Sitting room
hot tubs

Elegant Country English inn on wooded gold mine site in historic California Gold Country. Near Yosemite, redwoods, skiing, fishing.

Lavender Hill B&B
683 S. Barretta St., 95370
209-532-9024
Alice J. Byrnes
All year

$$ B&B
3 rooms, 1 pb
C-no/S-ltd/P-no/H-no

Full breakfast
Sitting room
porch swing

Restored Victorian in historic Gold Country. Antique furnishings, lovely grounds, porch swing and unmatched hospitality. Walk to town. Near Yosemite.

SONORA

Lulu Belle's B&B
85 Gold St., 95370
209-533-3455
Janet & Chris Miller
All year

$$ B&B
5 rooms, 5 pb
Visa, MC, AmEx •
C-yes/S-ltd/P-no/H-no
German, Spanish

Full breakfast
Afternoon tea, snacks
Library, A/C, bicycles
hot tubs (avail. 4/90)
music room, dinner pckgs

Historic 103-year-old Victorian with beautiful gardens and Lulu Belle's famous hospitality. Enjoy nearby theater, antiquing, boating, horseback riding and Gold Rush towns.

Ryan House
153 S. Shepherd St., 95370
209-533-3445
Nancy & Guy Hoffman
All year

$$ B&B
4 rooms, 2 pb
Visa, MC •
C-yes/S-no/P-no/H-no

Full breakfast
Afternoon tea, sherry
Sitting room
all queen-sized beds

Gold Rush romance in historic Mother Lode, close to fine dining and antique shops — we make you kindly welcome!!!

Serenity
15305 Bear Club Dr., 95370
209-533-1441
Fred & Charlotte Hoover
All year

$$$ B&B
4 rooms, 4 pb
Visa, MC •
C-no/S-ltd/P-no/H-no

Full breakfast
Comp. tea, wine
Sitting room
piano

Enjoy relaxed elegance in period home. Large rooms, library, veranda, and wooded grounds add to the serene ambience.

Via Serena Ranch
18007 Via Serena Dr., 95370
209-532-5307
Beverly Ballash
All year

$$ B&B
3 rooms
C-15+/S-no/P-no/H-no

Full breakfast
Sitting room
large deck

In the country, all amenities, fireplaces, electric blankets, air conditioning, large deck, tall pines and live oaks. A western welcome awaits all.

STINSON BEACH

Casa Del Mar
P.O. Box 238, 94970
37 Belvedere Ave.
415-868-2124
Rick Klein
All year

$$$ B&B
4 rooms, 4 pb
Visa, MC •
C-yes/S-no/P-no/H-no

Full breakfast
Afternoon tea
Comp. wine
Sitting room, library
garden

Nestled in the lap of Mount Tamalpais overlooking the ocean, a Mediterranean villa rises above a terraced garden. And what a garden!

SUTTER CREEK

Gold Quartz Inn
15 Bryson Dr., 95685
209-267-9155
Wendy Woolrich
All year

$$$ B&B
24 rooms, 24 pb
Visa, MC
S-no/P-no/H-yes

Full breakfast
Afternoon tea, beverages
Food catered for groups
Porch, picnics, A/C
TV in rm, conference rm.

Tucked away in charming Gold Country town. Step back 100 years. Rooms are decorated with antique furniture, prints and charming small touches, and have private porches.

SUTTER CREEK

Sutter Creek Inn	$$ B&B	Full breakfast
P.O. Box 385, 95685	19 rooms, 19 pb	Comp. refreshments
75 Main St.	C-15+/S-ltd/P-no/H-no	Sitting room, piano
209-267-5606		library, fireplaces
All year		handwriting analysis

Lovely country inn known for swinging beds and fireplaces. Beautiful grounds with hammocks and chaise lounges. Air conditioning and electric blankets.

TAHOE CITY

Mayfield House	$$ B&B	Continental plus
P.O. Box 5999, 95730	6 rooms	Comp. wine
236 Grove St.	Visa, MC •	
916-583-1001	C-10+/S-ltd/P-no/H-yes	
All year		

Within walking distance to shops and restaurants—each room individually decorated—"spit-spat" clean—convenient shuttle to skiing.

TAHOMA

Captain's Alpenhaus Inn	$$ B&B	Full breakfast
P.O. Box 262, 95733	14 rooms, 12 pb	Lunch/dinner, restaurant
6941 W. Lake Blvd.	Visa, MC, AmEx •	Bar, sitting room, pool
916-525-5000	C-yes/S-yes/P-ltd	hot tubs, Ping-Pong
Joel & Phyllis Butler	Spanish	volleyball, horseshoes
All year		

Our European-style country inn is across the street from Lake Tahoe and only minutes from Sierra ski resorts.

THREE RIVERS

Cort Cottage	$$ B&B	Continental plus
P.O. Box 245, 93271	1 rooms, 1 pb	Fully equiped kitchen
209-561-4671	•	Hot tubs outside
Gary & Catherine Cort	C-yes/S-ltd/P-no/H-ltd	living room
All year		

Contemporary, cozy cottage nestled into hillside, panoramic view of Sierra foothills, seasonal wild-flower path to creek, minutes away from Sequoia National Park.

TWAIN HARTE

Twain Harte's B&B	$ B&B	Full breakfast
P.O. Box 1718, 95383	6 rooms, 2 pb	Comp. wine
18864 Manzanita Dr.	Visa, MC •	Sitting room, piano
209-586-3311	C-yes/S-yes/P-no/H-yes	
El & Pat Pantaleoni		
All year		

Quaint mountain hideaway in wooded setting. Close to winter and summer recreation. Antique furnished and near fine dining. Family suite available.

VALLEY FORD

Inn at Valley Ford	$$ B&B	Continental plus
P.O. Box 439, 94972	4 rooms	Comp. tea, wine
14395 Hwy 1	Visa, MC	Hot tub
707-876-3182	C-no/S-ltd/P-no/H-ltd	bicycles
N. Balashov, S. Nicholls	French	sitting room
All year		

Comfortable Victorian farmhouse furnished with antiques, books and flowers. Located in pastoral hills, minutes from the Pacific and Sonoma Wine Country.

VENTURA

"La Mer" Bed & Breakfast	$$$ B&B	Full breakfast
411 Poli St., 93001	5 rooms, 5 pb	Comp. wine
805-643-3600	Visa, MC •	Library, sitting room
Michael & Gisela Baida	C-14+/S-no/P-no/H-no	
All year	German, Spanish	

Authentic European style in old Victorian. Ocean view. Three blocks to beach. Private entrances and private baths. Complimentary wine.

Bella Maggiore Inn	$$ B&B	Full breakfast
67 S. California St., 93001	32 rooms, 32 pb	Snacks
805-652-0277/800-523-8479	AmEx, Visa, MC •	Sitting room
Thomas Wood	C-13+/S-yes/P-no/H-no	grand piano
All year		spas in some rooms

Walk to beach from historic landmark inn. Enjoy European elegance—garden courtyard, chandeliers, antiques, original artwork, grand piano in lobby.

VOLCANO

St. George Hotel	$$$ MAP	Full breakfast
Main St., P.O. Box 9, 95689	20 rooms, 6 pb	Dinner included, bar
209-296-4458	C-ltd/S-no/P-ltd/H-ltd	Sitting room
Charles & Marlene Inman		pianos
Wed—Sun, mid-Feb.—Dec.		

Elegant Mother Lode hotel built in 1862. Maintains a timeless quality. Quiet area.

WALNUT CREEK

Mansion at Lakewood	$$$ B&B	Continental plus
1056 Hacienda Dr., 94598	7 rooms, 7 pb	Afternoon tea, snacks
415-946-9075	Visa, MC, AmEx	Sitting room, library
M. & S. McCoy, A. Johnson	C-12+/S-no/P-no/H-no	suite with fireplace &
All year		jacuzzi

19th-century country retreat for the 20th-century urban traveler. Elegantly restored 1861 estate with 3 acres of gardens. 7 extraordinary rooms. Hospitality unsurpassed!

WESTPORT

Bowen's Pelican Lodge	$ B&B	Continental breakfast
P.O. Box 35, 95488	6 rooms, 4 pb	Dining room, cocktails
38921 N. Hwy. 1	Visa, MC •	Sitting room, piano
707-964-5588	C-16+/S-yes/P-no/H-no	
Velma Bowen		
All year		

A small Victorian western country inn located 200 yards from the ocean in a small village with secluded beaches.

DeHaven Valley Farm	$$$ B&B	Full breakfast
39247 N. Hwy 1, 95488	8 rooms, 6 pb	Restaurant, lunch (res.)
707-961-1660	Visa, MC	4-course dinner Wed-Sat
Jim & Kathy Tobin	C-yes/S-no/P-no	Beer/wine, sitting room
All year		Library, hot tubs

1885 farmhouse and cottages on 20 acres of hills, meadows and streams, next to Pacific Ocean. Horses, donkeys, sheep and more. Explore Mendocino, tide pools, redwood forests.

78   California

WESTPORT ─────────────────────────────────

Howard Creek Ranch	$$ B&B	Full ranch breakfast
P.O. Box 121, 95488	6 rooms, 3 pb	Comp. tea
40501 N. Hwy 1	•	Hot tub, sauna
707-964-6725	C-ltd/S-ltd/P-ltd/H-ltd	swimming pool
Charles & Sally Grigg	Ger., Fr., Ital., Dutch	sitting room, piano
All year		

Historic farmhouse filled with collectibles, antiques & memorabilia, unique health spa with privacy and dramatic views adjoining a wide beach. Award-winning flower garden.

WHITTIER ─────────────────────────────────

Coleen's California Casa	$$ B&B	Full gourmet breakfast
P.O. Box 9302, 90601	3 rooms, 3 pb	Lunch & dinner on requ.
11715 S. Circle Dr.	•	Comp. wine, tea, snacks
213-699-8427	C-yes/S-yes/P-ltd/H-yes	Sitting room, patio
Coleen Davis	some Spanish	deck overlooking city
All year		

Beautifully decorated hillside home with sweeping view and lush landscaping. Wine & cheese await your return from sightseeing. Just 5 minutes from the 605 freeway.

WILLIAMS ─────────────────────────────────

Wilbur Hot Springs	$$$ EP	Kitchen privileges
Star Route, 95987	15 rooms, 2 pb	Sitting room, piano
916-473-2306	Visa, MC	swimming pool, hot tub
Richard & Ezzie Davis	C-ltd/S-ltd/P-no/H-ltd	entertainment
All year		

A peaceful rural retreat; no traffic, clean air, incredibly starry nights; naturally hot mineral baths; large country kitchen; turn-of-the-century hotel.

WINDSOR ─────────────────────────────────

Country Meadow Inn	$$$ B&B	Full breakfast
11360 Old Redwood Hwy, 95492	5 rooms, 5 pb	Afternoon tea, snacks
707-431-1276	Visa, MC •	Sitting room, A/C
Barry & Sandy Benson-Weber	C-yes/S-ltd/P-no/H-yes	hot tubs in room only
All year		reading materials

An informal country setting. Romantic & comfortable. Fireplaces, whirlpool tubs, decks, flower gardens, swimming and a freshness that extends to the abundant gourmet breakfast.

YOUNTVILLE ─────────────────────────────────

Burgundy House Country Inn	$$$ B&B	Full breakfast
P.O. Box 3156, 94599	5 rooms, 5 pb	Comp. wine
6711 Washington St.	•	Air conditioned
707-944-0889	C-no/S-no/P-no/H-no	Mobil 4-star rated
Dieter & Ruth Back	French, German	
All year		

1870 rustic country French stone house with Old World appeal. Furnished with country antiques. Perfect location in beautiful Napa Valley.

Oleander House	$$$ B&B	Full breakfast
P.O. Box 2937, 94599	4 rooms, 4 pb	Comp. beverages
7433 St. Helena Hwy (#29)	credit cards accepted •	Sitting room
707-944-8315	C-no/S-no/P-no/H-no	
Jonh & Louise Packard	Spanish	
All year		

Country French charm—antiques, brass beds—private decks, baths, fireplaces. Laura Ashley fabrics and wallpapers. Wine and cheese in afternoon.

More Inns...

Wool Loft   32751 Navarro Ridge Rd., Albion 95410   707-937-0377
Kenton Mine Lodge   P.O. Box 942, Alleghany 95910   916-287-3212
Cedar Creek Inn   P.O. Box 1466, Alpine 92001   619-445-9605
Dorris House   P.O. Box 1655, Alturas 96101   916-233-3786
Culbert House Inn   P.O. Box 45, Amador City 95601   209-267-0440
Cooper House B&B Inn   P.O. Box 1388, Angels Camp 95222   209-736-2145
Lady Anne Victorian Inn   902-14th St., Arcata 95521   707-822-2797
Guest House   120 Hart Lane, Arroyo Grande 93420   805-481-9304
Village Inn   407 El Camino Real, Arroyo Grande 93420   805-489-5926
Dry Creek Inn   13740 Dry Creek Rd., Auburn 95603   916-878-0885
Old Auburn Inn   149 Pleasant, Auburn 95603   916-885-6407
Hotel Villa Portofino   P.O. Box 127, Avalon 90704   213-510-0555
Inn at Mt. Ada   P.O. Box 2560, Avalon 90704   213-510-2030
Mavilla Inn   P.O. Box 2607, Avalon 90704   213-510-1651
Zane Grey Pueblo Hotel   P.O. Box 216, Avalon 90704   213-510-0966
San Luis Bay Inn   Box 188, Avila Beach 93424   805-595-2333
Helen K Inn   2105-19th St., Bakersfield 93301   805-325-5451
Star Route Inn   825 Olema-Balinas Road, Balinas 94924   415-868-2502
Thomas' White House Inn   118 Kale Road, Balinas 94924   415-868-0279
Ballard Inn   2436 Baseline, Ballard 93463   805-688-7770
Bayview House   1070 Santa Lucia Ave., Baywood Pk. 93402   805-528-3098
Fairview Manor   P.O. Box 74, Ben Lomond 95005   408-336-3355
Union Hotel   401 First St., Benicia 94510   707-746-0100
Delphinus B&B   1007 Leneve, El Cerrito, Berkeley 94530   415-527-9622
French Hotel   1538 Shattuck Ave., Berkeley 94709   415-548-9930
Gramma's B&B Inn   2740 Telegraph, Berkeley 94705   415-549-2145
Victorian Hotel   2520 Durant Ave., Berkeley 94704   415-540-0700
Gold Mountain Manor Inn   P.O. Box 2027, Big Bear City 92314   714-585-6997
Knickerbocker Mansion   869 S. Knickerbocker, Big Bear Lake 92315   714-866-8221
Deetjen's Big Sur Inn   Hwy. 1, Big Sur 93920   408-667-2377
Lucia Lodge   Big Sur 93920   408-667-2391
Taylor's Estero Vista Inn   P.O. Box 255, Bodega 94922   707-876-3300
Bodega Harbor Inn   P.O. Box 161, Bodega Bay 94923   707-875-3594
Bolinas Villa   P.O. Box 40, Bolinas 94924   415-868-1650
Wharf Road B&B   11 Wharf Rd., Bolinas 94924   415-868-1430
Anderson Creek Inn   P.O. Box 217, Boonville 95415   707-895-3091
Colfax's Guest House   Redwood Ridge Road, Boonville 95415   707-895-3241
Furtado's Hideaway   P.O. Box 650, Boonville 94515   707-895-3898
Bridgeport Hotel   Main Street, Bridgeport 93517   619-932-7380
Burbank/Belair   941 N. Frederic, Burbank 91505   818-848-9227
Burlingame B&B   1021 Balboa Avenue, Burlingame 94010   415-344-5815
Cora Harschel   8 Mariposa Ct., Burlingame 94010   415-697-5560
Brandy Wine Inn   1623 Lincoln Avenue, Calistoga 94515   707-942-0202
Brannon's Loft   P.O. Box 561, Calistoga 94515
Calistoga Country Lodge   2883 Foothill Blvd, Calistoga 94515   707-942-5555
Elms   1300 Cedar St., Calistoga 94515   707-942-9476
Golden Haven Hot Springs   1713 Lake St., Calistoga 94515   707-942-6793
Hideaway Cottages   1412 Fairway, Calistoga 94515   707-942-4108
Inn on Cedar Street   1307 Cedar St., Calistoga 94515   707-942-9244
La Chaumiere   1301 Cedar Street, Calistoga 94515   707-942-5139
Larkmead Country Inn   1103 Larkmead Ln., Calistoga 94515   707-942-5360
Le Spa Francais   1880 Lincoln Ave., Calistoga 94515   707-942-4636
Mountain Home Ranch   3400 Mountain Home, Calistoga 94515   707-942-6616

Quail Cottage   4698 Silverado Tr., Calistoga 94515   707-942-9030
Silver Rose Inn   351 Rosedale Rd., Calistoga 94515   707-942-9581
Washington Street Lodging   1605 Washington St., Calistoga 94515   707-942-6968
Wayside Inn   1523 Foothill Blvd., Calistoga 94515   707-942-0645
Country Bay Inn   34862 S. Coast Hwy., Capistrano Beach 92624   714-496-6656
Summer House B&B   216 Monterey Way, Capitola Valley 95010   408-475-8474
Pelican Cove Inn   320 Walnut Ave., Carlsbad 92008   619-434-5995
Colonial Terrace Inn   P.O. Box 1375, Carmel 93921   408-624-2741
Happy Landing Inn   P.O. Box 2619, Carmel 93921   408-624-7917
Mission Ranch   26270 Dolores, Carmel 93923   408-624-6436
San Antonio House   P.O. Box 2747, Carmel 93921   408-624-4334
Sandpiper Inn-At-the-Beach   2408 Bay View Ave., Carmel 93923   408-624-6433
Sea View Inn   P.O. Box 4138, Carmel 93921   408-624-8778
Sundial Lodge   P.O. Box J, Carmel 93921   408-624-8578
Forest Lodge   Ocean Ave. and Torres, Carmel-by-the-Sea 95903   408-624-7023
Pines Inn   P.O. Box 250, Carmel-by-the-Sea 93921   408-624-3851
Cazanoma Lodge   P.O. Box 37, Cazadero 95421   707-632-5255
Ten Aker Wood   P.O. Box 208, Cazadero 95421   707-632-5328
Timberhill Ranch Resort   35755 Hauser Bridge Rd, Cazadero 95421   707-847-3258
Drakesbad Guest Ranch   Warner Valley Rd., Chester 96020   (916) Drakes
White Sulphur Springs Rnch   P.O. Box 136, Clio 96106   916-836-2387
Crocker Country Inn   26532 River Rd., Cloverdale 95425   707-894-3911
Vintage Towers Inn   302 N. Main St., Cloverdale 95425   707-894-4535
Brookhill   Box 1019, 17655 HWY 17S, Cobb 95426   707-928-5029
Bear River Mt. Farm   21725 Placer Hills Rd., Colfax 95713   916-878-8314
Coloma Country Inn   P.O. Box 502, Coloma 95613   916-622-6919
Sierra Nevada House   P.O. Box 268, Coloma 95613   916-622-5856
O'Rourke Mansion   1765 Lurline Rd., Colusa 95932   916-458-5625
Carolyn's B&B Homes   P.O. Box 943, Coronado 92118   207-548-2289
Jeffrey Hotel   P.O. Box 4, Coulterville 95311   209-878-3400
Partridge Inn   521 First St., Davis 95616   916-753-1211
Dorrington Hotel   P.O. Box 4307, Dorrington 95223   209-795-5800
Lamplighters   7724 E Cecilia St, Downey 90241   213-928-8229
Sierra Shangri-La   P.O. 285, Rt. 49, Downieville 95936   916-289-3455
Brookside Farm B&B Inn   1373 Marron Valley Rd., Dulzura 92017   619-468-3043
Lion's Head Guest House   Box 21203, El Cajon 92021   619-463-4271
Green Dolphin Inn   P.O. Box 132, Elk 95432   707-877-3342
Greenwood Lodge   P.O. Box 172, Elk 95432   707-877-3422
Scott Valley Inn   P.O. Box 261, Etna 96027   916-467-3229
Eagle House Victorian Inn   139 2nd St., Eureka 95501   707-442-2334
Heuer's Victorian Inn   1302 E Street, Eureka 95501   707-445-7334
Iris Inn   1134 H Street, Eureka 95501   707-445-0307
Stevens House   917 3rd St., Eureka 95501   707-444-8062
Freitas House Inn   744 Jackson St., Fairfield 94533   707-425-1366
Narrow Gauge Inn   48571 Hwy. 41, Fish Camp 93623   209-683-7720
Folsom Hotel   703 Sutter Street, Folsom 95630
Plum Tree Inn   307 Leidesdorff St., Folsom 95630   916-351-0116
Avalon House   561 Stewart St., Fort Bragg 95437   707-964-5555
Blue Rose Inn   520 North Main St., Fort Bragg 95437   707-964-3477
Cleone Lodge   24600 N Hwy. 1, Fort Bragg 95437   707-964-2788
Colonial Inn   P.O. Box 565, Fort Bragg 95437   707-964-9979
Country Inn   632 N. Main St., Fort Bragg 95437   707-964-3737
Glass Beach B&B Inn   726 N. Main St., Fort Bragg 95437   707-964-6774
Oceanview Lodge   1141 N. Main St., Fort Bragg 95437   707-964-1951

Orca Inn   31502 N. Hwy 1, Fort Bragg 95437   707-964-5585
Pine Beach Inn   P.O. Box 1173, Fort Bragg 95437   707-964-5603
Pudding Creek Inn   700 N. Main St., Fort Bragg 95437   707-964-9529
Roundhedge Inn   159 N. Whipple St., Fort Bragg 95437   707-964-9605
Marlahan House   9539 No. Hwy 3, Fort Jones 96032   916-468-5527
Patrick Creek Lodge   Gasquet 95543   Dial 0 Idlew
Isis Oasis Lodge   20889 Geyserville Ave., Geyserville 95441   707-857-3524
Gaige House   13540 Arnold Dr., Glen Ellen 95442   707-935-0237
Stonetree Ranch   7910 Sonoma Mt. Road, Glen Ellen 95442   707-996-8173
Tanglewood House   250 Bonnie Way, Glen Ellen 95442   707-996-5021
Watermans, A B&B   12841 Dunbar Rd., Glen Ellen 95442   707-996-8106
Annie Horan's B&B   415 W. Main St., Grass Valley 95945   916-272-2418
Domike's Inn   220 Colfax Ave., Grass Valley 95945   916-273-9010
Golden Ore House B&B   448 S. Auburn St., Grass Valley 95945   916-272-6870
Holbrooke Hotl/Purcell Hse   212 W. Main St., Grass Valley 95945   916-273-1353
Murphy's Inn   318 Neal St., Grass Valley 95945   916-273-6873
Hotel Charlotte   Rt. 120, Groveland 95321   209-962-6455
Gualala Country Inn   P.O. Box 697, Gualala 95445
Old Milano Hotel   38300 Hwy 1, Gualala 95445   707-884-3256
Saint Orres   P.O. Box 523, Gualala 95445   707-884-3303
Camelot Resort   P.O. Box 467 4th & Mill, Guerneville 95446   707-869-2538
Creekside Inn & Resort   P.O. Box 2185, Guerneville 95446   707-869-3623
River Lane Resort   16320 1st Street, Guerneville 95446   707-869-2323
Willows   P.O. Box 465, Guerneville 95446   707-869-3279
Irwin Street Inn   522 N. Irwin, Hanford 93230   209-584-9286
Belle de Jour Inn   16276 Healdsburg Ave., Healdsburg 95448   707-433-7892
Grape Leaf Inn   539 Johnson St., Healdsburg 95448   707-433-8140
L'Auberge du Sans-Souci   25 W. Grant St., Healdsburg 95448   707-431-1110
Hudson   1740 N. Hudson Ave, Hollywood 90028   213-469-5320
Rockwood Lodge   P.O. Box 226, Homewood 95718   916-525-4663
Sorensen's Resort   Highway 88, Hope Valley 96120   916-694-2203
Thatcher Inn   13401 Hwy. 101, Hopland 95449   707-744-1890
Wilkum Inn   P.O. Box 1115, Idyllwild 92349   714-659-4087
Alder House   105 Vision Rd. P.O. Box 6, Inverness 94937   414-669-7218
The Ark   Box 273, Inverness 94937   415-663-9338
Gray Whale Upstairs   12781 Sir Francis Drake, Inverness 94937   415-669-1330
Inverness Valley Inn   13275 Sir Francis Drake, Inverness 94937   415-669-7250
MacLean House   P.O. Box 651, Inverness 94937   415-669-7392
Manka's Inverness Lodge   P.O. Box 126, Inverness 94937   415-669-1034
Ann Marie's Lodging   410 Stasel St., Jackson 95642   209-223-1452
Court Street Inn   215 Court St., Jackson 95642   209-223-0416
Jamestown Hotel   P.O. Box 539, Jamestown 95327   209-984-3902
Palm B&B   10382 Willow Street, Jamestown 95327   209-984-3429
Murphy's Jenner Inn   P.O. Box 69, Jenner 95450   707-865-2377
Salt Point Lodge   23255 Coast Hwy One, Jenner 95450   707-847-3234
Stillwater Cove Ranch   Jenner 95450   707-847-3227
Julian Lodge   P.O. Box 1930, Julian 92036   619-765-1420
Pine Hills Lodge   P.O. Box 701, Julian 92036   619-765-1100
Shadow Mountain Ranch   2771 Frisius Rd., Julian 92036   619-765-0323
Villa Idalene   P.O. Box 90, Julian 92036   619-765-1252
B&B Inn at La Jolla   7753 Draper Ave., La Jolla 92037   619-456-2066
Hotel California   1316 S. Coast Highway, Laguna Beach 92651   714-497-1457
Lakeview Lodge   28051 Highway 189, Lake Arrowhead 92352   714-337-6633
Saddleback Inn   300 S. State HWY 173, Lake Arrowhead 92352   714-336-3571

Bell Glen Eel River Inn   70400 Highway 101, Leggett 95455   707-925-6425
Fools Rush Inn   7533 N. Highway One, Little River 95456   707-937-5339
Glendeven   8221 N. Hwy. 1, Little River 95456   707-937-0083
Mercy Hot Springs   P.O. Box 1363, Los Banos 93635
Courtside   14675 Winchester Blvd., Los Gatos 95030   408-395-7111
La Hacienda Inn   18840 Los Gatos Road, Los Gatos 95030   408-354-9230
Los Gatos Hotel   31 E. Main St., Los Gatos 95030   408-354-4440
Country Cottage   2920 Grand Ave. Box 26, Los Olivos 93441   805-688-1395
Los Olivos Grand Hotel   2860 Grand Avenue, Los Olivos 93441   805-688-7788
Red Rooster Ranch   P.O. Box 554, Los Olivos 93441   805-688-8050
Zaca Lake   P.O. Box 187, Los Olivos 93441   805-688-4891
Geralda's B&B   1056 Bay Oaks Drive, Los Osos 93402   805-528-3973
Big Canyon Inn   P.O. Box 1311, Lower Lake 95457   707-928-5631
Chalet on the Mount   4960 Usona Rd., Mariposa 95338   209-966-5115
Dick & Shirl's B&B   4870 Triangle Rd., Mariposa 95338   209-966-2514
Vista Grande B&B   4160 Vista Grande Way, Mariposa 95338   209-742-6206
B.G. Ranch & Inn   9601 N. Hwy 1, Mendocino 95460   707-937-5322
Bay Company Inn   P.O. Box 817, 571 Ukiah, Mendocino 95460   707-937-5266
Blackberry Inn   44951 Larkin Road, Mendocino 95460   707-937-5281
Blue Heron Inn B&B   390 Kasten St.,POB 1142, Mendocino 95460   707-937-4323
Hill House Inn   P.O. Box 625, Mendocino 95410   707-937-0554
Mama Moon Gardens   P.O. Box 994, Mendocino 95460   707-937-4234
Mendocino Hotel   P.O. Box 587, Mendocino 95460   707-937-0511
Mendocino Tennis Club/Ldge   43250 Little Lake Road, Mendocino 95460   707-937-0007
Rachel's Inn   Box 134, Mendocino 95460   707-937-0088
Sea Gull Inn   P.O. Box 317, Mendocino 95460   707-937-5204
Sea Rock B&B Inn   P.O. Box 286, Mendocino 95460   707-937-5517
Sears House Inn   Main St. P.O. Box 844, Mendocino 95460   707-937-4076
Harbin Hot Springs   P.O. Box 782, Middletown 95461   707-987-2477
Nethercott Inn   P.O. Box 671, Middletown 95461   707-987-3362
Happy Medium   P.O. Box 10, Midpine, Midpine 95345   209-742-6366
Homestead Guest Ranch B&B   P.O. Box 13, Midpines 95345   209-966-2820
Sierra Bed & Breakfast   Box 221, Midpines 95345   209-966-5478
Sycamore House   99 Sycamore Ave., Mill Valley 94941   415-383-0612
Hotel Leger   P.O. Box 50, Mokelumne Hill 95245   209-286-1401
Farallone Hotel   1410 Main, Montara 94037   415-728-7817
House of a 1000 Flowers   P.O. Box 369, Monte Rio 95421   707-632-5571
Huckleberry Springs Inn   P.O. Box 400, Monte Rio 95462   707-865-2683
Del Monte Beach Inn   1110 Del Monte Ave., Monterey 93940   408-649-4410
Merritt House   386 Pacific St., Monterey 93940   408-646-9686
The Monterey   406 Alvarado St., Monterey 93940   408-375-3184
Mt. Shasta House B&B   113 South "A" St., Mt. Shasta 96067   916-926-5089
Murphys Hotel   P.O. Box 329, 457 Main, Murphys 95247   209-728-3444
Arbor Guest House   1436 G Street, Napa 94559   707-252-8144
Beazley House   1910 First St., Napa 94559   707-257-1649
Black Surrey Inn   1815 Silverado Tr., Napa 94558   707-255-1197
Brookside Vineyard B&B   3194 Redwood Road, Napa 94558   707-944-1661
Churchill Manor   485 Brown St., Napa 94559   707-253-7733
Crystal Rose Victorian Inn   7564 St. Helena Hwy., Napa 94558   707-944-8185
Elm House   800 California, Napa 94559   707-255-1831
Goodman House   1225 Division St., Napa 94558   707-257-1166
Hennessey House B&B   1727 Main Street, Napa 94559   707-226-3774
La Belle Epoque   1386 Calistoga Ave., Napa 94558   707-257-2161
La Residence Country Inn   4066 St. Helena Hwy. N., Napa 94558   707-253-0337

Magnolia Hotel P.O. Box M, Yountville, Napa 94599 707-944-2056
Oak Knoll Inn 2200 E. Oak Knoll Ave., Napa 94558 707-255-2200
Old World Inn 1301 Jefferson St., Napa 94559 707-257-0112
Rockhaven 7774 Silverado Trail, Napa 94558 707-944-2041
Sybron House 7400 St. Helena Hwy, Napa 94558 707-944-2785
Trubody Ranch B&B 5444 St. Helena Hwy, Napa 94558 707-255-5907
Yesterhouse Inn 643 Third Street, Napa 94559 707-257-0550
Flume's End 317 S. Pine, Nevada City 95959 916-265-9665
Doryman's Inn 2102 W. Oceanfront, Newport Beach 92663 714-675-7300
Norden House Box 94, Norden 95724 916-426-3326
Ye Olde South Fork Inn P.O. Box 731, North Fork 93643 209-877-7025
Rockridge B&B 5428 Thomas Ave., Oakland 94618 415-655-1223
Ojai Bed & Breakfast 921 Patricia Ct., Ojai 93023 805-646-8337
Theodore Woolsey House 1484 E. Ojai Ave, Ojai 93023 805-646-9779
Olema Inn P. O. Box 10, Olema 94950 415-663-8441
Point Reyes Seashore Lodge 10021 Coastal Highway 1, Olema 94950 415-663-9000
Christy Hill Inn Box 2449, Olympic Valley 95730 916-583-8551
Red Lion Inn 222 N. Vineyard Road, Ontario 91764 714-983-0909
Down Under Inn 157 15th St., Pacific Grove 93950 408-373-2993
Maison Bleue French B&B P.O. Box 51371, Pacific Grove 93950 408-373-2993
Old St. Angela Inn 321 Central Ave., Pacific Grove 93950 408-372-3246
Ingleside Inn 200 W. Ramon Rd., Palm Springs 92262 619-325-0046
Le Petit Chateau 1491 Via Soledad, Palm Springs 92262 619-325-2686
Crown B&B Inn 530 S. Marengo, Pasadena 91101 818-792-4031
Donnymac Irish Inn 119 N. Meridith, Pasadena 91106 818-440-0066
Pismo Landmark B&B 701 Price St, Pismo Beach 93449 805-773-5566
Chichester House B&B 800 Spring St., Placerville 95667 916-626-1882
Fleming Jones Homestead 3170 Newtown Rd., Placerville 95667 916-626-5840
Historic Combellack-Blair 3059 Cedar Ravine, Placerville 95667 916-622-3764
James Blair House 2985 Clay St., Placerville 95667 916-626-6136
Rupley House Inn P.O. Box 1709, Placerville 95667 916-626-0630
Point Arena Lighthouse Box 11, Point Arena 95468 707-882-2777
Ferrando's Hideaway P.O. Box 688, Point Reyes 94956 415-663-1966
Quinta Quetzalcoati P.O. Box 27, Point Richmond 94807 415-235-2050
James Creek Ranch B&B 2249 James Crk., Pope Valley 94567
Olson Farmhouse B&B 3620 Road B, Redwood Valley 95470 707-485-7523
Auberge du Soleil 180 Rutherford Hill Rd., Rutherford 94573 707-963-1211
Rosi's of Rutherford B&B P.O. Box 243, Rutherford 94573 707-963-3135
Briggs House 2209 Capitol Ave., Sacramento 95816 916-441-3214
Driver Mansion Inn 2019 21st Street, Sacramento 95818 916-455-5243
Ambrose Bierce House 1515 Main St., Saint Helena 94574 707-963-3003
Creekwood 850 Conn Valley Rd., Saint Helena 94574 707-963-3590
Harvest Inn One Main St., Saint Helena 94574 707-963-9463
Thorn Mansion P.O. Box 1437, San Andreas 95249 209-754-1027
Casa Tropicana 610 Avenida Victoria, San Clemente 92672 714-492-1234
San Clemente Hideaway 323 Cazador Ln., San Clemente 92672 714-498-2219
Balboa Park Inn 3402 Park Blvd., San Diego 92103 619-298-0823
Edgemont Inn 1955 Edgemont St., San Diego 92102 619-238-1677
Frances Williamson 2156 Becky Place, San Diego 92104
Keating House Inn 2331 Second Ave., San Diego 92101 619-239-8585
"No Name B&B" 847 Fillmore St., San Francisco 94117 415-931-3083
Adelaide Inn 5 Adelaide Place, San Francisco 94102 415-441-2261
Ansonia B&B Inn 711 Post St., San Francisco 94109 415-673-2670
Aurora Manor 1328 16th Ave., San Francisco 94122 415-564-2480

Bock's Bed and Breakfast 1448 Willard St., San Francisco 94117 415-664-6842
Clementina's Bay Brick 1190 Folsom St., San Francisco 94103 415-431-8334
Comfort B&B 1265 Guerrero St., San Francisco 94110 415-641-8803
Commodore International 825 Sutter St. at Jones, San Francisco 94109 415-885-2464
Dolores Park Inn 3641 Seventeenth St., San Francisco 94114 415-621-0482
Edward II Inn & Suites 3155 Scott St & Lombard, San Francisco 94123 415-922-3000
Emperor Norton Inn 615 Post St., San Francisco 94109 415-775-2567
Fay Mansion Inn 834 Grove St., San Francisco 94117 415-921-1816
Hermitage House 2224 Sacramento St., San Francisco 94115 415-921-5515
Hotel Louise 845 Bush St., San Francisco 94108 415-775-1755
Inn at Union Square 440 Post St., San Francisco 94102 415-397-3510
Jackson Court 2198 Jackson St., San Francisco 94115 415-929-7670
Le Petit Manoir 468 Noe St., San Francisco 94114 415-864-7232
Lyon Street B&B 120 Lyon St., San Francisco 94117 415-552-4773
Mansion Hotel 2220 Sacramento, San Francisco 94115 415-929-9444
Masonic Manor 1468 Masonic Ave., San Francisco 94117 415-621-3365
Millefiori Inn 444 Columbus, San Francisco 94133 415-433-9111
Pacific Heights Inn 1555 Union St., San Francisco 94123 415-776-3310
Pensione San Francisco 1668 Market St., San Francisco 94102 415-864-1271
Riley's B&B 1322-24 6th Ave., San Francisco 94122 415-731-0788
Spencer House 1080 Haight St., San Francisco 94117 415-626-9205
Stanyan Park Hotel 750 Stanyan St., San Francisco 94117 415-751-1000
Stewart-Grinsell House 2963 Laguna St., San Francisco 94123 415-346-0424
Washington Square Inn 1660 Stockton St., San Francisco 94133 415-981-4220
O'Neill's Private Accom. 11801 Sharon Dr., San Jose 95129 408-996-1231
B&B San Juan P.O. Box 613, San Juan Bautista 95045 408-623-4101
Heritage Inn 978 Olive St., San Luis Obispo 93401 805-544-2878
Ole Rafael B&B 528 C St., San Rafael 94901 415-453-0414
Old Oak Table 809 Clemensen Ave., Santa Ana 92701 714-639-7798
Arlington Inn 1136 De La Vina, Santa Barbara 93101 805-965-6532
Brinkerhoff B&B Inn 523 Brinkerhoff Ave., Santa Barbara 93101 805-963-7844
Harbor Carriage House 420 W. Montecito St., Santa Barbara 93101 805-962-8447
Inn at Two Twenty Two 222 W. Valerio, Santa Barbara 93101 805-687-7216
Red Rose Inn 1416 Castillo, Santa Barbara 93101 805-966-1470
Tiffany Inn 1323 De la Vina, Santa Barbara 93101 805-963-2283
Upham Hotel 1404 De La Vina St., Santa Barbara 93101 805-962-0058
Villa Rosa 15 Chapala St., Santa Barbara 93101 805-966-0851
Villa d'Italia 780 Mission Canyon Rd., Santa Barbara 93105 805-687-6933
Cliff Crest B&B Inn 407 Cliff St., Santa Cruz 95060 408-427-2609
Pleasure Point Inn B&B 2-3665 East Cliff Dr., Santa Cruz 95062 408-474-4657
Santa Maria Inn 801 S. Broadway, Santa Maria 93454 805-928-7777
Sovereign at Santa Monica 205 Washington Ave., Santa Monica 90403 800-331-0163
Lemon Tree Inn 299 W. Santa Paula St., Santa Paula 93060 805-525-7747
Belvedere Inn 727 Mendocino Ave., Santa Rosa 95401 707-575-1857
The Gables 4257 Petaluma Hill Rd., Santa Rosa 95404 707-585-7777
Melitta Station Inn 5850 Melita Rd., Santa Rosa 95409 707-538-7712
Eden Valley Place 22490 Mt. Eden Rd., Saratoga 95070 408-867-1785
Alta Mira Continental Hote P.O. Box 706, Sausalito 94966 415-332-1350
Scotia Inn P.O. Box 248, Scotia 95565 707-764-5683
Sea Ranch Lodge P.O. Box 44, Sea Ranch 95497 707-785-2371
O'Hagin's Guest House P.O. Box 126, Sebastopol 95472 707-823-4771
Strout House 253 Florence Ave., Sebastopol 95472 707-823-5188
Spring Creek Inn 15201 Hwy 299 W., Box 1, Shasta 96087 916-243-0914
Consciousness Village Box 234, Sierraville 96126 916-994-8984

Sunflower House   243 Third St., Solvang 93463   805-688-4492
Ranch at Somis   6441 La Cumbre Rd., Somis 93066   805-987-8455
Au Relais Inn   681 Broadway, Sonoma 95476   707-996-1031
Austin Street Cottage   739 Austin St., Sonoma 95476   707-938-8434
Country Cottage   291 1st St. East, Sonoma 95476   707-938-2479
El Dorado Inn   405 First Street West, Sonoma 95476   707-996-3030
Hidden Oak   214 E. Napa Street, Sonoma 95476   707-996-9863
Kate Murphy's Cottage   43 France St., Sonoma 95476   707-996-4359
Overview Farm B&B Inn   15650 Arnold Dr., Sonoma 95476   707-938-8574
Thistle Dew Inn   P.O. Box 1326, Sonoma 95476   707-938-2909
Trojan Horse Inn   P.O. Box 1663, Sonoma 95476   707-996-2430
Vineyard Inn   P.O. Box 368, Sonoma 95476   707-938-2350
JVB Vineyard   P.O. Box 997, Sonoma-Glen Ellen 95442   707-996-4533
Gunn House   286 S. Washington, Sonora 95370   209-532-3421
Oak Hill Ranch B&B   P.O. Box 307, Tuolumne, Sonora 95379   209-928-4717
Sonora Inn   160 S. Washington, Sonora 95370   209-532-7468
Willow Spgs. Country Inn   20599 Kings Ct., Soulsbyville 95372   209-533-2030
Christiana Inn   Box 18298, South Lake Tahoe 95706   916-544-7337
Strawberry Lodge   Hwy 50, South Lake Tahoe 95720   916-659-7200
Bale Mill Inn   3431 N St. Helena Hwy., St. Helena 94574   707-963-4545
Bell Creek B&B   3220 Silverado Tr., St. Helena 94574   707-963-2383
Chestelson House   1417 Kearney St., St. Helena 94574   707-963-2238
Creekwood   850 Conn Valley Rd., St. Helena 94574   707-963-3590
Farmhouse   300 Turpin Rd., St. Helena 94574   707-944-8430
Judy's Ranch House   701 Rossi Road, St. Helena 94574   707-963-3081
Prager Winery B&B   1281 Lewelling Ln., St. Helena 94574   707-963-3713
Spanish Villa Inn   474 Glass Mtn. Rd., St. Helena 94574   707-963-7483
Valley Knoll Vineyard   Highway 29, St. Helena 94574   707-963-7770
White Ranch   707 White Lane, St. Helena 94574   707-963-4635
Old Victorian Inn   207 W Acacia St., Stockton 95203   209-462-1613
Figs Cottage   3935 Rhodes Avenue, Studio City 91604   818-769-2662
Summerland Inn   2161 Ortega Hill Rd,B12, Summerland 93067   805-969-5225
Sunnyside Inn   435 E. McKinley, Sunnyvale 94086   408-736-3794
Sunset B&B Inn   P.O. Box 1202, Sunset Beach 90742   213-592-1666
Botto Country Inn   11 Sutter Hill Rd, Sutter Creek 95685   209-267-5519
Foxes in Sutter Creek   P.O. Box 159; 77 Main St., Sutter Creek 95685   209-267-5882
Hanford House   P.O. Box 1450, Sutter Creek 95685   209-267-0747
Nancy & Bob's Inn   P.O. Box 386, Sutter Creek 95685   209-267-0342
Lakeside House   P.O. Box 7108, Tahoe City 95730   916-683-8796
River Ranch   P.O. Box 197, Tahoe City 95730   916-583-4264
Country House Inn   91 Main St., Templeton 93465   805-434-1598
Quail Country B&B   1104 Old Monticello Roa, Thomasville 31792   912-226-7218
Byron Randall's Victorian   25 Valley St., Tomales 94971   707-878-9992
Lost Whale Inn   3452 Patrick's Point Dr, Trinidad 95570   707-677-3425
Trinidad Bed & Breakfast   P.O. Box 849, Trinidad 95570   707-677-0840
Hilltop at Truckee   Box 8579, Hwy. 267, Truckee 95737   916-587-2545
Mountain View Inn   P.O. Box 2011, Truckee 95734   916-587-5388
Sanford House   306 S. Pine, Ukiah 95482   707-462-1653
Narrows Lodge   5670 Blue Lake Road, Upper Lake 95485   707-275-2718
Venice Beach House   15 30th Ave., Venice 90291   213-823-1966
Baker Inn   1093 Poli St., Ventura 93001   805-652-0143
Clocktower Inn   181 E. Santa Clara St., Ventura 93001   805-652-0141
Roseholm   51 Sulphur Mt. Rd., Ventura 93001   805-649-4014

Volcano Inn   P.O. Box 4, Volcano 95689   209-296-4959
Gasthaus zum Baren   2113 Blackstone Dr., Walnut Creek 94598   415-934-8119
Hendrick Inn   2124 E. Merced Ave., West Covina 91791   818-919-2125
Westport Inn B&B   Box 145, Westport 95488   707-964-5135
Doll House B&B   118 School St., Willits 95490   707-459-4055
Napa Valley Railway Inn   6503 Washington St., Yountville 94559   707-944-2000
Webber Place   6610 Webber St., Yountville 94599   707-944-8384
Harkey House B&B   212 C Street, Yuba City 95991   916-674-1942
Wick's   560 Cooper Ave., Yuba City 95991   916-674-7951

Colorado

ALAMOSA

Cottonwood Inn
123 San Juan, 81101
719-589-3882
Julie & George Sellman
All year

$ B&B
5 rooms, 2 pb
Visa, MC •
C-12+/S-ltd
Spanish

Full bkfst (summ, wkend)
Cont. plus (fall, wkday)
Comp. wine, library
Nutragena soaps & creams
turndown service

Charming inn. Artwork and antiques adorn cozy guest rooms. Biking, hiking, dune walking, fishing, bird-watching & skiing. Historically furnished dining room. Gourmet breakfast.

ASPEN

Christmas Inn B&B
232 W. Main St., 81611
303-925-3822
Barbara Fasching
All year

$ B&B
23 rooms, 23 pb
Visa, MC, AmEx •
C-yes/S-yes/P-no/H-ltd

Full breakfast
Sitting room
phones in each room
hot tub, sauna

Attractive, cozy, clean rooms with extra-long beds. Excellent location. Cheerful lobby and sitting room for spectacular view of Aspen ski mountains.

Hearthstone House
134 E. Hyman St., 81611
303-925-7632
Irma Prodinger
Summer & winter

$$$ B&B
17 rooms, 17 pb
Visa, MC, AmEx •
C-5+/S-ltd/P-no/H-no
French, German

Full breakfast
Afternoon tea
Hot tub, bed turndown
service, sitting room,
fireplace, herbal bath

The preferred place to stay! Distinctive lodge with the hospitality and services in the finest tradition of European luxury inns.

Innsbruck Inn
233 W. Main St., 81611
303-925-2980
Karen & Heinz Coordes
6/1—10/15, 11/23—4/15

$$ B&B
30 rooms, 30 pb
Visa, MC, AmEx, DC, CB •
C-yes/S-yes/P-no/H-no
German

Full breakfast
Comp. wine (winter)
Afternoon tea (winter)
Sitting room, library
hot tub, sauna, pool

Tyrolean charm and decor; located at ski shuttle stop, 4 blocks from malls. Sunny breakfast room, generous buffet, apres-ski refreshments, fireside lobby.

Gosby House Inn, Pacific Grove, CA

ASPEN

Snow Queen Victorian Lodge	$$ B&B	Cont. plus (winter only)
124 E. Cooper, 81612	7 rooms, 3 pb	Outdoor hot tub
303-925-8455/303-925-6971	AmEx •	parlor w/fireplace,
Norma Dolle & Larry Lediugham	C-yes/S-yes/P-no/H-no	color TV, walk to ski
All year	Spanish	lifts

We specialize in a friendly congenial atmosphere with western hospitality & inexpensive rates. Rooms named after famous silver mines in town. Easy walk to center of town.

Ullr Lodge	$$ B&B	Continental breakfast
520 W. Main St., 81611	25 rooms, 25 pb	Hot tub, sauna
303-925-7696	Visa, MC, AmEx, DC, Ch •	swimming pool
Anthony Percival	C-yes/S-yes/P-no/H-no	sitting room
All year	Dutch, Flemish	

Small European-style lodge offering rooms and condominiums. Free shuttle to ski route. Walking distance to music festival and Aspen Institute.

BOULDER

Pearl Street Inn
1820 Pearl St., 80302
303-444-5584
Yossi Shem-Avi
All year

$$$ B&B
7 rooms, 7 pb
Visa, MC, AmEx, Diners •
C-yes/S-yes/P-yes/H-no
French

Continental plus
Comp. wine, bar service
Sitting room
entertainment
TV in most rooms

A rare combination of European inn and luxury hotel. Near Boulder's pedestrian mall. Refreshing breakfast and evening bar in garden courtyard.

BUENA VISTA

Adobe Inn
P.O. Box 1560, 81211
303 N. Hwy 24
719-395-6340
Paul & Marjorie Knox
All year

$ B&B
5 rooms, 5 pb
Visa, MC
C-yes/S-no/P-no/H-no
some Spanish

Full gourmet breakfast
Comp. beverages
Restaurant, sitting room
Library, piano, solarium
2 suites, jacuzzi

Santa Fe-style adobe hacienda. Indian, Mexican, antique, wicker & Mediterranean rooms. Indian fireplaces. Gourmet breakfast. Jacuzzi. Majestic mountain & river scenery.

Trout City Inn
Box 431, 81211
719-495-0348
Juel & Irene Kjeldsen
June—October 15

$ B&B
4 rooms, 4 pb
Visa, MC •
C-10+/S-no/P-no/H-no

Full breakfast
Box lunch, snacks
Comp. non-alc. wine
Library, bicycles, pool
hiking, gold panning

Historic railway station on mountain pass in national forest. Our own railroad, trout stream, beaver ponds, goldmine. Grand mountain view.

COLORADO SPRINGS

Holden House-1902
1102 W. Pikes Peak Ave., 80904
719-471-3980
Sallie & Welling Clark
All year

$$ B&B
3 rooms, 3 pb
Visa, MC •
C-no/S-no/P-no/H-no

Full breakfast
Comp. sherry
Sitting room w/TV
living room
fireplace

Charming 1902 Victorian home filled with antiques and family heirlooms. Located in historic "Old Colorado City" area. Close to restaurants and shops.

DENVER

Queen Anne Inn
2147 Tremont Pl., 80205
303-296-6666
Ann & Chuck Hillestad
All year

$$ B&B
10 rooms, 10 pb
Visa, MC, AmEx •
C-15+/S-no/P-no/H-no

Continental plus
Lunch, dinner avail.
Afternoon tea, snacks
comp. wine, sitting room
Bicycles, flower garden

Elegant. Urbane. Close to everything, but far from clamor. Located in beautiful, residential 1870s district in heart of downtown. Fresh flowers, original art, chamber music.

Seventh Ave. Manor
722 E. 7th Ave., 80203
303-832-0039
Te Brown
All year

$$ B&B
7 rooms, 7 pb
Visa, MC, AmEx •
C-ltd/S-no/P-no/H-no
German, some Spanish

Continental plus
Can cater lunch & dinner
Comp. tea, wine, cheese
Sitting room, library
terraced garden, balcony

Originally part of the fabulous Ferguson Estate. Today Seventh Ave. Mansion's central location and attention to comfort provide a perfect destination for travelers.

DURANGO

Blue Lake Ranch
16919 State Hwy. 140, 81326
Hesperus
303-385-4537
David & Lucretia Alford
May 1—September 30

$$$ B&B
1 rooms, 1 pb
•
C-ltd/S-no/P-no/H-no

Continental plus
Afternoon tea
Sitting room
bicycles, lake
sauna, gardens, fishing

Victorian farmhouse surrounded by gardens of flowers, vegetables and herbs. Spectacular lake & mountain views, trout-stocked lake, meals of homegrown ingredients.

River House B&B Inn
495 Animas View Dr., 81301
303-247-4775
Crystal Carroll
Exc. Oct. 15—Nov. 15, Apr.

$$ B&B
6 rooms, 6 pb
Visa, MC •
C-yes/S-no/P-yes/H-no

Full gourmet breakfast
Comp. wine & snacks
Massage & hypnosis sess.
snooker table, fish pond
928 sq. ft. atrium

Enjoy breakfast in spacious skylighted atrium. View the Animas River Valley. Hear the haunting steam whistle of historic narrow-gauge train. Special menus available.

Scrubby Oaks B&B Inn
1901 Florida Ave., 81301
P.O.Box 1047
303-247-2176
Mary Ann Craig
All year

$$ B&B
7 rooms, 3 pb
•
C-yes/S-no/P-no/H-no

Full breakfast
Comp. wine, snacks
Sitting room, library
sauna, pool table, TV
close to skiing

Spectacular views of Animas River Valley and mountains on 10 acres; antique furnishings, artworks, books, patios framed by gardens, fireplaces. Close to Mesa Verde Nat'l Park.

Vagabond Inn B&B
P.O. Box 2141, 81301
2180 Main Ave.
303-259-5901, ext. 23
Ace K. Hall
All year

$$$ B&B
28 rooms, 24 pb
Visa, MC, AmEx, DC, CB •
C-yes/S-yes/P-no/H-yes

Continental breakfast
Comp. wine
Sitting room, hot tubs
BBQ grill, deck, patio
fireplaces, bridal suite

Attractions include the historic train, Purgatory Ski Area, Mesa Verde National Park, a national scenic highway, many other activities, fine dining, and entertainment.

ESTES PARK

Anniversary Inn
1060 Mary's Lake Rd., 80517
Moraine Rt.
303-586-6200
Bruce & Janie Hinds
All year

$$ B&B
4 rooms, 1 pb
C-no/S-no/P-no/H-no

Full gourmet breakfast
Lunch, tea
snacks
Sitting room
library

Turn-of-the-century log house, moss-rock fireplace. Hearty breakfast served on wraparound porch. Half-mile to Rocky Mountain National Park.

Baldpate Inn
P.O. Box 4445, 80517
4900 S. Hwy 7
303-586-6151
Mike, Lois, Jenny & MacKenzie
End May—early October

$$ B&B
12 rooms, 5 pb
Visa, MC, personal chck
C-yes/S-no/P-no

Full breakfast
Restaurant, snacks
Lunch, dinner, library
Key collection, views
native stone fireplaces

Adjacent to Rocky Mountain National Park. Spectacular views, charming guest rooms, scrumptious food, and world-famous key and photograph collections.

90   Colorado

ESTES PARK ────────────────────────────────

Cottenwood House	$$ B&B	Full breakfast
P.O. Box 1208, 80517	2 rooms, 1 pb	Afternoon tea
540 Big Horn Dr.	•	Comp. wine, snacks
303-586-5104	C-8+ / S-ltd	Sun porch
Ron & Kathleen Cotten		
All year		

1920s mountain home offering old-fashioned hospitality, with country furnishings and antiques. Country-style breakfast served on wicker and flower-filled sun porch.

Emerald Manor	$ B&B	Full breakfast
P.O. Box 3592, 80517	4 rooms, 4 pb	Comp. sherry
441 Chiquita Lane	Visa, MC •	Sitting room, library
303-586-8050	C-15+	tennis courts, sauna
Reggie & Moira Fowler		swimming pool, game room
All year		

Romantic Irish manor nestled in the Rocky Mountains. Beautiful indoor swimming pool and sauna. Full hearty Irish breakfast. Incredible views!

Wanek's Lodge at Estes	$ B&B	Continental breakfast
P.O. Box 898, 80517	3 rooms	Lunch, dinner, BYOB
560 Ponderosa Dr.	C-10+ / S-no/P-no/H-no	Piano
303-586-5851	German	sitting room
Jim & Pat Wanek		
All year		

A modern mountain inn, old-fashioned hospitality, great food, unparalleled panoramas; Rocky Mountains National Park, fish, golf, swim, tennis, hike, ski nearby.

FORT COLLINS ────────────────────────────────

Elizabeth St. Guest House	$ B&B	Full breakfast
202 E. Elizabeth St., 80524	3 rooms	Comp. coffee, tea, wine
303-493-2337	Visa, MC •	Sitting room
Sheryl & John Clark	C-4+ / S-ltd/P-no/H-no	desk, phone
All year		refrigerator

Beautifully restored 1905 American four-square brick home furnished with antiques. Located one block east of Colorado State University.

GEORGETOWN ────────────────────────────────

Hardy House B&B Inn	$ B&B	Full breakfast (winter)
P.O. Box 0156, 80444	3 rooms, 1 pb	Cont. breakfast (summer)
605 Brownell	Visa, MC dep. only •	dinner on request, wine
303-569-3388	C-10+ / S-no/P-no/H-no	Sitting room
Sarah M. Schmidt		tandem bicycles
All year		

Rocky Mountain Victorian 50 minutes from Denver. Special breakfasts of fresh trout, scrambled eggs, pancakes and coffee cakes. Shopping, hiking, skiing, fishing and cycling.

GRAND JUNCTION ────────────────────────────────

Gate House Bed & Breakfast	$ B&B	Full breakfast
2502 N. First St., 81501	4 rooms, 2 pb	Library
303-242-6105	Visa, MC	
Rhonda & Garrett McClary	C-10+	
All year		

The Gate House is elegantly decorated and has beautiful surroundings. We serve gourmet breakfasts. Centrally located to area attractions.

GREEN MOUNTAIN FALLS

Outlook Lodge	$ B&B	Continental plus
P.O. Box 5, 80819	11 rooms, 2 pb	Sitting room, library
6975 Howard St.	Visa, MC •	tennis courts
719-684-2303	C-yes/H-yes	swimming pool, skiing
Rod & Sherri Ramsey		
All year		

Historic Victorian inn located in a secluded mountain village at the foot of Pikes Peak. Reminiscences of the past rekindled to the present. Swimming, fishing, horses, tennis.

GUNNISON

Mary Lawrence Inn	$ B&B	Full breakfast
601 N. Taylor, 81230	6 rooms, 2 pb	Candlelight dinner RSVP
303-641-3343	Visa, MC •	Comp. wine
Leslie A. Bushman	C-yes/S-no/P-no/H-no	Sitting room, books
All year		tandem bicycles

Our renovated home is inviting and comfortable; delectable breakfasts. Gunnison country offers marvelous outdoor adventures; super Crested Butte ski package.

LIMON

Midwest Motel/Country Inn	$ EP	Coffee & tea
795 Main St., Box X, 80828	32 rooms, 32 pb	Restaurant-1 block
719-775-2373	Visa, MC, AmEx •	Sitting room, gift shop
Harold & Vivian Lowe	C-yes/S-yes/P-no/H-no	"listening" waterfall
All year		& "watching" fountain

Beautiful rooms, oak antiques, stained glass, elegant wallpapered bathrooms, near I-70—1½ hours from Denver and Colorado Springs.

LOVELAND

The Lovelander	$ B&B	Full gourmet breakfast
217 W. 4th St., 80537	9 rooms, 7 pb	Aftn. tea, comp. wine
303-669-0798	Visa, MC, AmEx •	Dinner by request only
Marilyn & Bob Wiltgen	C-10+/S-no/P-no/H-ltd	Sitting room, library
All year		1 whirlpool/deluxe room

Victorian grace and old-fashioned hospitality from the heart of the Sweetheart City: a community of the arts. Gateway to the Rockies.

MINTURN

Eagle River Inn	$$ B&B	Continental plus
P.O. Box 100, 81645	12 rooms, 12 pb	Comp. wine & cheese
145 N. Main St.	Visa, MC, AmEx •	Sitting room, patio
303-827-5761/800-344-1750	C-12+/S-no/P-no/H-no	hot tub, backyard
Beverly Rude		alongside Eagle river
Exc. May & mid-Oct.		

Quiet mountain inn nestled alongside the Eagle River minutes from Vail Ski Resort. Furnished in southwest decor. Romantic riverside setting catering especially to couples.

OURAY

St. Elmo Hotel	$ B&B	Full breakfast
426 Main St., Box 667, 81427	11 rooms, 7 pb	Restaurant on premises
303-325-4951	Visa, MC •	Sitting room, TV, piano
Dan & Sandy Lingenfelter	C-yes/S-ltd/P-no/H-no	sauna, outdoor hot tub
All year		meeting room

Hotel & Bon Ton Restaurant surrounded by beautiful, rugged 14,000-ft. peaks. Furnished with antiques, stained glass & brass; honeymoon suite. Hot springs, jeeping, x-c skiing.

92   Colorado

SILVER PLUME ─────────────────────────────────

Brewery Inn B&B
P.O. Box 473, 80476
246 Main St.
303-674-5565
Mary P. Joss
All year

$ B&B
4 rooms, 1 pb
Visa, MC
C-yes/S-yes/P-no/H-yes

Continental plus
Comp. sherry
Sitting room
paperback library

Cozy restored Victorian home offers mountain refuge in tiny historic mining community. Close to Denver and ski areas. Restaurant & saloon next door.

SILVERTON ─────────────────────────────────

Alma House
P.O. Box 780, 81433
220 E. 10th St.
303-387-5336
Don & Jolene Stott
Mem. Day—Labor Day

$ EP
10 rooms, 1 pb
Visa, MC, AmEx, Disc •
C-yes/S-no/P-no/H-no

Coffee & tea
Sitting room
in-house movies

Completely restored 1898 Colorado mountain town hotel featuring soft water, huge towels, clock-radio, cable color TV, Beautyrest Queen in each room. Beautiful views.

Christopher House B&B
821 Empire St., Box 241, 81433
303-387-5857
Howard & Eileen Swonger
June—mid-September

$ B&B
3 rooms, 1 pb
•
C-yes

Full breakfast
Afternoon tea
snacks
Sitting room, library
hot tubs

Charming 1894 Victorian home with golden oak woodwork and sturdy antiques. Guests welcomed with mints, fresh wildflowers and homebaked cookies. Breakfast served to Irish music.

Teller House Hotel
P.O. Box 2, 81433
1250 Greene St.
303-387-5423
Fritz Klinke & Loren Lew
All year

$ B&B
9 rooms
credit cards accepted •
C-yes/S-yes/P-yes/H-ltd

Full breakfast
Lunch, dinner, bar
Piano in 1 room
Bakery on premises, ski
rentals, lift discounts

Step back 100 years in the heart of the San Juans, the "Mining Town that Never Quit."

TELLURIDE ─────────────────────────────────

Dahl Haus B&B
122 S. Oak St. Box 695, 81435
303-728-4158
Michael & Christine Courter
11/25—4/10; 5/20—10/7

$ B&B
9 rooms, 1 pb
•
C-yes/S-yes/P-no/H-no

Continental plus
Sitting room

Built in the 1890s as a boarding house for the Telluride hard-rock miners. Offers rooms with antique furnishings, parlor with TV, books and games.

New Sheridan Hotel
P.O. Box 980, 81435
231 W. Colorado
303-728-4351
Steve Hannon
All year

$ EP
30 rooms
Visa, MC, AmEx •
C-yes/S-yes/P-no/H-no
Spanish, French

North Italian restaurant
Dinner, bar
Hot tub

Victorian elegance, relaxed, restored comfort, situated in the heart of Telluride—a national historic landmark, just minutes from Telluride Ski Area.

TELLURIDE ───

Pennington's Mnt. Vllg Inn	$$$ B&B	Full breakfast
100 Pennington Court, 81435	12 rooms, 12 pb	Aftn. tea, comp. wine
P.O. Box 2428, Mtn. Vllge	Visa, MC, AmEx, other •	Bar service, happy hour
303-728-5337	C-yes/S-yes/P-no/H-yes	Library, pool table
Steve & Edie Pennington		hot tubs, guest laundry
All year		

Mountain retreat surrounded by Aspens, ski area and proposed golf course. Full country breakfast, Happy Hour, spa, pool table, library, and many other amenities.

San Sophia	$$ B&B	Full breakfast
330 W. Pacific Ave., 81435	16 rooms, 16 pb	Comp. wine, snacks
P.O. Box 1825	Visa, MC, AmEx •	Sitting room, library
800-537-4721	C-10+/S-no/P-no/H-no	hot tubs, dining deck
Dianne & Garg Eschman		ski storage, boot dryers
All year		

Elegant new inn with all luxurious rooms. Gourmet breakfast; spectacular views of surrounding mountains. One block from historic downtown district.

More Inns. . .

Allenspark Lodge   Colorado Hwy. 7-Bus., Allenspark 80510   303-747-2552
Lazy H Ranch   Box 248, Allenspark 80510   303-747-2532
Alpina Haus   935 E. Durant, Aspen 81611   800 24A-SPEN
Aspen Ski Lodge   101 W. Main St., Aspen 81611   303-925-3434
Brass Bed Inn   926 E. Durant, Aspen 81611   303-925-3622
Copper Horse Guest House   328 W. Main, Aspen 81611   303-925-7525
Hotel Lenado   200 S. Aspen St., Aspen 81611   303-925-6246
Little Red Ski Haus   118 E. Cooper, Aspen 81611   303-925-3333
Molly Gibson Lodge   120 W. Hopkins, Aspen 81611   303-925-2580
Mountain House B&B   905 East Hopkins, Aspen 81611   303-920-2550
Pomegranate Inn   Box 1368, Aspen 81612   800-525-4012
Sardy House   128 E. Main St., Aspen 81611   303-920-2525
Tipple Inn   747 S. Galena St., Aspen 81611   800-321-7025
Deer Valley Resorts   P.O. Box 796, Bayfield 81122   303-884-2600
Parrish's Country Squire   2515 Parrish Rd., Berthoud 80513   303-772-7678
Briar Rose B&B Inn   2151 Arapahoe, Boulder 80302   303-442-3007
Fireside Inn   P.O. Box 2252, Breckenridge 80424   303-453-6456
Blue Sky Inn   719 Arizona St., Buena Vista 81211   303-395-8865
Golden Rose Hotel   Central City 80427   303-582-5060
Two-Ten Casey   P.O. Box 154, 210 Casey, Central City 80427   303-582-5906
Home Ranch   Box 822, Clark 80428   303-879-1780
1894 Victorian   P.O. Box 9322, Colorado Springs 80932   719-630-3322
Griffin's Hospitality Hse   4222 N Chestnut, Colorado Springs 80907   303-599-3035
Katies Korner   P.O. Box 804, Colorado Springs 80901   303-630-3322
Pikes Peak Paradise   Box 5760, Woodland Park, Colorado Springs 80866   719-687-6656
Brumder Hearth   P.O. Box 1152, Crested Butte 81224   303-349-6253
Claim Jumper   704 Whiterock, Box 1181, Crested Butte 81224   303-349-6471
Forest Queen Hotel   Box 127 2nd & Elk Ave, Crested Butte 81224   303-349-5336
Nordic Inn   P.O. Box 939, Crested Butte 81224   303-349-5542
Purple Mountain Lodge   P.O. Box 897, Crested Butte 81224   303-349-5888
Imperial Hotel   123 N. Third St., Cripple Creek 80813   303-689-2713
Balloon Ranch   Box 41, Del Norte 81132   303-754-2533
Windsor Hotel B&B Inn   P. O. Box 762, Del Norte 81132   719-657-2668

Cambridge Club Hotel   1560 Sherman, Denver 80203   303-831-1252
Victoria Oaks Inn   1575 Race Street, Denver 80206   303-355-1818
Silverheels   Box 367, 81 Buffalo Dr., Dillon 80435   303-468-2926
Tall Timber   Box 90G, Durango 81301   303-259-4813
Victorian Inn   2117 W. 2nd Ave., Durango 81301   303-247-2223
Victorian Veranda B&B   P.O. Box 361, Eaton 80615   303-454-3890
Aspen Lodge & Guest Ranch   Longs Peak Rt. 7, Estes Park 80517   303-586-8133
Riversong   P.O. Box 1910, Estes Park 80517   303-586-4666
Wind River Ranch   P.O. Box 3410, Estes Park 80517   303-586-4212
Helmshire Inn   1204 S. College, Fort Collins 80524   303-493-4683
Hideout   1293-117 Road, Glenwood Springs 81601   303-945-5621
Talbott House   928 Colorado Ave., Glenwood Springs 81601   303-945-1039
Dove Inn   711 14th St., Golden 80401   303-278-2209
Drowsy Water Ranch   Box 147A, Granby 80446   303-725-3456
Junction Country Inn B&B   861 Grand Ave., Grand Junction 81501   303-241-2817
Tumbling River Ranch   Grant 80448   303-838-5981
Waunita Hot Springs Ranch   8007 Country Rd. 877, Gunnison 81230   303-641-1266
7-W Guest Ranch   3412 County Rd. 151, Gypsum 81637   303-524-9328
Sweetwater Creek Guest Ran   2650 Sweetwater Road, Gypsum 81637   303-524-9301
Midway Inn   1340 Hwy 133, Hotchkiss 81419   303-527-3422
Kelsall's Ute Creek Ranch   2192 County Rd. 334, Ignacio 81137   303-563-4464
Ute Creek Ranch   2192 County Rd. 334, Ignacio 81137   303-563-4464
1899 Inn   314 S. Main, La Veta 81055   303-742-3576
Crystal Lodge   Lake City 81235   303-944-2201
Delaware Hotel   700 Harrison Ave., Leadville 80461   303-486-1418
Nippersink   106 Spencer Ave., Manitou Springs 80829   303-685-9211
Diamond J Guest Ranch   26604 Frying Pan Rd, Meredith 81642   303-927-3222
Deer Valley Ranch   Box Y, Nathrop 81236   303-395-2353
Baker's Manor   317 Second St., Ouray 81427   303-325-4574
Weisbaden Spa & Lodge   Box 349, Ouray 81427   303-325-4347
Davidson's Country Inn   Box 87, Pagosa Springs 81147   303-264-5863
E.T.'s Bed & Breakfast   1608 Sage Lane, Paonia 81428   303-527-3300
Aspen Canyon Ranch   13206 Country Rd. #3, Parshall 80468   303-725-3518
Bar Lazy J Guest Ranch   BOX N, Parshall 80468   303-725-3437
Jackson Hotel   220 S. Main St., Poncha Springs 81242   303-539-3122
Historic Redstone Inn   82 Redstone Blvd., Redstone 81623   303-963-2526
MacTiernan's San Juan   2882 Highway 23, Ridgway 81432   303-626-5360
Pueblo Hostel & Cantina   P.O. Box 346, Ridgway 81432   303-626-5939
Coulter Lake Guest Ranch   P.O. Box 906, Rifle 81650   303-625-1473
Poor Farm Country Inn   8495 C.R. 160, Salida 81201   719-539-3818
Sweet Adeline's B&B Inn   949 "F" St., Salida 81201   719-539-4100
North Fork Ranch   Box B, Shawnee 80475   303-838-9873
Alpen Hutte   471 Rainbow Dr., Box 91, Silverthorne 80498   303-468-6336
Fool's Gold   1069 Snowden, Silverton 81433   303-387-5879
Wyman Hotel   1371 Greene St., Silverton 81433   303-387-5372
Bear Pole Ranch   Star Rt. 1, Box BB, Steamboat Springs 80487   303-879-0576
Crawford House   Box 775062, Steamboat Springs 80477   303-879-1859
Harbor Hotel   P.O. Box 4109, Steamboat Springs 80477   800-543-8888
House on the Hill   POB 770598, Steamboat Springs 80477   303-879-1650
Inn at Steamboat   3070 Columbine Dr., Steamboat Springs 80477   303-879-2600
Sky Valley Lodge   Box 2153, Steamboat Springs 80477   303-879-5158
Vista Verde Guest Ranch   Box 465, Steamboat Springs 80477   303-879-3858
Scandinavian Lodge   Box 5040, Steamboat Village 80449   303-879-0517
Johnstone Inn   P.O. Box 546, Telluride 81435   303-728-3316
Skyline Guest Ranch   7214 Highway 145, Telluride 81435   303-728-3757
Woodland Hills Lodge   P.O. Box 276, Woodland Park 80863   800-621-8386

Connecticut

BOLTON

Jared Cone House
25 Hebron Rd., 06043
203-643-8538
Jeff & Cinde Smith
All year

$$ B&B
3 rooms, 1 pb
C-yes/S-no/P-no/H-no

Full breakfast
Comp. wine
Sitting room
bicycles
canoe available

Enjoy the charm of our home with scenic views of the countryside; spectacular foliage; berry farms; antiquing. Full breakfast featuring our own maple syrup when available.

BRISTOL

Chimney Crest Manor B&B
5 Founders Dr., 06010
203-582-4219
Dan & Cynthia Cimadamore
All year

$$ B&B
4 rooms, 4 pb
Visa, MC •
C-ltd/S-ltd/P-no/H-no

Full breakfast
All rooms are suites
sitting room, piano
wading pool, 3 mi. to
Hershey, Lake Compounce

32-room Tudor mansion located in the historical area of Bristol. Six fireplaces. Twenty minutes from Hartford, Litchfield and Waterburg. Unique architecture.

DEEP RIVER

Riverwind Inn
209 Main St., 06417
203-526-2014
Barbara & Bob Barlow
All year

$$$ B&B
8 rooms, 8 pb
Visa, MC
C-no/S-yes/P-no/H-no

Full breakfast
Comp. sherry
8 common rooms
piano, classic British
limousine service

Furnished in country antiques. Smithfield ham with breakfast, fireplace in dining room. New England charm and southern hospitality.

EAST HADDAM

Bishopsgate Inn
Goodspeed Landing, 06423
P.O. Box 290-7 Norwich Rd
203-873-1677
Dan & Molly Swartz
All year

$$$ B&B
6 rooms, 6 pb
C-6+/S-yes/P-no/H-ltd

Full breakfast
Comp. wine
Dinner
Piano, sauna
sitting room

1818 colonial home with 6 charming guest rooms, open fireplaces, period pieces and fine antiques, near famous Goodspeed Opera House.

GLASTONBURY

Butternut Farm
1654 Main St., 06033
203-633-7197
Donald B. Reid
All year

$$ B&B
4 rooms, 2 pb
C-yes/S-ltd/P-no/H-no

Full breakfast
Comp. wine
Piano, library
sitting rooms
bicycle

An 18th-century jewel furnished with period antiques. Attractive grounds with herb gardens and ancient trees, dairy goats and prize chickens.

Green Gables Inn, Pacific Grove, CA

IVORYTOWN

The Copper Beech Inn
Main Street, 06442
203-767-0330
Eldon & Sally Senner
Except Mondays

$$$ B&B
13 rooms, 13 pb
major credit cards
C-ltd/S-yes/P-no/H-yes

Continental plus
Lunch, dinner, bar
Bicycles, jacuzzi
piano, TV, decks
entertainment

A hostelry where even a short visit is a celebration of good living. The only 4-star restaurant in Connecticut. The feel of the entire inn is elegant country.

LITCHFIELD

Tollgate Hill Inn
P.O. Box 1339, 06759
Rt. 202 & Tollgate Rd.
203-567-4545
Frederick J. Zivic
Exc. last 3 weeks Mar

$$$ B&B
10 rooms, 10 pb
C-yes/S-yes/P-yes/H-no

Continental breakfast
Lunch, dinner, bar
Sitting room
piano, tennis
weekend entertainment

Restored 1745 inn listed on National Register of Historic Places. Luncheon, dinner, cocktails, over-night accommodations in beautifully decorated guest rooms.

MADISON

Madison Beach Hotel
94 West Wharf Road, 06443
203-245-1404
The Cooneys,The Bagdasarians
April 1—January 1

$$$ B&B
32 rooms, 32 pb
Visa, MC, AmEx, DC •
C-yes/S-ask/P-no/H-ask

Continental breakfast
Lunch, dinner, bar
Sitting room
entertainment
right on beach

Victorian beach hotel furnished with oak and wicker antiques. Seafood tops the menu at the attached restaurant. Weekend entertainment.

MIDDLEBURY

Tucker Hill Inn
96 Tucker Hill Rd., 06762
203-758-8334
Susan & Richard Cebelenski
All year

$$ B&B
4 rooms, 2 pb
Visa, MC •
C-yes/S-ltd/P-no/H-no

Full breakfast
Sitting room
library
TV room

Large colonial-style inn near the Village Green. Our period rooms are large and spacious. Hearty full-course breakfast. Convenient to sights and sports.

MOODUS

Fowler House
P.O. Box 432, Plains Rd, 06469
203-873-8906
Barbara Ally, Paul Seals
All year

$$ B&B
6 rooms, 4 pb
Visa, MC, AmEx •
C-12+/S-ltd/P-no/H-ltd

Continental plus
Dinner, Comp. tea, wine
Sitting room, library
bicycles
near swimming & tennis

1890 Queen Anne Victorian furnished with antiques. Close to Goodspeed Opera House, fine restaurants, antiquing. Enjoy afternoon tea on porch.

MYSTIC

Adams House
382 Cow Hill Rd., 06355
203-572-9551
Maureen & Ron Adams
All year

$$ B&B
5 rooms, 3 pb
Visa, MC
C-no/S-no/P-no/H-no

Continental
Sitting room, TV room
swimming pool
fireplaces

1790 home; 3 fireplaces; private setting; in-ground swimming pool; approximately 1½ miles from downtown Mystic. Surrounded by lush greenery and flower beds.

Comolli's Guest House
36 Bruggeman Pl., 06355
203-536-8723
Dorothy Comolli
All year

$$ EP
2 rooms, 1 pb
C-no/S-yes/P-no/H-no

Continental plus
Kitchen privileges
TV in rooms

Country setting on top of dead-end street overlooking Mystic seaport; immaculate and quiet. Within walking distance of everything.

Harbour Inne & Cottage
RFD #1, Box 398, 06355
Edgemont St.
203-572-9253
Charles Lecouras, Jr.
All year

$ EP
5 rooms, 5 pb
no credit cards •
C-yes/S-yes/P-yes/H-no
Greek

Kitchen privileges
Sitting room
canoe and row boats
cable TV, A/C

Small inn plus 3-room cottage on Mystic River. Walk to seaport & all attractions. Waterfront tables, cable TV, kitchen privileges, canoeing and boating.

Palmer Inn
25 Church St., Noank, 06340
203-572-9000
Patricia White Cornish
All year

$$$ B&B
6 rooms, 6 pb
Visa, MC
C-no/S-ltd/P-no/H-no

Continental plus
Comp. sherry, tea
Sitting room
bicycles, games
fireplaces, flowers

Elegant 1907 mansion with antique furnishings. Quiet charm of New England fishing village, 2 miles to historic Mystic. Thanksgiving & Victorian Christmas weekends.

NEW HAVEN

Inn at Chapel West
1201 Chapel St., 06511
203-777-1201
Steven G. Schneider
All year

$$$ B&B
10 rooms, 10 pb
Visa, MC, AmEx, DC •
C-yes/S-yes/P-ltd/H-yes

Continental plus
Lunch & dinner (by resv)
Comp. wine, tea
Sitting room
tennis/golf/pool nearby

Nineteenth-century residence with 10 distinctive guest rooms and conference facilities. Downtown location adjacent to Yale campus, fine dining and shopping.

NEW LONDON

Queen Anne Inn
P.O. Box 647, 06320
265 Williams St.
203-447-2600
Beth Slevers, Morgan Beatty
All year

$$ B&B
9 rooms, 9 pb
Visa, MC, AmEx •
C-12+/S-ltd/P-no/H-no

Full buffet breakfast
Afternoon tea
Sitting room
hot tub, sauna
tennis, massage

Elegant lodging near the historically rich Mystic-Groton-New London waterfront resort area. Massages. Free Health and Racquet Club.

NEW MILFORD

Homestead Inn
5 Elm St., 06776
203-354-4080
Rolf & Peggy Hammer
All year

$$ B&B
14 rooms, 14 pb
Visa, MC, AmEx •
C-no/S-no/P-ltd/H-ltd

Continental plus
Sitting room, piano
front porch, gardens
near trout fishing

Small country inn in picturesque New England town next to village green, near shops, churches, restaurants, antiques, galleries, hiking, crafts.

NEW PRESTON

Inn on Lake Waramaug
06777
203-868-0563/212-724-8775
Richard B. Combs
All year

$$ MAP
25 rooms, 25 pb
Visa, MC, AmEx, DC
C-yes/S-yes/P-no/H-yes

Full breakfast
Luncheon, dinner, bar
Pool, sauna, tennis
sitting room, piano
entertainment

Authentic colonial (1790) restored and furnished with pine and cherry antiques. Complete resort, private beach, indoor pool, Showboat Cruises, sleigh rides.

NORFOLK

Manor House
P.O. Box 447, 06058
Maple Ave.
203-542-5690
Hank & Diane Tremblay
All year

$$ B&B
8 rooms, 4 pb
Visa, MC •
C-12+/S-ltd/P-no/H-ltd
French

Full breakfast
Comp. tea, wine
Sitting room
piano
bicycles, lake

Historic Victorian mansion furnished with genuine antiques, on 5 acres. Romantic and elegant bedrooms, several with fireplaces. Sleigh & carriage rides. Concert series.

OLD LYME

Bee and Thistle Inn
100 Lyme St., 06371
203-434-1667
Bob/Penny Nelson
All year

$$ EP
11 rooms, 9 pb
Visa, MC, AmEx
C-yes/S-yes/P-no/H-no

Lunch, dinner, bar
Bicycles
2 parlors, piano
harpist Saturdays

An inn on 5½ acres in historic district. On the Lieutenant River set back amidst majestic trees. Sophisticated country cuisine.

Connecticut   99

OLD LYME

Old Lyme Inn
P.O. Box 787, 06371
85 Lyme St.
203-434-2600
Diana Field Atwood
All year

$$$ B&B
13 rooms, 13 pb
major credit cards •
C-yes/S-yes/P-ltd/H-yes

Continental plus
Lunch, dinner
Sitting room
telephones & TV in rooms
banister porch

19th-century colonial residence in Old Lyme's historic district. Given three stars by the New York Times *on three separate visits. Empire and Victorian furnishings.*

OLD MYSTIC

Old Mystic Inn/Carriage Hs
58 Main St., Box 318, 06372
203-572-9422
Lois & Karl Taylor
All year

$$$ B&B
8 rooms, 8 pb
Visa, MC, AmEx
C-6+/S-no/P-no/H-no

Full country breakfast
Afternoon team
Comp. wine & snacks
Sitting room
bicycles

Located minutes from Mystic Seaport and Aquarium, this charming inn offers a complete country breakfast to guests.

Red Brook Inn
P.O. Box 237, 06372
2750 Goldstar Hwy
203-572-0349
Ruth Keyes
All year

$$$ B&B
9 rooms, 9 pb
Visa, MC
C-9+/S-no/P-no/H-no

Full breakfast
Comp. wine, tea
Sitting room, library
bicycles, patio
whirlpool

The inn strikes a nice balance between authentic handsome furnishings and comfort. Surrounded by wooded acres, convenient to old New England sights.

PLAINFIELD

French Renaissance House
550 Norwich Rd., 06374
203-564-3277
Lucile & Ted Melbur
All year

$$ B&B
4 rooms, 1 pb
Visa, MC •
C-yes

Full breakfast
Comp. tea and snacks
Sitting room
library

1871 Victorian French Renaissance Second Empire architecture; listed on Historic Register. Large rooms; rounded arched windows; high ceilings; charming atmosphere.

RIDGEFIELD

West Lane Inn
22 West Lane, 06877
203-438-7323
Maureen Mayer
All year

$$$ B&B
20 rooms, 20 pb
Visa, MC, AmEx, DC
C-yes/S-yes/P-no
Spanish

Continental breakfast
Afternoon tea, snacks
Comp. wine
Bicycles
tennis nearby

Colonial elegance framed by majestic old maples and flowering shrubs. Breakfast served on the veranda. Always a relaxing atmosphere.

RIVERTON

Old Riverton Inn
P.O. Box 6, Rt. 20, 06065
203-379-8678
All year

$$ B&B
10 rooms, 10 pb
Visa, MC, AmEx, DC
C-yes/S-yes/P-no/H-yes

Full breakfast
Lunch, dinner, bar
Sitting room
piano
entertainment

Hospitality for the hungry, thirsty and sleepy since 1796. Originally a stagecoach stop. Overlooking West Branch of Farmington River.

100   Connecticut

SALISBURY

Under Mountain Inn
Under Mountain Rd., 06068
Route 41
203-435-0242
Marged K. Higginson
Exc. mid-Dec. & 3/15-5/15

$$$ MAP
7 rooms, 7 pb
Visa, MC, AmEx
C-6+/S-ltd

Full breakfast
Dinner, tea
Restaurant, bar service
Sitting room
library

British-flavored hospitality in an 18th-century farmhouse. A proper cup of tea, The Manchester Guardian, *steak and kidney pie. Close to music festival, boating, swimming.*

STORRS

Farmhouse on the Hill
418 Gurleyville Rd., 06268
203-429-1400
Elaine & Bill Kollet
All year

$$ B&B
4 rooms, 2 pb
•
C-yes/S-yes/P-no/H-no

Full breakfast
Dinner by arrangement
Quiet room
piano
bicycles, A/C

Elegant farmhouse in college town; close to Sturbridge, MA, & Mystic & Hartford, CT. Raise Columbia sheep; heart of historic Gurleyville. Playhouse and auditorium at U. Conn.

TOLLAND

Tolland Inn
P.O. Box 717, 06084
63 Tolland Green
203-872-0800
Susan & Steve Geddes-Beeching
All year

$$ B&B
5 rooms, 3 pb
Visa, MC, AmEx
C-ltd/S-no/P-no/H-no

Continental plus
Sitting room

Historic inn on New England village green. Short drive from I-84—convenient to Hartford, Sturbridge, Brimfield and University of Connecticut.

WATERBURY

Parsonage Bed & Breakfast
18 Hewlett St., 06710
203-574-2855
Lonetta Baysinger
All year

$$ B&B
4 rooms, 1 pb
Visa, MC •
C-yes

Full breakfast
Sitting room, library
near tennis, park,
amusement park, antiques

Fifteen-room Victorian with carefully restored decor in quiet t storic area. Gourmet breakfasts. Great antique area. Midway between N.Y.C. and Boston.

WESTBROOK

Captain Stannard House
138 S. Main St., 06498
203-399-7565
Ray & Elaine Grandmaison
All year

$$ B&B
9 rooms, 9 pb
Visa, MC, AmEx
C-6+/S-ltd/P-no/H-no

Continental plus
Sitting room
bicycles

Charming country inn/antique shop in interesting seafaring village. Furnished in New England antiques. Homemade breakfast in large, sunny breakfast room.

More Inns...

Sandford/Pond House   P.O. Box 306, Bridgewater 06752   203-355-4677
Inn at Chester   318 W. Main St., Chester 06412   203-526-4961
Hayward House Inn   35 Hayward Avenue, Colchester 06415   203-537-5772
Austin's Stonecroft Inn   17 Main St., East Haddam 06423   203-873-1754
Gelston House   Goodspeed Landing, East Haddam 06423   203-873-1411
Stonecroft Inn   17 Main St., East Haddam 06423   203-873-1754
Whispering Winds Inn   93 River Rd., East Haddam 06423   203-526-3055
Griswood Inn   Essex 06426   203-767-0991

Homestead Inn   420 Field Point Rd., Greenwich 06830   203-869-7500
Stanton House Inn   17 Mead Ave., Greenwich 06830   203-869-2110
Shore Inne   54 E. Shore Rd., Groton Long Point 06340   203-536-1180
1741 Saltbox Inn   P.O. Box 677, Kent 06757   203-927-4376
B&B at Laharan Farm   350 Rt. 81, Killingworth 06417   203-663-1706
Killingworth Inn   249 Rt. 81, Killingworth 06417   203-663-1103
Wake Robin Inn   Rt. 41, Lakeville 06039   203-435-2515
Wake Robin Inn   Rt. 41, Lakeville 06039   203-435-2515
Applewood Farms Inn   528 Col. Ledyard Hwy., Ledyard 06355   203-536-2022
Dolly Madison Inn   73 W. Wharf Rd., Madison 06443   203-245-7377
Red Brook Inn   2800 Gold Star Hiway, Mystic 06372   203-572-0349
Whaler's Inn   Box 488-T, Mystic 06355   203-536-1506
Whaler's Inn   P.O. Box 488, Mystic 06355   800-243-2588
Maples Inn   179 Oenoke Ridge, New Canaan 06840   203-966-2927
Highland Farm B&B   Highland Ave., New Hartford 06057   203-379-6029
Birches Inn   West Shore Rd., New Preston 06777   203-868-0229
Hopkins Inn   Hopkins Rd., New Preston 06777   203-868-7295
Hawley Manor Inn   19 Main St., Newtown 06470   203-426-4456
Blackberry River Inn   Route 44, Norfolk 06058   203-542-5100
Greenwoods Gate B&B Inn   P.O. Box 662, Norfolk 06058   203-542-5439
Mountain View Inn   Route 272, Box 467, Norfolk 06058   203-542-5595
Weaver's House   P.O. Box 336, Rt. 44, Norfolk 06058   203-542-5108
Silvermine Tavern   Silvermine Ave., Norwalk 06850   203-847-4558
Harbor House Inn   165 Shore Rd., Old Greenwich 06870   203-637-0145
Croft   7 Penny Corner Rd, Portland 06480   203-342-1856
Felshaw Tavern   Five Mile River Road, Putnam 06260   203-928-3467
Elms Inn   500 Main St., Ridgefield 06877   203-438-2541
Stonehenge Inn   P.O. Box 667, Ridgefield 06877   203-438-6511
White Hart Inn   Village Green, Salisbury 06068   203-435-2511
Yesterday's Yankee   Route 44 East, Salisbury 06068   203-435-9539
Simsbury 1820 House   731 Hopmeadow St., Simsbury 06070   203-658-7658
Inn at Woodstock Hill   P.O.Box 98,Plaine Hill, South Woodstock 06267   203-928-0528
Winterbrook Farm   Beffa Rd., Staffordville 06076   203-684-2124
Lasbury's B&B   24 Orchard St., Stonington Village 06378   203-535-2681
Hedgerow House   Box 265, Thompson 06227   203-923-9073
Samuel Watson House   Rt. 193, Thompson 06277   203-923-2491
Old Babcock Tavern   484 Mile Hill Rd., Rt. 31, Tolland 06084   203-875-1239
Mayflower Inn   Route 47, Washington 06793   213-868-0515
Costwold Inn   76 Myrtle Ave., Westport
Provincial House   151 Main St., Winsted 06098   203-379-1631
Curtis House   506 Main St. S., Woodbury 06798   203-263-2101

Delaware

BETHANY BEACH

Sea-Vista Villas
Box 62, 19930
773-C Salt Pond Circle
302-539-3354
Dale M. Duvall
April—Thanksgiving

$$ B&B
3 rooms, 3 pb
C-ltd/S-yes/P-no/H-no

Full breakfast
Comp. cocktails
Swimming pool
tennis courts
bicycles

This bed and breakfast at Sea-Vista Villa offers a housekeeping villa for delightful beach and lakeside holiday in serene setting.

LAUREL

Spring Garden B&B
P.O. Box 283A, 19956
Rt. 1, Delaware Ave. Ext.
302-875-7015
Gwen North
All year

$$ B&B
6 rooms, 2 pb
•
C-10+ /S-ltd/H-yes
Spanish

Continental plus
Comp. wine, snacks
Bar service set-ups
Sitting room, library
bicycles, historic tours

Get away to a Colonial National Registry country plantation home near Atlantic beaches & Chesapeake Bay. Enjoy casual elegance, friendliness and charm of the Eastern shore.

MILFORD

Towers Bed & Breakfast
101 N.W. Front St., 19963
302-422-3814
Michael Real
All year

$$$ B&B
6 rooms, 4 pb
Visa, MC •
C-12+ /S-ltd/P-no/H-no
Spanish

Full breakfast
Afternoon tea
Comp. wine
Sitting room
library, bicycles

A whimsical Victorian dream. Unique Steamboat Gothic Victorian mansion. Suites with fireplaces, furnishings in the French Victorian manner. Rehoboth and beaches nearby.

NEW CASTLE

David Finney Inn
216 Delaware St., 19720
P.O. Box 207
302-322-6367
Judy Piser
All year

$$ B&B
20 rooms, 20 pb
Visa, MC, AmEx, Disc •
C-yes/S-yes/P-no/H-yes
Spanish

Continental plus
Luncheon, dinner,
bar, piano
Living room, bike paths
entertainment

Restored 1685 inn in unique historic village 35 minutes south of Philadelphia. Thirteen rooms, four suites, private baths. Gourmet restaurant, tavern.

Jefferson House B&B
The Strand at the Wharf, 19720
302-322-8944/302-323-0999
C. Bechstein or Dr. Rosenthal
All year

$$ B&B
3 rooms, 3 pb
•
C-yes/S-yes

Full breakfast
Restaurant, lunch,dinner
Comp. wine, aftn. tea
Room w/porch river view
one room with kitchen

Charming 200-year-old riverfront hotel, center of historic district. Furnished with antiques or in a country motif. Original wood floors & millwork. William Penn landed here.

NEW CASTLE

William Penn Guest House	$ B&B	Continental breakfast
206 Delaware St., 19720	4 rooms	Living room
302-328-7736	C-no/S-no/P-no/H-no	
Irma & Richard Burwell	Italian	
All year		

This house was built about 1682, and William Penn stayed overnight! Restored and located in the center of the Square.

REHOBOTH BEACH

Corner Cupboard Inn	$$$ B&B/MAP	Full breakfast
50 Park Ave., 19971	18 rooms, 18 pb	Dinner (summer season)
302-227-8553	Visa, MC, AmEx	Restaurant
Elizabeth G. Hooper	C-yes/S-yes/P-yes/H-no	Sitting room, piano
All year		beach

The inn that was in before inns were in! Fifty years at 50 Park Ave. as a summer retreat for Baltimore and Washington. B&B mid-Sept. to Mem. Day, MAP otherwise.

Tembo Guest House	$$ B&B	Continental plus
100 Laurel St., 19971	6 rooms, 1 pb	Use of kitchen
Don & Gerry Cooper	C-6+/S-no/P-ask/H-no	Sitting room w/fireplace
All year		enclosed porch

Warm hospitality in cozy beach cottage furnished with antiques, fine art, braided rugs. Short walk to beach, quality shops, restaurants. Nonsmoking.

WILMINGTON

Small Wonder B&B	$$ B&B	Full breakfast
213 W. Crest Rd., 19803	2 rooms, 1 pb	Comp. beverages, fruit
302-764-0789	Visa, Mc, AmEx •	Sitting room, library
Dot & Art Brill	C-9+/S-ltd/P-no/H-no	music room, rec. room
All year		VCR, TV, pool, hot tub

Well-appointed, traditional suburban home. Award-winning landscaping. Very close to I-95, museums, corporations, colleges and historical attractions. First class.

More Inns...

Addy Sea   P.O. Box 275, Bethany Beach 19930   302-539-3707
Homestead Guests   721 Garfield Pkwy, Bethany Beach 19930   (302)539-724
Biddles B&B   101 Wyoming Ave, Dover 19901   302-736-1570
Noble Guest House B&B   33 South Bradford St., Dover 19901   302-674-4084
Savannah Inn   330 Savannah Road, Lewes 19958   302-645-5592
Beach House   15 Hickman St., Rehoboth Beach 19971   302-227-7074
Beach House Bedroom   Box 138, Rehoboth Beach 19971   302-227-0937
Gladstone Inn   3 Olive Avenue, Rehoboth Beach 19971   302-227-2641
Lord Baltimore Lodge   16 Baltimore Ave., Rehoboth Beach 19971   302-227-2855
Pleasant Inn Lodge   31 Olive Ave. @ 1st St., Rehoboth Beach 19971   302-227-7311

Florida

AMELIA ISLAND

1735 House
584 S. Fletcher Ave., 32034
904-261-5878
Gary & Emily Grable
All year

$$ B&B
5 rooms, 5 pb
Visa, MC, AmEx •
C-yes/S-yes/P-no/H-no

Continental breakfast
Comp. newspaper
comp. beach towels
surf cast fishing
private lighthouse

White frame house overlooking the Atlantic Ocean. Breakfast served with morning newspaper. Accommodations in suites (up to 4) or Lighthouse (up to 6).

CEDAR KEY

Historic Island Hotel
P.O. Box 460, 32625
Main St.
904-543-5111
Marcia Rogers
All year

$$ B&B
10 rooms, 6 pb
•
C-yes/S-ltd/P-no/H-ltd
Spanish, Mandarin

Full breakfast
Full menu, cafe
Sitting & dining room
jazz duo, murals
Bicycle-built-for-2

1850 Jamaican architecture in historic district. Antiques. Gourmet natural foods specializing in original recipes, seafood and vegetarian, poppy-seed bread.

CORAL GABLES

Hotel Place St. Michel
162 Alcazar Ave., 33134
305-444-1666
Stuart N. Bornstein
All year

$$$ B&B
28 rooms, 28 pb
Visa, MC, AmEx, DC, CB •
C-yes/S-yes/P-no/H-no
Fr, Span, Ger, It, Port

Continental breakfast
Lunch, dinner, bar, deli
Sitting room, piano
entertainment

Charming small European-style hotel filled with English & French antiques, featuring the best service and friendly atmosphere. Award-winning restaurant.

DAYTONA BEACH

Captain's Quarters Inn
3711 S. Atlantic Ave., 32019
904-767-3119
Becky Sue Morgan & sons
All year

$$$ B&B
25 rooms, 25 pb
Visa, MC, AmEx •
C-yes/S-yes/P-ask/H-yes

Full breakfast
Lunch, comp. wine
Sitting room, ice cream
socials, turn-down serv.
swimming pool, bicycles

Daytona's first new B&B inn, directly on the world's most famous beach. Old-fashioned coffee shop. Unique antique shoppe—all-suite inn—private balconies. AAA "excellent."

EDGEWATER

Colonial House
110 E. Yelkca Terrace, 32132
904-427-4445
Eva Brandner
All year

$ B&B
5 rooms, 4 pb
•
C-7+/S-yes
German, French, Italian

Full breakfast
Comp. snacks on arrival
Guest refrigerator, A/C
washing machine, TV
pool, hot tub

Colonial-style home with year-round heated pool and hot tub close to one of Florida's finest beaches and attractions.

FERNANDINA BEACH ────────────────────────────

Bailey House	$$$ B&B	Continental plus
P.O. Box 805, 32034	4 rooms, 4 pb	Tandem bicycle
28 S. 7th St.	AmEx •	old pump organ, victrola
904-261-5390	C-ltd/S-no/P-no/H-no	sitting room
Tom & Diane Hay	French	A/C, heat, beach towels
All year		

Elegant 1895 Queen Anne Victorian on National Register, in historic district. Walk to shopping, restaurants, marina, dining. Near state park beach.

FORT LAUDERDALE BEACH ────────────────────────

Casa Alhambra B&B Inn	$ B&B	Continental plus
3029 Alhambra St., 33304	6 rooms, 4 pb	Comp. drink on arrival
305-467-2262	•	Tea, sitting room
Vicky G. Feaman	C-10+/S-yes/P-no/H-no	Library, sauna
All year		bicycles

Just off Ft. Lauderdale Beach. Minutes from restaurants, shopping, theatre. Elegant and charming restored 1930s Florida beach house with garden/deck area.

HOLMES BEACH ────────────────────────────────

Harrington House B&B	$$$ B&B	Full breakfast
5626 Gulf Dr., 34217	5 rooms	Sitting room
813-778-5444	Visa, MC •	bicycles
Betty & Walt Spangler	C-12+/S-no/P-no	swimming pool
All year		

Charming restored 1920s-style home reflects a "casual elegance" on the beach. Antiques, balconies, great rooms, swimming pool, peace and quiet. Near major attractions.

JACKSONVILLE ────────────────────────────────

House on Cherry Street	$$ B&B	Full breakfast
1844 Cherry St., 32205	4 rooms, 2 pb	Comp. wine, snacks
904-384-1999	•	Sitting room
Carol Anderson	C-9+/S-yes/P-no/H-no	bicycles
All year		

In historic Riverside, a restored colonial house filled with period antiques, decoys and country collectibles. On beautiful St. John's River.

KEY WEST ─────────────────────────────────────

Colours Key West	$$ B&B	Continental plus
410 Fleming St., 33040	12 rooms, 11 pb	Comp. sunset cocktail
305-294-6977	Visa, MC, AmEx •	Direct dial phones
James Remes	C-no/S-ltd/P-no/H-no	movie library, video
All year		lounge, swimming pool

For the avant-garde, celebrate your life-style in our Victorian mansion in the heart of Old Towne with very personal attention.

Duval House	$$ B&B	Continental plus
815 Duval St., 33040	25 rooms, 22 pb	Comp. wine
305-294-1666	Visa, MC, AmEx	Sitting room
Scott & Shannon Zurbrigen	C-15+/S-yes	TV lounge
All year		swimming pool, gardens

A restored guest house (circa 1885) offering fine lodging. Ideally located in historic Old Key West. Tropical gardens and a laid-back atmosphere.

KEY WEST ──

Eaton Lodge
511 Eaton St., 33040
305-294-3800
Denison Tempel
All year

$$$ B&B
11 rooms, 11 pb
Visa, MC, AmEx •
C-ltd/S-yes/P-no/H-no
French, Italian

Continental plus
Refrigerators
Hot tub
sitting room

Handsome Victorian home, in historic downtown, tastefully adapted; paddle fans and verandas; lush tropical gardens, whirlpool-spa & secluded terrace.

Eden House
1015 Fleming St., 33040
305-296-6868/800-533-KEYS
Michael Eden
All year

$$$ EP
41 rooms, 41 pb
Visa, MC, AmEx •
C-yes/S-yes/P-no/H-no
some Spanish

Restaurant
Guest discount at cafe
Swimming pool
snorkeling, scuba diving
sailing & jet ski nearby

In old Key West. Ceiling fans and white wicker. Sip a cool drink under our poolside gazebo, lounge on the veranda or dine in our garden cafe. Join us on a sunset sail.

Heron House
512 Simonton St., 33040
305-294-9227
Fred Gribelt
All year

$$ B&B
23 rooms, 21 pb
Visa, MC, AmEx •
C-15+/S-yes/P-no/H-yes

Continental breakfast
Full breakfast twice
weekly
Swimming pool

Old island charm situated in location central to all the main tourist attractions. Pool, sun deck, gardens and gym.

Nassau House
1016 Fleming St., 33040
305-296-8513
J. Greg Henley
All year

$ EP
6 rooms, 6 pb
Visa, MC, AmEx •
C-ltd/S-yes/P-no/H-no
Continental breakfast

Full kitchens in ea unit
Swimming pool
air conditioning

Located in "Old Town". Six intimate units all fully furnished with white wicker furniture, plants, A/C, color cable TV, private deck. Pool is lagoon style with waterfall.

Popular House/Key West B&B
415 William St., 33040
305-296-7274
Jody Carlson
All year

$$ B&B
7 rooms, 2 pb
Visa, MC, AmEx •
S-yes

Continental plus
Sitting room
hot tubs, sauna
sun deck

In the heart of the Historic Preservation District, a 100-year-old Victorian located within walking distance to everything. Sun deck, sauna, jacuzzi for your relaxation.

Watson House
525 Simonton St., 33040
305-294-6712
Ed Czaplicki, Joe Beres
All year

$$$ B&B
3 rooms, 3 pb
Visa, MC •
S-yes
Spanish

Continental breakfast
Veranda, heated spa
swimming pool
wicker/rattan furniture

Small, quaint award-winning inn with fully furnished guest suites in a lush, tropical garden setting. Located in the Historic Preservation District.

LAKE BUENA VISTA

Casa Adobe	$$ B&B	Full breakfast
9107 SR 535 North, 32830	3 rooms, 2 pb	Lunch, dinner, aftn. tea
P.O. Box 22088	•	Comp. wine, hot tubs
407-876-5432	C-yes/S-yes/P-yes/H-yes	Library, pool, bikes
All year		boats, fishing poles

Lakefront inn and country hideaway just minutes from Disney World and all major attractions. Great fishing and sailing or quiet relaxation by pool or spa.

LAKE WALES

Chalet Suzanne Country Inn	$$$ MAP	Continental plus
P.O. Drawer AC, 33859	30 rooms, 30 pb	Full breakfast $
US Hwy 27 & CR 17A	Major credit cards •	restaurant, lounge
813-676-6011/800-288-6011	C-yes/S-yes/P-yes/H-ltd	pool on lake, airstrip
Carl & Vita Hinshaw	German, French	gift shops
All year		

Unique country inn centrally located for Florida attractions. Gourmet meals; award-winning restaurant. Ranked one of 10 most romantic spots in Florida. A memorable experience.

MARATHON

Hopp-Inn Guest House	$$ B&B	Full breakfast
5 Man-O-War Dr., 33050	5 rooms, 5 pb	Televisions
305-743-4118	•	Bahama fans
Joe & Joan Hopp	C-yes/S-yes/P-no/H-ltd	air-conditioning
October—August	German	

Three rooms with private entrances and baths. Located on the ocean with tropical plants and many palm trees. Two ocean view villas sleep 2-6.

Pygmalion House B&B, Santa Rosa, CA

108   Florida

MAYO ——————————————————————————

Jim Hollis' River Rendez.
Route 2, Box 60, 32066
904-294-2510
Rosa Falconer, Jim Hollis
All year

$ EP
23 rooms, 24 pb
Visa, MC, AmEx, DC
C-yes/S-yes/P-ltd/H-yes

Full breakfast from menu
Restaurant, bar
Hot tubs, steam room
natural spring, bicycles
game room, canoe rentals

Nestled on the beautiful Suwannee River—a unique experience for a hideaway. "Once is not enough."

MIAMI ——————————————————————————

Miami River Inn
118 SW South River Dr., 33130
305-325-0045
Jaime Caceres
All year

$$ B&B
41 rooms, 39 pb
Visa, MC •
C-yes/S-yes/P-no/H-no
Spanish

Continental plus
Afternoon tea
Sitting room, library
hot tubs, swimming pool
croquet, table games

A cluster of historic buildings, carefully restored and furnished in period. Right next to downtown Miami but a world apart.

MIAMI BEACH ——————————————————————

Cavalier Hotel/Cabana Club
1320 Ocean Dr., 33139
305-534-2135
Don Meginley
All year

$$$ B&B
44 rooms, 46 pb
Visa, MC, AmEx, Enroute •
C-yes/S-yes/P-no/H-no
Spanish, French, German

Continental plus
Restaurant next door
Sitting room
ocean front
historic district

In the heart of the historic "Art Deco District," recalling a less hurried time of a '30s seaside resort. Home for the well-traveled. Ultimate symbol of "tropical deco."

OCKLAWAHA ——————————————————————

Lake Weir Inn
Rt. 2, 12660 SE Hwy 25, 32179
904-288-3723/904-629-0134
Al & Myrtle Flechas
All year

$ B&B
8 rooms, 8 pb
Visa, MC •
C-ask/S-no/P-no/H-yes

Continental breakfast
Sand bottom lake
boating, fishing
swimming, etc.

Beautiful two-story hideaway on 6000-acre lake. Charming country resort community. Grocery, restaurant and boat ramp nearby. Ample parking available.

PENSACOLA ——————————————————————

Liechty's Homestead Inn
7830 Pine Forest Rd., 32506
904-944-4816
Neil & Jeanne Liechty
All year

$$ B&B
5 rooms, 5 pb
AmEx, Visa, MC •
C-12+/S-ltd/P-no/H-no

Full 6-course breakfast
Evening dessert included
Lunch, dinner, tea
Sitting room, hot tub
beautiful garden

Featuring Lancaster Pennsylvania Amish-Mennonite recipes at our restaurant. Our rooms have wood floors, poster beds, fireplaces and garden tubs.

SAINT AUGUSTINE ——————————————————

Casa De La Paz B&B Inn
22 Avenida Menendez, 32084
904-829-2915
Harry Stafford, Brenda Sugg
All year

$$$ B&B
5 rooms, 5 pb
Visa, MC, AmEx, Disc •
C-8+/S-no/P-no/H-no
French

Continental plus
Comp. wine & chocolates
Sitting room, library
room service, courtyard
veranda, carriage tours

On the bayfront in the Historic District, this elegant Mediterranean-style home (1915) offers the finest accommodations in a beautiful, central location.

SAINT AUGUSTINE ──────────────────────────

Kenwood Inn	$$ B&B	Continental breakfast
38 Marine St., 32084	15 rooms, 15 pb	Swimming pool
904-824-2116	Visa, MC	sitting room
The Constant Family	C-6+ /S-yes/P-no/H-no	piano
All year		

19th-century inn located in historic district of our nation's oldest city. Walk to attractions: beautiful beaches 5 minutes away.

St. Francis Inn	$ B&B	Continental plus
279 St. George St., 32084	11 rooms, 11 pb	Bicycles
904-824-6068	•	free passes to Oldest
Marie Register	C-yes/S-yes/P-no/H-no	House
All year		

Built in 1791, located in Historic District, one block west of the "Oldest House in USA." New owner, many improvements.

Victorian House B&B	$$ B&B	Continental plus
11 Cadiz St., 32084	6 rooms, 6 pb	Sitting room
904-824-5214	Visa, MC	
Daisy Morden	C-ltd/S-yes/P-no/H-no	
All year		

Located in the heart of the historic area. Enjoy canopy beds, stenciled walls. Explore the charm of St. Augustine from the Victorian House.

SAINT PETERSBURG ──────────────────────────

Bayboro House on Tampa Bay	$$ B&B	Continental plus
1719 Beach Dr. SE, 33701	4 rooms, 4 pb	Comp. wine/cocktails
813-823-4955	Visa, MC •	Veranda
Gordon & Antonia Powers	C-no/S-ltd/P-no/H-no	player piano
All year		

Walk out the door to sunning and beachcombing from a turn-of-the-century Queen Anne house. Florida B&B-ing at its best.

STUART ──────────────────────────

The Homeplace	$$$ B&B	Continental plus
501 Akron, 34994	3 rooms, 3 pb	Comp. wine, fruit/cheese
407-220-9148	Visa, MC	Sitting room, library
Jean Bell, Jim Smith	C-12+ /S-ltd/P-no/H-no	bicycles, hot tubs, pool
All year		city walking tour

Welcomed back in time, to a period much softer. Guests enjoy the quiet hospitality and fresh-baked "old Florida" recipes.

TARPON SPRINGS ──────────────────────────

Spring Bayou Inn	$$ B&B	Continental plus
32 W. Tarpon Ave., 34689	5 rooms, 3 pb	Comp. wine
813-938-9333	C-no/S-no/P-ask/H-no	Library
Ron & Cher Morrick		sitting room
October 1—August 1		baby grand piano

Elegant Victorian with modern conveniences. Walk to shops, bayou, restaurants, sponge docks. Golf, beaches, tennis, and fishing nearby.

110   Florida

VENICE ───

Banyan House
519 S. Harbor Dr., 34285
813-484-1385
Chuck & Susan McCormick
All year

$ B&B
9 rooms, 7 pb
C-12+ / S-ltd

Continental breakfast
Continental plus (wint.)
Sitting room
bicycles, hot tubs
swimming pool

Historic Mediterranean-style home. Enormous Banyan tree shades courtyard, pool and spa. Centrally located to shopping, restaurants, beaches and golfing.

More Inns...

Gibson Inn   P.O. Box 221, Apalachicola 32320   904-653-2191
Barnacle   Route 1 Box 780A, Big Pine Key 33043   305-872-3298
Gasparilla Inn   Boca Grande 33921   813-964-2201
Cabbage Key Inn   Cabbage Key 33924   813-283-2278
Pelican Inn   Dog Island, Carrabelle 32322   800-451-5294
Sprague House   125 Central Avenue, Crescent City 32012   904-698-2430
Jean Hutchison   811 N.W. 3rd Ave., Delray Beach 33444   407-276-7390
Lemon Bay B&B   12 Southwind Dr., Englewood 33533   813-474-7571
Rod & Gun Club   P.O. Box G, Everglades City 33929   813-695-2101
Greyfield Inn   P.O. Drawer B, Fernandina Beach 32034   904-261-6408
Wind Song Garden   5570-4 Woodrose Court, Fort Myers 33907   813-936-6378
Yearling Cabins   Rt. 3, Box 123, Hawthorne 32640   904-466-3033
Seminole Country Inn   15885 Warfield Blvd., Indiantown 33456   305-597-3777
Crown Hotel   109 N. Seminole Ave., Inverness 32650   904-344-5555
Jules' Undersea Lodge   P.O. Box 3330, Key Largo 33037   305-451-2353
Coconut Grove Guest House   817 Fleming St., Key West 33040   305-296-5107
Cypress House   601 Caroline St., Key West 33040   305-294-6969
Ellie's Nest   1414 Newton St., Key West 33040   305-296-5757
Garden House   329 Elizabeth St., Key West 33040   305-296-5368
Gideon Lowe House   409 William St., Key West 33040   305-294-5969
Island City Guesthouses   411 William St., Key West 33040   305-294-5702
Island House   1129 Fleming St., Key West 33040   305-294-6284
Marquesa Hotel   600 Fleming St., Key West 33040   305-292-1919
Merlinn Guesthouse   811 Simonton St., Key West 33040   305-296-3336
Oasis Guest House   823 Fleming St., Key West 33040   305-296-2131
Palms of Key West Resort   820 White St., Key West 33040   305-294-3146
Pines of Key West   521 United St., Key West 33040   305-296-7467
Simonton Court   320 Simonton St., Key West 33040   305-294-6386
Sunrise Sea House B&B   39 Bay Drive, Key West 33040   305-745-2875
Wicker Guesthouse   913 Duval St., Key West 33040   305-296-4275
Unicorn Inn   8 So. Orlando Ave., Kissimmee 31724   305-846-1200
Feller House   2473 Longboat Dr., Naples 33942   813-774-0182
Doll House B&B   719 S.E. 4th St., Ocala 32671   904-351-1167
Ritz-Ocala's Historic Inn   1205 E. Silver Springs, Ocala 32632   904-867-7700
Orange Springs   1 Main St., P.O. Box 550, Orange Springs 32682   904-546-2052
Alpen Gast Haus   8328 Curry Ford Rd., Orlando 32822   305-277-1811
Avonelle's   4755 Anderson Rd., Orlando 32806   305-275-8733
Meadow Marsh   940 Tildenville School, Orlando 32787   305-656-2064
Norment-Parry Inn   211 N. Lucerne Cir. E., Orlando 32801   407-648-5188
Rinaldi House   502 Lake Ave., Orlando 32801   407-425-6549
Robin Dodson   11754 Ruby Lake Road, Orlando 32819   305-239-0109
Spencer Home B&B   313 Spencer St., Orlando 32809   407-855-5603
Five Oaks Inn   1102 Riverside Drive, Palmetto 34221   813-723-1236
New World Inn   6000 South Palafox St., Pensacola 32501   904-432-4111

North Hill Inn   422 N. Baylen St., Pensacola 32501   904-432-9804
Sunshine   508 Decatur Ave., Pensacola 32507   904-455-6781
Westcott House   146 Avenida Menendez, Saint Augustine 32084   904-824-4301
Walters House   1115 Boca Ciega Island, Saint Petersburg Beach 33706   813-360-3372
Kona Kai Motel   1539 Periwinkle Way, Sanibel 33957   813-472-1001
Carriage Way B&B   70 Cuna St., St. Augustine 32084   904-829-2467
Wakulla Springs & Lodge   One Springs Drive, Wakulla 32305   904-561-7215
Fortnightly Inn   377 E. Fairbanks Avenue, Winter Park 32789   407-645-4440

Georgia

ATLANTA

Bessie's Bed & Breakfast	$$ B&B	Full breakfast
223 Ponce de Leon Ave., 30308	11 rooms, 6 pb	Afternoon tea
404-875-9449	•	Sitting room
The Joneses	C-yes/S-yes/P-no/H-no	hot tubs, porches
All year		movies/TV in parlor

Southern hospitality in the heart of Atlanta! Old Victorian home, formerly a bordello. Antiques, full Southern breakfast, hot tubs, hot-air ballooning available.

Beverly Hills Inn	$$ B&B	Continental plus
65 Sheridan Dr., 30305	18 rooms, 18 pb	Comp. wine
404-233-8520	Visa, MC, AmEx •	Sitting room, library
Bonnie & Lyle Kleinhans	C-yes/S-yes/P-no/H-no	piano, health club priv.
All year		London taxi shuttle

Charming city retreat, fine residential neighborhood. Close to Lenox Square, Historical Society and many art galleries. 15 min. to downtown. Shuttle to nearby attractions.

Shellmont B&B Lodge	$$$ B&B	Continental plus
821 Piedmont Ave. NE, 30308	4 rooms, 4 pb	Afternoon tea
404-872-9290	Visa, MC •	Sitting room
Edward & Debbie McCord	C-ltd/S-ltd/P-no/H-yes	bicycles
All year		

Small by intent, located near historic theater, cultural and restaurant district. Independently listed National Register property.

AUGUSTA

Telfair Inn	$$ B&B	Full Southern breakfast
326 Greene St., 30901	AmEx, Visa, MC, DC •	Restaurant, bar service
404-724-3315	C-yes/S-yes/P-sml/H-yes	Sitting room, concierge
Greg Ray		conference ctr, hot tub
All year		tennis courts, pool

Historic District; near downtown and airports; restored houses; full complimentary breakfast, whirlpool baths, canopied beds. Special packages.

BRUNSWICK ─────────────────────────────

Rose Manor Guest House	$ B&B	Full breakfast
1108 Richmond St., 31520	5 rooms, 3 pb	Picnic lunch, high tea
at Hanover Square	•	Comp. wine, refreshments
912-267-6369	C-yes/S-ltd/P-no/H-no	Sitting room, library
Rachel Rose	some French	bicycles, croquet
All year		

Southern Victorian, elegantly restored, resplendent English gardens, gracious amenities. Historic Port City, Wardo's Spring Capital, gateway to Georgia's Golden Isles.

CLARKESVILLE ─────────────────────────

Burns-Sutton House	$$ B&B	Full breakfast
P.O. Box 992, 30523	7 rooms, 4 pb	Snacks
124 S. Washington St.	Visa, MC	Restaurant nearby
404-754-5565	C-yes/S-no/P-no/H-no	Sitting room
John & JoAnn Smith		cable TV
All year		

Historic Victorian home elegantly restored. Furnished in antiques. At the foothills of the mountains, close to nature activities and antiquing.

Glen-Ella Springs Inn	$$ B&B	Continental plus
Route 3, Box 3304, 30523	16 rooms, 16 pb	Lunch, dinner, snacks
Bear Gap Rd.	Visa, MC, AmEx •	Restaurant, conf. room
404-754-7295/800-552-3479	C-ltd/S-yes/P-no/H-yes	Sitting room, library
Barrie C. Aycock		pool, hiking, gardens
All year		

100-year-old inn in northeast Georgia. Award-winning restoration in 1987. Gourmet dining room features fresh seafood, prime rib and many specialties.

CLAYTON ───────────────────────────────

English Manor Inns	$$ B&B	Continental plus
P.O. Box 1605, 30525	60 rooms, 60 pb	Lunch & tea (on request)
US Hwy. 76 East	Visa, MC •	dinner (for groups)
800-782-5780	C-yes/S-yes/P-yes	appetizers, comp. wine
Susan & English Thornwell	French, Spanish, German	Tennis courts, sauna
All year		

Seven inns, all furnished in exquisite antiques, reflecting the charm of an earlier era with all the amenities of today.

COLUMBUS ──────────────────────────────

De Loffre House	$$ B&B	Continental breakfast
812 Broadway, 31901	5 rooms, 5 pb	Comp. sherry
404-324-1144/404-324-1146	Visa, MC, AmEx •	Sitting room
Shirley & Paul Romo	C-12+/S-yes/P-no/H-no	
All year		

An 1863 town house, elegantly restored & modernized, where guests may enjoy Victorian charm and gracious hospitality of the South.

DAHLONEGA ─────────────────────────────

Laurel Ridge	$ B&B	Continental breakfast
P.O. Box 338, 30533	2 rooms, 2 pb	Comp. fruit on arrival
Ben Higgins Rd.	C-yes/S-no	Wooded walking trails
404-864-7817		
Glenda & Nick Pender		
All year		

Rustic warmth in peaceful, wooded setting. Nestled in foothills of the Appalachian Mountains near Appalachian Trail, rivers and gold panning.

DARIEN

Open Gates Bed & Breakfast $ B&B Full breakfast
P.O. Box 1526, 31305 5 rooms, 3 pb Boxed lunch
Vernon Square • Sitting room, library
912-437-6985 C-ask/S-no/P-no/H-no bicycles, pool, antiques
Carolyn & Philip Hodges Steinway piano, sailing
All year

Timber baron's gracious home on oak-shaded historic square. Access to untrammeled barrier islands, including Sapelo and the Altamaha Delta rice culture.

GAINESVILLE

Dunlap House $$ B&B Continental breakfast
635 Green St., 30501 11 rooms, 11 pb Comp. tea
404-536-7933 Visa, MC, AmEx • Sitting room
C. Dunlap, L. Sigler C-ask/S-yes/P-no/H-yes bicycles
All year Spanish

Luxurious historic accommodations. Breakfast in bed or on the veranda. Restaurant and lounge across the street. Lodging and dining excellence.

HAMILTON

Wedgwood Bed & Breakfast $$ B&B Full breakfast
P.O. Box 115, 31811 3 rooms, 1 pb Snacks
Hwy 27 & Mobley • Living room, library
404-628-5659 C-ask den with TV & VCR
Janice Neuffer bicycle, gazebo
March—December

Callaway Gardens in 6 miles north. Your hostess makes you feel at home in this beautiful 1845 southern home.

HELEN

Hilltop Haus B&B $ B&B Full country breakfast
P.O. Box 154, 30545 2 rooms, 3 pb Afternoon coffee
Chattahoochee St. • Bicycles
404-878-2388 C-ltd/S-ltd/P-no/H-yes sitting rooms
Frankie Tysor w/fireplaces
All year

Located within walking distance of alpine village, Helen. Country-style breakfast with buttermilk biscuits, Appalachian Trail nearby.

MACON

1842 Inn $$ B&B Continental plus
353 College St., 31201 22 rooms, 22 pb Afternoon tea
912-741-1842 Visa, MC, AmEx • Bar service
Aileen Hatcher C-yes/S-yes/H-yes Sitting room
All year whirlpools

Antebellum mansion and Victorian cottage furnished with fine antiques. All rooms have private baths, air conditioning and color televisions.

MOUNTAIN CITY

York House $$ B&B Continental plus
P.O. Box 126, 30562 15 rooms, 15 pb Honeymoon suite
York House Rd. Visa, MC • Sitting room, piano
404-746-2068 C-yes/S-ltd/P-no/H-yes fireplaces, earn credit
James H. Smith for free stays
All year

Est. 1896. Tranquil lodging and antiques. Breakfast served in room. Rafting, skiing, rocking on porch, picnic area. Featured in movie Deliverance.

114   Georgia

SAINT MARY'S

Riverview Hotel
105 Osborne St., 31558
912-882-3242
Jerry Brandon
All year

$ EP
18 rooms, 18 pb
Visa, MC, AmEx, Dis, CB •
C-yes/S-yes/P-no/H-no

Restaurant
Breakfast/lunch/dinner
Bar service
Sitting room

Overlooking the St. Mary's River, the recently renovated Riverview features Seagle's Restaurant. Famous for its great seafood and unique atmosphere.

SAINT SIMONS ISLAND

Little St. Simons Island
P.O. Box 1078, 31522
912-638-7472
Ben & Laura Gibbens
Mid-Feb.—mid-Nov.

$$$ AP
12 rooms, 12 pb
Visa, MC •
C-yes/S-yes/P-no/H-ltd

Full breakfast
Lunch/dinner/snacks incl
Swimming pool
sitting room
bicycles, horses

A 10,000-acre undeveloped barrier island with early 1900's lodge and guest cottages. Southern cuisine. Professional naturalists and activities included.

SAUTEE

Stovall House
Route 1 Box 1476, 30571
Hwy. 225 N.
404-878-3355
Hamilton & Kathy Schwartz
All year

$$ B&B
6 rooms, 6 pb
C-yes/S-yes/P-no/H-ltd
Spanish

Continental breakfast
Restaurant
Lunch, dinner
Sitting room

Award-winning restoration of 1837 farmhouse on 28 serene acres; mountain views; a country experience. One of top 50 restaurants in Georgia. National Register.

SAVANNAH

Ballastone Inn
14 E. Oglethorpe Ave., 31401
912-236-1484
Richard Carlson, Tim Hargus
All year

$$$ B&B
18 rooms, 18 pb
Visa, MC, AmEx •
C-no/S-yes/P-no/H-yes

Continental plus
Comp. sherry, cognac
Full service bar
Elevator, VCRs
parlor, courtyard

Closest B&B inn to the Savannah Riverfront. 1853 Mansion with beautiful antiques and courtyard. Fireplaces, jacuzzis. Recommended by the New York Times.

Bed & Breakfast Inn
117 W. Gordon St., 31401
at Chatham Sq.
912-238-0518
Bob McAlister
All year

$ B&B
7 rooms, 4 pb
Visa, MC •
C-yes/S-yes/P-ltd/H-no
German, French, Spanish

Full homestyle breakfast
Comp. wine in suites
Sitting room
library
garden

Restored 1853 Federal-style townhouse in heart of historic Savannah; amidst museums, restaurants & antique shops; walk to major attractions. Personalized hospitality.

Charlton Court
403 Charlton St. E., 31401
912-236-2895
Mr. & Mrs. J.H. Reeves
All year

$$$ B&B
1 rooms, 1 pb
C-yes/S-yes/P-no/H-no

Continental plus
Comp. wine
Suite
sitting room
bicycles

Private carriage house, c. 1850, in midst of Historic District. Extraordinary accommodations including wine, bicycles, breakfast.

SAVANNAH

Eliza Thompson House
5 W. Jones St., 31401
912-236-3620/800-348-9378
David A. Barrow
All year

$$$ B&B
25 rooms, 25 pb
Visa, MC, AmEx •
C-yes/S-yes/P-no/H-yes

Continental breakfast
Champagne on arrival
Parlor
imported wine daily

Regally restored home in the heart of the Historic District. Elegant parlor, beautifully landscaped courtyard with splashing fountains. Serene.

Foley House Inn
14 W. Hull St., 31401
912-232-6622/800-647-3708
Susan Steinhauser
All year

$$$ B&B
20 rooms, 20 pb
Visa, MC, AmEx •
C-yes/S-yes/P-no/H-no

Continental plus
Comp. wine
Hot tub, newspaper
shoes shined on request
VCR & film lib. in rooms

A restored antebellum mansion, furnished with antiques, 5 jacuzzi rooms, in-room video disc players. Turndown service, fireplace rooms. Truly the best of two worlds.

Forsyth Park Inn
102 West Hall St., 31401
912-233-6800
Hal & Virginia Sullivan
All year

$$$ B&B
10 rooms, 10 pb
Visa, MC, AmEx
C-yes/S-yes
French (limited)

Continental plus
Comp. wine
Sitting room
tennis courts, hot tubs
piano music nightly

An elegantly restored Victorian mansion in the historic district. Rooms feature fireplaces, whirlpool tubs, antiques and 16-foot ceilings.

The Gastonian
220 E. Gaston St., 31401
917-232-2869
Hugh & Roberta Lineberger
All year

$$$ B&B
13 rooms, 13 pb
Visa, MC, AmEx
C-yes/S-yes/P-no/H-yes

Full breakfast
Comp. wine, tea
Sitting room
bicycles
hot tub

1868 southern elegance! Large rooms and suites have antiques, canopied beds and whirlpool tubs. Hot tubs on the sun deck. Luxurious.

Greystone Inn
214 E. Jones St., 31401
912-236-2442/800-348-9378
All year

$$ B&B
7 rooms, 7 pb
Visa, MC, AmEx
C-ltd/S-yes/P-no/H-no

Continental plus
Comp. wine
Sitting room

The "inn" place to stay in historic Savannah. 1858 Federal-style home furnished with antiques.

Haslam-Fort House
417 E. Charlton St., 31401
912-233-6380
Alan Fort
All year

$$$ B&B
1 rooms, 1 pb
•
C-yes/S-yes/P-yes/H-yes
Ger, Norw, Span, French

Self-serve guest kitchen
Comp. wine
Private living room
books, games, TV
radio, garden

A personal, private 2-bedroom suite with "all the comforts of home." Ideal for two to four persons. Charming antiques! Prestigious location with private parking & patio.

Jesse Mount House
209 W. Jones St., 31401
912-236-1774
H. Crawford, L. Bannerman
All year

$$$ B&B
2 rooms, 2 pb
•
C-yes/S-yes/P-ltd/H-yes

Continental plus
Comp. wine/fruit/candies
Garden with fountains
full kitchen
bicycles

Circa 1854 elegant Greek Revival house. Two luxurious 3-bedroom suites for one to six persons in a party. Cable TV. Rare antiques, gilded harps.

116   Georgia

Liberty Inn 1834
128 W. Liberty St., 31401
912-233-1007/800-637-1007
Frank & Janie Harris
All year

$$$ B&B
7 rooms, 7 pb
Visa, MC, AmEx •
C-yes/S-yes/P-no/H-yes

Continental breakfast
Kitchen
Comp. coffee
Receiving twin parlor
spa, hot tub

1834 inn located in heart of historic Savannah, near the waterfront & shops. Garden, super spa, parking, continental breakfast. Peach cordial in each suite.

Olde Harbour Inn
508 E. Factors Walk, 31401
912-234-4100/800-553-6533
Pamela L. Barnes
All year

$$ B&B
24 rooms, 24 pb
Visa, MC, AmEx •
C-yes/S-yes/P-no/H-ltd

Continental plus
Comp. wine, cheese,
crackers & ice cream
Sitting room, library
kitchens in suites

Our traditionally renovated inn, built in 1892, offers spacious suites complete with kitchens and river views in Savannah's Historical District.

Presidents' Quarters
225 E. President St., 31401
912-233-1600/800-233-1776
Muril Broy
All year

$$$ B&B
16 rooms, 16 pb
Visa, MC, AmEx, DC •
C-yes/S-ltd/P-no/H-yes

Continental plus
Comp. wine, tea, snacks
Ltd. bar, sandwiches
Sitting room, courtyard
jacuzzi, pool

Newly restored 1885 home in the heart of Historic District offering jacuzzi bathtubs, gas log fireplaces, period reproductions. Deluxe but affordable accommodations.

Pulaski Square Inn
203 W. Charlton St., 31401
912-233-5797/800-227-0650
J.B. & Hilda J. Smith
All year

$$ B&B
9 rooms, 5 pb
Visa, MC, AmEx •
C-ltd/S-yes/P-no/H-no

Continental breakfast
Sitting room
fireplaces

Distinctive inn on a lovely square in historic downtown. Continental breakfast in room or garden. Beautiful antiques, oriental rugs, fireplaces.

Remshart-Brooks House
106 W. Jones St., 31401
912-234-6928
Anne & Ewing Barnett
All year

$$ B&B
1 rooms, 1 pb
Visa, MC •
C-6+/S-yes/P-no/H-ltd

Continental breakfast
Sitting room
terrace garden

Experience the charm and hospitality of historic Savannah while being "at home" in the garden suite of Remshart-Brooks House—built in 1854.

The Veranda
P.O. Box 177, 30276
252 Seavy St.
404-599-3905
Jan & Bobby Boal
All year

$$$ B&B
8 rooms, 8 pb
Visa, MC, Discover •
C-ltd/S-ltd/P-no/H-yes
German

Full breakfast
Lunch, dinner by res.
Library, conference fac.
sitting room, organ
tennis courts nearby

Historic inn furnished with antiques and fascinating collections of Victorian memorabilia. Delicious meals and gourmet dining beautifully served in an Old South setting.

THOMASVILLE ─────────────────────────────────

Neel House	$$ B&B	Continental plus
P.O. Box 2906, 31792	2 rooms, 2 pb	Restaurant, bar service
502 S. Broad St.	Visa, MC, AmEx, DC	Snacks, lunch, dinner
912-228-6500	C-yes/S-yes	
Brad Koeneman		
All year		

A Neo-Classical mansion located in the historic district. Period antiques featured throughout the inn. Close to many sites and landmarks.

Susina Plantation Inn	$$$ MAP	Full breakfast
Rt. 3 Box 1010, 31792	8 rooms, 7 pb	Dinner complimentary
912-377-9644	C-yes/S-yes/P-yes/H-no	Swimming pool
Anne-Marie Walker		tennis, bicycles
All year		sitting room

Greek Revival mansion built 1840 and furnished in antiques; a real southern "Tara."

More Inns...

Augusta House P.O. Box 40069, Augusta 30904   404-738-5122
Charm House Inn   Box 392, Highway 441, Clarkesville 30523   404-754-9347
LaPrade's Rt. 1, Hwy 197N, Clarkesville 30523   404-947-3312
Rusharon P.O. Box 273, Cleveland 30528   404-865-5173
Towering Oaks B&B Lodge #5 Box 5172, Cleveland 30528   404-865-6760
Forest Hills Mt. Resort Rt. 3, Dahlonega 30533   404-864-6456
Mountain Top Lodge Rt. 3, Box 173, Dahlonega 30533   404-864-5257
Smith House 202 S. Chestatee St., Dahlonega 30533   404-864-3566
Worley Homestead Inn 410 West Main St., Dahlonega 30533   404-864-7002
Dillard House Inn P.O. Box 10, Dillard 30537   404-746-5349
Hartwell Inn 504 W. Howell Street, Hartwell 30643
Helendorf Inn P.O. Box 305, Helen 30545   404-878-2271
Anapauo Farm Star Rt., Box 13C, Lakemont 30522   404-782-6442
Lake Rabun Inn Lakemont 30552   404-782-4946
Arden Hall 1052 Arden Dr. SW, Marietta 30060   404-422-0780
Marlow House/Stanley House 192 Church St., Marietta 30060   404-426-1887
Olena's Guest House Rt. 26, Montezuma 31063   912-472-7620
Buckley's Cedar House Route 10, Box 161, Ringgold 30736   404-935-2619
Woodhaven Chalet Rt. 1, Box 39, Sautee 30571   404-878-2580
17 Hundred 90 Inn 307 E. President St., Savannah 31401   912-236-7122
Comer House 2 East Taylor St., Savannah 31401   912-234-2923
East Bay Inn 225 East Bay St., Savannah 31401   912-238-1225
Magnolia Place Inn 503 Whitaker St., Savannah 31401   912-236-7674
Mary Lee's House P.O. Box 607, Savannah 31402   912-232-0891
Morel House 117 W. Perry St., Savannah 31401   912-234-4088
Oglethorpe Inn P.O. Box 9803, Savannah 31412   912-232-2700
Royal Colony Inn 29 Abercorn St., Savannah 31401   912-232-5678
Stoddard-Cooper House 19 W. Perry St., Savannah 31401   912-233-6809
Timmons House 407 E. Charlton St., Savannah 31401   912-233-4456
'417' Haslam-Fort House 417 E. Charlton St., Savannah 31401   912-233-6380
Culpepper House B&B 35 Broad St., Senoia 30276   404-599-8182
King's on the March 1776 Demere Rd., St. Simons Isl. 31522   912-638-1426
Edenfield House Inn Box 556, Swainsboro 30401   912-237-3007

118

Hawaii

ANAHOLA, KAUAI ─────────────────────────────

Mahina Kai	$$ B&B	Continental plus
P.O. Box 699, 96703	4 rooms, 2 pb	Kitchenette facilities
4933 Aliomanu	•	Sitting room
808-822-9451	S-yes	library, bicycles
Dave Matlock	Italian, French	art collection
All year		

Asian-Pacific beach villa and tropical gardens overlooking secluded bay. Separate guest wing with ethnic art collected by artist/owner.

BIG ISLAND ─────────────────────────────

Volcano Heart Chalet	$$ B&B	Continental breakfast
P.O. Box 404, 96713	3 rooms, 2 pb	Exercise
11th Ave.	•	laundry
808-248-7725	C-no/S-no/P-no/H-no	light cooking
JoLoyce & John Kaia		
All year		

Cozy, comfy cedar retreat surrounded by exotic native flora. A good base for exploring nearby national parks and many other attractions.

HAIKU, MAUI ─────────────────────────────

Haikuleana B&B Inn	$$ B&B	Continental breakfast
69 Haiku Rd., 96708	2 rooms	Afternoon tea
808-575-2890	•	Sitting room
Denise & Clark Champion	C-yes/S-yes/P-yes/H-no	15 min. from airport
All year		

Hawaiian country life with waterfalls, beaches and quiet relaxation, built amongst pineapple fields and pine trees in the time of King Kamehameha.

HANA, MAUI ─────────────────────────────

Kaia Ranch & Co.	$$ B&B	Full breakfast
P.O. Box 404, 96713	1 rooms	Sitting room, library
Ulaino Rd.	•	walk & picnic in flower
808-248-7725	C-no/S-no/P-no/H-no	& fruit gardens
JoLoyce & John Kaia		
All year		

A country farm. The real Hawaii which few see. Animals, gardens, and friends you'll never forget. Hana is a unique experience.

HONOLULU, OAHU ─────────────────────────────

John Guild Inn	$$ B&B	Continental plus
2001 Vancouver Dr., 96822	8 rooms, 2 pb	Comp. wine
808-947-6019	Visa, MC	Sitting room
Peter Johnson	C-no/S-ltd/P-no/H-no	piano
All year		

1919 restored historic mansion furnished with antiques. Intimate and peaceful hideaway, conveniently located; generous continental breakfast, amenities.

HONOLULU, OAHU

Manoa Valley Inn
2001 Vancouver Dr., 96822
99-969 Iwaena St. Aiea HI
808-947-6019/800-634-5115
Marianne Schultz
All year

$$$ B&B
8 rooms, 5 pb
Visa, MC, AmEx, CB •
C-14+/S-ltd/P-no/H-no

Continental plus
Aftn. tea
Sitting room
conference room
tour/dining information

Hawaii's intimate country inn located in lush Manoa Valley, two miles from Waikiki Beach. Daily afternoon fresh tropical fruits, wine & cheese tastings on the shady lanai.

KAILUA, OAHU

Pacific-Hawaii B&B
19 Kai Nani Pl., 96734
808-262-6026/800-999-6026
Doris Epp
All year

$$$ EP
2 rooms, 1 pb
•
C-yes/S-yes/P-yes/H-yes
German, Spanish

Cooking facilites
Barbecue facilites
TV
sleeps 4-5 if necessary

Oceanfront home on white sand beach. Perfect for swimming or walking for miles. Quiet residential area. Close to small shopping center. TV, microwave in room.

KAMUELA

Upcountry Hideaways
P.O. Box 563, 96743
808-885-7441/808-885-4550
Barbara Campbell
All year

$$ B&B
3 rooms, 3 pb
personal checks •
C-yes/S-no/P-no/H-yes

Full breakfast
Sitting room, library
beach towels, backrests,
coolers for beach trips

A trio of B&B cottages. Centrally located for touring Kailua-Kona & Volcano; minutes to white-sand beaches, horseback riding, restaurants. In one of the most charming towns.

KANEOHE, OAHU

Emma's Guest Rooms
47-600 Hui Ulili St., 96744
808-239-7248
Emma Sargeant
All year

$ EP
5 rooms, 2 pb
•
C-yes/S-no/P-no/H-no
German

Guest kitchenette
Dining room, library
TV lounge

Cool windward location, private entrance, fully equipped kitchen, tropical garden view dining, convenient shopping, beaches and all Oahu island attractions.

KAPAA

Kay Barker's B&B
P.O. Box 740, 96746
3rd St. off Crossley
808-822-3073
Kay Barker
All year

$ B&B
4 rooms, 4 pb
•
C-yes/S-yes/P-no/H-yes

Continental plus
Sitting room, library
restaurant, tennis
beaches & river 10 min.

Lovely home in a garden setting, with mountain and pasture views. Ten minutes from beaches, restaurants, golf, tennis and shopping.

KOLOA, KAUAI

Poipu B&B Inn
2720 Hoonani Rd., 96756
808-742-1146/800-347-6548
Dotti Cichon, B. Young
All year

$$$ B&B
6 rooms, 6 pb
Visa, MC •
C-yes
French, German

Continental plus
Afternoon tea, snacks
Sitting room, library
swimming pool
tennis courts

Lovingly restored plantation house, one block from beach, includes two oceanfront rooms. Furnished in white wicker, pine antiques and carousel houses.

Gold Quartz Inn, Sutter Creek, CA

KULA, MAUI

Kula Lodge & Restaurant	$$$ B&B	Full breakfast
RR 1 Box 475, 96790	5 rooms, 5 pb	Lunch, dinner, snacks
808-878-2517/808-878-1535	Visa, MC •	Bar & restaurant
Fred Romanchak	C-yes/S-yes/P-no/H-yes	Sitting room
All year		

On the slopes of Haleakala Crater. . .out in the country, away from the frantic pace of the cities . . .rustic and romantic. Cool & quiet at 3,500 feet above sea level.

LAHAINA, MAUI

Plantation Inn	$$$ B&B	Full tropical buffet
174 Lahainaluna Rd., 96761	10 rooms, 10 pb	Dinner
800-433-6815/808-667-9225	•	Sitting room, TV
Jim & Julie Follett	C-no/S-no/P-no/H-no	garden, large tiled pool
All year		spa, barbecue area

The rooms are spacious and have soundproofing, oak floors w/area carpets, brass beds, 10' ceilings, A/C, lanais (decks), fridges. Inn is located one block from the beach.

Lahaina Hotel	$$$ B&B	Continental
127 Lahainaluna Rd., 96761	12 rooms, 12 pb	Restaurant
99-969 Iwaena St. Aiea HI	Visa, MC •	Bar service
808-661-0577	C-no/S-yes/P-no/H-no	Balcony lanais in rooms
Ken Eisley		ocean & mountain views
All year		

Located in heart of historic Lahaina town. Completely restored & redecorated in 1988-89. Each guest room is furnished with authenic turn-of-the century antiques.

LAWAI, KAUAI

Victoria Place	$$ B&B	Continental plus
P.O. Box 930, 96765	3 rooms, 1 pb	Lunch & dinner nearby
3459 Lawai Loa Lane	•	Large library
808-332-9300	H-yes	swimming pool
Edee Seymour		lanai overlooking mtns.
All year		

Jungle and ocean view—all rooms open onto pool—near beaches, golf, tennis. We pamper: flowers, chocolates, homemade muffins and aloha.

NAPILI, MAUI

Coconut Inn $$$ B&B   Continental breakfast
181 Hui Rd. "F", 96761   41 rooms, 41 pb   Welcome MaiTai Party Fri
808-669-5712/800-367-8006   •   Snorkel classes, pool
Cindy Vee   C-yes/S-yes/P-no/H-yes   spa, BBQ grills, tennis
All year   beach, golf nearby

This country inn nestled in pineapple fields is only a short stroll to a beautiful beach. Fully equipped kitchens and daily maid service.

PAHOA

Kalani Honua $ EP   Full service cafe, bar
Box 4500, Ocean Hwy 137, 96778   31 rooms, 10 pb   Lunch, dinner, comp.cof.
808-965-7828/800-367-8047   AmEx, Visa, MC •   Sitting room, library
Richard Koob & Madalyn Sandra   C-yes/S-ltd/P-no/H-yes   hot tub, sauna, pool
All year   Fr., Ger., Sp., Japanese   tennis, bicycles

Hike into underground hot springs, dance homage to Volcano goddesses, bake on black beaches. Sweet dreams, tender moments, delicious and healthful meals.

POIPU, KAUAI

Gloria's Spouting Horn B&B $$ B&B   Continental
4464 Lawai Beach Rd., 96756   5 rooms, 4 pb   Comp. wine
808-742-6995   •   Beach mats, coolers
Gloria & Bob Merkle   & towels provided
All year

Oceanfront accommodations with surf 40 ft. away; relax in hammocks under cocopalms on secluded beach. Charming cottage antiques. Romantic Tea House. Tropical breakfast.

VOLCANO

Guesthouse at Volcano $$ B&B   Continental plus
P.O. Box 6, 96785   1 rooms, 1 pb   Cottage with kitchen
11-3733 Ala Ohia   TV, telephone
808-967-7775   C-yes/S-yes   children bicycles
Bonnie Goodell   Span, some Greek, Mandr.   extensive library
All year

Cozy cottage with kitchen on 6 acres of orchards and pristine native forest, nest to National Park and Volcano Golf Course.

Kilauea Lodge $$$ B&B   Full breakfast
P.O. Blx 116, 96785   12 rooms, 12 pb   Lunch, dinner
808-967-7366   Visa, MC, AmEx   Restaurant, full bar
All year   C-ask/S-no/P-no/H-no   Sitting room, bicycles
                                             German   Volcanoes National Park

Mountain lodge with full service restaurant. Rooms with fireplace. One mile from spectacular Volcanoes National Park. 28 miles from Hilo.

More Inns...

Alohaland Guest House   98-1003 Oliwa St., Aiea 96701   808-487-0482
Adriennes B&B Paradise   RR 1, Box 8E, Captain Cook 96704   808-328-9726
Manago Hotel   Box 145, Captain Cook 96704   808-323-2642
Heavenly Hana Inn   P.O. Box 146, Hana, Maui 96713   808-248-8442
Aha Hui Hawaiian   Box 10, Hawi 96719   808-889-5523
B&B Waikiki Beach   P.O. Box 89080, Honolulu 96830   808-923-5459
Hawaiian Bed & Breakfast   876 Kaahue St., Honolulu 96825   808-395-5183
Kahala Hibiscus Inn   1030 Kealaolu Ave., Honolulu 96816   808-732-5889

Hawaii Kai   876 Ka'ahue Street, Hononlulu 96825   808-395-8153
Hale Kipa O Kiana   RR 2, Box 4874, Kalapana Shores 96778   808-965-8661
Pau Hana Inn   P.O. Box 546, Kaunakakai, Molokai 96748   800-367-8047
My Island B&B   Box 100, Volcano 96785

Idaho

BONNER'S FERRY

Deep Creek Inn	$ B&B	Continental breakfast
83805	12 rooms, 12 pb	Lunch, dinner, bar
208-267-2373	Visa, MC	Swimming pool
Sue Boardman	C-yes/S-yes/P-yes/H-yes	bicycles, coffee shop
All year		piano

Sleep and eat by the creek. Country setting just as pretty in winter as summer, and fall is enchanting!

COEUR D'ALENE

Greenbriar B&B Inn	$$ B&B	Full 4-course breakfast
315 Wallace, 83814	7 rooms, 4 pb	Gourmet dining by resv.
208-667-9660	Visa, MC, AmEx •	Library, sitting room
C. Soucy, K. McIlvenna	C-yes/S-no/P-no/H-no	hot tub, bicycles
All year	French	tandem bikes, canoes

Coeur d'Alene's only historic residence, 4 blocks from lake front, shopping area. Gourmet cuisine, antiques, down comforters. European-style country inn.

HORSESHOE BEND

Riverside Bed & Breakfast	$ B&B	Full breakfast
Highway 55, 83629	2 rooms, 2 pb	Restaurant, lunch,dinner
Route 1, Box 14A	Visa, MC	Comp. wine
208-793-2408	C-yes/S-yes/P-yes/H-no	Flower/gift shop
Joan & Jim Cochrane		spaces for RVs
May—September		

Enjoy staying in an updated depot on the banks of Payette River; situated close to both city and outdoor activities.

IDAHO CITY

Idaho City Hotel	$ B&B	Full breakfast
P.O. Box 70, 83631	5 rooms, 5 pb	Lounge, cable TV
215 Montgomery St.	Visa, MC, AmEx •	telephones in each room
208-392-4290	C-yes/S-yes/P-yes/H-no	near hot springs
Don & Pat Campbell	German	
All year		

Old west hotel furnished with genuine antiques, in old mining town just 45 minutes from Boise.

IRWIN

McBride's B&B Guesthouse
P.O. Box 166, 83428
102 Valley Dr.
208-483-4221
Deanna & Craig McBride
All year

$ B&B
1 rooms, 1 pb
Visa, MC •
C-yes/S-yes/P-yes

Full breakfast
Comp. wine
Beautiful yard in
mountains
barbecue grill

Private guest house in a high mountain valley. Year-round sportsman's paradise with easy access to Snake River, Tetons, Yellowstone Park.

KETCHUM

River Street Inn
Box 182, Sun Valley, 83353
100 River St. W.
208-726-3611
Virginia Van Doren
All year

$$$ B&B
8 rooms, 8 pb
Visa, MC, AmEx •
C-yes/S-no/P-no/H-no

Full breakfast
Sitting room w/fireplace
skiing

Located on Trail Creek, mountain views, spacious rooms with shower and Japanese soaking tub. Walk to athletic club, night life, shopping, ski lifts.

MOSCOW

Twin Peaks Inn
2455 W. Twin Rd., 83843
208-882-3898
Dennis & Tricia Horn
All year

$$ B&B
3 rooms, 2 pb
•
C-yes/S-ltd/P-yes/H-no

Full breakfast
Dinner by request
Comp. wine, tea, snacks
Hot tubs, near hiking,
Univ. of ID & WA State U

Enjoy our log cottage, antiques, quilts, hot tub, peaceful country atmosphere, breathtaking views, genuine hospitality, and famous multi-course gourmet breakfasts!

NORTHFORK

Indian Creek Guest Ranch
Route 2 Box 105, 83466
call Salmon, ask for ring
Jack & Lois Briggs
April 1—November 1

$$ B&B
4 rooms, 4 pb
•
C-yes/S-yes/P-yes/H-no

Full breakfast
Meals served
Sitting room
piano
horseback, jeep trips

Restful small mountain ranch. We never take more than ten people at a time. Private baths; home-grown and homemade foods.

POCATELLO

Holmes Retreat
178 N. Mink Creek Rd., 83204
208-232-5518
Shirley & Acel Holmes
All year

$/$$ B&B
2 rooms, 1 pb
Visa, MC •
C-yes/S-ltd/P-ltd/H-yes

Full gourmet breakfast
Meals served, lemonade
Sitting room with plants
piano, garden w/fountain
library, nature walk

6.4 acres nestled in the mountains, beside scenic Mink Creek. Hummingbird haven, fishing, croquet, volleyball. Special bed turndown service. Gracious hosts.

SANDPOINT

Old McFarland Inn
227 S. First Ave., 83864
208-265-0260
Bonnie & William Gall
All year

$$ B&B
6 rooms, 2 pb
Visa, MC, AmEx •
C-no/S-ltd/P-no/H-no

Full gourmet breakfast
Comp. wine & cheese
Living & dining room
bikes, wraparound porch
garden sitting area

1909 inn known as the "finest house in town." Antiques, baby grand piano, formal dining room. Atmosphere of an English country estate. Near beaches, shopping, dining, skiing.

124　Idaho

SHOUP ————————————————————————

Smith House B&B $ B&B Full breakfast
49 Salmon River Rd., 83469 5 rooms, 1 pb Comp. wine
208-756-2098 Visa, MC Sitting room, library
Aubrey & Marsha Smith C-yes/S-no/P-yes/H-no hot tubs, organ
All year   gift shop, float trips

Rustic, country setting with all the comforts of home. Enjoy sightseeing, hunting, hiking or just relaxing. Delicious breakfasts!

STANLEY ————————————————————————

Redfish Lake Lodge $ EP Full menu dining room
P.O. Box 9, 83278 35 rooms, 24 pb Bar service
208-774-3536 Visa, MC Lake swimming
Jack & Patty See C-yes/S-yes/P-yes/H-yes bicycles
Memorial Day—Oct. 3

Reasonably priced rustic inn on Redfish Lake.

More Inns...

Idaho Heritage Inn 109 West Idaho, Boise 83702 208-342-8066
Sunrise 2730 Sunrise Rim Road, Boise 83705 208-345-5260
Blackwell House 820 Sherman Ave., Coeur d'Alene 83814 208-664-0656
Tulip House 403 S. Florence St., Grangeville 83530 208-983-1034
Comfort Inn Box 984, Hailey 83333 208-788-2477
Ellsworth Inn 715 3rd Ave. S., Hailey 83333 208-788-2298
MaryAnne's HCR 1, Box 43E, Harrison 83833 208-245-2537
Peg's Bed 'n Breakfast Pla P.O. Box 144, Harrison 83833 208-689-3525
Dorsett House 305 South Division, Kellogg 83837 208-786-2311
Busterback Ranch Star Rt., Ketchum 83340 208-774-2217
Lift Haven Inn Box 21, 100 Lloyd Drive, Ketchum 83340 208-726-5601
Powderhorn Lodge Box 3970, Ketchum 83340 208-726-3107
Looking Glass Guest Ranch HC-75, Box 32, Kooskia 83539 208-926-0855
River Birch Farm P.O. Box 87, Laclede 83841 208-263-4033
Home Place 415 W Lake Hazel Rd., Meridian 83642 208-888-3857
Hillcrest House 210 Hillcrest Dr., Pinehurst 83850 208-682-3911
Whitaker House 410 Railroad Ave, #10, Sandpoint 83864 208-263-0816
Knoll Hus P.O. Box 572, St. Maries 83861 208-245-4137
Idaho Rocky Mtn. Ranch HC 64 Box 9934, Stanley 83278 208-774-3544
Jameson B&B 304 Sixth St., Wallace 83873 208-556-1554
Pine Tree Inn 177 King St., Box 1023, Wallace 83873 208-752-4391

Illinois

DECATUR

Hamilton House B&B Inn
500 W. Main St., 62522
217-429-1669
Nancy C. Phillips
All year

$ B&B
5 rooms, 1 pb
Visa, MC, AmEx •
C-yes/S-yes/P-no/H-no
German, Dutch

Full breakfast
Comp. tea, wine
Restaurant, Bar
Sitting room
gift shop

Built in 1892, this Victorian mansion is on the National Register of Historic Places. Guest rooms filled with antique furniture.

EVANSTON

Charles & Barbara Pollard
2633 Poplar, 60201
312-328-6162
Charles & Barbara Pollard
All year

$ B&B
2 rooms, 1 pb
C-yes/S-yes/P-ltd

Continental breakfast

Casual comfort and the location's a plus! 3 blocks to Northwestern University's Dyche Stadium; walk to transportation, Lake Michigan, antiques, restaurants, movies and more!

The Homestead
1625 Hinman Ave., 60201
708-475-3300
David T. Reynolds
All year

$$ EP
35 rooms, 35 pb
C-yes/S-yes/P-no/H-ltd

French restaurant

Historic residential neighborhood; two blocks from Lake Michigan & Northwestern Univ.; 30 minutes from Downtown Chicago by car or rail; French restaurant serves dinner.

GALENA

Aldrich Guest House
900 Third St., 61036
815-777-3323
Judy Green
All year

$$ B&B
5 rooms, 3 pb
Visa, MC
C-6+/S-ltd/P-no/H-no

Full breakfast
Comp. beverages
Sitting room w/fireplace
piano, screened porch

Elegant Greek Revival furnished with fine antiques. Breakfast in dining room or screened porch served formally yet unfussily. Central air-conditioning.

Avery Guest House B&B
606 S. Prospect St., 61036
815-777-3883
Flo & Roger Jensen
All year

$ B&B
4 rooms
Visa, MC
C-yes/S-no/P-no/H-no

Continental plus
Afternoon tea or cider
Library
sitting room
porch swing

Enjoy historic Galena, scenic beauty, fine restaurants, antiques. Comfortable 1840s house, homey hospitality, porch swing, piano and sunny dining room.

GALENA

Comfort Guest House
1000 Third St., 61036
815-777-3062
Connie & Tom Sola
All year

$$ B&B
3 rooms
C-14+/S-ltd/P-no/H-no

Continental plus
Sitting room w/fireplace
front porch

Riverfront town, home of Ulysses S. Grant. 1856 guest house. Stroll to downtown antique shops. Quilts, country breakfasts. Golf, skiing, biking nearby.

Hellman Guest House
318 Hill St., 61036
815-777-3638
Merilyn Tommaro
All year

$$ B&B
4 rooms, 4 pb
Visa, MC, AmEx
C-12+/S-ltd/P-no/H-no

Continental plus
Comp. wine
Sitting room, library
golf, horseback riding,
and skiing nearby

Elegant 19th-century Victorian—featuring stained-glass windows, fireplaces, pocket doors. Inviting parlor, library and porch with spectacular views of Galena.

Mars Avenue Guest Home
515 Mars Ave., 61036
815-777-3880
Joanne Bielenda
February—December

$$ B&B
4 rooms
Visa, MC
C-12+/H-yes

Continental plus
Afternoon tea
Sitting room

Relax in a country home in old Galena. Stenciling throughout. Near quaint shops, antiques and riverboat rides.

Stillman's Country Inn
P.O. Box 272, 61036
513 Boothillier
815-777-0557
Bill & Pamela Lozeau
All year

$$ B&B
5 rooms, 5 pb
Visa, MC
C-ltd/S-yes/P-no/H-no
German

Continental breakfast
2 Victorian dining rooms
2 cocktail lounges
Nightclub
color cable TV

Stillman Manor Estate, 1858. General Grant was a regular guest. Antiques and fireplaces, crystal, porcelain. Riverboats.

Stillwaters Country Inn
7213 W. Buckhill Rd., 60613
815-777-0223
Honora Simon
All year

$$ B&B
3 rooms, 3 pb
•
C-yes/S-yes/P-no/H-no

Continental breakfast
Kitchens
Sitting room
sauna
special packages avail.

Unique guest suites in charming country hideaway—located on 17 secluded wooded acres only 5 miles from Galena, Illinois.

GENEVA

Oscar Swan Country Inn
1800 W. State St., 60134
312-232-0173
Nina Heymann
All year

$$$ B&B
8 rooms, 4 pb
Visa, MC •
C-yes/S-no/P-no/H-no
German

Full breakfast
Snacks
Sitting room, library
tennis courts, pool
X-C skiing on 7 acres

Country hideaway on 7 private acres. Fireplaces, cozy kitchen, hearty breakfast, wonderful River Town, antiques, bike paths. The New England of the Midwest.

GOODFIELD ───────────────────────────────────

The Brick House B&B $ B&B / $$ MAP   Full breakfast
P.O. Box 301, 61742   4 rooms   Dinner-theater (MAP)
RR 1, Conklin Court   S-yes   Sitting room
309-965-2545   riding stable nearby
Mary Simon & Chaunce Conklin
All year

Built in 1857; many of the original furnishings are still in the home where Abe Lincoln once spent his time. Dinner-theater in old round roofed barn. In rural setting.

NAPERVILLE ───────────────────────────────────

Harrison House B&B $ B&B   Full breakfast (wkends)
26 N. Eagle St., 60540   4 rooms, 2 pb   Continental breakfast
25 W 135 Essex Ave.   Visa, MC, AmEx •   Comp. wine, tea, snacks
708-420-1117 / 709-355-4665   S-ltd   Sitting room, bicycles
Carolyn Harper   Spanish   tennis & pool nearby
All year

25 miles west of Chicago. Walk to quaint shops, restaurants. Antique guest rooms; Victorian Room has jacuzzi. Scrumptious breakfast and gracious hospitality.

ROCK ISLAND ───────────────────────────────────

Potter House B&B $ B&B   Full breakfast
1906—7 Ave., 61201   4 rooms, 3 pb   Afternoon tea
309-788-1906   Visa, MC •   Library
Nancy & Gary Pheiffer   C-yes   tennis courts, pool
All year   & restaurant nearby

Historic landmark, circa 1907. Close to Mississippi River attractions. Breakfast served in mahogany paneled dining room or elegant sunporch.

Top O' The Morning B&B $ B&B   Full breakfast
1505 19th Ave., 61201   2 rooms, 2 pb   Sitting room, library
309-786-3513   C-yes / S-ltd / P-no / H-no   piano, bicycles
Sam & Peggy Doak   tennis, hot tubs
All year   A/C in all bedrooms

Brick mansion on 3½ acres in the center of town. Large porch, grand piano, formal dining. Irish hospitality. Champagne, flowers & breakfast in bridal suite for honeymoons.

More Inns...

Haagen House B&B   617 State Street, Alton 62002   618-462-2419
Wright Farmhouse   RR 3, Carthage 62321   217-357-2421
Davidson Place B&B   1110 Davidson Drive, Champaign 61820   217-356-5915
River View Guest House   507 East Everett, Dixon 61021   815-288-5974
Hobson's Bluffdale   Eldred-Hillview Rd, Eldred 62027   217-983-2854
Corner Nest B&B   3 Elm St., P.O. Box 22, Elsah 62028   618-374-1892
Green Tree Inn   P.O. Box 96, 15 Mill St., Elsah 62028   618-374-2821
Bedford House   Route 20 West, Galena 61036   815-777-2043
Belle Aire Mansion   Rt. 20 West, Galena 61036   815-777-0893
Chestnut Mountain Resort   8700 W. Chestnut Road, Galena 61036   800-435-2914
Mother's Country Inn   349 Spring St., Galena 61036   815-777-3153
Robert Scribe Harris House   713 S. Bench St., Galena 61036   815-777-1611
Ryan Mansion Inn   Route 20 West, Galena 61036   815-777-2043
Victorian Mansion   301 High St., Galena 61036   815-777-0675
Stolz Home   RR 2, Box 27, Gibson City 60936   217-784-4502
Mansion of Golconda   P.O. Box 339, Golcanda 62938   618-683-4400
Colonial Inn   Rock & Green Sts., Grand Detour 61021   815-652-4422

Bennett Curtis House   302 W. Taylor, Grant Park 60940   815-465-6025
Annie Tique's Hotel   378 Main St., Marseilles 61341   815-795-5848
Carr Mansion Guest House   416 E. Broadway, Monmouth 61462   309-734-5573
Die Blane Gaus   95265 Route 59, Naperville 60565   312-355-0835
Inn-on-the-Square   3 Montgomery St., Oakland 61943   217-346-2289
Barber House Inn   410 W. Mason, Polo 61064   815-946-2607
Victoria's B&B   201 North Sixth St., Rockford 61107   815-963-3232
Mischler House   718 South 8th St., Springfield 62703   217-523-3714
Stage Coach Inn   41 W. 278 Whitney Road, St. Charles 60174   312-584-1263
Maple Lane   3115 Rush Creek Road, Stockton 61085   815-947-3773
Wheaton Inn   301 W. Roosevelt Rd., Wheaton 60187   815-690-2600
Bundling Board Inn   222 E. South St., Woodstock 60098

Indiana

BEVERLY SHORES

Dunes Shore Inn	$ B&B	Continental plus
Box 807, 46301	12 rooms	Comp. cider & cookies
Lakeshore County Rd.	Visa, MC	Library, sitting room
219-879-9029	C-yes/S-ltd/P-no/H-no	bicycles
Rosemary & Fred Braun	German	outdoor grill, tables
All year		

Located one block from Lake Michigan and surrounded by the National Lakeshore and Dunes State Parks, this inn is an oasis for nature lovers. One hour from Chicago.

COLUMBUS

Lafayette Street B&B	$ B&B	Full breakfast
723 Lafayette St., 47201	2 rooms, 1 pb	Aftn. tea by request
812-372-7245	C-yes/S-no/P-no/H-no	Snacks
Patti March, Mike Mullett		restaurant, tennis &
All year		library nearby

Charming, comfortable Queen Anne Victorian with period architectural features and antique furnishings. Over 40 outstanding examples of contemporary architecture nearby.

CONNERSVILLE

Maple Leaf Inn B&B	$ B&B	Continental plus
831 N. Grand Ave., 47331	4 rooms, 1 pb	Snacks
317-825-7099	Visa, MC	Sitting room
Gary & Karen Lanning	C-yes/S-ltd/P-no/H-no	bicycles
All year		

1860's home furnished with antiques; pictures by local artists; nearby are antique shops, state parks, nature trails, restored canal town.

CORYDON

Kinter House Inn	$$ B&B	Full breakfast
101 S. Capitol Ave., 47112	16 rooms, 16 pb	Snacks
P.O. Box 414	Visa, MC, AmEx, DC •	Tennis courts
812-738-2020	C-yes	golf arrangements
Mary Jane Bridgewater		swimming
Exc. Thanksgiving, Xmas		

National Historic Registry—14 guest rooms in Victorian and country decor. Full breakfast. Located in downtown historic Corydon. 2 miles south of I-64.

CRAWFORDSVILLE

Davis House	$ B&B	Continental plus
1010 W. Wabash Ave., 47933	3 rooms, 3 pb	Snacks
317-364-0461	Visa, MC, AmEx •	Sitting room
Jan Stearns	C-yes/S-yes/P-no/H-no	library
All year		

Victorian mansion with country atmosphere near canoeing, hiking, and historical sites. Complimentary snacks. Homemade coffee cakes and breads for breakfast.

EVANSVILLE

Brigadoon B&B Inn	$ B&B	Full breakfast
1201 S.E. Second St., 47713	4 rooms, 2 pb	Stained glass
812-422-9635/812-425-1696	Visa, MC •	Library, sitting room
Kathee Forbes	C-yes/S-yes/P-yes/H-yes	meeting rooms for
All year		parties, etc.

Romantic, lace-filled, river city Victorian. Picket fence, gingerbread porch, parquet floors, four fireplaces. Hearty breakfast, homemade breads.

FORT WAYNE

Candlewyck Inn	$$ B&B	Continental plus (wkdys)
331 W. Washington Blvd., 46802	5 rooms	Full breakfast (wkends)
219-424-2643	Visa, MC, AmEx •	Comp. wine & cheese
Bob & Jan Goehringer	C-no/S-ltd/P-no/H-no	Sun porch, cable TV
All year		bicycles

Charming, historical inn close to convention center and public library. Five lovely rooms, beautiful decor. Hearty continental breakfast.

GOSHEN

Checkerberry Inn	$$$ B&B	Continental breakfast
62644 County Road 37, 46526	12 rooms, 12 pb	Lunch/dinner, restaurant
219-642-4445	Visa, MC, AmEx •	Sitting room, library
John & Susan Graff	C-yes/S-ltd/H-yes	tennis courts, pool
Closed January		croquet court

European-style country inn surrounded by Amish farmland, 100 acres of fields and woods. French country cuisine, luxuriously comfortable decor.

HAGERSTOWN

Teetor House	$$$ B&B	Full breakfast
300 West Main St., 47346	4 rooms, 4 pb	Lunch & dinner (groups)
317-489-4422	Visa, MC	Afternoon tea, snacks
Jack & Joanne Warmoth	C-yes/S-ltd	Sitting room, library
All year		tennis courts, pool

Elegance and charm in a peacefully rural setting near unique shops and restaurants. Air conditioned. 5 miles from I-70. Golf courses nearby. Horse and buggy rides available.

INDIANAPOLIS

Barn House	$ B&B	Continental plus
10656 E. 63rd St., 46236	2 rooms, 1 pb	Kitchen
317-823-4898	C-6+/S-yes/P-no/H-no	
Dr. Joe & Bettye Miller		
All year		

Charming, spacious guest house-living room, kitchen, bath, 2 bedrooms. Peace and quiet within half-hour of Indianapolis.

130   Indiana

INDIANAPOLIS ———————————————————————

Hollingsworth House Inn	$$$ B&B	Continental plus
6054 Hollingsworth Rd., 46254	5 rooms, 5 pb	Soft drinks
317-299-6700	AmEx, Visa, MC •	Sitting room
Susan Muller, Ann Irvine	C-no/S-yes/P-no/H-no	
All year		

Country hideaway within the city; 1854 brick farmhouse furnished with antiques, beautiful linens and china. Listed on the National Register of Historic Places.

Nuthatch Bed & Breakfast	$$ B&B	Full breakfast
7161 Edgewater Pl., 46240	2 rooms, 2 pb	Snacks
317-257-2660	•	Sitting room, deck
Joan H. Morris	C-12+/S-ltd/P-no/H-no	picnic table, swing
All year		canoe rental nearby

1920s country French architecture in a resort river setting minutes from downtown Indianapolis. Breakfast is an honest home-cooked celebration.

KNIGHTSTOWN ———————————————————————

Old Hoosier House B&B	$ B&B	Full breakfast
Route 2, Box 299-1, 46148	4 rooms, 3 pb	Afternoon tea, snacks
Greensboro Pike & CR 750S	•	Sitting room
317-345-2969	C-yes/S-ltd/P-no/H-no	library, bicycles
Tom & Jean Lewis		special golf rates
May 1—November 1		

1840 country home near Indianapolis; popular antique area; comfortable homey atmosphere; delicious breakfasts on patio overlooking Royal Hylands Golf Club.

LA GRANGE ———————————————————————

The 1886 Inn	$$ B&B	Continental plus
212 W. Factory St., 46761	3 rooms, 3 pb	Sitting room
P.O. Box 5	Visa, MC	bicycles
219-463-4227	C-yes/S-no/P-no/H-no	
Duane & Gloria Billman		
All year		

Step back in time to the 19th-century style of living. Only 10 minutes from Shipshewana Auction and Flea Market in Indiana's Amish country.

METAMORA ———————————————————————

Publick House	$ B&B	Continental breakfast
P.O. Box 219, 47030	6 rooms, 4 pb	
28 Duck Creek Crossing	Visa, MC, D •	
317-647-6235	C-yes/S-yes/P-ltd/H-yes	
Fred & Fern Betz		
April 15—December 24		

Circa 1850 frontier architecture, in a small country town. Enjoy the quiet atmosphere; walk to over 100 crafts and gift shops.

MIDDLEBURY ———————————————————————

Bee Hive Bed & Breakfast	$ B&B	Continental plus
P.O. Box 1191, 46540	3 rooms	Snacks
219-825-5023	C-yes/S-no	Sitting room
Herb & Treva Swarm		restaurant nearby
All year		

A country home in a relaxing atmosphere. Located in Amish Country with plenty of local attractions. Ski trails nearby. Easy access to Indiana Toll Road.

Emerald Manor, Estes Park, CO

MIDDLEBURY

Patchwork Quilt Country Inn	$$ B&B	Continental plus
11748 C.R. #2, 46540	3 rooms	Lunch, dinner
219-825-2417	C-12+ / S-no / P-no / H-no	Sitting room
Maxine Zook		piano
All year		Amish tours

Prepare to be pampered in gracious country home; patchwork quilts on all beds. In Amish country. Near Shipshewana Flea Auction. Award winning Amish Backroad Tours.

MISHAWAKA

Beiger Mansion Inn	$$ B&B	Full breakfast
P.O. Box 1106, 46544	10 rooms, 4 pb	Dinner by prior arrang.
317 Lincoln Way E.	Visa, MC, AmEx, Disc •	Comp. wine, snacks
219-256-0365	C-yes / S-no / P-no / H-no	Bicycles, rooms with A/C
Ron Montandon, Phil Robinson		art gallery, gift shop
All year		

This 22,000-sq.-ft. mansion built in 1903; perfect example of neoclassical limestone architecture. Close to restaurants, golf, U. Notre Dame. Art gallery with gift shop.

MORGANTOWN

Rock House	$ B&B	Full breakfast
380 W. Washington St., 46160	6 rooms, 4 pb	Afternoon tea, snacks
812-597-5100	C-yes	Sitting room
Doug & Marcia Norton		
All year		

Circa 1894. Unusual Victorian home built of concrete block embedded with treasures: dishes, doorknobs, dice, marbles! Located at "The Gateway to Brown County."

NAPPANEE ————————————————————————————

Victorian Guest House $ B&B   Continental breakfast
302 E. Market, 46550   4 rooms, 3 pb   Afternoon tea
219-773-4383/219-773-7034   Visa, MC, AmEx •
Kris Leksich   C-yes/S-yes/P-no/H-no
All year

This 100-year-old Victorian is in the Amish countryside. 30 minutes from South Bend and Elkhart on Route #6.

NASHVILLE ————————————————————————————

Allison House Inn $$$ B&B   Continental plus
P.O. Box 546, 47448   5 rooms, 5 pb   Library
90 S. Jefferson St.   C-6+/S-no/P-no/H-no   sitting room
812-988-0814
Bob & Tammy Galm
All year

In the heart of Brown County, the center for the arts and craft colony. Coziness, comfort and charm.

PERU ————————————————————————————————

Rosewood Mansion Inn $$ B&B   Full breakfast
54 N. Hood, 46970   5 rooms, 5 pb   Lunch/dinner on request
317-472-7151   Visa, MC, AmEx •   Snacks, sitting room
Zoyla & Carm Henderson   C-ltd/S-ltd/H-no   Library, bicycles
All year   Spanish   swimming pool

Quiet, elegant surroundings. Large, comfortable guest rooms. Gourmet breakfast. Many nearby attractions. Three blocks from downtown. We cater to businessmen.

PLYMOUTH ————————————————————————————

Driftwood $$$ B&B   Continental breakfast
P.O. Box 16, 46563   3 rooms, 3 pb   Sitting room
4604 Westshore Dr.   C-ltd/S-ltd/P-no/H-no   Fireplace, TV in rooms
219-546-2274   swimming, canoeing,
May—October   biking & hiking nearby

Lakefront home decorated in casual nautical style with beautiful beach and summer recreation.

SHIPSHEWANA ————————————————————————————

Green Meadow Ranch $$ B&B   Continental plus
R 2, Box 592, 46565   7 rooms   Sitting room
219-768-4221   C-ltd/S-no/P-no/H-no
Paul & Ruth Miller   Penn. Dutch
Closed Jan & Feb

Country home decorated with antiques, near famous flea market in Amish area. Miniature horses and donkeys, folk art.

SOUTH BEND ————————————————————————————

Queen Anne Inn $$ B&B   Full breakfast
420 W. Washington, 46601   5 rooms, 5 pb   Snacks
219-234-5959   Visa, MC, AmEx •   Sitting room, library
Pauline & Bob Medhurst   C-yes/S-ltd/P-no/H-no   phones in rooms
All year   conference room (15-25)

Relax in a charming 1893 Victorian home with Frank Lloyd Wright influence—near city center and many good restaurants. Private phones in each room.

SYRACUSE ───────────────────────

Anchor Inn Bed & Breakfast $ B&B   Continental breakfast
Rt. 4, Box 208-A, 46567   5 rooms   Adjacent to golf course
State Road #13   Visa, MC   Across from
219-457-4714   C-yes/S-no/P-no/H-no   Lake Wawasee
Robert & Jean Kennedy
All year

Turn-of-the-century home filled with period furniture. Close to Amish communities & several antique shops. Many lakes in the area & adjacent to 18-hole public golf course.

WESTFIELD ───────────────────────

Camel Lot $$ B&B   Full breakfast
4512 W. 131st St., 46074   1 rooms, 1 pb   Sitting room
317-873-4370   C-10+/S-yes/P-no/H-yes   piano
Moselle Schaffer
All year

Have breakfast on the terrace overlooking the Siberian tiger's quarters—photograph zebras, llamas, deer at this exotic animal breeding ranch.

More Inns. . .

Open Hearth B&B   56782 SR 15, Bristol 46507   219-825-2417
Gray Goose Inn B&B   350 Indian Boundary Rd., Chesterton 46304   219-926-5781
Wingfield's Inn B&B   526 Indian Oak Mall, Chesterton 46304   702-348-0766
Sycamore Spring Farm   Box 224, Churubusco 46723   219-693-3603
Cragwood Inn   303 N. Second St., Decatur 46733   219-728-9388
Timberidge B&B   16801 SR 4, Goshen 46526   219-533-7133
River Belle B&B   P.O. Box 669, Hwy 66, Grandview 47615   812-649-2500
1900 House (The)   50777 Ridgemoor Way, Granger 46530   219-277-7783
De'Coy's B&B   1546 W. 100 N., Hartford City 47348   317-348-2164
Pairadux Inn   6363 N. Guilford Ave., Indianapolis 46220   317-259-8005
Ye Olde Scotts Inn   RR 1, Box 5, Leavenworth 47137   812-739-4747
Cliff House   122 Fairmount Drive, Madison 47250   812-265-5272
Millwood House   512 West St., Madison 47250   812-265-6780
Thorpe House   Clayborne St., Metamora 47030   317-647-5425
Creekwood Inn   Rt. 20-35, Michigan City 46460   219-872-8357
Duneland Beach Inn   3311 Potawatomi, Michigan City 46360   219-874-7729
Coneygar   54835 C.R. 33, Middlebury 46540   219-825-5707
Essenhaus Country Inn   240 US 20, Middlebury 46540   219-825-9471
Indiana Amish Country B&B   1600 W. Market St., Nappanee 46550   219-773-4188
McGinley's Vacation Cabins   Rt. 3, Box 332, Nashville 47448   812-988-7337
Seasons   P.O. Box 187, Nashville 47448   812-988-2284
Story Inn   P.O. Box 64, Nashville 47448   812-988-6516
Sunset House   RR 3 Box 127, Nashville 47448   812-988-6118
Country Homestead Guest Ho   Rt. 1, Box 353, Richland 47634   812-359-4870
Jelley House Country Inn   222 S. Walnut St., Rising Sun 47404   812-438-2319
Victorian House   RR 1 Box 27, Roachdale 46172   317-522-1225
Jamison Inn   1404 N. Ivy Rd., South Bend 46637   219-277-9682
Mayor Wilhelm's Villa   428 N. Fifth St., Vincennes 47591   812-882-9487
Hilltop House B&B   88 W. Sinclair St., Wabash 46992   219-563-7726
Amish Acres, Inc.   160 W. Market, Wappanee 46550   219-773-4188
Candlelight Inn   503 E. Fort Wayne St., Warsaw 46580   219-267-2906
Country Roads Guesthouse   2731 West 146th St., Westfield 46074   317-846-2376

Iowa

ANAMOSA

Inn at Stone City
52205
319-462-4733
Michael Roberts
All year

$-87
6 rooms
Visa, MC
C-yes/S-yes/P-yes/H-no
Spanish

Full breakfast
Lunch, dinner, bar
Bicycles, jacuzzi
cross-country skiing
canoe rentals

Beautiful stone mansion and estate in former artists colony, Stone City. We take pride in our varied menus and personal service.

AVOCA

Victorian B&B Inn
P.O. Box 249, 51521
425 Walnut St.
712-343-6336/800-397-3914
Jan & Gene Kuehn
All year

$ B&B
4 rooms
Visa, MC •
C-12+/S-no/P-no/H-no

Full breakfast
Lunch, dinner by arr.
Snacks, comp. wine
Sitting room
farm tours arranged

1904 Queen Anne Victorian home located in quiet farming community; furnished with antiques, handsewn quilts; gourmet meals are innkeeper's specialty.

BELLEVUE

Mont Rest
300 Spring St., 52031
319-872-4220
Robert & Christine Gelms
Exc. XMas & New Years

$$ B&B
5 rooms
Visa, MC, AmEx •
C-yes/S-ltd

Full breakfast
Restaurant, lunch/dinner
Sitting room, library
bicycles, tennis courts
sauna, swimming pool

Mont Rest is a fully restored Victorian mansion perched on 9-acre bluff with a breathtaking view of Mississippi River. Country breakfast. Charm abounds.

CALMAR

Calmar Guesthouse
RR 1, Box 206, 52132
319-562-3851
Lucille B. Kruse
All year

$ B&B
5 rooms, 1 pb
C-yes/S-ltd/P-no/H-no
German

Full breakfast
Sitting room

Beautiful, fully restored Victorian. Breakfast served in formal dining room. Near Norwegian Museum. Bily Clocks, Luther College, NITI College, golf, canoeing, fishing.

COUNCIL BLUFFS

Robin's Nest Inn B&B
327—9th Ave., 51503
712-323-1649
Dorethea Smith & Wendy Storey
All year

$ B&B
4 rooms
Visa, MC
C-yes/S-no/P-no/H-no

Full breakfast
Dinner upon request
Sitting room
TV
weekend theme packages

Stately brick Victorian with romantic country furnishings; country breakfast, fresh breads and pastries; walking distance to historic Dodge house and Haymarket square.

DUBUQUE

The Redstone Inn
504 Bluff St., 52001
319-582-1894
Deborah Griesinger
All year

$$ EP
15 rooms, 15 pb
Visa, MC, AmEx •
C-yes/S-yes/P-no/H-no

Cont. plus/Full breakfst
Wine & beer
Afternoon tea June—Oct.
Sitting room
hot tub, hair dryers

Genuine antique furniture used throughout this professionally decorated chateau-style inn. Located in center of the Cathedral National Register District.

Stout House B&B
504 Bluff St., 52001
319-582-1894
Tom & Mary Mowbray
All year

$$$ B&B
5 rooms, 1 pb
Visa, MC, AmEx •
C-yes/S-yes/P-no/H-no

Continental breakfast
Library
sitting room

Romanesque stone mansion, former home of archbishop, highlighted by gleaming wood, stained glass, library, original art. Near tourist attractions in historic Dubuque.

HOMESTEAD

Die Heimat Country Inn
Main St., 52236
319-622-3937
Don & Sheila Janda
All year

$ B&B
19 rooms, 19 pb
Visa, MC
C-yes/S-yes/P-no/H-no

Continental breakfast
Beer & wine
Sitting room

Stay overnight at our century-old restored inn. All rooms have private baths furnished with Amana furniture and antiques.

KEOSAUQUA

Mason House/Bentonsport
RR 2, Box 237L, 52565
319-592-3133
Sheral & Bill McDermet
All year

$ B&B
10 rooms, 2 pb
C-no/S-ltd/P-no/H-yes

Full breakfast
Dinner by reservation
Bicycles

Historic inn built in steamboat era located in designated National Historic District. Quiet, comfortable escape to bygone era.

LANSING

FitzGerald's Inn
P.O. Box 157, 52151
160 N. Third St.
319-538-4872
Jeff & Marie FitzGerald
All year

$ B&B
5 rooms, 4 pb
•
C-ltd/S-ltd/P-no/H-no

Full breakfast
Sitting room
gazebo

Charming country inn located in hilly northeastern Iowa. Spacious grounds rise to spectacular bluff-top view of the Mississippi River.

NEWTON

La Corsette Maison Inn
629 First Ave. East, 50208
515-792-6833
Kay Owen
All year

$$ B&B
4 rooms, 4 pb
Visa, MC
C-yes/S-ltd/P-ask/H-no

Full breakfast
Gourmet dinner
Restaurant
Sitting room

Historic turn-of-the-century mission style mansion. Charming French bedchambers, beckoning hearths. 30 minutes from Des Moines on I-80. Near I-35.

SPENCER

Hannah Marie Country Inn
RR 1, Hway. 71 S., 51301
712-262-1286/712-332-7719
Mary Nichols
May—November

$$ B&B
3 rooms, 3 pb
Visa, MC •
C-13+/S-ltd/P-no/H-no
Basic Sign Language

Full breakfast
Comp. wine
Tea, refreshments
Sitting room, library
whirlpool

A lovingly restored Iowa farm home offering romantic country strolls, a good night's rest and a hearty country breakfast. Air conditioned.

SPILLVILLE

The Old World Inn
331 S. Main St., 52168
319-562-3739
Juanita J. Loven
All year

$ B&B
4 rooms, 4 pb
Visa, MC •
C-yes/S-no/P-no/H-no

Full breakfast
Restaurant
Beer & wine
Sitting room, library
tennis courts nearby

1971 National Register building renovated in 1987 as an historic inn. Located near the famous Bily/Clocks/Antonin Dvorak Museum in picturesque Czech village in scenic NE Iowa.

TIPTON

Victorian House
508 E. 4th St., 52772
319-886-2633
Robert & Christine Gelms
Exc. Xmas, New Year's

$$ B&B
5 rooms
Visa, MC, AmEx •
C-yes/S-ltd

Full breakfast
Restaurant, bar service
Aftn. tea, lunch, dinner
Library, bicycles
tennis, sauna, pool

Victorian House is an Eastlake-style mansion built in 1883, fully furnished in period antiques. Near I-80, Herbert Hoover Presidential Library and Amana Colonies.

More Inns...

Walden Acres B&B   RR 1, Box 30, Adel 50003   515-987-1567
Hotel Brooklyn   154 Front St., Brooklyn 52211   515-522-9229
Budget Inn   Box 102, Clear Lake 50428
River Oaks Inn B&B   1234 E. River Drive, Davenport 52803   319-326-2629
Montgomery Mansion   812 Maple Avenue, Decorah 52101   319-382-5088
Orval & Diane Bruvold   Rt. 1, Decorah 52101   319-382-4729
Hancock House   1105 Grove Terrace, Dubuke 52001   319-557-8989
Rainbow H. Lodging House   RR 1, Box 89, Elk Horn 51531   712-764-8272
Travelling Companion   4314 Main St., Elk Horn 51531   712-764-8932
Little House Vacations   Elkader 52043   319-783-7774
Cloverleaf Farm   Route 2, Box 140A, Fort Atkinson 52144   319-534-7061
LaVerne & Alice Hageman   Route 2, Box 104, Fort Atkinson 52144   319-534-7545
Larson House B&B   300 N 9th St., Fort Dodge 50501   515-573-5733
Lansing House   Box 97, 291 N. Front St, Lansing 52151   319-538-4263
Heritage House   RR 1, Leighton 50143   515-626-3092
Decker House Inn   128 N. Main, Maquoketa 52060   319-652-6654
Apple Orchard Inn B&B   RR 3 Box 129, Missouri Valley 51555   712-642-2418
Loy's B&B   RR 1, Morengo 52301   319-642-7787
Historic Harlan Hotel   122 N. Jefferson St., Mt. Pleasant 52641   319-385-3126
Strawtown Inn & Lodge   1111 Washington St., Pella 50219   515-628-2681
Terra Verde Farm   Rt. 1, Box 86, Swisher 52338   319-846-2478

Kansas

CONCORDIA

Crystle's Bed & Breakfast
508 W. 7th St., 66901
913-243-2192
Carrie Lee Warren
All year

$ B&B
5 rooms, 1 pb
Visa, MC
C-yes/S-no/P-no/H-no
Spanish

Full breakfast
Afternoon tea, snacks
Sitting room, library
tennis, swimming pool,
and golf nearby

Hospitality and charm overflowing! A beautiful 1880 home with original antiques decorating unique and creative rooms. Enjoy a breakfast and discover historic Concordia.

COUNCIL GROVE

Cottage House Hotel
25 N. Neosho, 66846
316-767-6828/800-888-8162
Connie Essington
All year

$ EP
Visa, MC, AmEx •
C-yes/S-yes/P-ltd/H-yes

Continental brkfst $2.50
Restaurant
Sitting room
hot tubs, sauna room
6 rooms w/whirlpool tubs

Beautifully restored Victorian hotel with all of the modern comforts. Lovely antique furnishings. Located in historic "Birthplace of the Santa Fe Trail."

MANHATTAN

Long's Country Inn
RR 1, Box 268, 66502
801 W. 54th Ave.
913-776-3212
Phyllis & Eric Long
All year

$ B&B
3 rooms
C-yes/S-no/P-yes/H-no
French

Continental breakfast
Afternoon tea
Sitting room, croquet
swimming pool, horseback
riding, hiking, fishing

Contemporary country inn, nestled in a lovely wooded valley overlooking a duck pond. Homemade breads and rolls served in a large family kitchen.

TONGANOXIE

Almeda's B&B Inn
220 S. Main, Box 103, 66086
913-845-2295
Almeda & Richard Tinberg
All year

$ B&B
7 rooms, 1 pb
C-ltd/S-ltd/P-no/H-no

Continental plus
Sitting room
organ
all rooms A/C

Dedicated as a historical site in 1983; in the '30s was the inspiration for the movie Bus Stop. *Decorated in country style with many antiques. Close to golf courses & pool.*

VALLEY FALLS

Barn Bed & Breakfast Inn
RR 2, Box 87, 66088
913-945-3303
Tom & Marcella Ryan
All year

$ B&B
9 rooms, 9 pb
•
C-yes/S-no/P-no/H-yes

Full breakfast &
Supper day of arrival
Lunch & dinner avail.
Sitting room, walking
fishing, hunting

A 93-year-old barn converted into a country inn. Offers peace, quiet and a very restful atmosphere. Come be a part of our family.

Inn at the Park	$$ B&B	Continental plus
3751 E. Douglas, 67218	12 rooms, 12 pb	Comp. wine, aftn. tea
316-652-0500	Visa, MC, AmEx •	Sitting room
Carrie Oliver	C-no/S-no/P-no/H-yes	library, hot tubs
All year	Spanish	tennis and pool nearby

A 1910 mansion, nestled on the edge of a park. 12 uniquely decorated suites. Close to fine dining, theater, business, shopping. Ideal for vacationers and corporate travelers.

Max Paul. . . An Inn	$$ B&B	Continental plus
3910 East Kellogg, 67218	14 rooms, 14 pb	Sitting room, library
316-689-8101	Visa, MC, AmEx, Diners	hot tub
Roberta & Jill Eaton	C-ask/S-yes/P-no/H-no	group facilities avail.
All year		pool & tennis nearby

Feather beds and antique furniture; fireplaces, decks, exercise/jacuzzi room opens on gardens and pond; close to park, shops and restaurant.

More Inns. . .

Cimarron Hotel & Restaurant   P.O. Box 633, Cimarron 67835   316-855-2244
Country Quarters   Rt. 5, Box 80, Fort Scott 66701   316-223-2889
Halcyon House   1000 Ohio, Lawrence 66044   913-841-0314
School House Inn   106 E. Beck, Melvern 66510   913-549-3473
Heritage House   3535 SW Sixth St., Topeka 66606   913-233-3800
Rock House B&B   201 Dogwood, Wakefield 67487   913-461-5732

Kentucky

Jailer's Inn	$ B&B	Continental breakfast
111 W. Stephen Foster, 40004	5 rooms, 1 pb	Sitting room
505-348-5551	Visa, MC	
Fran McCoy	C-yes/S-ltd/H-yes	
March—December		

Jailer's Inn was once a jail (1819) then a Jailer's residence (1874-1987) and is now completely remodeled and attractively decorated with antiques and oriental rugs.

Talbot Tavern/McLean House	$$ B&B	Continental breakfast
107 W. Stephen Foster, 40004	11 rooms, 11 pb	Lunch, dinner, bar
502-348-3494	Visa, MC, AmEx, DC	Entertainment
Bill & Jimmy Kelley	C-yes/S-yes/P-no/H-no	gift shop
All year		

1779 stone inn, one of first hostelries west, each room original, fireplaces, antiques. Wall paintings done by guest Prince Louis Phillipe of France.

BRANDENBURG

Doe Run Inn
Rt. 2, 40108
502-422-2982
Lucille S. Brown
All year

$-87
14 rooms, 5 pb
Visa, MC
C-yes/S-yes/P-no/H-no

Full breakfast
Lunch, dinner
Sitting room

Quiet country inn beside a running brook. Antiques. Breakfast, lunch & dinner daily, smorgasbords Friday night & Sunday noon. 1,000 acres to wander in.

FRANKFORT

Olde Kentucke B&B Inn
210 E. Fourth St., 40601
502-227-7389
Patty Smith
All year

$ B&B
4 rooms, 3 pb
Visa, MC, AmEx •
C-15+/S-yes/P-no/H-no

Continental plus
Afternoon tea
Sitting room, ceiling
fans, clawfoot tubs
third night free

Cheerful, old-fashioned boarding house atmosphere in historic district of Frankfort, which is nestled among the rolling hills of the Bluegrass region. 3rd night free policy.

Taylor-Compton House
419 Lewis St., 40601
502-227-4368
Barri Christian
March—mid-December

$ B&B
2 rooms
C-yes/S-no/P-yes/H-no

Continental plus
Living room & den
TV, movies

Elegant Victorian residence located next to Old Capitol Building and near historic specialty shops. Furnished with period antiques. Relive history!

GEORGETOWN

Log Cabin Bed & Breakfast
350 N. Broadway, 40324
502-863-3514
Janis & Clay McKnight
All year

$$ B&B
2 rooms, 1 pb
C-yes/S-yes/P-yes/H-yes

Continental plus
Complete kitchen
Entire cabin filled with
interesting amenities
fireplace, A/C

Authentic log cabin (1809); antique furnishings, complete kitchen, 2 bedrooms, fireplace, air conditioning; located 2 miles north of Lexington, 1.7 miles off I-75.

HARRODSBURG

Beaumont Inn
638 Beaumont Dr., 40330
606-734-3381
Chuck,Helen,Bud & Mary Dedman
March—November

$$ EP
29 rooms, 29 pb
Visa, MC
C-yes/S-yes/P-no/H-no

Full breakfast $
Luncheon, dinner
Swimming pool
tennis courts
sitting room, piano

Country inn built in 1845 in the heart of Kentucky's Bluegrass Region, furnished with antiques, serving traditional Kentucky southern cuisine.

LEXINGTON

Rokeby Hall
318 S. Mill St., 40508
606-254-5770
Amy Hackett
All year

$$$ B&B
4 rooms, 4 pb
Visa, MC, AmEx
C-yes/S-yes

Full breakfast
Lunch & dinner on requ.
Comp. wine, tea, snacks
Cable TV, fireplaces
off-street parking

Elegantly restored 19th-century home in the historic South Hill District of downtown Lexington—a real taste of Bluegrass hospitality.

More Inns...

Bowling Green B&B   659 E. 14th Avenue, Bowling Green 42101   502-781-3861
Broadwell B&B   Rt. 6, Box 58, Cynthiana 41031   606-234-4255
Canaan Land Farm B&B   4355 Lexington Rd., Harrodsburg 40330   606-734-3984
Ehrhardts B&B   285 Springwell Drive, Paducah 42001   502-554-0644

Louisiana

JEANERETTE

B&B on Bayou Teche	$ B&B	Continental plus
2148½ W. Main, 70544	1 rooms, 1 pb	Kitchenette, freezer
318-276-5061	•	Laundry facilities
Warren & Barbara Patout	C-yes/S-yes/P-no/H-yes	barbecue pit
All year	French	TV, radio, phone, A/C

Guest cottage with kitchen on large wooded lot. Bayou Teche—in heart of Cajun country, near many tourist attractions. Weekly rates on request.

NAPOLEONVILLE

Madewood Plantation House	$$$ B&B/MAP	Full breakfast (MAP)
Rt. 2, Box 478, Hwy 308, 70390	8 rooms, 8 pb	Cont. breakfast (B&B)
504-369-7151	•	Dinner, wine & cheese
Keith & Millie Marshall	C-yes/S-ltd/P-ltd/H-no	Sitting room, piano
All year	some French	canopied beds

Greek Revival mansion. Canopied beds, antiques, fresh flowers, wine and cheese, dinner by candlelight in formal family dining room.

NEW ORLEANS

Cornstalk Hotel	$$$ B&B	Continental breakfast
915 Royal St., 70116	14 rooms, 14 pb	Comp. tea & wine
504-523-1515	Visa, MC, AmEx •	Stained-glass windows
Debi & David Spencer	C-yes/S-yes/P-no/H-no	oriental rugs
All year	French, German	fireplaces

Small, elegant hotel in heart of French Quarter. All antique furnishings. Complimentary wine/liqueurs upon check-in. Recent renovation.

Dauzat Guest House	$$$ B&B	Continental plus
337 Burgundy St., 70130	5 rooms, 5 pb	Lunch, dinner
504-524-2075	none •	Comp. coffee, tea
R. Nicolais, D. Dauzat	C-12+ /S-ltd	Private courtyard w/pool
All year		

Innovative and historic guest house; fresh flowers and tasty muffins or croissants served with room service. Antiques and original artwork, featured in Architectural Digest.

NEW ORLEANS

Dusty Mansion
2231 Gen. Pershing, 70115	$ B&B	Continental plus
504-891-6061	4 rooms, 2 pb	Sunday champagne brunch
Cynthia Tomlin Riggs	•	Comp. wine, set-ups
All year	C-yes/S-yes/P-no/H-no	Sitting room
	Spanish, French	pool table, sun deck

Charming turn-of-the-century home, spacious, comfortable. Near St. Charles Street Car; easy access to French Quarter. Southern hospitality!

Grenoble House Inn
329 Dauphine St., 70112	$$$ EP	Fully equipped kitchens
504-522-1331	17 rooms, 17 pb	Comp. sherry
Carol Ann Chauppette	Visa, MC, AmEx •	Swimming pool
All year	C-yes/S-yes/P-no/H-yes	spa

Renovated and restored buildings in New Orleans' French Quarter. All suites have antique furniture, modern appointments.

Lamothe House Hotel
621 Esplanade Ave., 70116	$$$ B&B	Continental breakfast
504-947-1161/800-367-5858	20 rooms, 20 pb	Pralines, comp. beverage
William Prentiss	Visa, MC, AmEx •	Sitting room, courtyard
All year	C-yes/S-yes/P-no/H-no	newspaper, parking
		AAA 4-Diamond rating

An elegantly restored historic old mansion located on the eastern boundary of the French Quarter. This old mansion surrounds a romantic courtyard.

Marquette House Hostel
2253 Carondelet St., 70130	$ EP	Guest kitchen & laundry
504-523-3014	6 rooms	80 hostel beds
Steve & Alma Cross	Visa, MC •	Sitting rooms, board
All year	C-yes/S-ltd/P-no/H-no	games, garden-patio
	Spanish	

Clean, simple, basic accommodation for the budget traveler in a 100-year-old antebellum home. Affiliated with American Hosteling Association.

Nine-O-Five Royal Hotel
905 Royal St., 70116	$$ EP	Kitchens in all rooms
504-523-0219/504-523-4068	10 rooms, 10 pb	
Mrs. J. Morell	C-yes/S-yes/P-no/H-no	
All year		

Quaint guest house built in the 1890's, located in the French Quarter. Nicely furnished, antiques, high ceilings. Kitchenettes and Southern charm.

Noble Arms Inn
1006 Royal St., 70116	$$ B&B	Continental breakfast
504-524-2222/800-255-2655	17 rooms, 17 pb	Afternoon tea
Sheri Dazet	Visa, MC, AmEx, CB, DC •	
All year	C-yes/S-yes/P-no/H-ltd	

Historic renovated twin townhouses built in 1820 offer accommodations with kitchenettes and lace wrought iron balconies. In the French Quarter.

NEW ORLEANS ───

Prytania Inn	$ B&B	Full gourmet breakfast
1415 Prytania St., 70115	17 rooms, 17 pb	Aftn. tea, comp. wine,
504-566-1515	Visa, MC •	sherry & biscuits
Sally & Peter Schreiber	C-ltd/S-ltd	Sitting room, library
All year	Arabic, Fr, Span, Greek	parking

Charming Victorian, patio; southern gourmet breakfast, tender care; street car one block. French quarter, Super-Dome 5 minutes.

Soniat House	$$$ B&B	Continental breakfast
1133 Chartres St., 70116	24 rooms, 24 pb	Bar service
504-522-0570	Visa, MC, AmEx •	Jacuzzis
Rodney & Frances Smith	C-yes/S-yes/P-no/H-no	
All year	Spanish	

A private hotel in the residential area of the French Quarter, furnished in period antiques offering modern amenities of telephones and jacuzzi baths.

House on Cherry Street, Jacksonville, FL

NEW ORLEANS ───────────────────────

St. Charles Guesthouse B&B $ B&B   Continental breakfast
1748 Prytania St., 70130   30 rooms, 22 pb   Swimming pool
504-523-6556   •   patio, side porch
Dennis & Joanne Hilton   C-yes/S-yes/P-no/H-no   bicycles
All year   Spanish, French

Guest house located in historic Lower Garden District, one block from famous St. Charles Streetcar. Pool and patio. Very nice hosts. Simple, cozy, affordable.

NEW ROADS ──────────────────────────

Pointe Coupee B&B $$ B&B   Full breakfast
P.O. Box 386, 70760   10 rooms, 8 pb   Kitchen facilities
605 E. Main St.   •   Sitting room
504-638-6254   C-yes/S-ltd/P-ltd/H-yes
Rev. & Mrs. Miller Armstrong
All year

Overnight accommodations in three restored homes in downtown New Roads, near beautiful False River and scenic, historic Point Coupee Parish.

SAINT FRANCISVILLE ──────────────────

Barrow House $$ B&B   Continental breakfast
P.O. Box 1461, 70775   5 rooms, 3 pb   Full breakfast $5
524 Royal St.   •   Dinner (res), comp. wine
504-635-4791   C-8+/S-yes/P-no/H-no   Sitting room, bicycles
Lyle & Shirley Dittloff   cassette walking tours
All year

Circa 1809, located in the historic district. Rooms with period antiques. Cassette walking tours and complimentary wine for guests.

SHREVEPORT ──────────────────────────

Columns on Jordan $$ B&B   Continental plus
615 Jordan, 71101   5 rooms, 4 pb   Comp. wine, snacks
318-222-5912   Visa, MC, AmEx   Sitting room
Judith & Edwin Simonton   C-no/S-yes/P-ltd/H-no   library, bicycles
All year   Spanish   spa, pool

Sleep in the splendor and comfort of an antique bed and have a leisurely breakfast in the morning room. Enjoy the elegance of Southern living.

Fairfield Place $$ B&B   Continental plus
2221 Fairfield Ave., 71104   6 rooms, 6 pb   Sitting room
318-222-0048   Visa, MC, AmEx •
Janie Lipscomb   C-ltd/S-ltd/P-ltd/H-no
All year

Casually elegant 1900s inn. European and American antiques, gourmet breakfast. Ideal for business travelers and tourists.

WHITE CASTLE ────────────────────────

Nottoway Plantation Inn $$$ B&B   Full breakfast
P.O. Box 160, 70788   13 rooms, 13 pb   Full service restaurant
Lousiana Hwy 1   Visa, MC •   Swimming pool
504-545-2730/504-545-2409   C-yes/S-yes/P-no/H-ltd   sitting room
Cindy A. Hidalgo   French   piano, tennis nearby
All year exc. Xmas Day

Fresh flowers in your room, chilled champagne, a wake-up call consisting of hot sweet potato biscuits, coffee and juice delivered to your room. Also a guided tour of mansion.

More Inns...

Tezcuco Plantation Village   3138 Hwy. 44, Darrow 70725   504-562-3929
Asphodel Village   Rt. 2, Box 89 Hwy 68., Jackson 70748   504-654-6868
Milbank-Historic House   102 Bank St., Box 1000, Jackson 70748   504-634-5901
Patout's Guest House   Rt. 1 Box 288, Jeanerette 70544   318-364-0644
Mintmere Plantation House   1400 E. Main St., New Iberia 70560   318-364-6210
Bougainvillea House   924 Governor Nicholls S, New Orleans 70116   504-522-5000
Chimes Cottages   1360 Moss St., Box 5225, New Orleans 70152   504-525-4640
Columns Hotel   3811 St. Charles Ave., New Orleans 70115   504-899-9308
Creole B&B   3650 Gentilly Blvd., New Orleans 70122
French Quarter Maisons   1130 Chartres St., New Orleans 70116   504-524-9918
Hedgewood Hotel   2427 St. Charles Ave., New Orleans 70130   504-895-9708
Hotel Maison de Ville   727 Toulouse St., New Orleans 70130   504-561-5858
Hotel Villa Convento   616 Ursulines St., New Orleans 70116   504-522-1793
Hotel—The Frenchmen   417 Frenchmen St., New Orleans 70116   504-948-2166
Josephine Guest House   1450 Josephine St., New Orleans 70130   504-524-6361
Lafitte Guest House   1003 Bourbon St., New Orleans 70116   504-581-2678
Longpre Garden's Gsthouse   1726 Prytania, New Orleans 70130   504-561-0654
Old World Inn   1330 Prytania, New Orleans 70130   504-566-1330
Parkview Guest House   7004 St. Charles, New Orleans 70118   504-861-7564
Rue Dumaine   731 Rue Dumaine, New Orleans 70116
Terrell House   1441 Magazine St., New Orleans 70130   504-524-9859
Estorge House   427 N. Market St., Opelousas 70570   318-948-4592
Myrtles Plantation   P.O. Box 1100, Saint Francisville 70775   504-635-6277
St. Francisville Inn   P.O. Box 1369, Saint Francisville 70775   504-635-6502
Cottage Plantation   Route 5, Box 425, St. Francisville 70775   504-635-3674
Oak Alley Plantation   Rt. 2 Box 10, Hwy. 18, Vacherie 70090   504-265-2151
Old Lyons House   1335 Harridge St., Vinton 70668   318-589-2903
Viroqua Heritage Inn   220 E. Jefferson Inn, Viroqua 54665   608-637-3306
Wakefield Plantation   P.O. Box 41, Wakefield 70784
Glencoe Plantation   P.O. Box 178, Wilson 70789   504-629-5387

Maine

BAR HARBOR

Bayview Inn
111 Eden St. (Rt. 3), 04609
207-288-5861/800-356-3585
Mr. & Mrs. John Davis, Jr.
All year

$$$ EP
6 rooms, 6 pb
Visa, MC, AmEx •
C-12+/S-yes/P-no
French, Spanish

Continental plus $
Lunch, dinner, bar
Sitting room, library
piano, pool, badminton
croquet, games, kayaks

Luxury 8-acre waterfront estate reminiscent of the gracious chateaux of southern France. Elegant, intimate hotel, townhouses also available.

Black Friar Inn
10 Summer St., 04609
207-288-5091
Barbara & Jim Kelly
May 1—October 31

$$ B&B
6 rooms, 3 pb
Visa, MC, AmEx
C-12+/S-no/P-no/H-no

Full breakfast
Aft. tea & refreshments
Sitting room, wint. address:
1109 Mason Av. Drex. Hill
PA 19026, 215-449-6114

Rebuilt in 1981 with architectural finds from Mt. Desert Island. Furnished with antiques, Victorian and country flavor. Close to Acadia National Park. Swimming and tennis.

BAR HARBOR

Castlemaine Inn
39 Holland Ave., 04609
207-288-4563
T. O'Connell, N. O'Brien
All year

$$$ B&B
12 rooms, 12 pb
Visa, MC, AmEx
C-10+ /S-ltd/P-no

Continental plus
Sitting room w/fireplace
2 day minimum July,
August & holidays

The inn is nestled on a quiet side street in Bar Harbor village, surrounded by the magnificent Acadia National Park. Rooms are well-appointed. Delightful buffet breakfast.

Graycote Inn
40 Holland Ave., 04609
207-288-3044
Bill & Darlene De Mao
May—November

$$ B&B
10 rooms, 4 pb
Visa, MC
C-yes/S-ltd/P-no/H-no

Full breakfast
Sitting room, fireplaces
king or queen-sized beds
in six rooms

This elegantly restored Victorian inn is located near Acadia National Park and Frenchman's Bay. Numerous shops & fine restaurants are within walking distance.

Hearthside Inn
7 High St., 04609
207-288-4533
Barry & Susan Schwartz
All year

$$ B&B
9 rooms, 7 pb
Visa, MC
C-10+ /S-no/P-no/H-no

Continental plus
Comp. tea, wine
Evening refreshments
porch, patio
parlor with fireplace

Small, gracious hostelry in a quiet in-town location; elegant & comfortable; furnished with a blend of antiques & traditional furniture. Visit Bar Harbor & Acadia Nat'l Park.

Holbrook House
74 Mt. Desert St., 04609
207-288-4970
Dorothy & Mike Chester
Mid-May—mid-October

$$$ B&B
12 rooms, 12 pb
AmEx, Visa, MC
C-8+ /S-ltd/P-no/H-no

Full breakfast
Afternoon refreshments
Old fashion porch-parlor
library, inn rooms
beautiful furnishings

A bright and airy restored Victorian summer home on Bar Harbor's Historic Corridor. Close to shops, restaurants, ocean and park. Off-street parking.

The Ledgelawn Inn
66 Mount Desert St., 04609
207-288-4596
Mike & Nancy Miles
April 1—November 30

$$$ B&B
33 rooms, 33 pb
MC, Visa, AmEx •
C-yes/S-yes/P-no/H-no

Continental plus
Bar service
Pool, sauna, bicycles,
tennis nearby, piano
sitting room, library

A graceful turn-of-the-century mansion with lots of charm, antiques, sitting areas, fireplaces, hot tub; in a quiet location only 5 minutes walk to downtown.

Manor House Inn
106 West St., 04609
207-288-3759
Mac Noyes
May—mid-October

$$ B&B
14 rooms, 14 pb
Visa, MC, AmEx
C-12+ /S-ltd/P-no/H-no

Continental breakfast
Afternoon tea
3 sitting rooms
swimming pool, piano
tennis, gardens

Lots of special touches. Restored Victorian, National Register, antique furniture, pool, tennis courts, near Acadia National Park. Airport transfer with 2 or more nights stay.

BAR HARBOR ──

Mira Monte Inn
69 Mt. Desert St., 04609
207-288-4263/207-846-1236
Marian Burns
Early May—late October

$$$ B&B
11 rooms, 11 pb
Visa, MC, AmEx •
C-yes/S-yes/P-no/H-ltd

Continental plus
Wine & cheese
Sitting room, piano
tennis, swimming for
guests at nearby club

Renovated Victorian estate; period furnishings, fireplaces, one-acre grounds; quiet, in-town location, two king beds, walk to waterfront.

BATH ──

Fairhaven Inn
RR 2, Box 85, 04530
North Bath Rd.
207-443-4391
George & Sallie Pollard
All year

$$ B&B
7 rooms, 4 pb
C-yes/S-yes/P-no/H-no

Full breakfast
Sitting room, piano
library, bicycles
hiking trail, X-C skiing
winter snowshoeing

Old country inn—antique bed sets, quilts, etc. Hiking, swimming, golf nearby. Gourmet breakfasts available.

BELFAST ──

Jeweled Turret Inn
16 Pearl St., 04915
207-338-2304
Carl & Cathy Heffentrager
All year

$$ B&B
7 rooms, 7 pb
C-yes/S-ltd/P-no/H-no

Full breakfast
Afternoon tea
Sitting rooms, parlors
antiques
tennis & pool nearby

Intimate, charming, romantic. Unique architectural features; turrets, verandas, fireplaces, beautiful woodwork. Walk to town, shops & harbor. On National Register.

Northport House B&B
City 1 Mounted Rt., 04918
US Rt. 1
207-338-1422
Peter & Mary Lou Manicevetch
All year

$ B&B
8 rooms, 5 pb
Visa, MC
C-yes/S-no/P-no/H-no

Full breakfast
Afternoon tea
Sitting room

Old Victorian house (circa 1873) in coastal community. Rooms are spacious and tastefully decorated in period pieces. Enjoy a large American gourmet breakfast each morning.

Penobscot Meadows Inn
Route 1, 04915
207-338-5320
Dini & Bernie Chapnick
All year

$$ B&B
7 rooms, 7 pb
Visa, MC •
C-yes/S-yes/P-ask/H-ltd
French, Spanish, Portug.

Continental breakfast
Lunch, dinner
Bar
Sitting room

Beautifully restored inn on Penobscot Bay convenient for touring mid-coast Maine; gourmet dining features homemade breads, pasta, ice cream & pate.

BINGHAM ──

Mrs. G's Bed & Breakfast
P.O. Box 389, 04920
Meadow St.
207-672-4034
Frances Gibson
May—October

$$ B&B
4 rooms, 2 pb
•
C-yes/S-yes/P-no/H-no
Italian

Full breakfast
Dinner by reservation
Tennis nearby
horseshoes
badminton

Old Victorian home with rocking chairs on front porch. Walking distance to churches, shopping and restaurants. Situated on scenic Kennebec River.

BLUE HILL ───────────────────────────

Blue Hill Farm Country Inn $$$ B&B/MAP   Full breakfast
P.O. Box 403, Union St., 04614   7 rooms, 7 pb   Dinner (MAP)
207-374-5126   Visa, MC •   Piano, library
Mary & Don Hartley   C-12+/S-no/P-no/H-no   sitting room
All year

In continuous operation since 1840; nestled in picturesque village at head of Blue Hill Bay; mouth watering Down East cooking. Special fall & winter packages.

BOOTHBAY HARBOR ───────────────────────────

Admiral's Quarters Inn $$ EP   Comp. coffee
105 Commercial St., 04538   7 rooms, 7 pb   Unsurpassed harbor view
207-633-2474   Visa, MC   and sea views
Jean & George Duffy   C-12+/S-yes/P-no/H-ltd decks
May 1—November 1

Commanding a view of the Harbor unsurpassed by all, this large old sea captain's house has pretty rooms, private baths and decks for viewing.

Anchor Watch B&B $$ B&B   Continental breakfast
3 Eames Rd., 04538   3 rooms, 1 pb   Fresh strawberries may
207-633-2284   C-12+/S-yes/P-no/H-no   be picked from garden
Diane Campbell   courtyard in season
All year

Scenic shore; winter ducks feed near the rocks; flashing lighthouses; lobstermen hauling traps, 5-minute walk to restaurants, shops, boats.

Atlantic Ark Inn $$ B&B   Full breakfast
64 Atlantic Ave., 04538   5 rooms, 5 pb   Afternoon tea
207-633-5690   C-ltd/S-ltd/P-no/H-no   Comp. wine or sherry
Donna Piggott   freshly baked breads
May—October   Sitting room

Quaint and intimate, this small inn offers lovely harbor views, antiques, private baths, gourmet breakfasts, flowers, wine. Short walk to town.

Captain Sawyer's Place $$ B&B   Continental plus
87 Commercial St., 04538   10 rooms, 10 pb
207-633-2290   Visa, MC
Doreen Gibson   C-12+
Mid-May—October

A warm Victorian sea captain's home, overlooking the bustling harbor. A few stops away from fine shops and restaurants.

Howard House $ B&B   Continental plus
Route 27, 04538   15 rooms, 15 pb   Full breakfast $2.50
207-633-3933   C-yes/S-yes/P-no/H-yes
The Farrin Family
All year

Relax in casual, quiet, countrylike ambience, away from crowds, but only about a mile from beautiful Boothbay Harbor.

BOOTHBAY HARBOR

Kenniston Hill Inn	$$ B&B	Full breakfast
P.O. Box 125, 04537	8 rooms, 8 pb	Comp. brandy
Route 27	Visa, MC •	Sitting room
207-633-2159	C-12+/S-yes/P-no/H-no	bicycles
Paul & Ellen Morissette		
April—November		

200-year-old colonial on 4 acres of gardens, lawns and woods. Quilts and fresh flowers. A full gourmet breakfast.

Seafarer Guest House	$$ B&B	Continental plus
38 Union St., 04538	5 rooms, 2 pb	Lunch (on request, $)
207-633-2116	•	Doll collection
Olga F. Carito	C-12+/S-no/P-no/H-no	
Call for opening dates	Italian	

Grand old Victorian sea captain's home; head of harbor; magnificent, majestic view; close to center. Antiques, doll collection add charm throughout house.

BRIDGTON

Noble House B&B Inn	$$$ B&B	Full breakfast
P.O. Box 180, 04009	7 rooms, 4 pb	Comp. cream sherry
37 Highland Rd.	•	Sitting room, library
207-647-3733	C-yes/S-ltd/P-no/H-no	baby grand piano, organ
The Starets Family	French	canoe, lake, lawn games
All year		

Majestic turn-of-the-century home on beautiful Highland Lake; four-season activities; antique and craft shops, summer theater, skiing, family suites, personal attention.

BRUNSWICK

Harriet Beecher Stowe Hse	$$ EP	Continental breakfast
63 Federal St., 04011	48 rooms, 48 pb	Lunch, dinner
207-725-5543	Visa, MC, AmEx, DC, CB •	Bar service
Peggy & Bob Mathews	C-yes/S-yes/P-yes/H-yes	Sitting room
All year		gift shop

Federalist residence of H.B. Stowe houses renowned restaurant. 48 rooms with all amenities were completely refurbished in 1988 in the attached wing.

Lookout Point House	$$ B&B	Full breakfast buffets
Box 806, Scarborough, 04074	12 rooms	Comp. wine
141 Lookout Point Rd.	Visa, MC •	Sitting room
207-833-5509	C-ltd/S-ltd/P-no/H-no	bicycles
The Sewall Family	Danish, Swedish, German	
All year		

Lush lawns slope to the sea, private dock. Enjoy boating, swimming, bicycling—or just relax. Gourmet restaurants and great shopping nearby.

BUCKSPORT

Old Parsonage Inn	$ B&B	Full breakfast
P.O. Box 1577, 04416	3 rooms, 1 pb	Kitchenette unit
190 Franklin St.	C-ltd/S-ltd	Sitting room
207-469-6477		
Brian & Judy Clough		
All year		

Historic home, winding stairway, private entrance, furnished with antiques and reproductions. Centrally located coastal village; walk to restaurants and waterfront.

CAMDEN ——

Blackberry Inn
82 Elm St., 04843
207-236-6060
Edward & Vicki Doudera
All year

$$ B&B
8 rooms, 6 pb
Visa, MC
C-yes/S-no/P-no/H-no
French, Italian

Full breakfast
Sitting room
library

A wonderfully ornate Victorian home furnished in period style; a short stroll from Camden's harbor, shops and restaurants.

Blue Harbor House
67 Elm St., Route 1, 04843
207-236-3196
Jody Schmoll, Dennis Hayden
All year

$$ B&B
6 rooms, 4 pb
Visa, MC
C-yes/S-no/P-no/H-no

Full gourmet breakfast
Sitting room
qtr. acre back yard
bicycles

Restored circa 1835 homestead, antique furnishings, authentic country charm, cozy, comfortable accommodations, warm friendly hospitality, convenient village location.

Edgecombe-Coles House
HCR 60 Box 3010, 04843
64 High St.
207-236-2336
Terry & Louise Price
All year

$$ B&B
6 rooms, 6 pb
Visa, MC, AmEx, DC •
C-8+/S-yes/P-no/H-no

Full breakfast
Sitting room
Piano, library
bicycles
tennis courts

Distinctive country inn with breathtaking views of Penobscot Bay. Antique furnishings, private baths, hearty breakfasts. Maine's most beautiful seaport.

Goodspeed's Guest House
60 Mountain St., 04843
207-236-8077
The Goodspeeds & the Smalls
June—October

$$ B&B
8 rooms, 1 pb
C-10+/S-yes/P-no/H-no

Continental breakfast
Sitting room
bicycles
library

Quiet location, large grounds, only 5 blocks from harbor. Restored farm house with antique furniture, clock collection, stained glass and plank floors.

Hartstone Inn
41 Elm St., 04843
207-236-4259
Sunny & Peter Simmons
All year

$$ B&B
9 rooms, 9 pb
Visa, MC, AmEx
C-yes/S-yes/P-no/H-no

Full breakfast
Dinner
Afternoon tea, snacks
Sitting room, fireplaces
library, TV room

Stately Victorian inn, centrally located in picturesque village, steps away from harbor. Hearty breakfasts, romantic dinners, friendly, relaxed atmosphere.

Hawthorn Inn
9 High St., 04843
207-236-8842
Pauline & Bradford Staub
All year

$$$ B&B
9 rooms, 6 pb
Visa, MC •
C-10+/S-no/P-no/H-no

Full breakfast
Comp. tea, wine
2 sitting rooms
piano, hot tub in suites
volley ball

Refurbished Victorian home with light, airy rooms. Views of either harbor or mountains. Just a 5-minute walk to shops and restaurants.

150   Maine

CAMDEN ─────────────────────────────────

Maine Stay Inn	$ B&B	Full breakfast
22 High St., 04843	8 rooms, 2 pb	Comp. wine, tea
207-236-9636	Visa, MC •	2 parlors with working
Peter & The Twins	C-10+ /S-no/H-no	fireplaces, barbershop
All year		quartet singers

A treasured colonial built in 1802, the inn is located in the center of the Historic District—a five-minute walk to the harbor and restaurants.

Norumbega Inn	$$$ B&B	Full breakfast
61 High St. Rt. 1, 04843	7 rooms, 7 pb	Comp. tea, wine
207-236-4646	C-12+ /S-yes/P-no/H-no	3 sitting rooms
Mark Boland		
All year		

Camden's "stone castle," built 1886. Magnificent oak woodwork, spectacular views of Penobscot Bay and islands. Four acres of private grounds.

Swan House	$$ B&B	Full breakfast
49 Mountain St. (Rt. 52), 04843	6 rooms, 2 pb	Sitting room
207-236-8275	Visa, MC	outdoor gazebo
Le Cinq, Louise Price	C-8+ /S-no/P-no/H-ltd	
May—October		

Located in a quiet neighborhood, a short walk from Camden's Harbor. Hearty breakfasts and country antiques. Enjoy the private backyard gazebo.

Windward House B&B	$$ B&B	Full gourmet breakfast
6 High St., 04843	5 rooms, 5 pb	Afternoon tea & cider
207-236-9656	Visa, MC	comp. wine, snacks
Jon & Mary Davis	C-10+ /S-no/P-no/H-no	Sitting rooms
All year		library

In Harbor Village; spacious historic 1854 colonial fully restored, beautifully decorated, furnished with fine antiques. Gracious hospitality. Full gourmet breakfast.

CAPE NEDDICK ─────────────────────────────

Cape Neddick House	$$ B&B	Full breakfast
1300 Route 1, Box 70, 03902	6 rooms	Comp. wine
207-363-2500	C-9+ /S-ltd/P-no/H-no	Parlor & living room
Dianne Goodwin & Family		bicycles
All year		guitar

Coastal country 4th-generation Victorian home. Close to beaches, antiques, outlet shops, boutiques. Cultural & historic opportunities. Award-winning Apple Butter Nut Cake.

CENTER LOVELL ─────────────────────────────

Center Lovell Inn	$$$ EP/MAP	Full breakfast
Route 5, 04016	11 rooms, 7 pb	Dinner, bar
207-925-1575	Visa, MC •	Sitting room
William & Susan Mosca	C-ltd/S-no/P-no/H-yes	antique shop in barn
May—Oct. 21, Dec. 20—Feb.	Italian, French, Spanish	

Country inn, family oriented, surrounded by White Mountain National Forest, near Saco River for canoeing, Kezar Lake, foliage, Fryeburg Fair.

CENTER LOVELL

Westways on Kezar Lake
Box 175, Route 5, 04016
207-928-2663/800-225-4897
Nancy C. Tripp
Closed April & November

$$$ B&B/MAP
7 rooms, 3 pb
Visa, MC
C-yes/S-yes/P-ltd/H-no

Full breakfast
Dinner, bar
Sitting room, piano
tennis courts

Enjoy the splendor of the White Mountains. . . Let the haunting melody of the loon lull you to sleep. Complete recreational facilities.

CHEBEAGUE ISLAND

Chebeague Island Inn
Box 492, 04017
207-846-5155
Susan Krinsky
May—September

$$ EP
21 rooms, 15 pb
Visa, MC •
C-yes/S-yes/P-no/H-no
French, Italian

Breakfast $
Lunch, dinner, bar
Sitting room, piano
bicycles

Beautiful island retreat. Wraparound porch overlooking Casco Bay. Local seafood and other specialties served. Remote yet convenient.

CORNISH

Cornish Inn
P.O. Box 266, 04020
Main St., Route 25
207-625-8501
Jim & Judie Lapak
May-Oct., Dec.-Mar. (wknds)

$ B&B
17 rooms, 10 pb
Visa, MC •
C-yes/S-yes/P-no/H-no

Full breakfast
Full dinner menu avail.
Comp. wine
Library, sitting room

Discover the charm of old New England. Antiques, stenciling, country crafts, old-fashioned hospitality abound. Swimming, shopping, outdoor activities nearby.

DAMARISCOTTA

Brannon Bunker Inn
HCR 64 Box 045, 04543
Route 129 #45, Walpole
207-563-5941
Joseph & Jeanne Hovance
All year

$ B&B
9 rooms, 4 pb
Visa, MC •
C-yes/S-ltd/P-ltd/H-ltd

Continental plus
Kitchen facilities
Sitting room
porch

Country B&B; charming rooms furnished with antiques; close to all mid-coast recreational facilities including ocean, beach, boating & golf; antiquing!

DEER ISLE

Pilgrim's Inn
Main St., 04627
207-348-6615
Jean & Dud Hendrick
Mid-May—mid-October

$$$ B&B/MAP
13 rooms, 8 pb
•
C-yes/S-no/P-yes/H-no

Full breakfast
Supper, tea, bar
Sitting room, piano
bicycles, library
deck, patio grill area

Idyllic location on Deer Isle. Elegant yet informal colonial inn, creative cuisine, rustic antique-furnished barn. Commons rooms with 8' fireplaces.

DENNYSVILLE

Lincoln House Country Inn
Routes 1 & 86, 04628
207-726-3953
Mary & Jerry Haggerty
All year by reservation

$$$ MAP
6 rooms
Visa, MC, AmEx
C-yes/S-yes/P-no/H-no

Full breakfast
Dinner included
Bar
Sitting room
piano

A lovingly restored colonial with 95 acres of hiking, birding and fishing. Centerpiece of northeastern corner of coastal Maine. Internationally acclaimed. National Register.

152   Maine

EAST BOOTHBAY

Five Gables Inn
Murray Hill Rd., 04544
207-633-4551/207-633-2159
Ellen & Paul Morissette

$$$ B&B
15 rooms, 15 pb
C-12+/S-no/P-no

Full breakfast
Sitting room
Fireplaces, games
wraparound verandah
pool & boating nearby

Charm and elegance of old Victorian decor and the convenience of spotless facilities. All 15 rooms have views of the bay. Each room has unique furnishings and a private bath.

EAST WATERFORD

Waterford Inne
P.O. Box 149, 04233
Chadbourne Rd.
207-583-4037
Barbara/Rosalie Vanderzanden
Exc. Mar., Apr., Thg. week

$$ EP
9 rooms, 6 pb
C-yes/S-yes/P-ask/H-no

Full breakfast $5
Dinner
Sitting room
library

Country inning at its best! The hospitality, food and lovely surroundings will bring you back again and again.

EASTPORT

Todd House
1 Capen Av, Todd's Head, 04631
207-853-2328
Ruth M. McInnis
All year

$ B&B
5 rooms, 1 pb
•
C-yes/S-ltd/P-ltd/H-yes

Continental plus
Sitting room
barbecue
picnic facilities

Step into the past in our revolutionary-era Cape with wide panorama of Passamaquoddy Bay. Breakfast in common room before huge fireplace.

Weston House B&B
26 Boynton St., 04631
207-853-2907
Jett & John Peterson
All year

$ B&B
5 rooms
C-no/S-ltd/P-no/H-no

Full breakfast
Comp. wine, tea, snacks
Picnic lunch & dinner
Sitting room, library
croquet, "secret garden"

1810 Federal located on a hill overlooking Passamaquoddy Bay. On National Register of Historic Places. Furnished with antiques, clocks and family treasures.

ELIOT

High Meadows B&B
Route 101, 03903
207-439-0590
Elaine Raymond
April—December

$$ B&B
5 rooms, 3 pb
C-no/S-yes/P-no/H-no

Full breakfast
Comp. tea, wine
Sitting room

1736 colonial house in the country. Walking & cross-country ski trails. 6½ miles to historic Portsmouth, New Hampshire; shopping, theater & fine dining.

FREEPORT

Bagley House
RR 3, Box 269C, 04032
207-865-6566
Sigurd A. Knudsen, Jr.
All year

$$ B&B
5 rooms, 2 pb
Visa, MC, AmEx •
C-yes/S-no/P-no

Full breakfast
Lunch picnics on request
Sitting room, library
X-C skiing (winter)
6-acre yard, BBQ avail.

Peace, tranquillity and history abound in this magnificent 1772 country home. A warm welcome awaits you. Minutes from downtown Freeport.

Open Gates Bed & Breakfast, Darien, GA

FREEPORT

Harraseeket Inn
162 Main St., 04032
207-865-9377
Paul & Nancy Gray
All year

$$$ B&B
6 rooms, 6 pb
Visa, MC, AmEx
C-10+/S-ltd/P-no/H-no

Full breakfast
Restaurant, tavern
Sitting room
some rooms with jacuzzi
tubs and fireplaces

Luxury B&B. Private baths (Jacuzzi or steam), cable TV, elegant Maine country breakfast. Two blocks north of L.L. Bean. Walk to famous factory outlet shops.

Isaac Randall House
Independence Dr., 04032
207-865-9295
Jim & Glynrose Friedlander
All year

$$ B&B
8 rooms, 6 pb
C-yes/S-ask/P-ask/H-ask
Spanish, French

Full breakfast
Comp. soft drinks/snacks
Sitting room, library
dining porch, piano
A/C in four rooms

A gracious country inn circa 1823, elegantly and comfortably furnished with antiques. Pond, woods, picnic areas. Walk to L.L. Bean.

White Cedar Inn
178 Main St., 04032
207-865-9099
Philip & Carla Kerber
All year

$$$ B&B
6 rooms, 4 pb
Visa, MC
C-10+/S-no/P-no/H-no

Full breakfast
Outdoor grill
Sitting room
picnic table
brick patio

Recently restored 100-year-old home with large uncluttered antique-furnished rooms. Located just 2 blocks from L.L. Bean.

154   Maine

FRYEBURG ──────────────────────────

Admiral Perry House $$$ B&B   Full breakfast
9 Elm St., 04037   4 rooms, 4 pb   Afternoon tea
207-935-3365   Visa, MC •   Sitting room, library
Nancy & Ed Greenberg   C-ltd/S-no/P-no/H-no   bicycles, tennis courts
May 15—Oct., Dec. 15—Mar.   French   hot tubs, billiards, A/C

Charming historical home in a picturesque White Mountain Village. Clay tennis court, skiing, canoeing, hiking, spacious grounds and perennial gardens.

GREENVILLE ──────────────────────────

Greenville Inn $ EP   Full breakfast $
P.O. Box 1194, 04441   9 rooms, 7 pb   Full supper menu
Norris St.   Visa, MC   Gourmet dining & lounge
207-695-2206   C-ltd/S-yes/P-ltd/H-ltd   Sitting room
The Schnetzer's   German
All year

Restored lumber baron's mansion with many unique features on a hill in town overlooking Moose-head Lake and Squaw Mountain. 8 miles to skiing at Squaw Mountain.

HANCOCK POINT ──────────────────────────

Crocker House Country Inn $$ B&B   Full breakfast
Hancock Point Rd., 04640   10 rooms, 10 pb   Restaurant, bar, dinner
207-422-6806   Visa, MC, AmEx   Sitting room
Richard S. Malaby   C-ltd/S-yes/P-ltd/H-no
May 1—Thanksgiving

Quiet traditional coastal inn offering simple elegant dining. A little out of the way, but way out of the ordinary. Recently renovated.

ISLE AU HAUT ──────────────────────────

Keeper's House $$$ AP   Full breakfast
P.O. Box 26, 04645   4 rooms   Lunch, dinner included
207-367-2261   C-yes/S-no/P-no/H-no   Snacks
Jeff & Judi Burke   Spanish   Hiking
May 1—October 31   ocean swimming

Operating lighthouse station on remote unspoiled island within Acadia National Park. Tiny fishing village, primitive spectacular natural surroundings. Arrive on mailboat.

KENNEBUNK ──────────────────────────

Arundel Meadows Inn $$ B&B   Full gourmet breakfast
P.O. Box 1129, 04043   6 rooms, 6 pb   Afternoon tea
Route 1, Arundel   Visa, MC   Set-ups, library
207-985-3770   C-12+/S-yes/P-no/H-ltd   Sitting room
Mark Bachelder, Murray Yaeger
All year

Rooms individually decorated with art, antiques. Some with fireplaces; all with private baths. Gourmet breakfasts and teas. Near shops and beaches.

Sundial Inn $$$ B&B   Continental plus
48 Beach Ave., Box 1147, 04043 34 rooms, 34 pb   Aftn. tea (winter)
207-967-3850   Visa, MC, AmEx •   Sitting room
All year   C-no/S-ltd/P-no/H-yes   whirlpool tubs
                               French   beach

Directly on Kennebunkport beach. Completely renovated with country Victorian antiques and designer linens. Beautiful ocean views. An elevator for your convenience.

KENNEBUNKPORT ────────────────────────

1802 House B&B Inn $$$ B&B Full breakfast
Locke St., Box 646 A, 04046 8 rooms, 8 pb Sitting room
207-967-5632 Visa, MC, AmEx • hearthside
Sal & Patricia Ledda C-12+/S-yes/P-no/H-no
All year

One of Kennebunkport's most popular inns; charming colonial decor, located next to a beautiful 18-hole golf course. Some working fireplaces. Honeymoon suite.

Breakwater Inn $$ B&B Cont./Full breakfast
Ocean Ave., 04046 20 rooms, 20 pb Restaurant, bar
207-957-3118 Visa, MC, AmEx • Afternoon tea
The Lambert's & Underwood's C-yes/S-yes/P-ask/H-no full dinner menu (My-Oc)
January 16—December 14 Sitting room

Two 19th-century seaside guest houses located in historic fishing village. Ocean or harbor views. Walk to beaches & shopping. Famous country gourmet and seafood specialties.

Bufflehead Cove $$$ B&B Full breakfast
Gornitz Lane, 04046 6 rooms, 6 pb Aftn. tea, wine, cheese
P.O. Box 499 C-yes/S-no/P-no/H-no Sitting room, deck
207-967-3879 Spanish boat access to
Harriett Gott tidal river
All year

Secluded hideaway on the Kennebunk Tidal River—views of busy colonial village of Kennebunkport. Antiques, fireplace, flowers, sunny veranda and delightful breakfast.

Captain Lord Mansion $$$ B&B Full breakfast
P.O. Box 800, 04046 18 rooms, 18 pb Afternoon tea
Pleasant & Green Sts. C-12+/S-ltd/P-no/H-no Sitting room
207-967-3141 piano
Ben Davis, Richard Litchfield
All year

An intimate Maine coast inn with working fireplaces in 11 guest rooms. Furnished with genuine antiques.

Dock Square Inn $$$ B&B Full gourmet breakfast
P.O. Box 1123, 04046 6 rooms, 6 pb Sitting room
Temple St. Visa, MC bicycles
207-967-5773 C-10+/S-ltd/P-no/H-no color cable TV
Frank & Bernice Shoby Italian
March—December

Gracious Victorian country inn—former shipbuilder's home located in the heart of historic Kennebunkport village. Warm congenial atmosphere.

Harbor Inn $$$ B&B Full buffet breakfast
P.O. Box 538A, 04046 9 rooms, 9 pb Comp. tea, wine
Ocean Ave. C-12+/S-yes/P-no/H-no Sitting room
207-967-2074 front porch w/wicker
Charlotte & Bill Massmann large lawn, cottage
May 15—November 1

Comfortably and elegantly furnished throughout with antiques, canopy and poster beds. "More than just a night's lodging, a delightful experience."

KENNEBUNKPORT ─────────────────────────────────

Inn at Harbor Head	$$$ B&B	Full gourmet breakfast
RR 2, Box 1180, 04046	4 rooms, 4 pb	Afternoon refreshments
Pier Rd., Cape Porpoise	Visa, MC •	snacks, comp. wine
207-967-5564	C-12+/S-no/P-no/H-no	Sitting room, library
Dave & Joan Sutter		salt water harbor
Closed November		

Tides rise and fall at waterfront inn. Art and antiques, photogenic breakfasts served outside by sea roses in summer, by glowing fire in winter.

Inn on South Street	$$$ B&B	Full breakfast
P.O. Box 478A, 04046	3 rooms, 3 pb	Comp. tea, wine
South St.	AmEx •	Sitting room
207-967-5151/207-967-4639	C-10+/S-no/P-no/H-no	fireplace
Jacques & Eva Downs	German, Spanish, Russian	garden
February—December		

Enjoy beautifully appointed rooms in a romantic 19th-century home. Convenient, quiet location. Sumptuous breakfast, fireplaces, gardens, fresh flowers.

Kennebunkport Inn	$$ B&B/$$$ MAP	Continental plus
Dock Sq., P.O. Box 111, 04046	34 rooms, 34 pb	Restaurant, dinner My-Oc
207-967-2621	Visa, MC, AmEx •	Victorian pub
Rick & Martha Griffin	C-yes/P-no/H-no	Pool, color TV
All year	French	golf & tennis nearby

Classic country inn in old sea captain's home. All rooms with private baths & color TV. Gourmet dining, turn-of-the-century bar, piano bar. Located in historic district.

Kylemere House 1818	$$ B&B	Full gourmet breakfast
P.O. Box 1333, 04046	5 rooms, 3 pb	Comp. tea, wine
South Street	AmEx	Sitting room
207-967-2780	C-12+/S-ltd/P-no/H-no	large porch & lawn
Mary & Bill Kyle		
April 15—December 15		

Charming federal inn in historic area located within a short walk to shops and beach. Warm, inviting rooms, traditional hospitality and "down east" breakfast.

Port Gallery Inn	$$$ B&B	Continental breakfast
P.O. Box 1367, 04046	7 rooms, 7 pb	Sitting room
Spring & Maine Sts.	Visa, MC, AmEx •	baby grand piano
207-967-3728	C-ltd/S-yes/P-no/H-no	phones in rooms
Francis & Lucy Morphy	French	cable TV in all rooms
All year		

1891 Victorian mansion set in a lovely garden in the village center. Ultra-comfortable rooms. Famous marine art gallery on the 1st floor features painter Lawrence E. Donnison.

Welby Inn	$$ B&B	Full breakfast
P.O. Box 774, 04046	7 rooms, 7 pb	Comp. wine
Ocean Ave.	AmEx	Sitting room
207-967-4655	C-10+/S-ltd/P-no/H-no	piano
David & Betsy Rogers Knox		bicycles
All year		

Gracious turn-of-the-century home in historic Kennebunkport. Walk to beach, marina and shops. Deep-sea fishing and harbor cruises available.

KENNEBUNKPORT

The White Barn Inn
Beach St, RR 3, Box 387, 04046
207-967-2321/207-967-5331
L. Bongiorno & C. Hackett
March—December

$$$ B&B
24 rooms, 24 pb
Visa, MC, AmEx •
C-yes/S-yes/P-no/H-ltd

Continental plus
Dinner, bar
Entertainment
bicycles
near beach & town square

Elegant Queen Anne antiques & reproductions. Dining room set with pewter silver & linen. Architecturally preserved barn. Casual elegance. Recipient of 1983 Silver Spoon award.

KITTERY

Melfair Farm B&B
365 Wilson Rd., 03904
207-439-0320
Claire Cane
March—December

$$ B&B
5 rooms, 1 pb
•
C-10+/S-yes/P-no/H-no
French

Full breakfast
Comp. tea, lemonade
Large sitting room, TV
piano

1871 New England farmhouse, pastoral setting. Minutes from fine shopping, beaches. Theater, gourmet dining in nearby historical Portsmouth, New Hampshire.

LUBEC

Home Port Inn
45 Main St., 04652
207-733-2077
Tim & Miyoko Carman
May—October 31

$$ B&B
6 rooms, 5 pb
Visa, MC
C-7+/S-ltd/P-no/H-no

Full breakfast
Lunch, dinner
Sitting room
whales, bird tours
bicycle rentals

Charming country inn featuring fine food, whale-watching, bird-watching; near parks, beaches and shops in quiet area of town.

MOUNT DESERT ISLAND

Pointy Head Inn
Rt. 102A, Bass Harbor, 04653
HCR 33, Box 2A
207-244-7261
Doris & Warren Townsend
Mid-May—October

$$ B&B
5 rooms, 1 pb
C-ltd/S-no/P-no/H-no

Full breakfast
Sitting room
porch & deck
piano & 2 organs

Located on Bass Harbor, adjacent to Acadia National Park. Hearty breakfast on deck overlooking harbor. Half-hour to Bar Harbor.

NAPLES

Augustus Bove House
RR 1, Box 501, 04055
Corner of Rts. 302 & 114
207-693-6365
David & Arlene Stetson
All year

$ B&B
12 rooms, 5 pb
Visa, MC, AmEx •
C-yes/S-ltd/P-yes/H-ltd

Full breakfast
Afternoon tea
Sitting room
veranda, lawn

Recently restored, the Augustus Bove House offers authentic colonial accomodations in a relaxing atmosphere. Located between two lakes and 20 min. from mountains for skiing.

NEW HARBOR

Gosnold Arms
HC 61, Box 161, 04554
Route 32, Northside Rd.
207-677-3727
The Phinney Family
Mid-May—October

$$$ MAP
26 rooms, 19 pb
Visa, MC
C-yes/S-ltd/P-no/H-ltd

Full breakfast
Dinner included
Cocktails
Sitting room
small wharf

Charming country inn and cottages. All-weather dining porch overlooking harbor. Beaches, lobster pounds, parks nearby.

NEWCASTLE ──

Captain's House B&B	$ B&B	Full Maine breakfast
P.O. Box 242, 04553	5 rooms	Comp. tea
19 River Rd.	C-yes/S-yes/P-no/H-no	Dinner (Winter)
207-563-1482		Sitting room
Joe Sullivan, Susan Rizzo		
All year		

Spacious colonial home overlooking the Damariscotta River offers sunny rooms furnished with antiques and delicious full Maine breakfast. Omelettes a specialty.

Mill Pond Inn	$$ B&B	More than full breakfast
RFD1, Box 245, 04553	5 rooms, 5 pb	Sitting room
Route 215, Damariscotta	Visa, MC	swimming/boating in lake
207-563-8014	C-5+/S-yes/P-no/H-ltd	canoe for guests
Bobby & Sherry Whear		hammock, horseshoes
All year		

Small, private inn with a water view from four rooms, across the road from Damariscotta Lake.

Newcastle Inn	$$$ B&B	Gourmet 4-course brkfast
River Rd., 04553	15 rooms, 15 pb	Afternoon tea
207-563-5685	•	Dinner
Ted & Chris Sprague	C-ltd/S-no/P-no/H-ltd	Sitting room
All year		screened porch

Fine dining and a pampering environment in an intimate, full-service, country inn on the Damariscotta River.

NORTH HAVEN ISLAND ───────────────────────────────

Pulpit Harbor Inn	$$ B&B	Continental plus
Crabtree Point Rd., 04853	6 rooms, 2 pb	Full breakfast $
207-867-2219	Visa, MC	Restaurant, bar service
Christie & Barney Hallowell	C-yes/S-ltd/P-ltd	Sitting room, library
All year		bicycles, farm animals

On North Haven, an unspoiled, noncommercial, rocky-coast island. Reached by 12 mile ferry ride. Island hospitality. Sheep, chickens, ducks, rabbit. Romantic Penobscot Bay.

NORTH WATERFORD ──────────────────────────────────

Olde Rowley Inn	$ B&B	Full breakfast
P.O. Box 87, 04267	5 rooms, 3 pb	Dinner, bar
Route 35 N.	Visa, MC	Sitting room
207-583-4143	C-ltd/S-yes/P-no/H-ltd	
Brian & Meredith Thomas		
All year		

The Olde Rowley Inn was built in 1790, and served as a stagecoach inn. 5 quaint, cozy guest rooms. Fine country breakfast or dinner.

OGUNQUIT ──

Beauport Inn	$$$ B&B	Continental plus
P.O. Box 1793, 03907	4 rooms, 2 pb	Sitting room
96 Shore Rd.	Visa, MC	piano, TV room
207-646-8680	C-12+/S-no	antique shop
Dan Pender		
All year		

Restored cape furnished with antiques. Pine paneled sitting room with fireplace. Walk to beach, Marginal Way and Perkins Cove.

OGUNQUIT

The Gazebo	$$$ B&B	Full gourmet breakfast
P.O. Box 668, Rt. 1 N., 03907	9 rooms, 7 pb	Sitting room
207-646-3733	Visa, MC	dining room
Tony Fontes	C-12+/S-yes/P-no/H-no	Heated swimming pool
Closed January		

150-year-old restored farmhouse serving full gourmet breakfast. Short walk to Ogunquit Beach. Afternoon tea and pate.

Hartwell House	$$$ B&B	Continental plus
116 Shore Rd., 03907	17 rooms, 17 pb	Swimming, tennis avail.
207-646-7210	Visa, MC, AmEx	air conditioning
Jim & Trisha Hartwell	C-14+/S-ltd/P-no/H-no	
All year		

Elegantly furnished in early American & English antiques. Set amid 2 acres of sculpted gardens, perfect for relaxing.

Morning Dove B&B	$$ B&B	Continental plus
P.O. Box 1940, 03907	7 rooms, 3 pb	Comp. wine
5 Bourne Lane	Visa, MC •	Sitting room
207-646-3891	C-12+/S-yes/P-no/H-no	
Peter & Eeta Sachon		
All year		

1860s farmhouse featuring modern baths, airy rooms, authentic antiques, fresh flowers. Walk to beaches, Perkins Cove, playhouse and art galleries, trolley.

Trellis House	$$ B&B	Continental plus
P.O. Box 2229, 03907	6 rooms, 6 pb	Afternoon beverages
2 Beachmere Pl.	Visa, MC	Sitting room
207-646-7909	C-no/S-ltd/P-no/H-no	porches, ocean views
Jim Pontolilo		trolley stop
All year		

A year-round inn close to all that is special to Ogunquit. Furnished with an eclectic blend of antiques, coupled with some ocean views and quiet surroundings.

PEMAQUID

Little River Inn	$ B&B	Full breakfast
Rt. 130, HC 62, Box 178, 04558	6 rooms, 2 pb	Sitting room
207-677-2845	Visa, MC	
All year	C-yes/S-yes/P-no/H-no	

1840 Cape farmhouse by the Pemaquid River with view to the cove. Delicious country breakfast.

PORTLAND

Inn on Carleton	$$ B&B	Continental plus
46 Carleton St., 04102	7 rooms, 3 pb	Sitting room
207-775-1910	C-ltd/S-no/P-no/H-no	
Susan Holland		
All year		

Restored Victorian townhouse in Portland's West End historic district—close to city museums, shops, restaurants and waterfront.

PROSPECT HARBOR

Oceanside Meadows Inn	$$ B&B	Full breakfast
P.O. Box 90, 04669	7 rooms, 1 pb	Sitting room
207-963-5557	Visa, MC	library
Marge Babineau	C-yes/S-no/P-yes/H-no	ocean & sandy beach
All year		

Charming 19th-century home; sandy beach and ocean across street; beautiful gardens. One hour from Bar Harbor and Acadia National Park.

SEARSPORT

College Club Inn	$$ B&B	Continental plus
P.O. Box 617, US Rt. 1, 04974	5 rooms, 3 pb	Sitting room
207-548-6575	Visa, MC	library
Mike Harrigan	C-ask/S-ltd/P-ask/H-no	antiques & gifts shop
June—October		

Breakfast, with our home-baked breads and muffins, is served on a glassed-in porch overlooking Penobscot Bay.

Homeport Inn	$$ B&B	Full breakfast
Route 1, E. Main St., 04974	11 rooms, 7 pb	Tea, wine, English pub
207-548-2259	Visa, MC, AmEx, DC, CB •	Soda fountain, garden
Dr. F. Goerge, Edith Johnson	C-yes/S-ltd/P-no/H-yes	Antique shop, ocean view
All year		bicycles, golf, tennis

Listed on the Historic Register. Ideal mid-coast location for an extended stay to visit coast of Maine. Victorian cottage also available by the week.

Thurston House B&B Inn	$ B&B	Full breakfast
8 Elm St., 04974	4 rooms, 2 pb	Snacks (sometimes)
P.O. Box 686	•	Sitting room
207-548-2213	C-6+/S-no/P-no/H-no	library
Carl & Beverly Eppig		tennis courts nearby
All year		

Circa 1830 Colonial in quiet village setting. Easy stroll to everything, including Maritime Museum, tavern, beach park on Penobscot Bay.

SOUTHPORT

Albonegon Inn	$$ B&B	Continental breakfast
Capitol Island, 04538	15 rooms, 3 pb	Afternoon tea
207-633-2521	Visa, MC	Sitting room, piano
Kim Peckham	C-yes	tennis court
July—mid October	Spanish	beaches

A very special place to relax. On a private island, perched on the edge of the ocean. Spectacular views! Hike, bird-watch, swim, beachcomb, tennis, sail. Golf nearby.

SOUTHWEST HARBOR

The Island House	$$ B&B	Full breakfast
P.O. Box 1006, 04679	5 rooms, 1 pb	Restaurants nearby
Clark Point Rd.	•	Sitting room, library
207-244-5180	C-12+	large garden, harbor
Ann R. Gill		fishing docks
May—October		

The Island House, a gracious, restful, seacoast home on the quiet side of Mount Desert Island. An efficiency apartment available.

SOUTHWEST HARBOR

Island Watch B&B	$ B&B	Full breakfast
P.O. Box 1359, 04679	6 rooms, 4 pb	Sitting room
Freeman Ridge Rd.	•	
207-244-7229	C-12+/S-no/P-no/H-yes	
All year		

Island Watch sits atop Freeman Ridge, overlooking the Mt. Desert Island Harbor, the distant mountains, and the towns below. Near Acadia National Park.

The Kingsleigh Inn	$$ B&B	Full breakfast
P.O. Box 1426, 04679	7 rooms, 5 pb	Afternoon tea
100 Main St.	C-12+/S-ltd/P-no/H-no	Sitting room w/fireplace
207-244-5302		library
Jim & Kathy King		
May—October		

A cozy intimate inn overlooking the harbor. Filled with many antiques, wing-back chairs and four-poster beds. Rooms with harbor views.

Lindenwood Inn	$$ B&B	Full breakfast
P.O. Box 1328, 04679	8 rooms, 3 pb	Sitting room
Clark Point Rd.	C-ltd/S-no/P-no/H-no	harpsichord, TV
207-244-5335		decks
Gardiner & Marilyn Brower		
All year		

A friendly, cozy inn on the quiet side of Mount Desert Island, where you can enjoy the island's many attributes year-round.

Penury Hall	$ B&B	Full breakfast
Main St., Box 68, 04679	3 rooms	Comp. tea, wine
207-244-7102	C-ltd/S-yes/P-no/H-no	Sauna
Toby & Gretchen Strong		sitting room
All year		boats

Comfortable rambling old home. Decor reflects hosts' interests in art, antiques, books, gardening, sailing. Water sports paradise.

SPRUCE HEAD

Craignair Inn	$$ B&B	Full breakfast
Clark Island Rd., 04859	21 rooms	Comp. wine, restaurant
207-594-7644	Visa, MC	Wine service
Norman & Terry Smith	C-yes/S-yes/P-yes/H-no	Sitting room
All year		library

Area is alive with history of quarrying days; one of the original boarding houses. Swimming in abandoned granite quarry is delightful. The old church and store still stand.

SUNSET

Goose Cove Lodge	$$$ B&B/MAP	Continental plus
Deer Isle,Goose Cove Rd, 04683	21 rooms, 21 pb	Dinner, beer & wine
207-348-2508	•	Beaches, sailboats
George & Eleanor Pavloff	C-yes/S-ltd/P-no/H-yes	piano, sitting room
May 1—mid-October	French, German, Spanish	bicycles, entertainment

Rustic retreat—sand beaches, rocky shores, spruce forest with moss-covered trails and open ocean at the End of Beyond. B&B in the spring and fall. MAP in the summer.

SURRY ───────────────────────────────────

Surry Inn	$$ B&B	Full breakfast
P.O. Box 25, Route 172, 04684	13 rooms, 11 pb	Dinner, bar; comp. tea
207-667-5091	Visa, MC	Canoes, private beach
Sarah & Peter Krinsky	C-5+/S-yes/P-no/H-ltd	croquet, horseshoes
All year	Fr., Rus., Ger., Czech.	sitting room, library

Coastal country inn offering excellent cuisine, rolling lawns, private beach, spectacular sunsets, stenciled walls, New England charm and comfort.

TOPSHAM ───────────────────────────────────

The Walker Wilson House	$$ B&B	Full breakfast
2 Melcher Pl., 04086	4 rooms	Snacks
207-729-0715	•	Sitting room
Skip & Annie O'Rourke	C-yes/S-yes	library
All year		

Outstanding example of 1803 Federal architecture. Unique, original moldings and intricate woodwork attributed to Sameul Melcher. Minutes to Bowdoin College and L.L. Bean.

WALDOBORO ───────────────────────────────────

Broad Bay Inn & Gallery	$ B&B	Full gourmet breakfast
P.O. Box 607, Main St., 04572	5 rooms, 3 pb	Dinner, picnics
207-832-6668	Visa, MC •	Comp. sherry, sitting rm
Jim & Libby Hopkins	C-12+/S-ltd/P-no/H-no	Player piano, X-C ski
All year	French	bikes, garden, sun deck

Built in 1830, this inn is centrally located mid-coast. Close to lake, Audubon Sanctuary, fishing villages, tennis nearby, library, theater, antiques, art gallery on premises.

WATERFORD ───────────────────────────────────

Kedarburn Inn	$$ B&B	Full breakfast
Box 61, 04088	7 rooms, 3 pb	Dinner, bar
Valley Rd., Route 35	Visa, MC •	Sitting room
207-583-6182	C-yes/S-yes/P-yes/H-no	piano
Margaret & Derek Gibson	French	lake
All year		

A wonderful old home built in 1858, situated on a beautifully landscaped knoll in the center of historic Waterford Village. A romantic country setting. Sunday Brunch.

WELLS BEACH ───────────────────────────────────

Bayview Inn B&B	$$ B&B	Continental plus
RR 2131 Webhannet Dr., 04090	5 rooms	Afternoon tea
207-646-9260	Visa, MC, AmEx	Sitting room
Michael & Patricia	C-6+/S-yes/P-no/H-no	bicycles
Memorial Day—Labor Day		ocean

Our B&B is a restored 1890s barn on the ocean. Sunrises on the ocean, seafood, antiquing, sightseeing. Rachel Carson bird sanctuary off the rear deck.

YORK ───────────────────────────────────

Dockside Guest Quarters	$ EP	Continental plus $
P.O. Box 205, 03909	21 rooms, 19 pb	Luncheon, dinner
Harris Island Rd.	Visa, MC •	Restaurant, bar room
207-363-2868	C-yes/S-no/P-ltd/H-ltd	Sitting room
The David Lusty Family	German	marina, boat rentals
Memorial Day—mid-Oct.		

Super-scenic location, several ocean beaches nearby, historic district within walking distance. Rated three diamonds by AAA.

YORK HARBOR ———————————————————————————

York Harbor Inn $$ B&B   Continental plus
P.O. Box 573, 03911   32 rooms, 26 pb   Lunch, dinner, bar
York St., Route 1A   Visa, MC, AmEx •   Sitting room, piano
207-363-5119   C-yes/S-yes/P-no/H-ltd   bicycles, banquet/conf.
The Dominguez Family   faclties, ocean swimming
All year

Quiet, authentic country inn (circa 1637) listed in National Register of Historic Places; overlooks the ocean and York Harbor Beach.

More Inns. . .

Olde Berry Inn   Kennebunk Road, P.O. Box 2, Alfred 04002   207-324-0603
Crosby's B&B   51 Green St., Augusta 04330   207-622-1861
Cloverleaf Cottages   RFD 1, Box 75, Bailey Island 04003
Atlantean Inn   11 Atlantic Ave., Dept., Bar Harbor 04609   207-288-3270
Cleftstone Manor   92 Eden St., Rt. 3, Bar Harbor 04609   207-288-4951
Primrose Cottage Inn   73 Mt. Desert St., Bar Harbor 04609   207-288-4031
Shady Maples   RFD #1, Box 360, Bar Harbor 04609   207-288-3793
Stratford House Inn   45 Mt. Desert St., Bar Harbor 04609   207-288-5189
Thornhedge Inn   47 Mt. Desert St., Bar Harbor 04609   207-288-5398
Town Guest House   12 Atlantic Ave., Bar Harbor 04609   207-288-5548
Moosehorn B&B   Rt. 1, Box 322, Baring 04694   207-454-8883
Bass Harbor Cottages   Route 102A, Bass Harbor 04653   207-244-3460
Bass Harbor Inn   Shore Rd., Bass Harbor 04653   207-244-5157
Glad II   60 Pearl St., Bath 04530   207-443-1191
Hiram Alden Inn   19 Church St., Belfast 04915   207-338-2151
Horatio Johnson House   36 Church St., Belfast 04915   207-338-5153
Londonderry Inn   Rt. 3, Belmont Ave., Belfast 04915   207-338-3988
Bakers B&B   Rt. 2, Box 2090, Bethel 04217   207-824-2088
Bethel Inn and Count   P.O. Box 26, Bethel 04217   800-654-0125
Chapman Inn   P.O. Box 206, Bethel 04217   207-824-2657
Douglass Place   Route 2, Box 90, Bethel 04217   207-824-2229
Four Seasons Inn   P.O. Box 390, Bethel 04217   207-824-2755
L'Auberge Country Inn   P.O. Box 21, Bethel 04217   207-824-2774
Norseman Inn   HCR-61 Box 50, Bethel 04217   207-824-2002
Pointed Fir B&B   Paradise Rd., Box 745, Bethel 04217   207-824-2251
Sudbury Inn   Lower Main Street, Bethel 04217   207-824-2174
Sunday River Inn   Sunday River Road, Bethel 04217   207-824-2410
Lodge   19 Yates, Biddefordpool 04006   617-284-7148
Arcady Down East   South St., Blue Hill 04614   207-374-5576
John Peters Inn   P.O. Box 916, Blue Hill 04614   207-374-2116
Boothbay Harbor Inn   37 Atlantic Ave. Box 4, Boothbay Harbor 04538   207-633-6302
Green Shutters Inn   P.O. Box 543, Boothbay Harbor 04538   207-633-2646
Harbour Towne Inn   71 Townsend Ave., Boothbay Harbor 04538   207-633-4300
Hilltop Guest House   44 McKown Hill, Boothbay Harbor 04538   207-633-2941
Thistle Inn   P.O. Box 176, Boothbay Harbor 04538   207-633-3541
Topside   McKown Hill, Boothbay Harbor 04538   207-633-5404
Welch House   36 McKown St., Boothbay Harbor 04538   207-633-3431
Westgate B&B   18 West St., Boothbay Harbor 04538   207-633-3552
Mountainside B&B   P.O. Box 290, Bridgton 04009   207-647-5091
North Woods B&B   55 No. High St., Bridgton 04009   207-647-2100
Tarry-a-While Resort   Box A, Bridgton 04009   207-647-2522
Middlefield Farm B&B   P.O. Box 4, Bristol Mills 04539   207-529-5439
Aaron Dunning House   76 Federal St., Brunswick 04011   207-729-4486
Brunswick B&B   165 Park Row, Brunswick 04011   207-729-4914

Dove B&B   16 Douglas St., Brunswick 04011   207-729-6827
Harborgate B&B   RD 2-2260, Brunswick 04011   207-725-5894
Samuel Newman House   7 South St., Brunswick 04011   207-729-6959
Jed Prouty Tavern   Box 550, Bucksport 04416   207-469-2371
Camden Harbour Inn   83 Bayview St., Camden 04843   207-236-4200
Chestnut House   69 Chestnut St., Camden 04843   207-236-6137
The Elms   84 Elm St., Route 1, Camden 04843   207-236-6250
High Tide Inn   Camden 04843   207-236-3724
Hosmer House B&B   4A Pleasant St., Camden 04843   207-236-4012
Lord Camden Inn   24 Main St., Camden 04843   207-236-4325
Maine Stay B&B   22 High St., Camden 04843   207-236-9636
Owl and The Turtle   8 Bay View St., Camden 04843   207-236-4769
Green Acres Inn   RFD #112, Canton 04221   207-597-2333
Crescent Beach Inn   Rt. 77, Cape Elizabeth 04107   207-799-1517
Sea Chimes B&B   RD 1, Shore Rd., Cape Neddick 03902   207-646-5378
Wooden Goose Inn   P.O. Box 195, Cape Neddick 03902   207-363-5673
Newagen Seaside Inn   Box H, Southport Island, Cape Newagen 04552   207-633-5242
Sugarloaf Inn   Carrabassett Vly., Carrabassett Valley 04947   207-237-2701
Castine Inn   P.O. Box 41, Main St., Castine 04421   207-326-4365
Manor   Box 276, Castine 04421   207-326-4861
Pentagoet Inn   P.O. Box 4, Castine 04421   207-326-8616
Ricker House   P.O. Box 256, Cherryfield 04622   207-546-2780
Claryknoll Farm   Rt. 215 Box 751, Coopers Mills 04341   207-549-5250
Elizabeth's B&B   HC 61, Box 004, Damariscotta 04543   207-563-1919
Yellow House B&B   Water St. Box 732, Damariscotta 04543   207-563-1388
Eggemoggin Inn   RFD Box 324, Deer Isle 04650   207-348-2540
Ben-Loch Inn   RFD #1 Box 1020, Dixmont 04932   207-257-4768
Foxcroft B&B   25 W. Main St., Dover-Foxcraft 04426   207-564-7720
Linekin Village B&B   Route 65, Box 776, East Booth Bay 04544   207-633-3681
Ocean Point Inn   Shore Road, East Boothbay 04544   207-633-4200
East River B&B   P.O. Box 205 High St., East Machias 04630   207-255-8467
Artists Retreat   29 Washington St., Eastport 04631   207-853-4239
Ewenicorn Farm B&B   116 Goodwin Rd. Rt. 10, Eliot 03903   207-439-1337
Victoria's B&B   58 Pine St., Ellsworth 04605   207-667-5893
Inn at Cold Stream Pond   P.O. Box 76, Enfield 04433   207-732-3595
Grey Havens Inn   Box 82, Five Islands 04546   207-371-2616
181 Main Street B&B   181 Main St., Freeport 04032   207-865-1226
Holbrook Inn   7 Holbrook St., Freeport 04032   207-865-6693
Old Red Farm   Desert of Maine Road, Freeport 04032   207-865-4550
Oxford House Inn   105 Main St., Fryeburg 04037   207-935-3442
Country Squire B&B   RR 1 Box 178 Mighty, Gorham 04038   207-839-4855
Sunset House   HCR #60, Box 62, Gouldsboro 04607   207-963-7156
Trebor Inn   P.O. Box 299, Guilford 04443   207-876-4070
Le Domaine Restaurant / Inn   US 1, Box 496, Hancock 04640   207-422-3395
Tolman House Inn   P.O. Box 551 Tolman Rd, Harrison 04040   207-583-4445
Island B&B   Box 275,Ltl. Cranberry, Isleford 04646   207-244-9283
Dark Harbor House Inn   Box 185, Islesboro 04848   207-734-6669
Islesboro Inn   Islesboro 04848   207-734-2222
Tootsie's B&B   Trynor Sq., RFD 1,Box 2, Jonesport 04649
Alewive House   1917 Alewive Rd., Rt 35, Kennebunk 04043   207-985-2118
Kennebunk Inn   45 Main St., Kennebunk 04043   207-985-3351
Captain Fairfield House   P.O. Box 202, Kennebunkport 04046   207-967-4454
Captain Jefferds Inn   Box 691, Kennebunkport 04046   207-967-2311
Chetwynd House Inn   P.O. Box 130, Kennebunkport 04046   207-967-2235
English Meadows Inn   RR 3, Box 135, Kennebunkport 04046   207-967-5766

English Robin   R1 Box 194, Kennebunkport 04046   207-967-3505
Farm House   RR 1, Box 656, Kennebunkport 04046   207-967-4169
Flakeyard Farm   RFD 2, Kennebunkport 04046   207-967-5965
Kilburn House   P.O. Box 1309, Kennebunkport 04046   207-967-4762
Lake Brook Guest House   RR 3, Box 218, Kennebunkport 04046   207-967-4069
Ocean View   72 Beach Ave., Kennebunkport 04043   207-967-2750
Old Fort Inn   P.O. Box M, Kennebunkport 04046   207-967-5353
Schooners Inn & Restaurant   P.O. Box 1121, Kennebunkport 04046   207-967-5333
Seaside Inn   Gooch's Beach, Kennebunkport 04046   207-967-4461
Tides Inn By-The-Sea   737 Goose Rocks Beach, Kennebunkport 04046   207-967-3757
Village Cove Inn   P.O. Box 650, Kennebunkport 04046   207-967-3993
Country Cupboard   RFD 1, Box 1270, Kingfield 04947   207-265-2193
Herbert Inn   P.O. Box 67, Kingfield 04947   207-265-2000
Three Stanley Avenue   P.O. Box 169, Kingfield 04947   207-265-5541
Winter's Inn   P.O. Box 44, Kingfield 04947   207-265-5421
Harbour Watch B&B   R.F.D. 1 Box 42, Kittery Point 03905   207-439-3242
Whaleback Inn B&B   Box 162 Pepperrell Rd., Kittery Point 03905   207-439-9560
Green Woods   R.F.D. No. 2, Lincolnvile 04849   207-338-3187
Cedarholm Cottages   Star Route, Lincolnville 04849   207-236-3886
Longville   P.O. Box 75, Rt. 1, Lincolnville 04849   207-236-3785
Red House   HC 60 Box 540, Lincolnville 04849   207-236-4621
Sign of the Owl   Rt. 1 Box 85, Lincolnville 04849   207-338-4669
Youngtown Inn   Rt. 52, Lincolnville 04849   207-763-3003
Old Tavern Inn   P.O. Box 445, Litchfield 04350   207-268-4965
Hugel Haus B&B   55 Main St., Lubec 04652   207-733-4965
Overview (The)   RD 2, Box 106, Lubec 04652   207-733-2005
Clark Perry House   59 Court St., Machias 04654   207-255-8458
Monhegan House   Monhegan 04852   207-594-7983
Island Inn   On the Harbor, Monhegan Island 04852   207-596-0371
Shining Sails Inc.   Box 344, Monhegan Island 04852   207-596-0041
Feather Bed Inn   Box 65, Mt. Vernon 04352   207-293-2020
Charmwoods   Naples 04055   207-693-6798
Songo B&B   Songon Locks Road, Naples 04055   207-693-3960
Bradley Inn   361 Pemaquid Pt., New Harbor 04554   207-677-2105
Southside-by the Harbor   Southside Rd.,Rt. 1, New Harbor 04554   207-677-2991
Elfinhill   P.O. Box 497, Newcastle 04553   207-563-1886
Glidden House   RR 1 Box 740, Newcastle 04553   207-563-1859
Markert House   P.O. Box 224 Glidden, Newcastle 04553   207-563-1309
Lake Sebasticook B&B   8 Sebasticook Ave., Newport 04953   207-368-5507
Oliver Farm Inn   Box 136 Old Rt. 1, Nobleboro 04555   207-563-1527
Norridgewock Colonial Inn   Upper Main St.,Rt. 2 & 20, Norridgewock 04957
   207-634-3470
Channelridge Farm   358 Cross Pt. Rd., North Edgecomb 04556   207-882-7539
Sebago Lake Lodge   White Bridge Rd., North Windham 04062   207-892-2698
Grey Rock Inn   Northeast Harbor 04662   217-276-9360
Harbourside Inn   Northeast Harbor 04662   207-276-3272
Pressey House-1850   85 Summer St., Oakland 04963   207-465-3500
Admiral's Inn   70 S. Main St., Ogunquit 03907   207-646-7093
Admiral's Loft   97 Main St., Ogunquit 03907   207-646-5496
Berwick   Box 261, Ogunquit 03907   207-646-4062
Blue Shutters   6 Beachmere Pl., Ogunquit 03907   207-646-2163
Blue Water Inn   Beach St., Ogunquit 03907   207-646-5559
Capt. Lorenz Perkins House   P.O. Box 2130, N Main, Ogunquit 03907   207-646-7825
Channing Hall   3 Pine Hill Rd., Ogunquit 03907   207-646-5222
Clipper Ship Guest House   46 N. Main St., Ogunquit 03907   207-646-9735
Hillcrest Inn Resort   Shore Road, Ogunquit 03907   207-646-7776

Inn at 77 Shore Road   77 Shore Rd., Ogunquit 03907   207-646-2933
Juniper Hill Inn   Route 1 North, Ogunquit 03907   207-646-4501
Leisure Inn   19 School St., Ogunquit 03907   207-646-2737
Lemon Tree Inn   50 Shore Rd., Ogunquit 03907   207-646-7070
Marimor Motor Inn   66 Shore Rd., Ogunquit 03907   207-646-7397
Ogunquit House   P.O. Box 1883, Ogunquit 03907   207-646-2967
Old Village Inn   30 Main St., Ogunquit 03907   207-646-7088
Seafair Inn   Box 1221, Ogunquit 03907   207-646-2181
Strauss Haus   Shore Road, Ogunquit 03907   207-646-7756
Terrace By the Sea   11 Wharf Lane, Ogunquit 03907   207-646-3232
Yardarm Village Inn   P.O. Box 773 130 Shore Rd, Ogunquit 03907   207-646-7006
Yellow Monkey Guest House   44 Main St., Ogunquit 03907   207-646-9056
Claibern's B&B   P.O. Box B, Oxford, Otisfield 04270   207-539-2352
Moonshell Inn   Island Ave., Peaks Island 04081   207-766-2331
Copper Light B&B   Box 67, Port Clyde 04855   207-372-8510
Ocean House   Box 66, Port Clyde 04855   207-372-6691
Carleton Gardens   43 Carleton St., Portland 04102   207-772-3458
Inn at Parkspring   135 Spring St., Portland 04101   207-774-1059
Davis Lodge   Rt. 4, Rangeley 04970   207-864-5569
Farmhouse Inn   P.O. Box 496, Rangeley 04970   207-864-5805
Northern Pines Health Rsrt   Raymond 04071   207-655-7624
Old Granite Inn   546 Main St., Rockland 04841   207-594-7901
Rosemary Cottage   Russell Avenue, Rockport 04856   207-236-3513
Sign of the Unicorn House   P.O. Box 99, Rockport 04856   207-236-4042
Allen's Inn   279 Main St., Sanford 04073   207-324-2160
Oakland House   Herricks Road, Sargentville 04673   207-359-8521
Higgins Beach Inn   Scarborough 04074   207-883-6684
Carriage House Inn   P.O. Box 238, Searsport 04974   207-548-2289
Rock Gardens Inn   Sebasco Estates 04565   207-389-1339
Sebasco Lodge   Sebasco Estates 04565   207-389-1161
Brick Farm B&B   RFD 1, Skowhegan 04976   207-474-3949
Breezemere Farm Inn   P.O. Box 290, South Brooksville 04617   207-326-8628
Buck's Harbor Inn   P.O. Box 268, South Brooksville 04617   207-326-8660
Migis Lodge   Route 302, South Casco 04077   207-655-4524
Thomas Inn & Playhouse   P.O. Box 128, South Casco 04077   207-655-7728
Alfred M. Senter B&B   Box 830, South Harpswell 04079   207-833-2874
Senter B&B   Route 123, South Harpswell 04079   207-833-2874
Weskeag Inn   Rt. 73, P.O. Box 213, South Thomaston 04858   207-596-6676
Claremont   Southwest Harbor 04679   207-244-5036
Harbor Lights Home   Rt. 102, Southwest Harbor 04679   207-244-3835
Widow's Walk   Box 150, Stratton 04982   207-246-6901
Sullivan Harbor Farm   Route 1, Sullivan 04682   207-422-3591
Time & Tide B&B   RR 1 Box 275B, Surry 04684   207-667-3382
East Wind Inn/Meeting Hse   P.O. Box 149, Tenants Harbor 04860   207-372-6366
Mill Pond House   Box 640, Tenants Harbor 04860   207-372-6209
Crab Apple Acres Inn   Rt. 201, The Forks 04985   207-663-2218
Bedside Manor Guest House   HCR 35 Box 100, Thomaston 04861   207-354-8862
Cap'n Frost's B&B   241 W. Main St., Thomaston 04861   207-354-8217
Gracie's B&B   52 Main St., Thomaston 04861   207-354-2326
River House B&B   HCR 35, Box 119, Thomaston 04861   207-354-8936
Middaugh B&B   36 Elm St., Topsham 04086   207-725-2562
Shepard Hill B&B   P.O. Box 338, Union 04862   207-785-4121
Fox Island Inn   P.O. Box 421, Vinalhaven 04863   207-863-2122
Le Vatout   Route 32, Box 375, Waldoboro 04572   207-832-4552
Letteney Farm Vacations   RFD 2, Box 166A, Waldoboro 04572   207-832-5143

Medomak House   P.O. Box 663 Friendship, Waldoboro 04572   207-832-4971
Roaring Lion (The)   Main St., P.O. Box 756, Waldoboro 04572   207-832-4038
Tide Watch Inn   Pine St. P.O. Box 94, Waldoboro 04572   207-832-4987
Bittersweet Inn   HCR 64, Box 013, Walpole 04573   207-563-5552
Windward Farm   Young's Hill Rd., Washington 04574   207-845-2830
Artemus Ward House   Waterford 04088   207-583-4106
Lake House   Rts. 35 & 37, Waterford 04088   207-583-4182
Kawanhee Inn   Route 142, Webb Lake, Weld 04285   207-585-2243
Weld Inn   Box 8, Weld 04285   207-585-2429
Grey Gull Inn   321 Webhannet Dr., Wells 04090   207-646-7501
The Haven   RR 4 Box 2270, Wells 04090   207-646-4194
Purple Sandpiper House   RR #3 Box 226, Wells 04090   207-646-7990
Bakke B&B   RD 1, Box 505A,Foster Pt, West Bath 04530   207-442-7185
New Meadows Inn   Bath Rd., West Bath 04530   207-443-3921
King's Inn   P.O. Box 92, West Bethel 04286   207-836-3375
Vicarage East Ltd   Box 368A, West Harpswell 04079   207-833-5480
Harbor Hill Inn   Box 280, Winter Harbor 04693   203-963-8872
Stacked Arms B&B   RFD 2 Box 146, Wiscasset 04578   207-882-5436
Homewood Inn   P.O. Box 196, Yarmouth 04096   207-846-3351
Scotland Bridge Inn   P.O. Box 521, York 03909   207-363-4432
Summer Place   RFD 1 Box 196, York 03909   207-363-5233
Wild Rose of York   78 Long Sands Road, York 03909   207-363-2532
Bennetts   3 Broadway, York Beach 03910   207-363-5302
Edwards Harbourside Inn   Stage Neck Road, York Beach 03910   207-363-3037
Jo-Mar B&B on the Ocean   P.O. Box 838, York Beach 03910   207-363-4826
Lighthouse Inn   Box 249, Nubble Road, York Beach 03910   207-363-6072
Lilac Inn   Box 1325, 3 Ridge Rd., York Beach 03910   207-363-3930
Nautilus B&B   7 Willow Ave., Box 916, York Beach 03910   207-363-6496
Inn at Harmon Park   York St. & Harmon, York Harbor 03911   207-363-2031

Maryland

ANNAPOLIS ───────────────────────────────────

Gibson's Lodgings	$$ B&B	Continental plus
110 Prince George St., 21401	14 rooms	Piano, conference fac.
301-268-5555	C-ltd/S-yes/P-no/H-no	daily maid service
Holly Perdue		parking
All year		

Located in historic district, near City Docks, adjacent to U.S. Naval Academy. Antique furnishings throughout. Offstreet parking. Daily maid service.

Jonah Williams Inn	$$ B&B	Continental plus
101 Severn Ave., 21403	4 rooms, 1 pb	Snacks, comp. wine
301-269-6020	•	Sitting room
Dorothy M. Robbins	C-no/S-no/P-no/H-no	library
All year	Ger. Fr. Ital. Span.	

Pleasant Laura Ashley decor newly and brightly renovated historic inn with plaque (1830). Parking; water view; close to city dock; water taxi service available to anywhere.

The Haslam-Fort House, Savannah, GA

ANNAPOLIS

Prince George Inn B&B	$$$ B&B	Continental plus
232 Prince George St., 21401	4 rooms	Refrigerator/ice/mix
301-263-6418	•	Parlor
Bill & Norma Grovermann	C-ltd/S-ltd/P-no/H-no	screened porch
All year		

A 100-year-old Victorian brick townhouse lovingly furnished with period antiques. Located in Historic District near Naval Academy and City Dock.

Shaw's Fancy B&B	$$ B&B	Continental plus
161 Green St., 21401	3 rooms, 1 pb	Afternoon wine & cheese
301-268-9750	No credit cards	Hot tubs
Jack House, Lilith Ren	C-10+/S-ltd/P-no/H-no	
All year		

Whimsical Victorian in the heart of historic Annapolis. Walk to naval academy, shops, restaurants. Gourmet breakfast in our lovely garden, or sherry on the porch swing.

William Page B&B Inn	$$ B&B	Continental plus
8 Martin St., 21401	5 rooms, 3 pb	Afternoon tea, snacks
301-626-1506	•	Wet bar set-up
Robert Zuchelli, Greg Page	C-no/S-no/P-no/H-no	Sitting room
All year		tennis and pool nearby

Circa 1908, furnished in genuine antiques and period reproductions. Featuring suite with private bath and whirlpool. Free off-street parking.

BALTIMORE ——————————————————————————————

Admiral Fell Inn
888 S. Broadway, 21231
301-522-7377/800-292-4667
Jim Widman
All year

$$$ B&B
37 rooms, 37 pb
Visa, MC, AmEx •
C-yes/S-yes/P-no/H-yes

Continental breakfast
Lunch, dinner, bar
Entertainment, hot tub
piano, cruises, parking
free van service

Beautiful urban inn located on the water in historic Fells Point section of Baltimore. Many activities within easy reach. Traditional Southern hospitality. Jacuzzis in 3 rooms.

Betsy's Bed & Breakfast
1428 Park Avenue, 21217
301-383-1274
Betsy Grater
All year

$$ B&B
3 rooms, 1 pb
Visa, MC •
C-yes/S-ltd/P-no/H-no

Continental plus
Comp. wine
Hot tub (by reservation)
piano, TV, bicycles
swim club privileges

This charming 100-year-old townhouse has a hallway floor laid in alternating oak and walnut strips, 6 carved marble fireplaces and handsome brass rubbings.

Celie's Waterfront B&B
P.O. Box 38241, 21231
1714 Thames St.
301-522-2323
Celie Ives
All year

$$$ B&B
7 rooms, 7 pb
Visa, MC, AmEx •
C-10+/S-no/P-no/H-yes

Continental plus
Kitchenettes
Private garden, A/C
bedroom fireplaces
whirlpool, parking

New antique-filled urban inn overlooking the water in maritime community of Fells Point. Minutes to Harbor Place by antique trolley or water taxi. Spectacular roof deck views.

Eagles Mere B&B
102 E. Montgomery, 21230
301-332-1618
Albert Strubinger
All year

$$ B&B
4 rooms
C-ltd/S-ltd/P-no/H-no

Continental plus
2 living rooms
library

Restored 1794 period-furnished home overlooking Inner Harbor. Seasonal fruit, bakery items, beverage. Cheerful tourist help, free parking, limo service.

Harborview Bed & Breakfast
112 E. Montgomery St., 21230
301-528-8692
Martin J. Mulligan
All year

$$$ B&B
3 rooms, 2 pb
Visa, MC •
C-yes/S-yes/P-no/H-no

Continental breakfast
Refrigerator
Sitting room
fireplaces in bedrooms

Circa 1796 National Historic home on Registry. Located less than a quarter-block to Baltimore's Inner Harbor. Home features magnificent harbor views and city light views.

Shirley Madison Inn
205 W. Madison St., 21201
301-728-6550
Herman Lantz
All year

$$ B&B
27 rooms, 27 pb
Visa, MC, AmEx, DC •
C-yes/S-yes/P-no/H-no

Continental breakfast
Comp. evening sherry
Tea, sitting room
Library
courtyard/backyard

Elegant 1880 Victorian mansion furnished with Victorian & Edwardian antiques. Short walk to Inner Harbor, cultural corridor, financial district. Charming & hospitable.

BALTIMORE ───────────────────────────────

Society Hill Hotel
58 W. Biddle St., 21201
301-837-3630
Kate C. Hopkins
All year

$$$ B&B
15 rooms, 15 pb
Visa, MC, AmEx •
C-yes/S-yes/P-ltd/H-no

Continental breakfast
Restaurant
Pianist
van service throughout
Baltimore City

Baltimore's first "urban inn." All guest rooms decorated with antiques, Victorian furniture. Fresh flowers, homemade candies.

Society Hill-Gov't House
1125 North Calvert St., 21202
301-752-7722
Peggy Bannester
All year

$$$ B&B
18 rooms, 18 pb
•
C-yes/S-yes/P-ltd/H-no

Continental breakfast
Van service throughout
Baltimore City

Lovely views from tastefully decorated Victorian rooms. Guests are pampered with European breakfast trays and excellent service.

Society Hill-Thompkins
404 St. Paul St., 21218
301-235-8600
Jo-Ann Fritz, Toni Pietrowitz
All year

$$$ B&B
26 rooms, 26 pb
•
C-yes/S-yes/P-ltd/H-no

Continental breakfast
Fruit, newspaper
Van service throughout
Baltimore
four meeting rooms

Delightful sunlit guest rooms lavished with art and antiques for the discerning traveler seeking an alternative to conventional lodging.

Twin Gates Bed & Breakfast
308 Morris Ave., 21093
Lutherville
301-252-3131/800-635-0370
Gwen & Bob Vaughan
All year

$$$ B&B
4 rooms, 2 pb
•
C-no/S-no/P-no/H-no

Full gourmet breakfast
Afternoon refreshments
Free winery tours

Elegant Victorian mansion in serene northern suburb. Twenty minutes to convention center, Harbor Place and National Aquarium. Excellent seafood restaurants, free winery tours.

BERLIN ───────────────────────────────

Atlantic Hotel Inn & Rest.
2 N. Main St., 21811
301-641-0189
Stephen T. Jacques
All year

$$ B&B
16 rooms, 16 pb
Visa, MC •
C-yes/S-yes/H-yes

Continental plus
Afternoon tea, dinner
Restaurant, bar service
Sitting room, library
lounge, parlor

Restored Victorian hotel, circa 1895, centrally located in historic Berlin. 16 bedrooms with antique furnishings, private baths and air-conditioning. Fine dining.

BUCKEYSTOWN ───────────────────────────

Inn at Buckeystown
3521 Buckeystown Pike, 21717
301-874-5755
Daniel R. Pelz
All year

$$$ MAP
10 rooms, 1 pb
Visa, MC •
C-no/S-ltd/P-no/H-no

Full breakfast
Dinner, comp. wine
Porch with rockers
antique & art collection
hot tub in cottage, A/C

Elegant mansion and historic church converted to cottage in Nationally Registered Historic Village. Victorian charm, antiques, on Monocacy River, great food.

CAMBRIDGE

Sarke Plantation B&B Inn
6033 Todd Point Rd., 21613
301-228-7020
Genevieve Finley
All year

$$ B&B
5 rooms, 3 pb
AmEx
C-ltd/S-yes/P-ltd/H-no

Continental breakfast
Fireplaces, stereo
swimming pool
sitting room, piano
pool table

Spacious & scenic country, waterfowl abundant on waterfront. Breakfast in simulated "sidewalk cafe" with paintings by local artists. Summer house for cards and games.

CHESTERTOWN

White Swan Tavern
231 High St., 21620
301-778-2300
Mary S. Maisel
All year

$$$ B&B
5 rooms, 5 pb
C-yes/S-yes/P-no/H-ltd

Continental breakfast
Afternoon tea, wine
Bicycles
sitting room
terrace

18th-century inn nestled in Maryland's historic eastern shore. Genuine antiques, homemade continental breakfast, tea, complimentary wine & fruit.

DENTON

Sophie Kerr House
Route 3, Box 7-B, 21629
Kerr & Fifth Aves.
301-479-3421
John & Thelma Lyons
All year

$ B&B
5 rooms
C-yes/S-yes/P-yes/H-no

Full breakfast
Afternoon tea, snacks
Comp. wine
Sitting room
swimming pool

Childhood home of Sophie Kerr, Eastern Shore writer. Centrally located on Maryland's Eastern Shore. Four star country French restaurant nearby.

EASTON

Hynson Tourist Home
804 Dover Rd., 21601
301-822-2777
Nellie R. Hynson
All year

$ EP
6 rooms, 2 pb
C-yes/S-ltd/P-ltd/H-no

Restaurants nearby
Piano

Located on the Eastern Shore, Easton is the site of the oldest Quaker Meeting House. Convenient to Washington, D.C., Annapolis and Baltimore. Your hostess welcomes you.

FREDERICK

Spring Bank
7945 Worman's Mill Rd., 21701
301-694-0440
Ray & Beverly Compton
All year

$$ B&B
6 rooms, 1 pb
AmEx
C-no/S-no/P-no/H-no

Continental plus
Comp. sherry
Double parlors
library
10 acres for roaming

On National Register; near Baltimore, Washington DC & Civil War battlefields. 2 mi. from Frederick with its colonial Victorian architecture & exceptional dining.

HAGERSTOWN

Lewrene Farm B&B
RD3, Box 150, 21740
Downsville Pike
301-582-1735
Lewis & Irene Lehman
All year

$ B&B
6 rooms, 3 pb
C-yes/S-no/P-no/H-no
Spanish, some German

Full breakfast
Snacks, sitting room
Piano, whirlpool tub
large farm, woodland
conference facility

Quiet farm, cozy colonial home with fireplace, antiques, candlelight breakfasts, Historic Antietam Battlefield, Harper's Ferry, outlets, restaurants, I-81 & I-70 nearby.

HAVRE DE GRACE

Vandiver Inn
301 S. Union Ave., 21078
301-939-5200
Charles T. Rothwell
All year

$$ B&B / $$$ MAP
10 rooms, 10 pb
Visa, MC, AmEx •
C-no/S-yes/P-no/H-no

Full breakfast
Sitting room, TV
Melodian, porches
bicycles, tennis
Chesapeake Bay cruises

Large detached Queen Anne cottage in historic town of Havre de Grace, nestled by the Chesapeake Bay. Complimentary country breakfast.

MCDANIEL

Wades Point Inn On The Bay
P.O. Box 130, 21647
Wades Point Rd.
301-745-2500
Betsy & John Feiler
March—December

$$ B&B
3 rooms, 3 pb
C-yes

Continental plus
Sitting room
Screened porches
fishing & crabbing dock

Wades Point Inn On The Bay is for those seeking the splendor of the country and the serenity of the Bay. Bird watching on 120 acres. Sightseeing nearby in quaint historic towns.

NEW MARKET

National Pike Inn
P.O. Box 299, 21774
9 W. Main St.
301-865-5055
Tom & Terry Rimel
All year

$$ B&B
5 rooms, 2 pb
Visa, MC
C-5+/S-ltd/P-no/H-no

Continental plus
Sitting room
Landscaped courtyard
tennis & golf nearby
shopping

Enjoy historic New Market, antique capital of Maryland. Federal town surrounded by rural farmland. One hour from Washington and Baltimore.

Strawberry Inn
P.O. Box 237, 21774
17 Main St.
301-865-3318
Jane & Ed Rossig
All year

$$ B&B
5 rooms, 5 pb
C-8+/S-yes/P-no/H-ltd

Continental plus
Sitting room, A/C
tennis nearby
small conference fac.

A country inn where the proprietor is host to his guests. A place of gracious hospitality, peace and quiet. Breakfast served to your room at your requested time.

OAKLAND

Red Run Inn
Rt. 5, Box 268, 21550
301-387-6606
Ruth M. Umbel
All year

$$ B&B
5 rooms, 5 pb
Visa, MC, AmEx •
C-yes/S-yes/P-no/H-no

Continental plus
Lunch, dinner, bar
Sitting room
tennis, entertainment
swimming pool

Tourist area, fourseason resort: skiing, water sports, fall foliage, fishing. The old barn dates back to the 1940s.

OLNEY

Thoroughbred B&B
16410 Batchellors Fores, 20832
301-774-7649
Helen Polinger
All year

$$ B&B
5 rooms, 3 pb
Visa, MC •
C-12+/S-no/P-no/H-ltd

Full breakfast
Sitting room, library
hot tubs, pool table
swimming pool
tennis courts nearby

Champion racehorses have been bred & raised here. 175 acres of rolling hills, only 12 miles from Washington D.C. Metro Transportation only 6 miles. Five lovely guest rooms.

OXFORD ──────────────────────────────

1876 House	$$$ B&B	Continental plus
P.O. Box 658, 21654	3 rooms, 1 pb	Comp. wine
110 N. Morris St.	C-14+/S-yes/P-no/H-no	Sitting room
301-226-5496		bicycles, transportation
Eleanor & Jerry Clark		to/from local marinas
Exc. Dec. 24—Jan. 1		

A relaxing and restful atmosphere in an elegantly restored 19th-century home. Wide planked floors, oriental rugs, 10' ceilings, Queen Anne reproduction furnishings.

SAINT MICHAELS ──────────────────────────────

Inn at Perry Cabin	$$$ B&B	Continental plus
21663	6 rooms, 6 pb	Lunch, dinner
301-745-5178	Visa, MC, AmEx	Bicycles
Ron Thomas	C-yes/S-yes/P-no/H-no	entertainment
All year		sitting room, piano

On the scenic Miles River in historic St. Michaels. Accessible to hunting, sailing, golfing and shopping. Seafood and wildlife abound.

Kemp House Inn	$$ B&B	Continental breakfast
412 S. Talbot St., 21663	7 rooms, 3 pb	Private cottage avail.
P.O. Box 638	Visa, MC	bicycles
301-745-2243	C-yes/S-yes/P-no/H-no	queen-sized beds
Stephen & Diane Cooper		
All year		

1805 Georgian house with four-poster beds and working fireplaces in historic eastern shore village; close to restaurants, museums, harbor.

Parsonage Inn	$$ B&B	Continental plus
210 N. Talbot, 21663	7 rooms, 7 pb	Comp. sherry, cookies
301-745-5519	Visa, MC •	Catered lunch for groups
Betty & Chuck Oler	C-yes/S-no/H-yes	aftn. tea (wint), parlor
All year		Library, bicycles

Unique brick Victorian, part of historic district. Walking distance to maritime museums, shops, restaurants. Working fireplaces and Laura Ashley linens.

SHARPSBURG ──────────────────────────────

Inn at Antietam	$$ B&B	Continental plus
P.O. Box 119, 21782	5 rooms, 5 pb	Afternoon tea
220 E. Main St.	AmEx •	Sitting room
301-432-6601	C-12+/S-ltd/P-no/H-no	piano
Betty Fairbourn		bicycles
Exc. Dec. 20—Jan. 2		

Lovely 1908 Victorian fully restored and furnished in antiques, on Antietam Battlefield in Civil War historic area. Special hospitality.

Piper House B&B Inn	$ B&B	Continental plus
Antietam Battlefield, 21782	4 rooms, 4 pb	Sitting room
301-797-1862	Visa, MC •	air conditioning
Douglass & Paula Reed	C-10+	
All year		

Located near Bloody Lane, this fully restored farmhouse once served as headquarters during the Civil War battle of Antietam. Period antiques; discreetly modernized; A/C.

SNOW HILL

Snow Hill Inn
104 E. Market St., 21863
301-632-2102
Terri & Robb Young
All year

$$ B&B
7 rooms, 2 pb
Visa, MC •
C-no/S-yes/P-no/H-no

Continental plus
Lunch, dinner
Restaurant, bar
Tennis nearby
pool nearby

Historic residence (circa 1790), converted into a lovely country inn and restaurant serving excellent fare. Golf and other activities nearby.

SOLOMONS ISLAND

Davis House
P.O. Box 759, 20688
Charles & Maltby Sts.
301-326-4811
Jack & Runa Howley
All year

$$ B&B
6 rooms
C-12+/S-ltd/P-no/H-no
Spanish, Swedish, French

Full breakfast
Afternoon tea
Comp. wine
Sitting room
library

Charming Victorian, furnished comfortably and stylishly, in front of the harbor, achieving a quality as the best of European inns. Golf, tennis, wind surfing, sailing nearby.

TANEYTOWN

Glenburn
3515 Runnymede Rd., 21787
301-751-1187
Elizabeth & Robert Neal
All year

$$$ B&B
3 rooms, 2 pb
C-yes/S-ltd/P-no/H-no

Full breakfast
Refrigerator, kitchen
2 bdr. cottage w/kitchen
swimming pool, porches
golf, A/C

Georgian house with Victorian addition, antique furnishings, featured in Maryland House & Garden Pilgrimage. Historic rural area close to Gettysburg.

UNIONTOWN

The Newel Post
3428 Uniontown Rd., 21157
301-775-2655
Roger & Janet Michael
All year

$$ B&B
4 rooms, 2 pb
•
French

Continental plus
Afternoon tea
comp. wine
Sitting room, bicycles
picnics in formal garden

An elegant Victorian in a historic tree-lined village; convenient to Baltimore, Washington, D.C. and Gettysburg. Enjoy picnicking in our country garden.

VIENNA

Tavern House
P.O. Box 98, 21869
111 Water St.
301-376-3347
Harvey & Elise Aitergott
All year

$$ B&B
3 rooms
Visa, MC •
C-12+/S-yes
Spanish, German

Full breakfast
Aftn. tea, comp. wine
Sitting room
tennis courts nearby

Restored Colonial tavern on Nanticoke River and Maryland's "Eastern Shore," the setting for Chesapeake. *Great for bicycling and bird-watching.*

More Inns...

Annapolis B&B   235 Prince George Sr., Annapolis 21401   301-269-0669
Bay View B&B   2654 Ogleton Road, Annapolis 21403   301-268-0781
Charles Inn   74 Charles St., Annapolis 21401   301-268-1451
Heart of Annapolis B&B   185 Duke of Gloucester, Annapolis 21404   301-267-2309
Maryland Inn   Church Circle, Annapolis 21401   800-638-8902
Reynolds Tavern   4 Church Cr., Annapolis 21401   800-638-8902
Robert Johnson House   23 State Cir., Annapolis 21401   800-638-8902

State House Inn   15 State Cir., Annapolis 21401   800-638-8902
Bolton Hill B&B   1534 Bolton St., Baltimore 21217   301-669-5356
Mulberry House   111 W. Mulberry St., Baltimore 21201   301-576-0111
Winslow Home   8217 Caraway St., Cabin John 20818   301-229-4654
Glasgow Inn B&B   1500 Hambrooks Blvd., Cambridge 21613   301-228-0575
Inwood Guest House   Box 378, Rt. 1, Cascade 21719   301-241-3467
Flyway Lodge   Rt. 1, Box 660, US Rt. 21, Chestertown 21620   301-778-5557
Great Oak Manor   Rt. 2 Box 766, Chestertown 21620   301-778-5796
Hill's Inn   114 Washington Ave., Chestertown 21620   301-778-INNS
Imperial Hotel   208 High St., Chestertown 21620   301-778-5000
Inn at Mitchell House   Box 329, R.D. 2, Chestertown 21620   301-778-6500
Radcliffe Cross   Rt. 3, Box 360, Chestertown 21620   301-778-5540
Tidewater Inn   Dover & Harrison St., Easton 21601   301-822-1300
Hayland Farm   5000 Sheppard Ln., Ellicott City 21043   301-531-5593
Trailside Country Inn   US 40, Flintstone 21530   301-478-2032
Tran Crossing   121 E. Patrick St., Frederick 21701   301-663-8449
Turning Point Inn   3406 Urbana Pike, Frederick 21701   301-874-2421
Freeland Farm   21616 Middletown Rd., Freeland 21053   301-357-5364
Kitty Knight House   Rt. 213, Georgetown 21930   301-648-5777
Nicholl's House   19217 Fox Chapel Dr., Germantown 90874
Beaver Creek House   Route 9, Box 330, Hagerstown 21740   301-797-4764
Country Inn   P.O. Box 397, McHenry 21541   301-387-6694
Castle   P.O. Box 578, Rt. 36, Mt. Savage 21545   301-759-5946
Westlawn Inn   7th St. and Chesapea, North Beach 20714   301-855-8410
Elmwood c. 1770 B&B   Locust Pt, P.O. Box 220, Princess Anne 21853   301-651-1066
Washington Hotel & Inn   Somerset Ave., Princess Anne 21853   301-651-2525
Strawberry Factory   Rt. 20, Gratitude, Rock Hall 21661   301-639-7468
Capt. & Ms. J's Guest House   P.O. Box 676, Solomons 20688   301-326-3334
Matoaka Cottages   P.O. Box 124, St. Leonard 20685   301-586-0269
Hambleton Inn   202 Cherry St., Box 299, St. Michaels 21663   301-245-3350
Two Swan Inn   P.O. Box 727, St. Michaels 21663   301-745-2929
Victoriana Inn   205 Cherry St., St. Michaels 21663   301-745-3368
Kent Manor Inn   Kent Island, Box 815, Stevensville 21666   301-643-5757
Harrison's Country Inn   P.O. Box 310, Tilghman 21671   301-886-2123
Governor's Ordinary   P.O. Box 156, Vienna 21869   301-376-3530
Nanticoke Manor House   P.O. Box 248, Vienna 21869   301-376-3530
Judge Thomas House 1893   195 Willis St., Westminster 21157   301-876-6686
Winchester Country Inn   430 So. Bishop St., Westminster 21157   301-876-7373
Rosebud Inn   4 N. Main St., Woodsboro 21798   301-845-2221

Massachusetts

ASHFIELD ───────────────────────────────

Ashfield Inn	$$$ B&B	Continental plus (wkdys)
P.O. Box 129, Main St., 01330	3 rooms	Full breakfast (wkends)
413-628-4571	Visa, MC, AmEx •	Afternoon tea
Scott & Stacey Alessi	C-yes/S-ltd	Sitting room, library
All year		recreational lake

Gracious Georgian mansion situated on nine acres overlooking lake; perfect year-round country hideaway; nearby swimming, golfing, tennis, skiing, antique shopping, etc . . .

AUBURN ───────────────────────────────

Capt. Samuel Eddy House	$$ B&B	Full breakfast
609 Oxford St. S., 01501	5 rooms, 5 pb	Dinner by reservation
508-832-5282/508-832-3149	Visa, MC •	Restaurant, aftn. tea
Jack & Carilyn O'Toole	C-yes/S-ltd/P-no/H-no	Sitting rm, country shop
All year		gardens, swimming pool

1765 Homestead, restored to its original era. Antiques, beehive fireplaces, queen canopies, bed chambers with private baths. Herb gardens & shop. Close to Boston & Sturbridge.

BARNSTABLE ───────────────────────────────

Ashley Manor	$$$ B&B	Full breakfast
P.O. Box 856, 02630	6 rooms, 6 pb	Comp. wine, sherry, port
3660 Main St. (Route 6A)	Visa, MC, AmEx •	Flowers, candy, fruit
805-362-8044	C-no/S-ask/P-no/H-no	Sitting room
Fay & Donald Bain		bicycles, croquet
All year		

1699 mansion in the historic district; rooms and suites have antiques, fireplaces and private baths; walk to beach, village and harbor. Fresh flowers and candy in rooms.

Beechwood Inn	$$$ B&B	Full gourmet breakfast
2839 Main St., 02630	6 rooms, 6 pb	Afternoon tea
508-362-6618	Visa, MC, AmEx	Comp. wine, Perrier
Anne & Bob Livermore	C-12+/S-ltd/P-no/H-no	Sitting room
All year		refrigerator

A romantic Victorian inn along the historic "Old King's Way." Spacious period-furnished guest rooms offer fireplaces and views of Cape Cod Bay. Walk to shops, beaches.

Cobb's Cove	$$$ B&B	Full breakfast
P.O. Box 208, 02630	6 rooms, 6 pb	Dinner, comp. wine
Powder Hill Rd.	•	Whirlpool tubs, robes
508-362-9356	C-no/S-ltd/P-no/H-no	toiletries, piano
Evelyn Chester, Henri Jean	French	sitting room, library
Closed Jan. & Feb.		

Secluded get away inn for couples. Located on Cape Cod's unspoiled North Shore overlooking Cape Cod Bay.

BARNSTABLE

Thomas Huckins House
P.O. Box 515, 02630
2701 Main St., Route 6A
508-362-6379
Eleanor Eddy
All year

$$ B&B
3 rooms, 3 pb
Visa, MC
C-6+/S-yes/P-no/H-no

Full breakfast
Sitting room
fireplaces

B&B in historic 1705 house on Cape Cod's picturesque northside. Fireplaces, antiques, canopy beds, privacy and charm. Walk to ocean and village.

BASS RIVER

Captain Isaiah's House
33 Pleasant St., 02664
508-394-1739
Alden & Marge Fallows
Late June—early Sept

$ B&B
8 rooms, 2 pb
C-5+/S-yes/P-no/H-no

Continental plus
Sitting room

Charming, restored old sea captain's house in historic Bass River area. Most rooms have fireplaces. Continental breakfast with homebaked breads, coffee cake.

BILLERICA

Billerica Bed & Breakfast
88 Rogers St., 01862
617-667-7317
Ted Barbour
All year

$$ EP
2 rooms, 2 pb
•
C-yes/S-yes/P-no/H-no

Lunch, dinner, snacks
Bar service
Library, sitting room
swimming pool

Quaint New England cape—charming decor—clean and quiet—convivial hosts—nice grounds with swimming pool—western suburbs of Boston near Rts. 3 & 495.

Haikuleana B&B Inn, Haiku, Maui, HI

BREWSTER

**Bramble Inn Restaurant
& Gallery**
Box 807, 02631
2019 Main St. Rt. 6A
508-896-7644
Ruth & Cliff Manchester
April—December

$$$ B&B
8 rooms, 8 pb
•
C-12+/S-yes/P-no/H-ltd

Full breakfast
Lunch, dinner
Sitting room
near beach, tennis

Romantic country inn in historic district of Cape Cod. Beach, tennis courts, and close to golf, fishing, and museums.

Captain Freeman Inn
15 Breakwater Rd., 02631
RR 4
508-896-7481
Barbara & John Mulkey
All year

$ B&B
10 rooms, 7 pb
Visa, MC, AmEx •
C-12+/S-no/P-no/H-no

Full breakfast
Afternoon tea
Sitting room
bicycles
swimming pool

A quiet, nonsmoking country inn in a charming old sea captain's mansion, with spacious rooms, canopy beds and romantic porch.

**Isaiah Clark House
& Rose Cottage**
1187 Main St., Rt. 6A, 02631
508-896-2223
C. Dicesare, R. Griffin
Mid-February—January 1

$$$ B&B
5 rooms, 5 pb
Visa, MC •
C-12+/S-ask/P-no/H-no
French, Italian

Full breakfast
Comp. tea
Library, sitting room
cable TV, records, tapes
bicycles

Charming 1780 captain's house set on five lush acres. Near the beach and all the Cape attractions. Warm New England hospitality.

Old Manse Inn
P.O. Box 839, 02631
1861 Main St.
508-896-3149
Sugar & Doug Manchester
March 1—December 31

$$$ B&B
9 rooms, 9 pb
Visa, MC, AmEx •
C-yes/S-yes/P-no/H-yes

Full breakfast
Gourmet dinner, bar
Sitting room, library
garden, patio, wine
air conditioned rooms

Enjoy the salt air from your room in this antique sea captain's home. Walk to Cape Cod's attractions. Dining by reservation; award-winning food.

Old Sea Pines Inn
2553 Main St., 02631
P.O. Box 1026
508-896-6114
Stephen & Michele Rowan
April 1—December 22

$ B&B
14 rooms, 9 pb
Visa, MC, DC, CB •
C-9+/S-yes/P-no/H-no
Italian, German

Full breakfast
Snacks, wine & beer
restaurant
Sitting room w/fireplace
parlor, deck

Newly redecorated turn-of-the-century mansion furnished with antiques. Near beaches, bicycle trails, quality restaurants and shops.

BROOKLINE

Beacon Inns
1087 & 1750 Beacon St., 02146
617-566-0088
Hy Gloth
All year

$ EP
25 rooms, 6 pb
Visa, MC
C-yes/S-yes/P-no/H-no

lobby fireplaces
Original woodwork

Large, comfortable furnished, sunny rooms provide pleasant accommodations at a surprisingly affordable price. Near subway line.

CHATHAM ———————————————————————————————

Bradford Inn & Motel	$$$ B&B	Full breakfast
P.O. Box 750, 02633	25 rooms, 25 pb	Snacks, bar service
26 Cross St.	Visa, MC, AmEx, Disc •	Sitting room, library
508-945-1030	C-8+ /S-yes	bicycles, tennis courts
William P. & Audrey E. Gray		heated swimming pool
All year		

Located off Main St., within Chatham's Historic District. Abundant amenities: fireplaces, 4-poster canopy beds, ac, refrigerator, cable TV. Rated Three Diamond by AAA.

Captains House of Chatham	$$$ B&B	Continental plus
369 Old Harbor Rd., 02633	14 rooms, 14 pb	Sitting room
508-945-0127	Visa, MC, AmEx	boat trips
David & Cathy Eakin	C-12+ /S-ltd/P-no/H-no	AAA 4-Diamond rating '87
Feb. 15—Dec. 1		

Antiques & Williamsburg wallpapers. Charming guest rooms have 4-poster beds, fireplaces. Private 2-acre estate of lawns and gardens. Quiet and elegant.

Chatham Town House Inn	$$$ B&B	Full gourmet breakfast
11 Library Lane, 02633	24 rooms, 24 pb	Scandinavian restaurant
508-945-2180	Major credit cards •	Liquor license
Russell & Svea Peterson	C-yes/S-ltd/P-no/H-no	Sitting room, cottages
Feb. 12—Dec. 7	Swedish, Spanish, German	international staff

Lodging and fine dining in an 1881 sea captain's mansion with that European touch. Fine dining; home-style breakfasts; Scandinavian hospitality. Cottages available.

Cranberry Inn at Chatham	$$$ B&B	Continental plus
359 Main St., 02633	14 rooms, 14 pb	Small Tap Room
508-945-9232	•	Phone and TV in rooms
Richard Morris, Peggy DeHan	C-12+ /S-ltd/P-no/H-no	individual A/C
March—mid-December		private baths

Conveniently located in the heart of Chatham's picturesque seaside village and historic district. Walk to beaches, shops, restaurants and Chatham's signature lighthouse.

Cyrus Kent House Inn	$$$ B&B	Continental plus
63 Cross St., 02633	8 rooms, 8 pb	Sitting room, fireplaces
508-945-9104	Visa, MC, AmEx •	porch, deck, antiques
Richard T. Morris	C-12+ /S-yes/P-no/H-no	ample parking, phones
March 15—December 15		art & antique gallery

A sea captain's house reborn in the heart of the quaint seaside village of Chatham.

CONCORD ———————————————————————————————

Hawthorne Inn	$$$ B&B	Continental plus
462 Lexington Rd., 01742	7 rooms, 7 pb	Comp. tea, wine
508-369-5610	•	Sitting room
Gregory Burch, Marilyn Mudry	C-yes/S-ltd/P-no/H-no	bicycles
All year		

On the "Battle Road" of 1775, furnished with antiques, quilts and artwork with the accent on New England comfort and charm.

COTUIT

Salty Dog Inn
451 Main St., 02635
508-428-5228
Jerry & Lynn Goldstein
All year

$ B&B
5 rooms, 1 pb
Visa, MC •
C-12+

Continental plus
Picnic tables
Parlor
bicycles
tennis nearby

Restored Victorian retaining the charm of turn-of-the-century homes. In the quiet seaside town of Cotuit, near the excitement of Hyannis and Falmouth and island boats.

CUMMINGTON

Cumworth Farm
RR 1, Box 110, 01026
Route 112
413-634-5529
Mary & Ed McColgan
All year

$$ B&B
6 rooms
C-yes/S-ltd

Full breakfast
Aftn. tea, snacks
Comp. wine
Sitting room
piano, bicycles

Big, 200-year-old farmhouse; sugarhouse on premises; sheep; berries—pick your own in season. Close to cross-country skiing, hiking trails. Quiet getaway.

Windfields Farm
RR 1, Box 170, 01026
Windsor Bush Rd.
413-684-3786
Carolyn & Arnold Westwood
Closed March & April

$$ B&B
2 rooms
C-12+/S-no/P-no/H-no

Full breakfast
Sitting room, piano
library
swimming pond

Secluded Berkshire Hills homestead. Equidistant to Tanglewood, Williamstown, Northampton. Hiking, skiing, swimming. Organic gardens, maple syrup, eggs, berries.

CUTTYHUNK

The Allen House Inn
P.O. Box 27, 02713
617-996-9292
Nina & Margo Solod
Memorial Day—Oct. 5

$$ B&B
15 rooms, 3 pb
Visa, MC
C-yes/S-no/P-no/H-no
French

Full breakfast off seas.
Lunch, dinner available
Sitting room, cottages
boat rental
fishing guides

A tiny island with quiet beaches. Enjoy fresh seafood and Atlantic breezes drifting through your open windows.

DENNIS

Isiah Hall B&B Inn
152 Whig St., 02638
508-385-9928
Marie & Dick Brophy
Mid-March—mid-November

$ B&B
11 rooms, 10 pb
AmEx, Visa, MC •
C-7+/S-ltd/P-no/H-no

Continental plus
Comp. tea
Library, gift shop
2 sitting rooms
innkeeping seminars

Enjoy our relaxing country ambience and hospitality in the heart of Cape Cod. Walk to beach, village, Playhouse and restaurants, from quiet residential neighborhood.

Soft Breezes Inn
158 Corporation Rd., 02638
508-385-5246
Lora J. Cobb
All year

$ B&B
6 rooms
Visa, MC •
C-yes/S-yes/P-ask/H-no

Continental plus
Sitting room
patio with gas grill

Located in historic district area with quiet home-style living. 2 minute walk to Corporation Beach. Close to all activities.

DENNISPORT

Rose Petal Bed & Breakfast
152 Sea St., Box 974, 02639
508-398-8470
Dan & Gayle Kelly
All year

$ B&B
4 rooms
Visa, MC
C-yes/S-ltd/P-no/H-no
some French

Full breakfast
Comp. wine, snacks
Guest refrg. on sun porch
Gas grill, lawn furnit.
sitting room, TV, piano

Inviting 1872 home, attractive yard, lovely accommodations, superb breakfasts with homemade pastries. In residential neighborhood, few blocks to sandy beach or Village center.

EAST ORLEANS

Nauset House Inn
P.O. Box 774, 02643
143 Beach Rd.
508-255-2195
Diane & Al Johnson
April 1—October 31

$$ EP
14 rooms, 8 pb
Visa, MC
C-12+/S-ltd/P-no/H-no

Full breakfast avail. $
Appetizers, tea, wine
Commons room
piano, conservatory
dining room

Intimate 1810 inn, unique turn-of-the-century conservatory, warm ambience, a short walk to the sea.

The Parsonage
P.O. Box 1016, 02643
202 Main St.
508-255-8217
Chris & Lloyd Shand
All year

$$ B&B
6 rooms, 2 pb
Visa, MC
C-6+/S-yes/P-no/H-no

Continental plus
Guest refrigerator

Experience a 1770 antique-furnished Cape home. Savor breakfast on the patio, walk to restaurants. Biking, golfing, fishing and beach nearby.

Ship's Knees Inn
P.O. Box 756, 02643
Beach Rd.
508-255-1312
Nancy & Carl Wideberg
All year

$ B&B
25 rooms, 11 pb
•
C-12+/S-yes/P-no/H-no

Continental breakfast
Sitting room
swimming pool
tennis courts

A restored sea captain's house; surrounded by the charm of yesterday while offering the convenience of today.

EAST SANDWICH

Wingscorton Farm Inn
Olde Kings Hwy, Rt. 6A, 02537
11 Wing Blvd.
508-888-0534
All year

$$$ B&B
4 rooms, 4 pb
Visa, MC, AmEx •
C-yes/S-yes/P-yes/H-yes

Full breakfast
Picnic basket lunch
Dinner, comp. wine
Library, bicycles
private ocean beach

A special retreat for couples seeking a private, intimate getaway. Eclectic mix of antiquity and modern convenience in the setting of a working New England farm. Private beach.

EASTHAM

Whalewalk Inn
169 Bridge Rd., 02642
508-255-0617
N. & V. de la Chapelle
April 1—December 1

$$$ EP/B&B
12 rooms, 12 pb
C-12+/S-yes/P-no/H-no

Full gourmet breakfast
Sitting room
suites, cottage
patio, bar, appetizers
lawn games, fireplaces

Elegant and sophisticated. Built in 1830's. Uniquely decorated and located on quiet road near bay and ocean. Rooms, suites, cottage.

EDGARTOWN

The Arbor
P.O. Box 1228, 02539	$$ B&B	Continental breakfast
222 Upper Main	10 rooms, 8 pb	Comp. tea
508-627-8137	Visa, MC •	Sitting room
Peggy Hall	C-12+ /S-ask/P-no/H-no	bicycle rack
May 1—October 30		courtyard

Turn-of-the-century home in historic Edgartown. Walk to town and harbor. The rooms are delight-fully and typically New England.

Captain Dexter House of Vineyard Haven
P.O. Box 2798, 02539	$$ B&B	Continental plus
35 Pease's Point Way	11 rooms, 11 pb	Afternoon tea
508-627-7289	Visa, MC, AmEx •	Comp. wine
Michael Maultz	C-12+ /S-ltd/P-no/H-no	Sitting room
All year		

Lovely 1840s home; romantic antique-filled guest rooms with canopied beds and working fire-places. Expensive landscaped gardens. Near the harbor, shops and restaurants.

Edgartown Inn
P.O. Box 1211, 02539	$$$ EP	Full or Cont. bkfast. $
56 N. Water St.	22 rooms, 13 pb	
508-627-4794	C-yes/S-yes	
Hwane & Earle Radford	French	
April 1—Nov. 1		

Historic inn where Nathaniel Hawthorne, Daniel Webster & John Kennedy stayed. Serving home-made cakes and breads for breakfast in the garden.

Point Way Inn
P.O. Box 128, 02539	$$ B&B	Continental breakfast
104 Main St.	15 rooms, 15 pb	Comp. wine, tea, snacks
508-627-8633	Visa, MC, AmEx •	Honor bar
Ben & Linda Smith	C-yes/S-yes/H-ltd	Sitting room, library
All year		croquet, gardens, gazebo

Located near center of town; 11 rooms with working fireplaces; no room phones or TVs. Inn is a former whaling captain's mansion.

Shiverick Inn
P.O. Box 640, 02539	$$$ B&B	Continental plus
Peases Point Wy-Pent Ln.	10 rooms, 10 pb	Snacks
508-627-3797	Visa, MC, AmEx	Sitting room, library
Claire & Juan del Real	S-ltd	dining room, parlor
All year		formal garden, bicycles

Exquisitely restored 19th-century mansion offering one-of-a-kind suites and guest rooms with fireplaces, library, formal parlor and garden.

ESSEX

George Fuller House
148 Main St., 01929	$$ B&B	Full breakfast
508-768-7766	5 rooms, 5 pb	Sitting room
All year	Visa, MC, AmEx	cruising sailboat avail.
	C-yes/S-ltd/P-no/H-no	

Federalist-style with antique furnishings, four fireplaces, color TV, full breakfast, marsh view. Located near antique shops and seafood restaurants.

FAIRHAVEN ───

Edgewater Bed & Breakfast $$ B&B Continental breakfast
2 Oxford St., 02719 5 rooms, 5 pb Sitting room
508-997-5512 C-4+ / S-yes / P-no / H-no library
The Reed Family spacious lawns
All year

Gracious waterfront mansion overlooking Bedford Harbor. Spacious accommodations; 2 suites w/fireplaces. 5 min. from I-195. Close to historic areas, beaches, factory outlets.

FALMOUTH ──

Captain Tom Lawrence House $$ B&B Full gourmet breakfast
75 Locust St., 02540 6 rooms, 6 pb Sitting room
508-540-1445 Visa, MC library
Barbara Sabo-Feller C-12+ / S-yes / P-no / H-no piano, TV
All year German porch, large yard

Newly redecorated Victorian captain's home close to village center, beaches, golf and island ferries. Quiet atmosphere. Breakfast with homemade bread from organic grain.

Mostly Hall B&B Inn $$$ B&B Full gourmet breakfast
27 Main St., 02540 6 rooms, 6 pb Lemonade, tea, sherry
508-548-3786 C-16+ / S-no / P-no / H-no Sitting room, piano
Caroline & Jim Lloyd German gazebo, veranda
Mid-Feb.—mid-Jan. bicycles, gardens

Falmouth's first summer residence built in southern style for New Orleans bride. Spacious corner rooms. Queen-sized four-poster canopy beds. Near beaches, shops, ferries.

Palmer House Inn $$$ B&B Full gourmet breakfast
81 Palmer Ave., 02540 8 rooms, 8 pb Hot mulled cider, ice
508-548-1230 Visa, MC • tea & lemonade
Bud & Phyllis Peacock C-14+ / S-ltd / P-no / H-no Sitting room
All year bicycles

Enjoy a romantic return to Grandma's day in this Victorian B&B. Antiques, private baths, full gourmet breakfast, bicycles.

Village Green Inn $$ B&B Full breakfast
40 W. Main St., 02540 5 rooms, 5 pb Seasonal beverages
508-548-5621 C-no / S-no / P-no / H-no Comp. wine
Linda & Don Long Sitting room, library
All year bicycles, open porches

Gracious old Victorian ideally located on Falmouth's historic green. Enjoy 19th-century charm and warm hospitality in lovely spacious rooms. Delightful breakfast served.

GREAT BARRINGTON ──────────────────────────────────

Round Hill Farm $$ B&B Full breakfast
17 Round Hill Rd., 01230 8 rooms, 3 pb Apartments,300-acre farm
413-528-3366 Visa, MC, AmEx • Parlor, library
Thomas & Margaret Whitfield C-16+ / S-no / P-ltd / H-no swimming hole, porches
All year French trout stream, X-C skiing

A haven for nonsmokers; classic New England hilltop guest house on dirt road; porches; privacy; the Berkshire Hills year-round. Jogging, bicycling, X-C skiing from the door.

184   Massachusetts

GREAT BARRINGTON ─────────────────────────────────

Seekonk Pines Inn $$ B&B   Full breakfast
142 Seekonk Cross Rd., 01230   7 rooms, 2 pb   Kitchenette avail
413-528-4192   C-yes/S-no/P-no/H-no Sitting room, bicycles
Linda & Christian Best   German   swimming pool
Exc. last 2 weeks Nov   baby grand piano

Country estate; close to Tanglewood, skiing, hiking. Hosts are artists/singers. Original artwork, homemade jams, produce for sale. Low-fat and low-cholesterol diets. Peaceful.

Turning Point Inn $$ B&B   Full breakfast
RD2 Box 140, 01230   8 rooms, 2 pb   Comp. tea, wine
3 Lake Buel Rd.   C-yes/S-no/P-no/H-no 2 sitting rooms
413-528-4777   piano, fireplaces
Shirley, Irving & Jamie Yost   bicycles, cottage
All year

We offer a natural environment: whole grain vegetarian breakfast; no smoking; hiking, skiing; comfort in 18th-century inn near Tanglewood, next to ski slopes.

HARWICH ──

Victorian Inn at Harwich $$$ B&B   Continental plus
P.O. Box 340, 02645   5 rooms, 4 pb   Picnic lunch by RSVP
102 Parallel St.   Visa, MC, AmEx •   Aftn. tea, snacks
508-432-8335   C-no/S-no/P-no/H-no Turned-down beds
Betty & Charlie Schneiderhan   Spanish, some Fr. & It. flowers, lawn chairs
All year

1866 Victorian home with rooms furnished in period antiques and reproductions. Art gallery in parlors. In historic Harwich Center, blocks away from shops, galleries, fairs.

HARWICH PORT ─────────────────────────────────────

Bayberry Shores $$ B&B   Continental plus
255 Lower County Rd., 02646   3 rooms, 3 pb   Efficiency w/fireplace
800-992-6550/508-432-0337   Visa, MC, AmEx •   Fireplaced common room
David & Kathleen Van Gelder   C-yes/S-yes/H-ltd   brick terrace with BBQ
All year   cable TV, beach, tennis

Brickfront Cape Cod house only 350 yards from beach. Attractive guest rooms with twin or king beds—one two-room suite perfect for families. Residential location.

Captain's Quarters $$ B&B   Continental plus
85 Bank St., 02646   5 rooms, 5 pb   Cottage, some cable T.V.
326 Lower County Rd.   Visa, MC, AmEx •   sitting room, porch
508-432-0337/800-992-6550   C-ltd/S-yes/P-no/H-ltd tennis & swimming nearby
David & Kathleen Van Gelder
All year

Classic 1850s Victorian with wraparound porch, turret, queen-sized brass beds. Walk to beach, shops, restaurants, bike rentals. Perfect for honeymooners!

Dunscroft by the Sea $$ B&B   Continental plus
24 Pilgrim Rd., 02646   9 rooms, 9 pb   Wine
508-432-0810   •   Sitting room, library
Alyce & Wally Cunningham   C-ltd/S-yes/P-no/H-no piano, sun porch
All year   cottage, brick terrace

Located 300 feet from a beautiful private beach on Nantucket Sound; walk to restaurants, shops and theaters. 2 efficiency apartments; 1 honeymoon cottage w/fireplace.

HARWICH PORT

Harbor Breeze
326 Lower County Rd., 02646
508-432-0337/800-992-6550
David & Kathleen VanGelder
March-November

$$ B&B
8 rooms, 8 pb
Visa, MC, AmEx •
C-yes/S-yes/P-ask/H-ltd

Continental plus
Comp. tea, coffee
Swimming pool, cable TVs
gardens,near free tennis
boat trips, picnic area

Walk to harbor, beach, shops, restaurants. Guestrooms each with private entrance around a garden courtyard—casual Cape Cod atmosphere. Some family suites. Children welcome.

Harbor Walk Guest House
6 Freeman St., 02646
508-432-1675
Preston & Marilyn Barry
May—October

$$ B&B
6 rooms, 4 pb
C-3+/S-no/P-no/H-no
some French

Continental plus
Sitting room
library
tennis & ocean nearby

Victorian charmer, featuring antiques and homemade quilts. Walk to beach and most photographed harbor on Cape Cod. Summer sports paradise.

Inn on Bank Street
88 Bank St., 02646
508-432-3206
Arky & Janet Silverio
April—mid-November

$$ B&B
6 rooms, 6 pb
Visa, AmEx •
C-ltd/S-ltd/P-no/H-yes
Italian, Spanish

Continental plus
Comp. tea, wine
Sitting room, piano
library
rental bicycles

The right place to get away to. Peaceful, private, comfortable and friendly. Walk to ocean beach, shops, restaurants and movie theater.

HOLYOKE

Yankee Pedlar Inn
1866 Northampton St., 01040
413-532-9494
Frank & Claire Banks
All year

$$ B&B
47 rooms, 47 pb
Visa, MC, AmEx, DC •
C-yes/S-ltd/P-no/H-ltd
French, Polish, Spanish

Continental breakfast
Lunch, dinner, bar
Piano
entertainment

Old Victorian mansion, antiqued bedrooms, many dining rooms including French restaurant and herb garden. Continental menu, live entertainment, outdoor cafe.

HYANNIS

Elegance by-the-Sea
162 Sea St., 02601
508-775-3595
Clark & Mary Boydston
All year

$$ B&B
6 rooms, 3 pb
Visa, MC, AmEx •
C-no/S-no/P-no/H-no
French

Full breakfast
Afternoon tea
Sitting room
bicycle rentals

Victorian captain's home offers hearty New England breakfast and romantic antique-furnished guest rooms. Walk to beach, golf or boats to Nantucket or Martha's Vineyard.

Inn on Sea Street
358 Sea St., 02601
508-775-8030
Lois Nelson & J.B. Whitehead
April 1—December 1

$$ B&B
5 rooms, 3 pb
Visa, MC, AmEx
C-16+/S-yes/P-no/H-no

Full breakfast
Fruit & cheese
Sitting room
library

Elegant Victorian inn, steps from the beach and Kennedy Compound. Antiques, canopy beds, fireplace, home-baked delights. Full gourmet breakfast, fruit and cheese.

HYANNIS PORT

Simmons Homestead Inn	$$$ B&B	Full breakfast
P.O. Box 578, 02647	9 rooms, 9 pb	Comp. wine and cheese
288 Scudder Ave.	•	Sitting room
508-778-4999	S-ltd	library, porch
Bill & Peggy Putman		huge yard, beaches
All year		

Beautifully restored 1820 sea captain's home abounds in art, priceless antiques, canopy beds. Lovely grounds. One of the most pleasant inns on the Cape.

LAKEVILLE

Pistachio Cove	$$ B&B	Lavish gourmet breakfast
229 County Rd., 02347	4 rooms, 1 pb	Boats, lake
Box 456, E. Freetown	C-yes/S-yes/P-yes/H-no	sitting room
617-763-2383	French	color TVs, phones
Ms. Dana Lapolla		
All year		

Savor country hospitality and informal elegance on scenic Lake Apponequet. Luxurious accommodations provide total relaxation.

LEE

Haus Andreas	$$ B&B	Continental breakfast
Stockbridge Rd., 01238	7 rooms, 5 pb	Guest pantry, library
413-243-3298	Visa, MC	Heated pool, tennis
Gerhard & Lilliane Schmid	C-10+/S-yes/P-no/H-no	bicycles, lawn sports
All year	French, German	sitting room, piano

Historic revolutionary setting, heated pool, golf, tennis, luxury, comfort, local fine restaurants. Complimentary breakfast. Relax in Old World charm.

LENOX

Amity House	$$$ B&B	Continental plus
15 Cliffwood St., 01240	7 rooms, 2 pb	Snacks
413-637-0005	C-7+	Sitting room
Rhoda M. Crowell		library
All year		bicycles

A unique country Victorian with Saratoga Front-Shaker & antique furnishings; close to Tanglewood, Jacob's Pillow. Complimentary snacks, etc.

Brook Farm Inn	$$ B&B	Full breakfast
15 Hawthorne St., 01240	12 rooms, 12 pb	Comp. tea
413-637-3013	Visa, MC •	Library
Bob & Betty Jacob	C-15+/S-no/P-no/H-no	sitting room
All year		swimming pool

There is poetry here: 650 volumes and 60 poets on tape with players available. 100-year-old inn.

Cornell Inn	$$ B&B	Continental breakfast
197 Main St., 01240	9 rooms, 9 pb	Comp. wine, snacks
413-637-0562	Visa, MC •	Afternoon tea, bar
David Rolland	C-12+/S-yes/P-no/H-no	Sitting room
All year		

We have X-C skiing and hiking in our backyard; luxury suites with kitchens, jacuzzis, fireplaces. Special weekend packages.

LENOX

Gables Inn
103 Walker St., 01240	$$ B&B	Continental plus
413-637-3416	14 rooms, 14 pb	Comp. wine
Mary & Frank Newton	Visa, MC, AmEx	Sitting room, library
All year	C-13+/S-yes/P-no/H-no	tennis courts
	Spanish	swimming pool

Built in 1885, this gracious "cottage" was the home of Edith Wharton at the turn of the century. Lovingly furnished in period style.

Garden Gables Inn
141 Main St., 01240	$$ B&B	Continental plus
P.O. Box 52	11 rooms, 11 pb	Sitting room, library
413-637-0193	Visa, MC	bicycles, tennis court
Mario & Lynn Mekinda	C-12+/S-ltd/P-no/H-no	pool, whirlpool
All year	German, French	

This 220-year-old gabled inn is located in the center of Lenox on four wooded acres. Furnished with antiques. One mile to Tanglewood and many other attractions.

Gateways Inn
71 Walker St., 01240	$$$ B&B	Continental breakfast
413-637-2532	8 rooms, 8 pb	Dinner
Vito Perulli, Brenda Mayberry	Visa, MC, AmEx, DC	Restaurant, bar
All year	C-10+/S-no/P-no/H-no	Sitting room
	French, German, Italian	tennis, pool nearby

Chef-owned Gateways Inn is Berkshire's only four-star restaurant. Elegant, luxurious townhouse in heart of Lenox.

Rookwood Inn
P.O. Box 1717, 01240	$$ B&B	Full breakfast
19 Old Stockbridge Rd.	16 rooms, 16 pb	Afternoon tea
413-637-9750	MC, AmEx •	Sitting room
Tom & Betsy Sherman	C-yes/S-no/P-no/H-no	library, verandas
All year		

Our romantic, antique-filled Painted Lady offers an ideal location—quiet, yet one block to village and all Berkshire activities.

Village Inn
P.O. Box 1810, 01240	$ EP	Restaurant, bar
16 Church St.	29 rooms, 27 pb	Afternoon tea
413-637-0020	Visa, MC, AmEx, Diners •	Sitting room, library
Clifford Rudisill	C-6+/S-yes/P-no/H-yes	lakes, mountain trails
All year	Spanish, French, German	parks & museums nearby

Historic 1771 inn reflecting charm and warmth of colonial New England. Rooms individually furnished in country antiques. Afternoon tea with homemade scones. American cuisine.

Whistler's Inn
5 Greenwood St., 01240	$$ B&B	Continental plus
413-637-0975	11 rooms, 11 pb	Comp. tea, sherry
Richard & Joan Mears	Visa, MC, AmEx	Sitting room, piano
All year	C-no/S-no/P-no/H-no	library, bicycles
	Spanish, Polish, French	air conditioned

Elegant, antique-filled Tudor mansion; cozy library and French salon with Steinway. Homebaked breads and muffins. Old World charm. Lake nearby.

Twin Peaks Inn, Moscow, ID

MARBLEHEAD

Harborside House	$$ B&B	Continental plus
23 Gregory St., 01945	2 rooms	Homebaked goods
617-631-1032	C-10+/S-no/P-ltd/H-no	Living room w/fireplace
Susan Blake		deck overlooking harbor
All year		sunny breakfast porch

C. 1850 colonial home offers antiques & modern amenities. Homemade baked goods. Sunny breakfast porch overlooks harbor. Close to historic sites, shops, beaches & restaurants.

Spray Cliff on the Ocean	$$$ B&B	Continental breakfast
25 Spray Ave., 01945	5 rooms, 5 pb	Sitting room
508-741-0680/800-446-2995	Visa, MC, AmEx, DC •	beach nearby
Richard & Diane Pabich	C-yes/S-no/P-no/H-no	
All year		

English Tudor mansion set high above the Atlantic. Views extend forever. Elegant bedrooms, cozy relaxed atmosphere; garden terrace. Come unwind.

MARTHA'S VINEYARD

Ashley Inn	$$$ B&B	Continental breakfast
P.O. Box 650, Edgartown, 02539	10 rooms, 8 pb	Sitting room
129 Main St., Edgartown	Visa, MC, AmEx •	
508-627-9655	C-10+/S-yes/P-no/H-no	
Jude Cortese, Fred Hurley		
All year		

Attractive 1800s sea captain's home with country charm, decorated with period antiques, brass and wicker. A leisurely stroll to shops, beaches, fine foods.

Massachusetts   189

MARTHA'S VINEYARD

Thorncroft Inn
278 Main St., 02568
P.O.Box 1022
508-693-3333
Karl & Lynn Buder
All year

$$$ B&B
13 rooms, 13 pb
•
C-12+/S-ltd/P-no/H-no

Full breakfast
3½ acres of
quiet grounds

Romantic, noncommercial atmosphere; fine antiques; fireplaces; central air-conditioning; luxury suites with jacuzzi; balconies.

NANTUCKET

Brass Lantern
11 N. Water St., 02554
508-228-4064
Stuart & Lee Gaw
April—December

$$ B&B
18 rooms, 14 pb
Visa, MC •
C-yes/S-yes

Continental breakfast
Afternoon tea

Renovated inn located in old historic district—canopied beds, antiques. Friendly. Romantic.

Carlisle House Inn
26 N. Water St., 02554
508-228-0720
Peter C. Conway
April 15—January 10

$$ B&B
14 rooms, 10 pb
C-10+/S-yes/P-no/H-no

Continental plus
Weekly special dinners
Weekly cookouts
Sitting room
private back lawn

Authentic 18th-century historic home in town, within a 10-minute walk to beach. Gracious living room and private yard. Elegant continetal breakfasts in the morning room.

Centerboard Guest House
P.O. Box 456, 02554
8 Chester St.
508-228-9696
Marcia Wasserman
All year

$$$ B&B
7 rooms, 7 pb
Visa, MC, AmEx •
C-12+/S-no/P-no/H-no

Cont. country breakfast
Comp. refreshments
Beach towels
library, sitting room
suite, jacuzzi

A Victorian guest house of quiet country elegance; lovingly renovated and restored in 1986-87; located in historic district, Nantucket Center; beaches nearby.

Century House
10 Cliff Rd., 02554
508-228-0530
Gerry & Jean Heron Connick
All year

$$$ B&B
9 rooms, 9 pb
•
C-ask/S-ltd/P-no/H-no
Fr, Rus, Ger, Jap, Chi

Continental plus
Nightly cocktail hour
munchies, set-ups incl.
Sitting room, veranda
H. Miller player piano

Historic sea captain's B&B inn serving the Nantucket traveler since the mid-1800s; minutes to beaches, restaurants, galleries & shops; antique appointments, L. Ashley decor.

Corner House
Box 1828, 02554
49 Centre St.
508-228-1530
John & Sandy Knox-Johnston
April 15—January 1

$$ B&B
14 rooms, 14 pb
Visa, MC •
C-8+/S-ltd/P-no/H-ltd
French, German

Continental plus
Afternoon tea, barbecue
Sitting rooms, conf. fac
screen porch w/wicker
library, beach towels

Especially charming and attractive antique-furnished 18th-century B&B inn in the heart of Nantucket's historic district, near wharf, shops, museums, beaches.

NANTUCKET

Four Chimneys
38 Orange St., 02554
508-228-1912
Betty York
Late April—late Dec.

$$$ B&B
10 rooms, 10 pb
Visa, MC, AmEx, DC, CB
C-no/S-yes/P-no/H-no

Continental breakfast
Sitting room
antiques

Distinctively Nantucket. Be a guest in a 1835 sea captain's mansion, the largest on this faraway island. Return to gracious living.

Jared Coffin House
29 Broad St., 02554
508-228-2405
Philip Whitney Read
All year

$$$ EP
Major credit cards
C-ltd/S-yes/P-ltd/H-no

Full menu, bar service
Sitting room
piano, meeting rooms
entertainment

Historically interesting collection of six buildings make up the inn. Convenient location in town near everything. Two excellent restaurants.

La Petite Maison
132 Main St., 02554
508-228-9242
Holli Martin
April 15—January 15

$$ B&B
4 rooms, 1 pb
C-8+ /S-yes/H-ltd
French

Continental plus
Afternoon tea
Food
Sitting room
dining room w/fireplace

Charming, antique-furnished European style guest house in a quiet town location. Continental breakfast served on the sun porch; peaceful garden; friendly atmosphere.

Quaker House Inn & Rest.
5 Chestnut St., 02554
508-228-0400
Caroline & Bob Taylor
Memorial Day wknd—Sept.

$$$ EP
9 rooms, 9 pb
Visa, MC •
C-ltd/S-ltd/P-no/H-no

Full breakfast $
Restaurant
Dinner, beer, wine
Sitting room

Located in the heart of Nantucket's historic district; each guest room decorated in 19th-century antiques.

Safe Harbor Guest House
2 Harbor View Way, 02554
508-228-3222
Sylvia & Larry Griggs
All year

$$$ B&B
5 rooms, 5 pb
•
C-10+
French, Spanish

Continental plus

Overlooking the harbor at Children's Beach, in the heart of Nantucket's historic district. Furnished with antiques. Renowned continental buffet. All rooms: harbor views.

Seven Sea Street Inn
7 Sea St., 02554
617-228-3577
Matthew S. Parker
All year

$$$ B&B
8 rooms, 8 pb
Visa, MC, AmEx •
C-yes/S-no/P-no/H-no

Continental plus
Sitting rooms
Jacuzzi
widow's walk

Red oak post and beam guest house with authentic Nantucket ambience. Romance, comfort and warmth best describe our colonial inn.

NANTUCKET

Ships Inn $$ B&B   Continental plus
13 Fair St., 02554   12 rooms, 10 pb   Dinner, restaurant
508-228-0040   Visa, MC, AmEx   Bar service
Joyce Berruet   C-3+ /S-yes/P-no/H-no   Sitting room
All year exc. Jan.—Feb.

Formerly a whaling captain's mansion, they are furnished accordingly. A bonus is their delightful restaurant and bar.

Woodbox Inn $$$ EP   Full breakfast avail. $
29 Fair St., 02554   9 rooms, 9 pb   Dinner
508-228-0587   C-yes/S-yes/P-ltd/H-yes   Sitting room
Dexter A. Tutein   French, German   fireplaces
June—mid-October

"Probably the best place to stay on Nantucket." Oldest inn (1709) furnished with period antiques. Breakfast 8:30-10:30; dinner—continental cuisine—7 and 9 p.m.

NANTUCKET ISLAND

Cobblestone Inn $$ B&B   Continental plus
5 Ash St., 02554   5 rooms, 5 pb   Sun porch, yard
508-228-1987   ●   living room
Robin Hammer-Yankow
All year

Circa 1725 home on quiet street in town. Relax in yard/sun porch/living room. Five rooms, all with private bath. Complimentary continental breakfast. Open year-round.

NEW MARLBOROUGH

Old Inn on the Green $$$ B&B   Continental plus
Star Rt. 70, 01230   6 rooms, 2 pb   Bar, dinner (Fri.-Sat.)
413-229-7924   C-yes/S-yes/P-no/H-no   Five public rooms
Bradford Wagstaff
All year

1760 colonial inn on historic landmark register. 3 public rooms downstairs. Parlor, dining room, old tavern. Inn furnished with antiques.

NEWTONVILLE

Sage and Thyme B&B $$ B&B   Full breakfast
P.O. Box 91, 02160   2 rooms   Air-conditioned
65 Kirkstall Rd.   C-yes/S-no/P-no/H-no
617-332-0695   Ger, Ital, Sp, Fr.
Edgar & Hertha Klugman
All year

Classic colonial in a quiet neighborhood. Downtown Boston only 5 miles away. Outstanding breakfasts and congenial hosts and cats.

NORTH EASTHAM

Penny House $$ B&B   Full breakfast
Rt. 6, Box 238, 02651   12 rooms   Sitting room
508-255-6632   Visa, MC   library
Paul & Barbara Landry   C-no/S-yes/P-no/H-no
All year   French

Experience the original Cape Cod charm and serenity of this 1751 bow roof rambling Cape conveniently located near all National Seashore Park activities.

NORTHAMPTON

The Knoll
230 N. Main St., 01060
Florence
413-584-8164
Lee Lesko
All year

$ B&B
3 rooms
C-no/S-no/P-no/H-no

Full breakfast
Afternoon tea

Large Tudor house in quiet rural setting on 16 acres. Near 5 colleges: Smith, Amherst, Mt. Holyoke, University of Massachusetts, Hampshire.

OAK BLUFFS

Oak House
P.O. Box 299, 02557
Seaview & Peguot Aves.
508-693-4187
Betsi Convery-Luce
May—mid-October

$$$ B&B
10 rooms, 10 pb
Visa, MC •
C-10+/S-yes/P-no/H-no

Continental breakfast
Afternoon tea
Sitting room, piano
sun porch, near beach
bicycles

Romantic Victorian inn on the beach. Richly restored 1872 Governor's home. Oak paneling, wide porches, balconies, leaded windows, water views. Walk to ferry, town, sights.

ORLEANS

Farmhouse at Nauset Beach
163 Beach Rd., 02653
508-255-6654
Don & Dot Standish
All year

$ B&B
8 rooms, 4 pb
Visa, MC
C-10+/S-yes/P-no/H-ltd

Continental plus
Sitting room
oceanview deck
picnic tables

19th-century farmhouse beautifully restored. Enjoy a unique blend of country life in a seashore setting. Short walk to Nauset Beach, breakfast on deck with ocean view.

PETERSHAM

Winterwood at Petersham
N. Main St., 01366
508-724-8885
Jean & Robert Day
All year

$$$ B&B
5 rooms, 5 pb
Visa, MC, AmEx •
C-yes/S-yes/P-no/H-no

Continental plus
Restaurant
Bar service
Sitting room, library
fireplaces

Sixteen-room Greek revival mansion—built as private summer home—on National Register of Historic Homes.

PLYMOUTH

Morton Park Place
1 Morton Park Rd., 02360
508-747-1730/800-698-1730
James & Janine Smith
All year

$ B&B
4 rooms, 2 pb
Visa, MC •
C-yes/S-yes/P-no/H-no
Spanish

Continental breakfast
Sitting room

One mile from Routes 3 and 44; Victorian charm in a park setting; 5 minutes from downtown and the waterfront. Individual rooms or suites available.

Two-Sixty-Four Sandwich
264 Sandwich St., 02360
508-747-5490
Julie Beach
April 15—November

$$ B&B
4 rooms, 1 pb
•
C-yes/S-yes/P-no/H-no

Full breakfast
Comp. wine, aftn. tea
Library, patio
lovely backyard
hammock for two

Two-Sixty-Four Sandwich is an antique cape filled with American antiques & English chintz. Close to all historical sites. Rooms are air-conditioned & beautifully decorated.

PRINCETON

Harrington Farm
178 Westminster Rd., 01541
508-464-5600
Victoria Morgan, John Bomba
All year

$$ B&B
8 rooms, 1 pb
Visa, MC •
C-yes/S-no/P-ltd/H-no
German

Full farm breakfast
Lunch, dinner
Snacks, afternoon tea
Sitting room
bicycles

1763 farmhouse on western slope of Mt. Wachusett. A century of inn-keeping tradition, full farm breakfast, skiing, hiking, breathtaking sunsets.

PROVINCETOWN

Branford Gardens Inn
178 Bradford St., 02657
508-487-1616
M. Susan Culligan
April—December

&&& B&B
12 rooms, 12 pb
Visa, MC, AmEx •
C-ask/S-ltd/P-no/H-no
French

Full breakfast

1820 Colonial antique-filled inn. Most rooms and cottages have fireplaces. Situated in beautiful gardens. Within a short walk to town center. Exceptionally clean & friendly.

Cape Codder Guest House
570 Commercial St., 02657
508-487-0131
Deborah Dionne
Mid-April—October

$ EP
15 rooms, 1 pb
Visa, MC
C-yes/S-ltd/P-ask/H-ltd

Continental breakfast $
1 apt. with private bath

Old-fashioned comfort in quiet area; private beach, sun deck; whalewatching and bicycling nearby; informal friendly atmosphere; resident marine biologists!

Fairbanks Inn
90 Bradford St., 02657
508-487-0386
Don Graichen
All year

$ B&B
14 rooms, 7 pb
Visa, MC •
C-no/S-yes/P-no/H-yes

Continental breakfast
Library, sitting room
sun deck, patio, porch
bicycles

A 1776 sea captain's house. Seven bedrooms with original working fireplaces. Warm, congenial atmosphere with typical New England charm.

Land's End Inn
22 Commercial St., 02657
508-487-0706
David Schoolman
All year

$$ B&B
14 rooms, 10 pb
C-no/S-yes/P-no/H-no

Continental breakfast
Sitting room

Victorian summer house set high on a hill overlooking Provincetown and all of Cape Cod Bay. With a homelike and friendly atmosphere.

Rose and Crown Guest House
158 Commercial St., 02657
508-487-3332
Preston S. Babbitt, Jr.
All year

$$ B&B
8 rooms, 5 pb
•
C-yes/S-yes/P-no/H-ltd

Continental breakfast
Sitting room

A relaxed, elegant 1780s captain's house. Rooms feature antiques in a homey atmosphere. An unusual eclectic living room is featured.

REHOBOTH ───────────────────────────────────

Perryville Inn
157 Perryville Rd., 02769
508-252-9239
Betsy & Tom Charnecki
All year

$ B&B
5 rooms, 4 pb
Visa, MC, AmEx •
C-yes/S-ltd/P-no/H-no

Continental plus
Comp. tea, wine
2 sitting rooms
piano, balloon rides
bicycles

Newly renovated 19th-century spacious farmhouse in quiet country setting. Centrally located between Boston, Newport, Providence. On National Register of Historic Homes

ROCKPORT ───────────────────────────────────

Addison Choate Inn
49 Broadway, 01966
508-546-7543
Peter & Chris Kelleher
All year

$$$ B&B
10 rooms, 10 pb
•
C-14+/S-ltd/P-no/H-yes
German

Continental breakfast
Swimming pool
sitting room
library

Remarkably fine small country inn. Cruise the coast on our private yacht, the Sweetwater. *Antiques, flowers, a surprise on your pillow!*

Inn on Cove Hill
37 Mt. Pleasant St., 01966
508-546-2701
John & Marjorie Pratt
April—October

$ B&B
11 rooms, 9 pb
C-16+/S-yes/P-no/H-no

Continental breakfast
Antique furnishings
view from porch

This 18th-century inn overlooks a historic harbor. Breakfast is served on fine china in the garden or in your room. Short walk to shops, Art Association, rocky seafront.

Mooringstone
12 Norwood Ave., 01966
508-546-2479
David & Mary Knowlton
May—October

$$ B&B
3 rooms, 3 pb
Visa, MC, AmEx
C-no/S-no/P-no

Continental plus
Aftn. tea, snacks
Restaurants close by

Quiet, central to beach and shops. Comfortable A/C ground-floor rooms. Cable TV, parking, refrigerators. Daily, weekly and offseason rates, without a room tax.

Old Farm Inn
291 Granite St., 01966
Route 127, Pigeon Cove
508-546-3237
The Balzarini Family
April—December

$$ B&B
13 rooms, 13 pb
Visa, MC
C-yes/S-yes/P-no/H-ltd

Continental plus
Sitting room
bicycles
queen or king beds

Relax by the fire, nap under a tree, wander on the rocky coastline. Unwind at our friendly, cozy, country farmhouse.

Rocky Shores Inn/Cottages
Eden Rd., 01966
508-546-2823
Gunter & Renate Kostka
April—October

$$$ B&B
22 rooms, 22 pb
C-10+/S-no/P-no/H-no
German

Continental plus
Sitting room
rooms w/full ocean views

Inn and cottages with unforgettable views of Thacher Island lights and open sea. Complete complimentary breakfast included.

ROCKPORT

Sally Webster Inn
34 Mt. Pleasant St., 01966
508-546-9251
The Webster Family
May—Oct., Feb.—Apr. wkends

$$ B&B
6 rooms, 6 pb
C-16+/S-yes/P-no/H-no

Continental plus
Comp. wine for anniver-
saries & honeymoons
Sitting room
piano

Historic, colonial home built in 1832. Antique decor. Walk to village and sea. Welcome to the charm of yesteryear.

Seacrest Manor
131 Marmion Way, 01966
508-546-2211
L. Saville, D. MacCormack, Jr
Exc. Xmas eve—mid-Feb.

$$ B&B
8 rooms, 6 pb
C-16+/S-ltd/P-no/H-no
some French

Full breakfast
Comp. tea
Library, sitting room
gardens, sun deck
bicycles

Decidedly small, intentionally quiet inn. Beautiful peaceful setting; lovely gardens overlooking woods and sea. Famous full breakfast included. 1988 INN OF THE YEAR!

Seafarer Inn
86 Marmion Way, 01966
508-546-6248
Leigh Reynolds
All year

$$ B&B
8 rooms, 8 pb
Visa, MC •
C-no/S-no/P-no/H-no
some French

Continental plus
Snacks
Sitting room

Small distinctive seaside inn; gourmet continental breakfast served overlooking the sea. All rooms have fabulous ocean views. Walk to historic Rockport.

Yankee Clipper Inn
P.O. Box 2399, 01966
96 Granite St.
508-546-3407
Bob & Barbara Ellis
Except Dec. 24-27

$$$ B&B
27 rooms, 27 pb
•
C-yes/S-ltd/P-no/H-no

Full breakfast
Gourmet dinner
Sitting room, weddings
small conference fac.
swimming pool, bicycles

Beautiful ocean-front grounds in picturesque Rockport. Accommodations in 3 converted estate buildings. Rooms furnished in antiques and named after clipper ships.

SALEM

Amelia Payson Guest House
16 Winter St., 01970
508-744-8304
Ada M. Roberts
All year

$$ B&B
4 rooms, 2 pb
Visa, MC, AmEx
C-12+

Continental plus
Restaurant nearby

Beautifully decorated rooms in an elegantly restored 1845 Greek Revival-style home; five-minute stroll finds restaurants, museums, shopping and train station.

Coach House Inn
284 Lafayette St., 01970
508-744-4092
Patricia Kessler
All year

$$ B&B
11 rooms, 10 pb
Visa, MC, AmEx
C-yes/S-yes/P-no/H-no

Continental breakfast

Return to elegance. Enjoy the intimacy of a small European-type inn. Victorian fireplaces highlight the charming decor of each room.

196   Massachusetts

Salem Inn
7 Summer St., 01970
508-741-0680
Diane & Richard Pabich
All year

$$$ B&B
23 rooms, 23 pb
Major credit cards •
C-yes/S-yes/P-no/H-no

Continental breakfast
Restaurant
Private garden
courtyard
color TV, phones, A/C

Spacious, luxuriously appointed rooms in elegantly restored Federal mansion. Some efficiencies & suites. In the heart of historic district, fine restaurants, harbor.

Stephen Daniels House
1 Daniels St., 01970
at 55 Essex St.
508-744-5709
Catherine Gill
All year

$$ B&B
5 rooms, 3 pb
•
C-yes/S-yes/P-yes/H-no

Continental plus
Sitting rooms
Walk-in fireplaces
private garden
bicycles

300-year-old house furnished with canopy beds, antiques throughout, fireplaces in every room. Lovely flower-filled shady English garden—private for guests.

SANDWICH

Capt. Ezra Nye House
152 Main St., 02563
508-888-6142
Harry & Elaine Dickson
All year

$$ B&B
6 rooms, 4 pb
Visa, MC, AmEx •
C-10+/S-no/P-no/H-no
Spanish

Continental plus
Comp. wine
Sitting room
library

1829 Federal home in the heart of historic Sandwich; nearby museums, antique shops, the ocean and world-famous Heritage Plantation.

Isaiah Jones Homestead
165 Main St., 02563
508-888-9115
Steve & Kathy Catania
All year

$$ B&B
4 rooms, 4 pb
Visa, MC, AmEx •
S-no

Continental plus
Afternoon tea or
bedside goodies
Gift shop
phones available

Victorian B&B; 4 rooms all with private baths & queen-sized beds, furnished with museum-quality antiques. Breakfast & afternoon tea or bedside goodies. Deluxe room.

SHEFFIELD

Centuryhurst Antiques B&B
P.O. Box 486, 01257
Main St., Route 7
413-229-8131
Ronald & Judith Timm
All year

$$ B&B
4 rooms
Visa, MC, AmEx
C-12+

Continental breakfast
Sitting room
Reading material
swimming pool
porch rockers

Circa 1800, colonial inn located in historic district. Furnishings reflect early 19th-century atmosphere. Summer and winter Berkshire attractions.

SOUTH CHATHAM

Ye Olde Nantucket House
P.O. Box 468, 02659
2647 Main St.
508-432-5641
Helen & Norm Anderton
All year

$$ B&B
5 rooms, 5 pb
Visa, MC •
C-8+/S-yes

Continental breakfast
Homebaked goods

Delightful 19th-century home with friendly, informal atmosphere. Close to Nantucket Sound beach. Fresh breads, muffins and crepes daily.

SOUTH EGREMONT

Egremont Inn
P.O. Box 418, 01258
Old Sheffield Rd.
413-528-2111
John Black
Exc. Mar. 15—April 15

$$$ B&B/MAP
21 rooms, 21 pb
Visa, MC •
C-8+/S-no/P-no/H-no

Continental breakfast
Dinner, bar
Swimming pool
tennis courts
sitting room, piano

One-of-a-kind authentic inn, built as an inn in 1780. Nothing like it in the Berkshires.

Weathervane Inn
Route 23, Main St., 01258
413-528-9580
Vincent & Anne Murphy
All year

$$$ B&B/MAP
10 rooms, 10 pb
Visa, MC •
C-7+/S-yes/P-no/H-yes

Full breakfast
Dinner by menu
Bar service
Sittng room, library
swimming pool

The Murphy family warmly greets you at the Weathervane, a 200-year-old hostelry with modern amenities. Hearty breakfasts and superb dining will make your stay memorable.

SOUTH YARMOUTH

Four Winds
345 High Bank Rd., 02664
508-394-4182
Mary & Walt Crowell
All year

$$ B&B
5 rooms, 4 pb
C-yes/S-yes

Continental plus

Four Winds is a 1712 sea captain's home in historic South Yarmouth near saltwater beaches and golf courses.

STERLING

Sterling Inn
P.O. Box 609, 01564
240 Worcester Rd., Rt. 12
508-422-6592
Mark & Patty Roy
All year

$ B&B
6 rooms, 4 pb
Visa, MC, AmEx
C-ltd/S-ltd/P-no/H-ltd

Continental plus
Lunch, dinner, bar
Sitting room
piano
entertainment

Turn-of-the-century setting, unique to the area. Near skiing. Private dining rooms. One hour to Boston.

STURBRIDGE

Publick House
P.O. Box 187, 01566
Rt. 131, on the Common
617-347-3313
Buddy Adler
All year

$$ EP
17 rooms, 17 pb
Major credit cards •
C-yes/S-yes/P-no/H-no
French

Comp. tea, wine
Swimming pool
sitting room, piano

Gracious 1786 country farmhouse with deluxe accommodations. Summit of Fiske Hill with commanding views. Publick House owned and operated.

Sturbridge Country Inn
P.O. Box 60, 01566
530 Main St.
508-347-5503
Kevin MacConnell
All year

$$$ EP
9 rooms, 9 pb
Visa, MC, AmEx •
C-yes/S-yes/P-no/H-yes

Restaurant, bar
Lunch, dinner, snacks
Comp. wine
Hot tubs

Close to Old Sturbridge Village lies our grand Greek Revival structure. Each room has period reproductions, fireplaces, and whirlpool tubs.

SUDBURY

Checkerberry Corner B&B $$ B&B Full breakfast
5 Checkerberry Circle, 01776 2 rooms Afternoon tea, snacks
508-443-8660 • Sitting room
Stu & Irene MacDonald C-yes swimming pool
All year

Charming colonial home located in heart of historic minutemen country; minutes from Concord, Lexington, Wayside Inn; easy access to Boston.

TOWNSEND

Wood Farm $ B&B Full breakfast
40 Worcester Rd., 01469 4 rooms Comp. wine
508-597-5019 C-ltd/S-no/P-ltd/H-no Sitting room
Debra Jones & Jim Mayrand French, Spanish bicycles
All year box stalls for horses

Restored 1716 Cape in antique country; country breakfast at working sheep farm; warm conversation by the hearth. Wooded trails and waterfall. Special theme weekends.

VINEYARD HAVEN

The Bayberry $$$ B&B Full gourmet breakfast
RFD 1 Box 546, 02568 5 rooms, 1 pb Comp. tea, wine
Old Courthse Rd.N.Tisbury Visa, MC Sitting room
617-693-1984 C-no/S-ltd/P-no/H-ltd piano
Rosalie Powell croquet, hammock
All year

Gourmet breakfast served before fireplace in charming country home on historic Martha's Vineyard Island. Antique furnishings, canopy beds, warm friendly atmosphere.

Captain Dexter House $$ B&B Continental plus
P.O. Box 2457, 02568 8 rooms, 8 pb Comp. sherry
100 Main St. Visa, MC • Library, fireplaces
508-693-6564 C-11+/S-yes/P-no/H-no sitting room, parking
Alisa Lengel fresh flowers
All year

Beautifully restored 1843 sea captain's home. Furnished with fine antiques. Some rooms have fireplaces and canopied beds. Walk to beach.

Lothrop Merry House $$ B&B Continental breakfast
Box 1939, Owen Park, 02568 7 rooms, 4 pb Terrace
508-693-1646 Visa, MC boat charters
Mary & John Clarke C-yes/S-no/P-no/H-no
All year

Charming 18th-century guest house. Harbor, view, beach front. Walk from ferry. Fireplaces, antiques. Home baked continental breakfast served.

WARE

Wildwood Inn $ B&B Full breakfast
121 Church St., 01082 5 rooms Tea, cider
413-967-7798 Visa, MC, AmEx Swimming hole, canoe
Margaret/Geoffrey Lobenstine C-6+/S-ltd/P-no/H-no tennis courts
All year sitting room

Relax! American primitve antiques, heirloom quilts, firm beds. Enjoy Sturbridge, Deerfield, Amherst. Canoe, swim, bike, hike. Outstanding foliage. We spoil you.

Madewood Plantation House, Napoleonville, LA

WEST BARNSTABLE

Honeysuckle Hill
591 Main St., 02668
508-362-4914
Bob & Barbara Rosenthal
All year

$$$ B&B
3 rooms, 3 pb
Visa, MC, AmEx •
C-ltd/S-yes/P-ltd/H-ltd
French, Italian

Full gourmet breakfast
Afternoon tea
Sitting room, library
croquet, bicycles, piano
cookies by bed

Victorian farmhouse with charming bed-sitting rooms recalls serenity of Cape Cod. Breakfast and afternoon tea served on spacious front porch.

WEST FALMOUTH

The Elms
P.O. Box 895, 02574
495 W. Falmouth Hwy
508-540-7232
Betty & Joe Mazzucchelli
All year

$$$ B&B
9 rooms, 7 pb
C-14+/S-ltd/P-no/H-no

Full gourmet breakfast
Comp. sherry
Living room, study
gardens, gazebo
bicycles

A refurbished Victorian home built in the 1800's, filled with antiques and plants and boasting cool breezes from Buzzard's Bay. Beach is half-mile away.

Sjoholm B&B Inn
P.O. Box 430, 02574
17 Chase Rd.
508-540-5706
Barbara Eck Menning
All year

$$ B&B
15 rooms, 5 pb
C-5+/S-ltd/P-no/H-no

Full breakfast buffet
Sitting room
TV, porch

Quiet country charm of an old restored farmhouse. Spectacular warm water beaches and golf nearby. Close to gourmet dining & ferries to Nantucket and Martha's Vineyard.

WEST HARWICH ————————————————————————————————

Cape Cod Sunny Pines B&B
P.O. Box 667, 02671
77 Main St.
508-432-9628
Eileen & Jack Connell
All year

$$$ B&B
6 rooms, 6 pb
AmEx, Visa, MC •
C-no/S-no/P-no/H-no

Gourmet Irish breakfast
Evening social with
Wine & hors d'oeuvres
Sitting room, library
porch, pool, gardens

Irish hospitality in a Victorian ambience. Central Cape Cod location. Walk to fine restaurants, shops, beach, biking and hiking trails.

Lion's Head Inn
P.O. Box 444, 02671
186 Belmont Rd.
508-432-7766
Kathleen & William Lockyer
All year

$$$ B&B
4 rooms, 4 pb
Visa, MC •
C-ltd/S-yes/P-no/H-ltd

Continental plus
Comp. tea, wine
Sitting room w/fireplace
croquet, bicycles, pool
private woods, T.V. room

Built as a Cape half-house in 1800; former sea captain's home; charming inn with a sense of history; furnished in period antiques; central Cape Cod location. Renovated in 1989.

WEST HYANNIS PORT ————————————————————————

Bed & Breakfast Cape Cod
P.O. Box 341, 02672
508-775-2772
Clark E. Diehl

$$
Visa, MC, AmEx

YARMOUTH PORT ————————————————————————————

Liberty Hill Inn
77 Main St., Route 6A, 02675
508-362-3976
Jack & Beth Flanagan
All year

$$$ B&B
5 rooms, 5 pb
Visa, MC •
C-no/S-yes/P-no/H-no

Full breakfast
Gourmet lunch
Candlelight dinner
Sitting room, cable TV
maid service, telephone

Liberty Hill is an elegant country inn in a gracious Greek Revival Manor house, circa 1825. Shopper's paradise, a romantic hideaway, antique furnishings. Near Cape Cod.

Wedgewood Inn
83 Main St., 02675
508-362-5157
Milt & Gerrie Graham
All year

$$$ B&B
6 rooms, 6 pb
Visa, MC, AmEx, DC •
C-10+/S-ltd/P-no/H-ltd

Full breakfast
Afternoon tea
Common room

Small romantic inn located in historic area of Cape Cod. Antiques, fireplaces, screened porches, wide board floors, pencil post beds.

More Inns. . .

Bull Frog B&B   Box 210, Star Route, Ashfield 01330   413-628-4493
Col. Blackinton Inn   203 North Main St., Attleboro 02703   617-222-6022
Goss House B&B   61 Pine Lane, Barnstable 02630   617-362-8559
Anchorage   122 South Shore Drive, Bass River 02664   617-398-8265
Belvedere B&B Inn   167 Main St., Bass River 02664   508-398-6674
Old Cape House   108 Old Main St., Bass River 02664   617-398-1068
Canterbury Farm B&B   Fred Snow Road, Becket 01223   413-623-8765
Stonehedge B&B   119 Sawyer Hill Road, Berlin 01503   617-838-2574

Bernardston Inn   P.O. Box 485, Bernardston 01337   413-648-9282
Tirnanoag-The McKenna Pl   Chester Road, Blandford 01008   413-848-2083
Terrace Townehouse   60 Chandler St., Boston 02116   617-350-6520
Bleu Auberge   5 Scar Hill Rd., Boylston 01505   617-869-2666
Inn of the Golden Ox   1360 Main, Brewster 02631   617-896-3111
Beacon Plaza   1459 Beacon St., Brookline 02146   617-232-6550
Brookline Manor Guest Hous   32 Centre St., Brookline 02146   617-232-0003
1797 House   Charlemont Road, Buckland 01338   413-625-2697
Scott House   Hawley Road, Buckland 01338   413-625-6624
Cambridge House B&B Inn   P.O. Box 211, Cambridge 02140   617-491-6300
Carver House   638 Main St., Centerville 02632   617-775-9414
Copper Beech Inn   497 Main St., P.O. Box 67, Centerville 02632   617-771-5488
Old Hundred House   1211 Craigville Beach R, Centerville 02632   617-775-6166
Terrace Gardens Inn   539 Main St., Centerville 02632   617-775-4707
Forest Way Farm   Route 8A (Heath), Charlemont 01339   413-337-8321
Gingerbread B&Brunch   RR 2 Box 542A Stafford, Charlton 01507   617-248-7940
Bow Roof House   59 Queen Anne Road, Chatham 02633   617-945-1346
Chatham Bars Inn   Shore Road, Chatham 02633   617-945-0096
Queen Anne Inn   70 Queen Anne Road, Chatham 02633   617-945-0394
Seafarer Motel   Main St., Chatham 02633   617-432-1739
Ship's Inn at Chatham   P.O. Box 468, Chatham 02659   508-945-5859
Pleasant Pheasant B&B   296 Heath St., Chestnut Hill 02167   617-566-4178
Grandmother's House   RR 1 Box 37, Colrain 01340   413-624-3771
Anderson-Wheeler Homestead   154 Fitchburg Turnpike, Concord 01742   617-369-3756
Colonel Roger Brown House   Damonmill Square, Concord 01742   617-369-9119
Colonial Inn   48 Monument Square, Concord 01742   617-369-9200
Hilltop B&B   Truce Road, Conway 01341   413-369-4928
Poundsworth B&B   Old Cricket Hill Road, Conway 01341
James & Ellen Allen B&B   60 Nickerson Ln, POB 22, Cotuit 02635   617-428-5702
Hill Gallery   Cole St., Cummington 01026   413-238-5914
Dalton House   955 Main St., Dalton 01226   413-684-3854
Four Chimneys Inn   946 Main St., Dennis 02638   617-385-6317
"By-the-Sea" Guests   57 Chase Avenue, Box 50, Dennisport 02639   617-398-8685
Winsor House Inn   P.O. Box 287 SHS, Duxbury 02331   617-934-0991
Ocean Gold Cape Cod B&B   74 Locust Lane Rt. 2, East Brewster 02631   617-255-7045
Peterson's B&B   226 Trotting Park, East Falmouth 02536   508-540-2962
Over Look Inn   P.O. Box 771, Eastham 02642   508-255-1886
Penny House Inn—Cape Cod   P.O. Box 238, Eastham 02651   508-255-6632
Chadwick House   Box 1035, Edgartown 02539   617-627-4435
Charlotte Inn   S. Summer St., Edgartown 02539   617-627-4751
Daggett House   P.O. Box 1333, Edgartown 02539   508-627-4600
Edgartown Heritage Hotel   227 Upper Main St., Edgartown 02539   617-627-5161
Governor Bradford Inn   P.O. Box 239, Edgartown 02539   617-627-9510
Katama Guest House   RFD #108,166 Katama Rd, Edgartown 02539   617-627-5158
Shiretown Inn   N. Water St., Box 921, Edgartown 02539   800-541-0090
Amherst   30 Amherst Avenue, Falmouth 02540   617-548-2781
Elm Arch Inn   Elm Arch Way, Falmouth 02540   617-548-0133
Gladstone Inn   219 Grand Avenue South, Falmouth 02540   617-548-9851
Grafton Inn   261 Grand Ave. S., Falmouth 02540   508-540-8688
Hastings By the Sea   28 Worcester Avenue, Falmouth 02540   617-548-1628
Moorings Lodge   207 Grand Avenue South, Falmouth 02540   617-540-2370
Wyndemere House   718 Palmer Avenue, Falmouth 02540   617-540-7069
Blue Shutters Inn   1 Nautilus Road, Gloucester 01930   617-281-2706
Williams Guest House   136 Bass Av., Gloucester 01930   617-283-4931

Whale Inn   Rt. 9, Main St., Box 6, Goshen 01032   413-268-7246
Bread & Roses   Star Route 65, Box 50, Great Barrington 01230   413-528-1099
Littlejohn Manor   Newsboy Monument, Rt. 23, Great Barrington 01230   413-528-2882
Red Bird Inn   Box 592, Gt. Barrington, Great Barrington 01230   413-229-2433
Thornewood Inn   453 Stockbridge Road, Great Barrington 01230   413-528-3828
Windflower Inn   Rt. 23, Box 25, Great Barrington 01230   413-528-2720
The Winstead   328 Bank St., Harwich 02645   508-432-4586
Country Inn Acres Inc.   86 Sisson Rd., Harwich Port 02646   617-432-2769
Alpine Haus   Mashapaung Rd, Box 782, Holland 01550   413-245-9082
Paulson B&B   Allen Coit Road, Huntington 01050   413-667-3208
Acorn House   240 Sea St., Hyannis 02601   617-771-4071
Captain Sylvester Baxter   156 Main St., Hyannis 02601   508-775-5611
Sea Breeze Inn   397 Sea St., Hyannis 02601   617-771-7213
Homestead   288 Scudder Ave., Hyannis Port 02647   508-778-4999
AMC-Bascom Lodge   P.O. Box 686, Lanesboro 01237   413-743-1591
1777 Greylock House   58 Greylock St., Lee 01238   413-243-1717
Ramsey House   203 West Park St., Lee 01238   413-243-1598
Apple Tree Inn   224 West St., Lenox 01240   413-637-1477
Birchwood Inn   P.O. Box 2020, Lenox 01240   413-637-2600
Blantyre   P.O. Box 995, Lenox 01240   413-637-3556
Candlelight Inn   53 Walker St., Lenox 01240   413-637-1555
Cliffwood Inn   25 Cliffwood St., Lenox 01240   413-637-3330
Strawberry Hill   P.O. Box 718, Lenox 01240   413-637-3381
Underledge Inn   76 Cliffwood St., Lenox 01240   413-637-0236
Walker House   74 Walker St., Lenox 01240   413-637-1271
Wheatleigh Inn   Lenox 01240   413-637-0610
Ashley's B&B   6 Moon Hill Road, Lexington 02173   617-862-6488
Halewood House   2 Larchmont Lane, Lexington 02173   617-862-5404
Sherman-Berry House   163 Dartmouth St., Lowell 01851   508-459-4760
10 Mugford Street B&B   10 Mugford St., Marblehead 01945   617-631-5642
Lindsey's Garrett   38 High St., Marblehead 01945   617-631-2653
Sea Street B&B   9 Gregory St., Marblehead 01945   617-631-1890
Farmhouse   State Road, Martha's Vineyard 02568   617-693-5354
Victorian Inn   P.O. Box 947, Martha's Vineyard 02539   617-627-4784
Beach Plum Inn   Box 98, Menemsha 02552   617-645-9454
Strawberry Banke Farm B&B   on Skyline Trail, Middlefield 01243   413-623-6481
Bay Breeze Guest House   P. O. Box 307, Monument Beach 02553
Anchor Inn   66 Centre St., Nantucket 02554   508-228-0072
Brant Point Inn   6 N. Beach St., Nantucket 02554   508-228-5442
Cliff Lodge B&B   9 Cliff Road, Nantucket 02554   617-228-9480
Cliffside Beach Club   P.O. Box 449, Nantucket 02554   617-228-0618
Dolphin Guest House   10 North Beach St., Nantucket 02554   617-228-4028
Easton House   Box 1033, Nantucket 02554   617-228-2759
Eighteen Gardner St. Inn   18 Gardner St., Nantucket 02554   508-228-1155
Fair Gardens   27 Fair street, Nantucket 02554   617-228-4258
Fair Winds   29 Cliff Road, Nantucket 02554
Four Ash Street   4 Ash St., Nantucket 02554   617-228-4899
Hawthorn House   2 Chestnut St., Nantucket 02554   617-228-1468
House of the Seven Gables   32 Cliff Road, Nantucket 02554   617-228-4706
Hussey House-1795   15 North Water St., Nantucket 02554   617-228-0747
India House   37 India St., Nantucket 02554   617-228-9043
Ivy Lodge   2 Chester St., Nantucket 02554   617-228-6612
Le Languedoc Inn   24 Broad St., Nantucket 02554   617-228-2552
Nantucket Landfall   4 Harbor View Way, Nantucket 02554   617-228-0500

Parker Guest House   4 East Chestnut St., Nantucket 02554   617-228-4625
Periwinkle Guest House   9 N. Water St., Nantucket 02554   617-228-9267
Rueben Joy Guest House   107 Main St., Nantucket 02554   617-228-6612
Ten Lyon Street Inn   10 Lyon St., Nantucket 02554   617-228-5040
Tuckernuck Inn   60 Union St., Nantucket 02554   617-228-4886
Wake Up On Pleasant Street   31 Pleasant St., Nantucket 02554   617-228-0673
West Moor Inn   Off Cliff Rd., Nantucket 02554   617-228-0877
Beachside   North Beach St., Nantucket Island 02554   617-228-2241
Carriage House   4 Ray's Court, Nantucket Island 02554   617-228-0326
Chestnut House   3 Chestnut St., Nantucket Island 02554   617-228-0049
Martin's Guest House   61 Centre St., Nantucket Island 02554   617-228-0678
Nesbitt Inn   21 Broad St., Nantucket Island 02554   617-228-0156
Roberts House   India & Centre St.s, Nantucket Island 02554   617-228-9009
Stumble Inne   109 Orange St., Nantucket Island 02554   617-228-4482
Wharf Cottages   New Whale St., Nantucket Island 02554   617-228-4620
Morrill Place Inn   209 High St., Newburyport 01950   617-462-2808
Windsor House   38 Federal St., Newburyport 01950   508-462-3778
Ted Barbour   88 Rogers St., North Billrtivs 01862   617-667-7317
Wingate Crossing   R 28A,190 N Falmouth Hy, North Falmouth 02556   617-540-8723
Autumn Inn   259 Elm St., Northampton 01060   413-584-7660
Centennial House   94 Main St., Northfield 01360   413-498-5921
Northfield Country House   RR 1 P.O. Box 79A, Northfield 01360   413-498-2692
Squaheag House (The)   RR 1, Northfield 01360   413-498-5749
Attleboro House   11 Lake Avenue, Oak Bluffs 02557   617-693-4346
Circuit House   Box 2422, 150 Circuit A, Oak Bluffs 02557   617-693-5033
Dockside Inn   Box 1206, Oak Bluffs 02557   617-693-2966
Narragansett House   62 Narragansett Avenue, Oak Bluffs 02557   617-693-3627
Nashua House   Kennebee and Park Ave., Oak Bluffs 02557   617-693-0043
Ship's Inn   Box 1483, Oak Bluffs 02557   617-693-2760
Osterville Fairways Inn   105 Parker Rd., Osterville 02655   617-428-2747
Chalet d'Alicia B&B   East Windsor Road, Peru 01235   413-655-8292
Another Place Inn   240 Sandwich St., Plymouth 02360   548-746-0126
Colonial House Inn   207 Sandwich St., Plymouth 02360   617-746-2087
Country Inn at Princeton   30 Mountain Rd., Princeton 01541   508-464-2030
Asheton House   3 Cook St., Provincetown 02657   617-487-9966
Bed 'n Breakfast   44 Commercial St., Provincetown 02657   617-487-9555
Captain Lysander Inn Ltd.   96 Commercial St., Provincetown 02657   617-487-2253
Lamplighter Guest House   26 Bradford St., Provincetown 02657   617-487-2529
Red Inn   15 Commercial St., Provincetown 02657   617-487-0050
Somerset House   378 Commercial St., Provincetown 02657   617-487-0383
Sunset Inn   142 Bradford St., Provincetown 02657   617-487-9810
Twelve Center Guest House   12 Center St., Provincetown 02657   617-487-0381
Victoria House   5 Standish St., Provincetown 02657   617-487-1319
Wave's Landing Guest House   158 Bradford St., Provincetown 02657   617-487-9198
White Wind Inn   Commercial at Winthrop, Provincetown 02657   617-487-1526
Windamar House   568 Commercial St., Provincetown 02657   617-487-0599
Cable House   3 Narwood Avenue, Rockport 01966   617-546-3895
Eden Pines Inn   Eden Road, Rockport 01966   617-546-2505
Lantana House   22 Broadway, Rockport 01966   617-546-3535
Leiden Tree Inn   26 King St., Rockport 01966   617-546-2494
Pleasant Street Inn   17 Pleasant St., Rockport 01966   508-546-3915
Seven South Street-The I   7 South St., Rockport 01966   617-546-6708
Tuck Inn   17 High Street, Rockport 01966   617-546-6252
B&B   One Hawes Road, Box 205, Sagamore Beach 02562   617-888-1559

Inn at Seven Winter St.   Seven Winter St., Salem 01970   617-745-9520
Stepping Stone Inn   19 Washington Sqaure N., Salem 01970   508-741-8900
Suzannah Flint House   98 Essex St., Salem 01970   508-744-5281
New Boston Inn   Routes 57 & 8, Sandisfield 01255   413-258-4477
Six Water Street   P.O. Box 1295, Sandwich 02563   508-888-6808
Colonel Ashley Inn   RR 1 Box 142, Bow Wow, Sheffield 01257   413-229-2929
Stagecoach Hill Inn   Route 41, Sheffield 01257   413-229-8585
Staveleigh House   P.O. Box 608, Sheffield 01257   413-229-2129
Unique B&B   Under Mountain Rd,POB 7, Sheffield 01257   413-229-3363
Country Comfort   15 Masonic Avenue, Shelburne Falls 01370   413-625-9877
Parson Hubbard House   Old Village Road, Shelburne Falls 01370   413-625-9730
Summer House   Box 313, Ocean Ave, Siasconset 02564   617-257-9976
House on the Hill   P.O. Box 51, 968 Main St., South Harwich 02661   617-432-4321
Merrell Tavern Inn   Rt. 102, Main St., South Lee 01260   413-243-1794
Hillbourne House B&B   Route 28, Box 190, South Orleans 02662   617-255-0780
Wayside Inn   South Sudbury 01776   617-443-8846
Langhaar House   P.O. Box 191, Southfield, Southfield 01259   413-229-2007
Inn at Stockbridge   Stockbridge 01262   413-298-3337
Olde Lamplighter   Church St., Stockbridge 01262   413-298-3053
Chamberlain   P.O. Box 187, Sturbridge 01566   617-347-3313
Commonwealth Inn   11 Summit Ave., Sturbridge 01518   508-347-7603
Country Motor Lodge   P.O. Box 187, Sturbridge 01566   617-347-3313
Sudbury B&B   3 Drum Lane, Sudbury 01776   617-443-2860
Parker House B&B   Route 6A, Box 114, Truro 02666   617-349-3358
Golden Goose   P.O. Box 336, Tyringham 01264   413-243-3008
Gazebo B&B   Edgartown Road, Vineyard Haven 02568   617-693-6955
Hanover House   Box 2107, Vineyard Haven 02568   617-693-1066
High Haven House   Box 289, Summer St., Vineyard Haven 02568   617-693-9204
Lambert's Cove Country Inn   Box 422, RFD, Vineyard Haven 02568   508-693-2298
Ocean Side Inn   Main St., Box 2700, Vineyard Haven 02568   617-693-1296
South Wind   Box 810, Vineyard Haven 02568   617-693-5031
Tuckerman House   45 William St, Box 194, Vineyard Haven 02568   617-693-0417
Inn at Duck Creeke   Main St., Box 364, Wellfleet 02667   617-349-9333
Rose Cottage   24 Worcester,Rts. 12 & 1, West Boylston 01583   617-835-4034
Brookfield House Inn   P.O. Box 796, West Brookfield 01585   617-867-6589
Beach House   61 Uncle Stephen's Rd., West Dennis 02670   617-398-8321
Lighthouse Inn   West Dennis 02670   508-398-2244
Old Silver Beach B&B   3 Cliffwood Lane, POB 6, West Falmouth 02574   617-540-5446
Barnaby Inn   P.O. Box 151, West Harwich 02671   508-432-6789
Stump Sprouts Guest Lodge   West Hill Road, West Hawley 01339   413-339-4265
Williamsville Inn   Rt. 41, West Stockbridge 01266   413-274-6118
Manor House   57 Maine Ave., West Yarmouth 02673   617-771-9211
Sunnyside Farm   11 River Road, Whately 01093   413-665-3113
Victorian   583 Linwood Ave., Whitinsville 01588   617-234-2500
B&B with Barbara & Bo   15 Three Rivers Road, Wilbraham 01095   413-596-6258
Carl & Lottie Sylvester   9 South St., Williamsburg 01096   413-268-7283
Twin Maples   106 South St., Williamsburg 01098   413-268-7925
Field Farm Guest House   554 Sloan Road, Williamstown 01267   413-458-3135
Le Jardin   777 Coldspring Road, Williamstown 01267   413-458-8032
River Bend Farm   643 Simonds Road, Williamstown 01267   413-458-5504
Steep Acres Farm   520 White Oaks Road, Williamstown 01267   413-458-3774
The House On Main Street   1120 Main St., Williamstown 01267   413-458-3031
Grey Whale Inn   565 Woods Hole Rd., Woods Hole 02543   617-548-7692
Marlborough   320 Woods Hole Rd., Woods Hole 02543   617-548-6218

Franklin Burrs   Kinne Brook Rd., Worthington 01098   413-238-5826
Inn Yesterday   Huntington Road, Rt. 11, Worthington 01098   413-238-5529
Worthington Inn   Route 143, Old North Rd, Worthington 01098   413-238-4441
Colonial House Inn   Rt. 6A, Old King's Hwy, Yarmouth Port 02675   617-362-4348
Crook' Jaw Inn   186 Main St., Route 6A, Yarmouth Port 02675   508-362-6111
Olde Captain's Inn   101 Main St., Rt. 6, Yarmouth Port 02675   617-362-4496
One Centre Street Inn   1 Centre St., Yarmouth Port 02675   508-362-8910
Joshua Sears Manor   4 Summer St & Route 6A, Yarmouthport 02675   508-362-5000

Michigan

ANN ARBOR

Urban Retreat $$ B&B   Full breakfast
2759 Canterbury Rd., 48104   2 rooms   Comp. wine/snacks, bar
313-971-8110   C-no/S-yes/P-no/H-no   Sitting room, library
Andre Rosalik & Gloria Krys   patio, picnic area
All year   gardens, bicycles, A/C

Charming 1950s ranch home on quiet tree-lined street; furnished with antiques; adjacent to 127-acre meadowland park; minutes from major universities.

ANN ARBOR-SALINE

Homestead Bed & Breakfast $ B&B   Full breakfast
9279 Macon Rd., 48176   6 rooms, 1 pb   Comp. wine & cheese
313-429-9626   Visa, MC, Diners •   Library
Shirley Grossman   C-12+/S-yes/P-no/H-no   sitting room
All year   A/C in some rooms

1851 brick farmhouse on 50-acre farm. Comfort, country and Victorian elegance. Superb breakfasts. Close to Ann Arbor, Ypsilanti, Greenfield Village, Detroit.

BAY CITY

Stonehedge Inn $$ B&B   Continental plus
924 Center Ave., 48708   7 rooms, 0 pb   Afternoon tea, snacks
517-894-4342   Visa, MC, AmEx •   Sitting room
Ruth Koerber, John Kleekamp   C-yes/S-yes/P-no/H-no   library
All year   bicycles

Elegant journey into the past; 1889 English Tudor home has original stained glass windows, nine fireplaces and a magnificent open staircase. Breakfast in formal dining room.

BROOKLYN

Chicago Street Inn $$ B&B   Continental plus
P.O. Box 546, 49230   4 rooms, 4 pb   Comp. wine
219 Chicago St.   Visa, MC •   Sitting room
517-592-3888   C-13+/S-ltd
Karen & Bill Kerr
All year

1886 Queen Anne Victorian home, furnished with antiques. Located in quiet village in the foothills of the Irish hills. Antique shops and hiking trails nearby.

CHARLEVOIX

Bridge Street Inn	$$ B&B	Continental plus
113 Michigan Ave., 49720	9 rooms, 3 pb	Close to beaches,
616-547-6606	•	restaurants, shopping,
Vera & John McKown	C-no/S-no/P-no/H-no	& boating
All year		

Recapture the grace and charm of a gentler era in this ca. 1895 colonial revival home. 3 stories decorated with unique and interesting antiques. Each room has different decor.

DETROIT

Blanche House Inn	$$ B&B	Continental plus
506 Parkview, 48214	8 rooms, 8 pb	Afternoon tea
313-822-7090	Visa, MC, AmEx •	Sitting room, hot tubs
S. Shannon, M. Shannon	C-yes/S-no/P-no/H-no	porches, hammocks
All year		fireplaces, suite

The Blanche House Inn boasts turn-of-the-century plastering, oak woodwork, etched glass, antique furnishings, located off the Detroit River.

FENNVILLE

Hidden Pond Farm	$$$ B&B	Full breakfast
5975 128th Ave., 49408	2 rooms, 2 pb	Guest use of home
616-561-2491	C-12+/S-yes/H-yes	
Edward X. Kennedy		
All year		

B&B accommodations of quiet elegance. Two rooms with private baths, plus five common rooms, on 28 acres of private ravined grounds.

FLINT

Avon House B&B	$ B&B	Full breakfast
518 Avon St., 48503	3 rooms, 1 pb	Sitting room
313-232-6861	C-yes/S-yes/P-no/H-no	A/C
Arletta Minore		extended stay rates
All year		

Enchanting Victorian home six blocks from Auto World & Water Street Pavilion. Music, fine dining, cultural center, performing arts close by.

HOLLAND

Dutch Colonial Inn	$$ B&B	Full breakfast
560 Central Ave., 49423	5 rooms, 3 pb	Afternoon tea, snacks
616-396-3664	Visa, MC	Sitting room
Pat Elenbaas	C-yes/S-no/P-no/H-no	bicycles
All year		whirlpool tubs

Lovely 1930 Dutch Colonial home. Touches of elegance and antiques. Air-conditioned. Whirlpool tubs for two in private baths; hideaway suite.

McIntyre Bed & Breakfast	$$ B&B	Continental breakfast
13 E. 13th St., 49423	3 rooms, 1 pb	Afternoon tea
616-392-9886	•	Sitting room with TV
Russ & Betty Jane McIntyre	C-5+/S-no/P-no/H-no	
All year		

Beautifully maintained home built in 1906. Antiques throughout. Air-conditioned rooms. Excellent beds. Off-street parking. Continental breakfast. Warm hospitality.

HOLLAND

Old Wing Inn
5298 E. 147th Ave., 49423
616-392-7362
Chuck/Chris Lorenz
May 1—November 1

$ B&B
5 rooms, 2 pb
Visa, MC
C-yes/S-ltd/P-no/H-no

Continental plus
Sitting room

Relax amidst rustic charm in Holland's oldest historic landmark home. Once an Ottawa Indian mission in 1839, this home was built in 1844-46. State & National Register.

LAKESIDE

Pebble House
15093 Lakeshore Rd., 49116
616-469-1416
Jean & Ed Lawrence
All year

$$$ B&B
8 rooms, 6 pb
C-12+/S-yes/P-no/H-ltd

Full breakfast
Library room, pergolas
Screen house w/hammocks
fireplace, bicycles
tennis courts, walkwys

Ca. 1910 decorative block & beach pebble house. Arts & Crafts furniture & decorative items. Fireplace, woodstove, rocking chairs and a lake view. Like going home to Grandma's.

LANSING

Maplewood B&B
15945 Wood Rd., 48906
517-485-1426
Patricia J. Bunce
All year

$ B&B
C-10+

Full breakfast
Comp. wine, tea, snacks
Sitting room, library
bicycles

Country house on 3-acre parcel; only minutes to state capitol and Michigan State University at East Lansing.

LEXINGTON

Governor's Inn
P.O. Box 471, 48450
7277 Simons St.
313-359-5770
Bob & Jane MacDonald
Memorial Day—Late Sep.

$ B&B
3 rooms, 3 pb
C-12+/S-yes/P-no/H-no

Continental plus
Sitting room

Governor's Inn re-creates the atmosphere of a turn-of-the-century summer home—wicker, iron beds, rockers on the shady porch.

LUDINGTON

B&B at Ludington
2458 S. Beaune Rd., 49431
616-843-9768
Grace & Robert Schneider
All year

$ B&B
4 rooms, 1 pb
Major credit cards
C-yes/S-no/P-yes/H-yes
French, Spanish

Full country breakfast
Afternoon tea
Sitting room
piano
hot tub

Two miles from Lake Michigan, we have 125 acres for hiking, skiing, snowshoeing (showshoes provided). Creek and trout pond. Also room in remodeled barn loft.

MACKINAC ISLAND

Haan's 1830 Inn, B&B
P.O. Box 123, 49757
Huron St.
906-847-6244/906-847-3403
The Haan Family
Mid-May—mid-October

$$ B&B
7 rooms, 5 pb
C-yes/S-ltd/P-no/H-no

Continental plus
Parlor

Historic Greek Revival home built in 1830, restored and furnished with beautiful antiques. Sit on our porches and enjoy Island ambience.

MANISTEE

Inn Wick-A-Te-Wah
3813 Lakeshore Dr., 49660
616-889-4396
Marge & Len Carlson
All year

$$ B&B
4 rooms, 1 pb
Visa, MC •
C-ltd/S-ltd/P-no/H-no

Full breakfast
Comp. wine
Sitting room
inner tubes, bicycles
sunfish (sailing)

Gorgeous view to Portage Lake and Lake Michigan Channel. All water sports, golf, and snow skiing nearby. Lovely, airy rooms with period furnishings.

MARQUETTE

Michigamme Lake Lodge
2403 US 41 West, 49855
906-225-1393
Frank & Linda Stabile
All year

$$$ B&B
9 rooms, 6 pb
Visa, MC •
C-no/S-no/P-no/H-no

Continental plus
Afternoon tea
Sitting room, porch
gift shop, canoes
1700 ft. of lake & beach

On the lake, sandy beach, canoes, stroll gardens and birch groves. Built in the 1930s. Quiet and secluded. Furnished with antiques.

MARSHALL

National House Inn
102 S. Parkview, 49068
616-781-7374
Mike & Betty McCarthy
Except Christmas Eve

$ B&B
16 rooms, 16 pb
Visa, MC, AmEx
C-yes/S-yes/P-no/H-no

Continental plus
Sitting room

Michigan's oldest inn lovingly restored with authentic antiques, located in Marshall, home of the Midwest's most striking examples of Victorian architecture.

NORTHVILLE

Atchison House
501 W. Dunlap St., 48167
313-349-3340
Don Mroz, Susan Lapine
All year

$$ B&B
5 rooms, 3 pb
Visa, MC, AmEx •
S-no/P-no/H-no
French, German

Continental plus
Full breakfast (Wednes.)
Comp. wine, tea, snacks

A magnificent 1882 Victorian Italianate furnished in period antiques. Located in the heart of the Historic District, just 4 blocks from downtown Northville.

PETOSKEY

Stafford's Bay View Inn
P.O. Box 3 G, 49770
613 Woodland Ave.
616-347-2771
Judy Honor
May—Nov./Xmas—March 30

$$$ B&B
20 rooms, 20 pb
Visa, MC, AmEx
C-yes/S-yes/P-no/H-yes

Full breakfast
Lunch, dinner, tea, wine
Sitting room
piano

Michigan Historic Site overlooking Little Traverse Bay. Victorian charm, exceptional cuisine, scenic drives, shopping, summer and winter recreation.

PORT HURON

Victorian Inn
1229 7th St., 48060
313-984-1437
Sheila Marinez
All year

$ B&B
4 rooms, 2 pb
Visa, MC, AmEx, Disc
C-13+/S-yes/P-no/H-no

Continental breakfast
Restaurant, pub
Lunch, dinner
Near museum, downtown,
civic center, marina

The Victorian Inn features fine dining with creative cuisine and guest rooms presenting a timeless ambience in authentically restored Victorian elegance.

PORT SANILAC ——————————————————————————

Raymond House Inn
111 S. Ridge St., 48469
313-622-8800
Shirley Denison
May—October

$ B&B
7 rooms, 7 pb
•
C-12+/S-ltd/P-no/H-no

Continental plus
Bicycles
sitting room
pottery studio

112-year-old Victorian home furnished in antiques; on Lake Huron; marina, boating, salmon fishing, swimming; owner-artist's gallery. New studio of handmade pottery.

SAGINAW ——————————————————————————

Brockway House B&B
1631 Brockway, 48602
517-792-0746
Dani & Rick Zuehlke
All year

$$ B&B
4 rooms, 3 pb
Visa, MC, AmEx •
C-yes/S-no/P-no/H-no

Gourmet breakfast
Comp. wine
Afternoon tea, snacks
Sitting room, library
king-sized beds

Share the enchantment of a classic B&B, a historic treasure for generations. Primitive antiques, gourmet breakfasts. 20 minutes from Frankenmuth.

SAINT IGNACE ——————————————————————————

Colonial House Inn
90 N. State St., 49781
906-643-6900
L. Hargrove, Marilyn Hurst
May—September

$ B&B
17 rooms, 12 pb
Visa, MC, AmEx
C-yes/S-yes

Continental plus
Comp. hors d'ouevres
Sitting room
library

Charming colonial revival-style home facing Mackinac Island, directly across from one of the ferries. Delightful breakfast served in parlor.

SAUGATUCK ——————————————————————————

Kemah Guest House
633 Pleasant, 49453
616-857-2919
Cindi & Terry Tatsch
All year

$$$ B&B
7 rooms
Visa, MC •
Spanish

Continental breakfast
Sitting room
library

Turn-of-the-century mansion sports a combination of Old World flavor, art deco and a splash of southwestern airiness.

Kingsley House
626 W. Main, Fennville, 49408
616-561-6425
David & Shirley Witt
All year

$$ B&B
5 rooms, 5 pb
•
C-8+/S-no

Full breakfast
Fireplaces
Sitting rooms
bicycles
porch swing

Elegant Queen Anne Victorian home, built in 1886. Country setting near beaches, cross-country skiing. Truly an unforgettable experience. Family antiques.

Maplewood Hotel
P.O. Box 1059, 49453
428 Butler St.
616-857-1771
David Cofield
All year

$ B&B
13 rooms, 13 pb
Visa, MC, AmEx
C-yes/S-yes/P-ltd/H-ltd

Continental breakfast
Restaurant, lunch by req.
Hors d'oeuvres, bar
Sitting room, library
pool, jacuzzi, tennis

Gracious Greek revival hotel is a gleaming tribute to the 19th century. Inside, crystal chandeliers, antiques and period furniture make the hotel a perennial favorite.

SAUGATUCK ─────────────────────────────────────

Twin Gables Country Inn	$ B&B	Continental plus
P.O. Box 881, 49453	10 rooms, 10 pb	Refreshments
900 Lake St.	Visa, MC •	Fireplace, hot tub
616-857-4346	C-ltd/S-ltd/P-no/H-yes	whirlpool, bicycles, A/C
Mike & Denise Simcik	Italian, French, Maltese	garden park, pond, pool
All year		

Country charm overlooking Kalamazoo Lake. 8 charming rooms, each in a delightful theme decor. Short walk to downtown. 3 cottages furnished in antiques also available.

Wickwood Inn	$$$ B&B	Continental breakfast
510 Butler, 49453	11 rooms, 11 pb	Comp. beverages
616-857-1097	Visa, MC, AmEx •	Sunday brunch
Sue & Stub Louis	C-no/S-yes/P-no/H-yes	Screened porch, patio
All year		4 common rooms

Truly elegant comfort in stately home on beautiful Lake Michigan yachting harbor. Laura Ashley decor, antiques, stunning common rooms. Featured in 9/86 Glamour Magazine.

SOUTH HAVEN ─────────────────────────────────────

Yelton Manor	$$ B&B	Continental plus
140 North Shore Dr., 49090	11 rooms, 11 pb	Snacks
616-637-5220	Visa, MC, AmEx	Sitting rooms, library
Jay & Joyce Yelton	C-16+/S-ltd/P-no/H-no	fireplace in parlor
All year		jacuzzis in some rooms

Country atmosphere. Within walking distance to lake, marina, shops, fine restaurants. 10 charming guest rooms with private bath, including a honeymoon suite.

Jeweled Turret Inn, Belfast, ME

TRAVERSE CITY

Linden Lea On Long Lake — $$ B&B — Full breakfast
279 S. Long Lake Rd., 49684 — 2 rooms, 1 pb — Snacks
616-943-9182 — • — Sitting room
Jim & Vicky McDonnell — C-yes — lake frontage, rowboat
All year — Spanish — sandy beach, raft

Wooded lakeside retreat with private sandy beach, rowboat & raft. Comfortable country furnishings, window seats, antiques & beveled glass throughout. Heavily wooded. Peaceful.

UNION CITY

Victorian Villa Guesthouse — $$$ B&B — Full breakfast
601 N. Broadway St., 49094 — 8 rooms, 6 pb — Full Victorian tea
517-741-7383 — Visa, MC • — Sitting rooms
Ron & Sue Gibson — C-yes/S-no/P-no/H-no — piano, bicycles
All year — 2 ac. landscaped grounds

Elegantly restored 1876 estate house with romantic accommodations. An opportunity to escape the 20th century. Special Victorian theme weekends.

More Inns...

Briaroaks Inn 2980 N. Adrian Hwy., Adrian 517-263-1659
Torch Lake B&B 10601 Coy Street, Alden 49612 616-331-6424
Winchester Inn 524 Marshall St., Allegan 49010 616-673-3621
Olde Bricke House P. O. Box 211, Allen 49227 517-869-2349
Old Lamplighter's Homestay 276 Capital Ave., N.E., Battle Creek 49017 616-963-2603
William Clements Inn 1712 Center (M-25), Bay City 48708 517-894-4600
Terrace Inn 216 Fairview Ave., Bay View 49770 616-347-2410
Brookside Inn US 31, Beulah 49617 616-882-7271
Windermere Inn 747 Crystal Drive, Beulah 49617 616-882-7264
Big Bay Lighthouse B&B No. 3 Lighthouse Road, Big Bay 49808 906-345-9957
PJ's B&B 722 North 29th St., Bilings 59101 406-259-3300
Silver Creek 4361 US-23, South, Black River 48721 517-471-2198
Celibeth House Blaney Park, Rt. 1, Box 5, Blaney Park 49836 906-283-3409
H. D. Ellis Inn 415 W. Adrian, US 223, Blissfield 49228 517-486-3155
Calumet House B&B P.O. Box 126, Calumet 49913 906-337-1936
Garden Gate B&B 315 Pearl St., Caro 48723 517-673-2696
Bay B&B Rt. 1, Box 136A, Charlevoix 49720 616-599-2570
Belvedere House 306 Belvedere Ave., Charlevoix 49720 616-547-4501
Channel View Inn 217 Park, Charlevoix 49720 616-147-6180
Chandelier Guest House 1567 Morgan Road, Clio 48420 313-687-6061
Oakbrook Inn 7256 E. Court St., Davison 48423 313-658-1546
Bannicks B&B 4608 Michigan Road, M-9, Dimondale 48821 517-646-0224
Rosemont Inn 83 Lake Shore Dr., Douglas 49406 616-857-2637
Sunrise B&B Box 52, Eastport 49627 616-599-2706
House on the Hill P.O. Box 206, Lake St., Ellsworth 49729 616-588-6304
B&B at Lynch's Dream 22177 80th Avenue, Evart 49631 616-734-5989
"Porches" 2297 70th St., Fennville 49408 616-543-4162
Pine Ridge N-10345 Old US 23, Fenton 48430 313-629-8911
Botsford Inn 28000 Grand River Ave., Framington Hills 40824 313-474-4800
B&B at the Pines 327 Ardussi St., Frankenmuth 48734 517-652-9019
Hotel Frankfort Main St., Frankfort 49635 616-882-7271
Trillium 611 South Shore Drive, Frankfort 49635 616-352-4976
Sylvan Inn 6680 Western Avenue, Glen Arbor 49636 616-334-4333
White Gull Inn P.O. Box 351, Glenn Arbor 49636 616-334-4486

Harbor House Inn   Harbor & Clinton St., Grand Haven 49417   616-846-0610
Highland Park Hotel B&B   1414 Lake Avenue, Grand Haven 49417   616-842-6483
Lakeview Inn   P.O. Box 297, Grand Marais 49839   906-494-2612
Fountain Hill   222 Fountain, NE, Grand Rapids 49503   616-458-6621
Wellock Inn   404 S. Huron Ave., Harbor Beach 48441   517-479-3645
Harbour Inn   Beach Drive, Harbor Springs 49740   616-526-2107
Red Geranium Inn   508 E. Main St., Box 61, Harrisville 48740   517-724-6153
Widow's Watch B&B   401 Lake St., Box 27, Harrisville 48740   517-724-5465
Parsonage 1908   6 E. 24th St., Holland 49423   616-396-1316
Grist Guest House   310 E. Main St., Homer 49245   517-568-4063
Hansen's Guest House   102 W. Adams, Homer 49245   517-568-3001
Wellman Accommodations   205 Main St., Horton 49246   517-563-2231
Chaffin Farms B&B   3239 W. St. Charles Rd., Ithaca 48847   517-463-4081
Munro House B&B   202 Maumee St., Jonesville 49250   517-849-9292
Hall House B&B   106 Thompson St., Kalamazoo 49007   616-343-2500
Kalamazoo House   447 W. South St., Kalamazoo 49007   616-343-5426
Stuart Avenue B&B   405 Stuart Ave., Kalamazoo 49007   616-342-0230
Creative Holiday Lodge   1000 Calumet St., Lake Linden 49945   906-296-0113
Stagecoach Stop B&B   Box 18, 4819 Leonard Rd, Lamont 49430   616-677-3940
Oak Cove Resort   58881 46th St., Lawrence 49064   616-674-8228
Springbrook B&B   28143 Springbrook Dr., Lawton 49065   616-624-6359
Riverside Inn   302 River St., Leland 49654   616-256-9971
Ludington House   501 E. Ludington Avenue, Luddington 49431   616-845-7769
White Rose Country Inn   6036 Barnhart Rd., Ludington 49431   616-843-8193
Bogan Lane Inn   P.O. Box 482, Mackinac Island 49757   906-847-3439
E. E. Douville House   111 Pine St., Manistee 49660   616-723-8654
Margaret's B&B   230 Arbutus, P.O. Box 344, Manistique 49854   906-341-5147
Country Cottage B&B   135 E. Harbor Hwy., Maple City 49664   616-228-5328
Leelanau Country Inn   149 E. Harbor Highway, Maple City 49664   616-228-5060
McCarthy's Bear Creek Inn   15230 C Drive North, Marshall 49068   616-781-8383
Helmer House Inn   Rt. 3, County Rd. 417, McMillan 49853   906-586-3204
Blue Lake Lodge B&B   P.O. Box 1, Mecosta 49332   616-972-8391
Mendon Country Inn   440 W. Main St., Mendon 49072   616-496-8132
Jay's B&B   4429 Bay City Road, Midland 48640   517-631-0470
Morning Glory Inn   8709 Old Channel Trail, Montague 49437   616-894-8237
Country Chalet   723 S. Meridian Rd., Mount Pleasant 48858   517-772-9269
Woods & Hearth B&B   950 S. Third St., Niles 49120   616-683-0876
Yesterday's Inn   518 N. 4th, Niles 49120   616-683-6079
Hutchinson's Garden B&B   P.O. Box 661, Northport 49670   616-386-5534
Old Mill Pond Inn   202 West 3rd St., Northport 49670   616-386-7341
Plum Lane Inn   P.O. Box 74, Northport 49670   616-386-5774
Vintage House B&B   Box 424, 102 Shabwasung, Northport 49670   616-386-7228
Wood How Lodge   Rt. 1 Box 44E, Northport 49670   616-386-7194
Stonegate Inn   10831 Cleveland, Nunica 49448   616-837-9267
Haus Austrian   4626 Omena Point Road, Omena 49674   616-386-7338
Mulberry House   1251 Shiawassee St., Owasso 48867   517-723-4890
Sylverlynd   3452 McBride Road, Owosso 48667   517-723-1267
Pentwater Inn   Box 98, Pentwater 49449   616-869-5909
Bear & The Bay   421 Charlevoix Avenue, Petoskey 49770   616-347-6077
Cozy Spot (The)   1145 Kalamazoo, Petoskey 49770   616-347-3869
Gull's Way   118 Boulder Lane, Petoskey 49770   616-347-9891
Pebble Beach   496 Rosedale Ave., Petoskey 49770   616-347-1903
Lake Street Manor   8569 Lake St. (M-53), Port Austin 49467   517-738-7720
Questover Inn   8510 Lake St., Port Austin 48467   517-738-5253
Webber House   527 James St., Portland 48875   517-647-4671

Country Heritage B&B   64707 Mound Rd., Romeo 48065   313-752-2879
Tall Trees   Rt. 2, 323 Birch Rd., Roscommon 48653   517-821-5592
Montague Inn   1581 S. Washington Ave., Saginaw 48601   517-752-3939
Jann's Guest House   132 Mason St., Box 3, Saugatuck 49453   616-857-8851
Kirby House   Box 1174, 294 W.Center, Saugatuck 49453   616-857-2904
Newnham Inn   Box 1106, 131 Giffith S, Saugatuck 49453   616-857-4249
Park House   888 Holland St., Saugatuck 49453   616-857-4535
Rummel's Tree Haven   41 N. Beck St., Sebewaing 48759   517-883-2450
A Country Place B&B   Rt. 5, Box 43, N. Shore, South Haven 49090   616-637-5523
Last Resort B&B Inn   86 North Shore Dr, South Haven 49090   616-637-8943
Old Harbor Inn   515 Williams St., South Haven 49090   616-637-8480
Ross B&B House   229 Michigan AVe, South Haven 49090   616-637-2256
Victoria Resort   241 Oak, South Haven 49090   616-637-6414
Alberties Waterfront   18470 Main St.-N. Shores, Spring Lake 49456   616-846-4016
Seascape B&B   20009 Breton, Spring Lake 49456   616-842-8409
Shifting Sands   19343 North Shore Drive, Spring Lake 49456   616-842-3594
Murphy Inn   505 Clinton Ave., St. Clair 48079   313-329-7118
Clifford Lake Hotel   561 W. Clifford Lake Dr., Stanton 48888   517-831-5151
Pink Palace Farms   6095 Baldwin Road, Swartz Creek 48473   313-655-4076
Boulevard Inn   904 W. Chicago Blvd., Tecumseh 49286   517-423-5169
Cider House B&B   5515 Barney Road, Traverse City 49684   616-947-2833
Hillside B&B   Rt. 1A, W. Lakeshore Rd, Traverse City 49621   616-228-6106
L'DA RU B&B   4370 N. Spider Lake Rd., Traverse City 49684   616-946-8999
Neahtawanta Inn   1308 Neahtawanta Road, Traverse City 49684   616-223-7315
Queen Anne's Castle   500 Webster, Traverse City 49684   616-946-1459
Warwickshire Inn   5037 Barney Rd., Traverse City 49684   616-946-7176
Bear Haven   2947-4th St., Trenton 48183   313-675-4844
Gordon Beach Inn   16240 Lakeshore Rd., Union Pier 49129   616-469-3344
Inn at Union Pier   P.O. Box 222, Union Pier 49129   616-469-4700
Walloon Lake Inn   P.O. Box 85, Walloon Lake Village 49796   616-535-2999
Green Inn   4045 West M-76, West Branch 48661   517-345-0334
River Haven   9222 St. Joe River Road, White Pigeon 49099   616-483-9104

Minnesota

CANNON FALLS

Quill & Quilt, B&B
615 W. Hoffman St., 55009
507-263-5507
D. Anderson, D. Karpinski
All year

$ B&B
4 rooms, 4 pb
Visa, MC •
C-12+ /S-ltd

Full breakfast
Dinner by arrangement
Comp. wine, sitting room
Library, cable TV, games
bikes, rec. room, deck

1897 colonial revival home. Four guest rooms, suite with whirlpool. In scenic Cannon River Valley; near biking, hiking, skiing, canoeing, etc. 1 hour from Minneapolis/St. Paul.

GRAND MARAIS

Pincushion Mountain B&B
P.O. Box 181, 55604
Gunflint Trail
218-387-1276/800-542-1226
Scott & Mary Beattie
Exc. April

$$ B&B
4 rooms, 1 pb
Visa, MC •
C-13+ /S-no/P-no/H-no

Full breakfast
Lunch, Aft. tea, snacks
Sitting room, library
hiking, fishing
X-C skiing

B&B sits on ridge of Sawtooth Mountains overlooking north shore of Lake Superior 1,000 feet below. Hiking & X-C ski trails at doorstep. 20 min. from Boundary Water Canoe Area.

HASTINGS

Thorwood Inn
4th & Pine, 55033
612-437-3297
Dick & Pam Thorsen
All year

$$ B&B
8 rooms, 8 pb
Visa, MC, AmEx •
C-yes/S-ltd/P-no/H-no

Full breakfast
Comp. evening snack
Sitting room, library
victrolas, fireplaces
whirlpools

1880 French Second Empire home, listed on National Register. Suite-size rooms, feather comforters, fine local wine with evening snack.

LAKE CITY

Red Gables Inn
403 N. High St., 55041
612-345-2605
Bill & Bonnie Saunders
All year

$ B&B
4 rooms, 2 pb
Visa, MC •
C-13+/S-ltd/P-no/H-no

Full breakfast
Comp. wine, snacks
Sitting room, library
bicycles
tennis nearby

Graciously restored 1865 Victorian on the shores of the Mississippi River. Enjoy antique decor, quiet elegance and Victorian breakfast. Sailing, swimming, skiing.

LANESBORO

Mrs. B's Lanesboro Inn
P.O. Box 411, 55949
101 Parkway
507-467-2154
The Bratruds

All year
9 rooms, 9 pb
S-ltd
some Norwegian, Hebrew

Full breakfast
Lunch & dinner by resv.
Comp. wine, snacks
Sitting room, library
tennis & golf nearby

Nestled deep in Root River Valley; 1872 limestone building in village on National Register. Serene; rural; famous for regional cuisine.

MINNEAPOLIS

Evelo's Bed & Breakfast
2301 Bryant Ave. S, 55405
612-374-9656
All year

$ B&B
3 rooms
•
C-yes/S-no/P-no/H-no

Full breakfast
TV, refrigerator
coffee maker

1897 Victorian, period furnishings. Located on bus line, walk to Guthrie Theater, Minneapolis Art Institute, children's theater. Near historic Lake District.

NEW PRAGUE

Schumacher's New Prague Hotel
212 W. Main St., 56071
612-758-2133/612-445-7285
John & Kathleen Schumacher
All year

$$$ EP
11 rooms, 11 pb
Visa, MC, AmEx •
C-no/S-yes/P-no/H-ltd

Restaurant, bar
Breakfast, lunch, dinner
Sitting room, piano
front porch, gift shop
whirlpools, fireplaces

Eleven European-decorated sleeping rooms named after the months of the year. Restaurant serves Czechoslovakian and German cuisine seven days a week.

RED WING

St. James Hotel
406 Main St., 55066
612-388-2846
Gene Foster
All year

$$$ EP
Visa, MC, AmEx, CB, DC
C-yes/S-yes/P-yes/H-yes

Veranda Cafe
Port of Red Wing Rest.
Sitting room
library

Restored Victorian hotel on National Register for Historic Places. Two restaurants, two lounges, 11 shops. Located in Mississippi River town surrounded by bluffs.

ROCHESTER

Canterbury Inn B&B	$$$ B&B	Full breakfast
723 2nd St. SW, 55902	4 rooms, 4 pb	Comp. tea, wine,
507-289-5553	Visa, MC, AmEx •	hors d'oeuvres
Jeffrey Van Sant, Mary Martin	C-ltd/S-ltd/P-no/H-no	Sitting room
All year	Italian	TV, stereo, cassettes

Victorian charm, modern comforts. Fireplace, a/c, phones. Gourmet breakfasts any time. Elegant "tea." Perfect for vacation, business visitors, Mayo Clinic.

SAINT PAUL

Chatsworth Bed & Breakfast	$$ B&B	Continental plus
984 Ashland Ave., 55104	5 rooms, 2 pb	Sitting room
612-227-4288	C-yes	library
Donna & Earl Gustafson		2 rooms with whirlpools
All year		

Peaceful retreat in city near Governor's Mansion. Whirlpool baths, down comforters, lace curtains. Excellent restaurants and unique shops within walking distance.

SAUK CENTRE

Palmer House Hotel	$ EP	Full service restaurant
500 Sinclair Lewis Ave., 56378	37 rooms, 4 pb	Tennis courts
612-352-3431	C-yes/S-yes/P-yes/H-no	sitting room, piano
Al Tingley	German	dinner theatre
All year		

Historic site—the "original Main Street" home of Sinclair Lewis—first American author to win the Nobel Prize for Literature.

SPRING VALLEY

Chase's	$$ B&B	Full farm breakfast
508 N. Huron Ave., 55975	5 rooms, 2 pb	Comp. tea
507-346-2850	Visa, MC •	Library
Bob & Jeannine Chase	C-yes/S-no/P-no/H-no	sitting room
May 1—November 1		crochet

Antiques throughout Chase's 19th-century mansion. Sleep in solitude, breakfast in quietness. Scenic southeastern Minnesota bluff country.

STILLWATER

Overlook Inn B&B	$$ B&B	Continental plus
210 E. Laurel, 55082	4 rooms, 2 pb	Comp. wine
612-439-3409	H-yes	Sitting room, library
David & Janel Belz		small wedding receptions
All year		large screened porch

An 1859 Victorian home overlooking the St. Croix River Valley. Each guest room has its own unique river view.

Rivertown Inn	$ B&B	Full breakfast
306 W. Olive St., 55082	9 rooms, 6 pb	Social hour in evenings
612-430-2955	Visa, MC •	Sitting areas, bicycles
Chuck & Judy Dougherty	C-12+/S-ltd/P-no/H-no	screen porch, gazebo
All year		ski packages

The perfect getaway for all seasons, within walking distance of historic Stillwater and the picturesque St. Croix River, 30 minutes from Minneapolis.

WALKER ───────────────────────────────────

Chase On The Lake Lodge	$$ B&B	Full breakfast
P.O. Box 206, 56484	20 rooms, 20 pb	Lunch, dinner
6th & Cleveland	Visa, MC, AmEx, D •	Restaurant, bar
218-547-1531	C-yes/S-yes/P-no/H-yes	Tennis nearby
James & Barb Aletto	Spanish, French	beach
All year		

Historic inn featuring fine dining with a spectacular view! Nightly entertainment in season.

More Inns...

Thayer Hotel　Hwy. 55, Annandale 55302　612-274-3371
Rainy River Lodge　Baudette 56623　218-634-2730
Grand View Lodge　Rt. 6, Box 22, Brainerd 56401　218-963-2234
Basswood Hill's Farm　Rt. 1, Box 331, Cannon Falls 55009　507-778-3259
Bluff Creek Inn　1161 Bluff Creek Drive, Chaska 55318　612-445-2735
Mansion　3600 London Rd., Duluth 55804　218-724-0739
Three Deer Haven　Hwy 169, Ely 55731　218-365-6464
Christopher Inn　201 Mill St., Excelsior 55331　612-474-6816
Murray Street Gardens B &　22520 Murray St., Excelsior 55331　612-474-8089
East Bay Hotel　Box 246, Grand Marais 55604　218-387-2800
Gunflint Lodge　Box 100 GT, Grand Marais 55604　800-328-3325
Naniboujou Lodge　Star Rt. 1, Box 505, Grand Marais 55604　218-387-2688
Young's Island　Gunflint Tr. 67-1, Grand Marais 55604　218-388-4487
Rahilly House　304 S. Oak St., Lake City 55041　612-345-4664
Cosgrove　228 S. Second St., Le Sueur 56058　612-665-2763
Pine Edge Inn　308 First St. SE, Little Falls 56345　612-632-6681
Grand Old Mansion　501 Clay St., Mantorville 55955　507-635-3231
American House　410 E. Third St., Morris 56267　612-589-4054
Schuyten Guest House　257 Third Ave., Newport 55055　612-459-5698
Archer House　212 Division St., Northfield 55057　507-645-5661
Lowell House　RR 2 Box 177, 531 Wood, Old Frontenac 55026　612-345-2111
Kettle Falls Hotel　Box 1272, Int'l Falls, Orr 55771　218-374-3511
Bunt's B&B　Lake Kabetogama, Ray 56669　218-875-3904
Pratt Taber Inn　706 W. 4th, Red Wing 55066　612-388-5945
Grant House　Box 87, Rush City 55069　612-358-4717
Country B&B　32030 Ranch Tr., Shafer 55074　612-257-4773
Kings Oakdale Park G.H.　6933 232nd Ave NE, Stacy 55029　612-462-5598
Driscolls for Guests　1103 South 3rd St., Stillwater 55082　612-439-7486
Lowell Inn　102 N. Second St., Stillwater 55082　612-439-1100
Hudspeth House B&B　21225 Victory Lane, Taylors Falls 55084　612-465-5811
Old Taylors Falls Jail　102 Government Road, Taylors Falls 55084　612-465-3112
Hotel & Zach's　129 W. Third Street, Winona 55987　507-452-5460

Mississippi

LORMAN

Rosswood Plantation
39096
601-437-4215
Jean & Walt Hylander
All year

$$$ B&B
4 rooms, 4 pb
Visa, MC •
C-yes/S-ltd/P-no/H-no

Full breakfast
Comp. tea/wine/cocktails
Sitting room, piano
Civil War library, TV
balconies

Classic 1857 mansion on a working plantation near Natchez. Ideal for honeymoons. Canopied beds, fine antiques, all conveniences. National Register, a Mississippi landmark.

NATCHEZ

The Burn
712 N. Union St., 39120
601-442-1344/800-654-8859
Loveta & Tony Byrne
All year

$$$ B&B
6 rooms, 6 pb
Visa, MC •
C-6+/S-yes/P-no/H-yes

Full breakfast
Comp. wine
Swimming pool
sitting room
piano, terraced gardens

The Burn (1832) is located in the oldest city on the Mississippi. Greek architecture. Once used as a hospital for Union soldiers.

Dunleith
84 Homochitto, 39120
601-446-8500/800-433-2445
Nancy Gibbs
Exc. last 2 weeks of year

$$$ B&B
11 rooms, 11 pb
Visa, MC, AmEx
C-14+/S-yes/P-no/H-no

Full Southern breakfast
Comp. wine, lemonade
Sitting room, conf. fac.
croquet, fishing
banquet facilities

Antebellum mansion used as backdrop for Huckleberry Finn *and* Showboat. *Member of Pilgrimage Garden Club. You are welcome!*

Hope Farm
147 Homochitto St., 39120
601-445-4848
Ethel G. Banta
All year

$$ B&B
4 rooms, 4 pb
•
C-6+/S-yes/P-no/H-no

Plantation breakfast
Comp. wine
Sitting room
library

Fine old southern mansion, circa 1775, on 20 acres including 10 acres of formal gardens. Antiques throughout.

PORT GIBSON

Oak Square Plantation
1207 Church St., 39150
601-437-4350
Mr. & Mrs. William Lum
All year

$$ B&B
8 rooms, 8 pb
Visa, MC, AmEx •
C-yes/S-ltd/P-no/H-ltd

Full breakfast
Comp. wine
Large sitting room
piano, TV
courtyard

Antebellum mansion in the town Gen. U.S. Grant said was "too beautiful to burn." Heirloom antiques. Canopied beds. National Register. AAA 4-diamond rated.

VICKSBURG

Anchuca
1010 First East St., 39180
601-636-4931/800-262-4822
May White
All year

$$$ B&B
9 rooms, 9 pb
Visa, MC, AmEx, Disc. •
C-yes/S-yes/P-ltd/H-no

Full breakfast
Comp. evening drinks
Turndown service
swimming pool, hot tub
sitting room, piano

Rooms furnished in beautiful antiques; sumptuous swimming pool, hot tub, breakfast served in magnificent dining room.

Cedar Grove Mansion
2300 Washington St., 39180
601-636-1605/800-862-1300
Estelle Mackey
All year

$$$ B&B
17 rooms, 17 pb
Visa, MC •
C-yes/S-ltd/H-yes
Spanish

Full breakfast
Comp. wine
Afternoon tea
bar service
Hots tubs, swimming pool

Antebellum mansion, ca. 1840. Exquisitely furnished with many original antiques, including gaslit chandeliers. Four acres of formal garden. Relive Gone With the Wind.

Corners Mansion
601 Klein St., 39180
601-636-7421/800-444-7421
Bettye & Cliff Whitney
All year

$$ B&B
7 rooms, 6 pb
Visa, MC •
C-yes/S-ltd/P-yes/H-yes

Full breakfast
Comp. wine
Afternoon tea
Sitting room, library
croquet

1872 mansion has original gardens; gallery offers a spectacular view of the mighty Mississippi. Period antiques. AAA four diamond rated.

The Duff Green Mansion
1114 First East St., 39180
P.O. Box 75
601-636-6968
Harry & Alicia Sharp
All year

$$$ B&B
7 rooms, 7 pb
Visa, MC, AmEx, Diners •
C-yes/S-yes/P-no/H-ltd
Spanish

Full breakfast
Lunch, dinner, bar
Library, sitting room
swimming pool
candlelight tours

Vicksburg's only true mansion, 12,000 sq. ft. of antique-filled rooms. Used as a hospital during the Civil War. Choice of drink on arrival. Two VIP suites.

More Inns...

Mount Holly   Box 140, Chatham 38731   601-827-2652
Antebellum Hmes   906 3rd Avenue, Columbus 39701   601-327-4064
Cartney-Hunt House   408 S. 7th St., Columbus 39701   601-327-4259
Springfield Plantation   Rt. 1 Box 201, Hwy 553, Fayette 39069   601-786-3802
Hamilton Place   105 E. Mason Ave., Holly Springs 38635   601-252-4368
Fairview   734 Fairview St., Jackson 39202   601-948-3429
Millsaps Buie House   628 N. State St., Jackson 39202   601-352-0221
Red Creek Colonial Inn   7416 Red Creek Rd., Long Beach 39503   601-452-3080
Linden   1 Linden Pl., Natchez 39120   601-445-5472
Monmouth Plantation   POB 1736, Natchez 39120   601-442-5852
Ravennaside   601 S. Union St., Natchez 39120   601-442-8015
Silver Street Inn   1 Silver St., Natchez 39120   601-442-4221
ISOM Place   1003 Jefferson Ave., Oxford 39655
Oliver-Britt House   512 Van Buren Av., Oxford 38655   601-234-8043
Turn of the Century   Rt. 4 Box 214, Menge, Pass Christian 39571   601-452-2868
Gray Oaks   4142 Rifle Range Rd., Vicksburg 39180   601-638-4424
Tomil Manor   2430 Drummond St., Vicksburg 39180   601-638-8893
Rosemont Plantation   Woodville 65247

Missouri

ARROW ROCK

By Hammer & Hand Antiques
Cedar Grove, 65320
816-837-3441
Kaye S. & David J. Perkins
All year

$ B&B
2 rooms
C-yes/S-ltd/P-no/H-no

Continental plus
Sitting room
library
yard w/swing

Visit our lovely guest house where you can relax and enjoy the charm of an historic small Missouri village. Fine antiques, crafts and gift shops within walking distance.

Down Over Inn
602 Main St., 65320
816-837-3268
John & Joy Vinson
April 15—December 15

$ B&B
2 rooms, 2 pb
C-yes/S-yes/P-no/H-no

Continental plus
Guest house
sitting room
piano, porch
bicycle-built-for-2

Enjoy Missouri small-town atmosphere. Playpen toys and swings for children. See Tom Sawyer, *which was filmed in Arrow Rock.*

BONNE TERRE

Lamplight Inn B&B
207 E. School St., 63628
314-358-4222
Jorgen & Krista Wibskov
All year

$$ B&B
6 rooms, 6 pb
Visa, MC, AmEx
C-yes/S-yes/P-no/H-no
Danish, German, Russian

Full breakfast
Lunch, dinner
restaurant, bar service
Sitting room
library

Award-winning restaurant; highly praised accommodations with a European flavor; elegant candlelit breakfasts; our guests are spoiled with attention.

Mansion Hill Country Inn
Mansion Hill Dr., 63628
314-358-3511
Doug & Cathy Goergens
All year

$$ B&B
7 rooms, 3 pb
Visa, MC, AmEx
C-yes/S-yes

Full breakfast
Restaurant
full pub
Sitting room
library

Relaxed getaway in turn-of-the-century English-style mansion on 130 acres with 45-mile view of Ozark Mountain foothills. Carriage rides, fishing, golf, cross-country skiing.

BRANSON

Branson House
120 4th Street, 65616
417-334-0959
Opal Kelly
April 1—November 30

$$ B&B
7 rooms, 7 pb
C-no/S-ltd/P-no/H-no

Full gourmet breakfast
Comp. wine
Sitting room
central A/C

Old home furnished with antiques. Breakfast served in the dining room or on the front porch. Overlooking downtown Branson and beautiful lake.

220   Missouri

EMINENCE ─────────────────────────────

River's Edge B&B Resort $ EP   Breakfast $
HCR 1, Box 11, 65466   15 rooms, 14 pb   Bubbling spa, Ping Pong
314-226-3233   •   Picnic area, hot tubs
Lynett Peters   C-yes/S-yes/P-no/H-yes   decks overlooking river
All year   color TV, inner tubes

In Eminence, where spring-fed rivers abound. Relax on private decks overlooking the river. Tubing and swimming in clear water. Private beach and riverfront. Perfect setting.

FULTON ─────────────────────────────

Loganberry Inn $ B&B   Full breakfast
310 W. 7th St., 65251   5 rooms, 3 pb   Comp. wine
314-642-9229   Visa, MC •   Snacks
Bob & Deb Logan   C-yes/S-yes/P-ask/H-no   Sitting room
All year

Antique-filled century-old English-style inn within walking distance of Churchill Memorial and quaint shops. Complimentary beverages served.

HANNIBAL ─────────────────────────────

Fifth Street Mansion $ B&B   Full breakfast
213 S. Fifth St., 63401   7 rooms, 2 pb   Comp. wine
314-221-0445   •   Sitting room
Donalene & Mike Andreotti   C-yes/S-yes/P-no/H-no   special event weekends
All year

Italianate Victorian brick mansion; National Historic Register home near historic district. Special events like mystery weekends, craft workshops, and art shows.

Garth Woodside Mansion $$ B&B   Full breakfast
RR 1 off Route 61, 63401   8 rooms, 4 pb   Comp. wine, aftn. tea
314-221-2789   Visa, MC •   Library, tour planning
Diane & Irv Feinberg   C-12+ /S-ltd   turndown service
All year   guest nightshirts

Mark Twain was a guest at this 39-acre country estate. Original Victorian furnishings, flying staircase. Pampered elegance, hospitality and a relaxing experience awaits you.

HERMANN ─────────────────────────────

Birk's Goethe St. Gasthaus $ B&B   Full breakfast
700 Goethe St., 65041   9 rooms, 7 pb   Comp. wine, coffee
314-486-2911   Visa, MC •   dining area, lounge
Gloria & Elmer Birk   C-no/S-no/P-no/H-no   Piano, sitting room
Closed Dec. 25—Jan. 1   porch w/gazebo

Original owner owned 3rd largest winery in the world, still in operation. Victorian furnishings, tubs w/gold-plated feet. Mystery weekends (2 each month). Grand place to stay.

Der Klingerbau Inn $ B&B   Full breakfast
108 E. 2d St., 65041   6 rooms, 4 pb   Fireside tea
314-486-2030   Visa, MC, AmEx   Sitting room
Betty Taylor   C-no/S-yes/P-no/H-no   piano
All year

Authentic original German village with 108 buildings on National Register of Historic Places in heart of "Rhine Country of Missouri." Restaurant, antiques.

Broad Bay Inn & Gallery, Waldoboro, ME

HERMANN

William Klinger Inn
P.O. Box 29, 65041
108 E. 2nd St.
314-486-5930
John & Nancy Bartel
All year

$$$ B&B
7 rooms, 7 pb
Visa, MC
C-no/S-no/P-no/H-no

Full gourmet breakfast
Lunch, dinner
Sitting room
patio
seminars

A 100-year-old Victorian home restored to its original elegance of 1879. Breakfast served by the fireside or on the patio. Weekday discounts.

INDEPENDENCE

Woodstock Inn B&B
1212 W. Lexington, 64050
816-833-2233
Lane & Ruth Harold
All year

$ B&B
11 rooms, 11 pb
Visa, MC •
C-yes/S-no/P-no/H-yes
German

Full breakfast
Afternoon tea
Snacks
Sitting room

Enjoy comfort, privacy and tastefully appointed rooms in this century-old renovated bed and breakfast. Individualized breakfasts. Truman, Missouri history sites nearby.

JAMESPORT

Richardson House B&B
P.O. Box 227, 64648
816-684-6664/816-684-6234
Mrs. Jayla Smith
All year

$$ B&B
4 rooms, 1 pb
Visa, MC •
C-yes/S-yes/P-ltd

Full breakfast
Lunch, dinner, snacks
Afternoon tea, library
Cable TV, picnic baskets
farm tours

Restored turn-of-the-century farmhouse furnished with antiques. Located near Amish community. Whole house rented—perfect for family adventure or romantic retreat.

KANSAS CITY

Doanleigh Wallagh Inn
217 E. 37th St., 64111
816-753-2667/800-255-0390
Ed & Carolyn Litchfield
All year

$$ B&B
5 rooms, 5 pb
Visa, MC •
C-ltd/S-ltd/P-no/H-no

Full breakfast, piano
Pump organ,big screen TV
Facilities for meetings,
parties, weddings, etc
TV & telephone in rooms

Turn-of-the-century mansion in the Hyde Park area. Minutes away from Country Club Plaza and Crown Center. Quiet elegance and superb food. Airport pickup arranged.

Dome Ridge
14360 N.W. Walker Rd., 64164
816-532-4074
Roberta & Bill Faust
All year

$ B&B
3 rooms, 3 pb
•
C-no/S-no/P-no/H-no

Full spcl.ord. breakfast
Library
hot tub, TV(each room)
bicycle, spa

Spacious dome home; soaring 30-ft. great room, wood ceiling. Nine acres of trees, ten minutes to airport, twenty to downtown.

MACON

Wardell Guest House
One Wardell Rd., 63552
816-385-4352
Larry & Marie Hyde
All year

$ B&B
3 rooms, 1 pb
Visa, MC •
C-yes/S-no/P-no/H-no

Full breakfast
Comp. wine
Snacks
Sitting room
library

Elegant 1890s National Register Victorian mansion in quaint peaceful town. Innkeepers serve up great food and true Southern hospitality.

MOUNTAIN VIEW

Jack's Fork Country Inn
Route 1 Box 347, 65548
417-934-1000
Michael & Shirlee Blue
All year exc. 2 wks Dec.

$ B&B
5 rooms, 5 pb
Visa, MC •
C-yes/S-ltd/P-yes/H-no

Full gourmet breakfast
Comp. wine, snacks
Sitting room
library, hot tubs
swimming pool

Charming country home with antiques throughout. Gardenlike setting with panoramic views. Perfect for the romantically inclined or sports enthusiast.

NEW HAVEN

Augustin River Bluff Farm
RR 1, Box 42, 63068
314-239-3452/314-237-3198
Robert & MaryLee Kliethermes
All year

$$$ EP
•
C-yes/S-yes

Continental breakfast
Dinner by arrangement
Comp. wine
Outside tub
Missouri River view

We rent to private parties of 1-8 people. Large 8-room home situated on a 99-acre river view estate. Family antiques; restored player piano. Deer, wild turkey. Secluded.

PARKVILLE

Down to Earth Lifestyles
Route 22, 64152
816-891-1018
Lola & Bill Coons
All year

$$ B&B
4 rooms, 4 pb
•
C-yes/S-yes/H-yes

Full breakfast
Comp. wine, tea
Sitting room, piano
organ, entertainment
indoor heated pool

Unique new earth-contact home designed for guests. Private baths, telephones, indoor pool. Closed-in country setting between KC and airport.

PLATTE CITY ─────────────────────────────────────

Basswood Country Inn B&B | $$ B&B | Continental plus
Route 1, Box 145B, 64079 | 5 rooms, 5 pb | Private entrances, decks
N. Winan & Interurban Rds | Visa, MC • | Fishing lakes, trails
816-431-5556 | C-7+ /S-yes/P-no/H-ltd | craft & gift store
Don & Betty Soper | American Sign Language | shuffleboard, horseshoes
All year

Historic Basswood Lakes; former millionaire's estate. 4 suites plus mother-in-law cottage—sleeps 6. Elegant country French; private baths, patios, refrig., microwaves & TV.

SAINT JOSEPH ────────────────────────────────────

Harding House B&B | $ B&B | Full breakfast
219 N. 20th St., 64501 | 4 rooms, 1 pb | Afternoon tea
816-232-7020 | Visa, MC, AmEx | Comp. wine
Glen & Mary Harding | C-yes | Sitting room, library
All year | | antique pump organ

Gracious turn-of-the-century home, furnished with antiques, offers you warm hospitality. Famous lemon bread and homemade coffee cakes.

SAINT LOUIS ──────────────────────────────────────

Coachlight B&B | $$ B&B | Continental breakfast
#1 Grandview Heights, 63131 | 3 rooms, 3 pb | Comp. wine, cheese
Res. Serv. (not address) | Visa, MC | & hot cider
314-965-5870/314-965-4328 | C-3+ /S-ltd | Sitting room
Susan & Chuck
All year

1904 World's Fair vintage brick home. Friendly ambience, charming, beautiful antiques. Generous breakfast. Historic neighborhood; walk to shops, restaurants, galleries.

Lafayette House | $ B&B | Full breakfast
2156 Lafayette Ave., 63104 | 5 rooms, 2 pb | Comp. wine, snacks
314-772-4429 | • | Sitting room
Sarah & Jack Milligan | C-yes/S-yes/P-no/H-no | library
All year | | cable TV, VCR

An 1876 Victorian mansion "in the center of things to do in St. Louis." Air conditioned. We have three cats. Children welcome.

SPRINGFIELD ──────────────────────────────────────

Walnut Street B&B | $$ B&B | Full breakfast
900 E. Walnut St., 65806 | 6 rooms, 6 pb | Dinner with reservation
417-864-6346 | Visa, MC | Comp. wine & cheese
Karol & Nancy Brown | C-10+ | high tea, bar service
All year | | Sitting rm, tennis nrby

Gracious 1894 Victorian inn in city's historic district. City's showcase home furnished with beautiful antiques. Gourmet breakfast in bed available.

WARRENSBURG ──────────────────────────────────────

Cedarcroft Farm B&B | $ B&B | Full breakfast
Route 3, Box 130, 64093 | 2 rooms | Lunch, dinner by arrang.
816-747-5728 | Visa, MC | Snacks
Bill & Sandra Wayne | C-yes/S-no/P-no/H-no | Sitting room, parlor
All year | | hiking nature trails

Real country hospitality at antique-filled 1867 farmhouse with 80 acres to roam. One hour from Kansas City, Truman Lake.

224 Montana

WASHINGTON

Schwegmann House B&B Inn $$ B&B — Continental plus
438 W. Front St., 63090 — 9 rooms, 7 pb — Bicycles
314-239-5025 — Visa, MC • — sitting room
Catherine Nagel — C-yes/S-yes/P-no/H-yes — piano
All year

A stately pre-Civil War Georgian-style brick residence overlooking the Missouri River in the heart of Missouri's wine country. Antique furnishings and quilts.

Washington House B&B Inn $$ B&B — Full or continental brkf
P.O. Box 527, 63090 — 4 rooms, 4 pb — Comp. wine
#3 Lafayette — • — comp. teas and coffees
314-239-2417 — C-yes/H-yes — Snacks, sitting room
Chuck & Kathy Davis
All year

Our historic 1837 inn on the Missouri River features antique furnishings and decor, canopy beds, river views and a country breakfast. Balcony and terrace on riverside.

More Inns...

Borgman's B&B   706 Van Buren, Arrow Rock 65320   816-837-3350
Ozark Mountain Country B&B   P.O. Box 295, Branson 65616   417-334-4720
Brewer's Maple Lane Farms   RR 1, Carthage 64836   417-358-6312
Eminence Cottage & Brkfst   P.O. Box 276, Eminence 65466   314-226-3642
Bordello House   111 Bird, Hannibal 63401   314-221-6111
Victorian Guest House   3 Stillwell, Hannibal 63401   314-221-3093
Frisco House   W. Hwy 38 & Church St., Hartville 65667   417-741-7304
Schmidt Guesthouse   300 Market, Hermann 65041   314-486-2146
Benner House B&B   645 Main St., Historic Weston 64098   816-386-2616
Doanleigh Wallagh Inn   217 E. 37th St., Kansas City 64111   816-753-2667
Faust Townhouse   8023 N. Stoddard, Kansas City 64152   816-741-7480
Parkview Farm   RR 1, Box 54, Lathrop 64465   816-664-2744
Wardell Guest House   1 Wardell Rd., Macon 63552   816-385-4352
Gramma's House   Rt. 3, Box 410, Marthasville 63357   314-433-2675
Boone's Lick Trail Inn   1000 S. Main St., St. Charles 63301   314-947-7000
Seven Gables Inn   26 N. Meramec, Saint Louis 63105   314-863-8400
Hotel Sainte Genevieve   Main & Merchant Sts., Ste. Genevieve 63670   314-883-2737
Inn St. Gemme Beauvais   78 N. Main, Box 231, Ste. Genevieve 63670   314-883-5744
Schuster-Rader Mansion   703 Hall St., St. Joseph 64501   816-279-9464
Zachariah Foss Guest House   4 Lafayette, Washington 63090   314-239-6499

Montana

ALBERTON

Johnson's Petty Creek Ranch $ B&B
Mail Box 195, 59820 — 3 rooms, 2 pb
406-864-2111
April—November

Lovely private ranch surrounded by national forest. Near Missoula and Glacier National Park. 7 miles to Interstate 90. Come visit us.

BIG SKY

Lone Mountain Ranch
P.O. Box 69, 59716
406-995-4644
B. & V. Schapp, M. Ankeny
All year

$$$ AP
20 rooms, 20 pb
Visa, MC, AmEx •
C-yes/S-no/P-no/H-ltd

All meals included
Bar service
Hot tub, jacuzzi, horses
sitting room, piano
winter sleigh ride dinner

Historic guest ranch offering family vacations and Nordic ski vacations near Yellowstone National Park. Beautiful log cabins with fireplaces, conveniences.

BIG TIMBER

Lazy K Bar Ranch
Box 550, 59011
406-537-4404
Van Cleve Family
June 23—Labor Day

$$$/wk AP
22 rooms, 22 pb
•
C-yes/S-yes/P-no/H-no

All meals included
Swimming pool
sitting room, piano
entertainment

100-year-old working dude ranch; isolated; totally different style. Rustic charm. Excellent service, horses, food and company! References required.

BIGFORK

O'Duachain Country Inn
675 Ferndale Dr., 59911
406-837-6851
Tom Margaret Doohan
All year

$$ B&B
5 rooms
Visa, MC •
C-yes/S-ltd/P-ltd/H-no

Full breakfast
Comp. wine
Sitting room
hot tubs
water sports

Elegant, rustic log home nestled in the woods and mountain meadows, antique furniture, original artwork, two huge stone fireplaces and manicured grounds.

BOZEMAN

Happy Acres Sun House B&B
9986 Happy Acres West, 59715
406-587-3651
Patricia Crowle
All year

$ B&B
4 rooms, 1 pb
Visa, MC •
C-yes/S-no/P-no/H-no

Full breakfast
Snacks
Sitting room
library, hot tubs
cross-country ski trails

Quiet, country retreat—a mountain hideaway near fishing, hiking, and skiing.

Silver Forest Inn
15325 Bridger Canyon Rd, 59715
406-586-1882
Kathryn & Richard Jensen
All year

$$ B&B
5 rooms, 2 pb
Visa, MC •
C-yes/S-ltd/P-ask/H-no
Spanish

Full breakfast
Catered lunch & dinner
Aftn. tea, comp. wine
Sitting room, 2 hot tubs
massage, TV, Ping-Pong

Romantic and historic mountain hideaway with panoramic vistas, year-round recreation, superb skiing, delicious breakfasts and friendly innkeepers.

Voss Inn Bed & Breakfast
319 S. Willson, 59715
406-587-0982
Bruce & Frankee Muller
All year

$$ B&B
6 rooms, 6 pb
Visa, MC, DC •
C-ltd/S-ltd/P-no/H-no

Full breakfast
Sitting room
piano

Warmly elegant historic Victorian mansion beautifully decorated with period wallpaper and furniture. Walk to university, museums, restaurants, shopping.

ESSEX

Izaak Walton Inn
Box 653, 59916
406-888-5569
Larry & Linda Vielleux
All year

$ EP
30 rooms, 7 pb
Visa, MC
C-yes/S-yes/P-no/H-no
Spanish

Full breakfast $
Dining car, bar
Sauna, bicycles
sitting room
piano

Wilderness inn; echoes past great days of transcontinental rail travel. Year-round retreat for hikers, cross-country skiers, rail fans; borders Glacier National Park.

NEVADA CITY

Nevada City Hotel
59755
406-843-5377
Nancy Mitman
June 1—Labor Day

$-87
14 rooms, 14 pb
Visa, MC
C-yes/S-yes/P-yes/H-no

Sitting room
piano

Truly western atmosphere of the Gold Rush Days. Two large rooms in the hotel are completely furnished in exquisite 19th-century decor.

RED LODGE

Pitcher Guest House
P.O. Box 3450, 59068
2 S. Platt
406-446-2859
All year

$$ EP
4 rooms, 2 pb
C-yes/S-yes/P-no/H-no

Restaurant nearby
Sitting room, library
Bicycles, tennis courts
hot tubs, cable TV
private phones, laundry

Nonhost, furnished home accommodating up to 8. Country-style decorating. 60 miles from Logan International Airport; 7 miles from ski lift. Three night minimum, advance deposit.

ROBERTS

Cottonwood Ranch Retreat
P.O. Box 1044, 59070
Star Route
406-445-2415/800-342-2345
Lynda Martinsen
All year

$ B&B
3 rooms
Visa, MC
C-yes/S-ltd/H-yes
some Spanish

Continental plus
Lunch, dinner, snacks
Comp. wine, aftn. tea
Sitting room
library

Real Western guest ranch! Two authentic Indian tipis for children's birthday parties, and almost any event can be hosted inside. Cross-country skiing offered!

SAINT IGNATIUS

Mission Mountain B&B
RR Box 183 A, 59865
190 Ansoneault Rd.
406-745-4331
Vic & Doris Peterson
All year

$ B&B
2 rooms
C-yes/S-no/P-no/H-no

Full breakfast
Lunch, dinner
Snacks
Library, TV
music, games

Comfortable ranch home with beautiful view of Mission Mountains. Fishing, skiing and other varied activities and sights in area.

WHITEFISH

Castle Bed & Breakfast
900 S. Baker, 59937
406-862-1257
Jim & Pat Egan
All year

$ B&B
3 rooms
Visa, MC •
C-yes/S-no/P-no/H-no

Full breakfast
Sitting room, library
piano, fireplace
video room, TV

Historic home in beautiful setting. Minutes from Big Mountain ski area and Glacier National Park. Tennis, golf, boating, hiking nearby.

More Inns...

Schwartz's B&B   890 McCaffery Rd., Bigfork 59911   406-837-5463
PJ's Bed & Breakfast   722 N. 29th St., Billings 59101   406-259-3300
Lehrkind Mansion   719 North Wallace, Bozeman 59715   406-586-1214
Torch & Toes B&B   309 S. Third Ave., Bozeman 59715   406-586-7285
Grave Creek B&B   P.O. Box 551, Eureka 59917   406-882-4658
Three Pheasant Inn   626 Fifth Avenue N., Great Falls 59401   406-453-0519
Whispering Pines   Box 36, Huson 59846   406-626-5664
Huckleberry Inn   1028 3rd Avenue West, Kalispell 59901   406-755-4825
Hibernation House   Whitefish, P.O. Box 1400 59937   406-862-3511
Ruth's B&B   802 7th. Ave, Polson 59860   406-883-2460
Maxwell's Mountain Home   606 S. Broadway, Red Lodge 59068   406-446-3052
Country Caboose B&B   852 Willoughby Rd., Stevensville 59870   406-777-3145
Camp Creek Inn   760 HC 105, Sula 59871   406-821-3508
Sacajawea Inn   P.O. Box 648, Three Forks 59752   406-285-6934
Hidden Hollow Hideaway   Box 233, Townsend 59644   406-266-3322
Foxwood Inn   Box 404, White Sulphur Springs 59645   406-547-3918
Duck Inn   1305 Columbia Avenue, Whitefish 59937   406-862-DUCK
Kandahar Lodge   P.O. Box 1659, Whitefish 59937   406-862-6098

Nebraska

BELGRADE ─────

Bel-Horst Inn
Marion at fountain, 68623
308-357-1094
Doris Brown
All year

$ EP
14 rooms, 14 pb
C-yes/S-yes/P-yes/H-no

Dining room (Fri.-Sun.)
Bar
Sitting room, piano
entertainment

Our authentically restored turn-of-the-century inn delights guests with its period items, wooden and brass furniture, and excellent cuisine.

GORDON ─────

Spring Lake Ranch
H.C. 84, Box 103, 69343
308-282-0835
Pat & Wendy Vinton
All year

$$ AP
3 rooms, 2 pb
•
C-yes/S-yes/P-yes/H-yes

Full breakfast
Lunch, dinner, snacks
Guided walking tour
4X4 tour, horseback rdng
hiking, picnics, hunting

Vast 18,000-acre sand hills ranch near South Dakota Black Hills & Badlands. Photographer's paradise. Ranch cooking. Sample our western hospitality. Complete vacation packages.

MADRID ─────

Clown 'N Country
RR Box 115, 69150
308-326-4378
Ford & Lou Cornelius
All year

$ B&B/MAP/AP
3 rooms, 1 pb
•
C-yes/S-ltd/H-yes

Full breakfast
Dinner, snacks
Sitting room
hot tubs, horseshoes
pool, croquet, badminton

Quiet country home in the heartland of Nebraska. We specialize in fun and friendliness with delicious food an added bonus. Clown collection.

More Inns...

Fort Robinson Inn   Box 392, Crawford 69339   308-665-2660
Rogers House   2145 B Street, Lincoln 68502   402-476-6961
Watson Manor Inn   410 S. Sycamore, North Platte 69103   308-532-1124

Nevada

CARSON CITY

Edwards House
204 N. Minnesota St., 89703
702-882-4884
Chris & Rick Broo
All year

$$ B&B
4 rooms
Visa, MC •

Full breakfast
Comp. wine
Sitting room
library
hot tub

In Carson City's historical district, this gracious sandstone 1882 Victorian will provide the peaceful rest and gourmet breakfast you need to explore Lake Tahoe & Reno.

IMLAY

Old Pioneer Garden Inn
Star Rt. Unionville #79, 89418
702-538-7585
Mitzi & Lew Jones
All year

$ B&B
11 rooms, 3 pb
•
C-ltd/S-yes/P-ltd/H-yes

Full breakfast
Other meals arranged
Sitting room
home movies

Ranch operating since 1861. We're proud of our pristine pure air, abundant fruit trees and trout stream through the property.

INCLINE VILLAGE

Haus Bavaria
P.O. Box 3308, 89450
593 N. Dyer Circle
702-831-6122/800-GO TAHOE
Wolfgang Zimmermann
All year

$$ B&B
5 rooms, 5 pb
•
C-10+/S-no/P-no/H-no
German

Full breakfast
Comp. wine
Large family room
TV, fireplace

There is much to do and see in this area, from gambling casinos to all water sports and golf, hiking, tennis and skiing at 12 different nearby sites.

VIRGINIA CITY

Edith Palmer's Country Inn
Box 756, South B St., 89440
702-847-0707
Norm & Erlene Brown
All year

$$ B&B
5 rooms, 1 pb
Visa, MC
C-no/S-no/P-no/H-no

Full breakfast
Sitting room
piano

1862 country home and wine cellar; walk to historic Virginia City; near Tahoe/Reno. Known for fine food, quiet comfort.

More Inns...

Elliot Chartz House   412 No. Nevada, Carson City 89701   702-882-5323
Oasis B&B   540 W. Williams, Fallon 89406
Sierra Spirit Ranch   3000 Pinenut Road, Gardnerville 89410   702-782-7011
Genoa House Inn   P.O. Box 141, 180 Nixon, Genoa 89411   702-782-7075
Orchard House   188 Carson St., Genoa 89411   702-782-2640
Breitenstein House (J-Bar)   Lamoille 89828   702-753-6356
Bed & Breakfast—Reno   136 Andrew Lane, Reno 89511   702-849-0772

Hardwicke House   P.O. Box 96, Silver City 89429   702-847-0215
Windybrush Ranch   Box 85, Smith 89430   702-465-2481
Blue Fountain B&B   1590 B Street, Sparks 89431   702-359-0359
Gold Hill Hotel   Box 304, Virginia City, Virginia City 89440   702-847-0111
Savage Mansion   P.O. Box 445, Virginia City 89440   702-847-0574
Robin's Nest Inn   130 E. Winnemucca, Winnemucca 89445   702-623-2410
Robric Ranch   P.O. Box 2, Yerrington 89447   702-463-3515

New Hampshire

ANDOVER

English House
P.O. Box 162, 03216
Main St.
603-735-5987
Ken & Gillian Smith
All year

$$ B&B
7 rooms, 7 pb
Visa, MC •
C-9+ /S-no/P-no/H-yes
French, German

Full breakfast
Afternoon tea
Sitting room
homemade jams,
breads & muffins

Elegant comfort of an old English country house set in the scenic beauty of New England. Breakfast and afternoon tea are rare treats.

ASHLAND

Glynn House Victorian Inn
P.O. Box 819, 03217
43 Highland St.
603-968-3775
Karol & Betsy Paterman
All year

$$ B&B
4 rooms, 2 pb
C-yes/S-yes/P-no/H-no
Polish, Russian

Full breakfast
Comp. wine, snacks
Sitting room, bicycles
tennis, lake
golf & skiing nearby

Fine example of Victorian Queen Anne architecture situated among the lakes and mountains. Antiques, gourmet breakfasts and hospitality are our specialities.

BARTLETT

Country Inn at Bartlett
P.O. Box 327, 03812
Route 302
603-374-2353
Mark Dindorf
All year

$$ B&B
17 rooms, 10 pb
Visa, MC, AmEx
C-yes/S-ltd/P-ltd

Full breakfast
Afternoon tea
Sitting room
hot tub
X-C ski trails

An inn for hikers and skiers in the White Mountains of New Hampshire. Enjoy mountain hospitality in a quiet country setting.

BETHLEHEM

Highlands Inn
P.O. Box 118C, 03574
Valley View Ln.
603-869-3978
Judi Hall & Grace Newman
All year

$ B&B
14 rooms, 10 pb
Visa, MC •
C-yes/S-yes/P-yes/H-no

Continental plus
Dinner for groups
Swimming pool
2 sitting rooms
piano

Set on 100 scenic acres, ½ mile off the highway. Charming rooms with beautiful views. Warm, friendly, relaxing atmosphere.

Shaw's Fancy B&B, Annapolis, MD

BRADFORD

Bradford Inn
Main Street, 03221
P.O. Box 40
603-938-5309
Tom & Connie Mazol
All year

$$ B&B
12 rooms, 12 pb
Visa, MC •
C-yes/S-yes/P-yes/H-yes
Arabic

Full breakfast
Restaurant
Bicycles, sitting room
library, meeting facils.

There's simply "nothing to do," but we have a fireplace, good books, three ski areas, and two lovely lakes nearby. Banquets available. Recent period renovations.

Mountain Lake Inn
P.O. Box 443, Rt. 114, 03221
Route 114
603-938-2136/800-662-6005
Carol & Phil Fullerton
All year

$$$ B&B
9 rooms, 9 pb
•
C-yes/S-yes/P-no/H-no

Full country breakfast
Dinner
Sitting room, library
full screened porch
piano, bicycles

165 acres of beautiful vacationland for any season. Built before the Revolution. Near all ski areas. Private sandy beach.

CENTRE HARBOR

Kona Mansion Inn
Box 458, 03226
Off Moutonboro Neck Rd.
603-253-4900
The Crowley family
May 25-October 12

$$
14 rooms, 14 pb
Visa, MC
C-yes/S-ask/P-ask/H-ltd

Full breakfast available
Dinner, bar service
Sitting room
tennis courts, golf
private beach on lake

Kona Mansion, built in 1900, is a peaceful get away from today's hectic pace. Serving superb cuisine.

CENTRE HARBOR

Red Hill Inn
RFD #1 Box 99M, 03226
Route 25B & College Rd.
603-279-7001
All year

$$ B&B
23 rooms, 23 pb
AmEx, Visa, MC •
C-ltd/S-yes/P-no/H-no

Full breakfast
Lunch (summer), dinner
Bar, Sunday brunch
Library, lake swimming
small conference center

Lovely restored mansion on fifty private acres overlooking Squam Lake (Golden Pond) and White Mountains. Excellent country gourmet cuisine, antiques.

CHICHESTER

The Hitching Post B&B
RFD #2, P.O. Box 790, 03263
Dover Rd., Chichester
603-798-4951
Lis & Gil Lazich
Feb.—Nov. & by reservation

$ B&B
4 rooms
•
C-12+/S-ltd/P-no/H-no
Scan., Slav., Fr., Sp.

Full gourmet breakfast
Comp. tea/wine
Parlor, piano
library, VCR
color TV

Cozy 1787 Colonial; Scandinavian hospitality; on US 4 & 202, heart of NH's Antique Row. 7.5 miles east of Concord; "en route to anywhere else"—lakes, mountains, or ocean.

CHOCORUA

Staffords in the Field
Box 270, 03817
603-323-7766
Fred & Ramona Staffora
All year

$$ MAP
16 rooms, 10 pb
Visa, MC •
C-10+/S-ltd/P-no/H-no

Full breakfast
Dinner
Parlor & library
tennis court (clay)

Secluded country setting, converted farmhouse completely furnished with antiques, family-run, superb gourmet food ranging from French to Mexican.

CHOCORUA VILLAGE

Farmhouse Bed & Breakfast
P.O. Box 14, 03817
Page Hill Rd.
603-323-8707
Kathy & John Dyrenforth
All year

$$ B&B
4 rooms
C-yes/S-yes/P-no/H-no

Full country breakfast
Comp. wine, aftn. tea
Sitting room, library
March maple sugaring
screened porch

Country charm, gracious hospitality. Pre-Civil War homestead. Lakes and mountains resort area. Breakfast features our own maple syrup and farm products.

CONWAY

Darby Field Inn
P.O. Box D, 03818
Bald Hill Rd.
603-447-2181/800-426-4147
Marc & Maria Donaldson
All year

$$$ MAP
16 rooms, 14 pb
Visa, MC, AmEx •
C-yes/S-yes/P-no/H-no
Spanish

Full breakfast
Dinner, bar, sitting rm.
Swimming pool
12 mi. X-country skiing
piano, entertainment

Cozy little country inn situated on the north face of Bald Hill, overlooking the Mt. Washington Valley and Presidential Mountains.

CORNISH

Chase House
RR 2, Box 909, 03745
Route 12-A
603-675-5391
Hal & Marilyn Wallace
All year

$$$ B&B
6 rooms, 4 pb
Visa, MC •
C-ltd/S-ltd

Full breakfast
Sitting room
library, bicycles
Canoeing, hiking
and X-C skiing on site

Meticulously restored 1775 federal-style house is national historic landmark. The Chase House boasts beautiful decor, extraordinary breakfasts and idyllic surroundings.

EAST HEBRON

Six Chimneys
Star Rt., Box 114, 03232
Newfound Lake
603-744-2029
Peter & Lee Fortescue
April 15—March 15

$ B&B
6 rooms, 3 pb
Visa, MC •
C-7+/S-ltd/P-no/H-no

Full breakfast
Dinner (winter)
Comp. wine/coffee/cider
Sitting room, X-C skiing
hiking trail, beach

A nostalgic trip to a 200-year-old coaching stop—relaxing atmosphere, cozy fires. Awaken to beguiling breakfast aromas. Central location for lake and mountain activities.

EASTON

Blanche's Bed & Breakfast
Easton Valley Rd, Rt116, 03580
RFD 1, Box 75, Franconia
603-823-7061
John Vail, Brenda Shannon
All year

$$ B&B
5 rooms
Visa, MC
C-yes

Full breakfast
Dinner (occasionally)
Sitting room

Victorian farmhouse restored to a glory it never had before. Located at the base of Kinsman Ridge. All outdoor activities nearby.

EATON CENTER

Inn at Crystal Lake
Box 12, 03832
Route 153
603-447-2120
Walter & Jacqueline Spink
All year

$$ MAP
11 rooms, 11 pb
AmEx, MC, Visa •
C-yes/S-ltd/P-no/H-no

Full country breakfast
Dinner, bar, parlor, TV
Fireplace, lounge, piano
lake swimming & boats
hiking & X-C ski nearby

Newly restored country inn—Greek revival with Victorian influence. Relaxing ambience, extraordinary international cuisine presented with elegant appeal. Be pampered!

EXETER

Exeter Inn
90 Front St., 03833
603-772-5901
J.H. Hodgins
All year

$$ EP
50 rooms, 50 pb
Visa, MC, AmEx, DC, Dsc •
C-yes/S-yes/P-yes/H-no
French, Spanish

Restaurant
Lunch, dinner
Afternoon tea, snacks
Bar service, sitting rm
library, sauna

Three story brick Georgian-style building; on the campus of Phillips Exeter academy; in the Revolutionary capital of New Hampshire.

FITZWILLIAM

Amos A. Parker House
Rt. 119 Box 202, 03447
603-585-6540
Freda B. Houpt
All year

$$ B&B
5 rooms, 3 pb
•
C-no/S-yes/P-no/H-no

Full breakfast
Comp. tea, wine
Library
sitting room

This 18th-century country home is elegant and cozy with antiques, orientals throughout. Six fireplaces, extensive gardens. Quintessential New England village.

FRANCONIA

Bungay Jar Bed & Breakfast
P.O. Box 15, 03580
Easton Valley Rd.
603-823-7775
Kate Kerivan, Lee Strimbeck
All year

$$ B&B
6 rooms, 4 pb
AmEx •
C-6+

Full breakfast
Dinner for groups by res
Afternoon tea, snacks
Library, sauna, decks
swimming hole, antiques

5½ miles south of Franconia Village. Crackling fire; mulled cider; popovers; homemade snacks. Mountain views on 8 private, quiet wooded acres with garden walks to river.

FRANCONIA

Franconia Inn
Easton Rd., 03580
603-823-5542
Alec & Richard Morris
Mem. Day—Oct., 12/15-4/1

$$ EP/MAP
35 rooms, 31 pb
Visa, MC, AmEx •
C-yes/S-yes/P-no/H-no

Full breakfast $ (EP)
Restaurant, full bar
Lounge w/movies, library
bicycles, pool, tennis
piano, sitting room

Located in the Easton Valley-Mount Lafayette and Sugar Hill. Riding stable, ski center. All rooms beautifully decorated. Sleigh rides, horseback riding, soaring.

GORHAM

Gorham House Inn
55 Main St., 03581
603-466-2271
Maggie Cook & Ron Orso
All year

$$ B&B
4 rooms
Visa, MC
C-yes/S-ltd/P-yes

Full breakfast
Homebaked goods
Sitting room
library

1891 Victorian on town common. Closest B&B to White Mountain National Forest & Mount Washington. Fine restaurants, golf, hiking, skiing, sightseeing nearby.

HAMPTON

Inn at Elmwood Corners
252 Winnacunnet Rd., 03842
603-929-0443
John & Mary Hornberger
All year

$$ B&B
7 rooms, 2 pb
Visa, MC
C-yes/S-ltd

Full breakfast
Catered dinner by arr.
Sitting room/library
wraparound porch

Memorable breakfasts in an 1870 home filled with quilts and country charm. 1½ miles from the ocean; short walk to a quaint village.

HAMPTON BEACH

The Oceanside
365 Ocean Blvd., 03842
603-926-3542
Skip & Debbie Windemiller
Mid-May—mid-October

$$$ B&B
10 rooms, 10 pb
Visa, MC, AmEx, Disc •
C-ltd

Continental plus
(off season, else EP)
Bar service
Sitting room, library
beach chair & towels

Directly across the street from sandy beach; beautiful ocean views. Active, resort-type atmosphere during mid-summer. All rooms recently renovated, many with antiques.

HANOVER

Trumbull House
Box C-29, 03755
Etna Village Rd.
603-643-1400
Ann & Mike Fuller
All year

$$$ B&B
5 rooms, 5 pb
C-10+/S-ltd/P-no/H-no
Spanish, French

Full breakfast
Tea, snacks
Sitting room, library
garden patio, porches
X-C skiing, hiking

Five minutes from Dartmouth College—relax in elegant English country rooms overlooking 16 acres of fields, stone walls and woodlands.

HART'S LOCATION

Notchland Inn
Rt. 302, 03812
603-374-6131
John & Pat Bernardin
All year

$$ B&B
11 rooms, 11 pb
Visa, MC, AmEx
C-yes/S-ltd/P-no/H-yes

Full breakfast
Dinner
Comp. wine
Sitting room, library
hot tubs, sauna, X-C skiing

A traditional country inn where hospitality hasn't been forgotten. Working fireplaces in every room, gourmet meals and spectacular mountain views.

HAVERHILL

Haverhill Inn
Dartmouth College Hwy, 03765
P.O. Box 95
603-989-5961
Stephen Campbell
All year

$$$ B&B
4 rooms, 4 pb
C-8+ /S-ltd/P-no/H-ltd
French

Full breakfast
Comp. tea, wine
Grand piano
sitting room
library, canoeing

An elegant federal colonial with working fireplaces in every room, and incomparable views of Vermont and New Hampshire hills.

HENNIKER

Colby Hill Inn
P.O. Box 778, 03242
3 The Oaks
603-428-3281
David Romin, Ruth Hannah
All year

$$$ B&B
16 rooms, 16 pb
Visa, MC, AmEx
C-6+ /S-yes/P-no/H-ltd

Full breakfast
Dinner, bar
Sitting room
tennis, bicycles
swimming pool

1800 country inn in quiet village. Antiques, fireplaces, down comforters. Classic Yankee cuisine. Swimming, hiking, skiing and bicycling.

Meeting House Inn
35 Flanders Rd., 03242
603-428-3228
J. & B. Davis, P. & C. Bakke
All year

$$ B&B
6 rooms, 6 pb
Visa, MC, AmEx
C-yes/S-ltd/P-no/H-no

Full breakfast
Lunch, dinner, lounge
Hot tub, sauna
bicycles
sitting room

A country retreat with cozy rooms and attention to detail. "Your place to return to again and again."

HOLDERNESS

Inn on Golden Pond
P.O. Box 680, 03245
Route 3
603-968-7269
Bill & Bonnie Webb
All year

$$$ B&B
8 rooms, 6 pb
Visa, MC •
C-no/S-no/P-no/H-no

Full breakfast
Piano

Located on 55 wooded acres across street from Squam Lake, setting for On Golden Pond. *Close to major attractions, skiing.*

Manor on Golden Pond
Box T, 03245
Route 3
603-968-3348
Andri Lamoureux
All year

$$ EP
29 rooms, 29 pb
Visa, MC, AmEx, CB, DC •
C-yes/S-yes/P-no/H-ltd
French, Spanish

Full breakfast $
Dinner, bar, sitting rm.
Entertainment, pool
tennis, canoes, rowboats
beach snack bar (summer)

Elegant 1903 English mansion overlooking "Golden Pond." Spectacular views, spacious grounds, private beach, romantic dining. Charming accommodations.

INTERVALE

Forest, A Country Inn
Route 16A, P.O. Box 37, 03845
800-448-3534
Ken & Rae Wyman
Exc. April

$ B&B
13 rooms, 7 pb
Visa, MC, AmEx •
C-yes/S-no/P-no/H-no

Full breakfast
Dinner by reservation
Afternoon tea
Swimming pool, piano, TV
X-C skiing, skating

Century-old inn furnished with antiques; nestled in peaceful woodlands. Near White Mountains attractions. Sleigh rides, fireplaces. Formerly known as Holiday Inn.

INTERVALE

Wildflowers Guest House
P.O. Box 802, 03845
N. Main St., (Route 16)
603-356-2224
Eileen Davis, Dean Franke
All year

$$ B&B
6 rooms, 2 pb
C-yes/S-yes/P-no/H-no

Continental breakfast
Full breakfast (opt.)
Sitting room

Century-old country home offering simplicity and charm of yesteryear; cozy parlor with wood-stove; dining room with fireplace.

JACKSON

Ellis River House B&B
P.O. Box 656, 03846
Route 16
603-383-9339
Barry & Barbara Lubao
All year

$$ MAP
6 rooms, 1 pb
Visa, MC
C-yes/S-yes/P-ask/H-ask
Polish

Full country breakfast
Dinner, snacks, wine
Sitting room, atrium
cable TV, VCR, whirlpool
hot tub, fishing

Turn-of-the-century house overlooking spectacular Ellis River. Working farm; full hearty country breakfast with homemade breads; jacuzzi spa. Trout fishing & X-C skiing.

Inn at Jackson
P.O. Box H, 03846
Thorne Hill Rd. & Rt. 16A
603-383-4321
Lori & Steve Tradewell
All year

$$ B&B
6 rooms, 6 pb
Visa, MC, AmEx
C-yes/S-ltd/P-no/H-no

Full breakfast
Lunch during ski season
Comp. wine
Sitting room
library

Spacious and gracious inn overlooking the best of the White Mountains and Jackson village. Away from the hustle and bustle.

Village House
P.O. Box 359, Route 16A, 03846
603-383-6666
Robin Crocker, Lori Allen
All year

$$ B&B
10 rooms, 8 pb
Visa, MC
C-yes/S-yes/P-no/H-no

Full breakfast (winter)
Cont. plus (spring/fall)
Swimming pool
tennis courts
living room w/fireplace

Beautiful village setting on 7 acres. Ten tastefully decorated rooms. Close to fine dining, hiking & golfing.

JAFFREY

Benjamin Prescott Inn
Route 124 E., 03452
603-532-6637
Barry & Jan Miller
All year

$$ B&B
11 rooms, 9 pb
Visa, MC •
C-5+ /S-ltd/P-no/H-no

Full breakfast
Sitting room
bicycles

RelaxIndulgeLess than two hours from Boston, the inn offers the opportunity to reset your pace and explore the Monadnock region.

Lilac Hill Acres B&B
5 Ingalls Rd., 03452
603-532-7278/617-729-2686
The McNeill's
All year

$$ B&B
6 rooms, 1 pb
C-12+ /S-ltd/P-no/H-no

Full breakfast
Comp. tea
Sitting room
piano, pond

Five-star service in a beautiful setting. Enjoy a bit of life on the farm with a warm personal touch. Join us year-round.

JEFFERSON

Davenport Inn
RFD 1 Box 93A, 03583
Davenport Rd.
603-586-4320
Janet J. Leslie
Closed April

$$ B&B
5 rooms, 5 pb
Visa, MC
C-yes/S-no/P-no/H-no
German, Spanish, Italian

Full breakfast
tea
Sitting room
library
porch, games

Charming colonial home with beautiful views; excellent hiking, fishing, golfing nearby; gourmet breakfast—northern and southern European homecooking on request.

Jefferson Inn
RFD 1, Box 68A, 03583
Route 2
603-586-7998
Bertie Koelewijn, Greg Brown
Exc. November, April

$ EP
10 rooms, 5 pb
Visa, MC, AmEx •
C-ltd/S-ltd
Dutch, German, French

Full breakfast $
Evening tea
Conference room
swimming pond, tennis
2 bdr. family suite

Uniquely furnished Victorian near Mount Washington; outdoor paradise including hiking, golf, theater, swimming pond; wraparound porch; 360-degree views; evening tea.

LINCOLN

Red Sleigh Inn B&B
P.O. Box 562, 03251
Pollard Rd.
603-745-8517
Bill & Loretta Deppe
All year

$$ B&B
8 rooms
Visa, MC, Discover •
C-10+ /S-ltd/P-no/H-no

Full hearty breakfast
Comp. tea, wine
Sitting room, library
indoor/outdoor pool
sauna, hot tubs, BBQs

The mountains surrounding us abound in ski touring trails. Bedrooms are tastefully decorated with many antiques. Panoramic view of surrounding mountains.

LISBON

Ammonoosuc Inn
Bishop Rd., 03585
603-838-6118
Steve & Laura Bromley
All year

$$ B&B
9 rooms, 9 pb
Visa, MC, AmEx •
C-yes/S-yes/P-no/H-no

Continental breakfast
Lunch, snacks
Restaurant, bar
Sitting room, pool
fishing, canoeing

1888 farmhouse, guesthouse w/private baths, outdoor swimming pool, tennis, 9-hole golf course. Public dining room, lunch and cocktails on porch overlooking Ammonoosuc River.

LITTLETON

Edencroft Manor
Route 135, Dalton Rd., 03561
RR# 1, Box 523
603-444-6776
Phil & Maryann Frasca
All year

$$ EP
6 rooms, 4 pb
Visa, MC, AmEx •
C-yes/S-ltd/P-yes/H-ltd

Full breakfast $
Dinner, bar
Sitting room
piano

Country inn with fireplaces. Lounge overlooking the mountains. Antiques, handmade comforters. Gourmet dinner, full breakfast, international coffees served.

LOUDON

Inn at Loudon Ridge
Box 195, 03301
Lower Ridge Rd.
603-267-8952
Liz & Carol Early
All year

$$ B&B
5 rooms, 2 pb
Visa, MC, AmEx
C-12+ /P-no

Full breakfast
Comp. wine
Sitting room, bicycles
tennis courts, pool
X-C ski trails

Rambling early American home surrounded by 33 secluded acres; close to White Mountains, NH Lake Region and historic seacoast. Lots of crafts and antiques nearby.

MARLBOROUGH

Peep-Willow Farm
Bixby St., 03455
603-876-3807
Ms. Noel Aderer
All year

$ B&B
3 rooms, 1 pb
•
C-yes/S-no/P-ask/H-yes

Full breakfast
Comp. wine
Snacks
Sitting room

I raise thoroughbred horses—you can help with chores (no riding), watch the colts play and enjoy the view all the way to Vermont's Green Mountains.

Thatcher Hill Inn
Thatcher Hill Rd., 03455
603-876-3361
Marge & Cal Gage
All year

$$ B&B
7 rooms, 7 pb
Visa, MC
C-6+/S-no/P-no/H-yes

Full breakfast
Sitting room
Library
hiking, X-C skiing
snowshoeing on grounds

Immaculate rooms, comfortable beds, engaging hospitality and a beautiful 60-acre setting near to the very heartbeat of New England.

MEREDITH

Nutmeg Inn
Pease Road, RFD #2, 03253
603-279-8811/800-642-9229
Daryl & Cheri Lawrence
All year

$$ B&B
8 rooms, 6 pb
Visa, MC, AmEx, DC, CB •
C-yes

Full breakfast
Afternoon tea, snacks
Sitting room
library
swimming pool

Lovingly restored country inn; something for everyone. Relax by our fire, or enjoy swimming, skiing, fishing, golfing, antiquing or the fall foliage.

NEW LONDON

New London Inn
P.O. Box 8, 03257
Main St.
603-526-2791
Maureen & John Follansbee
All year

$$ B&B
30 rooms, 30 pb
Visa, MC •
C-ask/S-yes/P-no/H-no

Full breakfast
All meals available
Bar service, library
Award-winning gardens
conference facilities

Conveniently located on Main Street in a lovely college town. This 1792 inn offers exceptional fireside dining and charming rooms.

NEWPORT

Inn at Coit Mountain
HCR 63 Box 3, Rt. 10, 03773
603-863-3583/800-367-2364
Dick & Jude Tatem
All year

$$$ B&B
5 rooms, 1 pb
Visa, MC
C-yes/S-ltd/H-yes

Full gourmet breakfast
Lunch, dinner
Sitting room, library
sleigh rides
airport pickup

Elegant country home with French charm and rooms with fireplaces. Year-round activities in the Lake/Mount Sunapee region.

NORTH CONWAY

Buttonwood Inn
P.O. Box 1817, 03860
Mt. Surprise Rd.
603-356-2625
Ann & Hugh Begley
All year

$$ B&B
9 rooms, 2 pb
Visa, MC, AmEx •
C-yes/S-yes/P-no/H-no

Full breakfast
Comp. wine
Sitting room, library
40-foot swimming pool
TV, lawn sports

Tucked away on Mt. Surprise. Quiet & secluded yet only 2 miles from town, excellent dining & shopping. Skiing & all outdoor activities nearby. Apres-ski game rm. w/fireplace.

NORTH CONWAY ————————————————————————————————

Center Chimney—1787
P.O. Box 1220, 03860
River Rd.
603-356-6788
Farley Ames Whitley
All year

$ B&B
4 rooms
C-yes/S-yes/P-no/H-no

Continental breakfast
Comp. hot cider (winter)
Sitting room, library
cable TV, piano
whirlpool

Charming early Cape, woodsy setting, just off Saco River and Main St. Easy walking to shops, restaurants; year-round sports.

Cranmore Mountain Lodge
P.O. Box 1194, 03860
Kearsarge Rd.
603-356-2044
Dennis & Judy Helfand
All year

$$ B&B
16 rooms, 5 pb
Visa, MC, AmEx
C-yes/S-yes/P-no/H-no

Full breakfast
Dinner, poolside BBQs $
Fireplace room
piano, hot tub
swimming, tennis

Authentic country inn located in the heart of the White Mts. Hearty country breakfast. Tennis court, pool, jacuzzi, tobogganing, skating, X-C skiing.

Nereledge Inn
River Rd., 03860
603-356-2831
Valerie & Dave Halpin
All year

$$ B&B
8 rooms
Visa, MC, AmEx
C-yes/S-ltd/P-no/H-no

Full breakfast
Dinner, pub
2 sittings rooms
piano

Cozy 1787 inn, five minutes walk from village, close to skiing areas, fishing, golf, climbing, canoeing. Home-cooked meals including country-style breakfast.

Old Red Inn & Cottages
Route 16, P.O. Box 467, 03860
603-356-2642
Don & Winnie White
All year

$$ B&B
17 rooms, 15 pb
Visa, MC, AmEx
C-yes/S-yes/P-ltd/H-no
French

Full breakfast
Kitchenettes
Living room w/woodstove
piano, herb garden
flower gardens

Four-season 1810 country inn with 10 cottages and award-winning gardens. Walking distance to village. Alpine skiing surrounds us! Spectacular mountain view.

Peacock Inn
P.O. Box 1012, 03860
Kearsarge Rd.
603-356-9041
Claire & Larry Jackson
All year

$$$ B&B
18 rooms, 16 pb
Visa, MC, AmEx, Disc. •
C-yes/S-yes/P-no/H-no

Full country breakfast
Comp. wine, tea, snacks
Sitting room, library
bicycles, tennis courts
sauna, pool, hot tubs

Recapture the romance at our intimate country inn. Enjoy a scrumptious country breakfast while overlooking the mountains. Then relax at the health club or in our indoor pool.

Sunny Side Inn
Seavey St., 03860
603-356-6239
Chris & Marylee Uggerholt
All year

$ B&B
11 rooms, 3 pb
Visa, MC
C-yes/S-ltd/P-no/H-yes
Spanish

Full breakfast
Living room w/TV
fireplace, porches

Small casual B&B offers good company by our woodstove or fireplace and hearty breakfasts to start the day right. Walk to town or Mt. Cranmore.

NORTH SUTTON

Follansbee Inn
P.O. Box 92, Keysar St., 03260
603-927-4221
Dick & Sandy Reilein
Exc. parts of Apr. & Nov.

$$ B&B
23 rooms, 11 pb
Visa, MC
C-10+/S-no/P-no/H-no

Full country breakfast
Dinner, bar, wine list
Sitting room, fireplaces
piano, lounge, paddle
boats, wind surfer pier

An authentic 1840 New England farmhouse with comfortable sitting rooms, old-fashioned porch and charming bedrooms. Located on peaceful Kezar Lake. Golf and tennis nearby.

NORTH WOODSTOCK

Mt. Adams Inn
RFD #1, Box 72, 03262
Route 3, S. Main St.
603-745-2711
Gloria & Joe Town
All year

$ B&B
20 rooms, 2 pb
Visa, MC
C-yes/S-no/P-no/H-no

Full breakfast
Dinner, lounge
Living room & lounge
both with fireplace
river, cottages

Warm hospitality, full country breakfast. Located on the edge of the village near trails and attractions. Unique rock formations along Moosalauki River.

NORTHWOOD

Lake Shore Farm
30 Jenness Pond Rd., 03261
603-942-5921
Eloise, Ellis & Harry Ring
All year

$ EP
32 rooms, 24 pb
C-yes/S-yes/P-yes/H-no

Full breakfast $3.50
All meals, bar
Sitting room, piano
library
tennis courts, lake

Nothing to do yet so much to do! Your home away from home; all home cooking, family-style service. Same family management since 1926.

Meadow Farm B&B
Jenness Pond Rd., 03261
603-942-8619
Janet & Douglas Briggs
All year

$$ B&B
3 rooms
C-yes/S-ltd/P-ltd/H-no

Full breakfast
Dinner on request
Sitting room

Restored charming 1770 colonial home—50 acres of fields, woods. Private beach on lake. Enjoy walks, cross-country skiing. Memorable breakfasts.

Nostalgia Bed & Breakfast
Box 520, Route 1, 03261
Route 4
603-942-7748
Pat & Bob Stead
All year

$ B&B
5 rooms
Visa, MC •
C-yes/S-ltd

All-you-can-eat brkfast
Afternoon tea
Patios, antique shop
woodstoves, games
color TV, VCR

Cozy 1830 colonial, furnished with antiques. 30 min. from Concord, Manchester, Portsmouth, 15 min. from UNH; in heart of "Antique Alley"—20 antique shops in 5-mile radius.

ORFORD

White Goose Inn
P.O. Box 17, Rt. 10, 03777
603-353-4812
Manfred/Karin Wolf
All year

$$ B&B
15 rooms, 13 pb
Visa, MC
C-8+/S-ltd/P-no/H-no
German

Full breakfast
Sitting room
swimming pond

Classic brick Federalist in country setting near Dartmouth College with 9 fireplaces, stenciled walls, country quilts, spring-fed pond and grazing sheep.

OSSIPEE

Acorn Lodge
P.O. Box 144, 03864
Duncan Lake
603-539-2151
Julie & Ray Terry
June 1—October 15

$ B&B
4 rooms, 4 pb
•
C-yes/S-ltd/P-no/H-yes

Continental breakfast
Sitting room
lake, boats, canoes
bicycles
badminton, fishing

Grover Cleveland's country hideaway, furnished with antiques and new beds. Continental breakfast served on our veranda overlooking Duncan Lake. Cottage available by the week.

PLYMOUTH

Crab Apple Inn
RR4, Box 1955, 03264
Route 25
603-536-4476
Carolyn & Bill Crenson
All year

$$ B&B
5 rooms, 2 pb
Visa, MC
C-10+/S-no/P-no/H-no

Full gourmet breakfast
Afternoon refreshments
Chocolates, fruit
Library, patio, croquet
bicycles, snow shoes

1835 brick federal with elegant guest rooms, down comforters, English gardens, classical music, brook in yard, fireplaces. 15 min. to mountain and lake attractions. Antiquing.

Northway House
RFD 1, US Route 3 N., 03264
603-536-2838
Micheline & Norman McWilliams
All year

$ B&B
3 rooms
C-yes/S-yes/P-ltd/H-no
French

Full breakfast
Comp. wine
Sitting room
cable TV

Hospitality plus awaits the traveler in this charming colonial. Close to lakes and mountains. Gourmet breakfast. Reasonable rates—children welcome.

PORTSMOUTH

Leighton Inn
69 Richards Ave., 03801
603-433-2188
Catherine Stone
All year

$$ B&B
5 rooms, 3 pb
Visa, MC
C-yes/S-yes/P-no/H-no
French, some German

Full breakfast
Comp. tea and coffee
Sitting room, library
bicycles
tennis & pool nearby

One of Portsmouth's finest federal mansions, exquisitely restored; period furnishings and fireplaces in every room; 5 minutes to Strawbery Banke/waterfront.

Martin Hill Inn
404 Islington St., 03801
603-436-2287
Jane & Paul Harnden
All year

$$ B&B
7 rooms, 7 pb
Visa, MC
C-12+/S-ltd/P-no/H-no

Full breakfast

1810 colonial has beautifully appointed rooms with period antiques. Elegant yet comfortable. Walk to waterfront. Lovely gardens.

RINDGE

Tokfarm Inn
P.O. Box 229, 03461
603-899-6646
Mrs. W.B. Nottingham
April—December

$ B&B
4 rooms
C-no/S-no/P-no/H-no
Ger., Fr., Dutch, Span.

Continental breakfast
Swimming hole
sitting room
antique organ

Charming century-old hilltop farmhouse on Christmas Tree Farm. Spectacular tri-state view. Cathedral of the Pines and all sports close by.

RYE ——————————————————————————————

Cable House $ B&B   Continental breakfast
20 Old Beach Rd., 03870 7 rooms, 2 pb   Sitting room
603-964-5000   C-2+/S-yes/P-no/H-no
Katherine Kazakis   Greek
June—Sept.

Named historical site, walk to beach. Landfall of first direct cable between Europe and the USA.

Rock Ledge Manor B&B $$ B&B   Full breakfast
1413 Ocean Blvd, Rt. 1A, 03870 4 rooms, 4 pb   Comp. wine
603-431-1413   C-11+/S-no/P-no/H-no Sitting room
Norman & Janice Marineau   piano
All year   bicycles

Seacoast getaway on the ocean, period furnishings, full memorable breakfast served in mahogany-ceilinged breakfast room. Near all NH and ME activities, University of NH.

SNOWVILLE ——————————————————————————

Snowvillage Inn $$$ B&B/MAP   Full country breakfast
P.O. Box 176 L, 03849   19 rooms, 19 pb   Dinner, box lunch, bar
603-447-2818   Visa, MC, AmEx •   Sauna, fireplace, piano
Peter/Trudy/Frank Cutrone   C-ltd/S-ltd/P-ltd/H-ltd tennis court, sitting rm
Closed April   German   X-C & Alpine skiing

Seclusion and peace amidst mountain magic. Warm old-country elegance, great food; dine in chalet with breathtaking view of Mt. Washington and glorious sunsets. Lovely gardens.

Spring Bank, Frederick, MD

242   New Hampshire

STRAFFORD ───

Province Inn $$ B&B   Full breakfast
P.O. Box 309, 03884   4 rooms   Guest refrigerator
Province Rd.   •   Sitting room, library
603-664-2457   C-yes/S-yes   bicycles, tennis, pool
Steve & Corky Garboski   private lake access
All year

Unspoiled country setting; 120 acres of hiking with waterfall; canoeing on beautiful non-commercial lake. Convenient to seacoast, mountains and lakes.

SUNAPEE ───

Haus Edelweiss B&B $$ B&B   Cont. or full breakfast
P.O. Box 609, 03782   5 rooms, 1 pb   Comp. wine, snacks
Maple St.   Visa, MC   Sitting room
603-763-2100   C-6+/S-ltd/P-no/H-no   porches, TV
Alan & Lillian McGonnigal   German   books, games
All year

Lovely, spacious Victorian located at Sunapee Harbor, minutes from Mt. Sunapee. Leisurely and unsurpassed breakfasts: traditional, Yankee, Bavarian or continental.

SUNCOOK ───

Suncook House $ B&B   Full breakfast
62 Main St., 03275   4 rooms, 2 pb   Comp. wine
603-485-8141   •   Sitting room
Gerry & Evelyn Lavoie   C-13+/S-no/P-no/H-no   piano
All year   French

Renovated Georgian brick home in town center. Three acres of lovely grounds. Warm hospitality and delicious breakfasts.

WARREN ───

Black Iris Bed & Breakfast $ B&B   Full breakast
P.O. Box 83, 03279   5 rooms   Afternoon tea, snacks
S. Main St.   C-10+   Sitting room
603-764-9366   bicycles
Kathy Maiorano, Kathy Aiello   bakery on premises
All year

Victorian bed and breakfast on 32 acres in the White Mountains. Recreational activities for all seasons close by. Warm, friendly, open atmosphere.

WATERVILLE VALLEY ─────────────────────────────────────

Silver Squirrel Inn $$$ B&B   Continental plus
Snow's Brook Rd., 03223   31 rooms, 31 pb   Bicycles
603-236-8325   Visa, MC, AmEx, DC   sitting room, library
Lisa Chavaree   C-yes/S-yes/P-no/H-no   18 clay tennis courts
All year   swimming pool, sauna

Modern 3-story country inn nestled in a secluded year-round resort setting surrounded by the White Mountain National Forest.

Snowy Owl Inn $$ B&B   Continental breakfast
P.O. Box 407, 03215   80 rooms, 80 pb   Comp. wine, sitting room
Village Rd.   Visa, MC, AmEx, DC •   Library, fitness center
603-236-8383   C-yes/S-yes/P-no/H-yes tennis crts, sauna, pool
Donald Hyde   hot tubs, golf, fishing
All year

Rustic country inn. Shady porch, scenic "Owl's Nest," sunken fireplace, and friendly staff round off a warm, relaxing vacation experience.

WENTWORTH

Mountain Laurel Inn
P.O. Box 147, 03282
Rt. 25 & Atwell Hill Rd.
603-764-9600
Don & Diane LaBrie
All year

$$ B&B
6 rooms, 6 pb
Visa, MC
C-ltd/S-no/P-no/H-ltd
French

Full breakfast
Comp. wine, snacks
Afternoon tea
Sitting room
air-conditioned

150-year-old Colonial in picturesque New England town on scenic route through White Mountains. Gracious hospitality. King-sized beds.

WEST CHESTERFIELD

Chesterfield Inn
Route 9, 03466
603-256-3211
Judy & Phil Hueber
All year

$$$ MAP
9 rooms, 9 pb
Visa, MC, AmEx, DC
S-yes/H-yes

Full breakfast
Dinner, restaurant
Snacks, bar service
Sitting room
2 rooms have balconies

Featuring opulent guest rooms and exciting cuisine, Chesterfield Inn is located 2 miles east of Brattleboro, VT, the gateway to southern Vermont & New Hampshire.

WOLFEBORO

Wolfeboro Inn
44 N. Main St., 03894
P.O. Box 1270
603-569-3016
Robin L. Schempp
All year

$$$ B&B
43 rooms, 43 pb
Visa, MC, AmEx, Disc •
C-yes/S-yes/P-no/H-yes
Spanish, French

Continental plus
Two restaurants and bars
Lunch, dinner, aftn. tea
Sitting rooms, library
bicycles, boat trips

The best of both worlds—the charm and personal attention of a country inn combines with the amenities and quality of service found in an elegant resort.

More Inns...

Stone Rest B&B   652 Fowler River Road, Alexandria 03222   603-744-6066
Darby Brook Farm   Hill Road, Alstead 03602   603-835-6624
Breezy Point Inn   RFD-1, Box 302, Antrim 03440   603-478-5201
Uplands Inn   Miltimore Rd., Antrim Center 03440   603-588-6349
Country Options   P.O. Box 736, Ashland 03217   603-968-7958
David's Inn   Bennington Sq., Bennington 03442   603-588-2458
Pasquaney Inn   Star Rt. 1 Box 1066, Bridgewater 03222   603-744-2712
Village Guest House   P.O. Box 222, Campton Village 03223   (603)726-444
Sleepy Hollow B&B   RR 1, Baptist Hill Rd., Canterbury 03224   603-267-6055
Lavender Flower Inn   P.O. Box 328, Main St., Center Conway 03813   603-447-3794
Hitching Post Village Inn   Old Rt. 16, Center Ossipee 03814   603-539-4482
Corner House Inn   Main St., POB 204, Center Sandwich 03227   603-284-6219
Dearborn Place   Box 997, Rt. 25, Centre Harbor 03226   603-253-6711
Poplars   13 Grandview St., Claremont 03743   603-543-0858
Wyman Farm   RFD 8, Box 437, Concord 03301   603-783-4467
Eastman Inn   Main St., Conway 03860   603-356-6707
Merrill Farm   RFD Box 151, N. Conway, Conway 03860   603-447-3866
Home Hill Country Inn   RFD 2, Cornish 03781   603-675-6165
Inn at Danbury   Route 104, Danbury 03230   603-768-3318
Delford Inn   Centre St., East Sullivan 03445   603-847-9778
Haley House Farm   RFD 1, North River Rd, Epping 03857   603-679-8713
Moose Mountain Lodge   Moose Mountain, Etna 03750   603-643-3529
G Clef Bed & Breakfast   10 Ashbrook Rd., Exeter 03833   603-772-8850
Fitzwilliam Inn   Fitzwilliam 03447   603-585-9000
Francestown B&B   Main Street, Francestown 03043   603-547-6333
Inn at Crotched Mountain   Mountain Rd., Francestown 03043   603-588-6840

Cannon Mt. Inn and Cottage   Easton Rd., Rt. 116, Franconia 03580   603-823-9574
Horse and Hound Inn   Cannon Mt., Franconia 03580   603-823-5501
Lovett's Inn   Franconia 03580   603-823-7761
Pinestead Farm Lodge   Rt. 116, RFD 1, Franconia 03580   603-823-5601
Shepherd's Inn   P.O. Box 534, Franconia 03580   603-823-8777
Sugar Hill Inn   Route 117 (Sugar Hill), Franconia 03580   603-823-5621
Freedom House B&B   Box 338, 1 Maple St., Freedom 03836   603-539-4815
Gunstock Inn   580 Cherry Valley Rd., Gilford 03246   603-293-2021
Hall's Hillside B&B   R.D. #4 Box GA372, Gilford 03246   603-293-7290
Historic Tavern Inn   P.O. Box 369, Gilmanton 03237   603-267-7349
Bernerhof Inn   Box 381, Rt. 302, Glen 03838   (603)383-441
Greenfield Inn   P.O. Bkox 156, Greenfield 03047   603-547-6327
Blue Heron Inn   124 Landing Rd., Hampton 03842   603-926-9666
Curtis Field House   735 Exeter Rd., Hampton 03842   603-929-0082
John Hancock Inn   Main Street, Hancock 03449   603-525-3318
Westwinds of Hancock   P.O. Box 635, Route 1, Hancock 03449   603-525-4415
Harrisville Squires' Inn   Box 19, Keene Road, Harrisville 03450   603-827-3925
Stonebridge Inn   Star Rt. 3, Box 82, Hillsborough 03244   603-464-3155
New England Inn   P.O. Box 100, Intervale 03845   603-356-5541
Riverside   Rt. 16A, Intervale 03845   603-356-9060
Christmas Farm Inn   Rt. 16B, POB 176, Jackson 03846   603-383-4313
Covered Bridge Motor Lodge   Box 277B, White Mt. Hwy, Jackson 03846   603-383-9151
Dana Place Inn   Rt 16, Pinkham Notch Rd, Jackson 03846   603-383-6822
Inn at Thorn Hill   Thorn Hill Rd. Box A, Jackson 03846   603-383-4242
Nestlenook Inn   P.O. Box Q, Jackson 03846   603-383-9443
Whitney's Inn   Route 16B, Jackson 03846   603-383-6886
Inn at Thorn Hill   Thorn Hill Road, Jackson Village 03846   603-383-4242
Wildcat Inn & Tavern   Box T, Main St., Jackson Village 03846   603-383-4245
Galway House B&B   247 Old Peterboro Rd., Jaffrey 03452   603-532-8083
Gould Farm   P.O. Box 27, Jaffrey 03452   603-532-6996
Jaffrey Manor Inn   13 Stratton Road, Jaffrey 03452   603-532-8069
Mill Pond Inn   50 Prescott Road, Jaffrey 03452   603-532-7687
Woodbound Inn   Post Office, Jaffrey 03452   603-532-8341
Monadnock Inn   Main St., Box 103, Jaffrey Center 03454   603-532-7001
Applebrook   Route 115A, Jefferson 03583   603-586-7713
289 Court   289 Court St., Kenne 03431   603-357-3195
Cartway House Inn   Box 575 RFD #5, Laconia 03246   603-528-1172
Hickory Stick Farm   R.F.D. #2, Laconia 03246   603-524-3333
Tin Whistle Inn   1047 Union Av., Laconia 03246   603-528-4185
1895 House   74 Pleasant St., Littleton 03561   603-444-5200
Beal House Inn   247 W. Main St., Littleton 03561   603-444-2661
Loch Lyme Lodge   RFD 278, Lyme 03768   603-795-2141
Lyme Inn   Route 10, Lyme 03768   603-795-2222
Manor on the Park   503 Beech St., Manchester 03104   603-669-8600
Hathaway Inn   RFD 4, Red Gate Lane, Meredith 03253   603-279-5521
Ram in the Thicket   Maple St., Milford 03055   603-654-6440
Olde Orchard Inn   RR, Box 256, Moultonboro 03254   603-476-5004
Backside Inn   P.O. Box 171, Mount Sunapee 03772   603-863-5161
Inn at New Ipswich   Porter Hill Rd., New Ipswich 03071   603-878-3711
Maple Hill Farm   RR1 Box 1620, New London 03257   603-526-2248
Helga's B&B   92 Packers Falls Rd., Newmarket 03857   603-659-6856
Indian Shutters Inn   Rt. 12, North Charlestown 03603   603-826-4445
1785 Inn   P.O. Box 1785, North Conway 03860   603-356-9025
Foothills Farm B&B   P.O. Box 1904, North Conway 03860   207-935-3799

Scottish Lion Inn   Rt. 16, Main St., North Conway 03860   603-356-6381
Stonehurst Manor   P.O. Box 1937, North Conway 03860   603-356-3271
Wyatt House English Inn   Route 16, North Conway 03860   603-356-7977
Cascade Lodge/B&B   Main St., POB 95, North Woodstock 03262   603-745-2722
Woodstock Inn   Rt. 3, Box 118, Main St, North Woodstock 03262   603-745-3951
Aviary   Bow Lake, Box 268, Northwood 03261   603-942-7755
Inn at Strawbery Banke   314 Court St., Portsmouth 03801   603-436-7242
Sheafe Street Inn   3 Sheafe St., Portsmouth 03801   603-436-9104
Theatre Inn   121 Bow Street, Portsmouth 03801   603-431-5846
Grassy Pond House   Rindge 03461   603-899-5166
Hide-Away Lodge   P.O. Box 6, New London, Springfield 03257   603-526-4861
Stoddard Inn   Route 123, Stoddard 03464   603-446-7873
Hilltop Inn   Main St., Rt. 117, Sugar Hill 03585   603-823-5695
Ledgeland   RR1, Box 94, Sugar Hill 03585   603-823-5341
Sunset Hill House   Sunset Road, Sugar Hill 03585   603-823-5522
Dexter's Inn   Stagecoach Rd., Sunapee 03782   603-763-5571
Inn at Sunapee   Box 336, Sunapee 03782   603-763-4444
Loma Lodge   RFD #1 Box 592, Sunapee 03782   603-763-4849
Old Governor's House   P.O. Box 524, Sunapee 03782   603-763-9918
Seven Hearths Inn   Old Route 11, Sunapee 03782   603-763-5657
Times Ten Inn   Rt. 103B Box 572, Sunapee 03782   603-763-5120
Tamworth Inn   Main Street, Tamworth 03886   603-323-7721
Birchwood Inn   Rt. 45, Temple 03084   603-878-3285
Black Swan Inn   308 W. Main St., Tilton 03276   603-286-4524
Country Place   RFD 2, Box 342, Tilton 03276   603-286-8551
Tilton Manor   28 Chestnut St., Tilton 03276   603-286-3457
Thirteen Colonies Farm   RFD Rt. 16, Union 03887   603-652-4458
Hobson House   Town Common, Wentworth 03282   603-764-9460
Partridge Brook Inn   P.O. Box 151, Westmoreland 03467   603-399-4994
Kimball Hill Inn   P.O. Box 74, Whitefield 03598   603-837-2284
Stepping Stones B&B   RFD #1, Box 208, Wilton Center 03086   603-654-9048
Inn of New Durham   RR 1, Middleton Rd., Wolfboro 03894
Tuc'Me Inn B&B   68 N. Main St., Wolfeboro 03894   603-569-5702

New Jersey

AVON-BY-THE-SEA ————————————

Cashelmara Inn
P.O. Box 223, 07717
22 Lakeside Ave.
201-776-8727
Martin J. Mulligan
All year

$$$ B&B
14 rooms, 14 pb
Visa, MC, AmEx
C-yes/S-yes/P-no/H-no

Full breakfast
Comp. wine
Sitting room

Oceanfront, lakeside charming Victorian inn with period antiques. Cozy rooms with private baths. Hearty breakfast served on enclosed oceanside veranda.

BAY HEAD ————————————

Bay Head Sands Inn
2 Twilight Rd., 08742
201-899-7016
Mary/Ken Glass
All year

$$ B&B
9 rooms, 5 pb
Visa, MC, AmEx
C-ltd/S-yes/P-no/H-no

Continental plus
Sunday full breakfast
Summer lunch
Summer weekends dinner
Sitting room, color TV

Friendly, romantic seaside getaway, Laura Ashley prints, antiques, iron beds, delicious home-baked treats. One block from beach. A special place.

Conover's Bay Head Inn
646 Main Ave., 08742
201-892-4664
Carl & Beverly Conover
Exc. wkdys/Dec.15-Feb. 15

$$ B&B
12 rooms, 6 pb
AmEx, Visa, MC
C-ltd/S-ltd/P-no/H-no

Continental plus, summer
Full breakfast, winter
Comp. tea, Oct-April
Sitting room, library
air-conditioned

Romantic seashore hideaway furnished with antiques, handmade pillows, bedcovers, crocheted washcloths, old family pictures. Quiet town on ocean at the bay head.

BEACH HAVEN ————————————

Magnolia House
215 Centre St., 08008
609-492-0398
Gail & Tom Greenwald
Spring, summer, fall

$$$ B&B
12 rooms, 12 pb
C-12+/S-no/P-no/H-no

Continental plus
Sitting room
beach tags & chairs
bicycles

Newly restored 120-year-old oceanside Victorian. Park and walk to white sand beaches and all historic Long Beach Island has to offer.

St. Rita Hotel
127 Engleside, 08008
609-492-9192/609-492-1704
Harold & Marie Coates
April—November

$$$ EP
22 rooms, 8 pb
Visa, MC, AmEx
C-yes/S-yes/P-no/H-no

Sitting room
wicker furnished porch

Half block from ocean; oldest hotel on Long Beach Island; within walking distance to restaurants, shops, amusements, fishing, etc.

CAPE MAY ————

7th Sister Guesthouse
10 Jackson Str., 08204
609-884-2280
JoAnne & Bob Myers
All year

$$ EP
6 rooms
C-7+/S-yes/P-no/H-no
Spanish, French, German

Sitting room, piano
rooms 100 ft. from beach
library

Original furniture plus an extensive wicker collection. Paintings by the owner/innkeeper, JoAnne Echevarria Myers, hang throughout. Ocean view rooms wonderfully furnished.

The Abbey
Columbia & Gurney Sts., 08204
609-884-4506
Jay & Marianne Schatz
April—December

$$ B&B
14 rooms, 11 pb
Visa, MC
C-12+/S-ltd/P-no/H-no

Continental plus (sum.)
Full brkfast (spr./fall)
Complimentary wine
2 parlors, piano, harp
off-street parking

Elegantly restored villa, with period antiques. Genuine merriment and a warm atmosphere are always present. One block from Atlantic Ocean.

Abigail Adams B&B
12 Jackson St., 08204
609-884-1371
Ed & Donna Misner
April—November

$$ B&B
5 rooms, 3 pb
Visa, MC
C-16+/S-no/P-no/H-no

Full breakfast
Comp. tea & wine
Sitting room

Intimate, elegant country charm, ocean views, gourmet breakfast all located in historic Cape May and within 100 feet of beach.

Barnard-Good House
238 Perry St., 08204
609-884-5381
Nancy & Tom Hawkins
April—November 15

$$$ B&B
5 rooms, 2 pb
Visa, MC
C-no/S-ltd/P-no/H-no

Full 4-course breakfast
Sitting room
antique organ

Victorian splendor in landmark-dotted town. Breakfast is a taste bud thrill. . .sumptuous, gourmet and lovingly created for you. Awarded best breakfast in N.J.

Bedford Inn
805 Stockton Ave., 08204
609-884-4158
Alan & Cindy Schmucker
March—December

$$$ B&B
11 rooms, 11 pb
Visa, MC
C-7+/S-no/P-no/H-no

Full breakfast
Continental plus (summ.)
Comp. wine
Set-up service
Sitting room

1880 Italianate seaside inn with unusual double staircase; offering lovely, antique-filled rooms and suites. Close to beach and shops.

Bell Shields House
501 Hughes St., 08204
609-884-8512
Lorraine Bell
February—October

$$ B&B
6 rooms, 1 pb
C-yes/S-ltd/P-no/H-no

Full breakfast
Comp. wine
Sitting room, TV
wraparound porch
parking

Restored Victorian house in middle of historic district. 2 blocks from beach and Victorian shopping mall. Delicious home-cooked breakfasts. Antiques.

CAPE MAY ——————————————————————————————————————

Brass Bed Inn
719 Columbia Ave., 08204
609-884-8075
John & Donna Dunwoody
All year

$$ B&B
8 rooms, 4 pb
Visa, MC
C-12 + /S-ltd/P-no/H-no

Full breakfast
Afternoon tea & snacks
Sitting room, library
outside enclosed shower
& dressing room

An eight guest room Gothic Revival "cottage" with wrap-around veranda and lovely gardens. Authentically furnished with an outstanding collection of brass beds in guest rooms.

Captain Mey's Inn
202 Ocean St., 08204
609-884-7793/609-884-9637
C. Fedderman, M. LaCanfora
All year

$$$ B&B
9 rooms, 2 pb
Visa, MC
C-12 + /S-ltd/P-no/H-no
Dutch, Italian

Full country breakfast
Afternoon tea
Victorian parlor
parking, beach equipment
veranda, courtyard

Turn-of-the-century inn with spacious rooms furnished in antiques, private Delft Blue collection, Dutch artifacts, European accents. Evening turndown service with mints.

Cliveden Inn
709 Columbia Ave., 08204
609-884-4516
Susan & Al DeRosa
May—November

$$ B&B
10 rooms, 8 pb
Visa, MC
C-12 +

Continental plus
Afternoon tea

Comfortable and attractive accommodations, centrally located in the primary historic district. Enjoy our "super-continental-plus breakfast" on the veranda each morning.

Columns by the Sea
1513 Beach Dr., 08204
609-884-2228
Barry & Cathy Rein
April—October

$$$ B&B
11 rooms, 11 pb
Visa, MC •
C-12 + /S-no/P-no/H-no
German

Full gourmet breakfast
Comp. tea
Sitting room
beach chairs & towels
bicycles free

Large, airy rooms, most with ocean views. Elegant turn-of-the-century mansion, decorated with Victorian antiques. Rockers on veranda. Gourmet breakfast.

Dormer House International
800 Columbia Ave., 08204
609-884-7446
Stephen & Ruth Fellin
All year

$$$ EP
8 rooms, 8 pb
C-yes/S-yes/P-no/H-no

Full kitchens in rooms
Sunporch
coin-op washer and dryer

All apartments are cheerfully decorated and maintained in superb condition—comfortable, attractive, sunny, light and airy. Full kitchen in each apartment. Linens not provided

Duke of Windsor Inn
817 Washington St., 08204
609-884-1355
Bruce & Fran Prichard
All year

$$ B&B
9 rooms, 7 pb
Visa, MC
C-12 + /S-ltd/P-no/H-no

Full breakfast 10/1-6/14
Cont. plus 6/15-9/30
Afternoon tea
Sitting rooms
bicycles, organ

Queen Anne bed and breakfast inn. Warm and friendly atmosphere, antiques. Close to beaches, restaurants, shopping area, historical area, tennis courts.

CAPE MAY ——————————————————————————————————————

Gingerbread House
28 Gurney St., 08204
609-884-0211
Fred & Joan Echevarria
All year

$$ B&B
6 rooms, 3 pb
C-7+ / S-yes / P-no / H-no

Continental breakfast
Porch
parlor with fireplace
Victorian antiques

The G.B.H. offers period furnished rooms—comfortable accommodations within walking distance to all major sights and restaurants. Half block from the beach.

Humphrey Hughes House
29 Ocean St., 08204
609-884-4428
Lorraine & Terry Schmidt
All year

$$$ B&B
12 rooms, 4 pb

Full breakfast
Afternoon tea
Sitting room
library
piano

Our inn is one of the most authentically restored bed & breakfast inns. Hospitality, Victorian charm, and casual, yet elegant, creature comforts are the hallmarks of our house.

Mainstay Inn & Cottage
635 Columbia Ave., 08204
609-884-8690
Tom & Sue Carroll
April—November

$$$ B&B
13 rooms, 9 pb
C-12+ / S-no / P-no / H-no

Full breakfst (spr / fall)
Cont. breakfast (summer)
3 sitting rooms
piano

Two wealthy 19th-century gamblers spared no expense to build this luxurious villa. Victorian furnishings, garden, afternoon tea.

Manor House
612 Hughes St., 08204
609-884-4710
Mary & Tom Snyder
All year exc. January

$$ B&B
9 rooms, 7 pb
C-ask / S-no / P-no / H-no

Full breakfast
Afternoon tea
Cookie fairy
Sitting room

Relaxing, comfortable setting in town center. Mirthfully served morning meal—four courses of "made from scratch" main dishes; great buns!

Mason Cottage
625 Columbia Ave., 08204
609-884-3358
Dave & Joan Mason
May—October

$$ B&B
5 rooms, 3 pb
Visa, MC •
C-12+ / S-no / P-no / H-ltd

Continental plus
Private outside shower
sitting room, veranda
games, reading material
parlor, bike rack

A mansard-style country Victorian located on a quiet, tree-shaded street in the center of the historic district, just a block from the ocean and the Victorian mall.

Mooring Guest House
801 Stockton Ave., 08204
609-884-5425
Harry & Carol Schaefer
April 3—December 30

$$$ B&B
12 rooms, 12 pb
Visa, MC
C-12+ / S-no / P-no / H-no

Full breakfast
Afternoon tea
Sitting room
mid-week discounts
Sept-Jan, March-June

Victorian mansard structure furnished in original period antiques. One block to ocean and easy walking distance to five different restaurants.

CAPE MAY ───

Poor Richard's Inn
17 Jackson St., 08204
609-884-3536
Richard & Harriett Samuelson
Valentine's—New Year's

$ B&B
9 rooms, 4 pb
C-ltd/S-yes/P-no/H-no

Continental breakfast
Sitting room
oriental rock garden

Classic gingerbread guest house offers accommodations with eclectic Victorian and country decor; near beach; friendly, unpretentious atmosphere.

Queen Victoria
102 Ocean St., 08204
609-884-8702
Joan & Dane Wells
All year

$$ B&B
12 rooms, 12 pb
Visa, MC, AmEx
C-ltd/S-ltd/P-no/H-ltd
French

Full buffet breakfast
Afternoon tea
Sitting room, bicycles
kitchen & whirlpool
2 luxury suites

A country inn located in the center of the nation's oldest seaside resort; specialty is comfort & service. Full a.m. & p.m. room cleanings. Large breakfast. Free bicycles.

Sand Castle Guest House
829 Stockton Ave., 08204
201-884-5451
Mark & Cathy Vitale
Mid-April—mid-October

$$ B&B
7 rooms, 1 pb
Visa, MC
C-ltd/S-ltd/P-no/H-no

Continental plus
Sitting room
Bicycles
beach passes

1873 carpenter gothic with country Victorian decor. Comfortable atmosphere, ocean view from wraparound veranda. Only a short block from the ocean.

Springside
18 Jackson St., 08204
609-884-2654
Meryl & Bill Nelson
All year

$$ EP
4 rooms
Visa, MC
C-5+/S-no/P-no/H-no

Sitting room
Library
King-sized beds
½ block from beach
½ block from mall

1890 Victorian beach house with bright, airy guest rooms with ocean views. Many creature comforts—big beds, ceiling fans, rockers on veranda, books and good music.

White House Inn
821 Beach Ave., 08204
609-884-5329
Shirley D. Stiles
April—October 20

$$ B&B
8 rooms
C-3+/S-ltd/P-no/H-no
some French

Full breakfast
Snacks
Sitting room

A bed & breakfast inn on the beach with a Victorian atmosphere. Wine and cheese each afternoon. Close to everything.

Windward House
24 Jackson St., 08204
609-884-3368
Owen & Sandy Miller
All year

$$$ B&B
8 rooms, 8 pb
Visa, MC
C-12+/S-yes/P-no/H-no

Full breakfast
Afternoon refreshments
Comp. sherry
Library, parking
bicycles, beach equip.

Edwardian shingle cottage; sun and shade porches; spacious antique-filled guest rooms; massive oak doors with stained and leaded glass.

CLINTON

Leigh Way Bed & Breakfast
66 Leigh St., 08809
201-735-4311
Peg & Bob Haake
April—December

$$ B&B
5 rooms, 3 pb
Visa, MC, AmEx
C-no/S-no/P-no/H-no
French

Continental plus (wkdys)
Full breakfast (wkends)
Restaurant nearby
Sitting room
fishing, sailing, tennis

Lovingly restored inn with cozy fireplace, porch swing and ferns. Authentic Victorian (c. 1862) located in picture-book Clinton, where small town America is alive and well.

FLEMINGTON

Jerica Hill-A B&B Inn
96 Broad St., 08822
201-782-8234
Judith S. Studer
All year

$$ B&B
5 rooms, 2 pb
Visa, MC, AmEx
C-12+/S-no/P-no/H-no

Continental plus
Comp. champagne
Picnic & wine tours
Bicycles
hot balloon flights

Gracious Victorian in heart of historic Flemington. Spacious, sunny guest rooms, antiques, living room with fireplace, wicker-filled screened porch.

MONTCLAIR

Marlboro Inn
334 Grove St., 07042
201-783-5300
Joan & John Rees
All year

$$$ B&B
Visa, MC, AmEx, DC •
C-yes/S-yes/P-no/H-yes
Spanish Italian

Continental plus
Full breakfast $
Full menu
Sitting room
piano

Turn-of-the-century Tudor mansion on a 3-acre estate, featuring luxury bedrooms and suites, each with private bath. Complimentary continental breakfast.

NORTH WILDWOOD

Candlelight Inn
2310 Central Ave., 08260
609-522-6100
Paul DiFilippo, Diane Buscham
Except January

$$ B&B
9 rooms, 7 pb
Visa, MC, AmEx •
C-no/S-ltd/P-no/H-no
French

Full breakfast
Afternoon refreshments
Sitting room, piano
hot tub, sun deck
getaway specials

Seashore B&B with genuine antiques, fireplace, wide veranda. Hot tub and sun deck. Getaway specials and murder mystery parties available. Close to beach and boardwalk.

OCEAN CITY

Enterprise Inn
1020 Central Ave., 08226
609-398-1698
Steve & Patty Hydock
All year

$$ B&B
11 rooms, 9 pb
Visa, MC •
C-yes/S-yes/P-no/H-no

Full breakfast
Comp. beach tags
Jacuzzi in one room
8 rooms, 3 apartments

A little bit of country at the shore! Home-cooked country breakfast; gingerbread; wicker. 15 minutes to Atlantic City. Rated "One of the Best Inns" (Atlantic City Magazine).

New Brighton Inn
519 Fifth St., 08226
609-399-2829
Daniel & Donna Hand
All year

$$ B&B
4 rooms, 2 pb
Visa, MC, AmEx
C-10+/S-ltd/P-no/H-no

Full breakfast
Afternoon tea
Sitting room
library
bicycles

Magnificently restored seaside Victorian filled with antiques. Close to beach, boardwalk, shopping district, restaurants. A charming and definitely romantic inn.

Bradford Inn & Motel, Chatham, MA

OCEAN GROVE

Cordova	$ B&B	Continental plus
26 Webb Ave., 07756	20 rooms, 3 pb	Communal kitchen
201-774-3084/212-751-9577	•	Sitting room
Doris & Vlad Chernik	C-yes/S-ltd/P-no/H-no	bicycles, yard
Mem. Day—Labor Day	French, Russian	BBQ, picnic tables

This century-old Victorian inn is located in a lovely historic beach community. At Cordova you feel like one of the family, experience old world charm, many amenities.

Pine Tree Inn	$$ B&B	Continental plus
10 Main Ave., 07756	13 rooms, 3 pb	Holistic therapies
201-775-3264	C-12+/S-no/P-no/H-no	Reflexology, jinshin
Karen Mason, Francis Goger		fresh flowers, TV lounge
All year		pillow mints, bicycles

Small inn furnished with Victorian antiques & collectibles. Ocean view from rooms & porches. Home-baked muffins. 40 yards to boardwalk & beach. Historic seaside town.

PRINCETON

Peacock Inn	$$$ B&B	Continental plus
20 Bayard Lane, 08540	17 rooms, 12 pb	French restaurant, bar
609-924-1707	Visa, AmEx	Lunch, dinner, snacks
Michael Walker/Canice Lindsay	C-yes/P-yes/H-no	Afternoon tea
All year	Czech, Spanish, French	Sitting room

Convenient to New York City and Philadelphia, near Princeton University. Newly renovated rooms, gourmet French restaurant. Available for groups or family reunions.

SEA GIRT

Holly Harbor Guest House	$$ B&B	Full buffet breakfast
112 Baltimore Blvd., 08750	12 rooms	Open porch
201-449-9731	AmEx	ocean swimming
Kim & Bill Walsh	C-yes/S-no/P-no/H-no	
All year	German	

Enjoy the friendly atmosphere in our redecorated turn-of-the-century inn nestled in quiet seashore community, eight houses from ocean.

SPRING LAKE ───────────────────────────

Ashling Cottage	$$ B&B	Continental plus buffet
106 Sussex Ave., 07762	10 rooms, 8 pb	AAA rated 3 diamonds
201-449-3553	C-no/S-ltd/P-no/H-no	Sitting room
Goodi & Jack Stewart	German	TV, VCR, bicycles
March—January 1		library, games

Victorian gem furnished with oak antiques and solarium breakfast room, a block from the ocean, in a storybook setting.

Chateau	$$$ EP	Cont. breakfast to room
500 Warren Ave., 07762	35 rooms, 35 pb	Sitting room
201-974-2000	•	bicycles
Scott & Karen Smith	C-yes/S-yes/P-no/H-ltd	cable color TV
April—November 10		

Turn-of-the-century inn, nestled between two parks, overlooking lake. Air-conditioning, TV, refrigerators, phones. AAA-rated 3 diamonds.

Johnson House Inn	$$$ B&B	Continental plus
25 Tuttle Ave., 07762	17 rooms, 8 pb	Sitting room with TV
201-449-1860	C-yes/S-yes	
The Gomboses & Desiderios	Hungarian, Finnish	
All year		

In days of old, the pineapple, a sign of comfort and hospitality, was a welcome sign for friend and weary traveler. Let us re-create that same atmosphere for you.

Normandy Inn	$$$ B&B	Full breakfast
21 Tuttle Ave., 07762	20 rooms, 15 pb	Comp. wine
201-449-7172	C-yes/S-ltd/P-no/H-no	Sitting room
Michael & Susan Ingino		bicycles, front porch
All year		side enclosed porch

A country inn at the shore, decorated with lovely Victorian antiques, painted with 5 different Victorian colors. Hearty breakfast included.

STANHOPE ───────────────────────────

Whistling Swan Inn	$$ B&B	Full breakfast buffet
P.O. Box 791, 07874	6 rooms, 6 pb	Comp. wine
110 Main St.	Visa, MC, AmEx •	Sitting room
201-347-6369	C-no/S-no/P-no/H-no	clawfoot tubs for two
Paula Williams, Joe Mulay		bicycles
All year		

Northwestern New Jersey's finest Victorian bed and breakfast guest house; 1½ miles from Waterloo Village, International Trade Zone, 20 miles to Delaware River.

WOODBINE ───────────────────────────

Henry Ludlam Inn	$$ B&B	Full gourmet breakfast
RD 3 Box 298,Woodbine, 08270	6 rooms, 2 pb	Comp. tea, wine
124 S. Delsea Dr., Rt. 47	•	Dinner winter Sat. nites
609-861-5847	C-12+/S-ltd/P-no/H-no	Sitting room
Ann & Marty Thurlow		piano
All year		

1804 home overlooking Ludlam Lake. All chambers decorated with antiques and fireplaces. Fishing, canoeing, delicious country breakfasts. Fireside picnics in winter.

More Inns...

Hudson Guide Farm   Andover 07821   201-398-2679
Sands B&B Inn   42 Sylvania Ave., Avon-by-the-Sea 07717   201-776-8386
Old Mill Inn   P.O. Box 423, Basking Ridge 07920   201-221-1100
Bayberry Barque B&B Inn   117 Centre St., Beach Haven 08008   609-492-5216
The Seaflower   110 Ninth Ave., Belmar 07719   201-681-6006
Alexander's Inn   653 Washington St., Cape May 08204   609-884-2555
Delsea   621 Columbia Avenue, Cape May 08204   609-884-8540
Hanson House   111 Ocean Street, Cape May 08204   609-884-8791
Heirloom B&B Inn   601 Columbia Ave., Cape May 08204   609-884-1666
Holly House   20 Jackson St., Cape May 08204   609-884-7365
John F. Craig House   609 Columbia Avenue, Cape May 08204   609-884-0100
Manse Inn   510 Hughes Street, Cape May 08204   609-884-0116
Perry Street Inn   29 Perry Street, Cape May 08204   609-884-4590
Summer Cottage Inn   613 Columbia Avenue, Cape May 08204   609-884-4948
Victorian Lace Inn   901 Stockton Avenue, Cape May 08204   609-884-1772
Victorian Rose   719 Columbia Avenue, Cape May 08204   609-884-2497
Wooden Rabbit B&B Country   609 Hughes St., Cape May 08204   609-884-7293
Woodleigh House   808 Washington St., Cape May 08204   609-884-7123
Publick House Inn   111 Main St., P.O. Box 85, Chester 07930   201-879-6878
National Hotel   31 Race St., Frenchtown 08825   201-996-4871
Old Hunterdon House   12 Bridge St., Frenchtown 08825   201-996-3632
Studio of John F. Peto   102 Cedar Ave., Island Heights 08732   201-270-6058
Coryell House   44 Coryell St., Lambertville 08530   609-397-2750
Winchester Hotel   1 S. 24 Street, Longport 08403   609-822-0623
Jeremiah J. Yercance House   410 Riverside Ave., Lyndhurst 07071   201-438-9457
Chestnut Hill on Delaware   P.O. Box N, Milford 08848   201-995-9761
Keswick Inn   32 Embury Ave., Ocean Grove 07756   201-775-7506
Shaloum Guest House   119 Tower Hill, Red Bank 07701   201-530-7759
Ma Bowman's B&B   156 Harmersville Peck-, Salem 08079   609-935-4913
The Kenilworth   1505 Ocean Ave., Spring Lake 07762   201-449-5327
Sandpiper Inn   71 Atlantic Ave., Spring Lake 07762   201-449-6060
Sea Crest of Spring Lake   19 Tuttle Avenue, Spring Lake 07762   201-449-9031
Stone Post Inn   115 Washington Ave., Spring Lake 07762   201-449-1212
Victoria House   214 Monmouth Ave., Spring Lake 07762   201-974-1882
Warren Hotel   901 Ocean Avenue, Spring Lake 07762   201-449-8800
Colligan's Stockton Inn   Rt. 29, Stockton 08559   609-397-1250
Woolverton Inn   6 Woolverton Rd., Stockton 08559   609-397-0802

New Mexico

CHIMAYO

La Posada de Chimayo
P.O. Box 463, 87522
El Rincon Rd.
505-351-4605
Sue Farrington
All year

$$$ B&B
2 rooms, 2 pb
C-yes/S-yes/P-ask/H-no
Spanish

Full breakfast
Private sitting rooms
fireplace

A traditional adobe guest house in beautiful northern New Mexico, thirty miles north of Santa Fe on High Road to Taos.

CLOUDCROFT

Lodge at Cloudcroft
P.O. Box 497, 88317
Corona Place
505-682-2566/800-842-4216
Mike Coy
All year

$$ EP/$$$ B&B
59 rooms, 59 pb
Visa, MC, AmEx, Dis, DC •
C-yes/S-ltd/P-no/H-no
Spanish

Continental breakfast
Aftn. tea, lunch, dinner
Restaurant & bar
Tennis, golf, skiing
hot tub, sauna, pool

Charming, historic railway lodge furnished in genuine antiques; gourmet dining above the clouds (9,200'); U.S. highest golf course and southernmost ski area.

LAS VEGAS

Plaza Hotel
230 Old Town Plaza, 87701
505-425-3591
David Fenzi
All year

$$ EP
37 rooms, 37 pb
AmEx, Visa, MC, DC •
C-yes/S-yes/P-yes/H-yes
Spanish

Lunch, dinner
Sitting room
personalized meeting
planner service

Center of activity on old-town plaza. Turn-of-the-century furnishings. Glass-enclosed brick conservatory for performers.

LOS ALAMOS

Casa del Rey
305 Rover, 87544
505-672-9401
Virginia King
All year

$ B&B
2 rooms, 1 pb
C-10+/S-no/P-no/H-no

Continental plus
Homemade breads, granola
Sitting room
patio, sun porch
tennis courts nearby

Quiet residential area, friendly atmosphere, beautiful mountain views from patios. Excellent library, restaurants and recreational facilities nearby.

Orange Street B&B
3496 Orange St., 87544
505-662-2651
Michael & Susanne Paisley
All year

$ B&B
5 rooms
•
C-no/S-no/P-no/H-no

Full breakfast
Sitting room, piano
bicycles, cable TV
tennis, swimming nearby

A delightful inn favoring Santa Fe-style and country charm offering sumptuous meals served with hospitality. Skiing, hiking, Santa Fe nearby.

NOGAL

Monjeau Shadows Inn $$ B&B   Continental plus
Bonito Route, 88341   5 rooms, 4 pb   Lunch/dinner by request
505-336-4191   Visa, MC •   Afternoon tea
The Cantrells & Alexanders   C-ltd/S-ltd/P-no/H-no   Sitting room
All year

Modern comforts in a charming Victorian-era farmhouse, graced by traditionally furnished guestrooms, fireplaces, located on ten wooded acres of pine forest.

PILAR

Plum Tree AYH-Hostel & B&B $ B&B   Continental breakfast
Box 1-A, 87531   5 rooms, 3 pb   Cafe
2886 State Rd. 68   Visa, MC, AmEx •   Hot tub, sauna
800-678-7586   C-yes/S-ltd/P-ltd/H-yes   kitchen
Dick Thibodeau, Robin Sandeen   Sitting room
All year

At the Plum Tree you can hike, bird-watch, rockhound, swim, X-C ski, raft, learn to kayak, see petroglyphs, study art, enjoy wholesome food. Nature program in the fall.

SANTA FE

Canyon Road Casitas $$$ B&B   Continental plus
652 Canyon Rd., 87501   2 rooms, 2 pb   Comp. bottle wine
505-988-5888   Visa, MC, AmEx, DC, Dis •   Guest robes
Trisha Ambrose   C-yes/S-no/P-no/H-yes   private walled courtyard
All year   bicycles

Awarded most spectacular B&B in N.M. by Rocky Mountain B&B. Decorated in the finest of Southwestern decor. European down quilts, down pillows, feather beds. Original artwork.

Casa De La Cuma B&B $$ B&B   Continental plus
105 Paseo De La Cuma, 87501   3 rooms, 1 pb   Afternoon tea/coffee
505-983-1717   C-13+/S-ltd/P-no/H-no   Solarium, garden
Norma & Al Tell   Spanish   patio with barbecue
All year   TV

Mountain views! CLOSE walking: downtown Plaza, shopping, restaurants, galleries, library, museums, banks. City sports facilities across street. Skiing 17 miles.

Dunshee's $$$ B&B   Full breakfast
986 Acequia Madre, 87501   1 rooms, 1 pb   Homemade cookies
505-982-0988   Visa, MC   Sitting room
Susan Dunshee   C-yes/S-no/P-no/H-no   refrig., microwave, TV
All year   patio, porch

Romantic hideaway in adobe home in historic zone, two-room suite furnished with antiques, folk art, fresh flowers, two fireplaces.

El Paradero $$ B&B   Full gourmet breakfast
220 W. Manhattan, 87501   14 rooms, 8 pb   Comp. tea, wine
505-988-1177   Visa, MC •   Gourmet picnic lunches
Ouida MacGregor, Thom Allen   C-yes/S-ltd/P-ltd/H-ltd   Television room
All year   Spanish   living room, piano

180-year-old adobe in quiet downtown location. Gourmet breakfasts, warm atmosphere, detailed visitor information. True southwestern hospitality.

SANTA FE ────────────────────────────────

Grant Corner Inn	$$ B&B	Full breakfast
122 Grant Ave., 87501	13 rooms, 7 pb	Comp. wine & cheese
505-983-6678	Visa, MC •	Gourmet picnic lunches
Louise Stewart, Pat Walter	C-6+/S-yes/P-no/H-yes	Private club access
All year	Spanish	(pool, sauna, tennis)

Elegant colonial home located in the heart of downtown Santa Fe, nine charming rooms furnished with antiques; friendly, warm atmosphere.

Inn of the Animal Tracks	$$$ B&B	Full breakfast
707 Paseo de Peralta, 87501	4 rooms, 4 pb	Afternoon tea
505-988-1546	Visa, MC, AmEx •	Sitting room
Daun Martin	C-yes/S-no/P-no/H-yes	
All year		

Full of humor and Southwest charm. Historic adobe style inn. 2½ blocks from city's 17th-century Plaza and close to ski slopes. Hearty breakfast and afternoon teas.

Polly's Guest House	$$ EP	House has kitchen
410 Camino Don Miguel, 87501	1 rooms, 1 pb	Coffee, tea, staples
505-983-9781	Visa, MC, checks	Private garden patio
Polly Rose	S-yes/P-ask	telephone
All year		

Adobe casita, comfortably furnished; Southwestern books, nice kitchen, cozy garden patio; Eastside neighborhood. Walk to Plaza, museums, restaurants, shopping, foothills.

Preston House	$ B&B	Continental plus
106 Faithway St., 87501	9 rooms, 7 pb	Comp. tea, wine
505-982-3465	Visa, MC •	Sitting room
Signe Bergman	C-ltd/S-ltd/P-no/H-no	lawn
All year		

Historic 100-year-old Queen Anne house on National Register with fireplaces and antiques; quiet location 3 blocks from Plaza.

TAOS ────────────────────────────────

Hacienda del Sol	$ B&B	Continental plus
P.O. Box 177, 87571	3 rooms, 3 pb	Comp. sangria, snacks
109 Mabel Dodge Lane	Visa, MC •	Robes for guest use
505-758-0287	C-5+/S-no/P-ltd/H-ltd	valet laundry service
Carol & Randy Pelton	Spanish, French	records, library, jacuzzi
All year		

180-year-old large adobe purchased as hideaway by Mabel Dodge for Indian husband, Tony. Adjoins vast Indian lands, yet close to Plaza. Tranquillity and mountain views.

La Posada de Taos	$ B&B	Full breakfast
P.O. Box 1118, 87571	5 rooms, 5 pb	Sitting room
309 Juanita Lane	•	piano
505-758-8164	C-yes/S-yes/P-yes/H-yes	
Sue Smoot		
All year		

Mountain views from this provincial adobe inn in artists' colony of Taos. Visit Indian pueblos and art galleries. Hearty breakfasts.

More Inns...

Adobe and Roses B&B 1011 Ortega Northwest, Albuquerque 87114 505-898-0654
Casita Chamisa B&B 850 Chamisal Rd. NW, Albuquerque 87107 505-897-4644
Sierra Mesa Lodge P.O. Box 463, Alto 88312 505-336-4515
All Season's B&B Swallow Pl., Box 144, Cloudcroft 88317 505-682-2380
Corrales Inn B&B P.O. Box 1361, Corrales 87048 505-897-4422
Blue Star Healing & Vacations P.O. Box 800, El Prado 87529 505-758-4634
Galisteo Inn Box 4, Galisteo 87540 505-982-1506
La Casita Rt. 10, Box 440, Glenwood 88039
Los Olmos Guest Ranch P.O. Box 127, Glenwood 88039 505-539-2311
Inn Of The Arts 618 S. Alameda Blvd., Las Cruces 88005 505-526-3327
Llewellyn House 618 S. Alameda, Las Cruces 88005 505-526-3327
Lundeen Inn of the Arts 618 S. Alemeda Blvd., Las Cruces 88005 505-526-3327
Carriage House B&B 925 6th Street, Las Vegas 87701 505-454-1784
Wortley Hotel Box 96, Lincoln 88338 505-653-4500
Los Alamos B&B P.O. Box 1212, Los Alamos 87544 505-662-6041
Walnut Executive Suite P.O. Box 777, Los Alamos 87544 505-662-9392
Meson de Mesilla P.O. Box 1212, Mesilla 88046 505-525-9212
Elms P.O. Box 1176, Mesilla Park 88001 505-524-1513
Broken Drum Guest Ranch Rt. 2 Box 100, Pecos 87552 505-757-6194
Hacienda de Las Munecas P.O. Box 564, Placitas 87043 505-867-3255
Ranchos Ritz B&B P.O. Box 669, Ranchos de Taos 87557 505-758-2640
El Western Lodge Box 301, Gilt Edge, Red River 87558 505-754-2272
Chinguague Compound P.O. Box 1118, San Juan Pueblo 87566 505-852-2194
The Pine Cone Inn Bed & Br Box 94, 13 Tejano Canyon, Sandia Park 87047 505-281-1384
Adobe Guest House P.O. Box 266, Santa Fe 87504 505-983-9481
Alexander's Inn 529 E. Palace Ave., Santa Fe 87501 505-986-1431
Inn of the Victorian Bird P.O. Box 3235, Santa Fe 87501 505-455-3375
Inn on the Alameda 303 E. Alameda, Santa Fe 87501
La Posada de Santa Fe 330 East Palace Avenue, Santa Fe 87501 800-621-7231
Pueblo Bonito B&B Inn 138 W. Manhattan, Santa Fe 87501 505-984-8001
Sunset House 436 Sunset, Santa Fe 87501 505-983-3523
Hotel St. Francis 210 Don Gaspar Avenue, Sante Fe 87501 505-983-5700
Inn of the Victorian Bird Box 3235, Arroyo Wyamun, Sante Fe 87501 505-455-3375
Bear Mtn. Guest Ranch P.O. Box 1163, Silver City 88062 505-538-2538
American Artists House P.O. Box 584, Taos 87571 505-758-4446
Brooks Street Inn P.O. Box 4954, Taos 87571 505-758-1489
Dasburg House & Studio Box 2764, Taos 87571 505-758-9513
Hotel Edelweiss P.O. Box 83, Taos 87571 505-776-2301
Las Palomas Conf. Center P.O. Box 6689, Taos 87571 505-758-9456
Mabel Dodge Lujan House P.O. Box 3400, Taos 87571 505-758-9456
Silvertree Inn P.O. Box 1528, Taos 87571 505-758-3071
Taos Inn 125 Paseo del Pueblo N., Taos 87571 505-758-2233
Amizette Inn P.O. Box 756, Taos Ski Valley 87525 505-776-2451
Rancho Encantado State Rd. 592, Tesuque 87501 505-982-3537
Rancho Arriba B&B P.O. Box 338, Truchas 87578 505-689-2374

New York

AMENIA ───────────────────────

Troutbeck
Box 26, Leedsville Rd., 12501
914-373-9681
J. Flaherty, K. Robinson
All year

$$$ AP
31 rooms, 26 pb
AmEx •
C-ltd/S-yes/P-no/H-no
Span., Port., Ital., Fr.

All meals included
Open bar
Public rooms, piano
tennis courts, library
year-round swimming pool

Historic English country estate on 422 acres, with indoor and outdoor pools, tennis courts, fine chefs, 12,000 books, lovely grounds. A quiet retreat.

AVERILL PARK ───────────────────────

Ananas Hus Bed & Breakfast
Route #3, Box 301, 12018
518-766-5035
T. Tomlinson, C. Tomlinson Jr
All year

$$ B&B
2 rooms
C-12+
Norwegian

Full breakfast
Afternoon tea, snacks
Sitting room
reading material
exercise bicycle

Hillside ranch home on 30 acres with panoramic view of Hudson River Valley midway between western Massachusetts and Capitol District. Walking, jogging, skiing & golf nearby.

Gregory House
P.O. Box 401, 12018
Route 43
518-674-3774
Bette & Bob Jewell
All year

$$ B&B
12 rooms, 12 pb
Visa, MC, AmEx, DC, CB •
C-6+/S-yes/P-no/H-no

Continental breakfast
Full breakfast $
Complimentary sherry
Common room w/fireplace
swimming pool (summer)

Gracious country charm centrally located—near Albany, Troy, Saratoga, Tanglewood, mountains, lakes and skiing. Vermont and Berkshires 45 min. away.

BOLTON LANDING ───────────────────────

Hilltop Cottage B&B
6883 Lakeshore Dr., 12814
P.O. Box 186
518-644-2492
Anita & Charles Richards
All year

$ B&B
4 rooms, 1 pb
C-yes/S-ltd/P-no/H-no
German

Full breakfast

Beautiful Lake George-Eastern Adirondack region. Clean, comfortable. Renovated farmhouse. Walk to beaches, restaurants, marinas. Friendly hosts knowledgeable about area.

BROOKLYN ───────────────────────

B&B on the Park
113 Prospect Park West, 11215
718-499-6115
Liana Paolella
All year

$$$ B&B
5 rooms, 2 pb
C-yes/S-ltd/P-no/H-no
French

Full breakfast
Sitting room
Victorian antiques
stained glass, woodwork

Beautifully appointed 1892 Victorian townhouse—a refuge minutes from Manhattan. Situated in Park Slope, a historic district of Brooklyn. Fabulous full breakfasts.

BURDETT

Red House Country Inn
Picnic Area Rd., 14818
Finger Lakes Nat'l Forest
607-546-8566
Joan Martin, Sandy Schmanke
All year

$$ B&B
5 rooms
Visa, MC, AmEx •
C-12+ / S-ltd

Full breakfast
Comp. wine
Oversized pool
sitting room, piano
nature trails

Within national forest; 28 miles of trails. Beautiful rooms in this gorgeous setting. Near famous Watkins Glen, east side of Seneca Lake. Over 30 wineries nearby.

CANANDAIGUA

Lakeview Farm B&B
4761 Rt. 364, Rushville, 14544
716-554-6973
Howard & Betty Freese
All year

$ B&B
4 rooms
•
C-ltd/S-ltd/P-no/H-no

Full breakfast
Upstairs sitting room
pond, lawn games
X-C skiing/walking trail

Antique-furnished, lake-view rooms in our country home overlooking Canandaigua Lake. Also waterfront rooms at our nearby lake house. Beach, lovely restaurant 1 mile.

CANDOR

Edge of Thyme B&B
6 Main St., 13743
607-659-5155
Eva Mae, Frank Musgrave
All year

$ B&B
6 rooms, 3 pb
•
C-yes/S-no/P-no/H-no

Full breakfast
Comp. tea, wine
Sitting room

Gracious Georgian home, antiques, gardens, arbor, leaded glass windowed porch. Finger Lakes, Cornell, Ithaca College, Watkins Glen, Corning, wineries nearby.

CAZENOVIA

Brae Loch Inn
5 Albany St., 13035
315-655-3431
H. Grey Barr, Doris L. Barr
All year

$$ B&B
12 rooms, 12 pb
Visa, MC, AmEx, DC •
C-yes/S-yes/P-no/H-yes

Continental breakfast
Restaurant, bar
Victorian lounge
fireplaces

Victorian inn built in 1805, decorated in a Scottish motif. Waitresses wear kilts and tams. Unique Scottish gift shop.

CHAPPAQUA

Crabtree's Kittle House
11 Kittle Rd., 10514
914-666-8044
John & Dick Crabtree
All year

$$$ B&B
11 rooms, 11 pb
Visa, MC, AmEx, DC
C-yes/S-yes/P-yes/H-yes
Spanish

Continental breakfast
Lunch, dinner
Restaurant, bar service
Snacks

Built in 1790, Crabtree's Kittle House maintains a distinctive blend of country-style comfort. Not to be missed are the dinner specialties of the house.

CHESTERTOWN

Balsam House
P.O. Box 171, 12817
Friends Lake
518-494-2828
Shawn & Alison Green
Closed April—mid-April

$$$ B&B/MAP
20 rooms, 20 pb
•
C-yes/S-yes/P-no/H-no

Full breakfast
Country French cuisine
Piano, entertainment
bicycles

Dramatically restored Victorian country inn, filled with antiques and wicker from 1900s. Fine wine list, superb dining, casual elegance, southern hospitality.

Harrington Farm, Princeton, MA

CLARENCE

Asa Ransom House	$$$ B&B	Full breakfast
10529 Main St. (Rt. 5), 14031	4 rooms, 4 pb	Dinner, bar
716-759-2315	•	Sitting room, library
Bob & Judy Lenz	C-yes/S-ltd/P-no/H-no	tap room, gift shop
Except January		herb garden, bicycles

Village inn furnished with antiques, period reproductions; tap room, gift shop, herb garden, regional dishes, homemade breads & desserts. 30 min. from Buffalo & Niagara Falls.

CLAYTON, 1000 ISLANDS

Thousand Islands Inn	$ EP	B&B available
P.O. Box 69, 13624	13 rooms, 13 pb	All meals served
335 Riverside Dr.	Visa, MC, DC, CB	Piano
315-686-3030	C-yes/S-yes/P-no/H-no	near public tennis
Allen & Susan Benas		courts and pool
Wed bef. Mem. Day—late Sept.		

The last full-service inn in the Islands. 1000 Islands salad dressing originated here in the early 1900s. Original recipe still used. 1987 was our 90th year!

COLD SPRING

One Market Street	$$ B&B	Continental breakfast
1 Market St., 10516	1 rooms, 1 pb	Complete kitchen
914-265-3912	Visa, MC	TV, air conditioning
Philip & Esther Baumgarten	C-yes/S-yes/P-no/H-no	sitting room
All year		one suite

Built ca. 1810; 1 block from Hudson River, Storm King Mt. & West Point nearby. Small suite includes double bed, bath, sitting room w/convertible couch, kitchen, TV, a/c.

Pig Hill Inn B&B	$$$ B&B	Full breakfast
73 Main St., 10516	8 rooms, 4 pb	Picnics packed
914-265-9247	Visa, MC, AmEx, DC	Sitting room
Wendy O'Brien	C-yes/S-no/P-no/H-no	fireplaces, garden
All year		heated towel racks

A newly renovated 1830s brick townhouse, filled with country elegance and whimsical details. Fireplaces, pretty garden and breakfast in bed.

COLDEN ───

Back of the Beyond	$ B&B	Full country breakfast
7233 Lower E. Hill Rd., 14033	3 rooms	Comp. wine, snacks
716-652-0427	C-yes/S-no/P-no/H-no	Kitchen, fireplace
Bill & Shash Georgi		pool table, gift shop
All year		swimming pond, X-C skiing

Charming mini-estate 50 miles from Niagara Falls, skiing, hiking, organic herb, flower and vegetable gardens. Breakfast served on deck/living room. Private chalet and cabin.

COOPERSTOWN ───

Angelholm	$$ B&B	Full breakfast
P.O. Box 705, 13326	4 rooms, 2 pb	Sitting room, porch
14 Elm St.	Visa, MC	piano
607-547-2483	C-yes/S-ltd/P-no/H-no	bicycles
George & Carolin Dempsey		
All year		

Historic 1815 colonial in town, with off-street parking. Walking distance to shops, restaurants and Hall of Fame Museum.

Hickory Grove Inn	$$ B&B	Continental plus
Rd. 2, Box 898, 13326	5 rooms, 3 pb	Dinner
Lake Rd. Six Mile Pt.	Visa, MC, AmEx	Restaurant, bar service
607-547-8100	C-yes/S-yes	Sitting room, piano
Karin & Vince Diorio		lakefront privilege
April October		

Charming 150-year-old country inn, built in 1805 as a stagecoach stop. Furnished with antiques. Wonderful Continental three-star restaurant. Lake swimming.

Hill & Hollow Farm B&B	$$ B&B	Full breakfast
RD 3, Box 70, 13326	3 rooms	Sitting room w/fireplace
State Route 28	C-8+/S-no/P-no/H-no	patio & picnic tables
607-547-2129		flower & herb gardens
Carolea Rooney		
All year		

Country atmosphere within easy reach of village and nearby colleges. Hearty breakfast in stenciled dining room. Furnished with antiques.

Inn at Cooperstown	$$$ B&B	Continental breakfast
16 Chestnut St., 13326	17 rooms, 17 pb	Sitting room
607-547-5756	Visa, MC, AmEx, DC •	1986 NY State Historic
Michael Jerome	C-yes/S-yes/P-no/H-yes	Presvtn. award winner
All year		

Restored Victorian inn providing genuine hospitality; close to Baseball Hall of Fame, Fenimore House and Farmer's Museum; open all year.

Litco Farms B&B	$ B&B	Full breakfast
P.O. Box 1048, 13337	4 rooms, 2 pb	Sitting room
Route 28, Fly Creek	C-yes/S-yes/P-no/H-no	library, pool
607-547-2501		X-C ski trails
Jim & Margaret Wolff		
All year		

Families and couples enjoy our 20'x40' pool, 70 acres and nature trails. Handmade quilts by our resident quilter. Warm hospitality and marvelous breakfasts are truly memorable.

CORNING

Rosewood Inn
134 E. First St., 14830
607-962-3253
Dick & Winnie Peer
All year

$$$ B&B
6 rooms, 4 pb
Visa, MC •
C-yes/S-ltd/P-ltd/H-ltd

Full breakfast
Sitting room
library

Elegantly appointed B&B in the Victorian manner. Walk to downtown Corning, Corning Glass Center, Corning Museum of Glass, theaters, museums and restaurants.

DE BRUCE

De Bruce Country Inn
RD 1, Box 286A, 12758
De Bruce Rd.
914-439-3900
Ron & Marilyn Lusker
All year

$$ B&B/MAP
15 rooms, 15 pb
•
C-yes/S-yes/P-yes/H-no
French

Full breakfast
Restaurant, bar, dinner
Library, sauna, pool
private preserve
trout pond, art gallery

Within the Catskill Forest Preserve with its trails, wildlife, famous trout stream, our turn-of-the-century inn offers superb dining overlooking the valley.

DEPOSIT

White Pillars Inn
82 Second St., 13754
607-467-4191/607-467-4189
Ms. Najla R. Aswad
All year

$$ B&B
5 rooms, 3 pb
Visa, MC, AmEx, DC, CB
C-yes/S-no/P-no/H-no

Full gourmet breakfast
Lunch & dinner by resv.
Comp. wine, snacks
Sitting room, library
portable TVs optional

Lavishly furnished 1820 Greek Revival mansion. Gourmet breakfast is the highlight of your stay. Antiquing, cycling or just a perfect place to do nothing at all.

DRYDEN

Sarah's Dream B&B
P.O. Box 1087, 13053
49 W. Main St.
607-844-4321
Judi Williams, Ken Morusty
All year

$$ B&B
7 rooms, 7 pb
Visa, MC •
C-10+/S-no/P-no/H-no

Full breakfast
Afternoon tea, snacks
Sitting room, library
airport pickup
room trays for weddings

On National Register of Historic Places. 1828 Greek Revival furnished with antiques. Subtly elegant, not pretentious. Nearby: golfing, sailing, skiing, antiquing.

DUNDEE

Country Manor B&B
4798 Dundee-Himrod Rd., 14837
RD 1, Box 16A
607-243-8628
Tricia & Jim Kidd
All year

$ B&B
3 rooms, 1 pb
C-yes/S-no/P-no/H-no

Full breakfast
Box lunches
Sitting room
library
card, puzzle room

Fifteen-room Victorian farmhouse on seven acres, including a ballroom. Full breakfast complemented by homemade jam from fruits grown on the grounds.

FAIR HAVEN

Frost Haven Resort B&B
West Bay Rd., 13064
315-947-5331
Brad & Chris Frost
All year

$$ B&B
4 rooms, 2 pb
Visa, MC, AmEx
C-yes/S-no/P-no/H-no

Full breakfast
Dockage for boat
Charter fishing

Located on beautiful Lake Ontario where nature and wildlife provide an ever-changing view. Area famous for trout and salmon fishing.

FOSTERDALE

Fosterdale Heights House	$ B&B	Full breakfast
RD 1, Box 198, 12726	12 rooms, 3 pb	Dinner, snacks
Mueller Rd.	Visa, MC	Sitting room, library
914-482-3369	C-no/S-yes/P-no/H-no	billiard room, piano
Roy & Trish Singer		X-C skiing, canoeing
All year		

Historic 1840 European-style country estate. Catskill Mountains, less than 2 hours from New York City. Gentle, quiet. Bountiful country breakfast.

FULTON

Battle Island Inn	$$ B&B	Full breakfast
RR 1, Box 176, 13069	6 rooms, 6 pb	Sitting room
315-593-3699	Visa, MC •	four acres of large
Richard & Joyce Rice	C-yes/S-no/P-no/H-no	flower & herb gardens
All year		

1840s farm estate furnished with period furnishings. Gourmet breakfast served in our elegant Empire Period dining room. Located across from golf course, X-C skiing.

GARRISON

Bird & Bottle Inn	$$$ B&B/MAP	Full breakfast
Route 9, 10524	4 rooms, 4 pb	Dinner, bar
Old Albany Post Rd.	Visa, MC, AmEx •	
914-424-3000	C-ltd/S-ltd/P-no/H-no	
Ira Boyar		
All year		

Established in 1761, the inn's history predates the Revolutionary War. Each room has a working fireplace and four-poster or canopy bed.

GENESEO

American House B&B Inn	$ B&B	Continental plus
39 Main St., 14454	6 rooms, 2 pb	Sitting room
716-243-5483	•	library
Harry & Helen Wadsworth	C-yes/S-yes	cable TV
All year		

1897 Victorian home offering distinctive lodging in the heart of village historic district. Comfortable, spacious rooms furnished with period antiques.

GENEVA

Inn at Belhurst Castle	$$ EP	Continental breakfast
P.O. Box 609, 14456	12 rooms, 12 pb	Lunch, dinner, bar
Lochland Rd.	Visa, MC, DC	Sitting room, piano
315-789-0359	C-yes/S-yes/P-no/H-no	
Robert & Nancy Golden	French, Arabic	
All year		

Elegant romanesque "castle" on 23-acre parklike setting on bluff overlooking Seneca Lake. Beautifully restored with antiques and modern baths.

GREENVILLE

Greenville Arms	$$ B&B	Full breakfast
South St., 12083	19 rooms, 13 pb	Dinner
30 mi. South of Albany	•	Library, piano
518-966-5219	C-yes/S-yes/P-ltd/H-no	swimming pool
Barbara & Laura Stevens		painting workshops
May 1—November 1		

A Victorian country inn found in a quiet village in the Hudson River Valley. The former house of William Vanderbilt.

GROTON

Benn Conger Inn
206 W. Cortland St., 13073
607-898-5817
Patricia & Mark Bloom
Closed Mondays & March

$$ B&B
4 rooms, 2 pb
Visa, MC, AmEx
C-12+/S-yes/P-no/H-no
Russian, Spanish

Full breakfast
Dinner, nightcap
Sitting room
library

Elegant and graceful Georgian-style mansion on quiet village side street. Original cuisine, distinctive accommodations. Convenient to I-81 (10 miles).

HADLEY

Saratoga Rose
4870 Rockwell St., 12835
P.O. Box 238
518-696-2861
Nancy & Anthony Merlino
All year

$$ B&B
5 rooms, 5 pb
Visa, MC, AmEx
C-no/S-ltd/P-no/H-no

Full breakfast
Restaurant, dinner
Bar service, sitting rm
Library, bicycles
in-room dining

Romantic Victorian inn/restaurant. Near Saratoga, Lake George, skiing, lakes, recreational activities. Fireplaces, antiques. Gourmet meals prepared by owner-chef.

HAMMONDSPORT

Laufersweilers Blushing Rose B&B
11 William St., 14840
607-569-3402
All year

$$ B&B
4 rooms, 4 pb
C-yes/S-yes/P-yes/H-no

Full country breakfast
Sitting room
bicycles
lake nearby

An 1843 Victorian Italianate located in heart of an historic town. Enjoy museums, wineries, Corning, swimming, boating or just strolling.

HAMPTON BAYS

House on the Water
Box 106, 11946
33 Rampasture Rd.
516-728-3560
Mrs. Ute Lambur
May—November

$$ B&B
2 rooms, 2 pb
•
C-no/S-ltd/P-no/H-no
German, Spanish, French

Full breakfast
Comp. coffee & tea
Kitchen privileges
Barbecue, windsurfer
sail/pedal boats, bikes

Seven miles to Southampton Village. Museum, art gallery, stores. Short drive to beaches. Breakfast on terrace, relax in garden, kitchen privileges (snacks).

HANCOCK

Sunrise Inn B&B
RD 1 Box 232B, 13783
Readburn Rd., Walton
607-865-7254
Adele & Jim Toth
All year

$ B&B
2 rooms
•
C-yes/S-no/P-no/H-no

Continental plus
Snacks
Sitting room, library
antique shop, gazebo
trout stream

Cozy 19th-century getaway in a quiet country setting. For nearby activities, enjoy fishing, canoeing, antiquing, golfing and fine dining.

HEMPSTEAD

Duvall Bed & Breakfast
237 Cathedral Ave., 11550
On the Garden City Line
516-292-9219
Richard & Wendy Duvall
All year

$$ B&B
4 rooms, 3 pb
•
C-yes/S-no/P-no/H-no
Spanish, German, French

Full breakfast
Comp. wine
Stereo
patio/backyard
color TV each room

Charming old Dutch colonial; close to New York City, beaches, airports and public transportation. Fifth Avenue of Long Island. Centrally located; near all tourist sights.

HILLSDALE

Swiss Hutte
Route 23, 12529
518-325-3333
Gert & Cindy Alper
April 15—March

$$$ MAP,EP avail
16 rooms, 16 pb
Visa, MC
C-yes/S-yes/P-yes/H-yes
German

Full breakfast
Lunch, dinner, noon tea
Restaurant, bar service
Sitting room
tennis, pool, skiing (W)

Swiss chef and owner. French continental decor. Indoor and outdoor patio dining. Nestled in a hidden valley among firs and hemlocks.

HUNTER

Washington Irving Lodge
P.O. Box 675, Rt. 23A, 12442
518-589-5560
Stefania & Mirko Jozic
All year

$ B&B
20 rooms, 7 pb
Visa, MC, AmEx
C-yes/S-yes/P-no/H-no
Serbocuoeshen

Full breakfast
Bar service
Sitting room
tennis courts, pool
near slopes, X-C skiing

The Lodge built in 1890 has the distinct charm of a Catskill country inn. Accommodations are homey and comfortable. A warm, informal atmosphere makes every guest feel welcome.

ITHACA

Glendale Farm B&B
224 Bostwick Rd., 14850
607-272-8756
Jeanne Marie Tomlinson
All year

$$ B&B
7 rooms, 4 pb
Visa, MC
C-yes/S-yes/P-yes/H-yes

Full breakfast
Sitting room
screened porch
organ, piano

Restored Victorian farmhouse furnished with antiques; full country breakfast. Near Buttermilk Falls State Park, in the heart of the Finger Lakes.

Peregrine House Inn
140 College Ave., 14850
133 Giles St. (M.A.)
607-277-3862
Nancy Falconer, Susan Vance
All year

$$ B&B
8 rooms, 4 pb
Visa, MC •
C-12+

Full breakfast
Afternoon tea, snacks
Comp. wine
Sitting room

Brick Victorian inn furnished with antiques, pretty linens, terry robes. In the heart of city, near Cornell campus. Air conditioned.

Rose Inn
P.O. Box 6576, 14851
813 Auburn Rd., Rt. 34 N.
607-533-7905
Sherry & Charles Rosemann
All year

$$$ B&B
12 rooms, 12 pb
AmEx •
C-12+ /S-no/P-no/H-no
German, Spanish

Full breakfast
Gourmet dinner by resv.
Sitting room, library
3 suites w/jacuzzis
piano, bicycles

1850s Italianate mansion with 3-story circular mahogany staircase. Furnished with period pieces, antique shop on premises. Twenty landscaped acres, orchard.

KEENE

Bark Eater Inn
Alstead Hill Rd., 12942
P.O. Box 139
518-576-2221
Joe Pete Wilson
All year

$$$ B&B
17 rooms, 4 pb
AmEx •
C-yes/S-yes/P-yes

Full breakfast
Comp. tea, wine
Sitting room
piano

Country inn from the stagecoach days, nestled in quiet valley in heart of Adirondack Mountains. Gracious hosts and gourmet food compliment your stay.

LAKE LUZERNE

Lamplight Inn	$$ B&B	Full breakfast
2129 Lake Ave., 12846	7 rooms, 7 pb	Comp. atmos
518-696-5294	•	Sitting room w/games, TV
Gene & Linda Merlino	C-12+ /S-ltd/P-no/H-no	porch w/swing, gardens
All year		lake swimming, bicycles

1890 restored Victorian mansion boasts four fireplaces, antiques and comfortable, romantic atmosphere. Southern Adirondacks, 10 min. to Lake George, 20 min. to Saratoga.

LAKE PLACID

Highland House Inn	$ B&B	Full breakfast
3 Highland Place, 12946	8 rooms, 5 pb	Sitting room
518-523-2377	Visa, MC	Bicycles, hot tubs, pool
Teddy & Cathy Blazer	C-yes/S-yes	and tennis all nearby
All year		

Renowned for blueberry pancakes. Glass enclosed garden dining during the summer. Central village location. Uniquely appealing. Fully efficient country cottage also available.

Interlaken Inn—Restaurant	$$$ B&B/MAP	Full breakfast
15 Interlaken Ave., 12946	12 rooms, 12 pb	Dinner, restaurant
518-523-3180	Visa, MC •	Bar service, sitting rm
Roy & Carol Johnson	C-7+ /S-yes/P-no/H-no	Volleyball, croquet &
Exc. April & November		badminton courts

Adirondack inn; heart of Olympic country; quiet setting— ½ block from Main St. Between Mirror Lake and Lake Placid; some rooms with balconies. Great food!

LIVINGSTON MANOR

Lanza's Country Inn	$$ B&B	Full breakfast
RD 2, Box 446, 12758	7 rooms, 7 pb	Lunch, dinner
Shandelee Rd.	Visa, MC, AmEx	Restaurant, bar service
914-439-5070	C-yes/S-yes	Sitting room
Dick, Pat & Mickey Lanza		
All year		

Guests lodging at the inn are treated to the warm, friendly, personal service of a family-operated B&B inn.

MAYVILLE

Plum Bush—A Victorian B&B	$$ B&B	Continental plus
Chautauqua-Stedman, RD2, 14757	4 rooms, 4 pb	Afternoon tea, snacks
716-789-5309	Visa, MC •	Sitting room
Sandra Green	C-12+ /S-no/P-no/H-no	library
All year		bicycles

Restored 1860s Italian villa country home; 125 acres; wildlife; cross-country; bicycles available; nearby lake, antiques, atmosries; One mile to Chautauqua Institute.

Village Inn B&B	$ B&B	Full breakfast
111 S. Erie St, Rt. 394, 14757	3 rooms	Comp. wine
716-753-3583	•	Sitting room
Dean Hanby	C-yes/S-yes	
All year	some Spanish	

Spacious Victorian home with woodwork by European artisans. Full breakfasts using family recipes. Near Chautauqua Institution, wineries, antique shops, X-C & downhill skiing.

MOUNT TREMPER

Mt. Tremper Inn
P.O. Box 51, 12457
Rt. 212 & Wittenberg Rd.
914-688-5329
Lou Caselli, Peter Lascala
All year

$$ B&B
23 rooms
C-no/S-ltd/P-no/H-no

Full breakfast
Comp. sherry
Elegant parlor, library
game room, reading room
comp. sundries

1850 Victorian mansion with Victorian antiques, classical music, gourmet breakfast, wraparound porch, large fireplace. Near Woodstock and all ski slopes.

MUMFORD

Genesee Country Inn
P.O. Box 340, 14511
948 George St.
716-538-2500
Glenda & Gregory Barcklow
All year

$$$ B&B
12 rooms, 12 pb
Visa, MC, AmEx, DC •
C-ltd/S-yes/P-no/H-ltd

Full breakfast
Afternoon tea
Common rooms, fireplaces
some canopy beds, TVs
A/C, flyfishing

17-room 1833 stone mill specializing in hospitality and quiet, comfortable retreats. Unique natural setting—woods, gardens, waterfalls. Near Village-Museum.

NEW ROCHELLE

Rose Hill Guest House
44 Rose Hill Ave., 10804
914-632-6464
Marilou Mayetta
All year

$$ B&B
2 rooms
•
C-yes/S-yes/P-no/H-no

Continental plus
Comp. wine, tea
Library, sitting room
bicycles, VCR/Cable TV

Beautiful Norman home 20 minutes from Manhattan or Greenwich. Enjoy "Big Apple" and country living in one. Bike and horse ride, golf, sailing, etc.

NEW YORK

Incentra Village House
32 8th Ave., 10014
212-206-0007
Gaylord Hoftiezer
All year

$$$ EP
10 rooms, 10 pb
Visa, MC, AmEx •
C-yes/S-yes/P-yes/H-no

Most rooms have kitchens
Fireplaces, A/C
sitting room

The Incentra Village House is a renovated 1841 townhouse centrally located in Greenwich Village. Most rooms are decorated in the period and include a fireplace and kitchenette.

NORTH HUDSON

Pine Tree Inn B&B
P.O. Box 555, 12855
Route 9
518-532-9255
Peter & Pat Schoch
All year

$ B&B
5 rooms
C-6+/S-ltd/P-no/H-no

Full breakfast
Dinner by resv. (winter)
Sitting room

Adirondack sturdy, converted 1920 hotel, country-comfortable furnishings (circa 1740-1956). Near Schroon Lake, Ft. Ticonderoga and Lake Placid.

OGDENSBURG

Maple Hill Country Inn
Box 21, 13669
Riverside Dr.
315-393-3961
All year

$$ B&B
4 rooms
C-yes/S-yes/P-yes/H-no

Full breakfast
Dinner on request
Comp. tea, wine, snacks
Library, sitting room
winter area tours

"More than a nice place to stay." We offer comfortable rooms, views of the St. Lawrence River and a hearty breakfast. Getaway weekends with special area tours during winter.

OLIVEREA ———

Slide Mountain Forest Hse
163 Oliverea Rd., 12462
914-254-5365
Ralph & Ursula Combe
All year

$ AP
21 rooms, 17 pb
Visa, MC
C-yes/S-yes/P-no/H-no
German

Full breakfast
Lunch, dinner
Bar service, sitting rm
Tennis courts, pool
hiking, fishing

Fresh air, nature and a touch of Old World charm await you at our German/American-style Catskill Mountains Inn.

RENSSELAER ———

Tibbitt's House Inn
100 Columbia Tpk., 12144
Routes 9 & 20
518-472-1348
Claire Rufleth
All year

$ EP
5 rooms, 1 pb
C-no/S-yes/P-no/H-no

Breakfast from menu $
Enclosed porch
one apartment

Comfortable, 126-year-old, antique-furnished farmhouse, 2 miles from Albany, State Museum, Hudson River, hiking/biking, old Dutch fort.

RHINEBECK ———

Village Victorian Inn
31 Center St., 12572
914-876-8345
Judy and Richard Kohler
All year

$$$ B&B
5 rooms, 5 pb
Visa, MC, AmEx •
S-yes
Italian

Full breakfast
Lunch & dinner (request)
Afternoon tea, snacks
Comp. wine
Sitting room

Our ambience is quite gentle, private and romantic. Come recapture a Victorian fantasy filled with antiques, laces and canopy beds.

RICHFIELD SPRINGS ———

Summerwood Bed & Breakfast
P.O. Box 388, 13439
72 E. Main St.
315-858-2024
Lona & George Smith
May—November

$$ B&B
4 rooms, 1 pb
•
C-yes/S-ltd/P-no/H-no

Full breakfast
Meals by arrangement
Comp. wine
Library, sitting room
TV, games, refrigerator

Restored Queen Anne listed on National and State Registries. Set on three acres, fifteen miles from Cooperstown and twelve miles from NY State Thruway. Weekend packages.

ROCHESTER ———

Dartmouth House B&B
215 Dartmouth St., 14607
716-271-7872/716-473-0778
Ellie & Bill Klein
All year

$$ B&B
2 rooms, 2 pb
•
C-ltd/S-no/P-no/H-no

Full breakfast
Snacks
Sitting room
grand piano and organ

Spacious Tudor home close to everything. Quiet, architecturally fascinating, residential neighborhood. Hosts are well traveled and love people! Great breakfasts!

Strawberry Castle B&B
1883 Penfield Rd., 14526
Penfield
716-385-3266
Cynthia & Charles Whited
All year

$$ B&B
3 rooms
Visa, MC, AmEx •
C-12+/S-yes/P-ask/H-no

Continental plus
Comp. wine
Sitting room, piano
swimming pool
bicycles

Landmark Victorian mansion on three acres. Large rooms and suites with antique furnishings. Small town advantages with convenience to Finger Lakes area.

ROME

Maplecrest Bed & Breakfast
6480 Williams Rd., 13440
315-337-0070
Diane Saladino
All year

$ B&B
3 rooms, 1 pb
Visa, MC, AmEx
C-yes/S-no/P-no/H-no
Italian

Full breakfast
Comp. wine
Sitting room, bicycles
refrigerator use
grill, picnic facilities

Modern split-level home. Formal country breakfast. Close to historic locations. Adirondack foliage, lakes, and skiing. Near Guffiss Air Force Base.

SARATOGA SPRINGS

Adelphi Hotel
365 Broadway, 12866
518-587-4688
Gregg Siefker
May—November

$$ B&B
20 rooms, 20 pb
Visa, MC, AmEx
C-yes/S-yes/P-no/H-no
sitting room
library, piano

Continental breakfast
Summer dinners, bar
Entertainment

Charming accommodations. Opulently restored high Victorian hotel located in the historic district of the renowned resort and spa of Saratoga Springs.

Saratoga Bed & Breakfast
Out Church St., Rt. 9N, 12866
518-584-0920
Kathleen & Noel Smith
All year

$$ B&B
14 rooms, 10 pb
Visa, MC
C-yes/S-yes/P-ltd/H-yes
French

Full breakfast
Dinner
Sitting room
piano
bicycles

Five pine-filled acres, large common rooms and terraces, full Irish breakfast, close to everything from summer thoroughbreds to winter skiing.

Six Sisters B&B
149 Union Ave., 12866
518-583-1173
Kate Benton, Steve Ramirez
All year exc. January

$$ B&B
4 rooms, 2 pb
C-12+/S-no/P-no

Full breakfast
Restaurant nearby
Sitting room
front porch
air-conditioning

Located within walking distance of Saratoga Race Track, museums, restaurants, historic Congress park and downtown. Late 1800s Victorian, full of charm.

Westchester House
P.O. Box 944, 12866
102 Lincoln Ave.
518-587-7613
Bob & Stephanie Melvin
All year

$$ B&B
7 rooms, 5 pb
Visa, MC, AmEx •
C-ltd/S-ltd/P-no/H-no
French, German

Continental plus
Complimentary beverages
Sitting room, library
wraparound porch, piano
X-C skiing, gardens

Gracious Queen Anne Victorian featuring elaborate fireplaces, beautiful wainscoting, antique furnishings and modern conveniences. Walk to all that historic Saratoga offers.

SOUTHAMPTON

Old Post House Inn
136 Main St., 11968
516-283-1717
Cecile & Edward Courville
All year

$$ B&B
7 rooms, 7 pb
Visa, MC, DC
C-13+/S-yes/P-no/H-no

Continental breakfast
Sitting room, library
tennis nearby
ocean nearby

Clean country charm less than two hours from Manhattan. National Register. Pristine Atlantic beaches one mile away. Complimentary van transport.

SOUTHOLD

Goose Creek Guesthouse
1475 Waterview Dr., 11971
P.O. Box 377
516-765-3356
Mary Mooney-Getoff
All year

$$ B&B
3 rooms, 1 pb
•
C-yes/S-no/P-ltd/H-no
Spanish

Full country breakfast
Tea, snacks
Homegrown vegetables &
fruit
Sitting room, library

Pre-Civil War farmhouse, secluded in 7 acres of woods, near golf, beaches and ferries. Gourmet country breakfasts, garden-fresh food.

SPENCERTOWN

Spencertown Guests
Box 122, Elm St & Rt203, 12165
518-392-2358
Mary/Isabel Zander
All year (ltd. Dec.—Mar.)

$ B&B
2 rooms
C-12+/S-ltd/P-ltd/H-no

Continental plus
Full breakfast $
Sitting room

Cozy 18th-century cottage furnished with antiques in historic hamlet. Near Tanglewood, summer theaters and Hudson River Valley attractions.

STONY BROOK

Three Village Inn
150 Main St., 11790
516-751-0555
All year except Xmas

$$$ EP
32 rooms, 32 pb
Visa, MC, AmEx
C-yes/S-yes/P-no/H-yes

Restaurant, bar service
Lunch, dinner, snacks
Live piano music Fri.-Sun.
Sitting room, library
beaches nearby

Three Village Inn offers historic Colonial charm with magnificent views of Stony Brook Harbor on the Long Island Sound. We offer the finest food, service, and hospitality.

SYRACUSE

Ivy Chimney
143 Didama St., 13224
315-446-4199
Elaine N. Samuels
All year

$ B&B
3 rooms
C-16+/S-no/P-yes/H-ltd

Continental plus

Clean, convenient, safe, reasonable. This is my own home. Very good for business travelers. Have cats in house. Easy drive to Syracuse University; walk to LeMoyne.

TANNERSVILLE

Eggery Country Inn
County Rd. 16, 12485
P.O. Box 4
518-589-5363
Abe & Julie Abramczyk
All year

$ P, $$$ B&B/MAP
15 rooms, 15 pb
Visa, MC
C-ltd/S-yes/P-no/H-yes

Full breakfast (B&B/MAP)
Dinner, wine list
Food service seasonal
Sitting room, cable TV
player piano, AAA app.

Majestic setting, panoramic views, dining in a garden setting, homelike personal atmosphere and individualized attention. Near Hunter Mt. ski slopes.

TERRYVILLE

Captain Hawkins Inn
321 Terryville Rd., 11776
516-473-8211
Ralph & Anne Cornelius
All year

$$ B&B
9 rooms, 6 pb
Visa, MC •
C-12+/S-ltd/P-no/H-ltd

Continental plus
Comp. wine on arrival
Afternoon tea, snacks
Sitting room
hot tubs, swimming pool

Quiet relaxed atmosphere; furnished in antiques and reproductions. Three villages, golf and tennis nearby; short ride to Long Island wine country; ferry to New England.

TRUMANSBURG

Taughannock Farms Inn
Route 89 at Taughannock, 14886
Falls State Park
607-387-7711
C. Keith & Nancy le Grand
March 15—December 15

$$$ B&B
10 rooms, 8 pb
C-yes/S-ltd/P-no/H-no
Dutch, German, French

Continental plus
Restaurant, bar
Sitting room, music box
honeymoon room
lake swimming, garden

Next to spectacular Taughannock Falls and Gorge. Hiking trails, boat rentals, picnic grounds, marina. Overlooking Cayuga Lake. 2-bedroom guest house available.

WARRENSBURG

Country Road Lodge
HCR 1 Box 227, 12885
Hickory Hill Rd.
518-623-2207
Steve & Sandi Parisi
All year

$$ B&B
4 rooms
•
C-no/S-yes/P-no/H-no

Full breakfast
AP Dec.-Apr.
Sitting room
piano, library

Quiet, idyllic setting in a clearing along Hudson River at the end of a country road. Discreetly sociable host. No traffic or TV. Near Lake George and garage sale country.

White House Lodge
53 Main St., 12885
518-623-3640
James & Ruth Gibson
All year

$$ B&B
5 rooms
Visa, MC
C-7+/S-yes/P-no/H-no

Continental breakfast
Comp. tea
Sitting room, TV
front porch

Pre-Civil War mansion, four miles from beautiful Lake George. Eight miles from Gore Mountain. Queen village of the Adirondacks.

Centuryhurst Antiques & B&B, Sheffield, MA

WEST SHOKAN

Haus Elissa B&B
P.O. Box 595, Rt. 28-A, 12494
914-657-6277
Gretchen & Helen Behl
All year

$ B&B
2 rooms
C-14+/S-ltd/P-no/H-no
German, Dutch, French

Full breakfast
Sitting room
library, piano
local history library

A blend of Catskill coziness and continental hospitality. Our own German pastries served with breakfast. Near fishing, hiking, skiing, fine dining.

WESTFIELD

William Seward Inn
S. Portage Rd., RD 2, 14787
716-326-4151
Peter & Joyce Wood
All year

$$ B&B
10 rooms, 10 pb
Visa, MC •
C-12+/S-no/P-no/H-yes
French

Full gourmet breakfast
Comp. wine
Wet bar available
Sitting room, library
bicycles

Country mansion with period antiques; complimentary full gourmet breakfast; close to major antique center, wineries, ski slopes and X-C, and charming Lake Chatauqua.

WESTHAMPTON BEACH

1880 Seafield House
P.O. Box 648, 11978
2 Seafield Lane
516-288-1559/800-346-3290
Elsie Pardee Collins
All year

$$$ B&B
3 rooms, 3 pb
•
C-no/S-no/P-no/H-no

Full breakfast
Sat. aft. tea & sherry
Sitting room, piano
tennis court, library
swimming pool

Country hideaway with three suites furnished in antiques—gourmet breakfast served in our lovely decorated dining room or enclosed porch overlooking the pool.

More Inns...

Providence Farm   11572 Hiller Road, Akron 14001   716-759-2109
Appel Inn   Route 146, Altamont 12009   518-861-6557
Mill-Garth-Mews Inn   P.O. Box 700, Amagansett 11930   516-267-3757
Marshfield B&B   RR 1, Box 432, Amenia 12501   914-868-7833
Green Acres   RD 1, Rt. 474, Ashville 14710   716-782-4254
Springside Inn   41 West Lake Road, Auburn 13021   315-252-7247
Aurora Inn   Main St. Rt. 90, Aurora 13026   315-364-8842
Mulligan Farm B&B   5403 Barber Rd., Avon 14414   716-226-6412
All Breeze Guest Farm   Haring Rd., Barryville 12719   914-557-6485
Bearsville B&B   P.O. Box 11, Bearsville 12409
Vrede Landgoed   Dug Rd., RD #2, Beaver Dams 14812   607-535-4108
Beaverbrook House   Duell Road, Bengall 12545   914-868-7677
Cold Brook Inn   P.O. Box 251, Boicerille 12412   914-657-6619
Four Seasons B&B   470 W. Lake Rd., Rt.54A, Branchport 14418   607-868-4686
Maple Ridge Inn   Rt. 372, RD 1, Box 391C, Cambridge 12816   518-677-3674
Tara Farm   Kiernan Rd., Campbell Hall 10916   914-294-6482
Inn at Shaker Mill Farm   Cherry Ln., Canaan 12029   518-794-9345
Thornberry Inn   Stony Kill Rd., Canaan 12029   518-781-4939
Inn a Still Woode   131 East St., Canandaigua 14424   716-394-0504
Wilder Tavern   5648 N. Bloomfield Rd., Canandaigua 14425   716-394-8132
Country House   P.O. Box 146 37 Mill St., Canaseraga 14822   607-545-6439
Locustwood Inn   3563 Route 89, Canoga 13148   315-549-7132
Eastwood House   45 So. Main Street, Castile 14427   716-493-2335
Ludwig's Kozy Kove   Box 866, Cayuga 13034   315-889-5940
Lincklaen House   79 Albany St., Cazenovia 13035   315-655-8171

Gasho Inn   Rt. 32 Box M, Central Valley 10917   914-928-2277
Banner House Inn   Chateaugay Lake 12920
Longfellow Inn   11 Roberts Ave, Box Y, Chautauqua 14722   716-357-2285
Friends Lake Inn   Friends Lake Rd., Chestertown 12817   518-494-4751
Maplewood   P.O. Box 40, Chichester 12416   914-688-5433
Clinton House   21 W. Park Row, Clinton 13323   315-853-5555
Bed & Breakfast   Sunset Trail, Clinton Corners 12514   914-266-3922
Hudson House, Country Inn   2 Main St., Cold Spring 10516   914-265-9355
Cooper Motor Inn   Chestnut St., Cooperstown 13326   607-547-2567
Phoenix Inn at River Road   R.D. #3, Box 150, Cooperstown 13326   607-547-8250
Tunnicliff Inn   34-36 Pioneer St., Cooperstown 13326   607-547-9611
Cecce Guest House   166 Chemung St., Corning 14830   607-962-5682
Laurel Hill B&B   2670 Powderhouse Rd., Corning 14830   607-936-3215
West Wind Farm B&B   402A Hornby Rd., Corning 14830   607-962-3979
33 South   33 South St., Cuba 14727   716-968-1387
1819 Red Brick Inn   Rd. 2, Box 57A, Dandee 14837   607-243-8844
Glenora Guests   Box 77, RD 1, Glenora, Dundee 14837   607-243-7686
Lakeside Terrace B&B   RD 1, P.O. Box 197, Dundee 14837   607-292-6606
Willow Cove   77 S. Glenora Rd., RD 4, Dundee 14837   607-243-8482
Big Moose Inn, Inc.   on Big Moose Lake, Eagle Bay 13331   315-357-2042
Roycroft Inn   40 S. Grove St., East Aurora 14052   716-652-9030
Holloway House   Routes 5 & 20, East Bloomfield 14443   716-657-7120
Highland Springs   Allen Rd., East Concord 14055   716-592-4323
1770 House   143 Main St., East Hampton 11937   516-324-1770
Bassett House   128 Montauk Hwy., East Hampton 11937   516-324-6127
Centennial House   13 Woods Lane, East Hampton 11937   516-324-9414
Hedges House   74 James Ln., East Hampton 11937   516-324-7100
Huntting Inn   94 Main St., East Hampton 11937   516-324-0410
Maidstone Arms   207 Main St., East Hampton 11937   516-324-5006
Caffrey House   Squires Avenue, East Quogue 11942   516-728-1327
Redcoat's Return   Dale Lane, Elka Park 12427   518-589-6379
Windswept B&B   County Rd. 16, Elka Park 12427   518-589-6275
Ellicottville Inn   4-10 Washington St., Ellicotville 14731   716-699-2373
Breinlinger's B&B   RD 3, Box 154 W. Hill, Elmira 14903   607-733-0089
Brown's Village Inn B&B   Box 378, Stafford St., Fair Haven 13064   315-947-5817
Issac Turner House   739 Main St., Fair Haven 13064   315-947-5901
Woods-Edge   P.O. Box 444, Fairport 14450   716-223-8510
Mansard Inn   Rd 1, Box 633, Falconer 14733
Runaway Inn   Main Street, Fleischmanns 12430   (914)-5660
Inn at Lake Joseph   P.O. Box 81, CR 108, Forestburgh 12777   914-791-9506
1870 House B&B   20 Chestnut St., Franklinville 14737   716-676-3571
White Inn   52 East Main Street, Fredonia 14063   716-672-2103
The Cobblestones   1160 Rts 5 & 20, Geneva 14456   315-789-1896
Geneva on the Lake   P.O. Box 929, Geneva 14456   315-789-7190
East Lake George House   492 Glen St., Glens Falls 12801   378-656-9452
Teepee   RD 1, Box 543, Gowanda 14070   716-532-2168
Grant Inn   Stormy Hill Road, Grant 13324   315-826-7677
Greenfield Pole & Hunt Club   Birchall Rd., Greenfield Park 12435   916-647-3240
Colgate Inn   Hamilton 13346   315-824-2134
Bowman House   61 Lake St., Hammondsport 14840   607-569-2516
Lake Keuka Manor   626 W. Lake Rd., Hammondsport 14840   607-868-3276
Wheeler B&B   RD #2 Box 455, Hammondsport 14810   607-776-6756
House on the Hill   Box 86 Old Rt. 213, High Falls 12440   914-687-9627
David Harum House   80 S. Main St., Homer 13077   607-749-3548

Le Chambord Inn   Rt. 52, Box 3, Hopewell Junction 12533   914-221-1941
Inn at Blue Stores   Box 99, Star Rt., Rt. 9, Hudson 12534   518-537-4277
Fala B&B   East Market Street, Hyde Park 12538   914-229-5937
Buttermilk Falls B&B   110 E. Buttermilk Falls, Ithaca 14850   607-273-3947
Elmshade Guest House   402 S. Albany St., Ithaca 14850   607-273-1707
Welcome Inn   529 Warren Rd., Ithaca 14850   607-257-0250
Champagne's High Peaks Inn   Rt. 73, POB 701, Keene Valley 12943   518-576-2003
Apple Muffin B&B   Rt. 9N, Keeserville 12944   518-834-7160
Rondout B&B   88 W. Chester St., Kingston 12401   914-331-2369
Corner Birches B&B Guests   86 Montcalm St., Lake George 12845   518-668-2837
Blackberry Inn B&B   59 Sentinel Rd., Lake Placid 12946   518-523-3419
Lake Placid Manor   Whiteface Inn Road, Lake Placid 12946   518-523-2573
South Meadow Farm & Lodge   Cascade Rd., Lake Placid 12946   518-523-9369
Horned Dorset Inn   Leonardsville 13364   315-855-7898
Napoli Stagecoach Inn   Napoli Corners, Little Valley 14755   716-938-6735
R.M. Farm   P.O. Box 391, Livingston Manor 12758   914-439-5511
Merryhart Victorian Inn   12 Front St., Marathon 13803   607-849-3951
Margaretville Mountain Inn   Margaretville Mtn., Margaretville 12455   914-586-3933
Inn at Hobnobbin Farm   P.O. Box 176, Rt. 17, Mayville 14757   716-753-3800
Calico Quail Inn   Route 44, Box 748, Millbrook   914-677-6016
Cottonwood Inn & Motel   Route 44, Millbrook 12545   914-677-3919
Mohonk Mountain House   Lake Mohonk, New Paltz 12561   914-255-1000
Nana's B&B   54 Old Ford Road, New Paltz 12561   914-255-5678
Nieuw Country Loft   41 Allhuson Road, New Paltz 12561   914-ALL-OLD
Ujjala's B&B   2 Forest Glen Road, New Paltz 12561
Chelsea Pines Inn   317 W. 14th St., New York 10014   212-929-1023
Historic Cook House   167 Main Street, Newfield 14867   607-564-9926
Garnet Hill Lodge   13th Lake Rd., North River 12856   518-251-2821
B&B of Long Island   P.O. Box 392, Old Westbury 11568   516-334-6231
Agnes Hall Tourist Home   94 Center St., Oneonta 13820   607-432-0655
Dannfield   50 Canada Road, Painted Post 14870   607-962-2740
Pearl's Place B&B   P.O. Box 465, Palenville 12463   518-678-5649
Canaltown B&B   119 Canandaigua Street, Palmyra 14522   315-597-5553
Finton's Landing   661 East Lake Road, Penn Yan 14527   315-536-3146
Fox Run Vineyards B&B   670 Rt. 14, RD 1, Penn Yan 14527   315-536-2507
Belleayre Youth Hostel   P.O. Box 665, Pine Hill 12465   914-254-4200
Pine Hill Arms   Pine Hill 12462   918-254-9811
Hammertown Inn   RD 2, Box 25, Pine Plains 12567   518-398-7539
Depot Inn   41 N. Main St., Pittsford 14534   716-381-9900
Oliver Loud's Inn   1474 Marsh Rd., Pittsford 14534   716-248-5200
Sunny Side Up B&B   RD 1, Box 58, Butler Rd, Plattsburgh 12901   518-563-5677
Genesee Falls Hotel   P.O. Box 396, Portageville 14536   716-493-2484
Inn at the Falls   50 Red Oaks Mill Rd., Poughkeepsie 12603   914-462-5770
Way Inn   7377 Salina Street, Pulaski 13142   315-298-6073
Living Springs Retreat   Rt. 3, Bryant Pond Rd., Putnam Valley 10579   914-526-2800
Red Hook Inn   31 S. Broadway, Red Hook 12571   914-758-8445
Beekman Arms   Rt. 9, Rhinebeck 12572   914-876-7077
Delamater House   44 Montgomery St., Rhinebeck 12572   914-876-7077
Don & Sally Kallop B&B   off Route 9, Rhinebeck 12572   914-876-4576
The Hellers   46C River Road, Rhinebeck 12572   914-876-3468
Mary Sweeney B&B   Asher Road, Rhinebeck 12572   914-876-6640
Montgomery Inn Guest House   67 Montgomery St., Rhinebeck 12572   914-876-3311
Sepascot Farms   60 Cedar Heights Road, Rhinebeck 12572   914-876-4592
Whistle Wood Farm   11 Pells Road, Rhinebeck 12572   914-876-6838

Rhinecliff B&B   Box 167 William, Rhinecliff 12574   914-876-3710
Rose Mansion & Gardens   625 Mt. Hope Ave., Rochester 14620   716-546-5426
Astoria Hotel   25 Main St., Rosendale 12472   914-658-8201
Klartag Farms B&B   West Branch Road, Rushford 14777   716-437-2946
Inn at Saratoga   231 Broadway, Saratoga Springs 12866   518-583-1890
Inn on Bacon Hill   RD #1, Box 1114A, Saratoga Springs 12871   518-695-3693
High Woods Inn   7472 Glasco Turnpike, Saugerties 12477   914-246-8655
House on the Quarry   7480 Pine Road, Saugerties 12477   914-246-8584
Sacks Lodge   Saugerties 12477   914-246-8711
Secret Garden   6071 Malden Tpk., Saugerties 12477   914-246-3338
Woods Lodge   Schroon Lodge 12870   518-532-7529
Auberge des Quatre Saisons   Route 42, Shandaken 12480   914-688-2223
Two Brooks B&B   SR 108, Route 42, Shandaken 12480   914-688-7101
Belle Crest House   P.O. Box 891, Shelter Island 11965   516-749-2041
Bowditch House   166 N. Ferry Rd., Shelter Island 11965   516-749-0075
Chequit Inn   23 Grand Ave., Shelter Island 11965   516-749-0018
Sherwood Inn   26 W. Genesee St., Skaneateles 13152   315-685-3405
Silver Waters Guest House   8420 Bay St., Sodus Point 14555   315-483-8098
Town & Country B&B   P.O. Box 208, South Dayton 14138   716-988-3340
Scenery Hill   North Cross Road, Staatsburg 12580   914-889-4812
Bluebird B&B   21 Harper St., Stamford 12167   607-652-3711
Lanigan Farmhouse   Box 399, RD 1, Stamford 12167   607-652-7455
Sixteen Firs   352 St. Paul Ave., Staten Island 10304   212-727-9188
Millhof Inn   Rt. 43, Stephentown 12168   518-733-5606
Bakers Bed & Breakfast   RD2 Box 80, Stone Ridge 12484   914-687-9795
Hasbrouck House Inn   Rt. 209, Box 76, Stone Ridge 12484   914-687-0055
Washington Irving Lodge   Rt. 23A, Tannersville 12485   518-589-5560
Le Muguet   2553 Church St., Three Mile Bay 13693   315-649-5896
Sage Cottage   Box 626, Trumansburg 14886   607-387-6449
Castle Hill B&B   Box 325, near Route 9D, Wappingers Falls 12590   914-298-8000
Evergreens   1248 Waterloo-Geneva Rd, Waterloo 13165   315-539-8329
Hist. James R. Webster   115 E. Main St., Waterloo 13165   315-539-3032
B&B of Waterville   211 White Street, Waterville 13480   315-841-8295
Center House Farm B&B   Box 64 RD #2, Watkins Glen 14891   607-535-4317
Buena Vista Manor   Rt. 9W, Box 144, West Camp 12490   914-246-6462
Glen Atty Farm   Box 578, West Shokan 12494   914-657-8110
Inn on the Library Lawn   1 Washington St., Westport 12993   518-962-8666
Chez Renux   229-C Budd Rd., Woodbourne 12788   914-434-1780
Fannie Schaffer's Veg. Hotel   P.O. Box 457 M, Woodridge 12789   914-434-4455

North Carolina

Wright Inn & Carriage Hse	$$ B&B	Continental breakfast
235 Pearson Dr., 28801	9 rooms, 9 pb	Afternoon tea, snacks
Mailing Add. 40 Cisco Rd.	Visa, MC	Sitting room
704-251-0789	C-ltd/S-no/P-no/H-no	
Ginger Cofield		
All year		

The elegantly restored Wright Inn offers the discriminating traveler the opportunity to step back to the peaceful and gracious time at the turn of the century.

ASHEVILLE ─────────────────────────────

Applewood Manor	$$ B&B	Full breakfast
62 Cumberland Circle, 28801	4 rooms, 4 pb	Picnic lunch basket $
704-254-2244	Visa, MC •	Aftn. tea, comp. wine
Jim & Linda LoPresti	C-12+/S-no/P-no/H-no	Sitting room, library
All year	Italian, Sign Language	badminton, croquet

Private baths, fireplaces, delicious breakfasts and afternoon tea. . . just to mention a few of the pleasures. Come romance yourselves with a stay.

Blake House Inn	$$ B&B	Full breakfast
150 Royal Pines Dr., 28704	5 rooms, 2 pb	Lunch, dinner (Thr-Sat)
Arden, South Asheville	Visa, MC •	Comp. wine, bar
704-684-1847	C-no/S-yes/P-no/H-yes	Sitting room, bicycles
Jack & Janet Bass		tennis & pool nearby

Mountains cradle our town with a protective embrace. Sip wine and dine in an intimate country inn on the edge of town.

Cairn Brae	$$ B&B	Continental plus
217 Patton Mountain Rd., 28804	3 rooms, 3 pb	Comp. wine, snacks
704-252-9219	Visa, MC	
Edward & Millie Adams	C-5+	
May—October		

Cairn Brae. The Scottish name "rocky mountain" describes the inn located on three acres of pines above Asheville.

Cedar Crest Victorian Inn	$$ B&B	Continental plus
674 Biltmore Ave., 28803	10 rooms, 8 pb	Afternoon tea
704-252-1389	Visa, MC	Comp. evening beverages
Jack & Barbara McEwan	C-12+/S-ltd/P-no/H-no	Sitting room, piano
All year		a/c, phones, desks

The essence of Victorian, opulent carved woodwork, beveled glass, period antiques. Breakfast and tea on veranda. Four blocks to Biltmore Estate.

ASHEVILLE ──

Cornerstone Inn	$$ B&B	Full breakfast
230 Pearson Dr., 28801	3 rooms, 3 pb	Comp. tea & snacks
704-253-5644	•	Sitting room
Lonnie & Evelyn Wyatt	C-10+ / S-no / P-no / H-no	A/C and phones in rooms
All year		

A historic Dutch Tudor home nestled among hemlocks, Cornerstone Inn combines fine antiques and collectibles to create country elegance.

Flint Street Inns	$$$ B&B	Full Southern breakfast
100 & 116 Flint St., 28801	8 rooms, 8 pb	Comp. wine
704-253-6723	Visa, MC, AmEx •	Sitting room, fireplaces
Rick, Lynne & Marion Vogel	C-12+ / S-yes / P-no / H-no	English style garden
All year		A/C, bicycles for guests

Charming, turn-of-the-century-style residences, located in historic district. Comfortable walking distance to town, restaurants, and shops.

Heritage Hill	$ B&B	Full breakfast buffet
64 Linden Ave., 28801	8 rooms, 6 pb	Afternoon tea
704-254-9336	Visa, MC •	Dinner Christmas Day
Linda & Ross Willard	C-12+ / S-no / P-no / H-no	Sitting room, library
All year incl. Christmas		color TV

Comfortable old tree-shaded Colonial. Wraparound porch, fireplaces in three rooms, handmade afghans on the beds. Lovely private grounds. Near Biltmore.

Old Reynolds Mansion	$$ B&B	Continental breakfast
100 Reynolds Heights, 28804	10 rooms, 7 pb	Comp. wine
704-254-0496	C-ltd / S-yes / P-no / H-no	Sitting room
Fred & Helen Faber		swimming pool
Exc. wkdys Dec.—Mar.		

A restored 1850 antebellum mansion in a country setting. Wide verandas, mountain views, wood-burning fireplaces, huge old swimming pool. On the National Register.

Ray House Bed & Breakfast	$ B&B	Continental breakfast
83 Hillside St., 28801	4 rooms, 2 pb	Library / music room
704-252-0106	C-yes / S-yes / P-ltd / H-no	grand piano
Alice & Will Curtis	French	
All year		

The Ray House is located in the city, yet hidden among spruces and native trees. Interior has English country home feel.

Reed House	$ B&B	Continental plus
119 Dodge St., 28803	4 rooms, 1 pb	Comp. wine
704-274-1604	Visa, MC	Sitting room
Marge Turcot	C-yes / S-yes / P-no / H-no	piano, pool table
May 1—November 1		play area for children

Children welcome in our Victorian home in Biltmore: fireplace in your room, breakfast on the porch, relaxing rocking chairs everywhere. Listed in the National Register.

ASHEVILLE ───────────────────────────────

Richmond Hill Inn	$$$ B&B	Full breakfast
87 Richmond Hill Dr., 27423	12 rooms, 12 pb	Restaurant, snacks
919-273-9409		Aftn. tea, comp. wine
All year		Extensive library
		turndown, conf. facil.

Warm service, remarkable scenery, magnificently renovated house will charm guests and meeting-goers alike. Meetings, seminars, weddings, banquets for up to 150 people.

BANNER ELK ───────────────────────────────

Archers Inn	$$ B&B	Full breakfast
Rt. 2, Box 56-A, 28604	14 rooms, 14 pb	Dinner served
Beech Mt. Parkway	Visa, MC •	Library
704-898-9004	C-yes/S-yes/P-no/ask	sitting room
Joe & Bonny Archer		
All year		

Quaint country inn with long-range view and fireplaces in most rooms. Two miles from the ski slopes. Dinners available.

BAT CAVE ───────────────────────────────

Old Mill Inn & Antiques	$$ B&B	Continental plus
P.O. Box 252, 28710	7 rooms, 4 pb	Restaurants next door
U.S. Hwy 64/74	Visa, MC •	Sitting room w/color TV
704-625-4256	C-yes/S-yes	library
Walt Davis	Spanish (limited)	antique shop on premises
February—December		

Quaint Bavarian-style chalet on the banks of a rushing stream in Hickory Nut Gorge. Relax to the sounds of the river. Close to Asheville, Chimney Rock, Lake Lure.

BEAUFORT ───────────────────────────────

Cedars Inn at Beaufort	$$$ B&B	Full breakfast
305 Front St., 28516	4 rooms, 4 pb	Dinner available, snacks
919-728-7036	Visa, MC, AmEx •	Bicycles, sail boats
Jackie Kwaak	C-ltd/S-yes/P-no/H-no	water skiing
Rest. clos. Jan. & Feb.	Spanish, French	harbor tours

1768 restored country home by the sea with antiques, fireplaces, rocking chairs, porches, sailboats and fine gourmet restaurant.

Langdon House B&B	$$$ B&B	Full breakfast
135 Craven St., 28516	4 rooms, 4 pb	Dinner reservations
919-728-5499	C-12+/S-ltd/P-no/H-no	Comp. wine, aftn. tea
Jimm Prest		Sitting room, bicycles
All year		fishing & beach supplies

Friends who help you make the most of your visit. Restored 18th-century home in historic seaside hamlet on the outer banks. Wonderful breakfasts—waffles are our specialty!

BOONE ───────────────────────────────

Grandma Jean's B&B	$ B&B	Continental plus
209 Meadowview Dr., 28607	4 rooms, 1 pb	Snacks
704-262-3670	•	
Dr. Jean Probinsky	C-yes/S-yes/P-no/H-no	
April—November 1	Spanish	

Old-fashioned country-style hospitality. The perfect stopover place. Within minutes to Appalachian State University and the scenic Blue Ridge Parkway.

BREVARD

The Inn at Brevard
410 E. Main St., 28712
704-884-2105
Eileen Bourget
March 1—December 31

$ B&B
13 rooms, 11 pb
C-ltd/S-ltd/P-no/H-no

Full breakfast
Lunch, dinner
Sunday brunch
Sitting room, color TV

Antique furnishings, gracious hospitality, restful beauty. Main building recently placed on the National Register of Historic Places.

Red House Inn
412 W. Probart St., 28712
704-884-9349
Marilyn Opaloyo Ong
All year

$ B&B
5 rooms, 3 pb
•
C-ltd/S-no/P-no/H-no

Full breakfast
Sitting room
porches

Lovingly restored antebellum home that has served as trading post, courthouse, school and more. Near park, theater and sights. Completely furnished in antiques.

BRYSON CITY

Folkestone Inn
767 W. Deep Creek Rd., 28713
704-488-2730
Norma & Peter Joyce
March—December

$$ B&B
6 rooms, 6 pb
•
C-yes

Full English breakfast
Comp. snacks, wine
Sitting room
library

Friendly atmosphere and gracious country living are offered at Folkestone Inn. Situated in a peaceful and secluded rural mountain setting.

Fryemont Inn
P.O. Box 459, 28713
704-488-2159
Sue & George Brown
April—November

$$$ MAP
36 rooms, 36 pb
Visa, MC
C-yes/S-yes/P-no/H-no

Full breakfast
Full dinner, wine
Library, sitting room
tennis courts
swimming pool

Located on a mountain shelf overlooking the Great Smoky Mountains National Park. A tradition in mountain hospitality since 1923.

Randolph House Country Inn
P.O. Box 816, 28713
Fryemont Rd.
704-488-3472
Bill & Ruth Adams
April—November

$$ B&B
6 rooms, 3 pb
Visa, MC, AmEx •
C-yes/S-yes/P-no/H-yes

Full country breakfast
Dinner, tea on request
Wine, set-ups
Sitting room
library, piano

Country inn circa 1895. Original furnishings; located in Smoky Mountains, close to Appalachian trails, whitewater rafting; ruby mines. Country gourmet food.

CANDLER

Mountain Springs Cottages
P.O. Box 2, 28715
Mt. Pisgah Rd.
704-665-1004
Sara Peltier
All year

$$ EP
9 rooms, 9 pb
C-yes/P-no/H-no

Cottages/chalets/cabins
Grills, picnicking
Fishing, swimming
horseback riding, hiking
badminton, horseshoes

The place you dream of but never expect to find. Porches overlooking mountain stream. Cottages furnished with a "Touch of Yesteryear." 15 miles west of Asheville.

CHAPEL HILL

Fearrington House Inn
Fearrington Village Ctr, 27312
Pittsboro
919-542-2121
Richard M. Delany
All year

$$$ B&B
14 rooms, 14 pb
Visa, MC •
C-12+/S-ltd/P-no/H-yes

Continental breakfast
Full breakfast $
Lunch & dinner served
Sitting room
swimming pool

Classic countryside elegance in suites furnished with English antiques. Charming courtyard and gardens. Delicately prepared regional cuisine. Member of Relais & Chateaux.

CHARLOTTE

Homeplace Bed & Breakfast
5901 Sardis Rd., 28226
704-365-1936
Peggy & Frank Dearien
All year

$$ B&B
4 rooms, 2 pb
Visa, MC, AmEx •
C-10+/S-no/P-no/H-no

Full breakfast
Afternoon tea
Refreshments, snacks
Sitting room, den w/TV
parlour, screened porch

The Homeplace offers country charm & Victorian elegance on 2½ acres with wraparound porch, garden gazebo, tin roof, and full homemade breakfast.

Inn on Providence
6700 Providence Rd., 28226
704-366-6700
Darlene & Daniel McNeill
All year

$$ B&B
5 rooms, 3 pb
Visa, MC •
C-12+/S-no/P-no/H-no

Full breakfast
Afternoon tea
Sitting room
library
swimming pool

Experience the grandeur of this large southern homestead and enjoy our attention to detail. Breakfast served on the veranda overlooking the pool.

New England Inn
3726 Providence Rd., 28211
704-362-0008
Jeanne & Ken England
All year

$$ B&B
4 rooms, 3 pb
Visa, MC
C-ltd/S-no/P-no/H-no

Full breakfast
Afternoon tea
Comp. wine, snacks
Sitting room, A/C
game room, piano

Warm southern hospitality abounds in large comfortable home; game room with pool table. Convenient to museums, shopping, downtown, interstate highways.

CHIMNEY ROCK

Gingerbread Inn
P.O. Box 187, Hwy 74, 28720
704-625-4038
Tom & Janet Sherman
All year

$ B&B
4 rooms
C-yes/S-yes/P-no/H-no

Continental breakfast
Sitting room

Our rooms are furnished with charming country furniture and home-sewn quilts. Relax in rocking chairs on deck overlooking the Rocky Broad River.

DURHAM

Arrowhead Inn
106 Mason Rd., 27712
919-477-8430
Jerry & Barbara Ryan
January—December 22

$$ B&B
6 rooms, 4 pb
Major credit cards •
C-yes/S-ltd/P-no/H-no
French

Full breakfast
Comp. wine, tea
Sitting room
piano

1775 manor house offers tasteful period rooms and private or shared bath. Full breakfast in dining rooms, continental in guest rooms.

EDENTON

Lords Proprietors' Inn
300 N. Broad St., 27932
919-482-3641
Arch & Jane Edwards
All year

$$ B&B
20 rooms, 20 pb
C-yes/S-yes/P-no/H-no

Continental plus
Full breakfast (Sundays)
Coff. placed outside rm.
Sitting room, bicycles
private pool privileges

Three restored houses in the historic district of "the South's prettiest town." Furnished by area antique dealers with all for sale.

Trestle House Inn
P.O. Route 4 Box 370, 27932
Soundside Rd.
919-482-2282
Peggy & Chuck Gregory
All year

$$ B&B
4 rooms, 4 pb
Visa, MC, AmEx •
C-9+ /S-ltd/P-no/H-no

Continental plus
BYOB, library
Sitting room, billiards
steam, exercise room
shuffleboard, fishing

Peaceful setting overlooking private 20-acre lake and 60 acres of trees. Five miles from historic town of Edenton.

FRANKLIN

Buttonwood Inn
190 Georgia Rd., 28734
704-369-8985
Liz Oehser
May—November

$$ B&B
4 rooms, 3 pb
Visa, MC
C-ltd/S-ltd/P-no/H-no

Full breakfast
Sitting room, TV
golf

Completely surrounded by tall pines, small and cozy Buttonwood will appeal to the person who prefers simplicity and natural rustic beauty.

Franklin Terrace
67 Harrison Ave., 28734
704-524-7907/800-633-2431
Helen Henson, Pat Reed
May—October

$ B&B
7 rooms, 7 pb
Visa, MC
C-no/S-ltd/P-no/H-no

Continental breakfast

All rooms furnished with antiques. First floor houses dessert shop with cheesecakes, home-made pies & cakes—also antique shop. In town. Beautiful views.

GRAHAM

Leftwich House
215 E. Harden St., 27253
919-226-5978
Carolyn L. Morrow
All year

$ B&B
3 rooms
•
C-yes

Full breakfast
Snacks
Sitting room
tennis, pool, golf,
& library nearby

Let us pamper you with Southern hospitality. Relax on the porch or browse through over 200 factory outlets nearby.

GREENSBORO

Greenwood Bed & Breakfast
205 N. Park Dr., 27401
919-274-6350
Jo Anne Green
All year

$$ B&B
5 rooms, 3 pb
Visa, MC, AmEx •
C-yes/S-yes/P-no/H-no

Continental plus
Comp. wine, cheese
Swimming pool
sitting room
cable TV

Three minutes from downtown Greensboro on park in historic district. Chalet-style home built in 1905. TV room, guest kitchen.

Dutch Colonial Inn, Holland, MI

HENDERSONVILLE

Claddagh Inn	$ B&B	Full breakfast
755 N. Main St., 28739	18 rooms, 18 pb	Dinner, comp. tea/sherry
704-697-7778/800-225-4700	Visa, MC, AmEx, Disc •	Sitting room, library
Fred & Marie Carberry	C-yes/S-yes/P-no/H-no	telephones in rooms, A/C
All year		tennis, shuffleboard

In National Registry of Historic Places. Beautiful country inn located in downtown Hendersonville, provides a homelike atmosphere where love and lasting friendships prevail.

Havenshire Inn	$$ B&B	Continental plus
Rt. 13, 28739	7 rooms, 4 pb	Afternoon tea
Box 366 Cummings Road	Visa, MC	Sitting room, organ
704-692-4096	C-yes/S-yes/P-no/H-no	pond, river, canoe
Lyra Picard	Spanish	Swedish massage
All year		

19th-century English country manor house. Rich furnishings lend to atmosphere of comfortable elegance. Horses; pond, canoeing, fishing, picnicing.

Waverly Inn	$ B&B	Full breakfast
783 N. Main St., 28792	22 rooms, 12 pb	Dinner (ltd)
704-692-1090/800-537-8195	Visa, MC •	Sitting room
John & Diane Sheiry	C-12+/S-yes/P-no/H-no	tennis courts
All year		

A landmark near downtown shopping park, quaint restaurants. Nominated for the National Register. Beautiful antiques. Spotlessly clean.

HICKORY

Hickory Bed & Breakfast	$ B&B	Full breakfast
464 7th St. SW, 28602	4 rooms, 1 pb	Comp. refreshment
704-324-0548	•	Two sitting rooms
Jane & Bill Mohney	C-yes/S-ltd/P-no/H-no	member NC B&B Ass'n.
All year		

A restful night in our home, followed by a specially cooked breakfast, guarantees a feeling of contentment. Come see us.

HIGH POINT

Premier Bed & Breakfast
P.O. Box 6222, 27262
1001 Johnson St.
919-889-8349
Alan Ferguson
All year

$$ B&B
6 rooms, 6 pb
Visa, MC, AmEx •
C-ltd

Full breakfast
Dinner by arrangement
Comp. wine, TV room

Delightfully and perfectly restored neo-colonial, eclectically furnished with everything from fine antiques to post modern accessories. In the world's furniture capital.

HIGHLANDS

Chandler Inn
P.O. Box 2156, 28741
Hwy 64 E. & Martha's Lane
704-526-5992
Lety Power
All year

$$ B&B
14 rooms, 14 pb
Visa, MC, AmEx •
C-yes/S-yes/H-yes
Spanish

Continental plus
Sitting room
trout stream
near golf courses

Romantic elegance! Brass headboards, eyelet sheets & comforters, pedestal sinks & country wallpaper. Gourmet coffees, homemade fruitbreads. Only a 10 min. walk to Main Street.

Colonial Pines Inn
Route 1, Box 22B, 28741
Hickory St.
704-526-2060
Chris & Donna Alley
All year

$$ B&B
7 rooms, 7 pb
Visa, MC
C-ltd/S-ltd/P-no/H-no

Full breakfast
Afternoon coffee & tea
Sitting room, kitchen
grand piano
picnic area

Two acres of lawn and trees, close-in, with mountain view from large veranda. Antique furnishings and country charm. Newly renovated guest house sleeps four.

Highlands Inn
P.O. Box 1030, 28741
4th & Main Sts.
704-526-9380/800-447-5873
Pat & Rip Benton
April—November

$$ B&B
28 rooms, 28 pb
Visa, MC, AmEx
C-yes/S-yes/P-no/H-yes

Continental plus
Restaurant, lunch/dinner
Comp. wine, aftn. tea
Sitting room, library
aviary room, golf priv.

Located in the heart of historic Highlands. Close to all outdoor activities. Highlands is noted for breathtaking mountain views, waterfalls and beautiful shops. Golf available.

Old Edwards Inn
P.O. Box 1778, 28741
4th & Main Sts.
704-526-5036/800-447-5873
Pat & Rip Benton
April—November

$$ B&B
20 rooms, 20 pb
Visa, MC, AmEx
C-no/S-yes/P-no/H-no

Continental plus
Restaurant, lunch/dinner
Comp. wine, snacks
Sitting room, golf priv.
Victorian side yards

Located in the heart of historic Highlands. Close to all outdoor activities. Highlands is noted for breathtaking mountain views, waterfalls and beautiful shops. Golf available.

KILL DEVIL HILLS

Ye Olde Cherokee Inn
Route 1, Box 315, 27948
500 N. Virginia Dare Tr.
919-441-6127
Phyllis & Robert Combs
April—November

$$ B&B
7 rooms, 7 pb
Visa, MC, AmEx, Choice •
C-no/S-ltd/P-no/H-ltd

Continental breakfast
Sitting room
overhead ceiling fans
Sr. citizen discount

Beach house with rustic cypress interior. Small, private, quiet. Near historic sites, shops and restaurants.

LAKE JUNALUSKA

Providence Lodge
One Atkins Loop, 28745
704-456-6486
Wilma & Ben Cato
June 1—September 30

$ MAP
16 rooms, 8 pb
C-yes/S-no/P-no/H-ltd

Full breakfast
Dinner
Sitting room
access to tennis,
swimming & boating

A touch of yesterday in an old, very rustic mountain lodge—where our food is our claim to fame.

LAKE LURE

Lodge on Lake Lure
Rt. 1 Box 529A, 28746
Charlotte Dr.
704-625-2789
Doris & Alan Carrington-Nunn
April 1—November 30

$$ B&B
11 rooms, 11 pb
Visa, MC, AmEx •
C-12+/S-no/P-no/H-no

Continental plus, Full
Breakfast $4, comp. wine
Sitting room, library
piano, lake swimming
tennis, golf nearby

Adult getaway in the Blue Ridge Mountains. Giant stone fireplace, breathtaking view of mountains and lake. Only public facility actually on Lake Lure.

LAKE TOXAWAY

Greystone Inn
P.O. Box 6, 28747
Greystone Lane
704-966-4700/800-824-5766
Tim & Harriet Lovelace
May—October

$$$ MAP
22 rooms, 22 pb
Visa, MC, AmEx •
C-yes/S-yes/P-no/H-no

Full breakfast
Gourmet dinner included
Sitting room, piano
swimming, tennis
daily lake tour, jacuzzi

Intimate historic mansion on a large mountain lake. Excellent golf, tennis, sailing, canoeing, water skiing. Country club membership during stay.

LITTLE SWITZERLAND

Big Lynn Lodge
P.O. Box 459, Hwy 226A, 28749
704-765-4257
Gale Armstrong
April 15—October

$$ MAP
38 rooms, 38 pb
Visa, MC, Disc •
C-yes/S-yes/P-no/H-ltd
German

Full breakfast
Dinner, snacks
Sitting room, library
player piano lounge
billards, shuffleboard

Old-fashioned country inn. Dinner and breakfast included with room. Cool mountain air. Elevation 3200 ft. Breathtaking view. Come and relax.

MANTEO

Tranquil House Inn
P.O. Box 2045, 27954
Queen Elizabeth Ave.
919-473-1404/800-458-7069
Margaret Buell
All year

$$ B&B
28 rooms, 28 pb
Visa, MC, AmEx •
C-yes/S-yes/P-no/H-yes

Continental plus
Afternoon tea, snacks
Comp. wine
Sitting room, library
bicycles

Minutes from the beach but a world apart. We offer accommodations in the tradition of the old Nags Head Inns.

MARS HILL

Baird House
P.O. Box 749, 28754
121 S. Main St.
704-689-5722
Yvette Wessel
All year ex. Dec.

$ B&B
5 rooms, 2 pb
•
C-yes/S-yes/P-no/H-no
French

Full breakfast
Sitting room
fireplaces

In a tiny village nestled in the hills of western North Carolina; traditional furnishings, open hearths, parlor, porches and garden.

286   North Carolina

MILTON

Woodside Inn
Box 197, 27379
Hwy. 57 South
919-234-8646
Lib/Tom McPherson
All year

$$ B&B
4 rooms, 4 pb
Visa, MC •
C-yes/S-yes/P-ltd/H-ltd

Full breakfast
Lunch, dinner avail.
Comp. wine, snacks
Sitting room
library

Greek revival plantation house provides elegant yet relaxed atmosphere, southern cuisine, period furnishings. Spacious wooded grounds for relaxed strolling and Piedmont vistas.

MOUNT AIRY

Pine Ridge Inn
2893 W. Pine St, Hwy 89, 27030
919-789-5034
Ellen & Manford Haxton
All year

$$ B&B
7 rooms, 5 pb
Visa, MC, AmEx •
C-yes/S-yes/P-no/H-yes

Continental breakfast
Full breakfast $5 extra
Comp. tea, wine
Sitting room, piano
hot tub, swimming pool

Elegant luxury at foot of Blue Ridge Mountains. A country inn with all the amenities of a grand hotel. All meals available on request.

NAGS HEAD

First Colony Inn
Route 1, Box 748, MP 16, 27959
6720 Va Dare Trail
919-441-2342/704-249-1114
The Lawrence Family
All year

$$$ B&B
26 rooms, 26 pb
Visa, MC, Discover •
C-yes/S-no/P-no/H-ltd

Continental plus
Aftn. tea, comp. wine
Sitting room, library
hot tubs, pool, croquet
ocean beach, fishing

The last remaining Old Nags Head inn is reborn to welcome guests to modern comfort while retaining all its charm.

NEW BERN

The Aerie
509 Pollock St., 28560
919-636-5553
Lois & Rick Cleveland
All year

$$$ B&B
7 rooms, 7 pb
AmEx, Visa, MC •
C-yes/S-ltd/P-no/H-no

Full country breakfast
Comp. beverages
Airport pickup
sitting room
player piano

Victorian home one block from Tryon Palace. Walk to shops and restaurants. Superb country breakfast; antique furnishings; modern amenities.

Harmony House Inn
215 Pollock St., 28560
919-636-3810
Diane & A.E. Hansen
All year

$$ B&B
9 rooms, 9 pb
Visa, MC, AmEx •
C-yes/S-ltd/P-no/H-no

Full breakfast
Comp. soft drinks/juices
Victorian pump organ
parlor

Unusually spacious circa 1850 home, rocking chairs on porch, lovely yard. In the historic district, near Tryon Palace, shops, fine restaurants.

King's Arms Inn
212 Pollock St., 28560
919-638-4409
David & Diana Parks
All year

$$ B&B
9 rooms, 9 pb
Visa, MC, AmEx •
C-yes/S-yes/P-no/H-no

Continental plus
Furnished with antiques
fireplaces

In heart of historic district. Delicious hot breakfast. Southern hospitality. Information on sightseeing and dining. Three blocks from Tryon Palace.

NEW BERN

New Berne House B&B
709 Broad St., 28560
800-842-7688
Joel & Shan Wilkins
All year

$$$ B&B
6 rooms, 6 pb
Visa, MC, AmEx •
C-yes/S-ltd/P-yes/H-no

Full gourmet breakfast
Comp. wine, tea, snacks
Bar set-ups/BYOB
Library
tennis, golf, pool near

Comfortable elegance and the warmth of southern hospitality in authentically restored B&B. Private, vintage baths; gourmet breakfast. Near Tryon Palace. AAA & AARP discounts.

OCRACOKE

Berkley Center Country Inn
Route 12, P.O. Box 220, 27960
919-928-5911
Wesley W. Egan, Sr.
March 1—December 1

$$ B&B
11 rooms, 9 pb
•
C-yes/S-yes/P-no/H-yes

Continental breakfast
Sitting room
bicycles

Beautifully restored estate on harbor of outer banks fishing village located in U.S. National Seashore. 19 miles of buildingless beach.

ORIENTAL

The Tar Heel Inn
P.O. Box 176, 28571
205 Church St.
919-249-1078
Dave & Patti Nelson
All year

$$ B&B
6 rooms, 6 pb
•
H-yes

Full breakfast
Restaurants nearby
Sitting room, library
bicycles, tennis courts
croquet, horseshoes

English-style country inn in quiet fishing village. Walk to shopping, fine restaurants. Sailing, fishing, golf, tennis & hunting! Oriental: 550 residents & 650 sailboats!

PILOT MOUNTAIN

Pilot Knob
P.O. Box 1280, 27041
919-325-2502
Jim Rouse
All year

$$$ B&B
5 rooms, 5 pb
•
C-no/S-yes/P-no/H-no
German

Continental plus
Bar in room
Library, sitting room
hot tub, sauna
swimming pool

The individual log cabins are 125-year-old tobacco barns nestled in a wooded setting. Pilot Mountain State Park, the Blue Ridge parkway and Old Salem can be explored.

PISGAH FOREST

Pines Country Inn
719 Hart Rd., 28768
Pisgah Forest
704-877-3131
Tom & Mary McEntire
May—October 31

$$ B&B/MAP
22 rooms, 19 pb
C-yes/S-yes/P-no/H-ltd

Full breakfast
Dinner (MAP, Wed-Sat)
Sitting room
piano

Quiet, homey country inn, fantastic view. Where you come as our guest and leave as our friend, part of our family.

POLKVILLE

Patterson's Carriage Shop
Hwy 10, P.O. Box 852, 28136
704-538-3929
Nancy Patterson
All year

$ B&B
4 rooms
C-12+/S-no/P-no/H-no

Full breakfast
Dinner by reservation
Sitting room, porch
grounds, carriage shop
horse accommodations

100-year-old farmhouse in quiet country setting. Full country breakfast served with 100% maple syrup. Carriage shop w/horse drawn vehicles for sale. Horse grazing pastures.

RALEIGH

Oakwood Inn
411 N. Bloodworth St., 27604
919-832-9712
Diane Newton
All year

$$$ B&B
6 rooms, 4 pb
Visa, MC •
C-12+/S-no/P-no/H-no

Full breakfast
Comp. refreshments
Sitting room

Charming inn in Victorian home built in 1871. On National Register and furnished with period antiques reflecting charm of yesteryear.

ROBBINSVILLE

Blue Boar Lodge
200 Santeetlah Rd., 28771
704-479-8126
Roy & Kathy Wilson
April—January 1

$$$ MAP
9 rooms, 9 pb
Visa, MC
C-yes/S-yes/P-no/H-no

Full breakfast
Dinner included
Sitting room, game room
lake swimming
boat rental, fishing

Secluded hideaway in the Smoky Mountains; near beautiful hiking trails and lake activities; family-style meals.

SALISBURY

Rowan Oak House
208 S. Fulton, 28144
704-633-2086
RuthAnn & Bill Coffey
All year

$$ B&B
3 rooms, 3 pb
•
C-12+/S-ltd
Spanish

Continental plus
Comp. wine, snacks
Afternoon tea
Sitting room, library
jacuzzi tub in one room

"Lavish, luxurious and unique" describes our Queen Anne home with antiques, flowers, porches, gardens, and historic Salisbury's small town atmosphere.

SOUTHERN PINES

Inn The Pines
1495 W. Connecticut Ave, 28387
919-692-1632
Louisa Jackson
All year

$$ B&B
4 rooms, 4 pb
C-yes/S-yes/P-no/H-no

Full breakfast
Comp. hors d'oeuvres
Late night dessert
and coffee
Sitting room with games

In the heart of the golf country. Wine and foodstuffs brought from Paris every week. House full of antiques.

SPRUCE PINE

Fairway Inn
110 Henry Lane, 28777
704-765-4917
Margaret & John Stevens
May 1—October 31

$$ B&B
5 rooms, 2 pb
•
C-ltd/S-ltd/P-no/H-no

Full breakfast
Comp. wine
Sitting room

Nestled in the Blue Ridge Mountains and overlooking the golf course, we offer attractive rooms and breakfast in your room.

Richmond Inn
101 Pine Ave., 28777
704-765-6993
Bill Ansley, Lenore Boucher
All year

$ B&B
7 rooms, 7 pb
Visa, MC
C-yes/S-yes/P-no/H-no
French, German

Full breakfast
Comp. tea, wine
Sitting room
piano

In the heart of the most spectacular mountain scenery. Close to Blue Ridge Parkway. Luxurious accommodations, Anglo/North Carolinian hosts. Cottages available.

TARBORO

Little Warren B&B
304 E. Park Ave., 27886
919-823-1314
Patsy & Tom Miller
All year

$$ B&B
3 rooms, 3 pb
Visa, MC
C-4+/S-yes/P-no/H-no
Spanish

Full breakfast
Comp. wine
Sitting room
tennis courts

Large, gracious family home historic district. Complimentary wine, fresh flowers. Choose from full English, American southern or full Continental breakfast.

TRYON

Mill Farm Inn
P.O. Box 1251, 28782
Hwy. 108 & Howard Gap Rd.
704-859-5656/800-547-1463
Chip & Penny Kessler
March 1—December 1

$ B&B
8 rooms, 8 pb
C-yes/S-yes/P-no/H-no
French

Continental plus
Sitting porch
large living room

Fine guest inn, including complimentary breakfast—homelike atmosphere, bird-watcher's paradise, plus cultural living experience.

Pine Crest Inn
P.O. Box 1030, 28782
200 Pine Crest Lane
800-633-3001/704-859-9135
Bob & Diane Johnson
All year

$$$ B&B
29 rooms, 29 pb
Visa, MC •
C-yes/S-yes/P-ltd/H-ltd

Full breakfast
Lunch, dinner, snacks
Restaurant, bar service
Comp. wine, sitting room
library, fireplaces

Pine Crest is the only full-service inn in area. Variety of rooms, suites and cabins, most with fireplaces. Moderately priced fine dining. Outstanding wine list.

VALLE CRUCIS

Mast Farm Inn
P.O. Box 704, 28691
704-963-5857
Sibyl & Francis Pressly
May—Oct., Dec. 26—Mar. 15

$$ MAP
12 rooms, 8 pb
Visa, MC
C-yes/S-no/P-no/H-yes
Portugese

Continental plus
Dinner included
Sitting room
setups

Inn on 18-acre farm in beautiful mountain valley near Boone. Ski, golf, fish, white water rafting. Country cooking. Vegetables from our farm.

WAYNESVILLE

Grandview Lodge
809 Valley View Circle, 28786
704-456-5212
Stan & Linda Arnold
All year

$$$ MAP
15 rooms, 15 pb
•
C-yes/S-yes
Polish, Russian, German

Full breakfast
Lunch (by special requ.)
Dinner, restaurant (Res)
Library, piano, golf
tennis, shuffleboard

Country inn located on rolling land, with an orchard and arbor. Breakfast features homemade jams & jellies. Dinner includes fresh vegetables, freshly baked breads & desserts.

Hallcrest Inn
299 Halltop Circle, 28786
704-456-6457
Russell & Margaret Burson
June—October

$$ MAP
12 rooms, 12 pb
•
C-yes/S-ltd/P-no/H-no

Full breakfast
Dinner
Eve. tea, coffee, choc.
Library, living room

Small country inn in 100-year-old farmhouse with adjacent modular unit. Family-style dining around lazy-susan tables and beautiful view of the mountain.

WAYNESVILLE

Haywood Street House B&B
409 S. Haywood St., 28780
704-456-9831
Jackie Stephens, Karen Kosec
All year

$ B&B
5 rooms, 1 pb
•
C-yes/S-yes/P-no/H-no

Continental plus
Snacks
Sitting room
library

Antique pieces, wainscoting and mantels; close to area attractions; view the Smoky Mountains from veranda; one block to Main St.

Heath Lodge
900 Dolan Rd., 28786
704-456-3333
David & Bonnie Probst
Mid-April—mid-November

$$$ MAP
22 rooms, 22 pb
C-yes/S-yes/P-ltd/H-ltd
Spanish

Full breakfast
Dinner included
Sitting room
2 pianos
color cable TV all rooms

Secluded on a wooded hillside, mountain inn offers unique lodging with beamed ceilings and country furnishings. Bountiful breakfasts and gourmet dinners.

Palmer House
108 Pigeon St., 28786
704-456-7521
Kris Gillet, Jeff Minick
All year

$ B&B
7 rooms, 7 pb
C-yes/S-yes/P-no/H-ltd

Continental plus
Comp. wine, juice &
Bedtime chocolates
Sitting room, library
piano, cafe, bookstore

Rambling old house with bookstore in rear. Small-town charm in the Smoky Mountains. Hiking, golf, skiing. Complimentary wine, bedtime chocolates. Discounts off-season.

Swag Country Inn
Route 2, Box 280-A, 28786
704-926-0430/704-926-3119
Deener Matthews
Memorial Day—October

$$$ AP
12 rooms, 12 pb
Visa, MC
C-ltd/S-yes/P-no/H-ltd

Full breakfast
Lunch & dinner (incl.)
Library, piano, sauna
racquetball, hiking
croquet field above pond

At 5,000 feet, hand-hewn log lodge. Elegant, intimate hideaway. Twelve unique bedrooms, excellent cuisine, breathtaking views. Executive retreat, honeymoon haven.

WEAVERVILLE

Dry Ridge Inn
26 Brown St., 28787
704-658-3899
John & Karen VanderElzen
All year

$$ B&B
5 rooms, 5 pb
Visa, MC
C-yes/S-ltd
Dutch

Full breakfast
Comp. wine
Sitting room
bicycles
gift shop

Convenient to Asheville and Blue Ridge Pkwy. with small town charm. Large comfortable guest rooms; antiques and homemade quilts.

WILMINGTON

Anderson Guest House
520 Orange St., 28401
919-343-8128
Connie Anderson
All year

$$ B&B
2 rooms, 2 pb
C-yes/S-yes/P-yes/H-no

Full breakfast
Comp. wine, snacks
Afternoon tea
Restaurant nearby
baby-sitting service

1851 Italianate townhouse with separate guest quarters overlooking private garden. Furnished with antiques, ceiling fans, fireplaces. Drinks upon arrival. Delightful breakfast.

WILMINGTON

Five Star Guest House

14 N. Seventh St., 28401	$$ B&B	Full breakfast
919-763-7581	3 rooms, 3 pb	Comp. wine, snacks
Alnn & Harvey Crowther	Visa, MC, AmEx	Sitting room
All year	C-ask/S-yes/P-no/H-no	library
		piano

Authentically restored, spacious guest rooms furnished with antiques. Private baths feature claw-footed tubs. Breakfast is served in our elegant dining room.

Inn on Orange

No. 410 Orange St., 28401	$$ B&B	Full breakfast
919-251-0863	3 rooms, 3 pb	Comp. wine, snacks, tea
Catherine Ackiss	Visa, MC, AmEx •	Bar service
All year	C-yes/S-yes/P-no/H-no	Sitting room, library
		swimming pool

In heart of the historical district. Experience the warm gracious hospitality and our tasty breakfasts. Near Wilmington attractions—beaches, shopping, museums, restaurants.

Murchison House B&B Inn

305 S. 3rd St., 28401	$$ B&B	Full breakfast
919-343-8580	3 rooms, 3 pb	Dinner by res.
Joseph Curry	Visa, MC, AmEx •	Fruit, coffee
All year	C-yes/S-yes/P-no/H-no	Sitting room
		library

Beautiful mansion and formal grounds in heart of historic district; near river, dining, entertainment. Antique furnishings, private baths, full breakfast.

Worth House—Victorian Inn

412 S. Third St., 28401	$$ B&B	Full breakfast
919-762-8562	4 rooms, 4 pb	Comp. wine, chocolates
Kate Walsh, Terry Meyer	C-no/S-yes/P-no/H-no	Coffee, newspaper
All year		piano, drawing room
		veranda, turndown serv.

Gracious Queen Anne in historic district of Wilmington, N.C. Walk to riverfront, restaurants, shops. Personalized attention, private porches, gourmet breakfast.

WINSTON-SALEM

Colonel Ludlow Inn

434 Summit St., 27101	$$ B&B	Continental plus
Summit & W. 5th Sts.	10 rooms, 10 pb	Comp. wine, snacks
919-777-1887	Visa, MC, AmEx •	Whirlpool tubs, library
Terri Jones & Ken Land	C-10+/S-no/P-no/H-no	bicycles, phones, cable
All year		sitting room w/piano

Historic National Register: 1887—unique guest rooms (private deluxe baths, some with two-person jacuzzi)—beautiful antiques. Restaurants, shops walking distance.

WRIGHTSVILLE BEACH

Edgewater Inn

10 W. Columbia St., 28480	$$ B&B	Continental breakfast
914-256-2914	11 rooms, 11 pb	Sitting room, porch
Debbie Tillery	Visa, MC •	private cottage and
All year	C-yes/S-no/P-no/H-no	fishing pier

Cozy, old-fashioned charm and Southern hospitality abound; join us on the front porch surrounded by cascading plants and rock away the evening, soothed by cool ocean breezes.

More Inns...

Walker Inn   39 Junaluska Rd., Andrews 28901   704-321-5019
Albemarle Inn   86 Edgemont Rd, Asheville 28807   704-255-0027
Lion & the Rose B&B   276 Montford Ave., Asheville 28801   704-255-7673
Balsam Lodge   P.O. Box 279, Balsam 28707   704-456-6528
Mountview Chateau   Rt. 1, Box 426, Banner Elk 28604   704-963-6593
Orig. Hickory Nut Gap Inn   P.O. Box 246, Bat Cave 28710   704-625-9108
Bath Guest House   So. Main Street, Bath 27808   919-923-6811
Captains' Quarters   315 Ann St., Beaufort 28516   919-728-7711
Inlet Inn   601 Front At Queen St., Beaufort 28516   919-728-3600
Shotgun House   406 Ann Street, Beaufort 28516   919-728-6248
River Forest Manor   600 E. Main St., Belhaven 27810   919-943-2151
B&B Over Yonder   269 N. Fork Rd., Black Mountain 28711   704-669-6762
Blackberry Inn   P.O. Box 965, Black Mountain 28711   704-669-8303
Red Rocker Inn   136 N. Dougherty St., Black Mountain 28711   704-669-5991
Gideon Ridge Inn   P.O. Box 1929, Blowing Rock 28605   704-295-3644
Hound Ears Lodge Club   P.O. Box 188, Blowing Rock 28605   704-963-4321
Maple Lodge B&B   P.O. Box 1120, Blowing Rock 28605   704-295-3331
Ragged Garden Inn   Box 1927, Blowing Rock 28605   704-295-9703
Sunshine Inn   P.O. Box 528, Sunset Dr., Blowing Rock 28605   704-295-3487
Womble Inn   P.O. Box 1441, Brevard 28712   704-884-4770
Hemlock Inn   Bryson City 28713   704-488-2885
Nantahala Village   P.O. Drawer J, Bryson City 28713   704-488-2826
Nu-Wray Inn   P.O. Box 156, Burnsville 28714   704-682-2329
Tom Jones B&B Inn   P.O. Box 458, Carthage 28327   919-947-3044
Caroline Inn   Box 1110, Chapel Hill 27514   919-933-2001
Hillcrest House   209 Hillcrest Rd., Chapel Hill 27514   919-942-2369
Inn at Bingham School   P.O. Box 267, Chapel Hill 27514   919-563-5583
Pineview Inn & Conf. Ctr.   Rt.10, Box 265, Chapel Hill 27514   919-967-7166
Fourth Ward B&B   523 N. Poplar St., Charlotte 28202   704-334-1485
Hampton Manor   3327 Carmel Rd., Charlotte 28211   704-542-6299
Morehead Inn   1122 E. Morehead St., Charlotte 28204   704-376-3357
Overcarsh House   326 West Eighth St., Charlotte 28202   704-334-8477
Esmeralda Inn   Box 57, Chimney Rock 28720   704-625-9105
Tanglewood Manor House   P.O. Box 1040, Clemmons 27012   919-766-0591
Jarrett House   P.O. Box 219, Dillsboro 28725   704-586-9964
Squire Watkins Inn   P.O. Box 430, Dillsboro 28725   704-586-5244
Sanderling Inn   SR Box 319Y, Duck 27949   919-261-4111
Woodfield Inn   P.O. Box 98, Flat Rock 28731   704-693-6016
Heritage Country Inn   7 Bates Branch Road, Franklin 28734   704-524-7381
Lullwater Farmhouse Inn   Rt. 5, Box 540, Franklin 28734   704-524-6532
Glendale Springs Inn   R 16, Milepost 259, Glendale Springs 28629   919-982-2102
Mountain View Lodge   P.O. Box 90, Glendale Springs 28629   919-982-2233
Mountain High   Big Ridge Rd., Glenville 28736   704-743-3094
Greenwich Inn   111 W. Washington St., Greensboro 27401   919-272-3474
Echo Mountain Inn   2849 Laurel Park Hwy., Hendersonville 28739   704-693-9626
Reverie   1197 Greenville Hwy, Hendersonville 28739   704-693-8255
Phelp's House   Route 1, Box 55, Highlands 28741   704-526-2590
Colonial Inn   153 W. King St., Hillsborough 27278   919-732-2461
Inn At Teardrop   175 W. King St., Hillsborough 27278   919-732-1120
Brookside Lodge   P.O. Box 925, Lake Junaluska 28745   704-456-8897
Sunset Inn   P.O. Box 548, Lake Junaluska 28745   704-456-6114
Fairfield Mountains   Rt. 1, Buffalo Rd., Lake Lure 28746   704-625-9111
Lawrences   Rt. 1, Box 641, Lexington 27292   704-249-1114
Mountainbrook Inn   P.O. Box 565 Hwy.19, Maggie Valley 28751   704-926-3962

Buntie's B&B   322 Houston St., Monroe 28110   704-289-1155
Oak Ridge Farm B&B   Rt. 5, Box 111,NC HWY 1, Mooresville 28115   704-663-7085
Courtland Manor B&B   #2 Courtland Blvd., Mountain Home 28758   800-544-9823
Carefree Cottages   Rt. 1 Box 748, Nags Head 27959   919-441-5340
Colony Beach Inn   P.O. Box 87, Nags Head 27959   919-441-3666
Blackbeard's Lodge   P.O. Box 37, Ocracoke 27960   919-928-3421
Boyette House   Box 39, Ocracoke 27960   919-928-4261
Ships Timbers B&B   Box 10, Ocracoke 27960   919-928-6141
Island Inn   Box 7, Ocracoke Island 27960   919-928-4351
Oscar's House   Box 206, Ocracoke Island 27960   919-928-1311
Inn at Old Fort   W. Main St., P.O. Box 111, Old Fort 28762   704-668-9384
Chinquapin Inn   P.O. Box 145, Penland 28765   704-765-0064
Magnolia Inn   Box 266, Pinehurst 28374   919-295-6900
Trent River Plantation   P.O. Box 154, Pollocksville 28573   919-224-3811
Snowbird Mountain Lodge   275 Santeetlah Rd., Robbinsville 28771   704-479-3433
Wilsons Tourist Home   P.O. Box 47, Robbinsville 28771   704-479-8679
Red Lion Inn   Star Route, Box 200, Rosman 28772   704-884-6868
Bear Creek Lodge   Rt. 1, Box 335, Saluda 28773   704-749-2272
Orchard Inn   P.O. Box 725, Saluda 28773   704-749-5471
Eli Olive's Inn   P.O. Box 2544, Smithfield 27577   919-934-9823
Jefferson Inn   150 W. New Hampshire, Southern Pines 28387   919-692-6400
Dosher Plantation House   Route 5, Box 100, Southport 28461   919-457-5554
Turby-Villa   East Whitehead St., Sparta 28675   919-372-8490
L'Auberge of Tryon   P.O. Box 1251, Tryon 28782   704-859-6992
Melrose Inn   211 Melrose, Tryon 28782   704-859-9419
Stone Hedge Inn   Box 366, Tryon 28782   704-859-9114
Mountainview Chateau   P.O. Box 723, Valle Crucis 28691   704-963-6593
C.W. Pugh's B&B   P.O. Box 427, Wanchese 27981   919-473-5466
Squire's Vintage Inn   Rt. 2 Box 130R, Warsaw 28398   919-296-1831
Way Inn   299 S. Main St., Waynesville 28786   704-456-3788
Graystone Guesthouse   100 S. Third St., Wilmington 28401   919-762-0358
Guest House—St. Thomas Ct.   101 S. 2nd St., Wilmington 28401   919-763-4933
Pilgrims Rest Inn   600 West Nash Street, Wilson 27893   919-243-4447
Brookstown Inn B&B   200 Brookstown Ave., Winston-Salem 27101   919-725-1120
Lowe-Alston House B&B   204 Cascade Ave., Winston-Salem 27127   919-727-1211

North Dakota

GRASSY BUTTE ─────────────────────────────

Long X Trail Ranch	$ B&B	Full breakfast
Box 157, 58634	11 rooms, 9 pb	Restaurant
701-842-2128	C-yes/S-yes/P-ltd/H-yes	Swimming pool, library
Merv & Doreen Wike		horses
All year		TV, rec room

A truly "real" Western experience—friendly hospitality—clean, quiet accommodations. Relax and enjoy nature at its finest in North Dakota badlands.

More Inns...

Farm Comfort   Kemare 58746   701-848-2433
Rough Rider Hotel   Medora 58505
Prairie View B&B   Route 2, Box 87, New Salem 58563   701-843-7236
Triple T Ranch   Rt. 1 Box 93, Stanley 58784   701-628-2418

Ohio

BELLVILLE ───────────────────────────────────

Frederick Fitting House
72 Fitting Ave., 44813
419-886-2863
Ramon & Suzanne Wilson
All year exc. Thnks/Xmas

$$ B&B
3 rooms, 1 pb
C-8+/S-ltd/P-no/H-no

Full breakfast
Lunch/dinner on request
Comp. wine, snacks
Sitting room, library
pool, tennis/golf nearby

1863 Victorian in charming country village. Gourmet breakfast in garden gazebo. Near Malabar Farm and Mohican State Parks. Canoeing, hiking, skiing nearby.

CENTERVILLE ───────────────────────────────────

Yesterday Bed & Breakfast
39 S. Main St., 45459
513-433-1660
Barbara Monnig
closed varied vacations

$$ B&B
3 rooms, 3 pb
C-12+/S-ltd

Continental plus
Beverage on arrival
Fruit bowl in parlor
Sitting room
one suite

Beautifully restored Victorian home in historic district. Short drive to downtown Dayton, Air Force Museum, King's Island Amusement Park, antique centers.

DAYTON ───────────────────────────────────

Price's Steamboat House
6 Josie St., 45403
513-223-2444
Ron & Ruth Price
All year

$$ B&B
3 rooms, 3 pb
•
C-12+/S-no/P-no/H-no

Full breakfast
Afternoon tea
Sitting room
library
tennis courts

On the National Register, this 1852 Victorian mansion, Steamboat Gothic, is furnished with exquisite antiques and overlooks downtown Dayton.

DELLROY ───────────────────────────────────

Pleasant Journey Inn
4247 Roswell Rd. SW, 44620
216-735-2987
Jim & Marie Etterman
All year

$ B&B
4 rooms, 1 pb
Visa, MC
C-10+

Continental plus
Sitting room

Restored Civil War mansion, furnished with antiques. Country charm close to swimming, boating, tennis and golf. Owners are retired Navy couple.

HURON ───────────────────────────────────

Captain Montague's B&B
229 Center St., 44839
419-433-4756
Shirley & Bob Reynolds
April—October

$$ B&B
6 rooms, 6 pb
C-no/S-no/P-no/H-no
English

Continental plus
Lunch (picnic basket)
Afternoon tea, snacks
Swimming pool, parlor
garden and gazebo

Captain Montague's Guest House is near a summer theater, waterfront parks, a boat harbor and Cedar Point. Ideal for reunions, weekend relaxing, or vacation travel.

KINSMAN

Hidden Hollow B&B
9340 State Route 5 N.E., 44428
216-876-8686
Rita White
All year

$ B&B
4 rooms, 3 pb
C-yes/S-yes/P-ask/H-no

Full breakfast
Comp. wine
Sitting room
swimming pool

Lovely setting. Breakfast by the pool or on the balcony overlooking Hidden Hollow. Gourmet snacks.

MEDINA

Oakwood Bed & Breakfast
226 N. Broadway, 44256
216-723-1162
Lonore & David Charbonneau
All year

$ B&B
2 rooms
C-12+/S-ltd/P-no/H-no

Continental plus
Comp. wine
Parlor
bicycles

Cozy country Victorian furnished with antiques, walking tour of restored Victorian village, antique shopper's paradise.

MOUNT VERNON

Russell-Cooper House
115 E. Gambier St., 43050
614-397-8638
Tim & Maureen Tyler
All year

$$ B&B
6 rooms, 6 pb
•
C-13+/S-ltd/P-no/H-no

Full breakfast
Comp. wine, tea
Tea room for party/mtgs.
Porch, museum & shop
recreational assistance

Victorian elegance abounds in restored Gothic mansion! Antiques, memorabilia, museum/shop, delightful breakfasts in Ohio's colonial city. Special weekenders with dinner.

NEWTOWN

Wind's Way Bed & Breakfast
3851 Edwards Rd., 45244
513-561-1933
Ray & Brenda Raffurty
All year

$$ B&B
4 rooms, 4 pb
Visa, MC •
C-yes/S-yes/P-no/H-no

Full breakfast
Comp. wine, aftn. tea
Sitting room, A/C
color tv in each room
antique shop

1840 restored mansion in a country setting, only 20 minutes from downtown Cincinnati. Antique shop on premises. Rooms furnished with antiques.

OLD WASHINGTON

Zane Trace Bed & Breakfast
Box 115, Main St., 43768
614-489-5970/301-757-4262
Ruth D. Wade
May 1—October 31

$ B&B
4 rooms
C-yes/S-yes/P-no/H-ltd

Continental breakfast
Sitting room
heated swimming pool

On historic national trail, this 1859 Victorian brick home has charm a plenty. Near Zane Grey Museum.

PICKERINGTON

Central House
27 W. Columbus St., 43147
Old Village Area
614-837-0932
Jim/Sue Maxwell, MaryLou Boyd
All year

$ B&B
4 rooms, 4 pb
•
C-yes/S-no/P-no/H-ltd

Full breakfast
Afternoon tea, snacks
Sitting room
library
tennis courts nearby

Total restoration of 1860 small-town hotel. Victorian ambience. Many unique shops in historic village near Columbus. Great cinnamon rolls!

Atchison House, Northville, MI

POLAND

Inn At The Green	$ B&B	Continental breakfast
500 S. Main St., 44514	4 rooms, 2 pb	Comp. wine
Youngstown	Visa, MC •	Sitting room, deck
216-757-4688	C-11+ /S-no/P-no/H-no	library, patio
Ginny & Steve Meloy		garden room
All year		

Authentically restored Victorian townhouse in preserved Western Reserve village near Youngstown. Convenient to Turnpike and I-80. Antiques, fireplace, oriental rugs, garden.

SANDUSKY

Pipe Creek Bed & Breakfast	$ B&B	Full breakfast
2719 Columbus Ave., 44870	3 rooms, 2 pb	Comp. wine
419-626-2067	C-12+ /S-yes/P-no/H-no	Sitting room
Carl & Beryl Dureck	some German	large library
Open May—Oct.		

Century-old Queen Anne Victorian, furnished in antiques, large comfortable rooms. Lake Erie islands, Cedar Point Amusement Park close by. Many trees, birds & wildlife.

Wagner's 1844 Inn	$$ B&B	Continental plus
230 E. Washington St., 44870	3 rooms, 3 pb	Comp. wine
419-626-1726	Visa, MC •	Chocolates
Walt & Barbara Wagner	C-no/S-ltd/P-no/H-no	Billard room with TV
All year		

Elegantly restored Victorian home. Listed on National Register of Historic Places. Near Lake Erie attractions. Air-conditioned rooms.

SPRING VALLEY —————————————————

3 B's Bed-n-Breakfast $ B&B   Full breakfast
103 E. Race St., 45370   5 rooms   Supper, tea, wine
513-862-4278/513-862-4241   C-yes/S-yes/P-yes/H-ltd   Sitting room
Patricia & Herb Boettcher   bicycles
All year   air-conditioned

Relax in this charming village home—owners retired Air Force couple. Twenty miles from Dayton's Air Force Museum, King's Island. Choice of Victorian or restored farmhouse.

TROY —————————————————

H.W. Allen B&B $$ B&B   Full breakfast
434 S. Market St., 45373   5 rooms, 4 pb   Comp. wine, aftn. tea
513-335-1181   Visa, MC, AmEx •   Self-serve snacks
Robert W. Smith   C-12+/S-ltd   Music room, bicycles
All year   front porch (smoking)

1874 restored Victorian mansion with antiques throughout, television, central A/C, 3 wineries, historic town, 15 minutes from Dayton Int. Airport; I-70 and I-75 access.

WEST MILTON —————————————————

Locust Lane Farm B&B $ B&B   Full breakfast
5590 Kessler Cowlesvlle, 45383   2 rooms, 1 pb   Afternoon tea
513-698-4743   C-yes/S-no/P-no/H-no   Library, sitting room
Ruth Shoup   screened porch
All year   bicycles

Comfort and hospitality in a tastefully decorated old home. Country farm setting. Gourmet breakfast served in dining room or screened porch.

ZOAR —————————————————

Cobbler Shop Inn $$ B&B   Full breakfast
#22, P.O. Box 511, 44697   5 rooms, 1 pb   Snacks
2nd & Main Sts.   Visa, MC, AmEx •   Sitting room
216-874-2600   C-6+/S-ltd/P-no/H-no
Marian Worley
All year

Original structure in historic village, furnished in 18th- and 19th-century antiques; close to local museum and a number of charming shops.

Inn at Cowger House #9 $$ B&B   Full country breakfast
#9 Fourth St., 44697   3 rooms, 3 pb   Lunch & dinner by resv.
216-874-3542   •   Entertainment
Mary & Edward Cowger   C-yes/S-yes/P-no/H-no   honeymoon suite with
All year   fireplace & jacuzzi

A little bit of Williamsburg. 1817 log cabin with 2-acre flower garden maintained by the Ohio Historic Society.

More Inns...

Portage House   601 Copley Rd., Akron 44320   216-535-1952
Rockledge Manor   Rt. 3, Possum Run Rd., Bellville 44813   419-892-3329
McNutt Farm II/Outdoorsman   6120 Cutler Lake Rd., Blue Rock 43720   614-674-4555
Chillicothe B&B   202 S. Paint St., Chillicothe 45601   614-772-6848
Tudor House   P.O. Box 18590, Cleveland 44118   216-321-3213
Slavka's B&B   180 Reinhard Ave., Columbus 43206   614-443-6076
White Oak Inn   29683 Walhonding Rd., Danville 43014   614-599-6107
Hill View Acres B&B   7320 Old Town Rd., East Fultonham 43735   614-849-2728

Granville Inn   314 E. Broadway, Granville 43023   614-587-3333
Beach House   213 Kiwanis Ave., Huron 44839   419-433-5839
Beatty House   South Shore Drive, Kelley's Island 43438   419-746-2379
Cricket Lodging   Lakeshore Dr., Kelley's Island 43438   419-746-2263
Quiet Country B&B   14758 TWP Rd 453, Lakeville 44638   216-378-3882
The White Fence Inn   8842 Denmanu Road, Lexington 44904   419-884-2356
Bells   Located in downtown, Logan 43138   614-385-4384
Log Cabin   7657 TWP Rd. 234, Logan 43138   614-385-8363
Blackfork Inn   303 N. Water St., Loudonville 44842   419-994-3252
Old Stone House Inn   133 Clemons St., Marblehead 43440   419-798-5922
Folger's Bantam Farm B&B   Rt 6, Mitchell Lane, Marietta 45750   614-374-6919
Oak Hill B&B   16720 Park Rd, Mount Vernon 43050   614-393-2912
Bayberry Inn B&B   25675 St., Rt. 41 N., Peebles 45660   513-587-2221
Centennial House   5995 Center St., Box 67, Peninsula 44264   216-657-2506
Old Island House Inn   102 Madison St., Port Clinton 43452   419-734-2166
Buckeye B&B   P.O. Box 130, Powell 43065   614-548-4555
Le Vent Passant   1539 Langram Road, Put-In-Bay 43456   419-285-5511
Big Oak   2501 S. Campbell St., Sandusky 44870
Bogart's Corner B&B   1403 E. Bogart Rd., Sandusky 44870   419-627-2707
Willowtree Inn   1900 W. State Route 571, Tipp City 45371   513-667-2957
Mansion View Inn   2035 Collingwood Blvd., Toledo 43620   419-244-5676
Governor's Lodge   SR 552, Waverly 45690   614-947-2266
Howey House   340 N. Bever St., Wooster 44691   216-264-8231
Worthington Inn   649 High Street, Worthington 43085   614-885-2600
Cider Mill B&B   P.O. Box 441, Zoar 44697   216-874-3133
Haven @ 4th & Park   P.O. Box 467, Zoar 44697   216-874-4672
Weaving Haus   P.O. Box 431, Zoar 77697   216-874-3318

Oklahoma

Harrison House $$ B&B   Continental plus
124 W. Harrison St., 73044   23 rooms, 23 pb   Comp. wine, snacks
405-282-1000   AmEx, Visa, MC •   Sitting room, gift shop
Phyllis Murray   C-yes/S-yes/P-ltd/H-no   bicycles, shoeshines
All year   games, theater next door

Turn-of-the-century charm with comfort of elegant 23-room restored hotel. Next to live theater, museums. Breakfast in Victorian parlor. Horseback riding, fishing.

More Inns...

Clayton Country Inn   Rt. 1, Box 8, Clayton 74536   918-569-4165
Edgewater Bed & Breakfast   P.O. Box 1746, Grove 74344   918-786-4116
Stone Lion Inn B&B   1016 W. Warner, Guthrie 73044   405-282-0012
Grandison B&B   1841 NW 15th, Oklahoma City 73106   405-521-0011
Drake House (The)   617 S. 93rd. E. Ave., Tulsa 74112   918-835-0752

Oregon

ASHLAND ─────────────────────────────────

Chanticleer Inn
120 Gresham St., 97520
503-482-1919
Nancy & Jim Beaver
All year

$$$ B&B
7 rooms, 7 pb
Visa, MC •
C-ltd/S-no/P-no/H-no

Full gourmet breakfast
Comp. wine, sherry,
Coffee, tea, cookies
Sitting room, fireplace
phones in all rooms, A/C

Fresh country charm, attention to detail. Antiques, fluffy comforters, garden patio and mountain views. Close to theaters. Discount ski lift tickets.

Hersey House B&B
451 N. Main St., 97520
503-482-4563
Lynn Savage & Gail Orell
Late April—October

$$ B&B
4 rooms, 4 pb
Visa •
C-12+/S-ltd/P-no/H-no

Full breakfast
Comp. tea, wine
Sitting room
player piano
English garden

Elegantly restored turn-of-the-century Victorian with family antiques, china, silver, linens, queen beds, central A/C, lovely English garden. Short walk to theaters.

Morical House
668 N. Main St., 97520
503-482-2254
Pat & Peter Dahl
All year

$$ B&B
5 rooms, 5 pb
Visa, MC •
C-ltd/S-ltd/P-no/H-no

Full breakfast
Comp. tea, wine
Sitting room, organ
putting green

An 1880s house, set in an acre of lawn and gardens, restored to the simple elegance of its Victorian heritage.

ASTORIA ─────────────────────────────────

Grandview Bed & Breakfast
1574 Grand Ave., 97103
503-325-0000/503-325-5555
Charleen Maxwell
All year

$ B&B
8 rooms, 6 pb
Visa, MC, Disc. •
C-10+

Continental plus
Lunch & dinner for conf.
Sitting room
books in room, bicycles
liquor not allowed

Light, airy, cheerful Victorian close to superb Maritime Museum, Lightship, churches, golf, clam-digging, fishing, beaches and rivers. Sleeps 21.

BEND ─────────────────────────────────

House at Water's Edge
36 NW Pinecrest Crt., 97701
503-382-1266
Sally Anderson, Samuel Plaut
All year

$$ B&B
2 rooms, 2 pb
C-no/S-no/P-no/H-no

Full breakfast
Afternoon tea
Comp. wine, snacks
Hot tubs
canoe

Casual elegance and cozy ambience. Overlooking Mirror Pond and Drake Park. 20 minutes to ski slopes. Tranquil, close to town.

300   Oregon

BEND

Mirror Pond House
1054 NW Harmon Blvd., 97701
503-389-1680
Beryl Kellum
All year

$$ B&B
2 rooms, 2 pb
C-12+/S-yes/P-no/H-no

Full breakfast
Comp. wine
Sitting room, fireplace
hammock, deck
guest canoe

Cape Cod at water's edge; a wildlife sanctuary near downtown and powdered ski slopes. Come share the friendly, relaxed tranquillity.

BROOKINGS

Chetco River Inn
21202 High Prairie Rd., 97415
503-469-2114, ext. 4628
Clayton, Dan & Sandra Brugger
All year

$$ B&B
3 rooms, 1 pb
Visa, MC •
C-ask/S-ltd/P-no/H-no

Full breakfast
Lunch, dinner with resv.
Aftn. snacks & beverages
Sitting room, library
games, hiking, river

Relax in peaceful seclusion of our private 35-acre forest, bordered on 3 sides by the Chetco River. Our inn is small, offering "Old World" hospitality, "New World" comfort.

COOS BAY

Captain's Quarters B&B
P.O. Box 3231, 97420
265 S. Empire Blvd.
503-888-6895
Jean & John Griswold
All year

$ B&B
3 rooms
C-10+/S-no/P-ltd/H-no
Spanish, German

Full breakfast
Snacks
Sitting room
library
athletic club nearby

1890 Victorian sea captain's home. Bay view, antiques, hotcakes, muffins, local berries and cheeses. Near beaches, boating, crabbing and clamming.

CORVALLIS

Huntington Manor
3555 NW Harrison Blvd., 97330
503-753-3735
Ann Sink
All year

$$ B&B
2 rooms, 2 pb
•
C-12+/S-yes

Full breakfast
Comp. wine, snacks
Sitting room

Huntington Manor boasts beautiful decor and lovely grounds. Only 4 blocks to Oregon State University; 1 hour to beaches.

Madison Inn B&B
660 SW Madison Ave., 97333
503-757-1274
Richard & Paige Down
All year

$$ B&B
7 rooms, 2 pb
Visa, MC
C-yes/S-yes/P-no/H-no

Full breakfast
Comp. wine
2 sitting rooms
piano

Historic Madison inn is ideally located one block from downtown Corvallis and two blocks from Oregon State campus.

ELMIRA

McGillivray's Log Home
88680 Evers Rd., 97437
503-935-3564
Evelyn R. McGillivray
All year

$ B&B
2 rooms, 2 pb
Visa, MC
C-yes/H-yes

Full breakfast

Enjoy hearty breakfasts in this secluded country home. Rooms feature king beds, private baths, and air-conditioning. 14 miles west of Eugene, Oregon.

EUGENE

Lorane Valley B&B
86621 Lorane Hwy., 97405
503-686-0241
Esther & George Ralph
All year

$$ B&B
1 rooms, 1 pb
Visa
C-12+

Full breakfast
Snacks, comp. wine
Sitting room, library
jacuzzi, cattle raising
wildflowers, bird-watching

Unique home on 22 acres with complete apartment which overlooks Lorane Valley. Air-conditioned, antiques, flowers, king/twin beds, private bath.

GOLD BEACH

Tu Tu Tun Lodge
96550 N. Bank Rogue, 97444
503-247-6664
Dirk & Laurie Van Zante
May 1—November 1

$$$ EP
18 rooms, 18 pb
Visa, MC •
C-yes/S-yes/P-yes/H-yes

Full breakfast
Lunch, dinner, bar
Swimming pool
library, sitting room
player piano, games

Secluded lodge nestled on banks of the Rogue River with "Country Inn" hospitality, gourmet meals, white water excursions, guided fishing.

GRANTS PASS

AHLF House Bed & Breakfast
762 NW 6th St., 97526
503-474-1374
B. Buskirk, R. Althaus
All year

$$ B&B
2 rooms
C-no/S-no/P-no/H-no

Full breakfast
Evening refreshments
Sitting room
bicycles

1902 Queen Anne Victorian furnished with fine collectibles and antiques is a step back in time. Close to town and Rogue River recreation trips.

JACKSONVILLE

Jacksonville Inn
P.O. Box 359, 97530
175 E. California St.
503-899-1900
Jerry & Linda Evans
All year

$$$ B&B
9 rooms, 9 pb
Visa, MC, AmEx, DC, Dis •
C-yes/S-yes/P-ltd/H-no
Greek

Full breakfast
Restaurant, bar service
Lunch, dinner, snacks
Luxurious cottage with
many amenities avail.

Built in 1863 and located in center of historic village. 8 rooms and one cottage. Private baths and award-winning restaurant with over 700 wines.

Livingston Mansion B&B
Box 1476, 97530
4132 Livingston Rd.
503-899-7107
Sherry Lossing
All year

$$ B&B
5 rooms, 3 pb
Visa, MC •
C-yes/S-ltd/P-no/H-no

Full breakfast
Comp. tea, wine
Sitting room
swimming pool

Sitting atop a hill overlooking the Rogue Valley, our inn offers a spectacular ever-changing view. Just two miles from historic Jacksonville.

LINCOLN CITY

Palmer House B&B Inn
646 N.W. Inlet, 97367
503-994-7932
Malcolm & Sally Palmer
All year

$$ B&B
3 rooms, 3 pb
Visa, MC •
C-no/S-ltd/P-no/H-no

Full breakfast
Comp. sherry
Dinner service for
groups renting entire
inn

Panoramic ocean view, excellent beach access highlight this contemporary inn. Robes, beach towels, kites, perfect breakfasts, elegant decor, super location.

MCMINNVILLE

Steiger Haus B&B Inn
360 Wilson St., 97128
503-472-0821
Doris & Lynn Steiger
All year

$$ B&B
3 rooms, 3 pb
•
Some German & French

Full breakfast
Comp. wine
Sitting room w/TV

In the heart of the Oregon wine country. Unique architecture in parklike town setting. Close to gour-
met restaurants. Charm and hospitality plus!

MERLIN

Morrison's Rogue River
8500 Galice Rd., 97532
503-476-3825/800-826-1963
B.A.& E. Hanten, M.& B. Ryan
May—November 15

$$$ MAP/AP
13 rooms, 13 pb
Visa, MC •
C-yes/S-yes/P-no/H-no

Full breakfast
Dinner, Lunch (fall)
Sitting room, pool
tennis, putting green
trails, fishing

Located on the banks of the Rogue River. Gourmet dinners served on deck overlooking river in
summer. Quiet country setting. White water raft trips available.

MYRTLE CREEK

Sonka Sheep Station Inn
901 NW Chadwick Lane, 97457
503-863-5168
Louis & Evelyn Sonka
All year

$ B&B
4 rooms, 2 pb
Visa, MC
C-12+/S-no/P-no/H-no

Full breakfast
Comp. tea, wine
Sitting room
bicycles

Working sheep ranch; house furnished in sheep country motif and antiques. Quiet setting along
river. Guests may partake of ranch activities as hosts and guests agree.

NEWBERG

Secluded Bed & Breakfast
19719 NE Williamson Rd., 97132
503-538-2635
Durell & Del Belanger
All year

$ B&B
2 rooms, 1 pb
•
C-10+/S-no/P-no/H-no

Full gourmet breakfast
Many restaurants nearby
Living room w/fireplace
library, A/C, VCR
hiking trails

Located in the heart of wine country! Antiques in every room; gourmet breakfast served; large
library. Hiking trails and seasonal wildlife. Air-conditioned home.

NEWPORT

Ocean House B&B
4920 N.W. Woody Way, 97365
503-265-6158/503-265-7779
Bob & Bette Garrard
Except 12/15—1/7

$$ B&B
4 rooms, 4 pb
Visa, MC
C-12+/S-no/P-no/H-no

Full breakfast
Snacks
Sitting room, library
beach trail, garden
gallery; golf nearby

Near the center of coastal activities and fun, this large comfortable home with beautiful surround-
ings overlooks gardens and surf. Unforgettable.

NORTH BEND

Sherman House B&B
2380 Sherman Ave., 97459
503-756-3496
Jennifer & Phillip Williams
All year

$ B&B
3 rooms, 1 pb
•
C-yes/S-yes/P-no/H-no

Full breakfast
Comp. wine, tea
Sitting room
kitchen privileges

A 1903 Pennsylvania Dutch home with extensive flower gardens, furnished with antiques and old
toys. Close to shopping, dunes and ocean.

OAKLAND

Pringle House B&B
P.O. Box 578, 97462
Locust & 7th Sts.
503-459-5038
Jim & Demay Pringle
All year

$ B&B
2 rooms
C-12+ /S-no/P-no/H-no
Spanish, French

Full breakfast from menu
Comp. wine
Sitting room
doll collection

Cozy, home comfort and Victorian charm in a peaceful historic town with antique shops, carriage works. Near wineries, golf and fishing.

PORT ORFORD

Home by the Sea Homestay
P.O. Box 606, 97465
444 Jackson St.
503-332-2855
Brenda & Alan Mitchell
All year

$ B&B
2 rooms, 2 pb
Visa, MC •
C-ltd/S-no/P-no/H-no

Full breakfast
Comp. wine, tea
Refrigerator, laundry
Beach access, ocean view
cable TV, phones, spa

Enjoy dramatic views of the ocean and miles of unspoiled public beaches in this quiet fishing village. Tennis and golf nearby.

PORTLAND

Cape Cod Bed & Breakfast
5733 SW Dickinson St., 97219
503-246-1839
Marcelle Tebo

$ B&B
2 rooms
C-no/S-no/P-no/H-no

Full breakfast
Family room, TV, VCR
Air-conditioned rooms
outdoor spa
enclosed garden

Relax in this charming Cape Cod home furnished with a beautiful mixture of antiques and traditionals. See the stars at night. Close to wineries, shopping and new Mormon Temple.

Corbett House B&B
7533 SW Corbett Ave., 97219
503-245-2580
All year

$$ B&B
3 rooms, 1 pb
Visa, MC, AmEx, DC •
C-10+ /S-ltd/P-no/H-no

Continental plus
Seasonal beverages
Living room
feather bed

Early 1920s art deco residence. Elegant hideaway with mountain and river views. Close to major arteries and downtown. Healthful gourmet foods. Feather bed in Etruscan Room.

General Hooker's B&B
125 SW Hooker, 97201
503-222-4435
Lori Hall
All year

$$ B&B
3 rooms, 1 pb
Visa, MC, AmEx •
C-13+ /S-no/P-no/H-no

Continental plus
TV, VCR, cable in rooms
air conditioning
sitting room, library
tennis, pool nearby

Elegantly refurbished Victorian in quiet, historic neighborhood within walking distance of downtown. Romantic amenities include 7-foot bed and skylight bath in Rose Suite.

John Palmer House
4314 N. Mississippi Ave, 97217
503-284-5893
Mary & Richard Sauter
All year

$ B&B
4 rooms, 1 pb
Visa, MC •
C-ltd/S-no/P-no/H-no
Sign Language

Full breakfast
High tea, chocolates
Comp wines, beer, snacks
Bathrobes, massages
bicycles, library, piano

Step back in time to the charm of 1890. High tea, gourmet summer breakfasts on the veranda. Flowers, wines, beer, chocolates. Victorian sleepwear may be rented for the stay.

Victorian Inn, Port Huron, MI

SANDLAKE

Sandlake Country Inn	$ B&B	Full breakfast
8505 Galloway Rd., 97112	2 rooms	Picnic lunch, dinner
503-965-6745	•	Aftn. tea, midni. snacks
Margo & Charles Underwood		Sitting room, croquet
All year		hammock by creek

Romantic, peaceful hideaway especially designed for making marriage memories. Coastal forest setting. Gourmet breakfasts served in your room or deck.

SEAL ROCK

Blackberry Inn B&B	$$ B&B	Full breakfast
P.O. Box 188, 97376	3 rooms, 3 pb	Comp. tea, wine
6575 NW Pacific Coast Hy	Visa, MC	Sitting room, library
503-563-2259	C-ask/S-no/P-no/H-no	color TV, victrola
Barbara Tarter		nature trail, crabbing
Exc. Nov. 15—Dec.		

Pamper yourself on the Oregon Coast. Fluffy comforters, antiques, hot tub, quiet beach, gourmet breakfast, farm critters, nature trails.

More Inns . . .

Farm "Mini Barn" Guest Hou   7070 Springhill Drive N, Albany 97321   503-928-9089
Ashland Guest Villa   634 Iowa St., Ashland 97520   503-488-1508
Ashland's Main St. Inn   142 W. Main St., Ashland 97520   503-488-0969
Auburn Street Cottage   549 Auburn St., Ashland 97520   503-482-3004
Columbia Hotel   262 ½ E. Main, Ashland 97520   503-482-3726
Country Walrus Inn   2785 E. Main St., Ashland 97520   503-488-1134
Country Willows Inn   1313 Clay St., Ashland 97520   503-488-1590
Cowslip's Belle   159 N. Main Street, Ashland 97520   503-488-2901
Edinburgh Lodge B&B   586 E. Main St., Ashland 97520   503-488-1050

Highland Acres   1350 E. Nevada Street, Ashland 97520   503-482-2170
Iris Inn   59 Manzanita St., Ashland 97520   503-488-2286
Lithia Rose Lodging on-the-Park   163 Granite St., Ashland 97520   503-482-1882
McCall House   153 Oak Street, Ashland 97520   503-482-9296
Mt. Ashland Inn   550 Mt. Ashland Road, Ashland 97520   503-482-8707
Neil Creek House   341 Mowetza Dr., Ashland 97520   503-482-1334
Oak Street Station B&B   239 Oak Street, Ashland 97520   503-482-1726
Parkside   171 Granite Street, Ashland 97520   503-482-2320
Queen Anne   125 N. Main Street, Ashland 97520   503-482-0220
Romeo Inn   295 Idaho St., Ashland 97520   503-488-0884
Shutes Lazy S   200 Mowetza Dr., Ashland 97520   503-482-5498
Stone House   80 Hargadine Street, Ashland 97520   503-482-9233
Treon's Country Homestay   1819 Colestin Road, Ashland 97520   503-482-0746
Winchester Inn   35 S. 2nd St., Ashland 97520   503-488-1113
Franklin House   P.O. Box 804, Astoria 97103   503-325-5044
Franklin St. Station B&B   1140 Franklin St., Astoria 97103   503-325-4314
Rosebriar Inn   636 14th Street, Astoria 97103   503-325-7427
Powder River B&B   HCR 87, Box 500, Baker 97814   503-523-7143
Cliff Harbor Guest House   P.O. Box 769, Bandon 97411   503-347-3956
Spindrift B&B   2990 Beach Loop Rd., Bandon 97411   503-347-2275
Heidi Haus   62227 Wallace Road, Bend 97701   503-388-0850
Lara House B&B   640 N.W. Congress, Bend 97701   503-388-4064
Holmes Sea Cove B&B   17350 Holmes Dr., Brookings 97415   503-469-3025
Sea Dreamer Inn   15167 McVay Ln. Box 184, Brookings 97415   503-469-6629
Ward House B&B   516 Redwood St., Box 86, Brookings 97415   503-469-5557
Tern Inn B&B   3663 S. Hemlock, Box 95, Cannon Beach 97110   503-436-1528
Oregon Caves Chateau   P.O. Box 128, Cave Junction 97523   503-592-3400
Hudson House   37700 Highway 101 S, Cloverdale 97112   503-392-3533
Wheeler's Bed & Breakfast   Box 8201, Coburg 97401   503-344-1366
This Olde House B&B   202 Alder St., Coos Bay 97420   503-267-5224
Wedgwood Inn   563 SW Jefferson Ave., Corvallis 97333   503-758-7377
Ivanoffs' Inn   3101 Bennett Creek Rd., Cottage Grove 97424
Lea House Inn   433 Pacific Hwy., Cottage Grove 97424   503-942-0933
Channel House B&B Inn   P.O. Box 56, Depoe Bay 97341   503-765-2140
Backroads B&B   85269 Lorane Hwy., Eugene 97405   503-485-0464
Campus Cottage B&B Inn   1136 E. 19th Ave., Eugene 97403   503-342-5346
Country Garden   245 Pearl St., Eugene 97403   503-345-7417
Country Lane   31180 Lane's Turn Road, Eugene 97401   503-686-1967
Griswold's B&B   552 W. Broadway, Eugene 97401   503-683-6294
House in the Woods   814 Lorane Hwy, Eugene 97405   503-343-3234
Shelley's Guest House   1546 Charnelton St., Eugene 97401   503-683-2062
Timewarp Inn   1006 Taylor St., Eugene 97402   503-344-5556
Johnson House   P.O. Box 1892, Florence 97439   503-997-8000
Guest House at Gardiner   401 Front St. P.O. Box 2, Gardiner 97441   503-271-4005
Dragovich House   P.O. Box 261, Gates 97346   503-897-2157
Bien Venue B&B   95629 Jerry Flat Rd., Gold Beach 97444   503-247-2335
Endicott Gardens   95768 Jerry's Flat Rd., Gold Beach 97444   503-247-6513
Fair Winds B&B   Box 1274, Gold Beach 97444   503-247-6753
Nicki's Country Place   31780 Edson Creek, Gold Beach 97444   503-247-6037
Handmaiden's Inn   230 Red Spur Dr., Grants Pass 97527   503-476-2932
Lawnridge House   1304 NW Lawnridge, Grants Pass 97526   503-476-8518
Mt. Baldy B&B   678 Troll View Road, Grants Pass 97527   503-479-7998
Paradise Ranch Inn   7000 Monument Dr., Grants Pass 97526   503-479-4333
River Banks Inn   8401 Riverbanks Rd., Grants Pass 97527   503-479-1118
Washington Inn   1002 NW Washington Blvd, Grants Pass 97526   503-476-1131

Clear Creek Farm B&B   Route 1, Box 138, Halfway 97834   503-742-2238
Barkheimer House/Lakecliff   1908 3820 Westcliff Dr., Hood River 97031   503-386-5918
Hackett House   922 State St., Hood River 97031   503-386-1014
Davidson House   887 Monmouth St., Independence 97351   503-838-3280
Out of the Blue B&B   386 Monmouth St., Independence 97351   503-838-3636
Judge Touvelle House   455 N. Oregon St., Jacksonville 97530   503-899-8223
McCully House Inn   P.O. Box 387, Jacksonville 97530   503-899-1942
Chandler's Bed, Bread, & T   Box 639, 700 E. Main, Joseph 97846   503-432-9765
The Bed, Bread & Trail   Rt. 1, Box 365, Joseph 97846   503-432-9765
Wallowa Lake Lodge   Joseph 97846   503-432-4082
Lands Inn B&B   Star Rt. #1, Kimberly 97848   503-934-2333
Thompson's B&B By the Lake   1420 Wild Plum Ct., Klamath Falls 97601   503-882-7938
Stange Manor   1612 Walnut, La Grande 97850   503-963-2400
A Gran-Mother's Home   12524 SW Bonnes Ferry, Lake Oswego 97034   505-244-4361
Country Lane B&B   P.O. Box Y, Lakeside 97449   503-759-3869
Lakeside Cottage   234 Pioneer So., Box 26, Lowell 97452   503-937-2443
Under the Greenwood Tree   3045 Bellinger Lane, Medford 97501   503-776-0000
Birch Tree Manor   615 S. Main St., Hwy 11, Milton-Freewater 97862   503-938-6455
Owl's View B&B   29585 NE Owls Ln., Newberg 97132   503-538-6498
Oar House   520 SW 2nd Street, Newport 97365   503-265-9571
Sylvia Beach Hotel   267 N.W. Cliff St., Newport 97365   503-265-5428
Highlands   608 Ridge Road, North Bend 97459   503-756-0300
Sleepy Hollow B&B   4320 Stearns Lane, Oakland 97462   503-459-3401
Three Capes B&B   1685 Maxwell Mnt. Rd., Oceanside 97134   503-842-6126
Pine Creek Guest House   Star Rt., Box 65, Pine Creek 97834   503-785-3320
Gwendolyn's B&B   735 8th, P.O. Box 913, Port Orford 97465   503-332-4373
Allenhouse B&B   2606 N.W. Lorejoy St., Portland 97210   503-227-6841
Clinkerbrick House   2311 N.E. Schuyler, Portland 97212   503-281-2533
Heron Haus   2545 NW Westover Road, Portland 97210   503-274-1846
Portland Guest House   1720 N.E. 15th Ave., Portland 97212   503-282-1402
Portland's White House   1914 N.E. 22nd Avenue, Portland 97212   503-287-7131
Baldwin Inn B&B   126 W. First St., Prineville 97754   503-447-5758
Tennyson Manor   P.O. Box 825, Rogue River 97537   503-582-2790
Harbison House   1845 Commercial S.E., Salem 97302   503-581-8118
State House B&B   2146 State St., Salem 97301   503-588-1340
Boarding House   208 N. Holladay Drive, Seaside 97138   503-738-9055
Gilbert House   341 Beach Dr., Seaside 97138   503-738-9770
Riverside Inn   430 S. Holladay St., Seaside 97138   503-738-8254
Victoriana B&B   606 12th Ave., Seaside 97138   503-738-8449
Lake Creek Lodge   Star Route, Sisters 97759   503-595-6331
Pioneer Bed & Breakfast   Star Route, Spray 97874   503-462-3934
Horncroft   42156 Kingston-Lyons Dr, Stayton 97383   503-769-6287
Steamboat Inn   Steamboat 97447   503-496-3495
Bigelow B&B   308 East Fourth St., The Dalles 97058   503-298-8239
Williams House Inn   608 W. 6th St., The Dalles 97058   503-296-2889
Blue Haven Inn   P.O. Box 1034, Tillamook 97141   503-842-2265
McKenzie River Inn   49164 McKenzie Hwy, Vida 97488   503-822-6260
Mountain Shadows B&B   Box 147, Welches 97067   503-622-4746
King Salmon Lodge   Ferry Road, Westport 97016
Key's B&B   5025 SW Homesteader Rd., Wilsonville 97070   503-638-3722
Wolf Creek Tavern   P.O. Box 97, Wolf Creek 97497   503-866-2474
Adobe   Yachats 97498   503-547-3141
Oceanaire Rest B&B   95354 Hwy 101, Yachats 97498   503-547-3782
Oregon House Inn   94288 Hwy 101, Yachats 97498   503-547-3329
Flying M Ranch   23029 NW Flying M Rd., Yamhill 97148   503-662-3222

Pennsylvania

ADAMSTOWN

Adamstown Inn
62 W. Main St., 19501
P.O. Box 938
215-484-0800
Thomas K. Berman
All year

$ B&B
4 rooms, 2 pb
Visa, MC
C-no/S-ltd/P-no/H-no

Continental plus
Afternoon tea, snacks
Sitting room
2-person whirlpool
public tennis and pool

Small charming Victorian inn located in the antique district and Pennsylvania Dutch countryside. Minutes from Reading/Lancaster factory outlets.

AIRVILLE

Spring House
Muddy Creek Forks, 17302
717-927-6906
Ray Constance Hearne
All year

$$ B&B
5 rooms, 2 pb
•
C-yes/S-no/P-no/H-yes
Spanish

Full breakfast
Comp. wine
Sitting room, piano
bicycles
creek swimming

Restored 18th-century stone house in pre-Revolutionary river valley settlement near Lancaster, York. Feather beds, gourmet country breakfast. Hiking, fishing, wineries.

ALLENTOWN

Coachaus
107-111 N. 8th St., 18101
215-821-4854
Barbara Kocher
All year

$$ B&B
24 rooms, 24 pb
Visa, MC, AmEx
C-ltd/S-ltd/P-ltd/H-no

Full breakfast
Comp. wine
Sitting room
exercise room

Lovingly restored; graciously appointed; blessed with amenities of the finest hotels. Fine dining, shops, theater nearby. 1-, 2-, 3-bedroom facilities, each with private bath.

Glasbern
RD 1 Box 250,Fogelsvlle, 18051
Pack House Rd. Fogelsvlle
215-285-4723
Beth & Al Granger
All year

$$$ B&B
20 rooms, 20 pb
Visa, MC, AmEx •
C-ltd/S-yes/P-no/H-ltd

Full breakfast
Lunch, dinner
Sitting room, fireplaces
conference room, pool
hiking trails, whirlpool

A simple elegance pervades this 19th-century bank barn, situated in a hidden pastoral valley. Creatively renovated. 16 acres of trails.

Salisbury House
910 E. Emmause Ave., 18103
215-791-4225
Ollie & Judith Orth
All year

$$$ B&B
5 rooms, 1 pb
Visa, MC, AmEx
C-no/S-yes/P-no/H-no

Full gourmet breakfast
Comp. wine
Library, sitting room
sun porch, nature trails
B&B seminars

Historic 1810 stone plantation house. Acres of formal gardens, lawn, woodland. Genuine antiques, 115 paintings. Gourmet breakfast on fine china. Gift certificates available.

BEACH LAKE

Beach Lake Hotel
P.O. Box 144, 18405
Main & Church
717-729-8239
Erika & Roy Miller
All year

$$$ B&B
6 rooms, 6 pb
Visa, MC •
C-no/S-ltd/P-no/H-no
Polish

Full breakfast
Dinner, aftn. tea
Restaurant, bar
A/C in guest rooms
antique store

1850s general store lovingly restored to Victorian splendor. Gourmet dinners. Your Pocono hideaway near the Delaware River.

BIRD IN HAND

Greystone Manor B&B
P.O. Box 270, 17505
2658 Old Philadelphia Pik
717-393-4233
Sally & Ed Davis
All year

$$ B&B
12 rooms, 12 pb
Visa, MC, AmEx •
C-ltd/S-ltd/P-no/H-no

Continental breakfast
Lobby, A/C
color cable TV
quilts & crafts shop

Victorian mansion and carriage house located on 2 acres close to Amish farms. Unique, air-conditioned rooms with private baths. Quilts & crafts shop in basement.

BLOOMSBURG

Inn at Turkey Hill
991 Central Rd., 17815
I-80 Exit 35 S
717-387-1500
Elizabeth & Andrew Pruden
All year

$$ MAP
18 rooms, 18 pb
Visa, MC, AmEx, DC •
C-yes/S-yes/P-yes/H-yes

Continental plus
Lunch, dinner
Bar service
library
tennis courts nearby

Nestled amid Pennsylvania's rolling hills & farmlands, the inn extends warmth, comfort, charm & hospitality. The inn is, as one guest says, "an unexpected find."

BLUE RIDGE SUMMIT

The Greystone
P.O. Box 280, 17214
717-794-8816
Patricia Melesky
All year

$$ B&B
14 rooms, 14 pb
Visa, MC, AmEx •
C-yes/S-yes/H-yes

Full breakfast
Dinner
Snacks, comp. wine avail
Bar service available

A quiet country inn amid historic surroundings. Skiers welcome, Appalachian trail nearby. Golf courses available. Restaurant services available.

BRACKNEY

Indian Mountain Inn B&B
RD 1 Box 68, 18812
Tripp Lake Rd.
717-663-2645
The Frierman's
All year

$$ B&B
10 rooms
Visa, MC, AmEx
C-yes/S-ltd

Full breakfast
Box lunch, dinner by res
Restaurant, bar service
Sitting room, hot tubs
lakes, swimming, boating

Nestled high in the Endless Mountains. Hundreds of acres for X-C skiing, hunting, fishing, hiking. Near Binghamton, N.Y. Dining room, liquor license.

CANADENSIS

Dreamy Acres
P.O. Box 7, 18325
Rt. 447 & Seese Hill Rd.
717-595-7115
All year

$ B&B
6 rooms, 4 pb
C-6+/S-yes/P-no/H-no

Continental plus
Sitting room, piano
color cable TV
air-conditioning

Dreamy Acres is situated in the "Heart of the Pocono Mountain Vacationland" close to stores, gift shops, churches and recreational facilities.

CANADENSIS

Nearbrook
RD 1, Box 630, 18325
717-595-3152
Barb & Dick Robinson
All year

$ B&B
3 rooms, 1 pb
C-yes/P-ask/H-yes

Full breakfast
Wooden train set
games, piano
art lessons

Rock garden paths, roses, woods and a mountain stream. Relaxing breakfast on the outdoor porch. Seven restaurants within four miles; hiking, skiing. Weekly rates.

Old Village Inn
Route 390 N. Box 404, 18325
717-595-2120
Otto & Vera Lissfeld
All year

$$ EP
11 rooms, 9 pb
Visa, MC, AmEx, Diners •
C-12+/P-no/H-no
German, French

Restaurant, bar
Sitting room
Comp. hors d'oeuvres
Porch, lawn games
maid nightly, turndown

Quiet elegance in the fine European tradition. Rooms furnished in antiques. Quaint restaurant offering a varied American and ethnic cuisine. Numerous outdoor activites.

Pine Knob Inn
Route 447, Box 275, 18325
717-595-2532
Annie & Scott Frankel
Exc. December 1-27

$$$ MAP
27 rooms, 18 pb
Visa, MC •
C-5+/S-no/P-no/H-no

Full breakfast
Dinner, bar
Sitting room, tennis
Steinway grand piano
swimming pool, hiking

The inn is in a lovely country setting in the Pocono Mountains. Antiques and art abound. Best of all, the food is scrumptious!

Pump House Inn
Sky Top Rd., 18325
717-595-7501
John Keeney
Except January

$$ B&B
6 rooms, 6 pb
Visa, MC, AmEx, DC
C-yes/S-yes/P-no/H-no

Continental breakfast
Dinner, bar
Private sitting rooms
piano

Relax at this charming inn surrounded by the beauty and quietude that is the Poconos. Enjoy exquisite gourmet French dining.

CHRISTIANA

Winding Glen Farm Home
107 Noble Rd., 17509
215-593-5535
Minnie & Robert Metzler
Exc. Jan. & Feb.

$ B&B
5 rooms
C-yes/S-ltd/P-no/H-ltd

Full breakfast
Sitting room
piano
slide shows

Working dairy farm situated in beautiful valley. Stores and quilt shops nearby. Handcrafted furniture made on premises.

COOKSBURG

Clarion River Lodge
River Rd., Cook Forest, 16217
P.O. Box 150
800-648-6743
E.F. (Skip) Williams
All year

$$ B&B
20 rooms, 20 pb
Visa, MC, AmEx •
C-yes/S-yes

Continental breakfast
Lunch & dinner
Bar service
Sitting room, library
adjacent to river

Small romantic inn along the gentle Clarion River in Northwestern Pennsylvania's great forest. Year-round outdoor activities. Fine lodging, dining and spirits.

COOKSBURG

Gateway Lodge & Cabins
Box 125 Route 36, 16217
814-744-8017/800-843-6862
Joseph & Linda Burney
All year

$$ EP
8 rooms, 3 pb
C-ltd/S-yes/P-ltd/H-ltd

Full breakfast $
Dinner, lunch
Piano, buggy rides
sitting room, hot tubs
swimming pool, gift shop

Colonial log cabin inn with large stone fireplace. Fine dining by lantern light. Heavy quilts on hand-hewn beds. Year-round activities. Indoor heated swimming pool.

COWANSVILLE

Garrott's Bed & Breakfast
RD 1, Box 73, 16218
412-545-2432
Denise Garrott
Exc. last two weeks Dec.

$$ B&B
3 rooms
C-8+/S-ltd/P-ltd

Full breakfast
Comp. wine, snacks
Sitting room, library
bicycles, hot tubs
hiking, fishing, gardens

Comfortable elegance in the heart of the country. A peaceful sanctuary surrounded by woods, fields, and gardens.

DANVILLE

Pine Barn Inn
#1 Pine Barn Pl., 17821
717-275-2071
Martin L. Walzer
All year

$ EP
75 rooms, 69 pb
Visa, MC, AmEx, DC, CB •
C-yes/S-yes/P-yes/H-ltd
Spanish

Full breakfast $
Lunch, dinner, bar
Dining patio

Main inn is 19th-century barn; guest rooms located in new lodge building. Located in residential part of community. Especially popular locally for fine food.

DOYLESTOWN

Inn at Fordhook Farm
105 New Britain Rd., 18901
215-345-1766
E. Romanella, B. Burpee Dohan
All year

$$$ B&B
6 rooms, 4 pb
Visa, MC, AmEx
C-12+

Full farm breakfast
Afternoon tea
Snacks
Sitting room
library

Burpee (seed) family estate with 60 acres of meadows and woodlands. 1760s home with grandfather clocks, majestic mirrors, fireplaces and balconies. On Natl. Historic Register

EAGLES MERE

Eagles Mere Inn
P.O. Box 356, 17731
Mary Ave.
717-525-3273
Lou & Joan Fiocchi
All year

$$ MAP
17 rooms, 17 pb
Visa, MC, AmEx
C-ltd/S-no/P-no/H-no

Full breakfast
Dinner included, bar
Entertainment
tennis, swimming pool
sitting room, piano

Charming country inn located in a quiet Victorian town high in the Endless Mountains. Superb food. Beautiful lake nearby.

Shady Lane Lodge
Allegheny Ave., 17731
717-525-3394
Lee & Alma Park
All year

$$ B&B
7 rooms, 7 pb
C-yes/S-yes/P-no/H-no

Full breakfast
Cont. plus (July-Aug.)
Two sitting rooms

Picturesque mountaintop resort close to excellent hiking, swimming, fishing, skiing and tobogganing. Eagles Mere: "the town time forgot." Summer craft and antique shops.

EAST BERLIN

Bechtel Mansion Inn	$$ B&B	Continental plus
400 W. King St., 17316	8 rooms, 7 pb	Comp. wine, aftn. tea
717-259-7760	Visa, MC, AmEx •	Sitting room, library
Ruth Spangler	C-yes/S-ltd/P-no/H-no	downhill/X-C skiing
All year		air-conditioned rooms

Restored Victorian mansion with fine antiques, in a Pennsylvania German National Historical District. Popular with honeymooners and Civil War and architecture buffs.

EAST STROUDSBURG

Inn at Meadowbrook	$$ B&B	Continental plus
RD 7, Box 7651, 18301	18 rooms, 12 pb	Dinner
Cherry Lane Rd.	Visa, MC •	Sitting room
717-629-0296	C-12+/S-yes/P-no/H-no	tennis, swimming pool
Robert & Kathy Overman		bicycles
All year		

Forty acres of meadows and woods located in the heart of the Poconos. Close to skiing and major attractions.

ELM

Elm Country Inn	$ B&B	Full breakfast
Box 37, 17521	3 rooms	Afternoon tea
Elm & Newport Rds.	Visa, MC	Sitting room
717-664-3623	C-yes/S-no/P-no/H-no	porch
Betty & Melvin Meck		
All year		

Charming 1860 house, warm hospitality, easy access to Amish country, Hershey and Gettysburg. Near Lititz, PA, in Lancaster County.

EPHRATA

Guesthouse at Doneckers	$$ B&B	Continental plus
318-324 N. State St., 17522	29 rooms, 27 pb	Restaurant, fireplaces
717-733-8696	AmEx, Visa, MC, DC, CB	Comp. tea, jacuzzis
Jan Grobengieser	C-yes/S-yes/P-no/H-yes	Sitting room, library
All year		porches, deck

Unique getaway with country simplicity and genteel luxury. Elegance with antiques and folk art; buffet breakfast; fine dining and splendid shopping.

Smithton Inn	$$ B&B	Full breakfast
900 W. Main St., 17522	7 rooms, 7 pb	Tea, bedtime snack
717-733-6094	Visa, MC	Sitting room, fireplaces
Dorothy Graybill	C-yes/S-no/P-yes/H-ltd	whirlpool baths
All year		library, canopy beds

Picturesque 1763 Penn. Dutch Country Inn. Fireplaces in parlor, dining and guest rooms. Chamber music; canopy four-poster beds, refrigerator, quilts and candles in each room.

ERWINNA

Evermay on-the-Delaware	$$ B&B	Continental plus
River Rd., 18920	16 rooms, 16 pb	Comp. tea, sherry
215-294-9100	Visa, MC	Bar, restaurant wkends
Ronald Strouse, Fred Cresson	C-no/S-ltd/P-no/H-yes	Sitting room, piano
Exc. December 24		

Romantic Victorian inn on 25 acres of gardens, woodlawn paths and pastures. Elegant dinner served Friday-Sunday & holidays. Rooms face the picturesque Delaware River.

ERWINNA

Golden Pheasant Inn	$$$ EP	Restaurant, dinner
River Rd., Route 32, 18920	5 rooms, 1 pb	Bar service
215-294-9595	Visa, MC	Delaware Canal & River
Barbara & Michel Faure	C-no/S-ltd/P-no	canoes
All year	French, Spanish, Italian	

1857 fieldstone inn situated between river and canal. Five rooms furnished with incredible blend of antiques. Quiet. Plant-filled solarium for romantic candlelight dining.

FRANKLIN

Quo Vadis Bed & Breakfast	$$ B&B	Continental plus
1501 Liberty St., 16323	6 rooms, 6 pb	Coffee, tea, cookies
814-432-4208	Visa, MC •	Sitting room, library
Amy & Bob Eisenhuth	C-12+/S-no/P-no/H-no	TV, dining room
All year exc. holidays		bathroom amenities

Queene Anne 1867 brick house, heirloom furnishings, quilts, and needlework. Located in Federal Registered Historic District, Franklin, America's Victorian City.

GETTYSBURG

Brafferton Inn	$$ B&B	Full breakfast
44 York St., 17325	8 rooms, 4 pb	Sitting room, library
717-337-3423	Visa, MC •	atrium, piano, old mags
Mimi & Jim Agard	C-7+/S-no/P-no/H-yes	hat collection
All year		primitive mural

Stone and clapboard inn circa 1786 near the center square of Gettysburg. The rooms have stenciled designs, antiques. Walk to battlefield and restaurants.

Hickory Bridge Farm	$$ B&B	Full breakfast
96 Hickory Bridge Rd., 17353	7 rooms, 6 pb	Saturday dinner
Orrtanna	Visa, MC	Sitting room
717-642-5261	C-yes/S-yes/P-no/H-no	bicycles, fishing,
Hammetts & Martins		pond swimming
All year		

Hickory Bridge Farm is a quiet retreat at the foot of the South Mountains, eight miles west of Gettysburg.

Keystone Inn	$$ B&B	Full breakfast from menu
231 Hanover St., 17325	4 rooms, 2 pb	Dinner (wkend Nov.-Mar.)
717-337-3888	Visa, MC	Afternoon tea
Doris Martin	C-yes	Sitting room, library
All year		tennis courts nearby

Unique decor—lots of natural chestnut and oak; comfort our priority. Area rich in history; antique lover's paradise. Country breakfast!

GORDONVILLE-INTERCOURSE

Osceola Mill House	$$ B&B	Full breakfast
313 Osceola Mill Rd., 17529	3 rooms	Comp. wine
717-768-3758	C-no/S-no/P-no/H-no	Sitting room
Barry & Joy Sawyer	German	bicycles nearby
Exc. Christmas & Easter		

Historic stone mill house built in 1766. Located in a scenic Lancaster County surrounded by Amish farms. Fireplaces and antiques throughout.

HANOVER

Beechmont Inn
315 Broadway, Route 194, 17331
717-632-3013
Monna Hormel
All year

$$ B&B
7 rooms, 3 pb
Visa, MC, AmEx
C-ltd/S-ltd/P-no/H-no

Full breakfast
Comp. tea
Library
sitting room
bicycles

Federal period elegance, echoes of Civil War memories, Beechmont is a refuge from the rush of the twentieth century—a bridge across time. Located near Gettysburg.

HAWLEY

Academy Street B&B
528 Academy St., 18428
717-226-3430/201-316-8148
Judith & Sheldon Lazan
May—October

$$ B&B
7 rooms, 2 pb
Visa
C-no/S-yes/P-no/H-no

Full breakfast
Comp. tea, wine
Sitting room, TV
A/C in all bedrooms

Magnificent Victorian in Poconos near Lake Wallenpaupack. European gourmet breakfast, afternoon coffee and cheesecake. Near restaurants, ALL activities.

Settlers Inn
4 Main Ave., 18428
717-226-2993/717-226-2448
Grant & Jeanne Genzlinger
All year

$$ B&B
18 rooms, 18 pb
Visa, MC, AmEx, DC •
C-yes/S-yes/P-ltd/H-no

Continental plus
Lunch, dinner, comp. tea
Bar, wknd entertainment
Sitting room, library
tennis, bicycles, piano

Delightful country inn of Tudor architecture, with gift shops and art gallery. Lake Wallenpaupack and shopping are nearby.

HESSTON

Aunt Susie's Country Vaca.
RD 1, Box 225, 16647
814-658-3638
John & Susan Wilson
All year

$ B&B
8 rooms, 2 pb
C-yes/S-no/P-no/H-no
French, German

Continental plus
Afternoon tea
Snacks
Sitting room

Experience country living in a warm friendly atmosphere; antiques, oil paintings. 28-mile-long Raystown Lake for recreation.

HOLICONG

Ash Mill Farm
P.O. Box 202, 18928
5358 Route 202
215-794-5373
Patricia & Jim Auslander
All year

$$ B&B
4 rooms
Visa, MC •
C-ltd/S-yes/P-no/H-no

Full breakfast
Tea & Perrier
Sitting room
tennis & swimming
nearby

18th-century farmhouse on 10 acres of rural countryside, adjacent to Peddlers' Village and convenient to all of Bucks County.

KANE

Kane Manor Bed & Breakfast
230 Clay St., 16735
814-837-6522
Laurie Anne Dalton
All year

$ B&B
10 rooms, 6 pb
Visa, MC, AmEx •
C-yes/S-ltd/P-no/H-yes

Continental (wkdays)
Full breakfast (wkends)
Afternoon tea
Bar on demand (fall/wint)
Sitting room, piano

Original Kane family home situated in the Allegheny National Forest, furnished with family furniture and artifacts. Summer recreation, cross-country skiing.

KENNETT SQUARE

Meadow Spring Farm	$$ B&B	Full breakfast
201 E Street Rd., 19348	5 rooms, 3 pb	Dinner upon request
215-444-3903	AmEx	Comp. wine, tea, snacks
Anne I. Hicks	C-yes/S-yes/P-no/H-no	Hot tubs, swimming pool
All year		pond for fishing

1836 farmhouse on working farm with sheep, pigs & cows; filled with antiques, dolls & teddy bears. Full country breakfast served on porch, spacious dining room or by the pool.

LAMPETER

Walkabout Inn	$$ B&B	Full breakfast
837 Village Rd., 17537	4 rooms, 2 pb	Afternoon tea
P.O. Box 294	Visa, MC, AmEx, Choice	Sitting room, library
717-464-0707	C-yes/S-yes/P-no/H-no	playground/picnic area
Richard & Maggie Mason		movies on Amish culture
All year		

Country-restored Mennonite home with large wraparound porch. Stenciling, cable TV, A/C, antiques, quilts, oriental carpets. Gift store on premises. AAA rated in AAA Guide Book.

LANCASTER

Churchtown Inn B&B	$ B&B	Full gourmet breakfast
Route 23, Churchtown, 17555	8 rooms, 6 pb	Arrange dinner with
M.A. Box 135 RD 3, Narvon	Visa, MC, AmEx •	Amish family, porch
215-445-7794	C-12+/S-ltd	piano, game room, parlor
Hermine/Stuart Smith, Jim Kent	German	boats and pool nearby
All year		

In the heart of Pennsylvania Dutch country. Historic circa 1735 federal colonial. Near tourist attractions, antiquing, farm markets and outlets. Completely restored.

Witmer's Tavern — 1725 Inn	$$ B&B	Continental breakfast
2014 Old Philadelphia, 17602	5 rooms	Pop corn and poppers
2014 Old Philadelphia Pk.	•	Antique shop, sitting rm
717-299-5305	C-yes/S-ltd/P-no/H-no	air field, canoeing
Brant, Pamela or Jeann Hartung		8 museums/sites nearby
All year		

Lancaster's only authentic pre-Revolutionary inn still lodging travelers. Fireplaces, flowers and antiques in every room. On National Register. Located in Amish country.

LANCASTER-WILLOW STREET

Apple Bin Inn	$ B&B	Full breakfast
2835 Willow Street Pike, 17584	4 rooms, 2 pb	Afternoon tea
717-464-5881	Visa, MC •	Snacks
Barry & Debbie Hershey	C-yes/S-no/P-no/H-no	Sitting room
All year		storage, bike accom.

Warm colonial charm with a country flavor. Located near Amish community, antique and craft shops, excellent restaurants and historical sites.

LEWISBURG

Brookpark Farm B&B	$ B&B	Full breakfast
100 Reitz Blvd., 17831	5 rooms	Sitting room
717-524-7733	Visa, MC •	
Frank & Rhea Belle Kuhn	C-yes/S-no/P-no/H-no	
All year		

Farm setting; outbuildings renovated to unique shops. Barn; Pennsylvania House Gallery; antique shops. 2 mi. to Bucknell Univ.; 1 mi. west on Rt. 15; beautiful Buffalo Valley.

LEWISBURG

Inn on Fiddler's Tract
Route 192 W., 17837
RD 2 Box 573A
717-523-7197
Tony & Natalie Boldurian
All year

$$ B&B
5 rooms, 5 pb
Visa, MC, AmEx •
C-12+ /S-ltd/P-no/H-no

Continental plus
Comp. wine
Party dining by adv.res.
Library, on premises
hiking & X-C skiing

Located on 33 acres, this 1810 stone mansion welcomes you to enjoy the tranquillity of the Susquehanna Valley and the charm of Victorian Lewisburg.

Pineapple Inn
439 Market St., 17837
717-524-6200
Charles & Deborah North
All year

$$ B&B
6 rooms, 2 pb
Visa, MC, DC, CB
C-ltd/S-ltd/P-no/H-no
German

Full breakfast
Comp. tea, snacks
All rooms A/C, tea room
piano, sitting room
tennis, pool nearby

This circa 1857 home of Federalist design is decorated with period antiques. Just blocks from Bucknell University. Full country breakfast. Upside-Down Shoppe.

LITITZ

Swiss Woods B&B
500 Blantz Rd., 17543
717-627-3358
Werner & Debrah Mosimann
All year

$$ B&B
5 rooms, 5 pb
Visa, MC
C-yes
German, Swiss German

Full breakfast
Lunch (picnic baskets)
Afternoon tea
Sitting room
bicycles

A chalet nestled in the woods overlooking Speedwell Fodge Lake. Swiss specialties and European decor. Queen beds and down comforters.

Tamworth Inn, Tamworth, NH

LOGANVILLE ───────────────────────────────

Country Spun Farm B&B $$ B&B   Full breakfast
P.O. Box 117, 17342   2 rooms, 2 pb   Afternoon tea
55 S. Main St.   Visa, MC, Disc •   Sitting room, library
717-428-1162   C-10+/S-no/P-no/H-no   wool shop
Martha Lau   1 suite, TV, A/C
All year

Beautiful setting, lovely gardens, Oxford shop, abundant hospitality in Pennsylvania Dutch area. Large, comfortable rooms have A/C and private baths.

LUMBERVILLE ───────────────────────────────

Black Bass Hotel $$ B&B   Continental breakfast
3774 River Rd., Rt. 32, 18933   7 rooms, 3 pb   Lunch, dinner
215-297-5770   Visa, MC, AmEx, DC   Piano
Herbert E. Ward   C-ltd/S-yes/P-yes/H-yes   entertainment
All year   Spanish

Classic country 250-year-old hotel on Delaware River. Service, American food. Same owner for 35 years.

MANHEIM ───────────────────────────────

Alden House $$ B&B   Continental plus
2256 Huber Dr., 17545   7 rooms, 5 pb   Tea, snacks
717-627-3363   Visa, MC •   Sitting room, library
Gloria Adams   C-11+/S-no/P-no/H-no   parking, AC
All year   TV, porches

Fully restored 1850 townhouse in center of historic area. All sites and shopping within walking distance.

Herr Farmhouse Inn $$ B&B   Continental plus
2256 Huber Dr., 17545   4 rooms, 2 pb   Snacks
717-653-9852   Visa, MC   Sitting room, library
Gloria Adams   C-6+/S-ltd/P-no/H-no   sunroom, fireplaces
All year   Amish dining 5 min. away

Relax in this 18th-century restored stone farmhouse situated on 26 acres of peaceful farmland located in Lancaster County.

MERCER ───────────────────────────────

Magoffin Inn $ B&B   Full breakfast
129 S. Pitt St., 16137   7 rooms, 7 pb   Lunch M-F
412-662-4611   Visa, MC, AmEx   Dinner Thur.-Sat.
J. McClelland, G. Slagle   C-yes/S-yes/P-no/H-no   Sitting room, library
All year   tennis courts & pool

1884 Queen Anne Victorian. Affordable elegance in ideal location. Outdoor activities abound: boating, fishing, golf, cross-country skiing. Near I-79 and I-80.

Stranahan House $$ B&B   Full breakfast
117 E. Market St., 16137   2 rooms, 1 pb   Comp. tea, wine, snacks
412-662-4516   •   Sitting room
Jim & Ann Stranahan   C-yes/S-no/P-no/H-no   screened porch
All year   bicycles

150-year-old colonial empire-style home furnished in antiques; historical area; Amish country; 5 minutes from I-79 and I-80.

MERCERSBURG

Mercersburg Inn	$$$ B&B	Full breakfast
405 S. Main St., 17236	15 rooms, 15 pb	6-course dinner
717-328-5231	Visa, MC, AmEx •	Bar service
Fran Guy	C-ltd/S-ltd/H-no	Sitting room
All year	Swiss, German, French	tennis courts nearby

Elegant, restored mansion in south central Pennsylvania. 90 minutes from Washington, D.C. Gourmet dining by candlelight. Handmade canopy beds, antiques and crackling fireplace.

MERTZTOWN

Longswamp Bed & Breakfast	$$ B&B	Full breakfast
RD2, Box 26, 19539	9 rooms, 5 pb	Picnics, comp. tea, wine
215-682-6197	C-yes/S-ltd/P-no/H-ltd	Sitting room, library
Elsa & Dean Dimick	French	piano, bicycles
All year		horseshoes, bocce court

Historic country farmhouse near Amish country and skiing. Tempting delicacies prepared by area chef. Book and music collection for guests' use.

MILFORD

Black Walnut Country Inn	$$ B&B	Full breakfast
RD 2 Box 9285, 18337	12 rooms, 8 pb	Comp. wine, sherry
717-296-6322	Visa, MC, AmEx	Sitting room
Stewart & Effie Schneider	C-ltd/S-ltd/P-no/H-no	pond
All year		piano

Large secluded estate for an exclusive clientele. Tudor-style stone house with historic marble fireplace, charming bedrooms with antiques and brass beds.

MONTOURSVILLE

Carriage House—Stonegate	$$ B&B	Continental plus
RD 1, Box 11A, 17754	2 rooms	Snacks, bar service
717-433-4340	•	Sitting room, library
Harold & Dena Mesaris	C-yes/S-yes/P-yes	bicycles, hiking
All year		tubing in creeks

Total privacy along the banks of Mill Creek, 30 yards from the main house in the beautiful Loyalsock Creek Valley.

MOUNT JOY

Cedar Hill Farm	$$ B&B	Continental plus
305 Longenecker Rd., 17552	4 rooms, 4 pb	Picnic table
717-653-4655	Visa, MC, AmEx	Sitting room, piano
Russel & Gladys Swarr	C-yes/S-no/P-no/H-no	separate guest entrance
All year		near golf, tennis, dining

Near Amish country. Stone farmhouse overlooking stream. Newly redecorated, air-conditioned, all private baths, antiques. Host born on this working farm.

NEW HOPE

Back Street Inn	$$$ B&B	Full gourmet breakfast
144 Old York Rd., 18938	7 rooms, 2 pb	Comp. wine
215-862-9571	Visa, MC	Sitting room
Robert Puccio, John Hein	S-yes	swimming pool
All year	German	croquet

There is New Hope in Bucks County, PA, a village of vitality and romance. 10 min. stroll into center of town. Swimming pool, A/C rooms & full gourmet breakfast in garden room.

NEW HOPE ————————————————————————————————

Centre Bridge Inn
Box 74 Star Route, 18938
Routes 32 & 263
215-862-9139/215-862-2048
Stephen R. DuGan
All year

$$$ B&B
9 rooms, 9 pb
Visa, MC
C-ltd/S-yes/P-no/H-no

Continental breakfast
Dinner, bar
Sitting room w/fireplace
riverside deck

Charming riverside country inn furnished with lovely period antiques; cozy old world restaurant with walk-in fireplace and alfresco dining in season.

Hotel du Village
N. River Rd., 18938
at Phillips Mill Rd.
215-862-9911
Barbara & Omar Arbani
All year

$$$ B&B
20 rooms, 20 pb
AmEx
C-ltd/S-yes/P-no/H-yes
French, Spanish

Continental breakfast
Dinner, bar
Swimming pool
tennis courts
sitting room

Intimate country dining & lodging in Bucks County, Pennsylvania.

Inn at Phillips Mill
North River Rd., 18938
215-862-9919
Joyce & Brooks Kaufman
Except Jan.—mid-Feb.

$ EP
5 rooms, 5 pb
C-8+/S-yes/P-no/H-no

Continental breakfast
Dinner
Sitting room

1750 renovated stone barn, 5 charming bedrooms, each with private bath. French cuisine, candlelit dining—by fire in winter, on flower-filled patio in summer.

Pineapple Hill
1324 River Rd., 18938
215-862-9608
Linda Chaize
All year

$$ B&B
5 rooms, 3 pb
AmEx
C-ltd/S-no/P-no/H-no

Continental plus
Aft./eve. refreshments
Parlor
swimming

Historic Bucks County farmhouse—primitive and country antiques, interesting stone ruins, five acres to roam. Shopping, restaurants & antiquing nearby.

Wedgewood B&B Inn
111 W. Bridge St., 18938
215-862-2570
Carl & Nadine Glassman
All year

$$ B&B
10 rooms, 8 pb
•
C-yes/S-ltd/P-ltd/H-ltd
Fr, Hebr, Dutch, Ger, Fr

Continental plus
Aftn. tea & refreshments
Victorian gazebo, parlor
horsedrawn carriage ride
club w/tennis, swimming

Victorian mansion in New Hope. Wedgewood china, fresh flowers & original art. Innkeepers on hand to make your stay as pleasant as the surroundings. OUR 1989 INN OF THE YEAR!

Whitehall Inn
RD 2 Box 250, 18938
1370 Pineville Rd.
215-598-7945
Mike & Suella Wass
All year

$$$ B&B
6 rooms, 4 pb
Visa, MC, AmEx, DC •
C-no/S-no/P-no/H-no

4-course candlelight bkf
High tea
Pool & rose garden
library, sun room
piano & pump organ

Experience our four-course candlelit breakfast using European china and crystal and heirloom sterling silver. Formal tea; fireplaces; working dressage horse farm.

NEWFOUNDLAND

White Cloud Sylvan Retreat
RD 1, Box 215, 18445
Panther Rd., Route 447
717-676-3162
George & Judy Wilkinson
All year

$ EP
20 rooms, 7 pb
Visa, MC, AmEx, DC •
C-yes/S-no/P-yes/H-no
French, German in summer

Full breakfast $
Lunch, dinner
Outdoor swimming pool
tennis courts
sitting room, piano

Country inn on fifty wooded acres, specializing in peace, quiet and good food. No TV; meatless, natural food meals.

NORTH EAST

Brown's Village Inn
51 E. Main St., 16428
814-725-5522
Rebecca Brown
All year

$$ B&B
3 rooms, 3 pb
Visa, MC •
C-yes/S-yes/P-ltd
Dutch, French

Full breakfast
Lunch/dinner, restaurant
Afternoon tea, snacks
Sitting room, library
golf, tennis, beach near

A restored 1832 federal-style house now is home for a fine restaurant and antique-appointed guest rooms. Only 1 mile to the Lake Erie shore. Experience a bit of yesteryear.

NORTH WALES

Joseph Ambler Inn
1005 Horsham Rd., 19454
Montgomeryville
215-362-7500
Steve & Terry Kratz
All year

$$$ B&B
28 rooms, 28 pb
Visa, MC, AmEx, DC, CB •
C-12+/S-yes/P-no/H-ltd
French, German

Full breakfast
Restaurant
3 sitting rooms
banquet/meeting room

1735 estate house set on 13 acres and furnished with antiques, four-poster beds, walk-in fireplace.

NOTTINGHAM

Little Britain Manor
20 Brown Rd., 19362
Village of Little Britain
717-529-2862
Fred & Evelyn Crider
All year

$ B&B
4 rooms
•
C-yes

Full breakfast
Dinner by request
Help with tours
2 rooms with A/C

A home away from home country farm furnished with antiques and country flair. See up close the unique culture of the Amish people and markets.

ORBISONIA

Salvino's Guest House
P.O. Box 116, 17243
Ridgely St.
814-447-5616
Elaine & Joe Salvino
All year

$ B&B
5 rooms
Visa, MC
C-yes/S-ltd/P-yes/H-no

Continental plus
Front porch w/swing
sitting room w/TV

Historic Orbisonia is home to EBT Steam Train & trolley museums & near Lake Raystown. Your hostess Elaine is an avid quilter and her Chatelaine Quilt Shop is right next door.

OXFORD

John Hayes House
8100 Limestone Rd., 19363
215-932-5347
Bill & Melissa Hostetter
All year

$$ B&B
3 rooms, 1 pb
•
C-no/S-no/P-no/H-no

Full breakfast
Afternoon tea
Sitting room
herb garden with
sitting area

Come experience the charm of an 18th-century farmhouse furnished with genuine antiques, located near Lancaster Country with working Amish farms in the area.

PARADISE

Maple Lane Farm	$ B&B	Continental plus
505 Paradise Ln., 17562	4 rooms, 2 pb	Sitting room
717-687-7479	C-yes/S-no/P-no/H-no	organ
Ed & Marion Rohrer		
All year		

Maple Lane Farm has air conditioning, antiques. Near Amish homesteads, museums, farmer's markets. Farm guest house plus 120-cow dairy, streams and woodland.

Neffdale Farm	$ EP	Coffee or tea
604 Strasburg Rd., 17562	6 rooms, 2 pb	Sitting room
717-687-7837/717-687-9367	C-yes/S-no/P-no/H-no	
Roy/Ellen/Charles/Glenda Neff		
All year		

Stay on a real working farm. Amish neighbors. Close to everything in the heart of Pennsylvania Dutch country.

PHILADELPHIA

Hotel La Reserve	$$ B&B	Continental plus
1804 Pine St., 19103	6 rooms, 2 pb	Afternoon high tea
215-735-0582	•	Complimentary wine
Karen & Gordon Andresen	C-no/S-yes/P-no/H-no	Salon area
All year	Spanish, French	

Four-story Victorian row home built in 1836. Renovated & decorated in French Country throughout. Conveniently located to historic areas, shopping, and "antique alley."

Society Hill Hotel	$$$ B&B	Continental breakfast
301 Chestnut St., 19106	12 rooms, 12 pb	Restaurant
215-925-1919	Visa, MC, AmEx, DC •	Piano bar
Jackie	C-yes/S-yes/P-ltd	telephones
All year		

An "urban inn" located in the midst of Philadelphia's Historic Park. Fresh flowers, chocolates and brass double beds grace each room.

Steele Away B&B	$$ B&B	Full breakfast (wkends)
7151 Boyer St., 19119	3 rooms	Continental plus (wkdys)
215-242-0722	C-5+/S-no/P-no/H-no	Afternoon tea, snacks
David & Diane Steele		Weaver's studio, TV, A/C
All year		veranda, kitchen avail.

Guests described this weaver and architect's Victorian home as a "slice of heaven," "piece of paradise." Scandanavian furnishings, stenciling, handwoven accents.

Thomas Bond House	$$$ B&B	Continental plus (wkdys)
129 S. Second St., 19106	12 rooms, 12 pb	Full breakfast (wkends)
215-923-8523	Visa, MC, AmEx •	Aftn. tea, comp. wine
Thomas F. Lantry	C-yes/S-yes/P-no/H-no	Wet bar, library
All year		whirlpool tubs, bicycles

Colonial period (c. 1770) guest house listed in National Register. Individually decorated rooms with hair dryers, TV, phones. Located in Independence National Historical Park.

PITTSBURGH

Priory—A City Inn
614 Pressley St., 15212
412-231-3338
Mary Ann Graf
All year

$$$ B&B
24 rooms, 24 pb
AmEx, Visa, MC •
C-yes/S-yes/P-no/H-yes

Continental plus
Comp. tea, wine
Sitting room, library
fireplace, courtyard
parking, shuttle

Newly restored historic Victorian Priory—antiques; courtyard or city view; neighborhood atmosphere; close to city. National Register district.

POINT PLEASANT

Tattersall Inn
P.O. Box 569, 18950
Cafferty & River Rds.
215-297-8233
Gerry & Herb Moss
All year

$$ B&B
6 rooms, 6 pb
AmEx, Visa, MC •
C-yes/S-yes/P-no/H-no

Continental plus
Comp. afternoon snacks
Library, sitting room
antique pinball machine

Historic lilac and cream mansion of the early 1800s. B&B in a village setting. Antique phonograph collection for your enjoyment.

QUAKERTOWN

Sign of The Sorrel Horse
P.O. Box 234, 18951
Old Bethlehem Rd.
215-536-4651
All year

$$$ EP/B&B
6 rooms, 6 pb
Visa, MC
C-no/S-no/P-yes/H-no
French, German

Continental plus
Restaurant, bar, dinner
Comp. sherry & fruits
Sitting room
skiing, fishing, boating

Built in 1749 as a stagecoach stop; secluded on 5 manicured acres; gracious country inn; six antique-filled guest rooms. A little bit of France in Bucks County.

QUARRYVILLE

**Runnymede Farm
Guesthouse**
1030 Robert Fulton Hwy., 17566
717-786-3625
Herb & Sara Hess
All year

$ EP
3 rooms
C-yes/S-no/P-no/H-no

Full country breakfast $
Piano
sitting room

Enjoy old-fashioned hospitality when you vacation in our clean, comfortable farm home. Full country breakfast available. Bicycling, hiking, picnicking.

SAINT MARYS

Towne House Inn
138 Center St., 15857
814-781-1556
Marianne Howell
All year

$ B&B/MAP
14 rooms, 14 pb
Visa, MC, AmEx, DC
C-yes/S-yes

Full breakfast
Lunch (Mon.-Fri.)
Tea & coffee service
Sitting room
refrigerators

Find Victorian grandeur at Towne House Inn. Home cooked breakfast & lunch. Guest rooms are uniquely decorated to complement the elegance found in our palatial Georgian mansion.

SELINSGROVE

Blue Lion inn
350 S. Market St., 17870
717-374-2929
Kent & Marilyn Thomson
All year

$ B&B
5 rooms, 1 pb
Visa, MC
C-5+/S-ltd

Full gourmet breakfast
Comp. wine, tea, snacks
Sitting room, library
jacuzzi suite, flowers
hand-dipped chocolates

Elegant circa 1849 inn furnished in antiques, wraparound porch, spacious landscaped grounds with historic tree. Restored Victorian, university town.

SEWICKLEY

Sewickley Bed & Breakfast	$$$ B&B	Full breakfast
222 Broad St., 15143	4 rooms	Comp. wine & sherry
412-741-0107	C-no/S-ltd/P-no/H-no	Snacks
Diane & Clark Race		Sitting room
All year		library

Romantic Victorian in quaint village on the Ohio River. Walk to restaurants, shops, art galleries. Sleep on feather beds. Enjoy personal attention. Close to Pittsburgh airport.

SLIPPERY ROCK

Applebutter Inn	$$$ B&B	Full breakfast
152 Applewood Lane, 16057	11 rooms, 11 pb	Afternoon tea, snacks
412-794-1844	Visa, MC	Sitting room
Gary & Sandra McKnight	C-yes/S-no/P-no/H-yes	library
All year		

Restored 1844 farmstead with fireplaces, canopy beds and genuine antiques; gourmet breakfasts; warm quiet atmosphere; close to university, parks.

SMOKETOWN

Homestead Lodging	$ EP	Comp. coffee
184 E. Brook Rd., 17576	4 rooms, 4 pb	Gift shop
717-393-6927	Visa, MC	air-conditioning
Robert & Lori Kepiro	C-yes/S-yes/H-yes	color TV w/stereo radio
All year		Amish country tours

Quiet country lodging in hand-stenciled rooms. Gift shop with local handcrafts. Located beside Amish farm. Walk to restaurants and outlets.

STARLIGHT

Inn at Starlight Lake	$$$ B&B	Full breakfast
18461	27 rooms, 21 pb	Luncheon, dinner $, bar
717-798-2519	Visa, MC	Sitting room, piano
Judy & Jack McMahon	C-yes/S-yes/P-no/H-no	tennis courts, boating
Except late Mar.-Apr. 16		bicycles, ski trails

A beautiful clear lake, setting of pastoral tranquillity, excellent food and spirits, recreation for every season, congenial and informal atmosphere.

STARRUCCA

Nethercott Inn	$ B&B	Full breakfast
P.O. Box 26, 18462	5 rooms, 3 pb	Sitting room
One Main St.	MC, Visa, AmEx	entertainment
717-727-2211	C-yes/S-ltd/P-no/H-no	antique shop on premises
Ned & Ginny Nethercott		
All year		

Victorian home built in 1893, furnished in antiques. Located in a quaint village in the Endless Mountains. Near golfing, fishing, hunting, skiing and snowmobiling.

STRASBURG

Decoy Bed & Breakfast	$ B&B	Full breakfast
958 Eisenberger Rd., 17579	4 rooms, 4 pb	Comp. wine
717-687-8585	C-yes/S-no/P-no/H-no	Sitting room
Deborah & Hap Joy		library, A/C
All year		bicycles tours

Spectacular view; quiet rural location in Amish farm country. Former Amish home. Bike touring paradise.

STRASBURG ───────────────────────────────

Limestone Inn B&B	$$ B&B	Continental plus
33 E. Main St., 17579	2 rooms	Sitting room
717-687-8392	AmEx	player piano
Jan & Dick Kennell	C-13+/S-ltd/P-no/H-no	library, patio
All year		

The Limestone Inn B&B (circa 1786) is listed in the National Register of Historic Places; situated in the heart of Lancaster's Amish country.

WASHINGTON CROSSING ────────────────────────

Woodhill Farms Inn	$$ B&B	Full breakfast (weekend)
150 Glenwood Dr., 18977	5 rooms, 5 pb	Continental plus (M-F)
215-493-1974	Visa, MC	Sitting room, piano
Don & MaryLou Spagnuolo	C-6+/S-ltd/P-no/H-no	entertainment
All year	German	use as small conf. ctr.

Nestled on ten wooded acres. Enjoy delicious breakfasts in rural, relaxing Bucks County. New York, Philadelphia, Princeton close by; New York—90 min.

WATERVILLE ───────────────────────────────

Point House	$ EP	Kitchen provided
P.O. Box 13, 17776	7 rooms, 1 pb	3 room suite avail.
Church St.	●	tent camping sites
717-753-8707	C-no/S-no/P-no/H-no	across creek
Brant Hartung		
All year		

Swimming, diving and fishing docks at foot of lawn. Boats available free of charge. Convenient to X-C and downhill skiing, camping and backpacking.

WEST CHESTER ────────────────────────────

Bankhouse Bed & Breakfast	$$ B&B	Full breakfast
875 Hillsdale Rd., 19382	2 rooms	Snacks
215-344-7388	C-12+/S-no/P-no/H-no	Sitting room, porch
Diana & Michael Bove		library
All year		private entrances

Charming 18th-century "bankhouse" located across from a 10-acre horse farm. Convenient to Longwood Gardnes, Wynthertur, etc. Quiet country setting.

WRIGHTSVILLE ────────────────────────────

Roundtop Bed & Breakfast	$ B&B	Full breakfast
RD #2 Box 258, 17368	6 rooms, 1 pb	Afternoon tea
717-252-3169	C-yes/S-yes/P-no/H-no	Sitting room
Judith Blakey, Joni Eberly		library
All year		hiking

Romantic 1880 stone home—unique setting—100 acres woodland, most spectacular view of Susquehanna River anywhere.

More Inns...

East Shore House   P.O. Box 12, Beach Lake 18405   717-729-8523
Jean Bonnet Tavern   R.D. 2, Box 724, Bedford 15522   814-623-2250
Grandmaw's Place Bunk & Board   R.D.2, Box 239, Benton 17814   717-925-2630
Ogline's B&B   1001 East Main St., Berlin 15530   814-267-3696
Sunday's Mill Farm   R.D.2, Box 419, Bernville 19506   215-488-7821
Twin Turrets Inn   11 E. Philadelphia Ave., Boyertown 19512   215-367-4513
Buck Hill Inn   Buck Hill Falls 18232   800-233-8113
Buffalo Lodge   R.D.1, Box 277, Buffalo Mills 15534   814-623-2207

Brookview Manor B&B   R.D. 1, Box 365, Canadensis 18325   717-595-2451
Canadensis Old Village Inn   P.O. Box 404, Canadensis 18325   717-595-2120
Laurel Grove Inn   Canadensis 18325   717-595-7262
Overlook Inn   RD 1, Box 680, Canadensis 18325   717-595-7519
Cedar Run Inn   Cedar Run 17727   717-353-6241
Cranberry B&B   P.O. Box 1009, Cranberry Township 16033   412-776-1198
La Anna Guest House   RD 2, Box 1051, Cresco 18326   717-676-4225
Pear & Patridge Inn   Dept. NT Old Easton Rd, Doylestown 18901   215-345-7800
Cherry Mills Lodge   Route 87S, RD 1, Dushore 18614   717-928-8978
Noon-Collins Inn   114 East High St., Ebensburg 15931   814-472-4311
Emig Mansion   Box 486, 3342 N.George, Emigsville 17318   717-764-2226
Covered Bridge Inn B&B   990 Rettew Mill Rd, Ephrata 17522   717-733-1592
Gerhard House B&B   287 Duke St., Ephrata 17522   717-733-0263
Hackman's Country Inn   140 Hackman Road, Ephrata 17522   717-733-3498
Duling-Kurtz House   146 S. Whitford Rd, Exton 19341   215-524-1830
Historic Fairfield Inn   15 W. Main St., Box 196, Fairfield 17320   717-642-5410
Herb Cottage Inn   Lincoln Hwy E., Rt.30, Fayetteville 17222   717-352-7733
Germantown B&B   5925 Wayne Avenue, Germantown 19144   215-848-1375
Bishop's Rocking Horse Inn   40 Hospital Road, Gettysburg 17325   717-334-9530
Cozy Comfort Inn   264 Baltimore St., Gettysburg 17325   717-337-3997
Dobbin House Tavern Gettysburg   89 Steinwehr Ave., Gettysburg 17325   717-334-2100
Swinn's Lodging   31 E. Lincoln Ave., Gettysburg 17325   717-334-5255
Log Cabin B&B   Box 393, Rt. 11, Hallstead 18822   717-879-4167
Horetsky's Tourist Home   217 Cocoa Avenue, Hershey 17033   000-533-5783
Shady Elms Farm B&B   Box 188, R.D. 1, Hickory 15340   412-356-7755
Barley Sheaf Farm   P.O. Box 10, Holicong 18928   215-794-5104
Yoder's B&B   R.D. 1, Box 312, Huntingdon 16652   814-643-3221
Das Tannen-Lied   Rt. 1, Jamestown 16134   412-932-5029
Villamayer   1027 East Lake Road, Jamestown 16134   412-932-5194
Harry Packer Mansion   Packer Hill, Jim Thorpe 18229   717-645-7965
Buttonwood Farm   231 Pemberton Rd., Kennett Square 19348   215-444-0278
Mrs. K's B&B   404 Ridge Ave., Kennett Square 19348   215-444-5559
Bucksville House   R.D. 2, Box 146, Kintnersville 18930   215-847-8948
Groff Tourist Farm Home   766 Brackbill Rd., Kinzer 17535   717-442-8223
Dingeldein House   1105 E. King St., Lancaster 17602   717-293-1723
Hollinger House B&B   2336 Hollinger Road, Lancaster 17602   717-464-3050
Landyshade Farms   1801 Colebrook Road, Lancaster 17601   717-898-7689
Lime Valley Cottage   1107 Lime Valley Rd., Lancaster 17602   717-687-6118
Ligonier Country Inn   P.O. Box 46, Rt. 30 E, Laughlintown 15655   412-238-3651
Loom Room   R.D. 1, Box 1420, Leesport 19533   215-926-3217
Grant House B&B   244 W. Church St., Ligonier 15658   412-238-5135
Royalview Dairy Farm   Box 93, Lincoln University 19352
General Sutter Inn   14 E. Main St., Lititz 17543   717-626-2115
1740 House   River Road, Lumberville 18933   215-297-5661
Three Center Square Inn   P.O. Box 428, Maytown 17550   717-426-3036
Guest Home   1040 Lincoln Way, McKeesport 15132   412-751-7143
Cliff Park Inn   Cliff Park Rd., Milford 18337   717-296-6491
Walnut Hill B&B   113 Walnut Hill Rd., Millersville 17551   717-872-2283
Montrose House   26 S. Main St., Montrose 18801   717-278-1124
Mount Gretna Inn   Kauffman & Pine, Mount Gretna 17064   717-964-3234
Brenneman Farm—B&B   Rd. 1, Box 310, Mount Joy 17552   717-653-4213
Cameron Estate Inn   R.D. 1, Box 305, Mount Joy 17752   717-653-1773
Nolt Farm Guest Home   South Jacob St. Farm, Mount Joy 17552   717-653-4192
Mountville Antiques B&B   407 East Main St.,Rt. 4, Mountville 17554   717-285-5956

Waltman's B&B   R.D. 1, Box 87, New Albany 18833   717-363-2295
Farm Fortune   204 Lime Kiln Rd., New Cumberland 17070   717-774-2683
Hacienda Inn   36 W. Mechanics St., New Hope 18938   215-862-2078
Logan Inn   10 W. Ferry St., New Hope 18938   215-862-5134
Tavern   Box 153 On the Square, New Wilmington 16142   412-946-2020
Windward Inn   51 Freeport Rd., North East 16428   814-725-5336
Rayba Acres Farm   183 Black Horse Rd., Paradise 17562   717-687-6729
Verdant View Farm   429 Strasburg Road, Paradise 17562   717-687-7353
Oakwood   235 Johnston Rd., Pittsburgh 15241   412-835-9565
Inn of Innisfree   Box 108, Point Pleasant 18950   215-297-8329
Coventry Forge Inn   R.D. 2, Pottstown 19464   215-469-6222
Fairway Farm   Vaughan Road, Pottstown 19464   215-326-1315
Riegelsville Hotel   10-12 Delaware Rd., Riegelsville 18077   215-749-2469
Candlelite Inn B&B   2574 Lincoln Highway E., Ronks 17572   717-299-6005
Millstone Inn   P.O. Box 279, Rt. 30, Schellsburg 15559   814-733-4864
Pine Wood Acres   Rt. 1 Box 634, Scottdale 15683   412-887-5404
Haag's Hotel   Main St., Shartlesville 19554   215-488-6692
Eagle Rock Lodge   River Road, Box 265, Shawnee-on-Delaware 18356   717-421-2139
Discoveries B&B   RD #1, Box 42, Sigel 15680   814-752-2632
Smoketown Village Tourist   2495 Old Phila. Pike, Smoketown 17576   717-393-5975
Holly Hedge Estate   P.O. Box 213, Solebury 18963   215-862-3136
Rambouillet at Hollyhedge   Box 213, Solebury 18963   215-862-3136
Sterling Inn   Route 191, South Sterling 18460   717-676-3311
Siloam   1430 Village Rd., Strasburg 17579   717-687-6231
Strasburg Village Inn   1 West Main St., Strasburg 17579   717-687-0900
Wye Oak Farm Tourists   RD #1, Box 152, Strasburg 17579   717-687-6547
Kaufman House   Box 183, Route 63, Sumneytown 18084   215-234-4181
Jefferson Inn   RD2, Box 36,Rt.171, Thompson 18465   717-727-2625
Victorian Guest House   118 York Av., Towanda 18848   717-265-6972
Tyler Hill B&B   P.O. Box 62, Route 371, Tyler Hill 18469   717-224-6418
Bridgeton House   P.O. Box 167, Upper Black Eddy 18972   215-982-5856
Tara   1 Bridgeton Hill, Upper Black Eddy 18972   215-982-5457
Upper Black Eddy Inn   Rt. 32-River Rd., Upper Black Eddy 18972   215-982-5554
Bennett's B&B   1700 Pennsylvania Ave E, Warren 16365   814-723-7358
Altheim B&B   104 Walnut Street, Waterford 16441
Jesse Robinson Manor   141 Main St., Wellsboro 16901   717-724-5704
Crooked Windsor   409 South Church St., West Chester 19382   215-692-4896
Highland Manor B&B   855 Hillsdale Road, West Chester 19382   215-686-6251
Reighard House B&B Inn   1323 E. Third St., Williamsport 17701   717-326-3593
Green Gables B&B   2532 Willow Street Pike, Willow Street 17584   717-464-5546
Woodward Inn   Box 177, Woodward 16882   814-349-8118
Wycombe Inn   P.O. Box 204, Wycombe 18980   215-598-7000
Cherry Mills Lodge   P.O. 6525, Wyomissing 19610   717-928-8978
Briarwold B&B   RD 24, Box 469, York 17406   717-252-4619
Fairhaven   RD 12 Box 445, Keller, York 17406   717-252-3726
Inn at Mundis Mills   R.D. 22, Box 15, York 17402   717-755-2002
Twin Brook Inn   Box 1042, R.D. 24, Kreut, York 17409   717-757-5384

Rhode Island

BLOCK ISLAND

Gothic Inn
P.O. Box 458, 02807
440 Dodge St.
401-466-2918
Bernadette Taylor
All year

$ B&B
9 rooms
Visa, MC
C-yes/S-no/P-no/H-ltd

Continental plus
Sitting room
outdoor fireplace

Turn-of-the-century Victorian inn. Spectacular views of sand and surf. Conveniently located in heart of historic district. Close to shops, restaurants, and ferries.

Hotel Manisses
P.O. Box I, 02807
401-466-2836/401-466-2421
Joan & Justin Abrams
April—November 1

$$$ B&B
18 rooms, 18 pb
Visa, MC, Amex •
C-10+/S-yes/P-no/H-yes
Spanish, Portuguese

Full buffet breakfast
Lunch & dinner, full bar
Comp. wine, appetizers
Elegant lobby, sitting
room, phones in all rms

1872 Victorian hotel—fully restored—some rooms with jacuzzi. Gourmet dining, High Tea served daily. Seafood Raw Bar.

GREEN HILL

Fairfield-by-The-Sea B&B
527 Green Hill Beach Rd, 02879
401-789-4717
Jeanne Ayers Lewis
All year

$$ B&B
2 rooms
C-ltd/S-ltd

Gourmet cont./Cont. plus
Comp. wine
Sitting room
library
tennis courts

Artist's contemporary house filled with art and books. Near ocean, great restaurants, historical places, Block Island, Newport, and Mystic. Fireplaces.

JAMESTOWN

Calico Cat Guest House
14 Union St., 02835
401-423-2641
Lori Lacaille
All year

$$ B&B
10 rooms
Visa, MC, AmEx •
C-yes/S-yes/P-sml/H-no

Continental breakfast
Sitting room
TV, books, A/C
baby-sitting avail.

Lovely old Victorian home with large rooms and high ceilings. Enjoy our lounge with TV, books, toys and games. Breakfast in sunny breakfast room.

MIDDLETOWN

Lindsey's Guest House
6 James St., 02840
401-846-9386
Dave & Anne Lindsey
All year

$ B&B
3 rooms
Visa, MC •
C-yes/H-yes

Continental plus
Sitting room
large yard, deck
ceiling fans in all rms

We are within a 10 min. walk to beaches and restaurants. One mile from Bellevue Ave. mansions. Two miles from downtown Newport harborfront. Off-street parking, large yard.

Brass Bed Inn, Cape May, NJ

NARRAGANSETT

The Richards
144 Gibson Ave., 02882
401-789-7746
Nancy & Steven Richards
All year

$$$ B&B
3 rooms, 2 pb
•
C-12+/S-no/P-no/H-no

Full gourmet breakfast
Library w/fireplace
tennis courts nearby
fireplaces in bedrooms

Gracious accommodations in a country setting. Awaken to the smell of gourmet coffee and freshly baked goods and then enjoy a refreshing walk to the beach.

Sea Gull Guest House
50 Narragansett Ave., 02882
401-783-4636
Kimber Wheelock
All year

$ EP
5 rooms
Visa, MC •
C-ltd/S-yes/P-no/H-no

Bar service
Library nearby
tennis courts nearby
ocean beach 1 block

Large rooms cooled by ocean breezes. Close to everything. Swim, sun, sail and fish in comfort that you can afford.

NEWPORT

Admiral Benbow Inn
8 Fair St. (mailing), 02840
93 Pelham St.
401-846-4256
Joan Fleming
February—December

$$ B&B
15 rooms, 15 pb
Visa, MC, AmEx •
C-yes/S-no/P-no/H-no

Continental plus
Breakfast/conf. room
Air conditioning
telephone service

Brass beds, antiques and atmosphere, deck and spectacular view of Narragansett Bay. Sir Francis Chichester stayed here.

NEWPORT

Admiral Farragut Inn
31 Clarke St., 02840
401-846-4256
Lillian Barnes
All year

$$ B&B
8 rooms, 8 pb
Visa, MC, AmEx •
C-yes/S-ltd/P-no/H-yes

Continental plus
Afternoon tea
Sitting room
air conditioning

Carefully restored 1702 colonial, furnished with exceptional antiques. All hand-made pencil four-poster beds, comfortable accommodations. Close to shop, wharf, Bellevue Ave.

Admiral Fitzroy Inn
398 Thames St., 02840
401-846-4256
Anita Gillin
All year exc. January

$$$ B&B
18 rooms, 18 pb
Visa, MC, AmEx •
C-yes/S-yes/H-yes

Full breakfast
Afternoon tea, snacks
Refrigerator, cable TV,
Telephone & coffee
maker in rooms

Brinley Victorian Inn
23 Brinley St., 02840
401-849-7645
Peter Carlisle, Amy Weintraub
All year

$$$ B&B
17 rooms, 12 pb
•
C-12+/S-yes/P-no/H-no

Continental breakfast
Sitting room
landscaped courtyard

Romantic Victorian uniquely decorated with antiques, period wallpapers. Brick courtyard planted with Victorian garden flowers. Park & walk to historic sites and beaches.

Cliff View Cottage
4 Cliff Terrace, 02840
401-846-0885
Pauline & John Shea
April 1—Nov. 15

$$ B&B
4 rooms, 2 pb
Visa, MC
C-yes/S-yes/P-no/H-no

Continental plus
Sitting room
piano

Two-story Victorian (circa 1871-1890). East side has view of Atlantic Ocean. Two porches, open sun deck. Walk to beach or Cliff Walk.

Cliffside Inn
2 Seaview Ave., 02840
401-847-1811
Kay Russell
May—October

$$ B&B
10 rooms, 10 pb
Visa, MC •
C-10+/S-yes/P-no/H-no

Continental breakfast
Afternoon ice tea
Guest living room
porch, piano
ceiling fans in rooms

Gracious, informal home furnished with antiques. Each room individually & tastefully decorated. Quiet home just off the Cliff Walk, 5-minute walk to beach.

Commodore Perry
8 Fair St., 02840
Side door 348 Thames St.
401-846-4256
All year

$ EP
•

Ark Restaurant below
Rooms are rented through
reservation office
downtairs and next
door to the inn

The inn is located above the Ark Restaurant and is decorated in Japanese motif. Very much in the hustle and bustle of Newport.

NEWPORT

Harborside Inn
Christie's Landing, 02840
401-846-6600/401-847-4638
Mary Comforti
All year

$$ B&B
14 rooms, 14 pb
Visa, MC, AmEx
C-yes/S-yes/P-no/H-no

Continental breakfast
Afternoon tea
Harbor Room
refrigerators, wet bars
TVs, decks

On Newport's historic waterfront, a new inn with each suite featuring a wet bar, refrigerator, color TV, sleeping loft, deck.

Melville House
39 Clarke St., 02840
401-847-0640
Rita & Sam Rogers
March 1—January 1

$ B&B
7 rooms, 5 pb
Visa, MC, AmEx
C-12+/S-yes/P-no/H-no

Continental plus
Comp. sherry
Sitting room
library
bicycles

1750 colonial inn, heart of historic district, close to shops, restaurants, wharfs. Off-street parking. Homemade granola, yogurt, and muffins for breakfast.

Merritt House Guests
57 2nd St., 02840
401-847-4289
Angela and Joseph Vars
All year

$$ B&B
2 rooms, 1 pb

Full breakfast
Snacks
Sitting room
private dining room
patio, glider in yard

Historic home in Point Section, two blocks from bay, 10 minutes from center of city, beaches & mansions. Nominated one of 100 Best B&B Homes in North America.

Mill Street Inn
75 Mill St., 02840
401-849-9500
J. Farrar, Ann Marie Puleo
All year

$$$ B&B
23 rooms, 23 pb
Visa, MC, AmEx, DC •
C-yes/S-yes/H-yes

Continental breakfast
Afternoon tea
Sun deck w/view
parking

Located in a 19th-century mill with panoramic view of Narragansett Bay. We combine affordable luxury with impeccable service.

Pilgrim House Inn
123 Spring St., 02840
401-751-8680
Maggie Pizzuti
All year

$ B&B
10 rooms, 8 pb
Visa, MC
C-no/S-yes/P-no/H-no

Continental breakfast
Deck
living room w/fireplace

Beautifully restored Victorian home in center of downtown historic district; magnificent rooftop deck with panoramic view of Newport Harbor.

Willows of Newport
8-10 Willow St., 02840
401-846-5486
Pattie Murphy
February—January 3

$$ B&B
5 rooms, 5 pb
C-no/S-ltd/P-no/H-no

Continental breakfast
Black tie brkfst in bed
Victorian parlor
wet bar
yard

Elegant breakfast in bed—cut flowers, mints on your pillow. Private parking and private bath, a/c. Featured nationally on 8/26/86 PM Magazine.

PROVIDENCE

Old Court Bed & Breakfast	$$$ B&B	Continental plus
144 Benefit St., 02906	10 rooms, 10 pb	Comp. tea
401-751-2002	Visa, MC, AmEx, Diners •	Sitting room, kitchen
Jon & Carol Rosenblatt	C-no/S-yes/P-no/H-no	antiques, washer/dryer
All year	French	apartment avail.

Historic Benefit Street mansion filled with antiques in a completely modernized environment. Views of the city.

WESTERLY

Shelter Harbor Inn	$$$ B&B	Full breakfast
10 Wagner Rd, Route 1, 02891	24 rooms, 24 pb	Lunch, dinner, bar
401-322-8883	Visa, MC, AmEx, DC •	Sitting room
Jim & Debbye Dey	C-yes/S-yes/P-no/H-no	library, hot tub
All year		paddle tennis

A charming country inn where the emphasis is on relaxation, superlative food, and a warm friendly atmosphere. Just a mile from the Rhode Island shore.

Woody Hill Bed & Breakfast	$$ B&B	Continental plus
RR #3 Box 676E, 02891	3 rooms, 1 pb	Extensive library
Woody Hill Rd.	C-yes/S-no/P-no/H-ltd	porch with swing
401-322-0452		sitting room
Dr. Ellen L. Madison		
All year		

Near beaches and Mystic Seaport, yet secluded country atmosphere. Handmade quilts, antiques, wide-board floors, gardens, casual Colonial feeling.

More Inns...

1661 Inn   Spring St., Block Island 02807   401-466-2421
Atlantic Inn   Box 188, Block Island 02807   401-466-2005
Barrington Inn   P.O. Box 397, Block Island 02807   401-466-5510
Blue Dory Inn, Ltd.   Box 488, Block Island 02807   401-466-2254
Driftwind Guests   High St., Block Island 02807   401-466-5548
Gables Inn   P.O. Box 516, Block Island 02807   401-466-2213
Guest House   P.O. Box 24, Center Road, Block Island 02807   401-466-2676
Island Manor Resort   Chapel St., Block Island 02807   401-466-5567
Mill Pond Cottages   Old Town Road, Block Island 02807   401-466-2423
New Shoreham House Inn   P.O. Box 356, Block Island 02807   401-466-2651
Old Town Inn   Old Town Road, P.O. Box 3, Block Island 02807   401-466-5958
Rose Farm Inn   Roselyn Road, Block Island 02807   401-466-2021
Sea Breeze Inn   Spring St., Box 141, Block Island 02807   401-466-2275
Seacrest Inn   207 High St., Block Island 02807   401-466-2882
Sheffield House   P.O. Box 836, Block Island 02807   401-466-2494
Willow Grove   P.O. Box 156, Block Island 02807   401-466-2896
Joseph Reynolds House   956 Hope St., Bristol 02809   401-254-0230
General Stanton Inn   Box 222, Rt. 1A, Old Post, Charlestown 02807   401-364-8888
King Tom Farm   P.O. Box 1440, Charlestown 02807   401-364-3371
Windswept Farm Inn   Rt. 1,Post Rd., Box 154, Charlestown 02807   401-364-6292
Mary W. Murphy   59 Walcott Avenue, Jamestown 02835   401-423-1338
Nordic Lodge   Pasquiset Pond Road, Kenyon 02836   401-783-4515
Ballyvoreen   78 Stone Church Road, Little Compton 02837   401-635-4396
Finnegan's Inn at Shadow L   120 Miantonomi Avenue, Middletown 02840   401-847-0902
Peckham's Guest Home   272 Paradise Av., Middletown 02840   401-846-2382

Andrea Hotel   89 Atlantic Avenue, Misquamicut 02891   401-348-8788
Ocean View   Atlantic Avenue, Misquamicut Beach 02891   401-596-7170
Chestnut House   11 Chestnut St., Narragansett 02882   401-789-5335
Duck Harbor   295 Boston Neck Road, Narragansett 02882   401-783-3495
Going My Way   75 Kingstown Road, Narragansett 02882   401-789-3479
Grinnell Inn   83 Narragansett Avenue, Narragansett 02882
Ilverthorpe Cottage   41 Robinson St., Narragansett 02882   401-789-2392
Kenyon Farms   P.O. Box 648, Narragansett 02882   401-783-7123
Mon Reve   41 Gibson Avenue, Narragansett 02882   401-783-2846
Murphy's B&B   43 South Pier Road, Narragansett 02882   401-789-1824
Narragansett Pier Inn   7 Prospect Ave., Narragansett 02882   401-783-8090
Phoenix House   29 Gibson Avenue, Narragansett 02882   401-783-1918
Southwest Wind Acres   8 Lindsley Road, Narragansett 02882   401-783-5860
Stone Lea   40 Newton Avenue, Narragansett 02882   401-783-9546
Summer House Inn   87 Narrangansett Ave., Narragansett 02882   401-783-0123
Aboard Commander's Quarter   54 Dixon St., Newport 02840   401-849-8393
Bellevue House   14 Catherine St., Newport 02840   401-847-1828
Blue Stone   33 Russell Avenue, Newport 02840   401-846-5408
Castle Keep   44 Everett, Newport 02840   401-846-0362
Cliff Walk Manor   82 Memorial Blvd, Newport 02840   401-847-1300
Covell Guest House   43 Farewell St., Newport 02840   401-847-8872
Guest House International   28 Weaver Ave., Newport 02840   401-847-1501
Inn at Castle Hill   Ocean Drive, Newport 02840   401-849-3800
Inn at Old Beach   19 Old Beach Rd., Newport 02840   401-849-8828
Inn of Jonathan Bowen on H   29 Pelham St., Newport 02840   401-846-3324
Inntowne   6 Mary Street, Newport 02840   401-846-9200
Jailhouse Inn   13 Marlborough St., Newport 02840   401-847-4638
La Forge cottage   96 Pelham St., Newport 02840   401-847-4400
Ma Gallagher's   348 Thames St., Newport 02840   401-849-3975
Ocean Cliff   Ocean Drive, Newport 02840   401-849-9000
Old Dennis House   59 Washington St., Newport 02840   401-846-1324
One Bliss   One Bliss Road, Newport 02840   401-846-5329
Queen Anne Inn   16 Clarke St., Newport 02840   401-846-5676
Sea Quest   9 Cliff Terrace, Newport 02840   401-846-0227
Spring Street Inn   353 Spring St., Newport 02840   401-847-4767
Thames Street Inn   400 Thames St., Newport 02840   401-847-4459
Wayside   Bellevue Ave., Newport 02840   401-847-0302
William Fludder House   30 Bellevue Ave., Newport 02840   401-849-4220
Sunset Cabins   1172 West Main Road, Portsmouth 02871   401-683-1874
Stone Bridge Inn   1 Lawton Ave., Tiverton 02878   401-624-6601
Larchwood Inn   176 Main St., Wakefield 02879   401-783-5454
Open Gate Motel   840 Quaker Lane, Warwick 02886   401-884-4490
Hartley's Guest House   Larkin Road, Watch Hill 02891
Inn at Watch Hill   Bay Street, Watch Hill 02891   401-596-0665
Watch Hill Inn   50 Bay Street, Watch Hill 02891   401-348-8912
Weekapaug Inn   Weekapaug 02891   401-322-0301
Cornerstone Inn   Rt. 1, Westerly 02891   401-322-3020
Inn on the Hill   29 Summer St., Westerly 02891   401-596-3791
J. Livingston's Guesthouse   39 Weekapang Road, Westerly 02891   401-322-0249
Sparrow's Nest   470 Annaquatucket Road, Wickford 02852   401-295-1142

South Carolina

Bay Street Inn
601 Bay St., 29902
803-524-7720
Gene/Kathleen Roe
All year

$$ B&B
6 rooms, 6 pb
Visa, MC •
C-yes/S-yes/P-no/H-no
French

Continental breakfast
Sherry, fruit, chocolate
Library
bicycles
air-conditioned

Antebellum cotton planter's home furnished with antiques; beautiful water views and fireplaces in every room; beaches, restaurants, golf and tennis nearby.

Old Point Inn
212 New St., 29902
803-524-3177
Charlie & Sandy Williams
All year

$$ B&B
3 rooms, 3 pb
Visa, MC, AmEx
C-yes/S-ltd

Continental plus
Sitting room
verandas

1898 Victorian with double verandas and hammock. Downtown historic residential district. River views. Delicious homemade breakfast breads. Relaxed, comfortable, friendly.

Rhett House Inn
1009 Craven St., 29902
803-524-9030
Marianne & Steve Harrison
All year

$$ B&B
5 rooms, 4 pb
Visa, MC, AmEx •
C-no/S-no/P-no/H-yes

Full breakfast
Comp. wine
Sitting room
central A/C

Restored, historic antebellum mansion. Courtyard with fountain. Walking distance to everything. Enjoy hammocks on a wide veranda.

Trescot Inn
500 Washington St., 29902
P.O. Box 2015
803-522-8552
All year

$$ B&B
5 rooms, 6 pb
Visa, MC, AmEx
C-12+/S-ltd/P-no/H-no

Continental plus
Comp. wine
Sitting room
bicycles

Old plantation home retains charm and hospitality of Old South while providing all modern conveniences.

Fripp House Inn
Bridge St., Box 857, 29910
803-757-2139
Dana Tuttle
All year

$ B&B
3 rooms, 3 pb
Visa, MC •
C-yes/S-ltd/P-no/H-no

Full breakfast
Snacks, set-up bar
Sitting room
bicycles, swimming pool
golf, beaches nearby

Historic landmark in a quiet village on the May River. Private gardens, fountains, fireplaces, antiques. Minutes from Hilton Head Island. Fine restaurants nearby.

CHARLESTON

1837 B&B & Tearoom
126 Wentworth St., 29401
803-723-7166
Sherri Weaver, Richard Dunn
All year

$ B&B
8 rooms, 7 pb
C-ltd/S-yes/P-no/H-no
French

Full gourmet breakfast
Afternoon tea
Comp. mint tea or coffee
Beer or wine avail. ($)
format dining room

Gracious southern home in historic Charleston. Breakfast in the formal dining room is festive; everyone visits & enjoys each other. Convenient to plantations and Fort Sumter.

Barksdale House Inn
27 George St., 29401
803-577-4800
Suzanne W. Chestnut
Closed Christmas day

$$$ B&B
10 rooms, 10 pb
Visa, MC •
C-ltd/S-yes/P-no/H-no

Continental breakfast
Comp. tea, wine
Sitting room
whirlpool baths
bicycle rental

Circa 1778, elegant inn with whirlpool baths, fireplaces, built-in dry bars, elaborate furnishings and antiques; adjacent to the historic shopping district.

Belvedere B&B
40 Rutledge Ave., 29407
803-722-0973
Jim Spell, Fran Oniffith
All year

$$$ B&B
3 rooms, 3 pb
C-12+/S-yes/P-no/H-no

Continental breakfast
Sherry
Sitting room, newspaper
TV, A/C, bicycles
porch with lake view

We offer hospitable accommodations in our gracious mansion overlooking beautiful Colonial Lake. We provide bicycles, sherry and other extras.

Cannonboro Inn
184 Ashley Ave., 29403
803-723-8572
James Hare, Robert Warley
All year

$$ B&B
6 rooms, 3 pb
•
C-yes/S-no/P-no/H-no
Italian

Full breakfast
Comp. wine
Sitting room
garden

Antebellum home in historic district. All rooms have fireplaces. Enjoy a full breakfast served on the columned piazza overlooking a low country garden.

Country Victorian B&B
105 Tradd St., 29401
803-577-0682
Diane Deardurff Weed
All year

$$ B&B
2 rooms, 2 pb
C-yes

Continental plus
Afternoon tea
Parking
TV, restaurants nearby

Private entrances, antique iron and brass beds, old quilts, antique oak and wicker furniture. Situated in a historic area. Walk to everywhere. Many extras.

Hayne House
30 King St., 29401
803-577-2633
Ben & Ann Chapman
All year

$$ B&B
3 rooms, 3 pb
C-ltd/S-ltd/P-no/H-no

Continental breakfast
Library

Fourth generation family home (1770/1840) in heart of residential historic district. Within walking distance of downtown. Furnished with antiques. Friendly hosts.

CHARLESTON ────────────────────────────────────

Indigo Inn
One Maiden Lane, 29401
803-577-5900/800-845-7639
Larry Deery
All year

$$$ B&B
40 rooms, 40 pb
Visa, MC, AmEx •
C-yes/S-yes/P-yes/H-yes

Continental plus
Comp. wine, aftn. tea
Bar service
Bicycles
hot tubs

Luxurious Old South charm furnished in 18th-century antiques and reproductions; famous Hunt breakfast. Close to open-air market, churches, mansions and restaurants.

John Rutledge House Inn
116 Broad St., 29401
803-723-7999/800-845-6119
Richard Widman
All year

$$$ B&B
19 rooms, 19 pb
Visa, MC, AmEx •
C-yes/S-ltd/P-no/H-yes

Continental plus
Comp. wine, bar service
Sitting room
hot tubs, concierge
turndown service

John Rutledge, one of the signers of the U.S. Constitution, built this elegant home in 1763. Now you can visit & relive history. Downtown location near shopping & historic sites.

Kings Courtyard Inn
198 King St., 29401
803-723-7000/800-845-6119
Laura Fox
All year

$$$ B&B
34 rooms, 34 pb
Visa, MC, AmEx •
C-yes/S-yes/P-no/H-yes

Continental plus
Comp. wine & sherry
Sitting room
bicycles, parking
hot tub, free parking

1853 historic inn, rooms with period furnishings, canopied beds, fireplaces, overlook two inner courtyards. Concierge service, evening turndown with brandy and chocolate.

Rutledge—Museum Inn
114 Rutledge Ave., 29401
803-722-7551
BJ, Jean, Jan & Mike
All year

$ EP/B&B
11 rooms
C-yes/S-ltd

Continental breakfast
Refrigerator
Porch, TV, parking
air-conditioning

Century-old Victorian house in Charleston's historic district. Rooms quaint, antique decor. Beautiful porch. Reasonable rates for historic district. Near all sightseeing.

Sword Gate Inn
111 Tradd St., 29401
803-723-8518
Walter & Amanda Barton
Except December 24—26

$$$ B&B
6 rooms, 6 pb
Visa, MC, AmEx
C-5+/S-yes/P-no/H-no

Full breakfast
Evening wine & cheese
Sitting room
piano
bicycles

Located in 18th-century home in the center of the historic district. Charleston's oldest inn. Generous Charleston breakfast of eggs, meat and pastries.

Villa de La Fontaine B&B
138 Wentworth St., 29401
803-577-7709
Aubrey Hancock, Bill Fontaine
All year

$$$ B&B
6 rooms, 6 pb
Visa, MC, AmEx •
C-9+

Full breakfast
Tennis courts nearby
garden, terraces
canopy beds

Southern colonial mansion, circa 1838, in historic district; half-acre garden; fountain and terraces. Furnished with 18th-century museum pieces. Walk to places of interest.

Hilltop Cottage B&B, Bolton Landing, NY

COLUMBIA

Claussen's Inn at 5 Points
2003 Greene St., 29205
803-765-0440/800-622-3382
Daniel Vance
All year

$$$ B&B
29 rooms, 29 pb
•
C-yes/S-yes/P-no/H-yes

Continental plus
Comp. wine & sherry
Morning paper
turndown service with
chocolate & brandy

Restored old bakery building close to the university, shops, dining, entertainment. Some rooms have kitchenettes.

GEORGETOWN

Shaw House
8 Cyprus Ct., 29440
803-546-9663
Mary Shaw
All year

$ B&B
3 rooms, 3 pb
•
C-yes/S-yes/P-no/H-ltd

Full breakfast
Comp. tea, wine
Sitting room
piano
bicycles

Spacious rooms furnished with antiques. Bird-watching from glassed-in den overlooking Willowbank Marsh. Walk to Historic District. Hostess loves pleasing her guests.

MCCLELLANVILLE

Laurel Hill Plantation
P.O. Box 182, 29458
8913 North Hwy 17
803-887-3708
Jackie & Lee Morrison
All year

$ B&B
4 rooms
C-6+/S-ltd/P-no/H-no

Full breakfast
Comp. wine, snacks
Sitting room
fishing boat trip
freshwater fish pond

Located with a view of salt marsh creeks and waterways, the 1850s house is furnished with country antiques.

MYRTLE BEACH

Serendipity, an Inn
407 71st Ave. N., 29577
803-449-5268
Cos & Ellen Ficarra
March—November

$$ B&B
15 rooms, 15 pb
Visa, MC, AmEx •
C-yes/S-ltd/P-no/H-no
Spanish, Italian

Continental plus
Sitting room
swimming pool
bicycles

Lovely Spanish mission style—winners of Myrtle Beach "Keep America Beautiful" Award. Two blocks to ocean. Squeaky clean.

PENDLETON ───────────────────────────────────

Liberty Hall Inn	$$ B&B	Continental plus
Business Hwy 28, 29670	10 rooms, 10 pb	Dinner, bar
803-646-7500	Visa, MC, AmEx, DC •	
Tom & Susan Jonas	C-ltd/S-ltd/P-no/H-no	
All year		

Lodge and dine in this classic 1840 Piedmont home, authentically restored, furnished in period antiques. In charming Pendleton National Historic District.

SPARTANBURG ─────────────────────────────────

Nicholls-Crook Plantation	$$ B&B	Full breakfast
P.O. Box 5812, 29304	3 rooms, 1 pb	Dinner by reservation
Plantation Dr.	•	Comp. sherry
803-583-7337	C-ltd/S-no/P-ltd/H-no	Sitting room, AC
Suzanne & Jim Brown	French, Spanish, German	fireplaces
All year		

Join us in our authentically restored, rare 18th-century plantation house, on National Register. Tranquil country setting, near I-26 and I-85.

More Inns...

Belmont Inn   106 E. Pickens St., Abbeville 29620   803-459-9625
Hair Residence   544 Magnolia Lane S.E., Aiken 29801
Holley Inn   235 Richland Ave.,W., Aiken 29801   803-648-4265
Pine Knoll Inn   305 Lancaster St. SW, Aiken 29801   803-649-5939
Willcox Inn   100 Colleton Ave., Aiken 29801   803-649-1377
Evergreen Inn   1109 South Main St., Anderson 29621   803-225-1109
Twelve Oaks Inn   P.O. Box 4126, Beaufort 29902   803-525-1371
Cedars Inn   1325 Williston Rd, POB 1, Beech Island 29841   803-827-0248
Fair Oaks   1308 Fair St., Camden 29020   803-432-1499
Inn on Broad   1308/10 Broad St., Camden 29020   803-425-1806
Ansonborough Inn   21 Hasell St., Charleston 29401   803-723-1655
Battery Carriage House   20 S. Battery, Charleston 29401   803-723-9881
Elliott House Inn   78 Queen St., Charleston 29401   803-723-1855
Holland's Guest House   15 New St., Charleston 29401   803-723-0090
Jasmine House   64 Hasell St., Charleston 29401   803-577-5900
Lodge Alley Inn   195 E. Bay St., Charleston 29401   800-845-1004
Maison DuPre   317 E. Bay St., Charleston 29401   803-723-8691
Palmer Home   87 Wentworth St., Charleston 29401   803-723-1574
Planters Inn   112 N. Market St., Charleston 29401   803-722-2345
Two Meeting Street Inn   2 Meeting St., Charleston 29401   803-723-7322
Vendue Inn   19 Vendue Range, Charleston 29401   803-577-7970
Spears B&B   501 Kershaw Street, Cheraw 29520   803-537-7733
Coosaw Plantation   Dale 29914   803-846-8225
John Lawton House   159 3rd St. E, Estill 29918   803-625-3240
1790 House   630 Highmarket St., Georgetown 29440   803-546-4821
Walton House   530 Prince St., Georgetown 29440   803-527-4330
Halcyon   Harbormaster 604, Hilton Head Island 29928   803-785-7912
Cox House Inn   P.O. Box 486, Johnston 29832   803-275-4552
Holly Hill   Rt. 1, Box 223, Landrum 29356   803-457-4010
Stella's Guest Home   P.O. Box 564, Little River 29566   803-249-1871
Annie's Inn   P. O. Box 311, Montmorenci 29839   803-649-6836
Guilds Inn   101 Pitt Street, Mount Pleasant 29464   803-881-0510
Webster's Manor   115 East James St., Mullins 29574   803-464-9632
Palmettos   P.O. Box 706, Sullivan's Island 29482   803-883-3389
Gadsden Manor Inn   Box 1710, Summerville 29484   803-875-1710

South Dakota

CANOVA ———————————————————

Skoglund Farm　$$ MAP　Full breakfast
Route 1, Box 45, 57321　6 rooms　Dinner included
605-247-3445　•　Sitting room, piano
Alden & Delores Skoglund　C-yes/S-ltd/P-yes/H-no　bicycles, horses
All year　Swedish

Return to your childhood, get away from it all at our farm—animals, horseback riding, country walking. Delicious home-cooked meals.

PHILIP ———————————————————

Thorson's Homestead　$ B&B　Full breakfast
HCR 2 Box 100, 57567　2 rooms　Comp. coffee
North Star Route　C-yes/S-ltd/P-yes/H-no
605-859-2120
Leonard & Phillis Thorson
All year

Close to the Badlands on historic Deadwood trail. Family-owned farm and ranch. Old-fashioned Western hospitality.

WEBSTER ———————————————————

Lakeside Farm B&B　$ B&B　Full breakfast
RR 2, Box 52, 57274　2 rooms　Other meals possible
605-486-4430　C-yes/S-no/P-no/H-no　Sitting room
Glenn & Joy Hagen　bicycles
All year　piano

A family-owned/operated dairy farm. Northeastern South Dakota lakes area. Fresh air. Open spaces. Fresh milk. Homemade cinnamon rolls.

YANKTON ———————————————————

Mulberry Inn　$ B&B　Full breakfast
512 Mulberry St., 57078　5 rooms, 1 pb　Comp. wine, snack
605-665-7116　Visa, MC　Afternoon tea
All year　C-yes/S-yes/P-ltd　Sitting room
　porch, parlors

Built in 1873. Beautiful hand-carved door, high ceilings and marble fireplaces. Very warm and homey with a quiet atmosphere.

More Inns...

State Game Lodge　Custer 57730　605-255-4541
Sylvan Lake Lodge　Box 752, Custer 57730　605-574-2561
Heart of the Hills B&B　517 Main St., Hill City 57745　605-574-2704
Fitch Farms　Box 8, Milesville 57553　605-544-3227
Roghair Herefords B&B　HCR 74 Box 16, Okaton 57562　605-669-2529

Tennessee

CHATTANOOGA

Alford House
2501 Lookout Mtn. Prkwy, 37419
Route 4
615-821-7625
Robert & Rhoda Alford
All year

$ B&B
3 rooms
•
C-yes

Full breakfast
Afternoon tea, snacks
Sitting room, gazebo
child care service
trails up Lake Mountain

Edge of national forest; minutes from attractions & downtown. Furnished in antiques (glass basket displayed). Coffee served at wakeup.

GATLINBURG

Buckhorn Inn
Route 3, Box 393, 37738
615-436-4668
John & Connie Burns
All year

$$ B&B
9 rooms, 9 pb
C-ltd/S-yes/P-no/H-no

Full breakfast
Dinner
Sitting room
piano

Quiet hilltop overlooking landscaped lawns and breathtaking views of highest peaks of the Smokies. Nearby golf course, Great Smoky Mountains National Park within 1 mile.

Mountainbrook Inn
Rt. 3, Hwy 321, Box 603, 37738
800-251-2811/800-451-0852
Joe Adair, Mary McCord
All year

$$ B&B
30 rooms, 30 pb
Visa, MC, AmEx •
C-yes/S-yes/P-yes/H-yes

Full country breakfast
Lunch & dinner by resv.
Restaurant, snacks
Golf/tennis/pool nearby
hot tubs, conf. fac.

Quiet country inn; breathtaking views; front porch rockers; hot tub; hiking trails. Full country breakfast, personal service and Southern hospitality.

Wind Hover
Route 4, Box 371, 37738
Campbell Lead
615-436-4068
Ruth M. Hunter
All year

$$ EP
5 rooms, 5 pb
•
C-yes/S-yes/P-no/H-no

Kitchens
Swimming pool
color TV
fireplaces

Secluded, private units with wood-burning fireplace, screened porch, kitchen, color TV, unsurpassed view of mountains and village. Swimming pool.

GREENVILLE

Big Spring Inn
315 N. Main St., 37743
615-638-2917
Jeanne Driese, Cheryl VanDyck
All year

$$ B&B
18 rooms, 4 pb
•
C-12+/S-yes

Full breakfast
Dinner by reservation
Snacks in room
sitting room
swimming pool

A unique, three-story turn-of-the-century home in a storybook town, nestled in the hills of East Tennessee.

HENDERSONVILLE

Monthaven
1154 W. Main St., 37075
615-824-6319
Hugh Waddell
All year

$ EP/B&B/$$$ MAP
4 rooms, 2 pb
Visa, MC, AmEx •
C-yes/S-no/P-yes/H-yes

Continental breakfast
Lunch, dinner
Afternoon tea, snacks
Bar, sitting room, bikes
tennis & pool nearby

On National Register; Monthaven offers both serene tranquillity of middle Tennessee & convenience; 15 mi. from downtown Nashville. True "Southern charm." Log cabin available.

HIGHLANDS

Phelp's House Inn
Rt. 1, Box 55, 28741
Main St.
704-526-2590
Carol C. Williams
All year

$ B&B
20 rooms, 20 pb
Visa, MC •
C-yes

Full breakfast
Dinner

100-year-old inn furnished with antiques and famous for its country cooking. Full breakfast included. Dinner served family style.

KNOXVILLE

Compton Manor
3747 Kingston Pike, 37919
615-523-1204
Brian & Hala Hunt
All year

$$ B&B
3 rooms, 1 pb
Visa, MC
C-no/S-no/P-no/H-no
Arabic

Continental plus
Afternoon tea
Sitting room, library
tennis, pool, Eng. darts
croquet, horseshoes

Elegant 1920s English Tudor near Utah. Antiques, Persian rugs, carved fireplace, leaded windows, solarium, paneled library and dining room with high tea on the terrace.

Graustein Inn
8300 Nubbin Ridge Rd., 37923
615-690-7007
Jim & Darlene Lara, V. Gwin
All year

$$ B&B/AP
5 rooms, 3 pb
Visa, MC •
C-13+/S-no/P-no/H-no
Spanish

Full breakfast
Lunch, dinner
Snacks
Sitting room
library, game room

Located on 20 wooded acres, the inn is furnished with 17th-and 18th-century antiques. Special areas include great room, library, breakfast porch and game room.

KODAK

Grandma's House
Route 1, Pollard Rd., 37764
615-933-3512
Hilda J. Hickman
All year

$$ B&B
3 rooms, 3 pb
C-15+/S-no/P-no/H-no

Full breakfast
Afternoon tea, snacks
Sitting room
bicycles
balcony

On a quiet country lane near Great Smoky Mountains. Hosts are both native East Tennesseans, always on premises. Hilda's special treats make up the Southern Farmstyle breakfast

MONTEAGLE

Edgeworth Inn
Box 340, Reppard Ave., 37356
in Monteagle Assembly
615-924-2669/615-924-2476
Merrily Teasley

$$ B&B
8 rooms, 8 pb
•
C-ltd/S-yes
French

Continental plus
Sitting room, library
Tennis courts, hiking
swimming pool (summer)
Chautauqua program (sum)

1896 historic mountaintop inn in southern Chautauqua. Rockers, rope hammocks and gingerbread porches; books, magazines and cheerful fire in the library.

MURFREESBORO

Clardy's Guest House
435 E. Main St., 37130
615-893-6030
Robert & Barbara Deaton
All year

$ B&B
4 rooms, 3 pb
•
C-yes/S-yes/P-no/H-no

Continental breakfast
Comp. beverages
Sitting room w/cable TV
porch

Built in 1898 during opulent and decorative times, the house is completely furnished with beautiful antiques. Murfreesboro is the south's antique center.

PIGEON FORGE

Hannah's House
Rt. 3, Middle Creek Rd., 37863
P.O. Box 674, Sevierville
615-428-2192
D. Alan Stott
All year

$$ B&B
3 rooms, 3 pb
Visa, MC •

Full breakfast
Picnic lunches
Sitting room
bicycles

Spend a day exploring the Smoky Mountains, then spend the night surrounded by Victorian furnishings, awakening to a southern breakfast.

ROGERSVILLE

Hale Springs Inn
110 W. Main, 37857
Town Square
615-272-5171
Ed Pace, Capt. & Carl Brown
All year

$ B&B
10 rooms, 10 pb
Visa, MC, AmEx
C-yes/S-yes/P-ltd/H-no

Continental breakfast
Restaurant
Sitting room
fireplaces, a/c

Restored 1824 brick. Fronts Village Green with other Antebellum buildings. Antiques, poster beds, working fireplaces, plush large rooms—near Gatlinburg.

RUGBY

Newbury House Inn
Hwy 52, P.O. Box 8, 37733
615-628-2430
Barbara Stagg
All year

$ B&B
8 rooms, 3 pb
Visa, MC
C-ltd/S-ltd/P-no/H-ltd

Full breakfast
Evening tea, restaurant
Victorian parlor
period library
games, fireplace

Unique 1880s Victorian village offers lodging in restored and antique-filled Newbury House and Pioneer Cottage, homestyle restaurant; near river gorges.

SEVIERVILLE

Kero Mountain Resort
Route 11, Box 380, 37862
615-453-7514
Grace Roblee, Lynn Brown
March—November

$ EP
6 rooms, 6 pb
C-yes/S-yes/P-yes/H-no

Brownies on arrival
Snacks
Lodge BYOB, jacuzzis
2 acre lake
bass fishing

Gatlinburg-Pigeon Forge area. 45 Acres of non-commercial mountain beauty. Fish or relax. Completely modern. In business 20 years. Brochure available.

Milk & Honey Country
P.O. Box 4972, 37864
Little Valley Rd.
615-428-4858
F. Miller, R. & L. Barnhart
All year

$$ B&B
6 rooms, 2 pb
Visa, MC
C-14+/S-no/P-no/H-no

Full breakfast
Afternoon tea, snacks
Sitting room
private sinks & vanities
whirlpool available

Heart of the Smokies, minutes from Gatlinburg/Pigeon Forge. Large porch with rockers. Cozy rooms of bygone era. Hearty country breakfast.

SEVIERVILLE ──────────────────────────────

Von-Bryan Inn	$$ B&B	Full breakfast
Rd. #4, Rt. 7, Box 91A, 37862	7 rooms, 5 pb	Lunch, dinner by request
Wears Valley	Visa, MC, AmEx •	Porches, decks, hot tubs
615-453-9832	C-ask/S-ltd/P-no/H-no	pool, garden room, views
D.J. & JoAnn Vaughn		hammocks, pool table
All year		

Lovely log home on a mountain top near the great Smoky Mountains, offering majestic views; private relaxed atmosphere; old-fashioned hospitality.

SWEETWATER ──────────────────────────────

Fox Trot Inn	$ B&B	Full breakfast
402 May St., 37874	4 rooms	Afternoon tea
615-337-4236	AmEx •	Sitting room, library
Lonnie & Merrill Jobe	C-6+/S-ltd/P-no/H-no	TV rm w/VCR & 100
		movies
All year exc. Thnks/XMas		terry robes for guests

Romantic getaway in 100-year-old Victorian house. Stained glass, fireplaces, ceiling fans, large front porch with rocking chairs. Convenient to Smoky Mountains.

More Inns...

Magnolia Manor B&B   418 N. Main St., Bolivar 38008   901-658-6700
Herbert's B&B   Box 2166, Brentwood 37027   615-373-9300
Hachland Hill Inn   1601 Madison St., Clarksville 37043   615-647-4084
Old Cowan Plantation B&B   Box 17, Rt. 2, Fayetteville 37334   615-433-0225
Barbara W. Humes B&B   1207 Holly Hill Drive, Franklin 37064
LeConte Lodge   P.O. Box 350, Gatlinburg 37738   615-436-4473
Jonesborough B&B   P.O. Box 722, Jonesborough 37659   615-753-9223
Mountain Breeze B&B   501 Mountain Breeze Ln., Knoxville 37922   615-966-3917
The Middleton   800 West Hill Avenue, Knoxville 37902   615-524-8100
Three Chimneys   1302 White Ave., Knoxville 37916   615-521-4970
River Road Inn   Rt.1, P.O. Box 372, Loudon 37774   615-458-4861
Lynchburg B&B   P.O. Box 34, Mechanic, Lynchburg 37352   615-759-7158
Lowenstein-Long House   1084 Poplar, Memphis 38105   901-527-7174
Parish Patch Farm & Inn   P.O. Box 27, Normandy 37360   615-857-3441
Homestead House Inn   P.O. Box 218, Pickwick Dam 38365   901-689-5500
Blue Mountain Mist Inn   P.O. Box 490, Sevierville 37862   615-428-2335
Cove Country Inn   Route 6, Box 197, Sevierville 37862   615-453-3997
Country Inn   Rt. 3, Chris Haven Dr., Seymour 37865   615-573-7170
Leawood-Williams Estate   P.O. Box 24, Shiloh 38376   901-689-5106
Flow Blue Inn   P.O. Box 495, Sweetwater 37874   615-442-2964
Tullahoma B&B   308 N. Atlantic St., Tullahoma 37388   615-455-8876
Nolan House Inn   P.O. Box 164, Waverly 37185   615-296-2511

342

Texas

AUSTIN

Brook House
609 W. 33rd St., 78705
512-459-0534
Sandy Hagler, Jim Bakken
All year

$$ B&B
4 rooms, 2 pb
Visa, MC •
C-yes/S-no/P-no/H-yes

Continental plus
Comp. wine
Sitting room
library
bicycles

1920s "petite" estates adjacent to University of Texas and capital. Beautifully decorated and landscaped. 2 private cottages and a friendly cat named Tony.

McCallum House
613 W. 32nd, 78705
512-451-6744
Roger & Nancy Danley
All year

$$ B&B
5 rooms, 5 pb
Visa, MC
C-8+/S-ltd/P-no/H-no

Full breakfast
Kitchen privileges
Private porches

Discover beautiful Austin from this historic, antique-filled late Victorian. We're ten blocks from Austin, 20 blocks from Capitol and downtown.

Southard-House
908 Blanco, 78703
512-474-4731
Jerry & Rejina Southard
All year

$ B&B
5 rooms, 5 pb
Visa, MC, AmEx •
C-ltd/S-yes/P-no/H-no

Continental plus (wkdys)
Full breakfast (wkends)
Comp. wine, sitting room
Player piano, library
garden, gazebo, porches

Elegant historic home. Clawfoot tub, cutwork linens. Dine by a roaring fire. Caring hosts in the grand Texas style. Downtown.

BACLIFF

Small Inn
4815 W. Bayshore Dr., 77518
713-339-3489
Harriet & George Small
All year

$$ B&B
1 rooms, 1 pb
•
C-yes/S-yes/P-yes/H-yes
Sign Language

Full breakfast
Lunch, dinner
Swimming pool, bicycles
sailing, deepsea charter
boat dock, fishing pier

Located on Galveston Bay halfway between Houston and Galveston. Owner is a caterer; gourmet breakfast served poolside. 12 minutes from NASA.

BIG SANDY

Annie's B&B Country Inn
P.O. Box 928, 75755
Hwy 155 N.
214-636-4355
Les & Martha Lane
All year

$ B&B
13 rooms, 8 pb
Visa, MC •
C-yes/S-no/P-no/H-yes

Full breakfast, Sun.-Fri.
Continental Sat.
Lunch, dinner
Sitting room, piano
library

Restored Victorian home with antiques and imported rugs; handmade quilts. Some rooms feature balconies overlooking beautiful flower and water gardens.

BOERNE ———————————————————————————

Borgman's Sunday House B&B $ B&B   Full breakfast
911 S. Main, 78006   12 rooms, 12 pb   Restaurant
512-249-9563   Visa, MC, AmEx, Disc •   Sitting room
Dale & Shannon Coryell   C-yes/S-ltd/P-no/H-ltd   private baths, A/C
All year   cable TV, telephone

On Main Street in a charming Texas hill country town. Antiques and vintage furnishings, craft shops, nature walks. 25 miles from San Antonio.

CANYON ———————————————————————————

Historical Hudspeth House $ B&B   Full gourmet breakfast
1905 4th Ave., 79015   8 rooms, 6 pb   Lunch & dinner (reserv.)
806-655-9800   Visa, MC •   Comp. wine, aftn. tea
Dave & Sally Haynie   C-yes/S-ltd   Sitting room
All year   health spa

Relaxing historical 1909 B&B featuring gourmet breakfasts, antiques and original stained glass. Close to musical drama "Texas," state park, Panhandle Plains Museum and WTSU.

CENTER ———————————————————————————

John C. Rogers House $ B&B   Full breakfast
416 Shebyville, 75935   5 rooms, 2 pb   Afternoon tea, snacks
409-598-3971   Visa, MC   Sitting room
All year   front porch
                                                        garden areas, sun porch

Late 1800 majestic home, 2 blocks from 103-year-old castle courthouse. Excellent biking, hiking and fishing with lush countryside.

Pine Colony Inn $ B&B   Full breakfast
500 Shelbyville St., 75935 12 rooms, 6 pb   Lunch & dinner
409-598-7700   Visa, MC •   Restaurant
R. Wright, M. Hughes   Sitting room
All year   fishing & hunting trips

Restored Old Country Hotel. Antiques throughout. Walk to many interesting shops and museums. Planned fishing, hunting and family excursions.

FREDERICKSBURG ———————————————————————————

Chemists Loft/Pape Danger $$$ B&B   Continental breakfast
242 W. Main St., 78624   3 rooms   Comp. wine for
512-997-8615   Visa, MC, AmEx   special occasions
Bill Varney   Gardens
All year

Both are Texas Historical Marker buildings made with native limestone and furnished with primitives. Charming, quiet gardens of herbs and natives. Walk to everything in town.

Country Cottage Inn $$ B&B   Continental breakfast
405 E. Main, 78624   5 rooms, 5 pb   Comp. wine
512-997-8549   Visa, MC •   Fireplaces
Jeffery Webb   C-yes/S-no/P-no/H-no   kitchens
All year   cable TV

Historic Texas stone home; built in 1850 by German pioneers; handcrafted woodwork, rafters, 24" walls; antique furnishings, king beds, jacuzzis; National Register.

FREDERICKSBURG ─────────────────────────

J Bar K Ranch B&B | $$ B&B | Full breakfast
HC-10, 53-A, 78624 | 2 rooms | Comp. wine
512-669-2471 | Visa, MC | Sitting room
Kermit & Naomi Kothe | C-10+ /S-yes/P-no/H-no | private kitchen
Mar.—Dec. | German | porch

Large historic German rock home on Texas hill country ranch; full country breakfast; 17 miles NW of Fredericksburg with German heritage and quaint shops.

HOUSTON ─────────────────────────

Durham House B&B | $$ B&B | Full breakfast
921 Heights Blvd., 77008 | 4 rooms, 3 pb | Comp. wine, snacks
713-868-4654 | Visa, MC • | Sitting room, gazebo
Marguerite Swanson | C-12+ | tandem bicycles
All year | German | weddings, receptions

Authentic Victorian on National Register of Historic Places. Antique furnishings; gazebo. Romantic getaway and wedding location. Very near downtown Houston.

Sara's Bed & Breakfast Inn | $ B&B | Continental plus
941 Heights Blvd., 77008 | 12 rooms, 3 pb | Sitting room
713-868-1130 | Visa, MC, AmEx, DC, CB • | hot tub, bicycles
Donna J. Arledge | C-ltd/S-ask/P-no/H-no
All year

Old-time hospitality in the heart of Houston. Twelve distinctive bedrooms are furnished with antiques. Only four miles from downtown Houston.

JEFFERSON ─────────────────────────

Austin Cottage | $$ B&B | Continental breakfast
P.O. Box 488, 75657 | 3 rooms, 3 pb | Snacks
406 Austin St. | Visa, MC, AmEx • | Full kitchen, sun room
214-938-5941/800-727-2204 | C-13+ /S-yes | Porch w/rockers
Tim & Cindy Edwards-Rinkle | | board games, A/C
All year

Lovingly restored 1923 batten board cottage decorated with a country flair & primitive antiques; enjoy homemade breakfast breads in the sun room or on the antique brick patio.

Hale House | $$ B&B | Full breakfast
702 S. Line St., 75657 | 7 rooms, 3 pb | Parlor
214-665-8877 | Visa, MC • | sun porch
L.D. & Joyce Barringer | C-yes/S-no/P-no/H-no | bicycles
All year

1890 Victorian home, overlooks park, historic churches. Charming guest rooms, antiques, large parlor & sunporch. Gourmet southern breakfast.

Pride House | $$$ B&B | Continental plus
409 Broadway, 75657 | 10 rooms, 10 pb | Sitting room
214-665-2675 | Visa, MC •
Ruthmary Jordan | C-ltd/S-yes/P-no/H-no
All year

Experience the charm of the Victorian era and the traditional legendary hospitality of the deep South in the oldest B&B in Texas.

MARBLE FALLS

La Casita Bed & Breakfast
1908 Redwood Dr., 78654
Granite Shoals
512-598-6443
Joanne & Roger Scarborough
All year exc. Christmas

$$ B&B
1 rooms, 1 pb
•
C-yes/S-ltd/P-no/H-yes

Full breakfast
Comp. wine on arrival
Refrigerator, sink
Library, bicycle
flowers, swimming

Private, hill country cottage west of Marble Falls, wildlife and wildflowers, near Lake LBJ, Vanishing Texas River Cruise and vineyards. Restaurant nearby.

MARSHALL

Ginocchio Hotel
707 N. Washington St., 75670
214-935-7635
Morris & Karon O'Tyson
All year

$$ B&B
8 rooms, 8 pb
Visa, MC •
C-9+/S-no/P-no/H-no

Full breakfast
All meals available
Bar, entertainment
Coffee & paper at door
Sitting room, library

Luxurious 1896 hotel, once called "the finest overnight hotel and eating establishment between New Orleans and Denver." Some of the rarest wood in the world. 1896 recaptured.

Three Oaks Bed & Breakfast
609 N. Washington Ave., 75670
214-938-6123
Bob & Sandra McCoy
All year

$$ B&B
1 rooms, 1 pb
C-9+/S-no/P-no/H-no

Full breakfast
7 room suite
Comp. wine
Evening dessert
Sitting room, bicycles

This 1895 Victorian with period antiques offers a full, elegant breakfast. The guest area includes piano and fireplace. Breakfast in bed.

NACOGDOCHES

Llano Grande Plantation
Route 4, Box 9400, 75961
409-569-1249
Ann & Charles Phillips
All year

$$ B&B
3 rooms, 3 pb
C-ask/S-yes/P-no/H-no

Full breakfast
Private kitchen
Sitting room
historic tours

Deep in the pine woods you will find the charming 1840s restored homestead of Tol Barret, who in 1866 drilled Texas' first producing oil well.

NEW BRAUNFELS

Prince Solms Inn
295 E. San Antonio, 78130
512-625-9169
Patrick A. Rousseau

$$ B&B
26 rooms, 26 pb
C-yes/S-yes/P-yes/H-no
Spanish

Full breakfast
Lunch, dinner, bar
Entertainment

Late 18th-century converted to motel in 1806, furnished with reproduction antique furnishings, turn-of-the-century; completely renovated and restored.

PORT ISABEL

Yacht Club Hotel
P.O. Box 4114, 78578
700 Yturria St.
512-943-1301
Ron & Lynn Speier
All year

$ EP
2 rooms, 1 pb
Major credit cards •
C-yes/S-yes/P-no/H-yes
Spanish

Continental breakfast
Dinner
Swimming pool

Quiet hideaway in the "shrimp capital of the world." Our restaurant specializes in local seafood. Just twenty minutes to Mexico.

RIO GRANDE

La Borde House
601 E. Main St., 78582
512-487-5101
Maria Sanchez
All year

$$ B&B
18 rooms, 18 pb
Visa, MC, AmEx •
C-yes/S-yes/P-no/H-yes
Spanish, French

Continental breakfast
Lunch, dinner, bar
Sitting room
entertainment

A faithful restoration dedicated to the proud past of all South Texas.

SAN ANTONIO

Bullis House Inn
P.O. Box 8059, 78208
621 Pierce St.
512-223-9426
Alma & Steve Cross
All year

$ B&B
7 rooms, 2 pb
Visa, MC, AmEx, Disc •
C-yes/S-yes/P-no/H-no
French, Spanish

Continental plus
Lunch, snacks, veranda
Guest kitchen, library
Swimming pool, Ping-Pong
king/queen/full beds

Historic white mansion minutes from Alamo, Riverwalk, downtown, with chandeliers, fireplaces, decorative 14-ft. ceilings, geometrically patterned floors of fine woods.

Falling Pines
300 W. French Place, 78212
512-733-1998
Grace & Bob Daubert
All year

$$ B&B
2 rooms, 2 pb
•
C-10+/S-no/P-no/H-no

Continental plus
Comp. wine
Sitting room, library
tennis courts
bicycles

Near downtown, riverwalk (5 minutes), three-story mansion in historic district with towering trees in parklike setting. Pristine restoration.

SAN MARCOS

Crystal River Inn
326 W. Hopkins, 78666
512-396-3739
Mike & Cathy Dillon
All year

$ B&B
8 rooms, 6 pb
Visa, MC •
C-8+/S-ltd/P-no/H-yes

Full breakfast (wkends)
Continental plus (wkdys)
Comp. desserts
Fireplaces, fountain
bicycles, piano

Romantic, luxurious Victorian capturing the matchless spirit of Texas' Hill Country. Fireplaces, fountain courtyards, fresh flowers, homemade biscuits.

TYLER

Rosevine Inn B&B
415 S. Vine, 75702
214-592-2221
Bert & Rebecca Powell
All year

$$ B&B
5 rooms, 5 pb
•
C-no/S-no/P-no/H-no
French

Full breakfast
Comp. wine
Sitting room, library
courtyard
hot tub & spa

Original bed and breakfast in the rose capital of the world. Pleasant accommodations with delicious breakfast. Friendly hosts make you feel at home.

WIMBERLEY

Old Oaks Ranch B&B
P.O. Box 912, 78676
County Rd. 221
512-847-9374
Bill & Susan Holt
All year

$$ B&B
2 rooms, 2 pb
Visa, MC •
C-no/S-no/P-no/H-no

Continental plus
Sitting room

Quiet, country inn furnished with antiques. Hiking. Cows, geese, deer. Hills and trees. Picturesque. Close to resort area. Golf & tennis available.

WIMBERLEY

Southwind Bed & Breakfast	$$ B&B	Full breakfast
Rt. 2, Box 15, 78676	2 rooms, 2 pb	Sitting room
512-847-5277	•	library
Herb & Carla Felsted	C-12+ /S-no/P-no/H-no	
All year	Spanish	

Rocking chairs on porch; 25 scenic hill country acres; hearty southwestern breakfasts; homemade bread and muffins. Convenient to Austin (40 min.) and San Antonio (1 + hour).

WINNSBORO

Thee Hubbell House	$$ B&B	Full breakfast
307 W. Elm, 75494	4 rooms, 4 pb	Afternoon tea, snacks
214-342-5629	Visa, MC •	Sitting room, library
Dan & Laurel Hubbell	C-yes	veranda, gallery
All year		piano, honeymoon pckages

1888 historic Georgian home, authentically restored and furnished in period antiques. Plantation or continental breakfast. Centrally located to other tourist areas.

More Inns...

Pfeiffer House   1802 Main Street, Bastrop 78602   512-321-2100
Pink Lady Inn   1307 Main Street, Bastrop 78602   512-321-6273
High Cotton Inn   214 S. Live Oak, Bellville 77419   409-865-9796
Knittel House   P.O. Box 261, Buchanan Dam 78639   512-793-6408
Landmark Inn   P.O. Box 577, Castroville 78009   512-538-2133
Browning Plantation   Rt. 1, Box 8, Chappell Hill 77426   409-836-6144
Gast Haus Lodge   Box 423, 952 High St., Comfort 78013   512-995-2304
Sand Dollar Hospitality   3605 Mendenhall, Corpus Christi 78415   512-853-1222
Reiffert-Mugge Inn   304 W. Prairie St., Cuero 77954   512-275-2626
Hill Top Cafe & Guesthouse   Fredericksburg Rt, Box 88, Doss 78618   512-997-8922
Farris 1912   201 N. McCarty, Eagle Lake 77434   409-234-2546
Red Rooster Square   Rt. 3, Box 3387, Edom 75756   214-852-6774
Gardner Hotel   311 E. Franklin Avenue, El Paso 79901   915-532-3661
Room with a View   821 Rim Rd., El Paso 79902   915-534-4400
New Canaan Farm   P.O. Box 1173-1, Elkhart 75839   214-764-2106
Country Place Hotel   P.O. Box 39, Fayetteville 78940   409-378-2712
Sutler's Limpia Hotel   P.O. Box 822, Fort Davis 79734   915-426-3237
Stockyards Hotel   Main & Exchange Sts., Fort Worth 76106   817-625-6427
Baron's Creek Inn   110 E. Creek St., Fredericksburg 78624   512-997-9398
Be My Guest   330 West Main, Fredericksburg 78624   512-997-7227
Gastehaus Schmidt   501 W. Main St., Fredericksburg 78624   512-997-5612
River View Farm   145 E. Main, Fredericksburg 78624   512-997-7227
Schmidt "Barn" B&B   Rt. 2, Box 112A3, Fredericksburg 98624   512-997-5612
Terrill's B&B   242 W. Main St., Apt. A, Fredericksburg 78624   512-997-8615
Victorian House   619 West Main, Fredericksburg 78624   512-997-4937
Dickens Loft   2021 Strand, Galveston 77550   409-762-1653
Gilded Thistle B&B   1805 Broadway, Galveston 77550   409-763-0194
Hazelwood House   1127 Church, Galveston 77550   713-762-1668
Key Largo   5400 Seawall Blvd., Galveston 77550   800-833-0120
La Quinta Inn   1402 Seawall Blvd., Galveston 77550   800-531-5900
Mather-Root Home   1816 Winnie, Galveston 77550   713-439-6253
Michael's-A B&B Inn   1715 35th St., Galveston 77550   409-763-3760
Tremont House   2300 Ship's Mechanic Rd, Galveston 77550   800-874-2300
Victorian Inn   511 17th St., Galveston 77550   409-762-3235
Matali B&B Inn   1727 Sealy, Galveston Island 77550   409-763-4526
Inn on the River   P.O. Box 1417, Glen Rose 76043   817-897-2101

White House Inn   P.O. Box 992, Goliad 77963   512-645-2701
Nutt House   Town Square, Granbury 76048   817-573-5612
Tarlton House   211 N. Pleasant St., Hillsboro 76645   817-582-7216
La Colombe d'Or   3410 Montrose Blvd., Houston 77226   713-524-7999
Woodlake House   2100 Tanglewilde, #371, Houston 77063
Excelsior House   211 W. Austin St., Jefferson 75657   214-665-2513
Gingerbread House   601 E. Jefferson, Jefferson 75657   214-665-8994
Magnolias Inn   209 E. Broadway, Jefferson 75657   214-665-2754
McKay House B&B Inn   306 E. Delta St., Jefferson 75657   214-665-7322
Stillwater Inn   203 E. Broadway, Jefferson 75657   214-665-8415
William Clark House   201 W. Henderson, Jefferson 75657   214-665-8880
Badu House   601 Bessemer, Llano 78643   915-247-4304
Harlyn House   508 Main St., Marble Falls 78654   512-693-7651
Cotten's Patch   703 E. Rusk, Marshall 75670   214-938-8756
Gregg-Plumb Home   1006 East Bowie, Marshall 75670   214-935-3366
La Maison Malfacon   700 East Rusk, Marshall 75670   214-935-6039
Meredith House   410 E. Meredith St., Marshall 75670   214-935-7147
Weisman-Hirsch-Beil Home   313 S. Washington, Marshall 75670   214-938-5504
Haden Edwards Inn   106 N. Lanana, Nacogdoches 75961   409-564-9999
Castle B&B   1403 E. Washington, Navasota 77868   409-825-8051
Comfort Common   240 South Seguin Avenue, New Braunfels 78130   512-995-3030
Gruene Mansion Inn   1275 Gruene Road, New Braunfels 78130   512-629-2641
Thomas J. Rusk Hotel   105 E. Sixth St., Rusk 75785   214-683-2556
Cardinal Cliff   3806 Highcliff, San Antonio 78218   512-655-2939
Mrs. Cauthorn's Inn   217 King William St., San Antonio 78204   512-227-5770
Aquarena Springs Inn   P.O. Box 2330, San Marcos 78666   512-396-8900
Lajitas on the Rio Grande   Box 400, Terlingua 79852   915-424-3471
Main House   3419 Main St., Texarkana 75503   214-793-5027
Big Thicket Guest House   Box 91, Village Mills 77663   409-834-2875
Weimar Country Inn   P.O. Box 782, Weimar 78962   409-725-8888
Rio Grande B&B   P.O. Box 16, Weslaco 78596   512-968-9646
Hygeia Health Retreat   439 Main St., Yorktown 78164   512-564-3670

Utah

CEDAR CITY

Meadeau View Lodge	$$ B&B	Full breakfast
P.O. Box 356, 84762	9 rooms, 9 pb	Dinner on request
Hwy 14-Duck Creek Village	Visa, MC	Snacks
801-682-2495	C-yes/S-ltd/P-no/H-yes	Sitting room
Vleria Torbenson		homelike atmosphere
All year		

Small, comfortable, scenic retreat in mountain setting (central to Zion and Bryce Parks). Fantastic scenery, hiking, fishing, boating, skiing, snowmobiling close by.

Paxman's Summer House	$$ B&B	Continental plus
170 N. 400W., 84720	4 rooms, 1 pb	Sitting room
801-586-3755	MC •	swimming pool
Karlene Paxman	C-yes/S-ltd/P-ltd/H-no	tennis courts
May—September		

Comfortable Victorian home, one block from Utah's Shakespearean Festival. Near Zion, Dixie and Bryce National Parks. Swimming, golf and tennis.

MIDWAY

The Homestead
P.O. Box 99, 84049
700 N. Homestead Dr.
801-654-1102/800-327-7220
Britt Mathwich
All year

$$ EP/$$$ B&B
97 rooms, 97 pb
Visa, MC, AmEx, Disc •
C-yes/S-ltd/P-no/H-yes
German, Spanish

Continental breakfast
Restaurant & bar
Sitting rm, water sports
tennis, skiing, golf
hot tubs, sauna, pool

Classic country inn located in gorgeous Heber Valley. Great country fare. Celebrated personal service. Charming accommodations. Tennis, golf, X-C skiing, fitness retreat.

MOAB

Sistelita B&B
Box 2105 CVSR, 84532
424 Amber Ln, Castle Vlly
801-259-6012/800-842-6622
Joe Makares
All year

$ B&B
4 rooms, 2 pb
•
C-ltd/S-yes/P-ltd/H-no

Continental breakfast
Full kitchen privileges
Comp. wine
Sauna, Roman jet bath
VCR, tour/trail planning

Secluded, scenic location close to Arches, Colorado River Canyon and Manti-La Sal Range. Artist's, naturalist's, as well as traveler's haven.

PARK CITY

Old Miners' Lodge B&B
P.O. Box 2639, 84060
615 Woodside Ave.
801-645-8068
Daniels, Sadowsky, Wynne
All year

$ B&B
10 rooms, 10 pb
Visa, MC, AmEx, Disc •
C-yes/S-ltd/P-no/H-no

Full country breakfast
Comp. wine
Organ, fireplace
sitting room, library
hot tub, games

An original miner's lodge—antique-filled rooms, feather beds, full breakfast, complimentary cocktails and fine hospitality; an unforgettable experience!

Snowed Inn
3770 N. Hwy 224, 84060
801-649-5713
Pat Glackin
All year

$$ B&B
10 rooms, 10 pb
Visa, MC, AmEx •
C-yes/S-ltd/P-no/H-yes

Continental plus
Lunch & dinner(seasonal)
Comp. sherry
Restaurant & bar
Sitting room, hot tub

All rooms have private bath, color TV, telephone, jacuzzi on back deck. We cater for business groups, retreats, wedding receptions.

Washington School Inn
P.O. Box 536, 84060
543 Park Ave.
800-824-1672/801-649-3800
Faye Slettom
All year

$$$ B&B
15 rooms, 15 pb
Visa, MC, AmEx •
C-12+/S-ltd/P-no/H-ltd

Full breakfast (winter)
Continental plus (summ.)
Comp. tea, wine
Sitting room, hot tub
sauna, steam showers

Original schoolhouse is now a unique country inn, antique furnishings, in the center of Park City. Many activities, including skiing.

SAINT GEORGE

Green Gate Village
76 W. Tabernacle, 84770
801-628-6999
Mark & Barbara Greene
All year

$ B&B
12 rooms, 9 pb
Visa, MC •
C-yes/S-no/P-yes/H-yes

Full breakfast
Lunch, Dinner
Afternoon tea, snacks
Sitting room, hot tubs
tennis courts, pool

Restored original pioneer home in a unique village close to downtown but in a quiet neighborhood. Close to Zion, Grand Canyon.

SAINT GEORGE

Seven Wives Inn	$ B&B	Full gourmet breakfast
217 N. 100 West, 84770	13 rooms, 13 pb	Comp. fruit
801-628-3737	Visa, MC •	Bicycles, hot tub
The Curtises and Bowcotts	C-ltd/S-no/P-ltd/H-ltd	sitting room, organ
All year		swimming pool

1870's pioneer home on National Register, furnished throughout in antiques, in heart of St. George—close to national parks.

SALT LAKE CITY

Brigham Street Inn	$$$ B&B	Continental breakfast
1135 E. South Temple, 84102	9 rooms, 9 pb	Comp. tea
801-364-4461	Visa, MC, AmEx •	Entertainment, piano
John & Nancy Pace	C-yes/S-yes/P-no/H-no	jacuzzi in 1 suite
All year		sitting room, library

National historic site, served as a designers' showcase in May 1982. Winner of several architectural awards. Near 7 major ski areas. Unique executive hotel.

National Historic B&B	$ B&B	Continental plus
936 E. 1700 South, 84105	5 rooms, 3 pb	Sitting room
801-485-3535	Visa, MC, AmEx •	bicycles
Lance & Sharon Davis	C-8+/S-ltd/P-no/H-no	entertainment room
All year		

San Francisco-style, 3-story Victorian inn offering fresh flowers, music and elegant breakfasts. Minutes from 7 ski resorts and downtown.

Spruces Bed & Breakfast	$$ B&B	Continental breakfast
6151 S. 900 East, 84121	4 rooms, 4 pb	Kitchens in 2 rooms
801-268-8762	•	Sitting room
Don & Lisa Fairbanks	C-yes/S-ltd/P-no/H-yes	
All year	Spanish	

Country setting among spruces with the amenities of the city close at hand. Nice accommodations, kitchens available for families or groups.

SANDY

Mountain Hollow B&B Inn	$$ B&B	Continental plus
P.O. Box 1841, 84092	9 rooms	Sitting rooms
10209 S. Dimple Dell Rd.	Visa, MC •	library
801-942-3428	C-14+/S-no/P-no/H-no	game room, hot tubs
Anne & Al Timpson		
All year		

Mountain hideaway, antiques, stream, peacocks, spa, recreation room, movies, room TVs, cathedral living room, relaxing atmosphere, close to downtown/skiing.

Quail Hills Guesthouse	$$ B&B	Continental plus
3744 E.N. Little Cttnwd, 84092	4 rooms, 2 pb	Sitting room
801-942-2858	•	bicycles
Jean Smith	C-12+	shuttle service
All year		

Small B&B located in Little Cottonwood Canyon; ten minutes from ski resorts. Summer affords swimming, hiking, enjoying canyon atmosphere.

SPRINGDALE ──────────────────────────

Zion House Bed & Breakfast $ B&B   Full breakfast
Box 323, 84767   3 rooms, 1 pb   Living room, dining room
801 Zion Park Blvd.   C-12+/S-no/P-no/H-no   rec room, library
801-772-3281
Lillie & Alan Baiardi
All year

Deluxe tri-level home surrounded by peaks of Zion National Park, within the "Golden Circle" of three National Parks and two National Monuments.

More Inns . . .

Bluff Bed & Breakfast   P.O. Box 158, Bluff 84512   801-672-2220
Recapture Lodge & Pioneer   Box 36, Bluff 84512   801-672-2281
Woodbury Guest House   237 S. 300 W., Cedar City 84720   801-586-6696
Birch Trees B&B   315 Boulevard, Logan 84321   801-753-1331
Center Street B&B Inn   169 E. Center St., Logan 84321   801-752-3443
Manti House Inn   401 North Main St, Manti 84642   801-835-0161
Canyon Country B&B   590 N. 500 West, Moab 84532   801-259-7882
Cedar Breaks Condos B&B   Center & 4th East, Moab 84532   801-259-7830
Peterson's Bed & Breakfast   P.O. Box 142, Monroe 84754   801-527-4830
Mansion House   298 South State St. #13, Mt. Pleasant 84647   801-462-3031
505 Woodside, B&B Place   P.O. Box 2446, Park City 84060   801-649-4841
Claimjumper Hotel   573 Main Street, Park City 84060   801-649-8051
Imperial Hotel   P.O. Box 1628, Park City 84060   801-649-1904
Star Hotel   227 Main Street, Park City 84060   801-649-8333
Chez Fontaine B&B   45 N. 300 E., Provo 84601   801-375-8484
Pullman B&B Inn   415 S. University Ave., Provo 84601   801-374-8141
Sundance   P.O. Box 837, Provo 84601   801-225-4100
Burr House B&B   190 W. Main St., Salina 84654   801-529-7320
Eller Bed & Breakfast   164 S. 900 E., Salt Lake City 84012   801-533-8184
Pinecrest B&B   6211 Emigration Canyon, Salt Lake City 84108   801-583-6663
Saltair B&B   164 South 900 East, Salt Lake City 84102   801-533-8184
Westminister B&B   1156 Blaine Avenue, Salt Lake City 84105   801-467-4114

Vermont

ARLINGTON ──────────────────────────

Arlington Inn $$ B&B   Continental plus
Historic Route 7A, 05250   13 rooms, 13 pb   Lunch (Summer & Fall)
802-375-6532   Visa, MC, AmEx •   Restaurant, bar service
Paul & Madeline Kruzel   C-yes/S-yes   Sitting room
All year   French   tennis courts

Antique-filled rooms in one of Vermont's finest Greek revival homes. Located in Norman Rockwell Country. Winner of 1988 Travel Holiday Dining Award & Taste of Vermont Award.

ARLINGTON

Hill Farm Inn
RR 2, Box 2015, 05250
Hill Farm Rd, Sunderland
802-375-2269
George & Joanne Hardy
All year

$$ B&B / $$$ MAP
13 rooms, 7 pb
Visa, MC, AmEx, Disc. •
C-yes/S-ltd/P-ltd/H-no

Full breakfast
Dinner, wine & beer
Comp. homemade jams
Sitting room, piano
fireplace, fruit baskets

1790 & 1830 farmhouses, an inn since 1905; pleasant mountain views, hearty home cooking, fish the Battenkill, hike country roads.

Shenandoah Farm
Box 3260 Route 313, 05250
802-375-6372
Diana & Woody Masterson
All year

$$ B&B
5 rooms, 3 pb
C-yes/S-yes/P-no/H-no

Full breakfast
Comp. wine, tea
Sitting room
piano, library

Beautifully restored 1820 colonial furnished with antiques, overlooking Battenkill River and rolling meadows. Near skiing, golf, tennis.

BENNINGTON

Four Chimneys Inn
21 West Rd., 05201
802-447-3500
Alex Koks
February 14—January 2

$$$ B&B
10 rooms, 10 pb
Visa, MC, AmEx, DC •
C-no/S-yes/P-ask/H-yes
French, German, Dutch

Continental plus
Restaurant, bar
Lunch, dinner
Sitting room, library
golf closeby

One of New England's premier inns. Classic French cuisine by master chef. Beautiful 11-acre estate, plush guest rooms with modern amenities and cocktail lounge.

Molly Stark Inn
1067 E. Main St., 05201
802-442-9631
Laurie & Reed Fendler
All year

$$ B&B
6 rooms, 6 pb
Visa, MC •
C-no/S-no/P-no/H-no

Full breakfast
Afternoon tea
Comp. wine
Color TV, bicycles
den with woodstove

Charming 1860 Victorian on Main Street, one mile from center. Decorated with country American, antiques, classical music playing. Gourmet breakfast served each morning.

BOLTON VALLEY

Black Bear Inn
Mountain Rd., 05477
802-434-2126/802-434-2920
Sue & Phil McKinnis
Dec.—April, May—Oct.

$$ EP
26 rooms, 26 pb
Visa, MC •
C-ltd/S-yes/P-no/H-no

Poolside breakfast $
Dinner, bar, Sun. brunch
Pool, entertainment
sitting room, piano
X-C & downhill skiing

Delightful mountaintop inn, many rooms with panoramic views. Hiking, tennis, golf, swimming and skiing. Indoor sport center available year-round.

BONDVILLE

Alpenrose Inn
P.O. Box 187, 05340
Winhall Hollow Rd.
802-297-2750
Bob & Rosemarie Strine
All year

$$$ B&B/MAP
9 rooms, 9 pb
Visa, MC
C-yes/S-ltd/P-no/H-no
German

Full breakfast
Guest refrig, MAP winter
Sitting room, piano
tennis, swimming
picnic area, pond

Located on quiet road, only minutes to slopes and Volvo tennis tournament. Cozy dining room and lounge with fireplace. Picnic area. Antiques.

BRANDON

Arches Country Inn
53 Park St., Route 73-E, 05733
802-247-8200
Jack & Ellen Scheffey
All year

$$ B&B
6 rooms, 6 pb
Visa, MC, AmEx •
C-yes

Full breakfast
Lunch & dinner
Restaurant, bar service
Sitting room
outdoor swimming pool

Stately colonial mansion within walking distance of downtown Brandon. Cross-country/down-hill skiing nearby. Hiking, cycling, golfing just minutes away.

Gazebo Inn
25 Grove St., Route 7, 05733
802-247-3235
Janet & Joel Mondlak
All year

$$ B&B
4 rooms, 4 pb
Visa, MC
C-yes/S-ltd
Spanish, Hebrew

Full breakfast
Dinner (limited)
Afternoon tea
Sitting rooms

Old World hospitality in a delightful 1860s home; perfectly located; surrounded by four-season activities. Lakes, golf, skiing, hiking, antiques.

Moffett House B&B
69 Park St., 05733
802-247-3843
Elliot & Nancy Phillips
All year

$$ B&B
6 rooms, 3 pb
C-yes/S-yes/P-ltd/H-no

Full breakfast
Comp. tea
Library, sitting room
tennis courts, bicycles
golf, skiing, gardens

Splendid Victorian bed & breakfast, perfect for a romantic getaway or family fun. Enjoy an elegant country breakfast and activities ranging from skiing to rocking.

BRIDGEWATER CORNERS

October Country Inn
Upper Rd., Box 66, 05035
802-672-3412
Richard Sims, Patrick Runkel
Dec.—mid-April/May—Nov.

$$ B&B, $$$ MAP
10 rooms, 7 pb
•
C-yes/S-no/P-no/H-ltd

Full breakfast
Dinner (MAP), wine
Sitting room
sun deck, pool

19th-century Vermont farmhouse. Meals include garden vegetables, freshly baked breads, desserts. Fireplace, antique wood stove, comfortable rooms, cozy living room.

BROOKFIELD

Green Trails Country Inn
Main St., 05036
802-276-3412
Pat/Peter Simpson
May 1—March 31

$$ B&B
15 rooms, 9 pb
•
C-yes/S-ltd/P-no/H-no
Swedish

Full breakfast
Dinner by res., tea
3 sitting rms., firepl.
swimming, canoeing
X-C skiing 34 km. trail

National Register of Historic Places. Located by the Floating Bridge. Decorated with quilts & antiques. Warm hospitality—like going home to Grandma's. Featured on Today show.

BURLINGTON

Howden Cottage B&B
32 N. Champlain St., 05401
802-864-7198
Bruce M. Howden
All year

$ B&B
2 rooms
Visa, MC
C-no/S-no/P-no/H-no

Continental breakfast
Sitting room
sinks in rooms

Howden Cottage offers cozy lodging and warm hospitality in the atmosphere of a private home. Owned and operated by a local artist, Bruce M. Howden. Reservations, please!

CHARLOTTE

Inn at Charlotte	$$ B&B	Full breakfast
RR1, Box 1188, 05445	5 rooms, 3 pb	Picnic lunch basket
State Park Rd.	Visa, MC •	Dinner on adv. request
802-425-2934	C-yes/S-no/P-no/H-no	Comp. wine, appetizers
Letty Ellinger	Philippine (Tagalog)	tennis courts, pool
All year		

Beautiful courtyard with flower gardens. Spacious rooms with country furniture. Breakfast served poolside. Picnic baskets and dinner available on request.

CHELSEA

Shire Inn	$$ B&B	Full breakfast
8 Main St., 05038	6 rooms, 6 pb	Dinner by reservation
802-685-3031	Visa, MC	Beer & wine
James & Mary Lee Papa	C-7+/S-no/P-no/H-no	Sitting room, fireplaces
All year		bicycles

Elegant country atmosphere; antique furnishings. Gracious candlelight dining. On White River with bridge to hiking trail. Cross-country skiing in winter.

CHESTER

Chester House	$$ B&B	Full breakfast
P.O. Box 708, 05143	4 rooms, 4 pb	Sitting room, library
Main St.	•	jacuzzi
802-875-2205	C-3+/S-yes	fireplaces in rooms
Irene & Norm Wright		
All year		

A southern Vermont B&B inn of extraordinary charm and hospitality. Beautifully restored, antique-furnished circa 1780 home in the National Register of Historic Places.

Greenleaf Inn	$$ B&B	Full breakfast
P.O. Box 188, 05143	4 rooms, 4 pb	Picnic box lunch $
Depot St.	C-7+/S-yes/P-no/H-no	Two large living rooms
802-875-3171		library
Dan & Elizabeth Duffield		bicycles nearby
All year		

Lovely 1880s village inn. Comfortable, large, airy rooms. Private baths. Big, puffy towels. Spotlessly clean. Beautifully furnished throughout. Two large living rooms.

Henry Farm Inn	$$ B&B	Full breakfast
P.O. Box 646, 05143	7 rooms, 7 pb	Afternoon tea
Green Mountain Trnpk	C-yes/S-ltd/P-no/H-ltd	Sitting room
802-875-2674		library
Jean Bowman		pond, hiking
All year		

1750s farmhouse in charming country setting in the glorious Green Mountains. Full country breakfast each morning. Extensive grounds available for your pleasure. Join us.

Hugging Bear Inn & Shoppe	$$ B&B	Full breakfast
Box 32, 05143	6 rooms, 6 pb	Afternoon tea
Main St.	Visa, MC	Sitting room
802-875-2412	C-yes/S-no/P-no/H-no	library
The Thomases	Russian	bicycles
All year		

Elegant Victorian in National Historic District, on the Village Green, thousands of Teddy Bears throughout, thousands in the shoppe. (3,609 at last count!) FUN!

Village Victorian Inn, Rhinebeck, NY

CHESTER

Inn at Long Last
Box 589, 05143
Main St.
802-875-2444
Jack Coleman
Exc. April

$$$ MAP
32 rooms, 28 pb
Visa, MC, AmEx •
C-yes/S-no/P-no/H-no

Full breakfast
Dinner, restaurant, bar
Sitting room, library
tennis courts, pool
planned drives

A Vermont inn where the guests are spoiled with warmth, whimsy and good food, but the village, one of New England's finest, is left unspoiled.

Rowell's Inn
RR1 Box 269 Simonsville, 05143
802-875-3658
Lee & Beth Davis
Exc. April

$$$ MAP
5 rooms, 5 pb
C-12+/S-yes/P-no/H-no

Full breakfast
Dinner included
Afternoon teas
Tavern
sitting room

1820 stagecoach hotel on National Register of Historic Places. Antique furnishings, hearty food. Rowell's Tavern offers Robert Haas wines and a variety of English beer.

Stone Hearth Inn
Route 11 W., 05143
802-875-2525
Janet & Don Strohmeyer
All year

$$ B&B
10 rooms, 8 pb
•
C-yes/S-ltd/P-ltd/H-ltd
Fr., Dutch, Flem., Ger.

Full breakfast
MAP only Sat. Fall/Wintr
Lunch, wine cellar, pub
Game room, library
pianos, whirlpool spas

Lovingly restored country inn built in 1810—beams, fireplaces, wide pine floors. Attached barn has game room, cozy pub. Family atmosphere.

CHITTENDEN

Mountain Top Inn
Mountain Top Rd., 05737
802-483-2311
Joan Hill
All year

$$$ MAP
33 rooms, 33 pb
Visa, MC, AmEx •
C-yes/S-yes/P-no/H-no
German

Full breakfast
Restaurant, bar
Lunch, dinner
Tennis, hot tub, sauna
pool, boating, skiing

This warm New England country inn steeped in the area's finest tradition, has been referred to as "Vermont's Best Kept Secret."

Tulip Tree Inn
Chittenden Dam Rd., 05737
802-483-6213
Ed & Rosemary McDowell
Exc. Apr. & Nov. to Thgvg

$$$ MAP
8 rooms, 8 pb
Visa, MC
C-ltd/S-ltd/P-no/H-no
German

Full breakfast
Dinner included, bar
Sitting room, library
some rooms w/jacuzzis
hot tub

Small, antique-filled country inn, hidden away in the Green Mountains. Gracious dining, home-made breads and desserts, liquor license, wine list. Newly redecorated.

CRAFTSBURY COMMON

Inn on the Common
Main St., 05827
802-586-9619/800-521-2233
Michael & Penny Schmitt
All year

$$$ B&B
18 rooms, 18 pb
Visa, MC
C-15+/S-yes/P-arr/H-no

Full breakfast
Dinner, bar
Swimming pool, sauna
tennis courts
library, sitting rooms

Superbly decorated, meticulously appointed, wonderful cuisine, complete recreation facilities. For the inn connoisseur, everything you could want.

CUTTINGSVILLE

Maple Crest Farm
Box 120, 05738
Lincoln Hill, Shrewsbury
802-492-3367
Donna & Bill Smith
All year

$ B&B
6 rooms, 3 pb
C-yes/S-yes/P-no/H-ltd

Full breakfast
Afternoon tea
Sitting room, piano
hiking, X-C skiing

Dairy farm located in beautiful mountain town of Shrewsbury. Lovingly preserved for five generations of Vermont tradition. Rutland area. Our 20th anniversary this year!

DANBY

Quail's Nest B&B Inn
P.O. Box 221, 05739
Main St.
802-293-5099
Chip & Anharad Edson
All year

$$ B&B
5 rooms, 3 pb
Visa, MC
C-ltd/S-yes/P-no/H-no

Full breakfast
Comp. tea
Sitting room w/fireplace
library, horseshoes
deck & garden, bicycles

Nestled among the Green Mountains in a quiet Vermont village; home-baked breakfasts followed by relaxing country fun!

Silas Griffith Inn
RR 1, Box 66F, 05739
S. Main St.
802-293-5567
Paul & Lois Dansereau
All year

$$ B&B
17 rooms, 11 pb
Visa, MC, AmEx •
C-yes/S-yes

Full breakfast
Restaurant, dinner
Aftn. tea, snacks, bar
Sitting room, library
swimming pool

Lovingly restored Victorian mansion and carriage house. Relax in antique-filled rooms; enjoy a quiet 19th-century village. Spectacular Green Mountain views.

DORSET

Barrows House
Rt. 30, 05251
802-867-4455
Tim & Sally Brown
All year

$$$ MAP
31 rooms, 29 pb
•
C-yes/S-yes/P-ltd/H-ltd
German

Full breakfast
Lunch, dinner, bar
Swimming pool, sauna
tennis courts, bicycles
sitting room, piano

Eight buildings on six parklike acres in picturesque Dorset, close to hiking, fishing, golf, horseback riding, shopping, X-C ski shop.

EAST BARNET

Inwood Manor
RD 1 Box 127, 05821
Lower Waterford Rd.
802-633-4047
R. Kaczor, P. Embarrato II
All year

$$ B&B
9 rooms
•
C-no/S-ltd/P-no/H-no
French, Spanish

Full breakfast
Dinner, wine & beer
Sitting room
library, piano
swimming/skating pond

Tastefully restored country inn, period antiques in all rooms. Small, intimate and personal. 20 private acres with waterfalls. Very private. Inn-to-inn canoeing.

EAST BURKE

Burke Green Guest House
RR 1, Box 81, 05832
802-467-3472
Beverly & Harland Lewin
All year

$ B&B
3 rooms, 1 pb
C-yes/S-yes/P-no/H-yes

Continental breakfast
Sitting room

Peaceful, comfortable home w/beautiful view of Burke Mt.; 1849 farmhouse on 25 acres. Relax by the fireplace or enjoy nearby skiing, hiking and lakes.

FAIR HAVEN

Maplewood Inn
RR 1, Box 4460, 05743
Route 22A S.
802-265-8039
Cindy & Paul Soder
All year

$$ B&B
5 rooms, 4 pb
Visa, MC •
C-6+/S-ltd

Full breakfast
Comp. wine, tea, cheese
BYOB tavern, chocolates
Sitting room, toiletries
library, TV room

Romantic, elegantly appointed rooms, suites and several common areas. In lakes region close to everything. We will pamper you!

FAIRLEE

Silver Maple Lodge & Cottages
RR 1, Box 8, 05045
S. Main St.
802-333-4326
Scott & Sharon Wright
All year

$ B&B
15 rooms, 7 pb
Visa, MC •
C-yes/S-yes/P-no/H-no

Continental breakfast
Sitting room, bicycles
lawn games
picnic area

Quaint country inn located in a scenic resort area; convenient to antique shops, fishing, golf, swimming, tennis and winter skiing.

GAYSVILLE

Cobble House Inn
P.O. Box 49, 05746
Childrens Camp Rd.
802-234-5458
Beau & Phil Benson
All year

$$$ B&B
6 rooms, 6 pb
Visa, MC •
C-5+/S-no/P-no/H-ltd

Full breakfast
Romantic restaurant
Afternoon hors d'oeuvres
2 sitting rooms, river
swimming, X-C skiing

Victorian mansion, 1864. Mountain views on the White River; country breakfasts; gourmet dinners; antique furnishings; private baths. Golf tours arranged.

GOSHEN

Blueberry Hill Inn	$$$ MAP	Full breakfast
RFD 3, 05733	8 rooms, 8 pb	Dinner, tea, wine
802-247-6735/800-448-0707	Visa, MC	Sitting room
Tony Clark	C-yes/S-ltd/P-no/H-yes	swimming pond
2/15—3/31; 6/1—10/31	French, Spanish	75 km X-C ski trails

1800 charming inn, gourmet cooking, dining by candlelight. Relax in an atmosphere of elegance and leisure. Fishing, swimming, hiking, X-C skiing.

GRAFTON

Inn at Woodchuck Hill Farm	$$ B&B	Continental plus
Middletown Rd., 05146	9 rooms, 7 pb	Dinner by reservation
802-843-2398	Visa, MC, AmEx	Comp. snacks, aftn. tea
Anne & Frank Gabriel	C-10+/S-yes/P-no/H-no	Sitting room, library
May thru October	French	swimming pond, trails

Lovely restored Colonial townhouse furnished with antiques. Spectacular view. Antique shop in barn. Auctions nearby. Hiking; walking trails on property.

Old Tavern at Grafton	$$ EP	Full breakfast
Main St., Box 009, 05146	Visa, MC, AmEx	Lunch & dinner avail.
802-843-2231	C-8+/S-ltd/P-ltd/H-yes	Bar, restaurant
Richard Ernst	French, Spanish, German	Library, bicycles
Exc. Dec. 24 & 25 & April		tennis, pool, game room

Village inn in tiny, picture-perfect Grafton. A virtual museum of antiquity with elegant yet comfortable rooms. Easy access to sports.

HYDE PARK

Fitch Hill Inn	$$ B&B	Full breakfast
RFD 1, Box 1879, 05655	4 rooms, 2 pb	Lunch & dinner on requ.
Fitch Hill	•	Sitting room
802-888-5941	C-ask/S-no/P-ltd/H-no	piano
Christa Wilkens	German	library
All year		

18th-century farmhouse close to Stowe and Northeast Kingdom, with extensive views of mountains, country antique decor, home cooking, informal atmosphere.

JAMAICA

Three Mountain Inn	$$$ MAP	Full breakfast
Box 180 BB, 05343	10 rooms, 8 pb	Dinner, bar
802-874-4140	C-yes/S-yes/P-no/H-no	Sitting room
Charles & Elaine Murray		bicycles
Exc. 4/15—5/15 & Nov.		swimming pool

Small romantic 1780 Colonial Inn. Charming rooms and fine food, X-C skiing & hiking in State Park; swimming pool; near 3 downhill ski areas.

JEFFERSONVILLE

Smuggler's Notch Inn	$$ B&B	Full breakfast
Church St., Box 280, 05464	11 rooms, 11 pb	Dinner, bar service
802-644-2412	Visa, MC •	Sitting room, bicycles
Virginia & Jeff Morgan	C-yes/S-yes/P-yes/H-no	tennis courts, pool
All year	French, Spanish	hot tub in guest room

Over 100 years of service to the Smugglers' Notch area. Maple floors, tin ceilings, screened porch, village setting. Enjoy our relaxing atmosphere.

JERICHO

Homeplace Bed & Breakfast
RR 2, Box 367, 05465
802-899-4694
Mariot G. Huessy
All year

$$ B&B
4 rooms, 1 pb
•
C-yes/S-no/P-no/H-no
German

Full breakfast
Aftn. tea, comp. wine
Sitting room, library
Perenial gardens, trails
tennis courts nearby

A quiet spot in a 100-acre wood, 1½ miles from Jericho. Our farm animals welcome you to their sprawling home, full of European antiques, Vermont craftwork and charm.

KILLINGTON

Inn at Long Trail
P.O. Box 267, 05751
Route 4, Sherburne Pass
802-775-7181
Kyran & Rosemary McGrath
Summer, Fall, Winter

$$ B&B Summer
20 rooms, 20 pb
Visa, MC •
C-yes/S-yes/P-no/H-ltd

Full breakfast
All meals, Irish pub
Sitting room
hot tub
weekend entertainment

Historic 1938 ski lodge, wood-paneled, candlelit dining, fieldstone fireplaces, adjacent to famous Appalachian and Long Trails for summer hiking.

Mountain Meadows Lodge
RR 1 Box 4080, 05751
Thundering Brook Rd.
802-775-1010
The Stevens Family
Exc. 4/15-6/1; 10/15-11/21

$$ B&B/MAP
18 rooms, 15 pb
Visa, MC •
C-yes/S-yes/P-ltd/H-ltd

Full breakfast
Dinner
Swimming pool
sitting room
mountain getaway pkges

A casual, friendly family lodge in a beautiful secluded mountain and lake setting. Complete cross-country ski center. Converted 1856 farmhouse and barn.

Vermont Inn
Route 4, Cream Hill Rd., 05751
802-775-0708/800-541-7795
Susan & Judd Levy
Mem. Day—10/25; 11/21—4/15

$$ MAP
16 rooms, 12 pb
Visa, MC, AmEx •
C-ltd/S-ltd/P-no/H-ltd
French, Spanish

Full breakfast (winter)
Continental plus (summ.)
Dinner included, bar
Library, piano, pool
tennis, sauna, whirlpool

Award-winning cuisine; fireside dining (winter), spectacular mountain views, secluded romantic stream. Minutes to Killington and Pico ski areas.

LINCOLN

Long Run Inn
RD 1 Box 560, Bristol, 05443
Lincoln Gap Rd.
802-453-3233
Michael & Beverly Conway
Mid-May—Oct./late Dec.—Mar.

$$ B&B/MAP
8 rooms
C-yes/S-ltd/P-no/H-no

Full breakfast
Dinner
Sitting room
old pump harmonium
swimming hole

Quiet location in center of quaint mountain village of Lincoln near Long Trail. Close to Sugarbush ski area, Middlebury College and Lake Champlain.

LONDONDERRY

Blue Gentian Lodge
Box 129 RR #1, 05148
Magic Mountain Rd.
802-824-5908
Richard Kidde
All year

$$ EP
14 rooms, 14 pb
•
C-yes/S-yes/P-ltd/H-no

Full breakfast $
Dinner
Sitting room
swimming pool

Mountain vista from secluded pool over pine-fringed pond. In the winter walk to ski lifts of Magic Mountain. Fine homemade meals, lounge with fireplace, game rooms.

LOWER WATERFORD

Rabbit Hill Inn	$$$ MAP	Full breakfast
Route 18, 05848	18 rooms, 18 pb	Restaurant, bar, dinner
802-748-5168	Visa, MC •	Aftn. tea, sitting room
Maureen & John Magee	C-no/S-no/P-no/H-no	Lawn games, canoeing
All year exc. April, Nov.	French	swimming pond, trails

Stylish country inn established 1795. Peaceful, storybook 15-acre setting. Heart-felt service and commitment to detail, dining, decor and music. Internationally acclaimed.

LUDLOW

Andrie Rose Inn	$$$ B&B	Full breakfast buffet
13 Pleasant St., 05149	8 rooms, 8 pb	Restaurant, lunch/dinner
802-228-4846	Visa, MC	Comp. hors d'oeuvres
Rick & Carolyn Bentzinger	C-no/S-no/P-no/H-no	Bar serivce, library
All year		hot tubs, bicycles

Elegant c. 1829 inn nestled in picturesque village. Fireside cocktails, complimentary hors d'oeuvres, whirlpool tubs. Minutes from skiing, lakes, shopping and restaurants.

Black River Inn	$$$ B&B/MAP	Full breakfast
100 Main St., 05149	10 rooms, 8 pb	5-course dinner
802-228-5585	Visa, MC, AmEx •	Full beverage service
Marilyn & Tom Nunan	C-no/S-ltd/P-no/H-no	Sitting room
Exc. April		

For couples only; specialized in romance & honeymoons. Antique furnished; candlelit; down comforters; breakfast in bed, brandy at bedside. 5 min. to downhill & X-C skiing.

Combes Family Inn	$$ B&B/MAP	Full breakfast
RFD 1 Box 275, 05149	12 rooms, 8 pb	Dinner
802-228-8799	Visa, MC, AmEx •	Sitting room, piano
Ruth & Bill Combes	C-yes/S-ltd/P-ltd/H-yes	bicycles
Except 4/15—5/15	French	

The Combes Family Inn is a century-old farmhouse located on a quiet country back road.

Governor's Inn	$$$ MAP	Full 5-course breakfast
86 Main St., 05149	8 rooms, 8 pb	6-course dinner, rest.
802-228-8830	Visa, MC, AmEx •	Afternoon tea, picnics
Charlie & Deedy Marble	C-no/S-ltd/P-no/H-no	Fireside hors d'oevres
All year exc. April		library, sitting room

A stylish, romantic, Victorian inn (circa 1890). Furnished with family antiques. Beautiful fireplaces. Warm, generous hospitality in a quiet VT town. OUR 1987 INN OF THE YEAR!

Okemo Inn	$$$ B&B/MAP	Full country breakfast
RFD #1, Box 133, 05149	12 rooms, 10 pb	Dinner (res.)
Rt. 103 & Rt. 100 N.	Visa, MC, AmEx, •	Fireside cocktail lounge
802-228-8834	C-6+/S-yes/P-no/H-no	Piano, swimming pool
Ron & Toni Parry		sauna, touring bikes
All year		

Fine food and lodging—lovely 1810 country inn where antiques set the mood. Convenient to all-season sports and activities. Biking and walking tours arranged.

LYNDONVILLE

Wildflower Inn
Darling Hill Rd., 05851
802-626-8310
Jim & Mary O'Reilly
All year

$$ B&B
16 rooms, 12 pb
Visa, MC
C-yes/S-ltd/P-no/H-ltd
Nepali

Full breakfast
Afternoon tea & snacks
Library, small conf. fac
pool, hot tub, sauna
trout pond, X-C skiing

Delightful family inn on 500-acre farm with working dairy operations. Homemade breads and snacks. Warm hospitality. Horse-drawn sleigh rides. Near Burke Mountain skiing.

MANCHESTER

1811 House
Box 39, Historic Rt. 7A, 05254
802-362-1811
P. & J. David, M. & J. Hirst
All year

$$$ B&B
14 rooms, 14 pb
Visa, MC, AmEx •
C-no/S-ltd/P-no/H-no

Full breakfast
Bar service
Sitting room, library
canopy beds
fireplaces

Unequaled charm in a Revolutionary War-era building furnished with English & American antiques. Walk to golf, tennis, swimming; near sailing, hiking, skiing.

Birch Hill Inn
P.O. Box 346, 05254
West Rd.
802-362-2761
Jim & Pat Lee
Exc. Nov.-Xmas, Apr.-late May

$$$ B&B
6 rooms, 6 pb
Visa, MC
C-6+/S-ltd/P-no/H-no

Full breakfast
Dinner, tea, wine
Swimming pool
sitting room, piano
trout pond

Small country inn, more than 15 kilometers of private cross-country ski trails through the woods; panoramic views, country cuisine; swimming pool; large fireplace.

Inn at Manchester
Box 41, Route 7A, 05254
802-362-1793
Harriet Rosenberg
All year

$$ B&B
21 rooms, 13 pb
Visa, MC, AmEx •
C-8+/S-ltd/P-no/H-no

Full breakfast
Comp. wine/beer (Sat.)
Sitting room, library
piano, swimming pool
3 lounge areas

Beautiful Victorian mansion restored by owners. Furnished with antiques. Delicious breakfasts. Golf, tennis, shopping, antiquing nearby. Country elegance.

Manchester Highlands Inn
P.O. Box 1754 B, 05255
Highland Ave.
802-362-4565
Robert & Patricia Eichorn
Exc. midweek in Apr. & Nov.

$$$ B&B
14 rooms, 10 pb
Visa, MC, AmEx •
C-8+/S-yes/P-no/H-no

Full breakfast
Tea, wine
Sitting room, piano
swimming pool

Romantic Victorian inn with 15 charming rooms. Homemade country breakfast in bed. Biking, hiking, golf, tennis, skiing, antiquing.

Village Country Inn
P.O. Box 408, 05254
Historic Route 7A
802-362-1792
Anne & Jay Degen
All year

$$$ MAP
30 rooms, 30 pb
Visa, MC •
C-ltd/S-yes/P-no/H-ltd

Full breakfast
Candlelight dinner
Tavern, sitting room
piano, swimming pool
tennis courts

In Vermont's Green Mountains on Route 7A. Comfortable and luxurious rooms, antiques, fireplaces. Convenient for summer and winter sports. 100 years old in 1989!

MANCHESTER CENTER

Brook-n-Hearth Inn	$ B&B	Full breakfast
Box 508 (SR 11 & 30), 05255	3 rooms, 3 pb	Gas BBQ grill
802-362-3604	AmEx	Sitting room, VCR
Larry & Terry Greene	C-yes/S-ltd/P-no/H-no	player piano
Exc. early Nov. & early May		library, swimming pool

Cozy early American decor, close to everything. Wooded pastoral setting, lawn games, walking or X-C skiing trails by brook.

MENDON

Red Clover Inn	$$$ MAP	Full breakfast
Woodward Rd., 05701	15 rooms, 11 pb	Dinner included, bar
802-775-2290	Visa, MC, AmEx, DC, CB •	Swimming pool
Ed & Judy Rup	C-12+/S-ltd/P-no/H-ltd	sitting room, piano
All year		

Beautiful country inn nestled in a hidden mountain valley. Wonderful breakfasts and dinners served in warm, friendly, gracious atmosphere. Named best restaurant in Killington.

MIDDLEBURY

Brookside Meadows	$$ B&B	Full breakfast
RD 3, Box 2460, 05753	5 rooms, 4 pb	Sitting room, piano
Painter Rd.	•	2 bedroom suite w/bath,
802-388-6429	C-5+/S-ltd/P-ltd/H-ltd	private entr., wdstove
Linda & Roger Cole		
All year		

Comfortable, gracious home in rural area, only 2½ miles from town and Middlebury College. Near Shelburne Museum. Hiking, X-C skiing on property.

Swift House Inn	$$ B&B	Full breakfast
25 Stewart Ln., Rt. 7, 05753	14 rooms, 14 pb	Restaurant, bar service
802-388-9925	Visa, MC, AmEx, D	Sitting room, library
Andrea & John Nelson	C-yes/S-yes/P-no/H-no	formal gardens
All year		whirlpool tubs in 3 rms

Warm and gracious lodging and dining in an elegant 1815 federalist estate furnished with antiques. Four of the bedrooms have working fireplaces.

NORTH HERO

North Hero House	$$ EP	Full breakfast $
P.O. Box 106, Route 2, 05474	32 rooms, 21 pb	Restaurant
Champlain Islands	C-yes/S-yes/P-no/H-yes	Lounge, sitting room
802-372-8237	Spanish, French	tennis, lake swimming
Apgar & Sherlock Families		bicycles, sauna
June 15—October 31		

Lake Champlain island inn (1890). Magnificent view of Mt. Mansfield and Green Mountains. Crystal-clear water for marvelous swimming, boating and fishing.

NORWICH

Norwich Inn	$$$ EP	Full breakfast & dinner
P.O. Box 908, 05055	22 rooms, 21 pb	Restaurant, bar service
Main St.	Visa, MC, AmEx •	Sitting room
802-649-1143	C-yes/S-yes/H-yes	library
Bob & Tammy Savidge		near Dartmouth College
All year		

Small town inn with country charm, personalized service and gourmet dining. Myriad cultural and recreational activities. Come relax. . .enjoy.

ORWELL

Historic Brookside Farms
Route 22A, 05760
802-948-2727
Joan & Murray Korda
All year

$$$ B&B
6 rooms, 2 pb
•
C-yes/S-yes/P-no/H-yes
Fr., Sp., Ger., Ital.

Full country breakfast
Lunch, dinner
Sitting room, library
music room
X-C skiing, skating

Enjoy country elegance in our National Register Greek revival mansion, set on 300 acres and furnished in period antiques. Antique shop on premises.

PERU

Johnny Seesaw's
P.O. Box 68, 05152
Route 11
802-824-5533
Gary & Nancy Okun
Exc. 4/1—5/30

$$ B&B/MAP
30 rooms, 27 pb
Visa, MC
C-yes/S-yes/P-yes/H-ltd

Full breakfast
Dinner (MAP winter)
Afternoon tea, full bar
Tennis, swimming pool
library, sitting room

Unique country lodge, rooms with private baths, cottages with king beds and fireplaces, licensed pub, full dining room, quarter-mile east of Bromley Mountain.

PITTSFIELD

Inn at Pittsfield
P.O. Box 526, 05762
Route 100
802-746-8943
Barbara Morris, Vikki Budasi
Exc. Nov., May

$$ MAP
10 rooms, 6 pb
Visa, MC •
C-yes/S-yes/P-no/H-no

Full breakfast
Dinner included, bar
Sitting room
piano
bicycles

Hideaway for the outdoor activities enthusiasts who do not want to compromise on the luxuries of fine food and accommodations. Bicycling and hiking tours.

POULTNEY

Lake St. Catherine Inn
P.O. Box 129, 05764
Cones Point Rd.
802-287-9347
Patricia & Raymond Endlich
May—October

$$ MAP
35 rooms, 35 pb
•
C-yes/S-yes/P-no/H-yes

Full breakfast
5-course dinner, bar
Piano, bicycles
free use of sailboats,
paddleboats & canoes

Rural country inn located among tall pines on the shores of Lake St. Catherine. Swimming, boating, fishing, and country dining.

Stonebridge Inn
Route 30, 05764
802-287-9849
Gail R. Turner
All year

$$ B&B
5 rooms, 2 pb
Visa, MC •
C-10+/S-ltd/P-no/H-no

Continental plus
Snacks
Tap room w/pool table
library w/40" TV
formal living room

A three-course European breakfast prepared by myself and served in the inn's dining room. Foyer and exquisitely designed stairway leading to the guest rooms on the 2nd floor.

PROCTORSVILLE

Golden Stage Inn
P.O. Box 218, 05153
Depot St.
802-226-7744
Kirsten Murphy, Marcel Perret
Exc. April & November

$$$ MAP
10 rooms, 6 pb
Visa, MC
C-yes/S-yes/P-no/H-no
Swiss, German, French

Full breakfast
Candlelight dinner, bar
Hors d'oeuvres by fire
Sitting room, pool
fabulous flower gardens

Country inn on 4 acres, Swiss specialities, sumptuous deserts, own baking, vegetable garden, colorful flowers, library, hiking, biking, skiing nearby.

Bechtel Mansion Inn, East Berlin, PA

PUTNEY

Hickory Ridge House
RFD 3, Box 1410, 05346
Hickory Ridge Rd.
802-387-5709
J. Walker, S. Anderson
All year

$ B&B
7 rooms, 3 pb
Visa, MC
C-yes/S-no/P-no/H-yes
French, German, Russian

Full breakfast
Dinner
Sitting room
piano
swimming hole

Gracious 1808 brick Federal with six fireplaces, rolling meadows, woods to explore on foot or skis. Our own breads, eggs, jams and honey for breakfast.

QUECHEE

**Quechee Inn-Marshland
Farm**
P.O. Box BB, 05059
Clubhouse Rd.
802-295-3133
Michael Maderia
All year

$$$ MAP
24 rooms, 24 pb
Visa, MC, AmEx •
C-yes/S-yes/P-no/H-ltd

Full breakfast
Dinner included, bar
Wine list, sitting room
Club membership (sauna,
swimming, tennis)

The beautifully restored 18th-century farmstead of Vermont's first lieutenant governor; nearby private Quechee Club for golf, tennis, swimming, boating, etc.

ROCHESTER

Liberty Hill Farm
Liberty Hill Rd., 05767
802-767-3926
Bob & Beth Kennett
All year

$$ MAP
5 rooms
•
C-yes/S-yes/P-no/H-no

Full breakfast
Dinner included
Sitting room
bicycles, babysitting
cribs, highchairs

Family dairy farm in Green Mtns. bounded by National Forest and White River. Hiking, X-C skiing from house. Major ski areas nearby. Farm breakfasts.

ROYALTON

Fox Stand Inn
RR 1, Box 108F, Rt. 14, 05068
802-763-8437
Jean & Gary Curley
All year

$ B&B
6 rooms
Visa, MC
C-yes/S-yes/P-no/H-no

Full breakfast
Lunch, dinner
Licensed restaurant
River swimming

Restored 1818 handsome brick building, family-owned and operated inn. Economical rates include full breakfast. Fishing, golf, X-C skiing nearby.

SAINT JOHNSBURY

Echo Ledge Farm Inn
Box 77, E. St Johnsbury, 05838
Route 2
802-748-4750
Rosina & Larry Greenwood
May—October

$ EP
6 rooms, 4 pb
Visa, MC
C-yes/S-yes/P-no/H-no
Spanish, German

Comp. tea, coffee, cookies
Sitting room
color TV

Come spend the night in the real Vermont at a farm settled in 1793. Recommended by National Geographic Traveler. Freshly papered or stenciled walls, hardwood floors.

SHREWSBURY

Buckmaster Inn B&B
RR #1, Box 118, 05738
Lincoln Hill Rd.
802-492-3485
Sam & Grace Husselman
All year

$ B&B
3 rooms, 1 pb
C-4+/S-ltd/P-no/H-ltd
Dutch

Full breakfast
Comp. tea
Sitting room, fireplace
porches, library
organ, bicycles

1801 historic stagecoach stop with spacious rooms, charm of family heirlooms in Green Mountains. Hike, bike, X-C ski from door. Nature paradise, relaxing atmosphere.

SOUTH WALLINGFORD

Green Mountain Tea Room
RR 1 Box 400, Route 7, 05773
802-446-2611
Candy & Ed Pino
All year

$$ B&B
6 rooms
C-yes/S-yes/P-yes/H-no

Full breakfast
Sunday brunch
Luncheon, tea
Sitting room, piano
6 ski areas nearby

Rural charm in an old stagecoach stop built in 1792. Canoe, fish, swim! Near 6 major ski areas. Gourmet dinner available.

SOUTH WOODSTOCK

Kedron Valley Inn
Route 106, 05071
802-457-1473
Max & Merrily Comins
All year

$$$ B&B/MAP
29 rooms, 29 pb
Visa, MC, DC •
C-yes/S-yes/P-yes/H-yes
French, Spanish

Full country breakfast
Dinner, bar
Sitting room, swim pond
piano, Franklin stoves
heirloom quilt display

Distinguished country inn built in 1822 in gentle valley. Full riding stables, hiking, X-C skiing. Nouvelle cuisine with local Vermont products. Canopy beds, fireplaces.

STOWE

1860 House
P.O. Box 276, 05672
School St.
800-248-1860
R. Hubbard, R. Matulionis
All year

$$$ B&B
5 rooms, 5 pb
Visa, MC •
C-yes/S-no/P-no/H-no
German

Full uncooked breakfast
Afternoon tea
Sitting room, piano
decks, terraces
sauna, jacuzzi, pool

Charming historic village inn. Decks & terraces overlooking flower gardens. Sauna, hot tub, steam room & outdoor pool nearby. Close to skiing, tennis, golf. National Register.

STOWE ————————————————————————————————————

Andersen Lodge—Austrian
RR 1, Box 1450, 05672
802-253-7336
Dietmar & Gertrude Heiss

$ EP/B&B/$$ MAP
17 rooms, 16 pb
credit cards accepted •
C-yes/S-yes/P-ltd/H-no
German, French

Full breakfast
Dinner
Sitting room, piano
game room, tennis court
heated pool, golf nearby

Set in relaxing surroundings with lovely view of mountains. Trout fishing, horseback riding, mountain hiking. Owners and hosts of Austrian background. Austrian chef.

Butternut Inn at Stowe
Mountain Rd., 05672
RD1, Box 950
802-253-4277
Jim & Deborah Wimberly
6/15—10/20, 12/18—4/20

$$ B&B, $$$ MAP
18 rooms, 18 pb
Visa, MC •
C-12+/S-no/P-no/H-no

Full country breakfast
Dinner (winter)
Afternoon tea
Sitting room, piano
swimming pool, courtyard

Landscaped grounds, mountain views, by mountain stream. Hospitality is a family tradition. Country wallpaper. Poolside breakfast and fireside dining. Couples retreat.

Edson Hill Manor
RR 1, Box 2480, 05672
802-253-7371
Anita & Larry Heath Jr.
All year

$$ MAP/EP summer
27 rooms, 22 pb
Visa, MC, AmEx •
C-yes/S-yes/P-no/H-no

Full breakfst ex. summer
Dinner/Lunch ex. summer
Swimming pool
sitting room
horseback riding all year

Country estate on 400 secluded acres. Cross-country skiing; gorgeous swimming pool, outdoor games, barbeques, horseback riding, hiking in summer. Sleigh rides.

Gables Inn
RR #1 Box 570, 05672
Mountain Rd.
802-253-7730
Lynn/Sol Baumrind
All year

$$ EP/$$$ MAP wt
16 rooms, 16 pb
•
C-yes/S-yes/P-ltd/H-no

Full breakfast
Winter MAP, Summer EP
Sitting room, piano
swimming pool
hot tub

Classic country inn—antiques, wide plank floors, panoramic view. Outstanding breakfast on lawn or porch (summer). Near golf, hiking, skiing.

Golden Kitz Lodge
RD 1 Box 2980, 05672
Rt. 108, Mountain Rd.
802-253-4217
Margie MacElwee Jones
All year

$ EP
16 rooms, 8 pb
Visa, MC, AmEx, CB
C-yes/S-ltd/P-ltd/H-ltd

Full breakfast $
Apres-ski wine/cheese
Sitting room, porch
piano, art studio
bicycles, riverside path

Share legendary Old World antique family treasures in cozy caring comfort. International 1747 Room. Yummy & chummy breakfasts unkink frazzled nerves.

Inn at the Brass Lantern
RR 2, Box 2610, 05672
Route 100 North
802-253-2229
Mindy & Andy Aldrich
All year

$$ B&B
9 rooms, 9 pb
Visa, MC, AmEx •
C-yes/S-ltd/P-no/H-no

Full bareakfast
Picnic lunches
Afternoon tea, snacks
Sitting room with piano
library, fireplaces, A/C

1800s farmhouse and carriage barn with antiques, handmade quilts, stenciled halls, patio and views. 1989 Award winning restoration by innkeepers. Apres-ski in winter.

STOWE ──

Logwood Inn & Chalets
Box 2290, Route 1, 05672
Edson Hill Rd.
800-426-6697/802-253-7354
Len & Ruth Shetler
All year

$$ B&B/MAP
23 rooms, 18 pb
Visa, MC, AmEx •
C-yes/S-yes/P-ltd/H-ltd

Full Vermont breakfast
MAP (winter)
Swimming pool, library
tennis court, game room
sitting room, piano, A/C

A warm welcome, tree-filled quiet oasis by mountain stream in scenic Stowe, Main lodge, balconies, apartment, 2 chalets. Home cooking with Pennsylvania Dutch accent.

Raspberry Patch
RR 2, Box 1915, 05672
Randolph Rd.
802-253-4145
Linda V. Jones
All year

$$ B&B
4 rooms, 3 pb
Visa, MC •
C-yes/S-ltd/P-ltd

Full breakfast
Aftn. tea, comp. wine
Snacks, BYOB bar
Bicycles, sun deck
croquet, badminton

Friendly hospitality, a peaceful mountain view. Immaculate, cozy rooms with antiques and down comforters await you at the Raspberry Patch.

The Siebeness
RR1 Box 1490, 05672
Mountain Rd.
802-253-8942/800-426-9001
Sue & Nils Andersen
All year

$$ B&B
10 rooms, 10 pb
Visa, MC, AmEx, DC, Dis •
C-yes/S-yes/P-no/H-no

Full breakfast
Dinner winter
Lounge, hot tub
bicycles, pool
X-C skiing

Charming country inn, newly renovated with antiques and quilts. Outstanding food served with mountain view. X-C skiing from door, near golf, tennis, skiing, recreation path.

Ten Acres Lodge
RR 3, Box 3220, 05672
Luce Hill Rd.
802-253-7638/800-327-7357
Dave & Libby Helprin
All year, excl. dining rm

$$ B&B
12 rooms, 9 pb
Visa, MC, AmEx, DC •
C-yes/S-ltd/P-ltd/H-no

Continental plus
Comp. aft. refreshments
Dinner, bar
Tennis court, sitting rm
swimming pool, hot tub

Stowe's favorite country inn and restaurant for over forty years. Close to ski trails, hiking, golf in New England ski capital. Hill house and cottages available.

Timberholm Inn
Cottage Club Rd., 05672
RR 1 Box 810
802-253-7603
Susan & Wes Jenson
All year

$$ B&B
10 rooms, 10 pb
Visa, MC •
C-yes/S-ltd/P-no/H-no

Full breakfast
Comp. wine, tea
Aftn. soups/refreshments
Sitting room
library

Country inn tucked in the woods. Beautiful mountain setting. Close to ski slopes, town of Stowe, shopping, activities. Rooms are tastefully decorated with antiques and quilts.

Ye Olde England Inne
Mountain Rd., Box 320, 05672
802-253-7558/802-253-7064
Christopher & Linda Francis
All year

$$ B&B
23 rooms, 23 pb
Visa, MC •
C-yes/S-yes/P-ltd/H-no
French, Arabic

Full breakfast, aftn tea
Dinner, valet parking
Library, piano, pool
pub, murder mystery wknd
polo & gliding packages

In Stowe Village, charming rooms Laura Ashley-style. Mr. Pickwick's Pub famous for food, atmosphere, ales, wines and entertainment amidst beams, brass, copper and stone.

SUNDERLAND

Inn at Sunderland	$$ B&B	Full breakfast
RR2 Box 2440, Arlington, 05250	10 rooms, 8 pb	Cider, hors d'oeuvres
Historic Route 7A	Visa, MC, AmEx	Sitting room, bicycles
802-362-4213	C-ltd/S-ltd/P-no/H-yes	wagon & sleigh rides
Tom & Peggy Wall		country club privileges
All year exc. April		

Country elegance in a B&B inn; beautifully restored Victorian farmhouse with antiques and fireplaces, double-decker porch with Green Mountains view. Your 4-season hideaway.

VERGENNES

Strong House Inn	$$ B&B	Full country breakfast
RD1, Box 1003, 05491	6 rooms, 2 pb	Dinner by reservation
82 W. Main St	Visa, MC, AmEx •	Catering available
802-877-3337	C-yes/S-ltd/P-ltd/H-ltd	Sitting room w/fireplace
Michelle & Ron Bring		piano
Exc. Nov., mid-Mar.—mid-Apr.		

Comfortably elegant lodging in a tastefully decorated historic home. Wonderful breakfasts. Convenient to Middlebury, Burlington, Lake Champlain. Superb cycling.

WAITSFIELD

Inn at Round Barn Farm	$$$ B&B	Full breakfast
The East Warren Rd., 05673	6 rooms, 6 pb	Afternoon tea, snacks
RR Box 247	Visa, MC, AmEx •	Sitting room, library
802-496-2276	C-no/S-no/P-no/H-no	bicycles, jacuzzi in rms
Jack, Doreen, Annemarie Simko	Hungarian	swimming pool
All year		

Sugarbush's most noted landmark; elegant inn; 85 acres for quiet walks, gourmet picnics, Bach, Mozart, and simple pleasures of unspoiled Vermont.

Lareau Farm Country Inn	$$ B&B	Full breakfast
Box 563, Route 100, 05673	10 rooms, 6 pb	Apres-ski hors d'oeuvres
802-496-4949	Visa, MC •	Dinner
Dan & Susan Easley	C-ltd/S-ltd/P-no/H-no	Sitting room
All year		

Nestled in a picturesque meadow beside the Mad River, our 150-year-old farmhouse is minutes from skiing and shopping.

Mad River Barn	$$ B&B	Full breakfast
P.O. Box 88, Route 17, 05673	15 rooms, 15 pb	Dinner (Dec.-Apr.), bar
802-496-3310	Visa, MC, AmEx •	Sitting room
Betsy Pratt	C-yes/S-yes/P-no/H-ltd	steam bath
All year		use of resort pool

Classic Vermont country lodge. Spacious rooms with private baths. Grand stone fireplace. Excellent hiking on our trails. One mile from ski area.

Millbrook Inn	$$ B&B$$$ MAP	Full breakfast from menu
RFD Box 62, 05673	7 rooms, 4 pb	Full dinner from rest.
802-496-2405	Visa, MC •	Sitting rooms (2)
Joan & Thom Gorman	C-ltd/S-ltd/P-no/H-ltd	piano
All year exc. May		

Charming hand-stenciled guest rooms with handmade quilts, country gourmet dining in our small candlelit restaurant, friendly, unhurried atmosphere.

WAITSFIELD

Tucker Hill Lodge
RD 1, Box 147 (Rt. 17), 05673
802-496-3983/800-451-4580
Chip & Meg Chapell
All year

$$ B&B
22 rooms, 16 pb
Visa, MC, AmEx, others •
C-yes/S-yes/P-no/H-no

Full breakfast
Dinner, bar service
Restaurant (exc. April,
May, Nov), sitting room
tennis courts, pool

Cozy country inn with award-winning New American/French restaurant. In Sugarbush/Mad River Valley, near skiing, hiking, biking, canoeing and golf.

Valley Inn
Route 100, RR 1, Box 8, 05673
802-496-3450
The Stinson Family
All year

$ B&B/MAP
20 rooms, 20 pb
Visa, MC, AmEx •
C-yes/S-yes/P-no/H-ltd
French

Full breakfast
Dinner included (MAP)
Sitting room, sauna
group-tour packages
soaring packages

An Austrian-style inn near Sugarbush and Mad River Ski Areas. Winter sports paradise, outstanding summer antiquing, golf and gliding.

Waitsfield Inn
Route 100, P.O. Box 969, 05673
802-496-3979
The Knapp Family
All year except May

$$ MAP
14 rooms, 14 pb
Visa, MC •
C-10+/S-ltd/P-no/H-no

Breakfast & dinner
Restaurant
Bar service
Sitting room
tennis & pool nearby

Gracious lodging and dining in an elegant 1825 parsonage in Vermont's beautiful Green Mountains. Skiing, summer activities, spectacular fall foliage.

WALLINGFORD

White Rocks Inn
RR1, Box 297, 05773
802-446-2077
June & Alfred Matthews
All year

$$ B&B
5 rooms, 5 pb
Visa, MC •
C-10+/S-no/P-no/H-no
some French, Spanish

Full breakfast
Aftn. tea, comp. wine
Sitting room
canoe rental

Ca. 1840 restored farmhouse with antiques, canopy beds. Listed in National Register of Historic Places. Close to 4 major ski areas.

WARREN

Beaver Pond Farm Inn
RD Box 306, 05674
Golf Course Rd.
802-583-2861
Betty & Bob Hansen
All year except May

$$ B&B
5 rooms, 3 pb
Visa, MC, AmEx •
C-yes/S-yes/P-no/H-no
French

Full breakfast
Comp. wine, tea
Sitting room
library
weddings

Beautifully restored Vermont farmhouse adjacent to golf course. Hiking, swimming and skiing nearby. Spectacular views from spacious deck; hearty breakfasts.

Sugartree—A Country Inn
RR Box 38, 05674
Sugarbush Valley
802-583-3211
Howard & Janice Chapman
All year

$$$ B&B
10 rooms, 10 pb
Visa, MC, AmEx •
C-5+/S-yes/P-no/H-yes

Full country breakfast
Living room w/fireplace
All rooms have brass,
antiques, or canopy beds

Beautifully decorated with unique country flair and antiques. Enchanting gazebo amid flower gardens. Breathtaking views of ski slopes or fall foliage.

WATERBURY

Grunberg Haus
RR 2, Box 1595, 05675
Duxbury
802-244-7726
Christopher Sellers
All year

$ B&B
10 rooms
Visa, MC, AmEx
C-6+/S-no/P-no/H-no

Full breakfast
Dinner by reservation
Self-serve pub
Bedtime liquor/chocolate
tennis court, sauna

Hand-built Tyrolian chalet secluded on 10 acres in the Green Mountains. Hiking trails, gardens, decks. Spontaneous personal attention. Near all the adventure Vermont offers.

Inn at Blush Hill
RR 1, Box 1266, 05676
Blush Hill Rd.
802-244-7529
Pamela & Gary Gosselin
All year

$$ B&B
6 rooms, 2 pb
•
C-yes/S-ltd/P-no/H-ltd

Full breakfast
Aftn. tea, sitting room
Library, fireplaces
piano, lawn games
electric mattress pads

Cozy, country, 1790s brick farmhouse, located across from 9-hole golf course, fifteen minutes to Sugarbush, Bolton, Stowe. Fireplaces, antiques. Swimming and boating nearby.

Inn at Thatcher Brook Flls
RD 2 Box 62, 05676
Route 100, (N. of I-89)
802-244-5911
Peter Varty & Kelly Fenton
All year

$$$ MAP
12 rooms, 12 pb
Visa, MC, AmEx •
C-5+/S-ltd/P-no/H-yes
French

Full breakfast
Dinner included, Pub
Restaurant, snacks
Private dining rooms
library, bicycles

Beautifully restored 1899 country Victorian mansion. Centrally located between renowned resorts of Stowe and Sugarbush. Exquisite lodging and superb gourmet dining!

WEST DOVER

Snow Den Inn
Route 100 Box 625, 05356
802-464-9355/802-464-5852
Andrew & Majorie Trautwein
June—April

$$$ B&B
8 rooms, 8 pb
Visa, MC, AmEx •
C-yes/S-yes/P-no/H-no

Full breakfast
Sitting room
fireplaces
color cable TV

Lovely country inn filled with antiques—fireplaces in five rooms. Close to golfing, swimming, tennis, skiing, hiking, antiquing, skating, boating.

Weathervane Lodge
HCR 63, Box 57, 05356
Dorr Fitch Rd.
802-464-5426
Liz & Ernie Chabot
All year

$$ B&B
11 rooms, 5 pb
C-yes/S-yes/P-no/H-no
French

Full breakfast
BYOB bar, lounge
Sitting room
piano
fireplaces

Mountainous country inn: Colonial antiques, lounge, recreation rooms with fireplaces. Ski, X-C, tennis, golf, swimming; bring children. Dinner winter, Sat. and holiday wks.

West Dover Inn
Box 506, Route 100, 05356
802-464-5207
Don & Madeline Mitchell
closed April—June

$$ B&B
10 rooms, 10 pb
Visa, MC, AmEx •
C-8+/S-yes/P-no/H-no

Full breakfast
Dinner plan (exc. Wed.)
Bar, lounge, library
2 suites w/fireplace
bicycles, organ

Historic inn. Handsomely appointed guest rooms with cozy quilts, antiques. Fine country dining. Golf, skiing, swimming, antiquing nearby. Register of Historic Places.

WEST RUTLAND

Silver Fox Inn	$$$ EP/B&B/MAP	Breakfast
RFD 1, Box 1222, 05777	7 rooms, 7 pb	Dinner, bar service
Rt. 133, Clarendon Ave.	Visa, MC •	Comp. hors d'oeuvres
802-438-5555	C-12+/S-ltd/P-no/H-no	Sitting room, library
Pam & Gerry Bliss		bicycles, tennis nearby
May—March		

Country elegance in a 1768 farmhouse. Mountain views galore. Hiking, fishing, biking, cross-country skiing, golf nearby. 20 minutes to Killington-Pico.

WEST TOWNSHEND

Windham Hill Inn	$$$ MAP	Full breakfast
RR 1, Box 44, 05359	15 rooms, 15 pb	Dinner included, bar
Off Rt. 30	Visa, MC	3 sitting rooms
802-874-4080	C-12+/S-yes/P-no/H-ltd	library, swimming pond
Ken & Linda Busteed		hiking, ski trails
Exc. Apr. & Nov. (open Thgv)		

Carefully restored 1825 farmhouse and barn offering warm, distinctive guest & public rooms, elegant dining, secluded hilltop setting, spectacular view. 1988 Best Inn—Innsider.

WESTON

1830 Inn on the Green	$$ B&B	Full breakfast
P.O. Box 104, Route 100, 05161	4 rooms, 3 pb	Afternoon tea
802-824-6789	Visa, MC	Snacks, comp. wine
Sandy & Dave Granger	C-14+/S-ltd	Sitting room
All year		

A small, romantic inn located on the Village Green. Recognized by the National Register of Historic Places.

Colonial House	$$ B&B	Full breakfast
RR 1, Box 138, Rt. 100, 05161	15 rooms, 9 pb	Dinner, comp. tea
802-824-6286	Visa, MC	Sitting room
John & Betty Nunnikhoven	C-yes/S-ltd/P-ltd/H-ltd	
All year		

Your country cousins are waiting with a warm welcome, old-fashioned meals and a relaxing living room for you while you visit the attractions of southern Vermont.

The Darling Family Inn	$$$ B&B	Full breakfast
Route 100, 05161	7 rooms, 7 pb	Dinner with notice
802-824-3223	C-ltd/S-yes/P-ltd/H-no	Complimentary tea, wine
Chapin & Joan Darling		Sitting room, cottages
All year		swimming pool

Restored Colonial in farmland and mountain setting with American and English country antiques. Closest inn to the famous Weston Priory.

WILLIAMSTOWN

Rosewood Inn	$$ B&B	Full gourmet breakfast
P.O. Box 31, 05679	5 rooms, 1 pb	Afternoon tea
Main St., Route 14	Visa, MC, AmEx •	Sitting room
802-433-5822	C-yes/S-yes/P-no/H-no	bicycles
Elaine & John Laveroni		
All year		

Elegant Victorian mansion. Charming country village. Awake to the aroma of our gourmet breakfast. Skiing, hunting, fishing all nearby.

WILMINGTON

Hermitage Inn &		
Brookbound	$$ MAP	Full breakfast
P.O. Box 457, 05363	29 rooms, 25 pb	Dinner incl. bar service
Coldbrook Rd.	AmEx, Visa, MC, DC	Tennis courts, sauna
802-464-3511	C-yes/S-yes/P-no/H-no	sitting room, swimming
Jim McGovern	French, Spanish	entertainment, piano
All year		

Specializing in home-raised gamebirds; over 1,200 selections on our award-winning wine list. Individually decorated guest rooms with fireplaces. 55 km of cross-country skiing.

Red Shutter Inn	$$ B&B	Full breakfast
P.O. Box 636, 05363	5 rooms, 5 pb	Restaurant, pub
Route 9 W.	Visa, MC	Snacks, sitting room
802-464-3768	C-14+/S-yes	fireplaces, guest suite
Max & Carolyn Hopkins		alfresco dining
Exc. early Nov. & April		

Congenial hillside inn (1894) at the village edge featuring candlelight dining. Fireplace suite. Golf, hike, ski amid mountains and valleys.

Trail's End	$$ B&B	Full breakfast
Smith Rd., 05363	22 rooms, 22 pb	Dinner, comp. tea
802-464-2727	C-yes/S-yes/P-no/H-no	Sitting room
Bill & Mary Kilburn		swimming pool, library
Exc. late Apr. & early Nov.		clay tennis court

Friendly inn tucked along a country road with English flower gardens, hiking trails, trout pond. Dramatic 2-story fireplace and loft. Skiing and golf nearby.

WOODSTOCK

Woodstocker B&B	$$ B&B	Continental plus
61 River St., 05091	7 rooms, 7 pb	Afternoon tea
802-457-3896	Visa, MC •	Sitting room
L. Deignan, R. Formichella	C-ltd/S-yes/P-no/H-yes	hot tub
All year exc. April		library

We enjoy making our guests feel at home. Within easy walking distance of shops and restaurants. Cross-country and downhill skiing close by.

More Inns . . .

Auberge Alburg   RD 1, Box 3, Alburg 05440   802-796-3169
Hillside   RR #1, Box 196, Andover 05143   802-875-3844
Evergreen   Sandgate, Box 2480, Arlington 05250   802-375-2272
Sycamore Inn   RD 2 Box 2485, Rt. 7A, Arlington 05250   802-362-2284
West Mountain Inn   Box 481, Arlington 05250   802-375-6516
Woodruff House   13 East Street, Barre 05641   802-476-7745
The Leslie Place   Box 62, Belmont 05730   802-259-2903
Parmenter House   POB 106, Church St, Belmont 05730   802-259-2009
Mt. Anthony Guest House   226 Main St., Bennington 05201   802-447-7396
South Shire Inn   124 Elm St., Bennington 05201   802-447-3839
Eastwood House   River Street, Bethel 05032   802-234-9686
Greenhurst Inn   Bethel 05032   802-234-9474
Poplar Manor   RD 2, Rts. 12 & 107, Bethel 05032   802-234-5426
Merry Meadow Farm   Lower Plain, Rt. 5, Bradford 05033   802-222-4412
Village Inn of Bradford   P.O. Box 354, Bradford 05033   802-222-9303

Beauchamp Place   31 Franklin St., Brandon 05733   802-247-3905
Brandon Inn   20 Park Green, Brandon 05733   802-247-5766
Churchill House Inn   RD 3, Route 73 East, Brandon 05733   802-247-3078
Inn at Tiffany Corner   RD 3, Blof Course Rd, Brandon 05733   802-247-6571
Old Mill Inn   Stone Mill Dam, Brandon 05733   802-247-8002
Mill Brook B&B & Gallery   P.O. Box 410, Brownsville 05037   802-484-7283
Yankee's Northview B&B   Lightening Ridge Road, Calais 05667   802-454-7191
Craftsbury Inn   Main St., Craftsbury 05826   802-586-2848
Derby Village Inn B&B   46 Main St., Derby Line 05830   802-873-3604
Cornucopia of Dorset   Route 30, Dorset 05251   802-867-5751
Dovetail Inn   Route 30, Main Street, Dorset 05251   802-867-5747
Little Lodge at Dorset   P.O. Box 673, Dorset 05251   802-867-4040
Marble West Inn   Box 22, West Road, Dorset 05251   802-867-4155
Village Auberge   P.O. Box 970, Dorset 05251   802-867-5715
Doveberry Inn   HCR 63 Box 9, Dover 05356   802-464-5652
Schneider Haus   Rt. 100, Duxbury 05676   802-244-7726
Garrison Inn   P.O. Box 177, East Burke 05832   802-626-8329
Old Cutter Inn   Burke Mt. Access Road, East Burke 05832   802-626-5152
Whispering Pines   East Fairfield 05448   802-827-3827
Brick House   Box 128, East Hardwick 05836   802-472-5512
Waybury Inn   Rt. 125, East Middlebury 05740   802-388-4015
Berkson Farms   RFD 1, Enosburg Falls 05450   802-933-2522
Fair Haven Inn   Fair Haven 05743   802-265-3833
Haven, est. 1948   1 Fourth St., Fair Haven 05743   802-265-3373
Vermont Marble Inn   12 W. Park Place, Fair Haven 05743   802-265-4736
Aloha Manor   Lake Morey, Fairlee 05045   802-333-4478
Old Town Farm Inn   Rt. 10, Gassetts 05143   802-875-2346
Laolke Lodge   P.O. Box 107, Gaysville 05746   802-234-9205
Hayes House   Grafton 05146   802-843-2461
Stronghold Inn   HCR 40, Rt. 121, Grafton 05146   802-843-2203
Highland Lodge   RR 1, Box 1290, Greensboro 05841   802-533-2647
Guildhall Inn   Box 129, Guildhall 05905   802-676-3720
Kincraft Inn   P.O. Box 96, Hancock 05748   802-767-3734
Tyler Place-Lake Champlain   Highgate Springs 05460   802-868-3301
Jay Village Inn   Rt. 242, Mountain Rd, Jay 05859   802-988-2643
Village Inn   Rt. 242, Jay 05859   802-988-2643
Woodshed Lodge   Jay 05859   802-988-4444
Windridge Inn B&B   Main St., Rt. 15 & 108, Jeffersonville 05464   802-644-8281
Eaton House B&B   P.O. Box 139, Jericho 05465   802-899-2354
Saxon Inn   RR 2, Box 4295, S. Orr, Jericho 05465   802-899-3015
Grey Bonnet Inn   Killington 05751   800-342-2086
Nordic Inn   Rt. 11, P.O. Box 96, Landgrove 05148   802-824-6444
Country Hare   Rt. 11 & Magic Mtn Rd., Londonderry 05148   802-824-3131
Highland House   Rt. 100, Londonderry 05148   802-824-3019
Village Inn   RFD Landgrove, Londonderry 05148   802-824-6673
Red Door   7 Pleasant St., Ludlow 05149   802-228-2376
Reluctant Panther Inn   Box 678, West Rd., Manchester 05254   802-362-2568
Sky Line Inn   Box 325, Manchester 05254   802-362-1113
Inn at Willow Pond   P.O. Box 1429, Rt. 7, Manchester Center 05255   802-362-4733
Longwood Inn   Rt. 9, POB 86, Marlboro 05344   802-257-1545
Middlebury Inn   P. O. Box 631, Middlebury 05753   800-842-4666
Middletown Springs Inn   Box 1068, Middletown Springs 05757   802-235-2198
Black Lantern Inn   Route 118, Montgomery Village 05470   802-326-4507
Nunts Hideaway   Rt. 111, Morgan 05872   802-895-4432

Seymour Lake Lodge   Rt. 111, Morgan 05853   802-895-2752
Austria Haus   Box 2, Austria Haus Rd., Mount Holly 05758   802-259-2441
Hound's Folly   Box 591, Mount Holly 05758   802-259-2718
A Century Past   P.O. Box 186, Route 5, Newbury 05051   802-866-3358
Four Columns Inn   Newfane 05345   802-365-7713
Old Newfane Inn   P.O. Box 101, Newfane 05345   802-365-4427
West River Lodge   RR 1, Box 693, Newfane 05345   802-365-7745
Charlies Northland Lodge   Rt. 2, Box 88, North Hero 05474   802-372-8822
Stone House Inn   Box 47, Rt. 5, North Thetford 05054   802-333-9124
Valley House Inn   4 Memorial Sq., Orleans 05860   802-754-6665
Peregrine's Rest   Upper Falls Rd., Perkinsville 05151   802-263-5784
Wiley Inn   Rt. 11, P.O. Box 37, Peru 05152   802-824-6600
Swiss Farm Lodge   Pittsfield 05762   802-748-8341
Fox Bros. Farm   Corn Hill Rd., Pittsford 05763   802-483-2870
Salt Ash Inn   Jct. Rts. 100 & 100A, Plymouth Union 05056   802-672-3748
Lake House Inn   Rt. 244, P.O. Box 65, Post Mills 05058   802-333-4025
Castle Inn   Box 157, Proctorsville 05153   802-226-7222
Okemo Lantern Lodge   P.O. Box 247, Proctorsville 05153   802-226-7770
Parker House   16 Main St., Box 0780, Quechee 05059   802-295-6077
Three Stallion Inn   RD 2 Stock Farm Rd., Randolph 05060   802-728-5575
Peeping Cow Inn   Rt. 106, P.O. Box 47, Reading 05062   802-484-5036
Old Coach Inn   RR 1 Box 260, Readsboro 05350   802-423-5394
Chipman Inn   Rt. 125, Ripton 05766   802-388-2390
Harveys Mt. View Inn   Rochester 05767   802-767-4273
New Homestead   Rochester 05767   802-767-4751
Echo Ledge Farm Inn   Box 77, E. St Johnsbury, Saint Johnsbury 05838   802-748-4750
Saxtons River Inn   Main St., Saxtons River 05154   802-869-2110
Shoreham Inn   Shoreham Village 05770   802-897-5861
Lindenwood—A Country Inn   916 Shelburne Rd., South Burlington 05403   802-862-2144
Londonderry Inn   Box 301, Rt. 100, South Londonderry 05155   802-824-3306
Inn at South Newfane   Dover Rd., South Newfane 05351   802-348-7191
Watercours Way   Route 132, South Strafford 05070   802-765-4314
Hartness House Inn   30 Orchard St., Springfield 05156   802-885-2115
Bellevue   9 Parsons Lane, St. Albans 05478   802-527-1115
Scarborough Inn   Rt. 100 HCR 65 Box 23, Stockbridge 05772   802-746-8141
Fiddler's Green Inn   Mountain Rd. Rt. 108, Stowe 05672   802-253-8124
Foxfire Inn   RR 2, Box 2180, Stowe 05672   802-253-4887
Grey Fox Inn   Stowe 05672   802-253-8921
Guesthouse Christel Horman   RR 1 Box 1635, Stowe 05672   802-253-4846
Innsburck Inn   RR 1, Box 1570, Stowe 05672   802-253-8582
Nichols Lodge   Box 1098, Stowe 05672   802-253-7683
Scandinavia Inn & Chalet   Stowe 05672   802-253-8555
Ski Inn   Rt. 108, Mountain Rd., Stowe 05672   802-253-4050
Spruce Pond Inn   Stowe 05672   802-253-4828
Stowehof Inn   P.O. Box 1108, Stowe 05672   802-253-9722
Applebutter Inn B&B   Happy Valley Rd., Taftville 05073   802-457-4158
Echo Lake Inn   Route 100, 05056, Tyson 05149   802-228-8602
Emersons' Guest House   82 Main St., Vergennes 05491   802-877-3293
Honeysuckle's Inn   P.O. Box 828, Waitsfield 05673   802-496-6200
Knoll Farm Country Inn   Bragg Hill Rd., Waitsfield 05673   802-496-3939
Mountain View Inn   Rt. 17, RFD Bx 69, Waitsfield 05673   802-496-2426
Snuggery Inn   Box 65, RR 1, Waitsfield 05673   802-496-2322
Wallingford Inn   Box 404, Wallingford 05773   802-446-2849
Inn at Weathersfield   P.O. Box 165, Weathersfield 05151   802-263-9217

Hunts' Hideaway   RR 1, Box 570, West Charleston 05872   802-895-4432
Deerhill Inn & Restaurant   P.O. Box 397, West Dover 05356   802-464-3100
Inn at Sawmill Farm   Box 8 (#100), West Dover 05356   802-464-8131
Shield Inn   Route 100, Box 366, West Dover 05356   802-464-3984
Waldwinkel Inn   West Dover 05356   802-464-5281
Lincoln Covered Bridge Inn   Route 4, RR 2, Box 40, West Woodstock 05091   802-457-3312
Inn at Weston   Route 100, P.O. Box 56, Weston 05161   802-824-5804
Wilder Homestead Inn   RR 1, Box 106D, Weston 05161   802-824-8172
Partridge Hill   P.O. Box 52, Williston 05495   802-878-4741
Brook Bound Building   Coldbrook Rd., Wilmington 05363   802-464-3511
Darcroft's Schoolhouse   Rt. 100, Wilmington 05363   802-464-2631
Fjord Gate Inn & Farm   Higley Hill Road, Wilmington 05363   802-464-2783
Misty Mountain Lodge   Wilmington 05356   802-464-3961
Nordic Hills Lodge   Wilmington 05356   802-464-5130
Nutmeg Inn   Box 818, Route 9W, Wilmington 05363   802-464-3351
On the Rocks Lodge   Wilmington 05363   802-464-8364
White House of Wilmington   Rt. 9 Box 757, Wilmington 05363   802-464-2135
Juniper Hill Inn   RR 1, Box 79, Windsor 05089   802-674-5273
3 Church Street B&B   3 Church St., Woodstock 05091   802-457-1925
Carriage House B&B   Woodstock 05091   802-457-4322
Lincoln Covered Bridge Inn   RR 2 Box 40, Woodstock 05091   802-457-3312
Village Inn of Woodstock   41 Pleasant St., Woodstock 05091   802-457-1255

Virginia

ABINGDON

Summerfield Inn
101 W. Valley St., 24210
703-628-5905
Champe & Don Hyatt
Apr. 1—Oct. 31

$$ B&B
4 rooms, 2 pb
Visa, MC •
C-12+/S-ltd/P-no/H-no

Continental plus
Set-ups
Sitting room
library
tennis courts

Excellent restaurants nearby. Barter Theater package available. Relax on the swing on our big front porch.

ARLINGTON

Memory House
6404 N. Washington Blvd, 22205
703-534-4607
Marlys McGrath
All year

$$ B&B
2 rooms, 1 pb
•
C-no/S-no/P-no/H-no

Continental plus
Two sitting rooms
one block from subway

Ornate 1899 Victorian decorated with antiques and collectibles. Convenient base for exploring nation's capital. Two blocks from I-66. Notable house-—featured on tours.

BASYE

Sky Chalet Country Inn
Route 263 West, 22810
703-856-2147
Ken & Mona Lesa Seay
All year

$ EP
12 rooms, 12 pb
Visa, MC •
C-yes/S-yes/P-yes/H-no

Restaurant, pub
All meals served
Gazebo, fireplaces, deck
nature, conference space
local airport pickup

Swiss-style mountaintop lodge hideaway in Shenendoah Valley of Virginia; spectacular mountain views; scrumptious dining; comfortable lodging; cozy pub.

CASTLETON

Blue Knoll Farm
Route 1, Box 171, 22716
Route 676
703-937-5234
Richard & Joy Brown
All year

$$$ B&B
3 rooms, 3 pb
C-no/S-no/P-no/H-no

Full breakfast
Afternoon tea
Sitting room

Charming 19th-century farmhouse in the foothills of Blue Ridge Mountains. 65 miles west of Washington, D.C., near Skyline Dr. and 5 star inn at Little Washington Restaurant.

CHARLES CITY

Edgewood Plantation
Route 2, Box 490, 23030
Rt 5 btwn Richmond&Willia
804-829-2962
Dot & Juilian Boulware
All year

$$$ B&B
6 rooms, 2 pb
Visa, MC
C-10+ /S-yes

Full breakfast
Comp. wine
Afternoon tea, snacks
hot tubs, swimming pool
gazebo

Sweetness, romance, uniqueness and charm fill each large antique bedroom. Breakfast in formal dining room or country kitchen. Pre-Civil War 1849 house filled with history.

North Bend Plantation B&B
P.O. Box 13A, Route 1, 23030
804-829-5176
George & Ridgely Copland
All year

$$$ B&B
3 rooms
•
C-yes
some French

Full breakfast
Comp. wine
Sitting room, library
game room w/pool table
piano, swimming pool

Virginia Historic Landmark circa 1819 located in the James River Plantation area. 25 min. to historic Williamsburg. Private, peaceful, surrounded by 250 acres of farmland.

Piney Grove B&B
Piney Grove, Route 615, 23030
16900 Gleveland(R1 Bx148)
804-829-2480
The Gordineers
All year

$$$ B&B
6 rooms, 4 pb
C-yes/S-no/P-no/H-no
German

Full breakfast
Picnic lunches (request)
Comp. wine & tea
Sitting room, library
swimming pool

National Registry property in James River Plantation Country—20 miles from Williamsburg. Two authentically restored and antique-filled antebellum houses.

CHARLOTTESVILLE

Woodstock Hall
Route 3, Box 40, 22901
804-293-8977
Jean Wheby, MaryAnn Elder
All year

$$$ B&B
4 rooms, 4 pb
C-8+ /S-no/P-no/H-no

Full breakfast
Afternoon tea
Dinner by prior arrange.
Sitting room, croquet
hiking, horseshoes

Historic landmark built circa 1757; 1808. Perfect for a relaxing, romantic getaway. Period furnishings; private baths; fireplaces; central air; full gourmet breakfasts.

CHINCOTEAGUE

Channel Bass Inn
100 Church St., 23336
804-336-6148
James S. Hanretta
All year

$$$ EP
10 rooms, 10 pb
Visa, MC, AmEx, DC •
C-no/S-yes/P-no/H-no

Full breakfast $
Dinner by reservation
Basque cuisine, bar
Room service
sitting rooms

Near Assateague seashore; elegant colonial atmosphere; all oversized beds; superb continental and classical cuisine. Art gallery specializing in 19th-century paintings.

Miss Molly's Inn
113 N. Main St., 23336
804-336-6686
Dr. & Mrs. James Stam
April 1—December 1

$$ B&B
7 rooms, 1 pb
C-12+/S-yes

Continental plus
Afternoon tea
Sitting room

Charming Victorian B&B inn over the bay. All rooms are air-conditioned & furnished with period antiques. Marguerite Henry stayed here while writing Misty of Chincoteague.

CLARKSVILLE

Needmoor Inn
P.O. Box 629, 23937
801 Virginia Ave.
804-374-2866
Lucy & Buddy Hairston
All year

$$ B&B
4 rooms, 3 pb
•
C-yes/S-ltd/P-ltd/H-no

Full gourmet breakfast
Aftn. tea, snacks
Comp. wine
Sitting room, library
bicycles, airport pickup

Heartfelt hospitality in the heart of Virginia's Lake Country. 1889 homestead amid 1½ acres of fruit trees and herb garden. Three blocks away from all water sports.

Witmer's Tavern—1725 Inn, Lancaster, PA

378 Virginia

CULPEPPER

Fountain Hall B&B Inn
609 S. East St., 22701
703-825-8200
Steve & Kathi Walker
All year

$$ B&B
5 rooms, 3 pb
Visa, MC, AmEx •
C-ltd/S-ltd/P-no/H-ltd

Continental plus
Comp. tea
3 sitting rooms, books
fireplaces, VCR, porches
golf nearby, bicycles

Gracious accommodations for business and leisure travelers. Centrally located in quaint historic Culpepper, between Washington, D.C., Charlottesville & Skyline Drive.

FLINT HILL

Caledonia Farm B&B
Route 1, Box 2080, 22627
703-675-3693
Phil Irwin
All year

$$ B&B
3 rooms, 1 pb
Visa, MC •
C-12+/S-no/P-no/H-yes
German, Danish

Full breakfast
Lunch, dinner available
Comp. wine, snacks
Evening social hour
sitting room, library

Beautifully restored 1812 stone farm home adjacent to Shenandoah National Park/Blue Ridge Mountains. 68 miles from Washington, D.C. Year-round hospitality.

FREDERICKSBURG

Fredericksburg Colonial
1707 Princess Anne St., 22401
703-371-5666
Robert S. Myers
All year

$ B&B
32 rooms, 32 pb
Visa, MC •
C-yes/S-yes/P-yes/H-yes

Continental breakfast

Rooms furnished in Victorian decor. Enjoy our antiques, prints, and museum. Inn located in historic district. Antique shops, restaurants nearby.

Kenmore Inn
1200 Princess Anne St., 22401
703-371-7622
Ed & Alice Bannan
All year

$$$ B&B
13 rooms, 12 pb
Visa, MC •
C-yes/S-yes/P-ltd/H-yes

Continental plus
Lunch, dinner, cocktails
Full service restaurant
Sitting room, lounge
antiques, bicycles

On the historic walking tour, elegant guest rooms with bath & air-conditioning, considered to be among Virginia's 5 most exclusive restaurants.

La Vista Plantation
Rt. 3, Box 1255, 22401
4420 Guinea Station Rd.
703-898-8444
Michele & Edward Schiesser
All year

$$ B&B
2 rooms, 2 pb
Visa, MC •
C-yes/S-yes/P-ltd/H-no

Full breakfast
Comp. beverages
Sitting room, library
bicycles, A/C, kitchen
TV, phone, wicker furn.

Lovely 1838 classical revival country home on 10 acres outside historic Fredericksburg. Antiques; fireplaces; old trees; pond. In the center of Virginia's historic triangle.

FRONT ROYAL

Chester House Inn
43 Chester St., 22630
703-635-3937
Bill & Ann Wilson
All year

$$ B&B
6 rooms, 2 pb
Visa, MC •
C-12+/S-ltd/P-no/H-no

Continental plus
Comp. wine, snacks
Living & dining room
lawns, gardens
television parlor

Quiet, elegant, relaxed atmosphere home reminiscent of a bygone era. Amidst formal boxwood garden and shade trees. Golf, tennis, horseback riding, hiking, canoeing nearby.

FRONT ROYAL

Constant Spring Inn
413 S. Royal Ave., 22630
703-635-7010
Betsy Qualls
ex. 2 weeks in January

$$ MAP
9 rooms, 9 pb
Visa, MC •
C-yes/S-yes/P-no/H-ltd

Continental plus
Dinner, tea, cider
Sitting room
bicycles
picnic baskets

Three blocks from Skyline Drive; parklike setting; heart of history land. Eighty minutes to Washington, D.C. Country cooking.

HILLSVILLE

Bray's Manor B&B Inn
Route 3, Box 210, 24343
703-728-7901
Dick & Helen Bray
March—January

$$ B&B
4 rooms, 2 pb
Visa, MC
C-yes/S-no/P-no/H-no

Full breakfast
Snacks
Sitting room with TV
parlor, library

Beautiful southwest Virginia; 12 miles north of Blue Ridge Parkway; croquet; badminton; rambling porch for sitting, sipping; near golf and crafts.

HOT SPRINGS

Vine Cottage Inn
P.O. Box 918, Rt. 220, 24445
703-839-2422
Wendell & Pat Lucas
All year

$$ B&B
14 rooms, 8 pb
Visa, MC, Choice
C-yes/S-yes/P-no/H-no

Continental plus
Sitting room, library
large veranda w/rockers
tennis nearby

A charming and relaxing turn-of-the-century inn located in a renowned mountain spa. Outdoorsmen delight in golfing, skiing, hunting, hiking, fishing and swimming.

LANCASTER

Inn at Levelfields
P.O. Box 216, 22503
State Route 3
804-435-6887
Doris & Warren Sadler
All year

$$$ B&B
4 rooms, 4 pb
Visa, MC
C-ltd/S-yes/P-no/H-no

Full breakfast
Lunch (Sun only), dinner
Bar, sitting room
Library, swimming pool
hair dryers, toiletries

Elegant accommodations and fine dining in antebellum plantation in Virginia's Northern Neck. Four spacious bedrooms, private baths, antique furnishings.

LEESBURG

Fleetwood Farm B&B
Route 1, Box 306-A, 22075
703-327-4325
Bill & Carol Chamberlin
All year

$$$ B&B
2 rooms, 2 pb
C-12+

Full abundant breakfast
Comp. wine, snacks, tea
Living room w/TV, stereo
library, games, jacuzzi
cook-out fac., canoe

1745 Virginia Hunt country manor house. Private rooms each with private baths, air-conditioning, fireplaces, antiques. Abundant breakfast.

LEXINGTON

Fassifern Bed & Breakfast
Rt. 5, Box 87, 24450
Rt. 39 at Rt. 750
703-463-1013
Ann Carol Perry
All year

$ B&B
6 rooms, 4 pb
Visa, MC, AmEx •
C-16+/S-ltd/P-no/H-no
some French, German

Continental plus
Comp. wine, snacks
Living room
conservatory
pond & lawn chairs

Comfortable 1867 manor house with antique furnishings in beautiful Shenandoah Valley near historic sites, Virginia Horse Ctr, and Blue Ridge Pkwy. Ambience is our trademark.

LEXINGTON

Llewellyn Lodge—Lexington	$$ B&B	Full breakfast
603 S. Main St., 24450	5 rooms, 5 pb	Comp. wine, snacks
703-463-3235	Visa, MC, Choice •	Sitting room
Ellen Thornber	C-yes/S-yes/P-no/H-no	tennis courts, pool,
All year		and golf nearby

Charming half-century-old colonial with a warm friendly atmosphere, where guests can relax after visiting this historic Shenandoah town. Gourmet breakfast.

LURAY

Boxwood Hill	$$$ B&B	4-course champagne bkfst
128 South Court, 22835	6 rooms, 5 pb	Dinner by reservation
703-743-9484/703-743-3550	•	Comp. wine, sitting rm
Eschi A. Warwick	C-yes/S-yes/P-ask	Library, hot tubs, pool
All year	German	volley ball, croquet

European service and ambience offering a relaxing atmosphere; on secluded mini-estate with antiques appointments; in historic Shenandoah Valley.

Ruffner House & Cottage	$$ B&B	Full breakfast
Box 620, Route 4, 22835	6 rooms, 5 pb	Fruit basket
703-743-7855	Visa, MC •	Sitting room, library
Mrs. Roman	C-12+/S-ltd	Arabian horses
All year	Fr, Ger, Rus, Pol, Czech	swimming pool

Historic (1739), elegant manor restored in period antiques, and a charming country retreat on 18-acre Arabian horse farm in Shenandoah Valley.

MATHEWS

Ravenswood Inn	$$$ MAP	Full breakfast,
P.O. Box 250, 23109	4 rooms, 4 pb	5-course French dinner
Poplar Grove lane	C-no/S-ltd/P-no/H-no	Comp. wine, living room
804-725-7272	Spanish	Hot tub, library
Peter & Sally Preston		sailboats, bicycles
Mid-Feb.—early Dec.		

Five-acre hideaway on Chesapeake's East River with focus on fine food and nesting; restored 1913 manor house with beautiful river views. A/C in rooms.

Riverfront House B&B	$$ B&B	Full breakfast
Route 14 E., 23109	7 rooms, 7 pb	Comp. wine
804-725-9975	•	Sitting room
Annette Goldreyer	C-7+/S-ltd/P-no/H-no	biking
April—November	Spanish	stocked fishing pond

An 1840 farmhouse in Chesapeake country setting of 7 acres amid age-old shade trees and tidal waters. Near Williamsburg.

MIDDLEBURG

Welbourne	$$$ B&B	Full breakfast
Route 743, 22117	10 rooms, 10 pb	Comp. wine
703-687-3201	•	Piano
Nathaniel & Sherry Morison	C-yes/S-yes/P-yes/H-ltd	sitting room
All year	French	

Antebellum home occupied by the same family for seven generations. In heart of Virginia's fox-hunting country. Virginia historic landmark.

MOLLUSK

Greenvale Manor
Route 354, Box 70, 22517
804-462-5995
Pam & Walt Smith
All year

$$ B&B
7 rooms, 7 pb
•
C-yes

Full breakfast
Lunch & dinner by
special arrangement
Sitting room, library
swimming pool, boating

Historical 1840 waterfront manor house with antiques, privacy, pool, dock, private beach, gorgeous sunsets and guest houses on a 13-acre peninsula. Charter boat available.

MOUNT CRAWFORD

Pumpkin House Inn, Ltd.
Route 2, Box 155, 22841
US 11 betw. exit 60 & 61
703-434-6963
Elizabeth Umstott
All year

$$ B&B
7 rooms, 3 pb
Visa, MC, AmEx
C-yes/S-yes/P-no/H-no

Continental plus
Comp. wine
Sitting room
fishing
walking

Restored 1847 brick home featuring Victorian and 18th-century rooms, some with private baths and working fireplaces. Furnished with antiques. Pumpkin patch in fall.

MOUNT JACKSON

Widow Kip's Country Inn
Route 1, Box 117, 22842
703-477-2400
Rosemary Kip
All year

$$ B&B
2 rooms, 2 pb
•
C-yes/S-yes/P-no/H-no

Full breakfast
Comp. sherry
Picnics & snacks
Sitting room, VCR
bicycles, swimming pool

1830 gracious colonial on 7 acres overlooking Shenandoah. Seven fireplaces. Chock-full of antiques and memories. Like visiting a grandmother's house. Near skiing.

NELLYSFORD

Trillium House
P.O. Box 280, 22958
Wintergreen Dr.
804-325-9126
Ed & Betty Dinwiddie
All year

$$$ B&B
12 rooms, 12 pb
Visa, MC •
C-yes/S-yes/P-no/H-yes

Full breakfast
Aftn. tea, bar
Dinner Fri. & Sat.
Sitting room, library
tennis, pool, golf nearby

Birds entertain at breakfast at this owner-designed inn in year 'round Wintergreen Resort. Fall and spring foliage are specialties.

NEW MARKET

A Touch of Country
9329 Congress St., 22844
703-740-8030
Dawn Kasow, Jean Schoellig
All year

$$ B&B
6 rooms, 2 pb
Visa, MC •
C-12+/S-ltd/P-no/H-no

Full breakfast
Comp. beverages
Sitting room with TV

A comfortable 1870s restored home decorated with antiques, collectibles, and a country flavor. Located in the beautiful Shenandoah Valley.

ONANCOCK

Colonial Manor Inn
P.O. Box 94, 23417
84 Market St.
804-787-3521
June & Jerry Evans
All year

$ EP
14 rooms, 5 pb
C-yes/S-yes/P-no/H-no

Comp. coffee
Sitting room
glassed-in porch
Victorian gazebo, TV

Family-owned business since 1936. At-home kind of atmosphere in a historic little town on the water; fine restaurants.

ORANGE

Hidden Inn	$$$ B&B/MAP	Full country breakfast
249 Caroline St., 22960	7 rooms, 7 pb	Aftn. tea, lunch (Tu-Sa)
703-672-3625	Visa, MC •	Dinner by reservation
Ray & Barbara Lonick	C-yes/S-no/P-no/H-no	Sitting room, jacuzzi
All year		air conditioned

Comfortably furnished country inn tucked away in rural community. Convenient to D.C., Charlottesville, Blue Ridge Mountains. Super breakfasts!

Mayhurst Inn	$$$ B&B	Full breakfast
P.O. Box 707, 22960	8 rooms, 8 pb	Comp. tea, wine
US Route 15 S.	•	Sitting room
703-672-5597	C-ltd/S-no/P-ask/H-no	fireplaces in rooms
Stephen & Shirley Ramsey		pond, 2 cottages
All year		

Exciting Italianate villa on 36 acres of pasture land. Rooftop gazebo, balconies for guests. Antique furniture. Special weekend packages available.

PALMYRA

Palmer Country Manor	$$$ B&B	Full breakfast
Route 2 Box 269, 22963	12 rooms, 10 pb	Comp. wine, tea, snacks
Northside of Route 640	Visa, MC, AmEx	Restaurant, sitting rm
804-589-1300	C-yes/S-ltd/P-no/H-no	Library, pool, fish pond
Gregg & Kathy Palmer	Spanish	trails, balloon rides
All year exc. last 2 wks.		

Beautifully restored 1834 plantation. Enjoy manicured gardens, acres of woods, pond fishing, river rafting, a heated pool, and hot air ballooning. A country resort.

PETERSBURG

High Street Inn	$$ B&B	Continental plus
405 High St., 23803	5 rooms, 3 pb	Comp. wine, tea
804-733-0505	Visa, MC •	Sitting room
Bruce & Candace Noe	C-yes/S-ltd/P-no/H-no	library
March—December	French, Spanish	films shown

Elegant Queen Anne mansion in heart of historic district. Period antiques and warm hospitality. Close to museums, shops and restaurants.

Mayfield Inn	$$ B&B	Full breakfast
P.O. Box 2265, 23804	4 rooms, 4 pb	Afternoon tea
W. Washington St.	Visa, MC, Choice	Two sitting rooms
804-861-6775/804-733-0866	C-yes/S-ltd/P-no/H-no	swimming pool
Jamie Caudle		
All year		

A 1750 house that has been completely and very beautifully restored, set in four tranquil acres. Close to historic Petersburg and battlefields.

RICHMOND

The Bensonhouse	$$ B&B	Continental plus
2036 Monument Ave., 23220	4 rooms, 4 pb	Natural cereals
804-353-6900	Visa, MC •	Large living room
Lyn M. Benson	C-12+/S-no/P-no/H-no	fireplace, library
All year		jacuzzi in large room

1914 Italian Renaissance with natural mahogany raised paneling, wainscoting, leaded glass windows, coffered ceilings with dropped beams. Private baths; one room has jacuzzi.

RICHMOND

Catlin-Abbott House
2304 E. Broad St., 23223
804-780-3746
Dr. & Mrs. James L. Abbott
All year

$$$ B&B
5 rooms, 3 pb
Visa, MC, AmEx •
C-13+ /S-yes/P-no/H-no

Full breakfast
Comp. wine

Retire in a four-poster bed in front of a romantic, burning fireplace—wake up to freshly brewed coffee served in your room.

Mr. Patrick Henry's Inn
2300 E. Broad St., 23223
804-644-1322
Lynn & Jim News
All year

$$$ B&B
3 rooms, 3 pb
Visa, MC, AmEx, DC
C-yes/S-yes/P-no/H-no

Full breakfast
Restaurant, bar service
Lunch, dinner
Sitting room, fireplaces
kitchenettes, balconies

A pre-Civil War inn. Walking distance to many tourist attractions. Featuring a gourmet restaurant, English pub and garden patio. Suites include fireplaces & full breakfast.

SCOTTSVILLE

High Meadows Inn
Rt. 4, Box 6, 24590
Rt. 20 S.
804-286-2218
Peter Sushka, Jae Abbitt
All year

$$$ B&B
6 rooms, 6 pb
•
C-8+ /S-ltd/P-ltd/H-no
French

Full breakfast
Candlelight dinner
Comp. wine, tea, snacks
Library, hot tub, pond
gazebo, bikes, vineyard

Enchanting historical landmark south of Charlottesville. Large, tastefully appointed rooms; fireplaces; period antiques. Private 23 acres for walking & picnics. Wine tasting.

SMITH MOUNTAIN LAKE

Holland-Duncan House
Route 5, Box 681, 24121
Route 122, Moneta
703-721-8510
Clint & Kathryn Shay
All year

$ B&B
3 rooms, 1 pb
C-yes/S-ltd/P-ask/H-no

Full gourmet breakfast
Comp. wine
Library, sitting room
tennis courts, boating
swimming, fishing, golf

This charming, historic antebellum mansion and its outbuildings are situated in a lake resort. It is a beautiful blend of old and new. Authentic log cabin also available.

Manor at Taylor's Store
Route 122, 24184
Rt. 1, Box 533, Wirtz
703-721-3951
Lee & Mary Lynn Tucker
All year

$$ B&B
4 rooms, 4 pb
Visa, MC
C-ltd/S-ltd/P-no/H-ltd
some German

Full breakfast
Comp. wine/tea, kitchen
Parlor, piano, library
exercise room, swimming
hot tub, fishing, hiking

Circa 1799, 100-acre estate offering elegant accommodations in antique-filled mansion. Cozy 3-bedroom cottage also offered. This country inn is a very special place!

SPERRYVILLE

Conyers House
Slate Mills Rd., 22740
703-987-8025
Sandra & Norman Brown
All year

$$$ B&B
9 rooms, 7 pb
C-ltd/S-ltd/P-ask/H-ltd
Fr., Ger., Ital., Arabic

Hearty gourmet breakfast
Comp. tea, wine
Candlelight dinner avail
Fireplaces, wood stoves
grand piano, porches

18th-century former country store graciously furnished with heirlooms and antiques. Outstanding hiking; foxhunting and trail rides. Candlelit dinner by reservation.

384 Virginia

STANLEY

Jordan Hollow Farm Inn
Route 2, Box 375, 22851
703-778-2209/703-778-2285
Marley & Jetze Beers
All year

$$ EP
16 rooms, 16 pb
Visa, MC, DC •
C-yes/S-yes/P-yes/H-no
Dutch, German, French

Full breakfast $
Restaurant & bar
Sitting room, game room
library, canoeing
horseback trail riding

A 200-year-old restored colonial horse farm. Friendly, informal atmosphere with spectacular views. Neaby Luray Caverns, Skyline Drive, canoeing.

STAUNTON

Frederick House
P.O. Box 1387, 24401
18 E. Frederick St.
703-885-4220
Joe & Evy Harman
All year

$ B&B
11 rooms, 11 pb
Visa, MC, AmEx, DC •
C-yes/S-no/P-no/H-no

Continental breakfast
Sitting room

Located in the oldest city west of the Blue Ridge Mountains of Virginia. Historic Staunton contains Woodrow Wilson birthplace, shops and restaurants.

SWOOPE

Lambsgate Bed & Breakfast
Route 1, Box 63, 24479
Corner Routes 254 & 833
703-337-6929
Daniel & Elizabeth Fannon
All year

$ B&B
3 rooms
C-yes/S-no/P-no/H-no

Full breakfast
Sitting room
veranda

Restored Shenandoah Valley farmhouse, circa 1816, on seven acres with mountain views and sheep. Hiking and historic sightseeing nearby. Six miles west of Staunton.

VIRGINIA BEACH

Angie's Guest Cottage
302 24th St., 23451
804-428-4690
Barbara G. Yates
April 1—October 1

$ B&B
7 rooms, 1 pb
C-ltd/S-ltd/P-ltd/H-no

Continental plus (sum.)
Kitchens
Sitting room, sun deck
BBQ pit, picnic tables
shaded porch, library

Located in the heart of the resort area by Atlantic Ocean. Guests have opportunity to meet visitors from other countries staying at our youth hostel.

WARM SPRINGS

Meadow Lane Lodge
Route 1, Box 110, 24484
Route 39 W
703-839-5959
Philip & Catherine Hirsh
April—December

$$$ B&B
10 rooms, 10 pb
Visa, MC, AmEx
C-ltd/S-ltd/P-ltd/H-no

Full breakfast
Tennis courts
sitting room

In the midst of 1,600 mountainous acres, scenic rivers stocked for trout fishing, golf, horseback riding, etc., are all nearby.

WASHINGTON

Foster-Harris House
P.O. Box 333, 22747
Main St.
703-675-3757
Camille Harris
All year

$$ B&B
3 rooms, 1 pb
Visa, MC •
C-yes/S-yes/P-ltd/H-no
Spanish, German

Cont., cont. plus or ful
Comp. wine, tea
Sitting room
fireplace stove
kennel, baby-sitting

Restored Victorian (circa 1900) house in historic "Little" Washington, Virginia. Antiques, fresh flowers, mountain views, three blocks from 5-star restaurant.

WHITE POST ────────────────────────────

L'Auberge Provencale $$$ B&B   Full gourmet breakfast
P.O. Box 119, 22663   6 rooms, 6 pb   Dinner, bar
Rt 340 1 mi S of Rt 50   Visa, MC, AmEx, DC   Comp. welcome drink
703-837-1375   C-10+/S-yes/P-no/H-no   Library, sitting room
Chef Alain/Celeste Borel   French   bicycles, gardens
Exc. Jan.—mid-Feb.

4th generation master chef Alain Borel, from Avignon, France, prepares nationally acclaimed cuisine moderne. Elegant overnight accommodations. Extensive wine list.

WILLIAMSBURG ────────────────────────────

Applewood Colonial B&B $$ B&B   Continental plus
605 Richmond Rd., 23185   4 rooms, 4 pb   Comp. wine
804-229-0205   Visa, MC •   Afternoon tea
F. Strout, M. & R. Jones   C-yes   Sitting room
All year

Elegant colonial decor. Walking distance to colonial Williamsburg & College of William and Mary. Fireplaces, antiques, apple collection and lots of comfort.

The Cedars $$ B&B   Continental breakfast
616 Jamestown Rd., 23185   9 rooms, 4 pb   Afternoon tea
804-229-3591   •   Screened porch
Gloria Molton   C-yes/S-ltd/P-no/H-yes   parlor with fireplace
All year

Brick Georgian colonial house, air-conditioned, antiques and canopy beds. Room for 22 guests, plus brick cottage with fully equipped kitchen for 6-8. $110 per night.

Liberty Rose Colonial B&B $$$ B&B   Full breakfast
1022 Jamestown Rd., 23185   5 rooms, 3 pb   Sitting room
804-253-1260   C-ltd   bicycles
Brad & Sandi Hirz
All year

A country French colonial lavishly decorated with a breakfast to match. Charming antiques. Join us for a traditional B&B experience!

Williamsburg Legacy Inn $$ B&B   Full breakfast
930 Jamestown Rd., 23185   3 rooms, 3 pb   Comp. wine
804-220-0524/800-WMBGS-BB   Visa, MC, AmEx •   Bar service
Ed & Mary Ann Lucas   C-13+   Library
All year   bicycles

Step back in time to the 18th century. Tall poster curtained beds. Fireplaces. Private baths. Bowl of fruit. Bicycles. Walk to historic Williamsburg. Owner occupied.

WOODSTOCK ────────────────────────────

Country Fare $$ B&B   Continental plus
402 N. Main St., 22664   3 rooms, 1 pb   Sitting room, patio
703-459-4828   Visa   comfortable chairs
Bette Hallgren   upstairs porch w/swing
All year

A charming log & brick colonial, circa 1772, affords cozy hand-stenciled bedrooms filled with Grandmother's antiques. A stay will surprise & delight you. Close to everything.

Maplewood Inn, Fair Haven, VT

WOODSTOCK

Inn at Narrow Passage	$$ B&B	Full breakfast
P.O. Box 608, 22664	12 rooms, 8 pb	Living room w/fireplace
US 11 S. (I-81, Exit 72)	Visa, MC •	fishing, swimming
703-459-8000	C-yes/S-ltd/P-no/H-no	rafting, small conf. fac.
Ellen & Ed Markel		
All year		

Historic 1740 log inn on the Shenandoah River. Fireplaces, colonial charm, close to vineyards. Civil War sites, hiking, fishing and caverns.

More Inns...

Maplewood Farm   Rt. 7, Box 272, Abingdon 24210
Little River Inn   P.O. Box 116, Rt. 50, Aldie 22001   703-327-6742
Alexandria Lodgings   10 Sunset Dr., Alexandria 22313   703-836-5575
Peaks of Otter Lodge   P.O. Box 489, Bedford 24523   703-586-1081
200 South Street Inn   200 South St., Charlottesville 22901   804-979-0200
Clifton—The Country Inn   Route 9, Box 412, Charlottesville 22901   804-971-1800
Silver Thatch Inn   3001 Hollymead Rd., Charlottesville 22901   804-978-4686
Sims-Mitchell House B&B   242 Whittle St. Box 846, Chatham 24531   804-432-0595
Little Traveller Inn   112 N. Main St., Chincoteague 23336   804-336-6686
Year of the Horse Inn   600 So. Main St., Chincoteuque 23336   804-336-3221
Buckhorn Inn   E Star Route, Box 139, Churchville 24421   703-337-6900
Mary's Country Inn   P.O. Box 4, Edinburg 22824   703-984-8286
Brookfield Inn   P.O. Box 341, Floyd 24091   703-763-3363
McGrath House   225 Princess Anne St., Fredericksburg 22401   703-371-4363
Richard Johnston Inn   711 Caroline St., Fredericksburg 22401   703-899-7606
Sleepy Hollow Farm B&B   Route 3, Box 43, Gordonsville 22942   703-832-5555
Hamilton Garden Inn   353 W. Colonial Highway, Hamilton 22068   703-338-3693
Tipton House   1043 N. Main St., Hillsville 24343   703-728-2351
Irish Gap Inns   Rt. 1, Box 40, Vesuvius, Irish Gap 24483   804-922-7701
King Carter Inn   P.O. Box 425, Irvington 22480   804-438-6053
Laurel Brigade Inn   20 W. Market St., Leesburg 22075   703-777-1010
Norris House Inn   108 Loudoun St. SW, Leesburg 22075   703-777-1806
Alexander-Withrow House   3 W. Washington, Lexington 24450   703-463-2044
McCampbell Inn   11 N. Main St., Lexington 24450   703-463-2044
Hawksbill Lodge   Luray 22835   703-281-0548

Cedar Point Country Inn   P.O. Box 369, North, Mathews 23128   804-725-9535
Shenandoah Valley Farm   Rt. 1, Box 142, McGaheysville 22840   703-289-5402
Evans Farm Inn   1696 Chain Bridge Rd., McLean 22101
Luck House   P.O. Box 919, Middleburg 22117   703-687-5387
Red Fox Inn & Tavern   P.O. Box 385, Middleburg 22117   703-687-6301
Wayside Inn since 1797   7783 Main St., Middletown 22645   703-869-1797
Fort Lewis Lodge   Millboro 24460   703-925-2314
Stuartfield Hearth   Rt. 1, Box 199, Mitchells 22729   703-825-8132
Highland Inn   P.O. Box 40, Monterey 24465   703-468-2143
Inn at Montross   P.O. Box 908, Montross 22520   804-493-9097
Sky Chalet   Star Rt., Box 28, Mount Jackson 22842   703-856-2147
B&B Larchmont   1112 Buckingham Ave., Norfolk 23508   804-489-8449
Rockledge—1758   Occoquau 22125   703-690-3377
Shadows B&B Inn   Route 1, Box 535, Orange 22960   703-672-5057
Ashby Inn   Rt. 1, Box 2/A, Paris 22130   703-592-3900
Abbie Hill B&B   P.O. Box 4503, Richmond 23220   804-353-4656
Mary Bladon House   381 Washington Ave. SW, Roanoke 24016   703-344-5361
Isle of Wight Inn   1607 S. Church St., Smithfield 23430   804-357-3176
Nethers Mill   Rt. 1, Box 62, Sperryville 22740   703-987-8625
Swift Run Gap B&B   Skyline Dr. & Rt. 33 E., Stanardsville 22973   804-985-2740
Belle Grae Inn   515 W. Frederick St., Staunton 24401   703-886-5151
Thornrose House   531 Thornrose Avenue, Staunton 24401   703-885-7026
Hotel Strasburg   201 Holliday St., Strasburg 22657   703-465-9191
Surrey House   Surrey 23883   804-294-3191
Grave's Mountain Lodge   Syria 22743   703-923-4231
Prospect Hill   Route 3 Box 30, Trevilians 23093   703-967-0844
1763 Inn   Rt. 1 Box 19 D, Upperville 22176   703-592-3848
Gibson Hall Inn   P.O. Box 25, Upperville 22176   703-592-3514
Sugar Tree Inn   Hwy. 56, Vesuvius 24483   703-377-2197
Inn at Gristmill Square   Box 229, Warm Springs 24484   703-839-2231
Three Hills Inn   P.O. Box 99, Warm Springs 24484   703-839-5381
Inn at Little Washington   Box 300, Middle & Main, Washington 22747   703-675-3800
Brass Lantern Lodge   1782 Jamestown Rd., Williamsburg 23185   804-229-9089
Newport House   710 S. Henry St., Williamsburg 23185   804-229-1775
Wood's Guest Home   1208 Stewart Drive, Williamsburg 23185   804-229-3376
Candlewick Inn   127 N. Church St., Woodstock 22664   703-459-8008

Washington

ANACORTES

Channel House
2902 Oakes Ave., 98221
206-293-9382
Dennis & Patricia McIntyre
All year

$$ B&B
6 rooms, 4 pb
Visa, MC •
C-12+/S-no/P-no/H-no

Full breakfast
Coffee, tea, cookies
Sitting room
hot tub
library, bicycle rentals

Gateway to the San Juan Islands; built in 1902; Victorian-style mansion; all antiques throughout. All rooms view San Juans and Puget Sound. Separate Rose Cottage.

BELLEVUE

Bellevue Bed & Breakfast
830 100th Ave. SE, 98004
216-453-1048
Cy & Carol Garnett
All year

$ B&B
2 rooms, 2 pb
Visa, MC, AmEx, Disc •
C-10+/S-no/P-no/H-yes

Full breakfast
Comp. wine
Sitting room
cable TV, telephone
microwave, laundry

Hilltop, mountain and city views from your private unit or single room. Gourmet coffee. Central location near Lake Washington. Reasonable rates. In Seattle "Best Places."

BELLINGHAM

Schnauzer Crossing B&B
4421 Lakeway Dr., 98226
206-733-0055
Vermont & Donna McAllister
All year

$$ B&B
2 rooms, 2 pb
Visa, MC
C-yes/P-ltd
Some Fr., Span., Ger.

Full gourmet breakfast
Sitting room w/lake view
tennis court
canoe for lake Whatcom

A luxury bed & breakfast set amidst tall evergreens overlooking Lake Whatcom. Master suite with jacuzzi. Private tennis court. Gourmet fare.

CATHLAMET

Country Keeper B&B Inn The
P.O. Box 35, 98612
61 Main St.
206-795-3030
Terry & Meredith Beaston
All year

$ B&B
4 rooms
Visa, MC •
C-yes/S-no/P-no/H-no

Full gourmet breakfast
Restaurant next door
Sitting room
library, bicycles
golf, tennis & pool near

Our stately 1907 home overlooks the scenic Columbia River and Puget Island. Candlelit breakfasts in elegant dining room. Historic area. Marina, ferry, and game reserve nearby.

DEER HARBOR

Palmer's Chart House
P.O. Box 51, Orcas Isl., 98243
206-376-4231
Majean & Donald Palmer
All year

$$ B&B
2 rooms, 2 pb
•
C-ltd/S-ltd/P-no/H-no
Spanish

Full breakfast
Dinner available
Library
travel slide shows

Fishing, hiking, golf, biking available nearby. Sailing on the Palmers' 33-foot sloop is $15 per person for a day sail.

EASTSOUND

Turtleback Farm Inn
Rt.1 Box 650, Orcas Isl, 98245
Crow Valley Rd.
206-376-4914
William & Susan Fletcher
All year

$$ B&B
7 rooms, 7 pb
Visa, MC •
C-ask/S-ltd/P-no/H-yes

Full breakfast
Tea, coffee, wine
Bar
Living room
fireplace

Charming country inn. 80 acres of meadows, forests and ponds. Furnished with fine antiques. Quiet comfort and warm hospitality. On Orcas Island.

EDMONDS

Pinkham's Pillow, Ltd.
202 3rd Ave. S., 98020
206-774-3406
L.Pinkham,T.Pixley,P.Hagerman
All year

B&B
5 rooms, 5 pb
Visa, MC
C-12+/S-ltd/P-no/H-yes

Full breakfast
Afternoon tea (Mondays)
Sitting room

Elegant, serene, relaxing, friendly. Light Victorian-style home. Walk to shopping, good restaurants, ferry, train, and trolley.

FERNDALE

Hill Top Bed & Breakfast
5832 Church Rd., 98248
206-384-3619
Paul & Doris Matz
April—October

$ B&B
3 rooms, 1 pb
Visa, MC
C-yes/H-ltd
some Norwegian

Continental plus
Sitting room
badminton, croquet
games, TV

Country hideaway furnished with colonial charm. Museum quality quilts and wall hangings. Magnificent views of Mt. Baker and the Cascade Mountain Range.

FREELAND

**Cliff House and
Seacliff Cottage**
5440 Windmill Rd., 98249
206-321-1566
Peggy Moore, Walter O'Toole
All year

$$$ B&B
3 rooms, 3 pb
C-no/S-no/P-no/H-no

Continental plus
Comp. wine
Hot tub, fireplace
sitting room, VHS
piano, stereo

A stunningly beautiful house, for one couple. Complete privacy in this forested hideaway with miles of beach. Beautiful, charming Sea Cliff Cottage with French country decor.

GREENBANK

Guest House B&B Cottages
835 E. Christenson Rd., 98253
Whidbey Island
206-678-3115
Mary Jane & Don Creger
All year

$$$ B&B
6 rooms, 6 pb
Visa, MC, AmEx, Disc •
S-no/P-no/H-ltd

Full breakfast in suites
Cont. plus in cottage
Comp. wine
Kitchens, microwaves
pool, hot tub, VCR in rm

Country hideaway; 3 secluded cottages, large log house; private pond. Farmhouse with guest suite on 25 wooded acres; charming antique decor. Only 4-diamond AAA B&B in WA & OR.

ISSAQUAH

Wildflower B&B Inn
25237 SE Issaquah Rd., 98027
Fall City Rd.
206-392-1196
Laureita Caldwell
All year

$ B&B
4 rooms, 3 pb
•
C-12+

Full breakfast
Afternoon tea, coffee
Snacks

Lovely log home in acres of evergreens offers quiet, relaxing country charm of years gone by. Delightful suburb of Seattle.

KIRKLAND

Shumway Mansion
11410—99th Pl. NE, 98033
206-823-2303
Richard & Salli Harris
All year

$$ B&B
7 rooms, 7 pb
Visa, MC •
C-12+/S-ltd/P-no/H-ltd

Full breakfast
Evening snack
Sitting room, piano
courtesy athletic club

Four-story mansion circa 1910. Beautiful views of lake and bay. Delicious breakfasts and afternoon treats. Walk to beach.

LANGLEY

Eagles Nest Inn B&B
3236 E. Saratoga Rd., 98260
206-321-5331
Nancy & Dale Bowman
All year

$$$ B&B
3 rooms, 3 pb
Visa, MC
S-no

Full breakfast
Snacks, cinnamon rolls,
chocolate chip cookies
Sitting room
library, hot tubs

Casual elegance in country setting on Whidbey Island two miles from seaside village of Langley. Breathtaking view of Saratoga Passage.

LANGLEY

Log Castle Bed & Breakfast	$$ B&B	Full breakfast
3273 E. Saratoga Rd., 98260	3 rooms, 3 pb	Sitting room
206-321-5483	Visa, MC •	rowboat
Senator Jack & Norma Metcalf	C-no/S-no/P-no/H-no	canoe
All year		

Unique waterfront log lodge on Whidbey Island. Turret bedrooms, secluded beach, fantastic view of mountains, 50 miles north of Seattle.

Lone Lake Cottage	$$$ B&B	Continental plus
5206 S. Bayview Rd., 98260	3 rooms, 3 pb	Canoes
206-321-5325	Visa, MC	bicycles
Dolores & Ward Meeks	C-no/S-no/P-no/H-no	mini tennis court
All year		14' sail boat

Whidbey's "Shangri-la"! Romantic, lovely cottages. Fireplaces, kitchens, beautiful beach. Complimentary snorkling trip in our 40-foot stern wheel boat.

Saratoga Inn	$$$ B&B	Continental plus
4850 S. Coles Rd., 98260	5 rooms, 5 pb	Sitting room
Whidbey Island	C-no/S-no/P-no/H-no	library
206-221-7526		
Debbie Jones		
All year		

The Saratoga Inn is nestled atop 25 scenic acres overlooking Sarataga Passage, yet minutes from the beach. Spacious, quiet rooms replete with fireplace, private bath.

LEAVENWORTH

Haus Rohrbach Pension	$$ B&B	Full breakfast
12882 Ranger Rd., 98826	10 rooms, 3 pb	Desserts offered
509-548-7024	Visa, MC •	Hot tub
Robert & Kathryn Harrild	C-yes/S-ltd/P-no/H-no	swimming pool
Nov.—Thanksgiving Fri.		sitting room

One-of-a-kind, European-style country inn, unequaled in the Pacific Northwest. Alpine setting, pool & hot tub. Year-round outdoor activities.

LOPEZ ISLAND

Inn at Swifts Bay	$$ B&B	Full breakfast
Route 2, Box 3402, 98261	4 rooms, 2 pb	Comp. wine
206-468-3636	Visa, MC	Sitting room
R. Herrman, C. Brandmeir	Portuguese, some Ger, Sp	video library, hot tub
All year		bicycle rentals

English country comfort in the San Juan Islands. Private separate beach. Delightful breakfasts. Bald eagles, Orca whales. Pastoral and restful.

LUMMI ISLAND

Shorebird House	$ B&B	Continental plus
2654 N. Nugent Rd, 98262	2 rooms, 1 pb	Lunch, dinner, tea
206-758-2177	Visa	Sitting room
Jan Bonaparte	C-yes/S-no/P-no/H-no	piano
All year		

Contemporary house on an island at the water's edge in the woods; Pritikin diet low cholesterol meals served; bird-watching paradise.

MONTESANO

Sylvan Haus Murphy B&B
P.O. Box 416, 98563
206-249-3453
Jo Anne Murphy
Exc. Nov.—Apr. (hike in)

$ B&B
3 rooms, 2 pb
Visa •
C-12+

Full gourmet breakfast
Country kitchen
Hot tubs
restaurant nearby
boating, swimming,hiking

A gracious family home surrounded by towering evergreens; secluded high hill overlooking valley. Dining room; 5 decks; hot tub; gourmet breakfast. 1 hour from Sea Tac Airport.

MOUNT VERNON

White Swan Guest House
1388 Moore Rd., 98273
206-445-6805
Peter Goldfarb
All year

$$ B&B
3 rooms
C-ltd/S-no/P-no/H-no

Continental plus
Cookies
Sitting room
library

A "storybook" Victorian farmhouse six miles from the historic waterfront village of La Conner. One hour north of Seattle. English gardens, farmland. A perfect romantic getaway.

OLYMPIA

Harbinger Inn
1136 E. Bay Dr., 98506
206-754-0389
David & Emmy Mathes
All year

$ B&B
4 rooms, 1 pb
Visa, MC, AmEx
C-ltd/S-no/P-no/H-no

Continental plus
Comp. wine, tea
Snacks
Sitting room
library

Restored turn-of-the-century home with beautiful water view; period furnishings; conveniently located for boating, bicycling, business and entertainment.

Puget View Guesthouse B&B
7924 61st Ave. NE, 98506
206-459-1676
Dick & Barbara Yunker
All year

$$ B&B
2 rooms, 1 pb
Visa, MC •
C-yes/S-yes/P-ask/H-no

Continental plus
Suite sleeps 4
Private dining area/deck
Books, games, canoe
100-acre park next door

Charming waterfront guest cottage suite next to host's log home. Breakfast to your cottage. Peaceful. Picturesque. A "NW Best Places" since 1984. Puget Sound 5 min. off I-5.

ORCAS

Orcas Hotel
P.O. Box 155, 98280
at the Ferry Landing
206-376-4300/206-376-4306
Barbara & John Jamieson
All year

$ B&B
12 rooms, 3 pb
AmEx, Visa, MC •
C-yes/S-yes/P-no/H-ltd
French, Spanish

Continental breakfast
Restaurant & bar
Sitting room, library
bicycle storage
music Saturday, Sunday

Beautifully restored Victorian inn above ferry landing, gorgeous view, fine dining, local seafood, cocktails, "White Pickets & Wicker," garden, antiques.

PORT TOWNSEND

Hastings House
313 Walker St., 98368
Walker & Washington Sts.
206-385-6753
Rob & Joanna Jackson
All year

$$ B&B
8 rooms, 8 pb
Visa, MC
C-8+/S-no/P-no/H-no

Full breakfast
Evening tea
Formal dining room
Parlors, grand piano
library, billiard room

Victorian decor that creates a nostalgia for great-grandmother's house! Cluttered elegance, romantic bedrooms—quiet and peaceful.

PORT TOWNSEND

Heritage House Inn
305 Pierce St., 98368
206-385-6800
J & P Broughton, B & C Ellis
All year

$$ B&B
6 rooms, 3 pb
C-8+ /S-no/P-no/H-ltd

Full breakfast
Coffee/tea/cider/cookies
Victorian parlor
bicycles

Unique combination of Victorian setting, unparalleled view of the bay, classic Italianate inn, quaint charm, warm traditional attention to comfort.

James House
1238 Washington St., 98368
206-385-1238
Lowell & Barbara Bogart
All year

$$ B&B
12 rooms, 6 pb
Visa, MC
C-12+ /S-ltd/P-ltd/H-ltd
French, Spanish

Continental plus
Comp. tea, wine
Sitting room, piano
library

1889 Queen Anne Victorian furnished in period antiques. First B&B in northwest, still the finest.

The Lincoln Inn
538 Lincoln St., 98368
206-385-6677
Joan & Robert Allen
Easter—Thanksgiving

$$ B&B
6 rooms, 6 pb
Visa, MC •
C-no/S-ltd/P-ltd/H-no
French, German

Full gourmet breakfast
Dinner, comp. wine
Sitting room
workout facilities
bicycles, tennis court

A small personally run inn offering a unique Victorian atmosphere and hospitality. Victorian antiques in all rooms. Leave the world behind you.

Starrett House Inn B&B
744 Clay St., 98368
206-385-3205
Edel & Bob Sokol
All year

$$ B&B
9 rooms, 3 pb
Visa, MC •
C-8+ /S-yes/P-no/H-ltd

Full breakfast
Dinner (Fri.-Mon.)
Baby grand piano
player piano
sitting room, jaccuzi

Port Townsend's only full-service Victorian inn. The most spectacular architectural achievement in the Pacific Northwest.

SEATTLE

Beech Tree Manor
1405 Queen Anne Ave. N., 98109
206-281-7037
Virginia Lucero
All year

$$ B&B
4 rooms
Visa, MC
C-yes/S-no/P-no/H-no

Continental plus
Comp. sherry
Sitting room, library
antique linen shop
porch w/wicker chairs

1904 mansion, near City Center, yet quiet; scrumptious breakfasts; sherry in Irish crystal; original art in all rooms; luxuriously comfortable.

Challenger Tugboat
809 Fairview Place N., 98109
206-340-1201
Jerry Brown
All year

$$ B&B
4 rooms, 1 pb
•
C-yes/S-yes/P-no/H-yes

Full gourmet breakfast
Self-serve bar
Sitting room, library
bicycles, fireplace
small boats

On board a fully functional, exceptionally clean, restored tugboat. Near downtown Seattle. Closed circuit TV. Carpeted throughout. Nautical antiques.

SEATTLE

Chambered Nautilus B&B Inn
5005 22nd Ave. NE, 98105
206-522-2536
Bunny & Bill Hagemeyer
All year

$$ B&B
6 rooms, 2 pb
Visa, MC, AmEx •
C-12+/S-no/P-no/H-no

Full breakfast
Buffet breakfast Sunday
Comp. wine & tea
Sitting room, phones
desks in rooms

Peaceful in-city retreat close to downtown, University of Washington and neighorhood parks. Gourmet breakfasts for business or vacation. Corporate rate offered.

Chelsea Station B&B Inn
4915 Linden Ave. N, 98103
206-547-6077
Dick & MaryLou Jones
All year

$$ B&B
5 rooms, 5 pb
Visa, MC, AmEx, DC •
C-10+/S-no/P-no/H-no

Full breakfast
Comp. wine, eve. snack
Sitting room, organ
kitchen suite
hot tub

Old world charm and tranquil country setting amidst the city's activity. Each room is a very private answer to a quiet getaway. Banana batter French toast: "Best in the West."

Emerald City Inn
1521 Bellevue Ave., 98122
206-587-6565
Bob Davis
All year

$$
9 rooms, 9 pb
Visa, MC, AmEx
C-no/S-yes/P-no/H-no

Continental breakfast
Comp. wine
Hot tub
gym
piano, wet bars

Nine suite guest house hotel in the modern 1960s style. Centrally located. A gem of a place to stay.

Galer Place B&B
318 W. Galer St., 98119
206-282-5339
Chris Chamberlain
All year

$$$ B&B
4 rooms, 2 pb
Visa, MC
C-12+/S-ltd/P-ask/H-no
French

Full breakfast
Sitting room

Turn-of-the-century inn, parking. Afternoon tea, fresh ground coffee and baked goods at breakfast. Near Seattle Center.

Mildred's B&B Inn
1202 15th Ave. E, 98112
206-325-6072
Mildred J. Sarver
All year

$$ B&B
4 rooms, 1 pb
•
C-yes/S-ltd/P-no/H-no

Full breakfast
Afternoon tea
Sitting room
library
tennis nearby

1890 Victorian. Wraparound veranda, lace curtains, red carpets, grand piano, fireplace. City location near bus, park and art museum.

Prince of Wales
133 13th Ave. E., 98102
206-325-9692
Naomi Reed, Bert Brun
All year

$$ B&B
3 rooms, 1 pb
Visa, MC •
C-13+/S-no/P-no/H-no

Full breakfast
Morning coffee to room
Sitting room
fireplaces
garden

Downtown one and a quarter miles away; on bus line; walk to convention center; turn-of-the-century ambience; panoramic view of city skyline.

SEATTLE

Seattle B&B Guest Cottage
2442 NW Market #300, 98107
206-784-0539
Inge Pokrandt
All year

$ EP/B&B
3 rooms, 2 pb
Visa, MC, AmEx •
C-ltd/S-no/P-no/H-yes
German

Some staple foods
Comp. tea, wine
Sitting rm, maid service
color cable TV, phone
kitchen, prvt. entrance

Private suite and cottage near downtown, parks, University. Relaxed atmosphere. Lots of tourist books/materials—hostess knowledgeable about area; a most hospitable home.

The Shafer Mansion
907 14th Ave. E., 98112
206-329-4628
H. Lee Vennes
All year

$$ B&B
5 rooms, 3 pb
AmEx •
C-yes

Continental plus
Sitting room
library

One of Seattle's greatest guest houses near Volunteer Park on beautiful tree-lined streets. Walk to unique restaurants and shops along 15th Ave. East and the popular Broadway.

Williams House B&B
1505 4th Ave. N., 98109
206-285-0810
Susan/Doug/Daughters Williams
All year

$$ B&B
5 rooms, 1 pb
Visa, MC, AmEx
C-yes/S-ltd/P-no/H-no

Full breakfast
Sitting room
piano

Views of Seattle, Puget Sound, mountains. One of Seattle's oldest neighborhoods. Very close to Seattle activities, parks, lakes.

SNOHOMISH

Countryman B&B
119 Cedar, 98290
206-568-9622
Larry & Sandy Countryman
All year

$$ B&B
3 rooms, 3 pb
Visa, MC •
C-yes/S-no/P-yes/H-no
German

Full breakfast
Afternoon tea
Sitting room
bicycles

1896 Queen Anne Victorian in National Historic district. One block from 300 antique dealers. The inn with the extras.

SOUTH CLE ELUM

Moore House Country Inn
P.O. Box 2861, 98943
526 Marie
509-674-5939
Monty & Connie Moore
All year

$ B&B
10 rooms, 4 pb
Visa, MC, AmEx •
C-yes/S-ltd/P-no/H-no

Full breakfast
Lunch & dinner avail.
Sitting room, hot tubs
1 caboose unit w/bath
winter sleigh rides

Old railroad hotel adjacent to Iron Horse State Park. Mountain location makes four seasons of activities possible from our doorstep.

SPOKANE

Fotheringham House B&B
2128 W. 2nd Ave., 99204
509-838-4363
Howard & Phyllis Ball
All year

$ B&B
8 rooms, 5 pb
AmEx, Visa, MC
C-12+/S-no/P-no/H-no

Continental plus
Comp. wine
Rolls Royce, living room
library, next to restnt.
near tennis & park

Victorian home located in historic Spokane District. Antique furnishings, queen beds, park across street. Next to restaurant in Victorian mansion.

Andrie Rose Inn, Ludlow, VT

SPOKANE

Whispering Pines B&B
E. 7504—44th, 99223
509-448-1433
The Campbells
All year

$ B&B
3 rooms, 1 pb
•

Full breakfast
Snacks
Sitting room
hiking

Fantastic view from luxury hideaway nestled in the trees. Birds and wildlife abound. Gourmet breakfast, air-conditioning. Minutes from town.

VASHON ISLAND

The Swallow's Nest
Route 3 Box 221, 98070
SW 248th St.,Maury Island
206-463-2646
Kathryn & Robert Keller
All year

$ EP
5 rooms, 3 pb
Visa, MC •
C-yes/S-no/P-ltd/H-ltd

Continental breakfast $
Fresh fruit in season
Hot tub
golf nearby

Get away to comfortable country cottages on the bluffs overlooking Puget Sound and Mt. Rainier. Optional breakfast brought to your cottage.

More Inns...

River Valley B&B   Box 158, Acme 98220   206-595-2686
Admiral's Hideaway   1318 30th St., Anacortes 98221   206-293-0106
Burrow's Bay B&B   4911 MacBeth Dr., Anacortes 98221   206-293-4792
Lowman House B&B   701 "K" Ave, Anacortes 98221   206-293-0590
Nantucket Inn   3402 Commercial Ave., Anacortes 98221   206-293-6007
Old Brook Inn   530 Old Brook Lane, Anacortes 98221   206-293-4768
White Gull   420 Commercial, Anacortes 98221   206-293-7011
Alexander's Country Inn   Hwy. 706, Ashford 98304   206-569-2300

Ashford Mansion   Box G, Ashford 98304   206-569-2739
Growly Bed & Breakfast   37311 SR 706, Ashford 98304   206-569-2339
Mountain Meadows Inn   28912 SR 706E, Ashford 98304   206-569-2788
Beach Cottage   5831 Ward Avenue, NE, Bainbridge Island 98110   206-842-6081
Bombay House   P.O. Box 11338, Bainbridge Island 98110   206-842-3926
Olympic View B&B   15415 Harvey Rd NE, Bainbridge Island 98110   206-842-4671
Lions Bed & Breakfast   803 92nd Avenue N.E., Bellevue 98004   206-455-1018
Petersen Bed & Breakfast   10228 S.E. 8th, Bellevue 98004   206-454-9334
De Cann House B&B   2610 Eldridge Ave, Bellingham 98225   206-734-9172
North Garden Inn   1014 N. Garden, Bellingham 98225   206-671-7828
Grand Old House   P.O. Box 667, Hwy. 14, Bingen 98605   509-493-2838
Carson Hot Springs Hotel   P.O. Box 370, Carson 98610   509-427-8292
Em's Bed & Breakfast Inn   P.O. Box 206, Chelan 98816   509-682-4149
Mary Kay's Whaley Mansion   Rt. 1, Box 693, Chelan 98816   509-682-5735
North Cascades Lodge   P.O. Box W, Chelan 98816   509-682-4711
Summer House   2603 Center Road, Chimacum 98325   206-732-4017
Home by the Sea   2388 E Sunlight Beach R, Clinton 98236   206-221-2964
Lake Side Manor B&B   Tiger Star Rt Box 194, Colville 99114   509-684-8741
Cascade Mountain Inn   3840 Pioneer Lane, Concrete Birdsview 98237   206-826-4333
Captain Whidbey Inn   2072 W. Whidbey Island, Coupeville 98239   206-678-4097
Colonel Crockett Farm B&B   1012 S. Fort Casey Rd., Coupeville 98239   206-466-3207
Fort Casey Inn   1124 S. Engle Road, Coupeville 98239   206-678-8792
Blue Heron   Rt. 1, Box 64, Eastsound 98245   206-376-2954
Kangaroo House B&B   P.O. Box 334, Eastsound 98245   206-376-2175
Outlook Inn   Box 210, Main Street, Eastsound 98245   206-376-2200
Rosario Resort Hotel   Eastsound 98245   206-376-2222
Old Mill House B&B   P.O. Box 543, Eatonville 98328   206-832-6506
Harrison House   210 Sunset Ave., Edmonds 98020   206-776-4748
Heather House   1011 "B" Avenue, Edmonds 98020   206-778-7233
Hudgrens Haven   9313 190th, SW, Edmonds 98020   206-776-2202
Anderson House B&B   P.O. Box 1547, Ferndale 98248   206-384-3450
Miller Tree Inn   P.O. Box 953, Forks 98331   206-374-6806
Pillars By The Sea   1367 E. Bayview, Freeland 98249   206-221-7738
Blair House B&B   345 Blair Ave., Friday Harbor 98250   206-378-5907
Collins House   225 A Street, Friday Harbor 98250   206-378-5834
Moon & Six Pence   3021 Beaverton Valley, Friday Harbor 98250   206-378-4138
Olympic Lights   4531A Cattle Point Rd., Friday Harbor 98250   206-378-3186
Tucker House B&B   260 B St., Friday Harbor 98250   206-378-2783
American Hearth B&B   7506 Soundview Dr., Gig Harbor 98335   206-851-2196
Olde Glencove Hotel   9418 Glencove Rd., Gig Harbor 98335   206-884-2835
Three Creeks Lodge   2120 Hwy 97 Satus Pass, Goldendale 98620   509-773-4026
Hopkinson House   862 Bumping River Rd., Goose Prairie 98929   509-248-2264
Smith House B&B   307 Maple St., Hamilton 98255   206-826-4214
San Juan Inn   P.O. Box 776, Harbor 98250   206-378-2070
Inn at Ilwaco   120 Williams Street N.E, Ilwaco 98624   206-642-8686
Bush House   P.O. Box 58, Index 98256   206-793-2312
Downey House   1880 Chilberg Road, La Conner 98257   206-678-3115
Heron in La Conner   Box 716 117 Maple St., La Conner 98257   206-466-4626
Katy's Inn   503 S. 3rd, Box 304, La Conner 98257   206-466-3366
La Conner Country Inn   P.O. Box 573, La Conner 98257   206-466-3101
Rainbow Inn   1075 Chilberg Rd,POB 16, La Conner 98257   206-466-4578
Whaley Mansion   415 Third St., Lake Cheelan 98816   509-682-5735
Orchard   619 3rd St., Langley 98260   206-221-7880
Whidbey Inn   P.O. Box 156, Langley 98260   206-221-7115

Bavarian Meadows B&B   11097 Eagle Creek Rd., Leavenworth 98826   509-548-4449
Brown's Farm B&B   11150 Hwy 209, Leavenworth 98826   509-548-7863
Edel Haus Pension   320 Ninth St., Leavenworth 98826   509-548-4412
Heaven Can Wait Lodge   12385 Shugart Flats Rd., Leavenworth 98826   206-881-5350
Hotel Europa   833 Front Street, Leavenworth 98826   509-548-5221
Mc Clain's B&B   1226 Front St., Leavenworth 98826   509-548-7755
Old Blewett Pass B&B   3470 Highway 97, Leavenworth 98826   509-548-4475
National Park Inn   Longmire 98398   206-569-2565
Betty's Place   P.O. Box 86, Lopez 98261   206-468-2470
MacKaye Harbor Inn   Rt. 1, Box 1940, Lopez Island 98261   206-468-2253
Willows Inn B&B   2579 West Shore Drive, Lummi Island 98262   206-758-2620
Le Cocq House   719 W. Edson, Lynden 98264   206-354-3032
Maple Valley B&B   20020 S.E. 228th, Maple Valley 98038   206-432-1409
Mazawa Country Inn   Mazawa 98833   509-996-2681
St. Helen's Manorhouse   7476 US Highway 12, Morton 98356   206-498-5243
Ecologic Place   10 Beach Dr., Nordland 98358   206-385-3077
Apple Tree Inn   43317 SE N.Bend Wy, North Bend 98045   206-888-3572
Hillwood Gardens B&B   41812 S. E. 142nd St., North Bend 98045   206-888-0799
Unicorn's Rest   316 E. 10th Street, Olympia 98501   206-754-9613
Woodsong Bed & Breakfast   P.O. Box 32, Orcas 98280   206-376-2340
Packwood Hotel   Rt. 256, Packwood 98361   206-494-5431
Amy's Manor B&B   P.O. Box 411, Pateros 98846   509-923-2334
French House B&B   206 W. Warren, Pateros 98846   509-923-2626
Old House   674 Kendor Road, Point Roberts 98281   206-945-5210
Bennett House B&B   325 E. 6th, Port Angeles 98362   206-457-0870
Glen Mar by the Sea   318 N. Eunice, Port Angeles 98362   206-457-6110
Harbour House   139 West 14th, Port Angeles 98362   206-457-3424
Lake Crescent Lodge   Star Route 1, Port Angeles 98362   206-928-3211
Tudor Inn   1108 S. Oak, Port Angeles 98362   206-452-3138
Ogle's B&B   1307 Dogwood Hill S.W., Port Orchard 98366   206-876-9170
Arcadia Country Inn   1891 S. Jacob Miller Rd, Port Townsend 98368   206-385-5245
Bishop Victorian Suites   714 Washington St., Port Townsend 98368   206-385-6122
Irish Acres   P.O. Box 466, Port Townsend 98368   206-385-4485
Lizzie's Victorian B&B   731 Pierce St., Port Townsend 98368   206-385-4168
Manresa Castle   P.O. Box 564, Port Townsend 98368   206-385-5750
Palace Hotel   1004 Water St., Port Townsend 98368   206-385-0773
Quimper Inn   1306 Franklin St., Port Townsend 98368   206-385-1086
Ravenscroft Inn Ltd.   533 Quincy St., Port Townsend 98368   206-385-2784
Manor Farm Inn   26069 Big Valley Rd., Poulsbo 98370   206-779-4628
Lake Quinault Lodge   P.O. Box 7, So. Shore Rd., Quinault 98575   206-288-2571
Hampton House B&B   409 Silverbrook Rd, Randle 98377
Cedarym, A Colonial B&B   1011 240th Ave. NE, Redmond 98053   206-868-4159
Roche Harbor Resort   Roche Harbor 98250   206-378-2155
Summer Song B&B   P.O. Box 82, Seabeck 98380   206-830-5089
Walton House   12340 Seabeck Hwy NW, Seabeck 98380   206-830-4498
Burton House   P.O. Box 9902, Seattle 98109   206-285-5945
College Inn Guest House   4000 University Way NE, Seattle 98105   206-633-4441
Hanson House B&B   1526 Palm Ave. SW, Seattle 98116   206-937-4157
Marit's B&B   6208 Palatine Ave. N., Seattle 98103   206-782-7900
Salisbury House   750 16th Ave. E, Seattle 98112   206-328-8682
Shelburne Country Inn   P.O. Box 250, Seaview 98644   206-642-2442
Margie's B&B   120 Forrest Road, Sequim 98382   206-683-7011
Twin River Ranch B&B   E 5730 Hwy 3, Shelton 98584   206-426-1023
Country Manner B&B   1120 First St., Snohowish 98290   206-568-8254

"Old" Honey Farm   8910 384th Ave. S. E., Snoqualmie 98065   206-329-4628
Blakely Estate B&B   E. 7710 Hodin Dr., Spokane 99212   509-926-9426
Durocher House B&B   W. 4000 Randolph Road, Spokane 99204   509-328-2971
Town & Country Cottage B&B   N7620 Fox Point Dr., Spokane 99208   509-466-7559
Tokeland Hotel   P.O. Box 117, Tokeland 98590   206-267-7700
Mio Amore Pensione   P.O. Box 208, Trout Lake 98650   509-395-2264
River Bend Inn   Rt. 2 Box 943, Usk 99180   509-445-1476
Island Inn B&B   Route 1, Box 950, Vashon Island 98070   206-567-4832
Rees Mansion Inn   260 E. Birch St., Walla Walla 99362   509-529-7845
Forget-Me-Not B&B   1133 Washington St., Wenatchee 98801   509-663-6114
Inn of the White Salmon   P.O. Box 1446, White Salmon 98672   509-493-2335
Orchard Hill Inn   Route 2, Box 130, White Salmon 98672   509-493-3024

Washington, D.C.

ARLINGTON, VA

Crystal Bed & Breakfast	$$ B&B	Full breakfast (wkends)
2620 S. Fern St., 22202	5 rooms, 1 pb	Continental plus (wkdys)
Arlington, VA	•	Tea, baked goods, fruit
703-548-7652	C-yes/S-yes/P-no/H-no	TV room, gardens
Susan Swain		handmade quilts each rm
All year		

Country in the city; breakfast served in lovely garden; country motif decor. Walk to subway; many restaurants nearby. 20 minutes to heart of D.C.; near Historic Alexandria.

WASHINGTON

Adams Inn	$$ B&B	Continental plus
1744 Lanier Pl. NW, 20009	11 rooms, 6 pb	Coffee, tea, donuts
202-745-3600	Visa, MC, AmEx •	Sitting room
Gene & Nancy Thompson	C-yes/S-no/P-no/H-no	library, TV lounge
All year		gardens, deck

Restored Edwardian townhouse; enjoy charm and quiet of residential street in the heart of the famous Adams-Morgan neighborhood. Shops and restaurants nearby. Walk to zoo.

Capitol Hill Guest House	$$ B&B	Continental breakfast
101 Fifth St. NE, 20002	10 rooms	Sitting room
202-547-1050	Visa, MC, AmEx •	
William Courville	C-12+/S-no/P-no/H-no	
All year	French	

Formerly home to US Congressional pages. Turn-of-the-century Victorian rowhouse with original woodwork and appointments. Ten moderately priced rooms in historic district.

WASHINGTON ─────────────────

Embassy Inn, Windsor Inn	$$ B&B	Continental breakfast
1627 16th St. NW, 20009	Visa, MC, AmEx •	Comp. sherry, snacks
1842 16th St. NW	C-yes/S-yes/P-no/H-no	Sitting room
202-234-7800/202-667-0300	Sp., Fr., Ch., Sign	
Susan Araujo		
All year		

Unique haven in the heart of the nation's capitol. Personalized service, complimentary evening sherry. Close to sights, museums, and restaurants.

Kalorama Guest House	$ B&B	Continental breakfast
1854 Mintwood Pl. NW, 20009	50 rooms, 50 pb	Comp. wine
202-667-6369	Visa, MC, AmEx, DC •	Sitting room
Tammi, Grace & Jonathon	C-yes/S-yes/P-no/H-no	
All year		

Charming European-style bed & breakfast in six turn-of-the-century townhouses. Period art, furnishings, brass beds, plants, outdoor landscaped garden, and hospitality.

Kalorama House / Woodley Prk	$ B&B	Continental breakfast
2700 Cathedral Ave., NW, 20008	19 rooms, 12 pb	Comp. sherry
202-328-0860	MC, Visa, AmEx, DC •	Parlor, sun room
Lynn Foley, Michael Gallagher	C-yes/S-yes/P-no/H-no	24-hour message service
All year		free local phone calls

Victorian townhouse decorated in period furnishings. Antique-filled, spacious rooms. Beautiful sun room for your morning breakfast. Charming, unique & inexpensive.

Swiss Inn	$$ EP	Kitchenettes
1204 Massachusetts NW, 20005	7 rooms, 7 pb	Library
202-842-0151	Visa, MC, AmEx •	
Ralph Nussbaumer	C-no/S-no/P-no/H-no	
All year	French, German, Italian	

Within walking distance to White House and Convention Center; all air-conditioned. Suites have private baths and fully equipped kitchenettes.

Victorian Accommodations	$$$ B&B	Full breakfast
1309 Rhode Island Av NW, 20005	15 rooms, 10 pb	Snacks, afternoon tea
202-234-6292/800-442-4884	•	Sitting room
Ronald D. Morgan	C-yes/S-yes	library
All year	some Spanish	organizing tours

Handcrafted Victorian elegance. Rooms with private bath, kitchen and fireplace; decorated with art and antiques. Near Washington, D.C., sights.

More Inns. . .

B&B Accom. of Washington   3222 Davenport St. NW, Washington, D.C. 20008   202-363-8909

Castlestone Inn   1918 17th St. NW, Washington, D.C. 20009   202-483-4706

Connecticut-Woodley House   2647 Woodley Rd.NW, Washington, D.C. 20008   202-667-0218

Meg's International House   1315 Euclid St., NW, Washington, D.C. 20009   202-232-5837

Morrison Clark Inn   Massachusetts & 11th., Washington, D.C. 20001   202-898-1200

Reeds   c/o Bed & Breakfast Ltd, Washington, D.C. 20005   202-328-3510

Victorian Accommodations   1309 Rhode Island Av NW, Washington, D.C. 20005   202-234-6292

Windsor Inn   1842 16th St. NW, Washington, D.C. 20009   202-667-0300

West Virginia

BERKELEY SPRINGS

Folkestone Bed & Breakfast
Route 2, Box 404, 25411
304-258-3743
Hettie Hawvermale
April—October

$$ B&B
2 rooms, 1 pb
C-15+/S-yes/P-no/H-no

Full breakfast
Sitting room
hot tub

An English Tudor home in 10 wooded acres, natural country setting. Famous spa baths in town. Rented to one group at a time, 1 to 5 persons.

Highlawn Inn
304 Market St., 25411
304-258-5700
Sandra Kauffman
All year

$$ B&B
6 rooms, 6 pb
Visa, MC
C-no/S-yes/P-no/H-ltd

Full country breakfast
Dinner for groups by res
Catering, weddings
TV, veranda, porch swing
golf, tennis, hiking

Restored Victorian; luxurious touches, solitude and antiques in quiet mountain town. Minutes from famous mineral baths. Winter Victorian escape packages. Thanksgiving feast.

CHARLES TOWN

Cottonwood Inn
Route 2, Box 61-S, 25414
Old Mill Rd.
304-725-3371
Colin & Eleanor Simpson
All year

$$$ B&B
6 rooms, 6 pb
Visa, MC, Choice
C-yes/S-yes/P-no/H-no

Full breakfast
Aftn. tea, snacks
Comp. wine
Sitting room, library
trout stream

Quiet country setting, stocked trout stream, near Harpers Ferry in historic Shenandoah Valley. Bountiful breakfast. Guest rooms have TV and air-conditioning.

Gilbert House B&B
P.O. Box 1104, 25414
Route 1, Middleway
304-725-0637
Jean & Bernie Heiler
All year

$$$ B&B
3 rooms, 3 pb
Visa, MC •
C-no/S-ltd/P-no/H-no
German, Spanish

Full gourmet breakfast
Comp tea/wine/champagne
Sitting room, library
piano, fireplaces
walking tour of village

Near Harper's Ferry, magnificent stone house on National Register in 18th-century village. Tasteful antiques, art treasures. Leisurely breakfast. Romantic.

DAVIS

Bright Morning
Route 32, William Ave., 26260
304-259-2719
Dr. & Mrs. George Bright

$$ EP
•

Full breakfast $
Restaurant
Box lunches

Former lumberjack boarding house in Davis, a small, rural town, renowned for its natural attractions. Historically authentic. A chance to experience a little history & charm.

ELKINS ——————————————

Tunnel Mountain B&B
Route 1, Box 59-1, 26241
304-636-1684
Robert & Paula Graglia
All year

$ B&B
3 rooms, 3 pb
Visa, MC •
C-10+/S-no/P-no/H-no

Full breakfast
Restaurant nearby
Sitting room w/fireplace
patio, wooded paths, A/C
scenic views, cable TV

Romantic country fieldstone B&B nestled in the scenic West Virginia. Mountains next to National Forest and recreational areas. Antiques, fireplaces, warm hospitality.

MARTINSBURG ——————————————

Dunn Country Inn
Route 3, Box 33J, 25401
304-263-8646
Prince & Dianna Dunn
All year

$$$ B&B
6 rooms, 2 pb
Visa, MC
C-12+/S-no/P-no/H-ltd

Full breakfast
Comp. wine, snacks
Sitting room

Country inn providing a tranquil setting—a welcome retreat from the city. Scrumptious and hearty breakfast. 1805 Home on National Register.

MATHIAS ——————————————

Valley View Farm
Route 1, Box 467, 26812
304-897-5229
Ernest & Edna Shipe
All year

$ B&B/AP
4 rooms
C-yes/S-no/P-no/H-no

Full country breakfast
All meals served
Sitting room
library
entertainment

A country hideaway easily accessible to eastern cities. Bountiful meals with homemade breads, sweets, fresh vegetables. Friendly country hospitality.

MOOREFIELD ——————————————

McMechen House Inn B&B
109 N. Main St., 26836
304-538-2417
Art & Evelyn Valloto
Exc. 12/24—1/15

$$ B&B
6 rooms, 6 pb
Visa, MC, AmEx
C-yes/S-ltd/P-ltd/H-no

Full breakfast
Sitting room
cable TV
air conditioning

Surrounded by majestic mountains, natural beauty. Built in 1853, furnished in period antiques, emphasis on hospitality and opportunities to see and do.

POMNEY ——————————————

Hampshire House 1884
165 N. Grafton St., 26757
304-822-7171
Jane & Scott Simmons
All year

$$ B&B/MAP/AP
5 rooms, 5 pb
Visa, MC, AmEx •
C-yes/S-no/P-no/H-no

Full breakfast
Lunch, dinner
Comp. wine, snacks
Sitting room, library
bicycles, tennis, pool

Completely renovated 1884 home. Period furniture, lamps, fireplaces. Gourmet dining. Quiet. Central heat and air. Therapeutic massage available.

SHEPHERDSTOWN ——————————————

Thomas Shepherd Inn
P.O. Box 1162, 25443
German & Duke Sts.
304-876-3715
Ed & Carol Ringoot
All year

$$ B&B
6 rooms, 4 pb
Visa, MC
C-12+/S-ltd/P-no/H-no
French, Flemish

Full breakfast
Comp. tea, wine
Living room w/fireplace
bicycles & picnics

1868 restored stately home in quaint historic Civil War town. Period antiques, very special breakfasts, fireside beverage, excellent restaurants.

SUMMIT POINT

Countryside	$ B&B	Continental plus to room
P.O. Box 57, 25446	2 rooms, 2 pb	Afternoon tea/snack
304-725-2614	Visa, MC	Sitting room, bicycles
Lisa & Daniel Hileman	C-yes/S-yes/P-yes/H-no	down comforters
All year		feather beds

Near historic Harper's Ferry; quiet and cozy country inn; hiking, cycling, antiquing, sightseeing. For romantic getaways, honeymoons, anniversary and birthday celebrations.

WHEELING

Stratford Springs Inn	$$$ AP	Continental plus
355 Oglebay Dr., 26003	3 rooms, 3 pb	Lunch & dinner included
304-233-5100	Visa, MC, AmEx	Restaurant, bar service
R.C. Wheat, Jr.	C-yes/S-yes/H-yes	Sitting room, gift shop
All year	Spanish, French, Italian	tennis courts, pool

Stratford Springs, with its gourmet dining, casual atmosphere, period antiques and luxurious lodging rooms, is West Virginia's best-kept secret. . . Only 10 minutes from I-70.

Yesterdays Ltd. B&B	$$ B&B	Full breakfast
827 Main St., 26003	12 rooms, 4 pb	Comp. wine, snacks
651, 811 & 817 Main St.	Visa, MC •	Sitting room
304-232-0864	C-yes/S-ltd/P-no/H-no	Whirlpool bath in
William & Nancy Fields		some rooms
All year		

Lovingly restored Victorian townhouses in historic district overlooking river. Antiques galore. Walk to downtown shopping and events. Perfect getaway or travel stopover.

More Inns. . .

Cabin Lodge   Box 355, Rt. 50, Aurora 26705   304-735-3563
Country Inn   207 So. Washington St, Berkeley Springs 25411   304-258-2210
Manor   P. O. Box 342, Berkeley Springs 25411   304-258-1552
Maria's Garden & Inn   201 Independence St., Berkeley Springs 25411   304-258-2021
Shelly's Homestead   Rt. 1, Box 1-A, Burlington 26710   304-289-3941
Greenbrier River Inn   Rt. 2 Box 96, Ronceverte, Caldwell 24925   304-647-5652
Carriage Inn   417 E. Washington Stree, Charles Town 25414   304-728-8003
Hillbrook Inn   Rt. 2, Box 152, Charles Town 25414   304-725-4223
Pennbrooke Farm B&B   Granny-she Run, Chloe 25235   304-655-7367
Twisted Thistle B&B   P.O. Box 480, Fourth St., Davis 26260   304-259-5389
Cheat River Lodge   Rt. 1, Box 116, Elkins 26241   304-636-2301
Prospect Hill B&B   P.O. Box 135, Gerrardstown 25420   304-229-3346
Glen Ferris Inn   US Rt. 60, Glen Ferris 25090   304-632-1111
Oak Knoll B&B   Crawley, Greenbrier County 24931   304-392-6903
Fillmore Street B&B   Box 34, Harpers Ferry 25245   301-337-8633
Beekeeper Inn   Helvetia 26224   304-924-6435
Current Bed & Breakfast   Box 135, Hillsboro 25946   304-653-4722
West Fork Inn   Rt. 2, Box 212, Jane Lew 26378   304-745-4893
General Lewis Inn   301 E. Washington, Lewisburg 24901   304-645-2600
Crawford's Country Corner   Box 112, Lost Creek 26385   304-745-3017
Guest House   Low-Gap, Lost River 26811   304-897-5707
Hickory Hill Farm   Rt. 1, Box 355, Moorefield 26836   304-538-2511
Maxwell B&B   Rt. 12, Box 197, Morgantown 26505   304-594-3041
Kilmarnock Farms   Rt. 1 Box 91, Orlando 26412   304-452-8319
Bavarian Inn & Lodge   Rt. 1, Box 30, Shepherdstown 25443   304-876-2551

Fuss 'N Feathers   Box 1088, 210 W. German, Shepherdstown 25443   304-876-6469
Little Inn   P.O. Box 219, Shepherdstown 25443   304-876-2208
Mecklenberg Inn   128 E. German St,Box 16, Shepherdstown 25443   304-876-2126
Shang-Ra-La B&B   Rt. 1, Box 156, Shepherdstown 25443   304-876-2391
Morgan Orchard   Route 2, Box 114, Sinks Grove 24976   304-772-3638
Cobblestone-on-The-Ohio   103 Charles St., Sistersville 26175   304-652-1206
Wells Inn   316 Charles St., Sistersville 26175   304-652-3111
Elk River Touring Center   Slatyfork 26291   304-572-3771
Garvey House   P.O. Box 98, Winona 25942   304-574-3235

Wisconsin

APPLETON

The Parkside
402 E. North St., 54911
414-733-0200
Bonnie Riley
All year

$$ B&B
1 rooms, 1 pb
C-no/S-yes/P-no/H-no

Full breakfast
Comp. wine, snacks
Sitting room, library
tennis
TV, A/C

Relax in Old World elegance. Private suite of rooms overlooks lovely city park. Walk to Lawrence University, museum or downtown.

BARABOO

Barrister's House
226 9th Ave., 53913
608-356-3344
Glen & Mary Schulz
Exc. weekdays Nov.—Apr.

$$ B&B
4 rooms, 4 pb
C-6+/S-no/P-no/H-no

Continental plus
Comp. wine & beverages
Sitting room, library
veranda, terrace
screened porch

Colonial charm and simple elegance in a parklike setting. Unique guest rooms, paneled library, fireplaces, screened porch and sitting room with game table and piano.

BAYFIELD

Greunke's Inn
17 Rittenhouse, 54814
715-779-5480
Judity Lokken-Strom
April—November

$ EP
7 rooms, 3 pb
Visa, MC
C-yes/S-no/P-no/H-no

Lunch, dinner, beer

Like stepping into one of Norman Rockwell's Saturday Evening Post *illustrations—little has changed here since the late 1940s. Old jukebox is a gathering place.*

Old Rittenhouse Inn
P.O. Box 584, 54814
301 Rittenhouse Ave.
715-779-5111
Jerry & Mary Phillips
All year

$$$ B&B
20 rooms, 20 pb
C-ltd/S-ltd/P-no/H-ltd

Continental plus
Full breakfast $
Dinner, wine
Sitting room, piano
entertainment, bicycles

Beautiful 30-room Victorian mansion, antiques and 12 working fireplaces. Guests relax on the porch. Overlooks Lake Superior. Also two lovely historic homes.

BELLEVILLE

Abendruh B&B Swiss-style
7019 Gehin Rd., 53508
608-424-3808
Franz & Mathilde Jaggi
All year

$ B&B
3 rooms, 2 pb
Visa, MC •
German, French, Swiss

Full breakfast
Afternoon tea, snacks
Comp. wine
Sitting room, library
hot tub

True European hospitality. Beautiful, quiet country getaway. Fireplaces, central A/C. Near X-C skiing, biking, nature trails. Many tourist attractions nearby.

CEDARBURG

Washington House Inn
W62 N573 Washington Ave, 53012
414-375-3550
Judith I. Drefahl
All year

$$ B&B
29 rooms, 29 pb
•
C-yes/S-yes/P-no/H-yes

Continental plus
Afternoon social
Sitting room, fireplaces
whirlpool baths, sauna
wet bars, bicycles

A country inn in the center of historical district. Breakfast served in charming gathering room. Shopping, golf, winter sports. Whirlpool baths and wet bars in each room.

COLUMBUS

By the Okeag
446 Wisconsin St., 53925
414-623-3007
Alton & Bernetta Mather
April—October 1

$$ B&B
1 rooms, 1 pb
Visa, MC
C-10+/S-no/P-no

Continental plus
Stocked refrigerator
Comp. wine, snacks
Private pier with
canoes and paddle boat

Beautifully decorated guest house by river. Quiet and private, landscaped with flower gardens & gazebo. Private pier with canoe & paddle boat. The perfect spot for relaxation.

Manchester Highlands Inn, Manchester, VT

ELLISON BAY

Griffin Inn
11976 Mink River Rd., 54210
414-854-4306
Laurie & Jim Roberts
All year

$$ B&B
10 rooms, 4 pb
C-7+ / S-ltd / P-no / H-no

Full breakfast
Lnch & din. by req.
Evening popcorn
Gathering rooms, library
bicycles, tennis court

A New England-style country inn on the Door County Peninsula, since 1910. Handmade quilts on antique beds. Full country breakfasts. Set on five lovely acres.

EPHRAIM

Eagle Harbor Inn / Cottages
P.O. Box 72, 54211
9914 Water St.
414-854-2121
Ronald & Barbara Schultz
All year

$$ B&B
9 rooms, 9 pb
Visa, MC •
C-15+ / H-yes

Full breakfast
Sitting rooms
fireplace room

An intimate New England styled country inn. Antique-filled; deluxe continental breakfast. Close to boating, beaches, golf course and parks.

Hillside Hotel
P.O. Box 17, 54211
9980 Hwy 42
414-854-2417 / 800-423-7023
David & Karen McNeil
May—Nov. 1, Jan.—Feb.

$$ B&B / MAP
12 rooms
Visa, MC, AmEx, Disc
C-yes / S-no / P-no / H-no

Full breakfast
6-course dinner, tea
Full service restaurant
Private beach, mooring
charcoaler for picnics

Country-Victorian hotel with harbor view, private beach, specialty breakfasts, gourmet dinners, original furnishings, spectacular views; near galleries, shops; in resort area.

FISH CREEK

Thorp House Inn
P.O. Box 90, 54212
4135 Bluff Rd.
414-868-2444
Christine & Sverre Pedersen
All year

$$ B&B
4 rooms
Norwegian

Continental plus
Sitting room w/ fireplace
library
bicycles

Antique-filled historic home backed by wooded bluff, overlooking bay. Walk to beach, park, shops and restaurants. Winter: cross-country skiing.

White Gull Inn
Box 175, 54212
414-868-3517
Andy & Jon Coulson
All year

$
16 rooms, 9 pb
C-yes / S-yes / P-no / H-ltd

Full breakfast
Lunch, dinner
Bicycles
entertainment
piano

Situated between the bluff and the bay in Fish Creek on Wisconsin's Door Peninsula; charming turn-of-the-century inn.

HARTLAND

Monches Mill House
W301 N9430 Hwy E, 53029
414-966-7546
Elaine Taylor
May—December

$$ B&B
4 rooms, 2 pb
C-yes / S-yes / P-yes / H-yes
French

Continental plus
Comp. wine
Sitting room
hot tub, bicycles
tennis, canoeing, hiking

House built in 1842, located on the bank of the mill pond, furnished in antiques, choice of patio, porch or gallery for breakfast enjoyment.

HUDSON

Jefferson-Day House	$$ B&B	Full breakfast weekends
1109 3rd St., 54016	4 rooms, 2 pb	Snacks
715-386-7111	•	Sitting room
The Millers	C-yes/H-yes	library
All year	Spanish	

1857 home just blocks away from beautiful St. Croix River. Skiing nearby. 15 minutes from St. Paul/Minneapolis. Antique collections. Three-course full breakfast.

JANESVILLE

Jackson Street Inn B&B	$ B&B	Full breakfast
210 S. Jackson St., 53545	4 rooms, 2 pb	Comp. tea, wine
608-754-7250	Visa, MC •	Sitting room, library
Ilah & Bob Sessler	C-yes/S-yes/P-no/H-no	fireplace, shuffleboard
All year		cable TV, putting green

Near I-90, home has spacious rooms, Old World charm. Full gourmet breakfast. Great golf, bike, ski trails. Brochure available.

KENOSHA

Manor House	$$$ B&B	Continental breakfast
6536 3rd Avenue, 53140	4 rooms, 4 pb	Meals upon arrangement
414-658-0014	Visa, MC,AmEx •	Complimentary wine
Ron & Mary Rzeplinski	C-12+/S-ltd/P-no/H-no	Sitting room, library
All year	French	piano, bicycles

Georgian mansion overlooking Lake Michigan. Furnished with 18th-century antiques. Formal landscaped grounds. Midway-Chicago & Milwaukee. National Register.

LAKE GENEVA

T.C. Smith Inn B&B	$$ B&B	Full buffet breakfast
865 Main St., 53147	9 rooms, 5 pb	Afternoon tea, snacks
414-248-1097	Visa, MC, AmEx •	Sitting room, library
The Marks Family	C-yes/S-yes/P-yes/H-no	bicycles, gift shoppe
All year		A/C, color televisions

Relax by the fireplaces to experience the romance and warmth of the Grand Victorian era in this downtown lakeview mansion of 1845. Listed on National Register.

MADISON

Annie's Hill House B&B	$$ B&B	Full breakfast
2117 Sheridan Dr., 53704	3 rooms, 1 pb	Snacks
608-244-2224	•	Library, tennis courts
Anne & Larry Stuart	C-yes/S-ltd/P-ltd/H-no	fishing, jogging, hiking
All year		boat rentals, X-C skiing

Beautiful country garden setting in the city, complete with romantic gazebo. Full recreational facilities. 10 min. to downtown and campus. Full breakfast every day. Enjoy!

Collins House B&B	$$ B&B	Full breakfast (wkends)
704 E. Gorham St., 53703	4 rooms, 4 pb	Cont. breakfast (wkdays)
608-255-4230	Visa, MC	Comp. chocolate truffles
Barbara & Mike Pratzel	C-yes/S-ltd/P-yes/H-no	Sitting room w/fireplace
All year		library, movies on video

Restored prairie school style. Overlooks Lake Mendota, near university and state capitol. Elegant rooms, wonderful gourmet breakfasts and pastries.

Wisconsin   407

MADISON

Plough Inn B&B
3402 Monroe St., 53711
608-238-2981
R. Ganser, K. Naherny
All year

$$ B&B
3 rooms, 3 pb
Visa, MC
C-no/S-no/P-no/H-no

Continental plus (wkday)
Full breakfast (weekend)
Comp. wine
Sitting room
new "tap" room added

Historic 1850s inn with 3 charming, spacious rooms. Arborview room has fireplace and whirl-pool bath. Across from arboretum, near university campus.

MENOMONEE FALLS

Dorshel's B&B Guest House
W140 N7616 Lilly Rd., 53051
414-255-7866
Dorothy Waggoner
All year

$$ B&B
3 rooms, 1 pb
C-6+/S-ltd/P-no/H-no

Continental plus
Comp. juices, snacks
Sitting room, pool table
library, game room
two screened porches

Lovely wooded residential area with access to major transporation. Contemporary home decorated with beautiful antiques in the traditional style. 20 min. to downtown Milwaukee.

MEQUON

Sonnenhof Inn
13907 N. Port Washington, 53092
414-375-4294
Georgia & Tom Houle
All year

$$ B&B
4 rooms, 1 pb
Visa, MC, AmEx
C-12+/S-no/P-no/H-no

Full breakfast
Fine restaurants nearby
Library, terrace, A/C
walking paths, pond
winter cross-country ski

A quiet, sunny home in the country. "It's like visiting Grandma's house," according to our guests. Historic Cedarburg 4 miles.

MERRILL

Candlewick Inn
700 W. Main St., 54452
715-536-7744
Dan & Loretta Zimmerman
All year

$ B&B
5 rooms, 3 pb
Visa, MC
C-12+/S-ltd/P-no/H-no

Full breakfast
Snacks, comp. wine
Restaurant nearby
Sitting room, library
bicycles, gift shop

Elegantly restored century-old mansion, appointed with fine antiques, and four fireplaces. Golf, water sports, downhill and cross-country skiing.

MINERAL POINT

Chesterfield Inn
20 Commerce St., 53565
608-987-3682
V. Duane Rath
All year

$ B&B
8 rooms
Visa, MC
C-yes/S-yes/P-yes/H-no

Continental breakfast
Lunch, dinner
Restaurant, bar service
Garden terrace
bicycles

Historic stone stagecoach inn in Cornish settlement. Charming outdoor dining with weekend entertainment. Plenty to do including antiquing, cycling, theater.

ONTARIO

Inn at Wildcat Mountain
P.O. Box 112, 54651
113 South St., Hwy 33
608-337-4352
Patricia & Wendell Barnes
All year

$ B&B
3 rooms
Visa, MC, AmEx •
C-10+/P-ltd

Full breakfast
Snacks, comp. wine
Parlor, library, porches
patio, on-premises shop
5 acres of grounds

Lovely 1910 Greek Revival home along Kickapoo River in Wisconsin's Hidden Valleys. . .at the entrance to Wildcat Mountain State Park & Amish Country. Wonderful full breakfasts.

OSHKOSH

Tiffany Inn
206 Algoma Blvd, 54901
414-426-1000
Linda Anderson
All year

$ B&B
12 rooms, 12 pb
Visa, MC
C-no/S-yes/P-no/H-yes

Continental plus
Library, sitting room
living room w/fireplace
games, books

Beautifully appointed rooms will help you step back in time. Close to downtown, the University of Wisconsin, the grand opera house, the museum and shopping.

POYNETTE

Jamieson House
P.O. Box 829, 53955
407 N. Franklin St.
608-635-4100
James/Carole Gacek
All year

$$ B&B
10 rooms, 10 pb
AmEx, DC
C-ltd/S-ltd/P-ltd/H-no

Full breakfast
Restaurant, bar
Garden room
piano, bicycles

The Jamieson House features intimate gourmet dining amid quiet Victorian elegance. Guest rooms have sumptuous velvet couches, sunken baths, antiques.

SISTER BAY

Renaissance Inn
414 Maple Dr., 54234
414-854-5107
John & Jodee Faller
May-Nov, Jan-Mar

$$ B&B
5 rooms, 5 pb
Visa, MC, AmEx
C-no/S-yes/P-no/H-no

Full breakfast
Lunch, dinner
Restaurant
Snacks
sitting room

Turn-of-the-century inn boasts chef as its host and an elegant creole dining room. Snug, pleasant rooms.

SPARTA

Franklin Victorian
220 E. Franklin St., 54656
608-269-3894
Jane & Lloyd Larson
All year

$$ B&B
4 rooms
C-10+

Full breakfast
Afternoon tea, snacks
Sitting room
library
canoe rental

Relax in quiet, gracious comfort—spacious rooms, fine woods. Delectable breakfasts. Surrounding area abounds with beauty. Recreation all four seasons.

STURGEON BAY

Gray Goose Bed & Breakfast
4258 Bay Shore Dr., 54235
414-743-9100
Jack & Jessie Burkhardt
All year

$$ B&B
4 rooms
Visa, MC, AmEx
S-ltd

Full breakfast
Snacks
Sitting room, library
full covered porch
cable TV, games

Comfortable Civil War home; genuine antiques. Quiet, wooded setting north of city. Wooded view. Full country breakfasts and personal attention.

Inn at Cedar Crossing
336 Louisiana St., 54235
414-743-4200
Terry Wulf
All year

$$ B&B
9 rooms, 9 pb
Visa, MC, DC
C-6+/S-ltd/P-no/H-no

Full breakfst (wint/spr)
Cont. plus (summer/fall)
Restaurant, snacks
Sitting room
whirlpools

1884 inn is situated in historic district close to shops, restaurants, museum, beaches. Country antique decor, fireplaces, whirlpools, common room.

STURGEON BAY

White Lace Inn
16 N. 5th Ave., 54235
414-743-1105
Bonnie & Dennis Statz
All year

$$ B&B
15 rooms, 15 pb
Visa, MC
C-no/S-ltd/P-no/H-ltd

Continental plus
Tea, coffee, chocolate
Sitting room
tandem bicycles

A Victorian country inn with romantic decor; 15 charming guest rooms, all with fine antiques, authentic Victorian or poster bed; 10 w/fireplace, 7 w/whirlpool and fireplace.

VIROQUA

Viroqua Heritage Inn B&B
220 E. Jefferson St., 54665
608-637-3306
Nancy L. Rhodes
All year

$ B&B
4 rooms
Visa, MC •
C-yes/S-ltd/P-no/H-no

Full breakfast
Baby grand piano
mystery weekends
near skiing, golf, hiking

Elegant Victorian home, lovingly restored by your innkeeper, offers a peaceful and romantic sojourn. Abundant breakfast served. Near sports, sightseeing.

WISCONSIN DELLS

Historic Bennett House
825 Oak St., 53965
608-254-2500
Gail & Rich Obermeyer
All year

$ B&B
4 rooms, 1 pb
C-no/S-no/P-no/H-no

Full breakfast
Snacks, sitting room
Nearby: golf, skiing,
Indian culture, parks,
railroad/circus museums

1863 home of pioneer photographer, on National Historic Register. Casual elegance, gourmet breakfasts, fireplaces, screened porch, relaxed conversation, and downtown.

More Inns...

Gallery House   215 North Main Street, Alma 54610   608-685-4975
Laue House Inn   Box 176, Alma 54610   608-685-4923
House of Seven Gables   Box 204, Baraboo 53913   608-356-8387
Cooper Hill House   P.O. Box 1288, Bayfield 54814   715-779-5060
Pinehurst Inn   Hwy 13, P.O. Box 222, Bayfield 54814   715-779-3676
Ty-Bach   2817, Beloit 53511   608-365-1039
Stagecoach Inn   W61 N520 Washington Ave, Cedarburg 53012   414-375-0208
Willson House   320 Superior St., Chippewa Falls 54729   715-723-0055
Son Ne Vale Farm B&B   Rt. 1 Box 132, Colfax 54730   715-962-4342
Creamery   Box 22, Downsville 54735   715-664-8354
Greystone Farms   770 Adam's Road, East Troy 53120   414-495-8485
Country Gardens B&B   6421 Hwy. 42, Egg Harbor 54209   414-743-7434
Proud Mary   P.O. Box 193, Fish Creek 54212   414-868-3442
Whistling Swan Inn   P.O. Box 193, Main St., Fish Creek 54212   414-868-3442
Strawberry Hill   Rt. 1, Box 524-D, Green Lake 54941   414-294-3450
McConnell Inn   497 S. Lawson Dr.,Box 6, Greenlake 54941   414-294-6430
Mustard Seed   205 California, Box 262, Hayward 54843   715-634-2908
Wisconsin House Stagecoach   2105 East Main, Hazel Green 53811   608-854-2233
Sandy Scott   1520 State Street, La Crosse 54601   608-784-7145
Trillium   Rt. 2, Box 121, La Farge 54639   608-625-4492
Chateau Madeleine   P.O. Box 27, La Pointe 54850   715-747-2463
OJ's Victorian Village   P.O. Box 98, Hwy 12, Lake Delton 53940   608-254-6568
Eleven Gables Inn on the L   493 Wrigley Drive, Lake Geneva 53147   414-248-8393
Elizabethian Inn   463 Wrigley Dr., Lake Geneva 53147   414-248-9131
Greene House B&B   RR2, Box 214, Hwy 12, Lake Geneva-Whitewater 53190   414-495-8771
Seven Pines Lodge   Lewis 54851   715-653-2323

Oak Hill Farm   9850 Highway 80, Livingston 53554   608-943-6006
Mansion Hill Inn   424 N. Pinckneg St., Madison 53703   608-255-3999
Lauerman Guest House Inn   1975 Riverside Avenue, Marinette 54143
Ogden House   2237 North Lake Drive, Milwaukee 53202   414-272-2740
Pfister Hotel   424 East Wisconsin Ave., Milwaukee 53202   414-273-8222
Duke House B&B   618 Maiden St., Mineral Point 53565   608-987-2821
Wilson House Inn   110 Dodge St., Mineral Point 53565   608-987-3600
Wm. A. Jones House   215 Ridge St., Hwy 1, Mineral Point 53565   608-987-2337
Inn   30 Wisconsin Avenue, Montreal 54550   715-561-5180
Rambling Hills Tree Farm &   8825 Willever Lane, Newton 53063   414-726-4388
St. Croix River Inn   305 River St., Osceola 54020   715-294-4248
Marybrooke Inn   705 W. New York Ave., Oshkosh 54901   414-426-4761
Halfway House B&B   Route 2, Box 80, Oxford 53952   608-586-5489
Limberlost Inn   2483 Hwy 17, Phelps 54554   715-545-2685
52 Stafford (Irish House)   P.O. Box 217, Plymouth 53073   414-893-0552
Breese Waye B&B   816 Macfarlane Rd., Portage 53901   608-742-5281
Country Aire   Rt. 2 Box 175, Portage 53901   608-742-5716
Mansion   323 S. Central, Richland Center 53581   608-647-2808
Just-N-Trails B&B   Route 1, Box 263, Sparta 54656   608-269-4522
Victorian Swan on Water   1716 Water St., Stevens Point 54481   715-345-0595
Stokstad's Bed & Breakfast   305 Hwy 51, Stoughton 53589   608-884-4941
Lake House   RR 2, Box 217, Strum 54770   715-695-3519
Bay Shore Inn   4205 Bay Shore Drive, Sturgeon Bay 54235   414-743-4551
Gandt's Haus und Hof   2962 Lake Forest Park, Sturgeon Bay 54235   414-743-1238
The Nautical Inn   234 Kentucky St., Sturgeon Bay 54235
Serendipity Farm   Route 3 Box 162, Viroqua 54665   608-637-7708
Rosenberry Inn   511 Franklin Street, Wausau 54401   715-842-5733
Westby House   State Street, Westby 54667   608-634-4112
Jesse's Wolf River Lodge   White Lake 54491   715-882-2182
Foxmoor Bed & Breakfast   Fox River Road, Wilmot 53192   414-862-6161
House on River Road   922 River Road, Wisconsin Dells 53965   608-253-5573
Sherman House   930 River Rd., Box 397, Wisconsin Dells 53965   608-253-2721
Nash House   1020 Oak St., Wisconsin Rapids 54494   715-424-2001

Wyoming

BIG HORN

Spahn's Big Horn Mountain	$ B&B	Full breakfast
P.O. Box 579, 82833	3 rooms, 3 pb	Lunch, Dinner available
Upper Hideaway Lane	•	Library, sitting room
307-674-8150	C-yes/S-ltd/P-yes/H-no	hot tub, baby-sitting
Ron & Bobbie Spahn		fishing
All year		

Secluded handcrafted log lodge on a high, pine-forested mountainside. Hundred-mile vista, hiking trails, deer and moose. Close to Interstate 90 and Sheridan.

CODY

Goff Creek Lodge
P.O. Box 155, 82414
995 N.F Hwy
307-587-3753
Gloria T. Schmitt
May 20—October 15

$$ EP
14 rooms, 14 pb
Visa, MC, AmEx •
C-yes/S-yes/P-yes/H-yes

Homebaked goods
Lunch, dinner, bar
Airport pickup
log units
wilderness activities

Horseback riding, campfire get-togethers, western hospitality, home-cooked meals. Just 10 miles from Yellowstone National Park.

Lockhart B&B Inn
109 W. Yellowstone Ave., 82414
307-587-6074
Mark & Cindy Baldwin
All year

$$ B&B
6 rooms, 6 pb
Visa, MC, CB, Diners •
C-4+/S-ltd/P-no/H-no

All you can eat breakfst
Comp. coffee/liquors
Sack lunch, sitting room
Cable color TV
phones

Historic home of famous western author Caroline Lockhart—featuring antiques, old-style comfort and hearty all-you-can-eat breakfast. Western hospitality. AAA-rated inn.

GLENROCK

Hotel Higgins
P.O. Box 741, 82637
416 W. Birch
307-436-9212
Jack & Margaret Doll
All year

$$ B&B
10 rooms, 7 pb
Visa, MC, AmEx
C-yes/S-yes/P-no/H-ltd

Full breakfast
Lunch, dinner, bar
Sitting room, small
intimate dining rooms
ceiling fans, piano

Charming old hotel filled with original turn-of-the-century furnishings. Personalized attention and service by owners. Nationally acclaimed restaurant.

JACKSON HOLE

Teton Tree House
P.O. Box 550, Wilson, 83014
6159 Heck of a Hill Rd.
307-733-3233
Chris & Denny Becker
All year

$$ B&B
6 rooms, 6 pb
Visa, MC, Discover
C-yes/S-no/P-no/H-no

Full breakfast
Fireplace
sitting room
library
slide shows

Helpful long-time mountain and river guides offer a rustic but elegant four-story open-beam home on a forested, wildflowered mountainside.

LANDER

Ituntry Fare B&B
904 Main St., 82520
307-332-9604
A.R. & Mary Ann Hoyt
All year

$ B&B
3 rooms, 1 pb
Visa, MC
C-7+

Full breakfast
English cream tea
Sitting room
airport pickup

Victorian house lovingly restored with English decor and antiques. Lander offers winter sports, hiking, fishing, hunting. Direct route to Yellowstone.

LARAMIE

Annie Moore's Guest House
819 University, 82070
307-721-4177
Diana Kopulos, David Garrett
All year

$ B&B
6 rooms
Visa, MC, AmEx •
C-no/S-no/P-no/H-no

Continental plus
Juice, tea
Sitting room
sun deck

Beautifully renovated post-Victorian Queen Anne. Cheerful parlor and second-story sun deck. Close to university, museums, downtown. Rocky Mountain recreational delight.

SARATOGA

Wolf Hotel
Box 1298, 82331
101 E. Bridge
307-326-5525
Doug & Kathleen Campbell
All year

$ EP
11 rooms, 7 pb
Visa, MC, AmEx, DC, CB
C-yes/S-yes/P-no/H-no

Lunch, dinner, bar

Hotel built in 1893 as a stage stop. Listed in National Register. Blue Ribbon fishing, golf, hot springs nearby. Dining room (AAA approved) & lounge redone in Victorian style.

SAVERY

Savery Creek Thoroughbred Ranch
Box 24, 82332
307-383-7840
Joyce B. Saer
All year

$ B&B
5 rooms, 5 pb
Major credit cards •
C-yes/S-yes/P-yes/H-no
Spanish, French

Full breakfast
All meals available
Sitting room, piano
tennis court, riding
river swimming, fishing

Real ranch with marvelous scenery and riding. Attractive old west cabins with private baths and fireplaces. Excellent meals.

WAPITI

Elephant Head Lodge
1170 Yellowstone Hwy, 82450
307-587-3980
Philip Lamb
May—October

$ B&B
10 rooms, 10 pb
Visa, MC •
C-yes/S-yes/P-yes/H-no

All meals available
Airport pick-up
Sitting room, library
bicycles, horses
tubing, fishing, TV

In spectacular Wapiti Valley, 40 miles west of Cody—11 miles east of Yellowstone Park. Great base for touring Yellowstone, the Tetons. American Plan available.

More Inns...

Shoshone Lodge Resort   P.O. Box 790BB, Cody 82414   307-587-4044
Akers Ranch B&B   81 Inez Rd., Rt. 1, Douglas 82633   307-358-3741
Bed & Breakfast at Akers R   81 Inez Rd., Douglas 82633   307-358-3741
Shoshone Lodge Resort   P.O. Box 790BB, Cody 82414   307-587-4044
Akers Ranch B&B   81 Inez Rd., Rt. 1, Douglas 82633   307-358-3741
Bed & Breakfast at Akers R   81 Inez Rd., Douglas 82633   307-358-3741
Big Mountain Inn   P.O. Box 7453, Jackson 83001   307-733-1981
Spring Creek Ranch   Box 3154, Jackson 83001   307-733-8833
Sundance Inn   135 W. Broadway, Jackson 83001   307-733-3444
Powderhorn Ranch   P.O. Box 7400, Jackson Hole 83001   307-733-3845
Bunkhouse   P.O. Box 384, Moose 83012   307-733-7283
Box K Ranch   Box 110, Moran 83013   307-543-2407
Fir Creek Ranch   P.O. Box 190, Moran 83013   307-543-2416
Ferris Mansion   607 West Maple, Rawlins 82301   307-324-3961
Mountain Shadows Ranch   Box 110BB, Wapiti 82450   307-587-2143
Heck of A Hill Homestead   P.O. Box 105, Wilson 83014   307-733-8023
Snow Job   P.O. Box 371, Wilson 83014   307-739-9695

Puerto Rico

CAROLINA

Duffys' Inn	$$ EP	Breakfast $
#9 Isla Verde Rd., 00913	14 rooms, 14 pb	Restaurant, lunch/dinner
809-726-1415	Visa, MC, AmEx •	Afternoon tea, snacks
Madeline Weihe	C-yes/S-yes/P-no/H-no	Across from one of the
All year	Spanish	finest beaches

A Spanish hacienda offers guests the Caribbean the way it was. Excellent food, reasonably priced, open 24 hrs. Near casinos. Across from one of the finest beaches in San Juan.

PATILLAS

Caribe Playa Resort	$$ EP	Full breakfast
HC 764 Buzon 8490, 00723	32 rooms, 32 pb	Lunch, dinner
809-839-6339	Visa, MC, AmEx •	Restaurant, bar service
Esther Geller	C-yes/S-yes/P-yes/H-yes	Sitting room, library
All year	Spanish	beach swimming, snorkel

Modern studios on private picturesque coconut beach on the Caribbean sea; swimming, snorkeling, fishing. Attentive owner/management.

SAN JUAN

El Canario Inn	$$ B&B	Continental plus
1317 Ashford Ave., 00907	25 rooms, 25 pb	Sitting room
Condado	Visa, MC, AmEx •	swimming pool
809-722-3861/800-533-2649	C-yes/S-yes/P-no/H-no	
Keith & Jude Olson	English, Spanish	
All year		

In heart of Condado, near beach, casinos, boutiques and fine restaurants. Freshwater jacuzzi pool, tropical patio and sun deck for sun, fun and relaxation.

Las Tres Palmas Guesthouse	$ B&B	Continental breakfast
2212 Park Blvd., 00913	7 rooms, 5 pb	Comp. pina colada
Puntas Las Marias	Visa, MC, AmEx •	Sitting room, cable TV
809-727-4617	C-ltd/S-ltd/P-no/H-no	library, sun deck
Francis & Eileen Walsh		pool, beach
All year		

Beachfront; casinos and gourmet restaurants five minutes away; airport and historic Old San Juan ten minutes.

Wind Chimes	$$ B&B	Continental breakfast
53 Calle Taft, 00911	12 rooms, 12 pb	Comp. welcome drink
809-727-4153	Visa, MC, AmEx •	Sitting room
Wayne Berry	C-yes/S-yes/P-no/H-no	swimming pool
All year	Spanish	

A charming Spanish-style villa with airy rooms, each with ceiling fan and private tile bath. Enjoy Caribbean trade winds on tropical patio.

More Inns...

Ceiba Country Inn   Carr 977 KM1.2 Barrio S, Ceiba 00635   809-885-0471
El Prado Inn   1350 Luchetti St., Condado, San Juan 00907   809-728-5526
Posada La Hamaca   68 Castelar Street, Culebra 00645   809-742-3516
Villa Boheme   P.O. Box 218, Culebra Island 00645   809-742-3508
La Casa Mathiesen   14 Calle Uno, Villamar, Isla Verde 00913   809-727-3223
La Playa   6 Amapola, Isla Verde 00630   809-791-1115
Parador Martorell   P.O. Box 384, Luquillo 00673   809-889-2710
Parador Hacienda Juanita   Box 838, Marico 00706   809-838-2550
Beach House   1957 Italia, Ocean Park 00913   809-727-5482
Buena Vista by-the-Sea   2218 Gen.Del Valle, Ocean Park, Santurce 00913   809-726-2796
La Condesa Inn   Cacique 2071, Ocean Park, Santurce 00911   809-727-3698
Safari on the Beach   Yardley Pl. #2, Ocean Park-San Juan 00911   809-726-0445
Horned Dorset Primavera Ho   Apartado 1132, Rincon 00743   809-823-4030
Parador Oasis   P.O. Box 144, San German 00753   809-892-1175
Arcade Inn Guest House   Taft St. #8 Condado, San Juan 00911   809-725-0668
Green Isle Inn   36 Cale Uno—Villamar, San Juan 00913   809-726-4330
Hosteria del Mar   5 Cervantes St., San Juan 00907   809-724-8203
Jewel's by the Sea   Seaview 1125-Condado, San Juan 00907   809-725-5313
San Antonio Guest House   1 Tapia, Ocean Park, San Juan 00752   914-727-3302
Bananas Guesthouse   P.O. Box 1300 Esperanza, Vieques 00765   809-741-8700
La Casa del Frances   Box 458, Esperanza, Vieques 00765   809-741-3751
Sea Gate Guest House   Barriada Fuerts, Vieques 00765   809-741-4661

Virgin Islands

SAINT THOMAS

Danish Chalet Inn	$$ B&B	Continental breakfast
P.O.Box 4319,Solberg Rd, 00803	15 rooms, 6 pb	Bar service
Frenchmen's Hill	Visa, MC •	Sitting room, library
809-774-5764/800-635-1531	C-yes/S-yes/P-no/H-no	jacuzzi, spa
Frank & Mary Davis	English	sun deck
All year		

Family inn overlooking Charlotte Amalie harbor, 5-minute walk to town, duty-free shops, restaurants. Cool breezes, honor bar, sun deck, jacuzzi. 15 min. to beaches.

Galleon House	$$ B&B	Continental plus
P.O. Box 6577, 00804	14 rooms, 7 pb	Refrigerators
800-524-2052/809-774-6952	•	A/C in rooms, pool
John & Donna Slone	C-yes/S-yes/P-no/H-no	snorkel gear/windsurfing
All year	English	veranda, beach towels

Visit historical Danish town. Superb view of harbor with city charm close to everything. Duty-free shopping, beach activities in 85-degree weather.

Mayhurst Inn, Orange, VA

SAINT THOMAS

Heritage Manor
P.O. Box 90, 00804
1A Snegle Gade
809-774-3003/800-776-0909
John & Diane Goh
All year

$$ B&B (winter)
7 rooms, 3 pb
credit cards •

Continental plus
Comp. wine upon check-in
Bar service
English high tea on req.
courtyard

Beautifully restored manor offers European country charm and simple elegance. Tastefully decorated rooms. Walk to duty-free shops, fine restaurants, sunset cruises, ferries.

Inn at Mandahl
P.O. Box 2483, 00803
Mandahl Beach 34B
809-775-2100
John Palmer
All year

$$ B&B
8 rooms, 8 pb
•
C-yes/S-yes/P-yes/H-yes
German, French, Spanish

Continental breakfast
Restaurant, lunch, dinner
Bar service, sitting rm
Tennis courts, pool
beach, private terraces

Every room has a king-size firm four-poster bed and a private terrace with lounges. View over ocean and 18 Bristish Islands. 8 hours of suntanning.

Island View Guest House
P.O. Box 1903, 00803
809-774-4270/800-524-2023
Barbara Cooper, Norman Leader
All year

$$ B&B
15 rooms, 13 pb
•
C-14+ /S-yes/P-no/H-no
Spanish

Continental breakfast
Full breakfast $
Sandwiches, bar
Gallery
freshwater swimming pool

Overlooking St. Thomas harbor, free continental breakfast, honor bar and freshwater pool. Spectacular harbor view from all rooms. Convenient to town and airport.

SAINT THOMAS ──

Maison Greaux Guest House $ EP Self-serve bar
P.O. Box 1856, 00803 , 4 pb Sitting room
23 Solberg •
809-774-0063 C-yes/S-yes/P-sml/H-no
Irene & Richard Cline
All year

Overlooking Frenchman's Hill with a 180-degree view of beautiful Charlotte Amalie; picturesque harbor bustling with cruise ships and sailboats. Walk to shops.

More Inns . . .

Pink Fancy Hotel 27 Prince St., Christiansted, St. Croix 00820 800-524-2045
Limestone Reef Terraces RD 4, Princeton, NJ, Princeton 08540 800-872-8784
Estate Zootenvaal Hurricane Hole, Saint John 00830 809-776-6321
Selene's P.O. Box 30, Cruz Bay, Saint John 00830 809-776-7850
Cruz Inn Box 566, Cruz Bay, St. John 00830 809-776-7688
Gallows Point Box 58, St. John 00830 809-776-6434
Intimate Inn of St. John POB 432, Cruz Bay, St. John 00830 809-776-6133
Raintree Inn Box 566, St. John 00830 809-776-7449
Hotel 1829 P.O. Box 1567, St. Thomas 00801 809-774-1829
Kyalami Estate Elizabeth No. 27, St. Thomas 11837 809-774-9980
Mafolie Hotel P.O. Box 1506, St. Thomas 00801 809-774-2790
Pavilions & Pools Hotel Rt. 6, St. Thomas 00802 800-524-2001
Pelican Beach Club Box 8387, St. Thomas 00801 809-775-6855
Twiins Guest House 5 Garden St,Charlotte A, St. Thomas 00801 809-776-0131
Villa Elaine 66 Water Island, St. Thomas 00802 809-774-0290

Alberta

CANMORE ──

Canadian Rocky Mountain $ B&B Full breakfast
Box 95, T0L 0M0 2 rooms, 2 pb Dinner can be arranged
1004 Larch Pl. Visa Both rooms w/sitting rm
403-678-6777 family room sleeps 5
Suzanne Stoeckle
All year

Nestled in the Rocky Mountains, close to four National Parks. Open beam cedar home offering spectacular mountain views. Quiet, restful environment close to town. Near skiing.

SEEBE ──

Brewster's Kananaskis Ranch $$$ B&B Full breakfast
General Delivery, T0L 1X0 27 rooms, 27 pb Lic. dining room, lounge
403-673-3737 Visa, MC • Seminar facility, golf
The Brewster Family C-yes/S-yes/P-no/H-yes whirlpool, horses
May 1—October 15 Western BBQs

Turn-of-the-century guest ranch; private cabins & chalet units; antique furniture. Operated by 5th-generation Brewsters. 45 miles west of Calgary, 30 miles east of Banff.

More Inns. . .

Crazee Akerz Farm   RR #1, Bentley T0C 0J0   403-843-6444
Cougar Creek Inn   240 Grizzly Cresent, Canmore T0L 0M0   403-678-4751
Haus Alpenrose Lodge   629 9th St., Box 723, Canmore T0L 0M0   403-678-4134
Mr. & Mrs. C.A. McMillan   512 54th Avenue W., Clausholm T0L 0T0
Edmonton Hostel   10422 91st Street, Edmonton   403-429-0140
Back Porch B&B   266 Northumberland St., Fredericton E3B 3J6   506-454-6875
Gwynalta Farm   Gwynne T0C 1L0   403-352-3587
Black Cat Guest Ranch   Box 6267, Hinton T7V 1X6   403-865-3084
Mesa Creek Ranch Vacation   General Delivery, Millarville T0L 1K0   403-931-3573
Broadview Farm   RR #2, Millet T0C 1Z0   403-387-4963
Timber Ridge Homestead   Box 94, Nanton T0L 1R0   403-646-5683
Wildflower Country House   Box 8, Site 1, R.R.2, Okotoks T0L 1T0
Rafter Six Ranch Resort   Seebe T0L 1X0   403-673-3622

British Columbia

CAMPBELL RIVER

April Point Lodge
Box 1, Campbell River, V9W 4Z9
April Pt. Rd., Quadra Isl
604-285-2222/604-285-2222
Eric Peterson
April 15—October 15

$$$ EP
36 rooms, 42 pb
Major credit cards •
C-yes/S-yes/P-ltd/H-ltd
Fr., Rus., Ger., Japan.

Full breakfast
Restaurant, bar
Sitting room, piano
entertainment (summer)
saltwater pool

Personal service is our pride. More than one staff member per guest. Saltwater pool, many languages spoken. One to five bedroom deluxe guest houses.

FORT STEELE

Wild Horse Farm
Box 7, Hwy 93/95, V0B 1N0
604-426-6000
Bob & Orma Termuende
May—October

$$ B&B
3 rooms, 3 pb
•
C-no/S-ltd/P-ltd/H-no

Full homebaked breakfast
Sitting room
standard & player pianos

Spacious early-1900s log-faced country manor nestled in the Rocky Mountains; extensive lawns, gardens, trees on grounds. Across from Fort Steele Historic Park.

GIBSON'S

Ocean View Cottage B&B
1927 Grandview Rd., V0N 1V0
RR 2, Site 46, C10
604-886-7943
Dianne Verzyl
April—mid-October

$$ B&B
1 rooms, 1 pb
C-yes/S-no/P-no/H-no
French, Dutch

Full breakfast
Coffee and tea anytime

Private, spacious, self-contained cottage on 3 acres, in quiet rural setting overlooking Vancouver Island and Georgia Strait. Golf, fishing, hiking, sandy beaches.

HORNBY ISLAND

Sea Breeze Lodge	$$ AP	Full breakfast
V0R 1Z0	11 rooms, 11 pb	All homecooked meals
604-335-2321	1	Sitting room, piano
Brian & Gail Bishop	C-yes/S-yes/P-yes/H-ltd	grass tennis courts
All year; AP 6/15—9/15	Spanish	hot tub, fishing guide

Sea Breeze Lodge—mentioned in 1983 edition of West World. Near the ocean. Breakfast, home-made pastries. Off season cottages set for housekeeping.

KLEENA KLEENE

Chilanko Lodge & Resort	$$$ B&B	Full breakfast
Gen. Delivery, Hwy 20, V0L 1M0	14 rooms, 7 pb	Lunch, dinner
604-Kleena K	Visa, MC •	Sitting room, library
Mark Sudweeks	C-yes/S-yes/P-yes/H-yes	hot tub, sauna, lake
All year		airstrip, horses

Pristine lakefront wilderness resort—wildlife abounds—world class fishing—amenities un-matched—beach—unparalleled professional staff—satisfaction guaranteed.

MAYNE ISLAND

Gingerbread House	$$ B&B	Full multi-course brkfst
Campbell Bay Rd., V0N 2J0	4 rooms, 2 pb	Fine dining by arrangmnt
604-539-3133	Visa, MC •	Sitting room, library
Ken & Karen Someroille	C-12+	bicycles, tennis courts
March 1—October 31		moorage & docking avail.

Completely restored heritage home (circa 1900). Antique-filled, color coordinated guest rooms emphasize comfort and elegance. Secluded setting.

MILL BAY

Pinelodge Farm B&B	$$ B&B	Full farm breakfast
3191 Mutter Rd., V0R 2P0	7 rooms, 7 pb	Sitting room
604-743-4083	•	museum
Cliff & Barbara Clarke	C-yes/S-ltd/P-no/H-no	antique sales
All year		

Our lodge is on a 30-acre farm with panoramic ocean views. Each room is furnished with exqui-site antiques and stained glass windows. Museum open to public. Antique sales.

NANOOSE BAY

The Lookout	$$ B&B	Full breakfast
Box 71,Blueback Dr,RR 2, V0R 2R0	3 rooms, 2 pb	Sitting room
3381 Dolphin Dr.	•	Library
604-468-9796	C-7+	fishing charter avail.
Marj & Herb Wilkie	Australian, American	golf course nearby
May—September		

Spectacular views of Georgia Strait, watch boats, eagles, cruise ships, maybe even Orca whales. Country breakfast on wrap around deck. Golf, fishing, marina nearby. Quiet.

NORTH VANCOUVER

Grouse Mountain B&B	$$ B&B	Full gourmet breakfast
900 Clements Ave., V7R 2K7	2 rooms, 1 pb	Sitting room
604-986-9630	•	piano
Lyne & John Armstrong	C-yes/S-no/P-yes/H-no	
All year	French, German	

Nestled in the foothills of Grouse Mountain, our comfortable, modern home awaits you. Features include large private rooms, warm hospitality.

NORTH VANCOUVER

Helen's Bed & Breakfast
302 E. 5th St., V7L 1L1
604-985-4869
Helen Boire
All year

$$ B&B
2 rooms, 2 pb
•
C-yes/S-ltd/P-no/H-no
French

Full breakfast
Sitting room
game room

Lovely, comfortable Victorian home. Views to ocean and city. Only five blocks to sea. Near all transport and attractions. Grouse Mountain skiing nearby.

Platt's Bed & Breakfast
4393 Quinton Pl., V7R 4A8
604-987-4100
Nancy & Elwood Platt
All year

$ B&B
2 rooms, 1 pb
C-no/S-no/P-no/H-no
English

Full breakfast
Homemade bread & jams

Quiet parklike area, homemade bread and jams. 15 minutes to heart of town and our famous Stanley Park.

Sue's Victorian B&B
152 E. 3rd, V7L 1E6
604-985-1523
Sue Chalmers
All year

$ EP/B&B
2 rooms, 1 pb
•
C-yes/S-no/P-no/H-no
English

Cont. & Full breakfast
Kitchen privileges
Piano, laundry
guest parking
baby-sitting by arrangmnt

Lovely restored 1909 home has gorgeous harbor view and individually keyed rooms. Centrally located for transportation, shopping, restaurants and tourist attractions.

VickeRidge Bed & Breakfast
2638 Lorraine Ave., V7R 4B8
604-985-0338
Borrie Vickers
All year

$ B&B
3 rooms, 1 pb
•
C-yes/S-no/P-no/H-no
French

Full breakfast
Dinner by prior arrang.
Comp. wine, snacks
Sitting room
library

Gracious accommodations, superb breakfasts, quiet alpine village, convenient to downtown, cruise ships, other destinations, cultural, recreational, business activities.

PENDER ISLAND

Corbett House B&B
Corbett Rd., V0N 2M0
604-629-6305
Linda Wolfe & John Eckfeldt
All year

$$ B&B
3 rooms, 3 pb
Visa, MC
C-no/S-no/P-no/H-no
English, French, Spanish

Full breakfast
Dinner by res., aft. tea
Sitting room, library
bicycles, canoe/kayak
fishing, golf nearby

Charming restored heritage farmhouse in the Gulf Islands. Quiet rural setting; close to ocean & ferry. Fine dining by reservation, eclectic library and music of your choice.

QUILCHENA

Quilchena Hotel
V0E 2R0
604-378-2611
Guyana Hilde Rose
Mid-April—mid-October

$$ EP
15 rooms
Visa, MC
C-yes/S-yes/P-no/H-no
German

Full breakfast $
Lunch, dinner, bar
Golf, lake swimming
riding, boating, fishing
sitting room, piano

If you're looking for a friendly atmosphere, good home cooking, old-fashioned comfort, then come stay at the Quilchena Hotel. General store, 2500' airstrip.

420 British Columbia

VANCOUVER

Diana Luxury Home B&B
1019 E. 38th Ave., V5W 1J4	$$ B&B	Continental breakfast
604-321-2855	8 rooms, 2 pb	Jacuzzi, garden
Diana Piwko	•	Sitting room, patio
All year	C-no/S-yes/P-yes/H-yes	baby-sitting avail.
	Polish,Russ,Yugos,Czech	TV, games, bicycles

Luxury home in a central area. Free airport pickup. Comfortable, friendly atmosphere. Accommodation right in downtown Vancouver also available.

Kenya Court Guest House
2230 Cornwall Ave., V6K 1B5	$$ B&B	Full breakfast
604-738-7085	5 rooms, 3 pb	Afternoon tea, snacks
Dr. & Mrs. H.R. Williams	US Cheque •	Sitting room, library
All year	C-10+/S-no/P-no/H-no	tennis courts
	Italian, French, German	glass solarium

Heritage guest house overlooking Kitsiland Beach, mountains, English Bay. Gourmet breakfast served in glass solarium with panoramic view. Minutes from downtown, Granville Isl.

Rose Garden Guest House
6808 Dawson St., V5S 2W3	$ B&B	Cont./Full breakfast
604-435-7129	2 rooms	Afternoon tea, snacks
Dwyla & Ed Beglaw	MC	Sitting room
All year	C-yes	

Warm hospitality, Canadian style. Eiderdown quilts, rose decor, TV, comp. snacks. Close to gardens, golf, downtown. Wholesome home baking every morning; vegetarian food avail.

Vincent's Guest House
1741 Grant St., V5L 2Y6	$ B&B	Full breakfast
604-254-7462	6 rooms	Sitting room
All year	•	TV, stereo, washer/dryer
	S-yes	bicycles
	Fr, Ital, Sp, Germ, Port	bus or airport pickup

Guest house, hostel style. International atmosphere; meet a lot of travelers, young and old. Excellent location; only 1 mile from downtown. Generous hospitality.

West End Guest House
1362 Haro St., V6E 1G2	$$ B&B	Continental plus
604-681-2889	7 rooms, 7 pb	Sitting room, library
C. Weigom, G. Christie	Visa, MC	parking, TV in lounge
All year	C-no/S-no/P-no/H-no	piano, phones in rooms
	English, French	

Walk to Stanley Park, beaches, Robson Street shops and restaurants; then enjoy the quiet ambience of our comfortable historic inn.

VERNON

Twin Willows By The Lake
Site 10, Comp 16, RR 4, VIT 6L7	$$ B&B	Full breakfast
7456 Kennedy Lane	2 rooms, 1 pb	Library, lake
604-542-8293	C-yes/S-no/P-yes/H-no	sailboat hire
Colleen & Rod Pringle	French, German, Spanish	wharf, swimming
May—October		

Spacious lakefront suite (bath & entrance) in sunny Okanagan. Every window lake view. Peaceful, private. Friendly hosts, delicious good. Swimming, moorage, hammock. Can sleep 6.

VERNON

Windmill House
5672 Learmouth Rd.
Lavington
604-549-2804
Rosemary & Jeremy Dyde
All year

$ B&B
4 rooms, 1 pb
C-yes/S-no/P-no/H-no

Full breakfast
Afternoon tea
Other meals by arrang.
Pickup from bus, airport
parking, craft shop

A unique experience. Sleep in an authentic windmill, set in pastoral Coldstream Valley. Easy access to fishing lakes, orchards, skiing on Silver Star and Hot Springs.

VICTORIA

"Our Home on the Hill" B&B
546 Delora Dr., V9C 3R8
604-474-4507
Grace Holman
All year

$ B&B
3 rooms, 2 pb
C-yes/S-no/P-no/H-no

Full breakfast
Afternoon tea
Sitting room
hot tub

Enjoy peaceful, treed seclusion; cozy, antique-accented bedrooms; a hearty breakfast; near beaches, parks and trails, 20 minutes from Victoria.

Abigail's Hotel
906 McClure Street, V8V 3E7
604-388-5363
Catherine Wollner
All year

$$$ B&B
16 rooms, 16 pb
Visa, MC •
C-yes

Full breakfast
Comp. sherry
Library
sitting room
bicycles

Completely updated classic Tudor building. Private jacuzzi tubs, fireplaces and goose down comforters. Walk to downtown. Delicious breakfast. First-class smiling hospitality.

Battery Street Guest House
670 Battery St., V8V 1E5
604-385-4632
Pamela Verduyn
All year

$$ B&B
6 rooms, 2 pb
C-ltd/S-no/P-no/H-no
Dutch

Full breakfast
Sitting room

Comfortable guest house (1898) in downtown Victoria. Centrally located; walk to town, sites, Beacon Hill Park and ocean. Ample breakfast. Host speaks Dutch as a first language.

Beaconsfield Inn
998 Humboldt St., V8V 2Z8
604-384-4044
Hazel Prior
All year

$$$ B&B
12 rooms, 12 pb
Visa, MC •
C-yes/S-ltd

Full breakfast
Comp. sherry
Sunroom, library
piano
bicycles

Award-winning restoration of an English mansion. Walk to downtown. Antiques throughout; rich textures, velvets, leather, warm woods. Delicious breakfast. Pampering service.

Captain's Palace Inn
309 Belleville St., V8V 1X2
604-388-9191
Florence Prior, Helen Beirnes
All year

$$$ B&B
14 rooms, 14 pb
Visa, MC, AmEx •
C-no/S-no/P-no/H-no

Full breakfast
Comp. wine

1897 mansion with crystal chandeliers, stained glass, antiques and restaurant; near heart of Victoria; full view of Inner Harbor; Christmas shop & chocolate factory to visit.

VICTORIA ──

Elk Lake Lodge B&B
5259 Patricia Bay Hwy, V8Y 1S8
604-658-8879
Marie McQuade
All year

$$ B&B
5 rooms, 3 pb
Visa, MC
C-ltd/S-ltd/P-ltd/H-no
French, Spanish

Full breakfast
Afternoon tea
Library and T.V.
large lounge
hot tub on patio

Formerly a unique 1910 monastery and church. Antique furnishings with bedrooms and living room overlooking Elk Lake. Ten minutes from the city center, ferries.

Hibernia Bed & Breakfast
747 Helvetia Cr., V8Y 1M1
604-658-5519
Aideen Lydon
All year

$ B&B
3 rooms
MC •
C-yes
French, Spanish, Gaelic

Full breakfast
Sitting room
large lawn with trees
vines

Peaceful. 15 minutes from Victoria, ferries, airport, Butchart Gardens, cul-de-sac; 5 minutes off Highway 17. Full Irish breakfast. Antique furnishings.

Holland House Inn
595 Michigan St., V8V 1S7
604-384-6644
Lance, Deborah, & Robin
All year

$$$ B&B
19 rooms, 19 pb
Visa, MC, AmEx, DC •
C-yes/S-no/P-no/H-yes

Full breakfast
Afternoon tea by request
Sitting room
library

A unique 19-room luxury inn furnished throughout with eclectic furnishings and original, contemporary art. Winter months include string quartets once a month.

Joan Brown's B&B
834 Pemberton Rd., V8S 3R4
604-592-5929
Joan Brown
March—December

$$$ B&B
6 rooms, 3 pb
•
C-yes/S-no/P-no/H-no

Full breakfast
Comp. sherry
Sitting room

1912 home in Victoria's Rockland District, 20 min. to downtown & beaches. Bedrooms with Laura Ashley touches, quilts, linens. A home filled with love and delicious breakfasts.

Portage Inlet B&B
993 Portage Rd., V8Z 1K9
604-479-4594
Jim & Pat Baillie
All year

$$ B&B
4 rooms, 3 pb
Visa, MC •
C-yes/S-ltd/P-no/H-yes

Full English breakfast

Acre of waterfront, 3 miles from city centre, located at mouth of salmon stream. Organic food; hearty breakfast. Ducks, swans, eagles, heron and other wildlife on property.

Sunnymeade House Inn
1002 Fenn Ave., V8Y 1P3
604-658-1414
Jack & Nancy Thompson
All year

$$ B&B
5 rooms, 1 pb
Visa, MC

Full breakfast
Restaurant, bar service
Afternoon tea
Sitting room
tennis courts

Village by the Sea—Walk to shops, restaurants, beach. Country style B&B inn. Beautiful decor and furnishings. Sumptuous full breakfast.

VICTORIA

Top o' Triangle Mountain
3442 Karger Terrace, V9C 3K5
604-478-7853
Henry & Pat Hansen
All year

$$ B&B
3 rooms, 3 pb
Visa, MC •
C-yes/S-ltd/P-no/H-yes
Danish

Full breakfast
Sitting room

Warm, solid cedar home tucked in among the firs. Breathtaking view. Clean, comfortable beds. Hospitality and good food are our specialties. One two-room suite available.

Tucker's Bed & Breakfast
5373 Pat Bay Hwy. #2, V8Y 1S9
604-658-8404
Michele & Ian MacDonald
All year

$ B&B
4 rooms, 2 pb
Visa, MC •
C-yes/S-ltd/P-no/H-no
French

Full country breakfast
Afternoon tea, snacks
Restaurants nearby
Sitting room, parlour
bicycles, piano

Country-style B&B; lakeside with swimming, parks and windsurfing; hearty home cooking; character rooms; close to Butchart Gardens and downtown Victoria.

More Inns. . .

Aguilar House Bamfield V0R 1B0   604-728-3323
Bobbing Boats Box 88, 7212 Peden Ln., Brentwood Bay V0S 1A0   604-652-9828
Brentwood Bay B&B Box 403, Brentwood Bay V0S 1A0   604-652-2012
Campbell River Lodge 1760 Island Hwy., Campbell River V9W 2E7   604-287-7446
Dogwoods 302 Birch Street, Campbell River V9W 2S6   604-287-4213
Grants RR 1, Chemainns V0R 1K0   604-246-3768
Moyers' B&B RR1, 10423 Chemainus Rd, Chemainus V0R 1K0   604-246-3991
Wilcuma Resort RR 3, Cobble Hill V0R 1L0   604-748-8737
Dahlia Patch 3675 Minto Rd., RR 6, Courtenay V9N 8H9
Denman Island Guest House Box 9, Denman Rd., Denman Island V0R 1T0   604-335-2688
Fairburn Farm RR 7, Duncan V9L 4W4   604-746-4637
Bradshaw's Minac Lodge On Canim Lake, Eagle Creek V0K 1L0   604-397-2416
Gimmy's Farm/Guesthouse SS2, Site 13, Comp. 11, Fort St. John V1J 4M7   604-787-9104
Surf Lodge Ltd. RR1, Site 1, Gabriola Island V0R 1X0   604-247-9231
Hummingbird Inn Sturdies Bay Road, Galiano Island V0N 1P0   604-539-5472
La Berengerie Montague Harbor Bl., Galiano Island V0N 1P0   604-539-5392
Woodstone Country Inn Galiano Island V0N 1P0   604-539-2010
Lord Jim's Resort Hotel RR #1, Ole's Cove Rd., Halfmoon Bay V0N 1Y0   604-885-7038
Blair House 1299 Rodondo Place, Kelowna V1V 1G6   604-762-5090
Cat's Meow 5299 Chute Lake Rd., Kelowna V1Y 7R3   604-764-7407
Gables Country Inn 2405 Bering Rd., Kelowna V1Y 7P8   604-768-4468
Manana Lodge Box 9 RR 1, Ladysmith V0R 2E0   604-245-2312
Yellow Point Lodge RR 3, Ladysmith V0R 2E0   604-245-7422
Heritage Inn 422 Vernon Street, Nelson   604-352-5331
B&B for Visitors 10356 Skagit Dr., North Delta V4C 2K9   604-588-8866
Laburnum Cottage 1388 Terrace Ave., North Vancouver V7R 1B4   604-988-4877
West Coast Contemporary RR 1, Site 116 C71, Parksville V0R 2S0   604-248-2585
Taliesin Guest House B&B Box 101, Parson V0A 1LO   604-348-2247
Rose Cottage 1362 Naish Dr., Penticton V2A 3B6   604-492-3462
Feathered Paddle B&B (The) 7 Queesto Drive, Port Renfrew V0S 1K0   604-647-5433
Ram's Head Inn Red Mt. Ski Area Box 63, Rossland VOG 1YO   604-362-9577
Cindosa B&B 3951 40th St. NE, Salmon Arm V1E 4M4   604-832-3342
Silver Creek Guest House 6820 30th Ave. SW, Salmon Arm V1E 4M1   604-832-8870
Hastings House Box 1110, Ganges, Salt Spring Island V0S 1E0   800-661-9255
Fen Mor Manor Box 453, Sicamous V0E 2V0   604-836-4994
Sooke Harbour House 1528 Whiffen Spit Rd., Sooke V0S 1N0   604-642-3421

Three Pines Lodge   So. 85, RR #2, Summerland V0H 1Z0   604-494-1661
Hirsch's Place   10336-145 A St., Surrey V3R 3S1   604-588-3326
Clayoquot Lodge   P.O. Box 188, Tofino V0R 2Z0   604-725-3284
Burley's Lodge   Box 193, Ucluelet V0R 3A0   604-726-4444
"The Cabin"   7603 Westkal Road, Vernon V1B 1Y4   000-542-3021
Five Junipers   3704 24th Ave., Vernon V1T 1L9   604-549-3615
Schroth Farm   Site 6, Comp 25, R.R.8, Vernon V1T 8L6   604-545-0010
Camelot   P.O. Box 5038, Stn. B, Victoria V8R 6N3   604-592-8589
Cherry Bank Hotel   825 Burdetl Avenue, Victoria V8W 1B3
Craigmyle B&B   1037 Craigdorroch Road, Victoria V8S 2A5   604-595-5411
Oak Bay Guest House   1052 Newport Ave., Victoria V8S 5E3   604-598-3812
Olde England Inn   429 Lampson Street, Victoria   604-388-4353
Oxford Castle Inn   133 George Road, East, Victoria V9A 1L1   604-388-6431
Wellington B&B   66 Wellington Ave., Victoria V8V 4H5   604-383-5976
Margit's Mountain Retreat   Box 466, Whistler V0N 1B0   604-932-5974
Sabey House   Box 341, Whistler V0N 1B0   604-932-3498

Manitoba

MORRIS

Deerbank Farm	$ B&B	Full breakfast
Box 23, RR 2, R0G 1K0	3 rooms	Supper by request
204-746-8395	C-yes/S-ltd/P-ask/H-no	Complimentray tea
Kathleen Jorgenson		Sitting room, piano
All year		bicycles, pool table

Working farm with extra animals for our guests. In heart of the Red River Valley, one hour to Winnipeg.

TREHERNE

Beulah Land	$ B&B	Full breakfast
Box 26, R0G 2V0	3 rooms	All meals
204-723-2828	C-yes/S-yes/P-no/H-no	Hot tub
Wilf. Eadie		sitting room
All year		

Beulah Land Farm is situated in the beautiful valley of the Assiniboine, in the centre of Manitoba. All meals are home-grown and home-cooked.

WINNIPEG

Chestnut House	$ B&B	Full breakfast
209 Chestnut St., R36 1R8	4 rooms	Sitting room
204-772-9788	•	
John & Louise Clark	C-yes/S-no	
All year		

Restored home in historic location, furnished with antiques. Close to downtown facilities, restaurants, antique shops. Full breakfast complemented by homemade baking.

More Inns . . .

Ernie & Tina Dyck   Box 1001, Boissevain R0K 0E0   204-534-2563
Casa Maley   1605 Victoria Ave., Brandon R7A 1C1   204-728-0812
Nancy & Geoff Tidmarch   330 Waverly St., Winnipeg R3M 3L3   204-284-3689

New Brunswick

ALBERT ───────────

Florentine Manor
R.R.2., E0A 1A0
506-882-2271
Mary & Cyril Tingley
All year

$ B&B
7 rooms, 1 pb
C-yes

Full breakfast
Lunch & dinner (request)
Two sitting rooms

Quiet, comfortable 1860s home furnished in genuine antiques. Ideal for outdoor enthusiasts bird-watchers, bicyclists, hikers, fishermen, golfers, sightseers & photographers.

CENTREVILLE ───────────

Reid's Farm Tourist Home
RR 1, E0J 1H0
506-276-4787
Ken & Shirley Reid
All year

$ B&B/MAP
4 rooms, 2 pb
C-yes/S-no/P-no/H-ltd

Full breakfast
Lunch, tea, dinner
Sitting room
bicycles

Enjoy a rural atmosphere and old-fashioned hospitality down on the farm. We have a lake stocked with trout. Also log cabin in the woods with 5 miles of X-C trails.

FREDERICTON ───────────

Happy Acres B&B
RR 4, E3B 4X5
Hwy 105
506-472-1819
Margaret & Angus Hamilton
All year

$$ B&B
4 rooms, 3 pb
C-yes/S-ltd/P-ask/H-yes
some French

Full breakfast
Afternoon tea, snacks
Sitting room, library
sauna, funny pool
whirlpool in one room

Enjoy peace and tranquillity in a rural setting just minutes from all the tourist attractions of the Fredericton area.

GRAND MANAN ISLAND ───────────

Shorecrest Lodge
North Head, E0G 2M0
506-662-3216
Jill Malins, Frank Longstaff
Mid-May—mid-October

$ B&B
15 rooms, 3 pb
Visa, MC •
C-yes/S-yes
some French

Continental plus
Lunch, seafood dinner
Afternoon tea
Library
tennis courts nearby

Excellent bird watching, whale watching and scenic hiking trails. Owners formerly organized tours for the Canadian equivalent of the National Audubon Society.

PLASTER ROCK ───────────

Northern Wilderness Lodge
Box 571, E0J 1W0
Highway #108
506-356-8327
William Linton
All year

$ EP
14 rooms, 14 pb
Visa, MC, AmEx •
C-yes/S-yes/P-no/H-yes
English

Full breakfast $
Restaurant, bar service
Tea, snacks
Sitting room
game room

Quiet, uniquely maritime—pleasant valley view—classy but country. Stroll around and through trails and forests. See country beauty for yourself.

Dunn Country Inn, Martinsburg, WV

RIVERSIDE

Cailswick Babbling Brook
Albert Co., Route 114, E0A 2R0
506-882-2079
Hazen & Eunice Cail
All year

$ B&B
5 rooms, 2 pb
C-yes/S-no/P-no/H-no
French

Country breakfast
Evening snack
Sitting room
TV

Country living. Quiet, serene and restful. Home-cooked meals. Century-old Victorian overlooking Shepardy Bay, running brooks, lovely grounds. Near Fundy National Park.

ROTHESAY

Shadow Lawn Country Inn
P.O. Box 41, E0G 2W0
3180 Rothesay Rd.
506-847-7539
Patrick & Margaret Gallagher
All year

$$ EP
8 rooms, 5 pb
C-yes/S-yes/P-yes/H-no
French

Full breakfast $
Dinner by reservation
Bar service
Sitting room, piano
tennis courts

Shadow Lawn in the village of Rothesay—next to golf, tennis, sailing. Gourmet dining, with silver service.

SAINT ANDREWS

Pansy Patch
P.O. Box 349, E0G 2X0
59 Carleton St.
506-529-3834/203-354-4181
Kathleen & Michael Lazare
May 15—October 1

$$ B&B
4 rooms
Visa, MC, AmEx •
C-yes/S-yes/P-no/H-no
English, French

Full breakfast
Picnic baskets w/notice
Sitting room, aftern tea
Snacks, library
tenn courts, swmng pool

Norman turreted home housing antique/book shop and B&B. Antique-furnished bedrooms. Gourmet breakfast in garden over Passamaquoddy Bay. Private bath in June & Sept.

More Inns...

Ingle-Neuk Lodge B&B   RR 3 Box 1180, Bathurst E2A 4G8   506-546-5758
Poplars—Les Peupliers   RR 1 Site 11 Box 16, Beresford E0B 1H0   506-546-5271
Victoriana Rose B&B   193 Church St., Fredericton E3B 4E1   506-454-0994
Compass Rose   North Head, Grand Manan E0G 2M0   506-662-8570
Cross Tree Guest House   Seal Cove, Grand Manan E0G 3B0   506-662-8263
Ferry Wharf Inn   North Head, Grand Manan E0G 2M0   506-662-8588
Grand Harbour Inn   Box 73, Grand Harbour, Grand Manan E0G 1X0   506-662-8681
Manan Island Inn & Spa   P.O. Box 15, Grand Manan E0G 2M0   506-662-8624
Eveleigh Hotel   Evandale, RR 1, Hampstead E0G 1Y0   506-425-9993
Woodsview II B&B   RR 5, Hartland E0J 1N0   506-375-4637
Dutch Treat Farm   RR 1, Hopewell Cape E0A 1Y0   506-882-2552
Mactaquac B&B   Mactaquac RR 1, Mactaquac E0H 1N0   506-363-3630
Governor's Mansion   Main Street, Nelson E0C 1T0   506-622-3036
Different Drummer   Box 188, Sackville E0A 3C0   506-536-1291
Marshlands Inn   Box 1440, Sackville E0A 3C0   506-536-0170
Shiretown Inn   Town Square, Saint Andrews E0G 2X0   506-529-8877
A Touch of Country B&B   61 Pleasant St., Saint Stephen E3L 1A6   506-466-5056
Puff'Inn   P.O. Box 135, St. Andrews E0G 2X0   506-529-4191
Andersons Holiday Farm   Sussex RR 2, Sussex E0E 1P0   506-433-3786
Chez Prime B&B   RR 3, Site 32, Losier St, Tracadie E0C 2B0   506-395-6884

Newfoundland

More Inns...

Chaulk's Tourist Home   P.O. Box 339, Lewisporte A0J 3AO   709-535-6305
Village Inn   Trinity A0C 2S0   709-464-3269

Northwest Territories

More Inns...

Harbour House   Box 54, #1 Lakeshore Dr., Hay River X0E 0R0   403-874-2233

Nova Scotia

ANNAPOLIS ROYAL

Garrison House Inn
P.O. Box 108, B0S 1A0
350 St. George St.
902-532-5750
Patrick & Anna Redgrave
May 15—November 1

$$ EP
7 rooms, 5 pb
Visa, MC
C-ltd/S-ltd/P-no/H-no
French

Full breakfast $
Intimate 16 seat pub
Licensed dining room
Picnic lunches
sitting room, bicycles

Restored 1854 Heritage House—early Canadian antiques, hooked rugs, quilts and folk art treasures. Dining room specializes in local seafood and produce.

GUYSBOROUGH COUNTY

Liscombe Lodge
Liscomb Mills, B0J 2A0
902-779-2307
David M. Evans
June—October

$$$ EP
Visa, MC, AmEx, Enroute •
C-yes/S-yes/P-ltd/H-yes

Restaurant, bar service
Afternoon tea, snacks
Sitting room, tennis
hiking, boat rentals
fishing equipment

A riverside resort, a get-away-from-it-all outdoor retreat for the entire family. Stay in chalets, cottages or the new lodge that overlooks our Marina.

HALIFAX

Apple Basket B&B
1756 Robie St., B3H 3E9
902-429-3019
Ms. Michal Crowe
All year

$ B&B
3 rooms
C-no/S-no/P-no/H-no

Continental plus

Turn-of-the-century Victorian furnished with antiques and art collection. Lovely homemade breakfast. Honeymoon special.

Queen Street Inn
1266 Queen St., B3J 2H4
902-422-9828
Alfred J. Saulnior
All year

$ EP
7 rooms, 1 pb
C-no/S-no/no

Old Halifax stone house built for a Nova Scotian Supreme Court Justice in 1870. Antique furnishings, in downtown Halifax.

HEBRON

Manor Inn
P.O. Box 56, Route 1, B0W 1X0
902-742-2487
Bev & Terry Grandy
May—December

$$ EP
Visa, MC, AmEx •
C-yes/S-yes/P-ltd/H-no
French

Full breakfast $
Lunch, dinner, bar
Entertainment
tennis courts, pool
putting green, croquet

Nine acres of landscaped grounds, formal rose garden, 3,000 feet of lake front. Magnificent old mansion and 24-unit motel. Boating, swimming, lawn games.

More Inns . . .

Amherst Shore Country Inn   RR #2, Amherst B4H 3X9   902-667-4800
Bread and Roses   P.O. Box 177, Annapolis Royal B0S 1A0   902-532-5727
Milford House   South Milford, RR #4, Annapolis Royal B0S 1A0   902-532-2617
Northhills Manor   Box 418, Annapolis Royal B0S 1A0   902-532-5555
Poplars B&B   124 Victoria St, Box 27, Annapolis Royal B0S 1A0   902-532-7936
Old Manse Inn   5 Tigo Park, Antigonish B2G 1L7   902-863-5696
Le Cape Pottery House   Queen St. P.O. Box 549, Baddeck B0E 1B0   902-295-3367
Telegraph House   Box 8, Baddeck B0E 1B0   902-295-9988
Lovett Lodge Inn   P.O. Box 119, Bear River B0S 1B0   902-467-3917
1850 House   Box 22, Main St., Canning, Kings County B0P 1H0   902-582-3052
Heart of Hart's T. H.   N.E. Margaree, Cape Breton B0E 2H0   902-248-2765
Kilmuir Place   NE Margaree, Cape Breton B0E 2H0   902-248-2877
Riverside Inn   Margaree Hrb., Cape Breton B0E 2B0   902-235-2002
McNeill Manor B&B   P.O. Box 565, Chester B0J 1J0   902-275-4638
Cobequid Hills Country Inn   Collingwood B0M 1E0   902-686-3381
Martin House   62 Pleasant St., Dartmouth B2Y 3P5   902-469-1896
Bayberry House   Box 114, Troop Ln., Granville Ferry B0S 1K0   902-532-2272
Shining Tides   RR #2, Granville Ferry B0S 1K0   902-532-2770
Seabright B&B   Seabright, Halifax County B0J 3J0   902-823-2987
Greta Cross B&B   81 Peperell St., Louisbourg B0A 1M0   902-733-2833
Boscawen Inn   P.O. Box 1343, Lunenburg B0J 2C0   902-634-3325
Cape Breton Island Farm   RR 2, Mabou B0E 1X0   902-945-2077
Camelot   Box 31, Rt. 7, Musquodoboit Harbour B0J 2L0   902-889-2198
Annfield Tourist Manor   RR 3, Bras D'or, North Sydney B0C 1B0   902-736-8770
L'Auberge   80 Front St., Box 99, Pictou B0K 1H0   902-485-6900
Westway Inn   Plympton B0W 2R0   902-837-4097
Blue Heron Inn   P.O. Box 405, Pugwash B0K 1L0   902-243-2900
Gramma's House   RR3, Shelburne B0T 1W0   902-637-2058
Harborview Inn   P.O. Box 35, Smith's Cove, Digby Co. B0S 1S0   902-245-5686
Lansdowne Lodge   Upper Stewiacke B0N 2P0   902-671-2749
Senator Guest House   Rt. 6, Sunrise Trail, Wallace B0K 1Y0   902-257-2417
Gilbert's Cove Farm   RR 3, Weymouth B0W 3T0   902-837-4505
Clockmaker's Inn B&B   1399 King Street, Windsor   902-798-5265
Blomidon Inn   P.O. Box 839, Wolfville B0P 1X0   902-542-9326
Victoria's Historic Inn   Box 819, 416 Main St., Wolfville B0P 1X0   902-542-5744

Ontario

BRAESIDE

Glenroy Farm
RR 1, K0A 1G0
613-432-6248
Noreen & Steve McGregor
All year

$ B&B
3 rooms, 1 pb
C-yes/S-yes/P-no/H-no

Full breakfast
Dinner $5.00
Sitting room, piano
bicycles

Century-old stone farmhouse on the Ottawa River, 50 miles to Canada's Capitol. Reservations 8 a.m. or 6 p.m. Rafting, full breakfast.

BURGESSVILLE

McMillen's Bed & Breakfast	$$ B&B	Full breakfast
P.O. Box 71, N0J 1C0	2 rooms, 1 pb	Afternoon tea (by req.)
41 Church St. E.		Air-conditioned home
519-424-9834		indoor swimming pool
All year		

McMillen's B&B is situated in a quiet village setting, close to a restaurant. Spacious bedroom. Only 10 minutes from 401. Short drive to Stratford Festival.

COBOURG

Northumberland Heights Inn	$$ EP	Full breakfast $
RR 5, K9A 4J8	14 rooms, 14 pb	Lunch, dinner, bar
Northumberland Heights Rd	Visa, MC, AmEx •	Hot tub, sauna
416-372-7500	C-yes/S-yes/P-no/H-yes	swimming pool
Mike & Veronica Thiele	German, French, Dutch	sitting room, piano
All year		

Situated on 100 acres of rolling countryside. Relaxing patio areas, miniature golf, outdoor checkers, trout pond, cross-country skiing, skating. Two night "Plan" available.

ELMIRA

Teddy Bear Bed & Breakfast	$$ B&B	Continental plus
RR #1, N3B 2Z1	3 rooms, 2 pb	Dinner with reservation
519-669-2379	Visa, MC •	Sitting room
Gerrie & Vivian Smith	C-yes/S-no/P-no/H-no	library
All year		bicycles

Hospitality abounds in this outstandingly beautiful countryside inn with Mennonite quilts, crafts, and antiques. Close to Elora, St. Jacob's, and Stratford.

GORE'S LANDING

Victoria Inn	$$ EP	Full breakfast $
County Rd. 18, K0K 2E0	9 rooms, 9 pb	Lunch, dinner, bar
416-342-3261	Visa, MC, AmEx	Sitting room, piano
Mid-May—mid-October	C-ltd/S-yes/P-no/H-yes	boat rental
		swimming pool

Restful waterfront estate, stained glass windows, fireplaces highlight quaint rooms. Veranda dining room with panoramic view of Rice Lake. Boat dockage.

MAYNOOTH

Bea's B&B House	$ B&B	Full breakfast
Box 133, K0L 2S0	4 rooms, 1 pb	Afternoon tea
613-338-2239	•	Sitting room, TV
Bea/Louie Leveque	C-10+/S-yes/P-no/H-no	
All year weekends only		

Older, well-built home. Quiet creek runs past house. Ample parking. Good food, home baking and cooked meals. Sauna under construction.

MCKELLER

Inn & Tennis Club—Manitou	$$$ AP	Full breakfast
McKellar Center Road, P0G 1C0	Visa, Mc, AmEx, checks •	Lunch & French dinner
251 Davenport Rd. M5R 1J9	C-yes/S-ltd	Stocked library, saunas
416-967-3466/705-389-2171	French	lake, hot tubs, pool
Ben & Sheila Wise		13 tennis courts
May—October		

Five star lakeside sophisticated Relais and Chateaux resort. Thirteen tennis courts, luxurious suites featuring skylit sumptuous washrooms with whirlpool baths and sauna.

NEW HAMBURG

Waterlot Inn
17 Huron St., N0B 2G0
519-662-2020
Gordon Elkeer
All year

$$ B&B
3 rooms, 1 pb
Visa, MC, AmEx
C-no/S-no/P-no/H-no

Continental breakfast
Lunch, dinner, bar
Gourmet shop

Just the place for a romantic gourmet. Quiet riverside escape. One of Ontario's finiest dining establishments.

OTTAWA

Albert House
478 Albert St., K1R 5B5
613-236-4479/800-267-1982
John & Cathy Delroy
All year

$$ B&B
17 rooms, 17 pb
Visa, MC, AmEx
C-yes/S-yes/P-no/H-no
French, ItWoian

Full breakfast
Sitting room
color cable TV in rooms
telephones

Fine restored Victorian residence designed by Thomas Seaton Scott in post-Confederate period. Complimentary breakfast, parking.

Australis Guest House
35 Marlborough Ave., K1N 8E6
613-235-8461
Carol & Brian Waters
All year

$ B&B
3 rooms, 1 pb
C-yes/S-yes/P-no/H-no

Full breakfast
Comp. tea
Sitting room, piano
bicycles
off-street parking avail

An older renovated antique-filled downtown home close to all attractions in an area of embassies, parks and the river. Family suite available.

Beatrice Lyon Guest House
479 Slater St., K1R 5C2
613-236-3904
Phyllis Beatrice Lyon
All year

$ B&B
3 rooms
C-yes/S-yes/P-yes/H-no
French

Full breakfast
Afternoon tea
Living room

A 100-year-old old-fashioned family home in downtown Ottawa. 5 minutes walk to Parliament buildings, shopping, National Library, art gallery and Arts Center.

Blue Spruces B&B
187 Glebe Ave., K1S 2C6
613-236-8521
Patricia & John Hunter
All year

$$ B&B
3 rooms, 1 pb
C-6+/S-ltd/P-no/H-no
French

Full breakfast
Afternoon tea
Sitting room

Elegant Edwardian home with antiques in downtown Ottawa. Home-cooked breakfasts. We enjoy talking with guests & helping them find memorable parts of Ottawa to explore.

Cartier House Inn
46 Cartier St., K2P 1J3
613-236-4667
Nicole Lalonde
All year

$$$ B&B
11 rooms, 11 pb
Visa,MC, AmEx •
C-ltd/S-ltd/P-no/H-no
English, Spanish, French

Continental plus
Afternoon tea/snacks
Jacuzzis in suites
morning paper, evening
chocolates

A "grand luxe" European inn which has been offering tranquillity and an attentive staff since the turn of the century. Near the Parliament, shops and restaurants.

OTTAWA

Doral Inn Hotel	$ EP	Full breakfast
486 Albert St., K1R 5B5	22 rooms, 22 pb	Continental restaurant
613-230-8055	Visa, MC, AmEx •	Indoor pool/spa access
Frank Baker	C-yes/S-yes/P-no/H-yes	sitting room, A/C
All year	French	parking, TV, phones

Restored 1879 Victorian heritage home furnished in antiques, fireplaces. Centrally located in downtown; walk to tourist attractions. 4-star inn. A warm welcome awaits you.

Gasthaus Switzerland	$ B&B	Swiss country breakfast
89 Daly Ave., K1N 6E6	17 rooms, 7 pb	Afternoon tea
613-237-0335	Visa, MC	TV room
Josef & Sabine Sauter	C-yes/S-yes/P-no/H-no	sitting room
All year	German, Serb., French	barbecue, garden

Warm Swiss atmosphere in Canada's beautiful capital; clean, cozy rooms; full Swiss-continental breakfast; close to tourist attractions; free parking. Warm, clean & cheery!

Rideau View Inn	$ B&B	Full breakfast
177 Frank St., K2P OX4	7 rooms	Sitting room
613-236-9309	Visa, MC, AmEx	bicycles
George W. Hartsgrove	C-ltd/S-ltd/P-no/H-no	tennis nearby
All year	English, French	

Large 1907 Edwardian home with very well-appointed guest rooms. Walking distance to Parliament Hill, Rideau Canal, fine restaurants, shopping and public transport.

Westminster Guest House	$ B&B	Full breakfast
446 Westminster Ave., K2A 2T8	3 rooms, 1 pb	Dinner by reservation
613-729-2707	C-ltd/S-ltd/P-ltd/H-no	Evening refreshments
E. Deavy, K. Mikoski	French	Sitting room, piano
All year		fireplace

A turn-of-the-century home in a peaceful setting just a short drive from Parliament Hill. Close to bicycle and walking trails along Ottawa River.

PORT CARLING

Sherwood Inn	$$$ MAP	Full breakfast
P.O. Box 400, P0B 1J0	29 rooms, 27 pb	Lunch, dinner, bar
705-765-3131	Visa, MC, AmEx, DC •	Tennis court
John & Eva Heineck	C-yes/S-yes/P-no/H-ltd	sitting room, piano
All year	German	

We have given every consideration to your leisure and recreational needs. All for your enjoyment, full breakfast, children welcome.

PORT STANLEY

Kettle Creek Inn	$$ B&B	Continental breakfast
Main St., N0L 2A0	10 rooms	Lunch, dinner, snacks
519-782-3388	AmEx, Visa, MC, EnRoute •	Tea, bar service
Gary & Jean Vedova	C-yes/S-yes/P-no/H-yes	Sitting room, library
All year		sauna, entertainment

Historic 1849 inn nestled in a quaint fishing village. Award winning dining—indoor or outdoor in our patio and gazebo. Lovely gardens. The perfect escape.

SAINT JACOBS

Jakobstettel Guest House	$$$ B&B	Continental plus
16 Isabella St., N0B 2N0	12 rooms, 12 pb	Tea, coffee, snacks
P.O. Box 28	Visa, MC, AmEx	Swimming pool, trail
519-664-2208	C-yes/S-ltd/P-no/H-no	tennis courts, bicycles
Ella Brubacher	Pennsylvania German	sitting room, library
All year		

Luxurious privacy set amidst 5 acres w/trees. Each room decorated with its own charm and Victorian features. Local artisan shops withing walking distance.

TORONTO

Ashleigh Heritage Home	$ B&B	Continental plus
Box 235 Station E, M6H 4E2	4 rooms	Sitting room, piano
42 Delaware Ave.	Visa •	bicycles, library
416-535-4000	C-yes/S-ltd/P-no/H-no	parking
Gwen Lee		
All year		

Restored 1910 home with interesting architectural details and a large garden. Just minutes from the University, the museum and government offices.

Burken Guest House	$$ B&B	Continental plus
322 Palmerston Blvd., M6G 2N6	8 rooms	Deck, garden
416-920-7842	Visa, MC •	parking
Burke & Ken	C-yes/S-yes/P-no/H-no	
All year	German, French	

Very attractive home in charming downtown residential area. Period furniture, close to Eaton Centre. Weekly rates available.

More Inns...

Horseshoe Inn   RR 2, Alton L0N 1A0   519-927-5779
Little Inn of Bayfield Ltd   P.O. Box 100, Bayfield N0M 1G0   519-565-2611
Landfall Farm   RR 1, Blackstock L0B 1B0   416-986-5588
Holiday House Inn   P.O. Box 1139, Bracebridge P0B 1C0   705-645-2245
Country Guest Home   RR 2, Bradford L3Z 2A5   416-775-3576
Caledon Inn   Caledon East L0N 1E0   416-584-2891
Chestnut Inn   9 Queen St., Cookstown L0L 1L0   705-458-9751
Sir Sam's Inn   Eagle Lake Post Office, Eagle Lake K0M 1M0   705-754-2188
Lucky Lancione's   635 Metler Rd. RR 3, Fenwick L0S 1C0   416-892-8104
Breadelbane Inn   487 St. Andrew St. W., Fergus N1M 1P2   519-843-4770
Bushland Meadows   Box 224, Flesherton N0C 1E0   519-924-2675
Glencairn Manor   P.O. Box 22, Glencairn L0M 1K0   705-424-6045
Cedarlane Farm B&B   R.R. 2, Iroquois K0E 1K0   613-652-4267
Prince George Hotel   200 Ontario St., Kingston K7L 2Y9   613-549-5440
Ivy Lea Inn   1000 Isl. Pkwy., Lansdowne K0E 1L0   613-659-2329
Rose Bed & Breakfast   526 Dufferin Ave., London N6B 2A2   519-433-9978
Minden House   P.O. Box 789, Minden K0M 2K0   705-286-3263
Sterling Lodge   Newboro K0G 1P0   613-272-2435
Kiely House Heritage Inn   P.O. Box 1642, Niagara-On-The-Lake L0S 1J0   416-468-4588
Angel Inn, Est. 1828   224 Regent St., Niagara-on-the-Lake L0S 1J0   416-468-3411
Kiely House Heritage Inn   209 Queen St. Box 1642, Niagara-on-the-Lake L2G 6R5
   416-468-4588
Paines' B&B   Carling Bay Road, RR 1, Nobel P0G 1G0   705-342-9266
Union Hotel   Box 38, RR 1, Normandale N0E 1W0   519-426-5568
Willi-Joy Farm   RR #3, Norwich N0J 1P0   519-424-2113
Al Leclerc's Residence   253-McLeod St., Ottawa K2P 1A1   613-234-7577
Constance House B&B   62 Sweetland Ave., Ottawa K1N 7T6   613-235-8888

Flora House   282 Flora St., Ottawa K1R 5S3   613-230-2152
Gwen's Guest Home   2071 Riverside Dr., Ottawa K1H 7X2   613-737-4129
Haydon House   18 Queen Elizabeth Drwy, Ottawa K2P 1C6   613-230-2697
O'Conner House Downtown   172 O'Conner St., Ottawa K2P 1T5   613-236-4221
Moses Sunset Farms B&B   RR 6, Owen Sound N4K 5N8   519-371-4559
Rebecca's B&B   P.O. Box 1028, Petrolia N0N 1R0   519-882-0118
Good Old British B&B   4 Ransford St., Port Franks N0M 2L0   519-243-3694
Arrowwood Lodge   P.O. Box 125, Port Severn L0K 1S0   705-538-2354
Houseboat Amaryllis Inn   General Delivery, Rockport K0E 1V0   613-659-3513
Unicorn Inn & Restaurant   RR 1, South Gillies P0T 2V0   807-475-4200
Burnside Guest Home   139 William St., Stratford N5A 4X9   519-271-7076
Shrewsbury Manor   30 Shrewsbury St., Stratford N5A 2V5   519-271-8520
Beaches Bed & Breakfast   Queen St. & Lee Ave., Toronto   416-465-9933
Mrs. Mitchell's   Violet Hill L0N 1S0   819-925-3672
Windermere House   Windermere P0B 1P0   705-769-3611
Old Bridge Inn   Young's Point K0L 3G0   705-652-8507

Prince Edward Island

CHARLOTTETOWN

Dundee Arms Inn
200 Pownal St., C1A 3W8
902-892-2496/800-565-7105
Don Clinton
All year

$$ EP
6 rooms, 6 pb
Visa, MC, AmEx, EnRoute •
C-no/S-yes/P-no/H-no
French

Continental breakfast
Luncheon, dinner, pub

A gracious Victorian Inn furnished in antiques. Famous for fine dining, charming atmosphere, and warm hospitality.

Stanhope by the Sea
P.O. Box 2109, C1A 7N7
Stanhope
902-672-2047/902-892-6008
Dr Alfy & Dr Constance Tadros
June—August

$$ EP
Visa, MC •
C-yes/S-yes/P-yes/H-no
French

Full breakfast
Lunch, dinner, bar
Sitting room, piano
entertainment, tennis
bikes, golf, surfing

Furnished with period antiques, resort setting, National Park beaches, sand dunes, windsurfing, bicycle packages and all-you-can-eat lobster smorgasbord daily.

KENSINGTON

Sherwood Acres Guest Home
RR 1, C0B 1M0
902-836-5430
Erma & James Hickey
All year

$ B&B
6 rooms, 1 pb
C-yes/S-yes/P-yes/H-yes

Full breakfast
Sitting room
piano

Near lovely sandy beaches, clam digging, country walks. Food is all homemade, including the bread and butter. Also private house available by the week.

MURRAY RIVER

Bayberry Cliff Inn B&B	$ B&B	Full breakfast
RR 4, Little Sands, C0A 1W0	7 rooms	Sitting room
902-962-3395	Visa, MC	library, craft shop
Nancy & Don Perkins	C-yes	Stairs down 400-ft.
May 15—September 30	Spanish	cliff to shore

Two remodeled post & beam barns 50 feet from edge of cliff. Furnishings: antiques, marine paintings. 8 minutes to W.I.'s ferry. Five levels.

SOUTH RUSTICO

Barachois Inn	$ EP	Full breakfast $
P.O. Box 1022, C1A 7M4	6 rooms, 1 pb	Sitting room
Church Rd., Rt. 243	C-yes/S-no/P-no/H-no	pump organ
902-963-2194	English, French	
Judy & Gary MacDonald		
May 1—October 31		

Victorian house offers lovely views of bay, river and countryside. Antique furnishings and modern comforts. Walk to seashore.

STANHOPE

Stanhope by the Sea	$$ EP	Restaurant, bar service
P.O. Box 2109	35 rooms, 35 pb	Lunch, dinner
Route 25	Visa, MC •	Sitting room, library
902-672-2047	C-yes/S-yes/P-ltd/H-yes	bicycles
June—September	French	tennis courts

Oldest summer resort on Prince Edward Island on the beach; golf next door; windsurfer paradise. Gourmet dining; a real treat for the entire family.

SUMMERSIDE

Silver Fox Inn	$ B&B	Continental breakfast
61 Granville St., C1N 2Z3	6 rooms, 6 pb	Sitting room
902-436-4033	Visa, MC, AmEx •	piano
Julie Simmons	C-no/S-yes/P-no/H-no	
All year		

Restored 1892 house with antique furnishings. Sunroom, sitting room with fireplace, and balcony for guests. Breakfast with homemade muffins, jams, farm eggs.

VERNON RIVER

Lea's Hobby Farm B&B	$ EP	Full breakfast $3.25
C0A 2E0	5 rooms, 1 pb	Continental plus $2
902-651-2501	C-yes/S-yes/P-no/H-no	Hot tub
Dora Lea		sitting room, piano
All year		

Small farm with beef cattle, pheasants, rabbits and a bird dog called Tipsy. Bedrooms with two double beds, some with one double bed. Country breakfasts.

More Inns...

Shore Farm B&B   Borden RR 1, Augustine Cove C0B 1X0   902-855-2871
Linden Lodge   RR 3, Belfast C0A 1A0   902-659-2716
Churchill Farm T.H.   RR 3, Bonshaw C0A 1C0   902-675-2481
Shaw's Hotel & Cottages   Brackley Beach C0A 2H0   902-672-2022
Windsong Farm   Rt. 6, RR 1, Winsloe, Brackley Beach C0A 2H0   902-672-2874
Allix's B&B   11 Johnson Av., Charlottetown C1A 3H7   902-892-2643
Just Folks B&B   RR 5, Charlottetown C1A 7J8   902-569-2089
Rosevale Farm B&B   Marshfield, RR 3, Charlottetown C1A 7J7   902-894-7821
Obanlea Farm Tourist Home   RR 4 North River PO, Cornwall C0A 1H0   902-566-3067

Chez-Nous B&B   Ferry Rd., RR 4, Corwan C0A 1H0   902-566-2779
Fralor Farm Tourist Home   RR 1, Kensington, Darnley C0B 1M0   902-836-5300
Beach Point View Inn   RR 5, Kensington C0B 1M0   902-836-5260
Blakeney's B&B   15 MacLean Ave, Box 17, Kensington C0B 1M0   902-836-3254
Murphy's Sea View B&B   Rt. 20, Kensington C0B 1M0   902-836-5456
Woodington's Country Inn   Sea View, RR 2, Kensington C0B 1M0   902-836-5518
Dalvay by the Sea Hotel   P. O. Box 8, Little York C0A 1P0   902-672-2048
Waugh's Farm B&B   Lower Bedeque C0B 1C0   902-887-2320
Carr's Corner Farm Tourist   Route 12, Miscouche C0B 1T0   902-436-6287
Brydon's B&B   Heatherdale RR 1, Montague C0A 1R0   902-838-4747
Harbourview B&B   RR 1, Murray Harbour C0A 1V0   902-962-2565
Laine Acres B&B   Cornwall RR 2, Nine Mile Creek C0A 1H0   902-675-2402
Joyce's Tourist Home   North Rustico C0A 1X0   902-963-2257
Smallman's B&B   Knutsford, RR 1, O'Leary C0B 1V0   902-859-3469
Partridge's B&B   RR 2, Montague, Panmure Island C0A 1R0   902-838-4687
MacCallum's B&B   Route 2, St. Peters Bay C0A 2A0   902-961-2957
Creekside Farm B&B   Stanley Bridge C0A 1E0   902-886-2713
Gulf Breeze   Stanley Bridge C0A 1E0   902-886-2678
Faye & Eric's B&B   380 Mac Ewen Road, Summerside C1N 4X8   902-436-6847
Harbour Lights T. H.   RR #2, Tignish C0B 2B0   902-882-2479
Doctor's Inn B&B   Tyne Valley C0B 2C0   902-831-2164
West Island Inn   Box 24, Tyne Valley C0B 2C0   902-831-2495
MacLeod's Farm B&B   UIGG, Vernon P.O., Vernon C0A 2E0   902-651-2303
Enman's Farm B&B   PO RR2 Vernon Bridge, Vernon Bridge C0A 2E0   902-651-2427
Victoria Village Inn   Victora by-the-Sea C0A 2G0   902-658-2288
Amber Lights B&B   P.O. Box 14, Rt. 26, York C0A 1P0   902-894-5868

Quebec

KAMOURASKA

Gite du Passant B&B
81 Ave. Morel, G0L 1M0
418-492-2921
Mariette Le Blanc
May—October

$ B&B
3 rooms, 3 pb
C-ltd/S-no/P-no/H-no
French

Full breakfast
Sitting room
piano

Venez voir notre beau village situe sur le bord du fleuve, dans une ancienne maison renove. Magnifique couche de soleil.

MONT TREMBLANT

Chateau Beauvallon, Inc.
Montee Ryan, Box 138, J0T 1Z0
819-425-7275
Judy & Alex Riddell
All year exc. mid-Oct.—Nov.

$$ B&B
14 rooms, 7 pb
•
C-yes/S-yes/P-ltd/H-ltd
French

Full breakfast
Dinner, bar
Sitting room, piano
bicycles
lake swimming

Country inn with home cooking, on a clear quiet mountain lake. Cycling, golf, tennis, windsurfing, all available within two-mile proximity.

MONTREAL

Ambrose Travel Lodge
3422 Stanley St., H3A 1R8
514-288-6922
Claude Jouhannet
All year

$ B&B
22 rooms, 17 pb
Visa, MC •
C-yes/S-yes/P-no/H-no
Eng., Fr., Span., Ger.

Continental breakfast
Phone in each room
cable TV, sitting room
air conditioning

Perfect location of this Victorian-style lodge close to McGill University, musee, restaurants, shopping center. Quiet surroundings and friendly home atmosphere.

Armor Inn
151 Sherbrooke E., H2X 1C7
514-285-0894
Annick Morvan
All year

$ EP
14 rooms, 7 pb
•
C-yes/S-yes/P-no/H-no
French

Comp. coffee

Once a fine Victorian townhouse in downtown Montreal. Fine woodwork in foyer and some guest rooms.

Auberge De La Fontaine
1301 E. Rachel St., H2J 2K1
514-597-0166
Celine Boudreau
All year

$$$ B&B
13 rooms, 13 pb
Visa, MC, AmEx •
C-12+/S-yes/P-no/H-yes
French

Continental plus
Afternoon tea

Facing Parc La Fontaine (84 acres), located near downtown area. A charming inn where you are welcomed as friends. Public transportation nearby. Warm and friendly staff.

Countryside, Summit Point, WV

NEW CARLISLE

Bay View Manor
P.O. Box 21, G0C 1Z0
395 Fauvel, Route 132
418-752-2725 / 418-752-6718
Helen Sawyer
All year

$ B&B
6 rooms, 2 pb
C-yes/P-no
French

Full breakfast
Lunch, dinner
Sitting room, library
tennis courts, pool
near golf, cottage avail

Seaside country haven, yet on a main highway. Fresh farm produce. August Folk Festival. Quilts, handicrafts and homebaking on sale. Cottage at $250 per week also available.

POINTE-AU-PIC

Auberge Donohue
145 Principale, CP 211, G0T 1M0
418-665-4377
Monique & Orval Aumont
All year

$$$ B&B
13 rooms, 13 pb
C-ltd/S-yes/P-no/H-no
French

Continental breakfast
Afternoon tea
Sitting room, piano
swimming pool
fireplaces

Cozy house situated right by the St. Lawrence River. Very large living room with fireplace. Every room has private bath; most rooms have view of the river.

PORT HILL

Senator's House
P.O. Box 63, Tyne Vally, C0B 2C0
Lady Slipper Dr.
902-831-2071 / 619-789-8355
Phyllis Baker
Mid-June—mid-September

$ EP
4 rooms, 4 pb
•
C-10+/S-ltd/P-no/H-no
French

Continental plus
Restaurant
Bar service
Sitting room
library

The Senator's House is the home of a Canadian statesman, restored and furnished with antiques and period reproductions. Close to parks, shopping malls and beaches.

PORTNEUF

Edale Place
Edale Pl., G0A 2Y0
418-286-3168
Mary & Tam Farnsworth
All year

$ B&B
4 rooms
C-yes/S-yes/P-no/H-no
French

Full breakfast
Afternoon tea
Sitting room
jacuzzi
15% reduction for skiers

Victorian country home. Beautiful, peaceful, quiet spot. 35-minute drive from Quebec City.

QUEBEC CITY

Au Manoir Ste-Genevieve
13 Ave. Ste-Genevieve, G1R 4A7
418-694-1666
Marguerite Coriveau
All year

$$ EP
9 rooms, 9 pb
C-yes/S-yes/P-no/H-no
French

Fresh cut flowers and
window boxes

Manor with modern facilities, furnished with antiques. Friendly and comfortable. Located behind Chateau Frontenac, on the St. Lawrence River. Walk to all points of interest.

Le Chateau De Pierre
17 Ave. Ste-Genevieve, G1R 4A8
418-694-0429
Lily Couturier
All year

$$$ EP
15 rooms, 15 pb
Visa, MC •
C-yes/S-ltd/P-no/H-no
French, Spanish

Kitchenettes in 2 units
Color TVs
air-conditioned

Old English colonial mansion with colonial charm. Fine appointments and distinctive atmosphere. Located in Old Quebec Uppertown. Walk to Citadell, shopping, historical points.

QUEBEC CITY

Maison Marie-Rollet
81, rue Ste-Anne, G1R 3X4
418-694-9271
Fernand Blouin
All year

$$ EP
10 rooms, 10 pb
Visa •
C-yes/S-yes/P-no/H-no
French

Well situated, in the center of Old Quebec facing the City Hall. Parking across the street. Quiet Victorian house.

SAINT ANNE DES MONT

Gite du Mont Albert
Case Postale 1150, G0E 2G0
418-763-2288/800-463-0860
Stephanie Barriere
March—January 3

$ B&B/MAP
Visa, MC, AmEx, Enroute •
C-yes/S-yes/H-yes
French

Full breakfast
Restaurant, bar service
Comp. wine, snacks
Pool, hot tubs, sauna
bicycles, fishing, ski

An inn renowned for its cuisine & its exceptional surroundings. Activities: hiking, fishing, canoeing & sailing, cycling in the mountains, nature interpretation, skiing.

SAINT ANTOINE DE TILLY

Auberge Manoir de Tilly
3854 Chemin de Tilly, G0S 2C0
418-886-2407
Jocelyne & Majella Gagnon
April 1—December 31

$$$ B&B/MAP
12 rooms, 7 pb
Visa, MC, AmEx, EnRoute •
C-yes/S-ltd/P-no/H-no
French, English

Full breakfast
Dinner available
Piano, swimming pool
bicycles, shuffleboard
golf, tennis nearby

200-year-old manor on St. Lawrence River shores. Furnished in antiques. Fifteen miles from Quebec Bridge (gate of Old City). Antique stores nearby.

SAINT SAUVEUR DES MONTS

Auberge St-Denis
61, St-Denis, CP 1229, J0R 1R0
514-227-4766/514-227-4602
Richard Desjardins
All year

$$$ B&B/MAP
23 rooms, 23 pb
Visa, MC, AmEx, DC •
C-ltd/S-ltd/P-no/H-ltd
French

Full breakfast
Lunch, dinner, tea, bar
Sitting room, garden
swimming pool, hot tub
phones, TV, wine cellar

Victorian-style inn built 1938, recently renovated. French owners, atmosphere. Chamber music ensemble Saturday nights. Gourmet breakfast, French cuisine. 18 fireplaces.

ST. MARC SUR RICHELIEU

Handfield Inn
555 Chemin du Prince, J0L 2E0
514-584-2226
Conrad Handfield
All year

$$ EP/MAP (wint)
53 rooms, 53 pb
Visa, MC, AmEx, DC •
C-yes/S-yes/P-no/H-yes
French

Full breakfast $
Restaurant, bar service
Aftn. tea, snacks,
Pool, horseback riding
tennis courts, marina

Country inn on the River Sibe. Ancestral house, 165 years old. All rooms decorated with antiques. Marina available for traveling sailors.

SUTTON

Schweizer Lodge
RR 2, J0E 2K0
514-538-2129
Pauline Canzani

$ MAP

Breakfast
Dinner

Simple lodging; two persons per room; beautiful 3 bedroom house available. Quiet mountain farm setting. Meals are just great—vegetarian food on request.

440   Quebec

More Inns. . .

La Maison Otis   23 R. St. Jean Baptiste, Baie St. Paul G0A 1B0   418-435-2255
Hostellerie Rive Gauche   1810 boul. Richelieu, Beloeil J3G 4S4   514-467-4650
Auberge La Pinsonniere   124 St. Raphael, Cap-a-l'Aigle G0T 1B0   418-665-4431
La Pinsonniere   124 St. Raphael, Cap-a-l'Aigle G0T 1B0   418-665-4431
Auberge Le Coin Du Banc   Rt. 132, Coin du Banc-Perce G0C 2L0   418-645-2907
Willow Inn   208 Main Rd., Como J0P 1A0   514-458-7006
Auberge La Martre   La Martre, Comte de Mantane G0E 2H0   418-288-5533
Maplewood   Malenfant Rd., Dunham J0E 1M0   514-295-2519
Henry House   105 DuParc, St. Simeon, Gaspesie G0C 3A0   418-534-2115
Georgeville Country Inn   CP P.O. Box 17, Georgeville J0B 1T0   819-843-8683
Hazelbrae Farm   1650 English River Rd., Howick J0S 1G0   514-825-2390
Otter Lake Haus   C.S. 29, CH Trudel, Huberdeau J0T 1G0   819-687-2767
Willow Place Inn   208 Main St., Hudson J0P 1A0   514-458-7006
Leduc   1128CH Riviere de Guerr, Huntington, St. Anicet J0S 1M0   514-264-6533
Chez les Dumas   1415 Chemin Royal, St., Ile d'Orleans G0A 3Z0   418-828-9442
Auberge Laketree   RR 2, Stage Coach Rd., Knowlton J0E 1V0   514-243-6604
Auberge Sauvignon   Rt. #327, Mont Tremblant J0T 1Z0   819-425-2658
Manoir des Erables   220 Du Manoir, Montmagny G54 V1G   418-248-0100
Antonio Costa   101 Northview, Montreal H4X 1C9   514-486-6910
Le Breton   1609 St. Hubert, Montreal East H2L 3Z1   514-524-7273
Auberge Hollandaise   Rt. 329, Morin Heights G0R 1H0   514-226-2009
Hotel la Normandie   P.O. Box 129, Perce, Gaspe Peninsula G0G 2L0   418-782-2112
France Beaulieu House   211 Chemin dela Travers, Portneuf G0A 2Y0   418-336-2724
B&B Bonjour Quebec   3765, BD Monaco, Quebec G1P 3J3   418-527-1465
Au Chateau Fleur de Lis   15 Ave. Ste. Genevieve, Quebec City G1R 4A8   418-694-1884
Auberge De La Chouette   71 Rue D'Auteuil, Quebec City G1K 5Y4   418-694-0232
Chateau de la Terrasse   6 Terrasse Dufferin, Quebec City G1R 4N5   418-694-9472
Memory Lane Farm   RR #1, Quyon J0X 2V0   819-458-2479
Maison sous les Arbres   145 Chemin Royal, St. Laurent G0A 3Z0   418-828-9442
Hostellerie Les Trois Till   290 rue Richelieu, St. Marc Sur Richelieu J0L 2E0   514-584-2231
Pelletier House   334 de la Seigneurie, St. Roch des Aulnaies G0R 4E0   418-354-2450
Auberge La Goeliche Inn   22 Rue du Quai, Ste. Petronille G0A 4C0   418-828-2248
Auberge SchweizerDUPLICATE   357 SchweizerOF 3119, Sutton J0E 2K0   514-538-2129
Auberge du Vieux Foyer   3167 Doncaster, Val David J0T 2N0   819-322-2686
Parker's Lodge   1340 Lac Paquin, Val David J0T 2N0   819-322-2026
Au Petit Hotel   3 Ruelle des Ursulines, Vieux-Quebec G1R 3Y6   418-694-0965
Perras   1552 RR 1, Waterloo J0E 1N0   514-539-2983

Saskatchewan

BULYEA

Hillcrest Hotel	$ EP	All meals, full bar
Box 98, S0G 0L0	7 rooms	Sitting room, piano
306-725-4874	C-yes/S-yes/P-yes/H-no	Entertainment
W. & A. Nosen	German	bicycles
All year		

Prairie inn and pub furnished in antiques, collectibles—10 minutes from Inland Lake. Ice fishing, hunting, boating, rodeos, country music festival.

BURSTALL

Tiger Lily Farm	$ B&B	Full breakfast
Box 135, S0N 0H0	3 rooms, 2 pb	All meals if ordered
306-679-4709	C-yes/S-yes/P-yes/H-yes	Hot tub, bicycles
Ray		sitting room
All year		library

Plenty of Canadian Geese in the Fall. Good meals.

TISDALE

Prairie Acres B&B	$ EP/$$ B&B/AP	Full breakfast
Box 1658, S0E 1T0	5 rooms, 2 pb	Lunch, dinner
306-873-2272	C-yes/P-ltd/H-yes	Afternoon tea, snacks
Kathleen & Clarence Reed		Library, bikes, hot tubs
All year		hiking trails, massage

Beautiful hillside setting, tall spruce trees, wild life, deer, Canada grass, beaver. Breakfast in beautiful flower garden. Relax in the hot tub.

More Inns...

Moldenhauer's Farm   Box 214, Allan S0K 0C0   306-257-3578
Ellis Farm   Box 84, Balcarres S0G 0C0   306-334-2238
Vereshagin's Country Place   Box 89, Blaine Lake S0J 0J0   306-497-2782
Sargent's Holiday Farm   Box 204, Borden S0K 0N0   306-997-2230
Magee's Farm   Box 654, Gull Lake S0N 1A0
Hearn's Manor House   Box 1177, Indian Head S0G 2K0   306-695-3837
Sugden Simmental Vacation   Box 2, Peebles S0G 3V0   306-697-3169
B & J's Bed & Breakfast   2066 Ottawa St., Regina S4P 1P8   306-522-4575
Turgeon International House   2310 McIntyre St., Regina S4P 2S2   306-522-4200
Dee Bar One   Box 51, Truax S0H 4A0   306-868-4614
Eastons' Farm   Box 58, Wawota S0G 5A0   306-739-2910
Pleasant Vista Angus Farm   Box 194, Wawota S0G 5A0   306-739-2915

Reservation Service Organizations

These are businesses through which you can reserve a room in thousands of private homes. In many cases, rooms in homes are available where there may not be an inn. Also, guest houses are quite inexpensive. RSOs operate in different ways. Some represent a single city or state. Others cover the entire country. Some require a small membership fee. Others sell a list of their host homes. Many will attempt to match you with just the type of accommodations you're seeking and you may pay the RSO directly for your lodging.

Reservation Service Organizations by Region—See main RSO listings under the state headings in this section for full description.

Northeast

Bed & Breakfast Ltd.
New Haven, CT

Covered Bridge B&B Res.
Norfolk, CT

Nutmeg B&B Agency
W. Hartford, CT

B&B of Delaware
Wilmington, DE

Bed & Breakfast of Maine
Falmouth, ME

Traveller in Maryland
Annapolis, MD

Amanda's B&B Reservation
Baltimore, MD

B&B Agency of Boston
Boston, MA

B&B Associates Bay Colony
Boston, MA

Host Homes of Boston
Boston, MA

Greater Boston Hospitality
Brookline, MA

B&B Cambridge & Gtr Boston
Cambridge, MA

Pineapple Hospitality Inc.
New Bedford, MA

House Guests Cape Cod
Orleans, MA

Be Our Guest B&B, Ltd.
Plymouth, MA

Berkshire Bed & Breakfast
Williamsburg, MA

B&B of New Jersey
Midland Park, NJ

B&B of Princeton
Princeton, NJ

Bed & Breakfast USA Ltd.
Croton-on-Hudson, NY

Bed & Breakfast Rochester
Fairport, NY

B&B Connections
Frankfort, NY

North Country B&B Reserv.
Lake Placid, NY

...Aaah! B&B #1, Ltd.
New York, NY

Abode Bed & Breakfast, Ltd.
New York, NY

B&B Network of New York
New York, NY

Bed & Breakfast (& Books)
New York, NY

New World Bed & Breakfast
New York, NY

Urban Ventures, Inc.
New York, NY

American Country Collection
Schenectady, NY

Elaine's B&B & Inn Reserv.
Syracuse, NY

B&B Connections
Devon, PA

B&B of Philadelphia
Gradyville, PA

B&B Lancaster County
Mountville, PA

B&B of Valley Forge
Valley Forge, PA

Pittsburgh Bed & Breakfast
Welford, PA

Guesthouses, Inc
West Chester, PA

Annas Victorian Connection
Newport, RI

B&B of Rhode Island
Newport, RI

Guest House Assoc.-Newport
Newport, RI

Newport Reservation Serv.
Newport, RI

B&B League/Sweet Dreams
Washington, DC

**Bed & Breakfast League
Sweet Dreams & Toast, Inc.**
Washington, DC

Bed 'n' Breakfast Ltd.
Washington, DC

Southeast

Bed & Breakfast Montgomery
Millbrook, AL

B&B of the Florida Keys
Marathon, FL

Central Florida B&B
Ocala, FL

B&B Suncoast Accommodations
Saint Pete Beach, FL

B&B Atlanta
Atlanta, GA

R.S.V.P. Savannah B&B
Savannah, GA

**Savannah Historic Inns
& Guest Houses**
Savannah, GA

Quail Country B&B, Ltd.
Thomasville, GA

Southern Comfort B&B Res.
Baton Rouge, LA

B&B of New Jersey
Midland Park, NJ

Charleston Society B&B
Charleston, SC

Historic Charleston B&B
Charleston, SC

Charleston East B&B League
Mount Pleasant, SC

Guesthouses B&B
Charlottesville, VA

B&B of Tidewater Virginia
Norfolk, VA

Bensonhouse of Richmond
Richmond, VA

Travel Tree
Williamsburg, VA

North Central

Bed & Breakfast/Chicago
Chicago, IL

B&B NW Suburban—Chicago
Hoffman Estates, IL

Bed & Breakfast In Iowa
Preston, IA

B&B Alliance of Kentucky
Danville, KY

Kentucky Homes B&B, Inc.
Louisville, KY

Bluegrass Bed & Breakfast
Versailles, KY

B&B in Michigan
Dearborn, MI

Ozark Mountain Country B&B
Branson, MO

B&B Kansas City
Lenexa, KS, MO

B&B of New Jersey
Midland Park, NJ

Private Lodgings, Inc.
Cleveland, OH

Private Lodgings, Inc.
Cleveland, OH

B&B Guest Homes
Algoma, WI

B&B of Milwaukee, Inc.
Mequon, WI

South Central

Bed & Breakfast Birmingham
Birmingham, AL

Arkansas & Ozarks B&B
Calico Rock, AR

B&B Alliance of Kentucky
Danville, KY

Southern Comfort B&B Res.
Baton Rouge, LA

New Orleans B&B
New Orleans, LA

Lincoln, Ltd. B&B Reserv.
Meridian, MS

Ozark Mountain Country B&B
Branson, MO

B&B of New Jersey
Midland Park, NJ

Bed & Breakfast in Memphis
Memphis, TN

B&B Hospitality Tennessee
Nashville, TN

B&B Country Style
Canton, TX

B&B of Fredericksburg
Fredericksburg, TX

Gasthaus Schmidt
Fredericksburg, TX

Northwest

**Accomodations Alaska Style
Stay with a Friend**
Anchorage, AK

**Alaska Private Lodgings
Anchorage B&B**
Anchorage, AK

Kodiak Bed & Breakfast
Kodiak, AK

B&B International
Albany, CA

B&B Exchange
Calistoga, CA

B&B Rocky Mountains
Colorado Springs, CO

Bed & Breakfast of Idaho
Boise, ID

B&B of New Jersey
Midland Park, NJ

NW B&B Travel Unlimited
Portland, OR

Pacific B&B Agency
Seattle, WA

Southwest

B&B In Arizona
Scottsdale, AZ

Valley o' the Sun B&B
Scottsdale, AZ

Mi Casa Su Casa
Tempe, AZ

Old Pueblo Homestays B&B
Tucson, AZ

B&B International
Albany, CA

Eye Openers B&B Res.
Altadena, CA

Digs West
Buena Park, CA

B&B Exchange
Calistoga, CA

Bed & Breakfast Homestay
Cambria, CA

**Carolyn's B&B Homes
of San Diego**
Chula Vista, CA

B&B of Southern California
Fullerton, CA

Mendocino Coast Reserv.
Mendocino, CA

B&B Exchange of Marin
San Anselmo, CA

B&B San Francisco
San Francisco, CA

Hospitality Plus
San Juan Capistrano, CA

Megan's Friends B&B Res.
San Luis Obispo, CA

Calif. Houseguests Intntl.
Tarzana, CA

B&B of Los Angeles
Westlake Village, CA

CoHost, America's B&B
Whittier, CA

Bed & Breakfast Colorado
Boulder, CO

B&B Rocky Mountains
Colorado Springs, CO

B&B Vail/Ski Areas
Vail, CO

B&B Honolulu (Statewide)
Honolulu, HI

B&B Pacific—Hawaii
Kailua, Oahu, HI

Bed & Breakfast Hawaii
Kapaa, Kauai, HI

B&B Maui Style
Kihei, Maui, HI

B&B Alliance of Kentucky
Danville, KY

Go Native . . . Hawaii
Lansing, MI

B&B of New Jersey
Midland Park, NJ

B&B of New Mexico
Santa Fe, NM

NW B&B Travel Unlimited
Portland, OR

B&B Texas Style
Dallas, TX

Eastern Canada

Calif. Houseguests Intntl.
Tarzana, CA

B&B of New Jersey
Midland Park, NJ

Niagara Region B&B Service
Niagara Falls, ON

Ottawa Area B&B
Ottawa, ON

Downtown Toronto Assoc.
Toronto, ON

Toronto B&B (1987) Inc.
Toronto, ON

Bed & Breakfast Montreal
Montreal, PQ

Downtown B&B Network
Montreal, PQ

Western Canada

Calif. Houseguests Intntl.
Tarzana, CA

B&B of New Jersey
Midland Park, NJ

NW B&B Travel Unlimited
Portland, OR

Born Free B&B of B.C. Ltd.
Burnaby, BC

Vancouver B&B Ltd.
Burnaby, BC

Old English B&B Registry
North Vancouver, BC

A B & C B&B of Vancouver
Vancouver, BC

Town & Country B&B in B.C.
Vancouver, BC

All Season B&B Agency
Victoria, BC

Garden City B&B Res. Serv.
Victoria, BC

B&B of Manitoba
Winnipeg, MB

International

Accommodations Alaska Style
Stay with a Friend
Anchorage, AK

Alaska B&B Association
Juneau, AK

Digs West
Buena Park, CA

Carolyn's B&B Homes
of San Diego
Chula Vista, CA

Calif. Houseguests Intntl.
Tarzana, CA

CoHost, America's B&B
Whittier, CA

B&B of the Florida Keys
Marathon, FL

Central Florida B&B
Ocala, FL

B&B Pacific—Hawaii
Kailua, Oahu, HI

Bed & Breakfast In Iowa
Preston, IA

B&B Alliance of Kentucky
Danville, KY

Southern Comfort B&B Res.
Baton Rouge, LA

Traveller in Maryland
Annapolis, MD

Pineapple Hospitality Inc.
New Bedford, MA

Go Native . . . Hawaii
Lansing, MI

Lincoln, Ltd. B&B Reserv.
Meridian, MS

Natchez Pilgrimage Tours
Natchez, MS

B&B of New Jersey
Midland Park, NJ

Bed & Breakfast USA Ltd.
Croton-on-Hudson, NY

. . . Aaah! B&B #1, Ltd.
New York, NY

Urban Ventures, Inc.
New York, NY

NW B&B Travel Unlimited
Portland, OR

B&B of Chester County
Kennett Square, PA

B&B of Valley Forge
Valley Forge, PA

Guesthouses, Inc
West Chester, PA

Charleston East B&B League
Mount Pleasant, SC

B&B Hospitality Tennessee
Nashville, TN

Gasthaus Schmidt
Fredericksburg, TX

Ottawa Area B&B
Ottawa, ON

ALABAMA ───────────────────────

Bed & Breakfast Birmingham 205-933-2487
P.O. Box 31328 $
Birmingham, AL 35222   Dep. 1 night or $40
                                + ans mach

Directory $2
Bmnghm, Mtgmry,
some other AL
& FL,TN
9:30-5:30 M-F

Bed & Breakfast Montgomery 205-285-5421
P.O. Box 886 $
Millbrook, AL 36054   Dep. $20

Free brochure
Alabama
24 hr. ans. mach.

ALASKA ───────────────────────

Accommodations Alaska Style 907-344-4006
Stay with a Friend $
3605 Arctic Blvd., Box 173 $35 dep. or Cr Cd
Anchorage, AK 99503   Visa, MC

Brochure SASE
Alaska
9-9, May-Oct.
9-12, Nov.-April

Alaska Private Lodgings   907-258-1717
Anchorage B&B $40-75
4631 Caravelle Dr.   Dep. 1 night
Anchorage, AK 99502   Ger,Fr, Sp

Free Brochure
Alaska
8am-5pm (M-F)

Alaska B&B Association   709-586-2959
P.O. Box 21890 $
Juneau, AK 99802   Dep. $40 or credit
                                card guarantee
                                Visa, MC, AmEx
                                Ger,Tlinget

Free Brochure
Alaska
Australia, Israel
24 hours, 7 days

Kodiak Bed & Breakfast   907-486-5367
308 Cope St. $$
Kodiak, AK 99615   Dep. $10
                                Visa, MC
                                Sp

Brochure
Alaska
Evenings
Weekends

ARIZONA ───────────────────────

B&B In Arizona   602-995-2831
4533 N Scottsdale Rd Ste 108 $
P.O. Box 8628   Dep. 1 night
Scottsdale, AZ 85252   Visa, MC, AmEx
                                Listing $3

Free brochure
All of Arizona
M-F 10am-6pm
Sat.-Sun. 10am-2pm

Valley o' the Sun B&B   602-941-1281
P.O. Box 2214 $
Scottsdale, AZ 85252   Dep. 1 night

Free Brochure
AZ
6 days 9am-5pm

Mi Casa Su Casa   602-990-0682
P.O. Box 950   800-456-0682
Tempe, AZ 85281 $
                                Dep. $25
                                Fr,Ger,Sp,It,Port,Ro

Directory $3
Arizona
New Mexico, Utah
8am-8pm daily

Old Pueblo Homestays B&B   602-790-2399
P.O. Box 13603 $
Tucson, AZ 85732   Dep. $25 to 25%

Brochure SASE
Arizona
24 hour ans. mach

More RSOs...
Bed & Breakfast Scottsdale   P.O. Box 3999, Phoenix 85302   602-776-1102

ARKANSAS

Arkansas & Ozarks B&B Route 1, Box 38 Calico Rock, AR 72519	501-297-8764 $ Dep. $20 Fr	Free Broch SASE Arkansas 6am-10pm

More RSOs...
B&B Reservation Services   11 Singleton, Eureka Springs 72632   501-253-9111

CALIFORNIA

B&B International 1181-B Solano Ave. Albany, CA 94706	415-525-4569 $ Dep. $25 Visa, MC, AmEx, Diners Club Fr,Ger,It,Ch,Jap,Sp	SASE brochure California Las Vegas, HI, NY 8:30-5pm Mon.-Fri. 8:30am-noon Sat.
Eye Openers B&B Res. P.O. Box 694 Altadena, CA 91003	213-684-4428 $ Dep. $25 Visa, MC Sp,Fr,Ger,Hun,Rus,He	List $1, SASE California 8am-6pm Mon.-Fri. 8am-noon Sat.
Unique Housing 81 Plaza Dr. Berkeley, CA 94705	415-658-3494	Berkeley, CA
Digs West 8191 Crowley Circle Buena Park, CA 90621	714-739-1669 $ Dep. 1 night Fr, Ger,Sp	Brochure SASE CA, especially Southern CA 8:30am-5:30pm M-F or ans. machine
B&B Exchange 1458 Lincoln Ave. Ste 3 Calistoga, CA 94515	707-942-5900 800-654-2992 $$ Dep. 1 night Visa, MC Sw,Ger,Fin,Lith	Free Brochure California M-F 8:30am-6pm Sat. 10a-12p, 2-6p
Bed & Breakfast Homestay P.O. Box 326 Cambria, CA 93428	805-927-4613 $$ Full deposit Du,Ger,It	Free brochure California 24 hrs, 7 days
Carolyn's B&B Homes of San Diego 416 Third Ave. Chula Vista, CA 92010	619-422-7009 $ Dep. 50% Sp, Ger	Brochure SASE Southern CA M-F 9am-6pm

B&B of Southern California 1943 Sunny Crest, #304 Fullerton, CA 92635	714-738-8361 714-441-1304 $ Dep. 20% Directory $5 Sp,Fr,Ger,Du,It,ASL	SASE brochure California 8:30-5:30 Mon.-Thu. 8:30-1:30pm Fri.
Mendocino Coast Reserv. 1001 Main St., Box 1034 Mendocino, CA 95460	707-937-1913 $ Dep. 3 nights full Visa, MC	Free brochure California 9am-6pm 7 days
B&B Hospitality Reserv. P.O. Box 2407 Oceanside, CA 92054	619-722-6694 $ Dep. 1 night, cash Sp,Heb,Ger,Fr,Jap,Sl	Free brochure California M-F 8am-6pm Sat 9-12 noon
B&B Exchange of Marin 45 Entrata Ave. San Anselmo, CA 94960	415-485-1971 $$ Dep. 1 night	Free brochure CA Marin County all hours
B&B San Francisco P.O. Box 349 San Francisco, CA 94101	415-931-3083 $$ Dep. 1 night Visa, MC, AmEx Free brochure Ger,Fr, Sp, Rus	Sample listing $1 California 9:30am-5pm M-F
Hospitality Plus P.O. Box 388 San Juan Capistrano, CA 92693	714-496-7050 $ Dep. 1 night	Free brochure CA Beach Cities 9am-5pm
Megan's Friends B&B Res. 1776 Royal Way San Luis Obispo, CA 93401	805-544-4406 $$ Dep. 20% Aus,Ger,Dut	SASE brochure California Central Coast 11am-4pm and 6pm-10pm daily
Calif. Houseguests Intntl. P.O. Box 643 Tarzana, CA 91356	818-344-7878 $ Dep. $25 Fr, Ger,Sp	SASE brochure CA, other states Canada, Mex, Eur answering machine prompt call back
B&B of Los Angeles 32074 Waterside Lane Westlake Village, CA 91361	818-889-8870 800-327-1111 $ Dep 20% or 1 night Visa, MC	Brochure $2 California 8am-8pm Mon-Fri also ans. machine
CoHost, America's B&B P.O. Box 9302 Whittier, CA 90608	213-699-8427 $$ Dep. $25	Listing $3 California 7am-7pm 7 days

More RSOs. . .

Napa Valley's Finest Ldgs.   1834 First St., Napa 94559   707-224-4667
Bed & Breakfast Almanac   P.O. Box 295, Saint Helena 94574   707-963-0852

COLORADO

Bed & Breakfast Colorado
P.O. Box 12206
Boulder, CO 80303

303-494-4994
800-373-4995
$
Dep. 25%
Visa, MC

Brochure $5
Colorado
8:30-5:30 Mon-Fri
9am-noon Sat

B&B Rocky Mountains
P.O. Box 804
Colorado Springs, CO 80901

719-630-3433
$
Dep. 1 night
Skiers %50
Visa, MC

Directory $4.50
CO/NM/WY/MT/UT
9am-5pm Mon-Fri
1pm-5pm (winter)

B&B Vail/Ski Areas
P.O. Box 491
Vail, CO 81658

303-949-1212
$
Dep. 50-100%
Visa, MC
Ger,Sp

Brochure $2
Colorado
Worldwide
M-F 10am-2pm summ
9am-6pm M-F wint.

CONNECTICUT

Bed & Breakfast Ltd.
P.O. Box 216
New Haven, CT 06513

203-469-3260
$$
Dep. 20%
Traveler's checks
Fr, Sp, Ger

List SASE
Connecticut
5-9:30 school dys
anytime summer

Covered Bridge B&B Res.
P.O. Box 447
Norfolk, CT 06058

203-542-5944
$$
Full deposit
Visa, MC, AmEx
Fr

Free list SASE
Connecticut,
MA/NY/RI
9am-6pm Mon.-Sat.

Nutmeg B&B Agency
P.O. Box 1117
W. Hartford, CT 06107

203-236-6698
$
Full deposit
Visa, MC, AmEx

Broch $2.50
Connecticut
& edge of RI
9am-5pm M-F

More RSOs...

Alexander's B&B Res. Serv.   Box 534, Salisbury 06068   203-435-9539
Four Seasons Int'l B&B   11 Bridlepath Rd., West Simsbury 06092   203-651-3045

DELAWARE

B&B of Delaware
3650 Silverside, Box 177
Wilmington, DE 19810

302-479-9500
$$
Dep. 20%

Free brochure
Delaware,Maryland
Pennsylvania
9am-9pm Mon.-Fri.

FLORIDA

B&B of the Florida Keys
5 Man-O-War Dr,Box 1373
Marathon, FL 33050

305-743-4118
$$
Dep. 1 night
Visa, MC
Ger

Free brochure
Florida Keys
England
8am-5pm Mon.-Fri.
9am-noon Sat.-Sun.

Central Florida B&B	904-351-1167	Free brochure
719 SE 4th St.	$	Central Florida
Ocala, FL 32671	Dep. 20%	8am-5pm 7 days

B&B Suncoast		
Accommodations	813-360-5245	Brochure SASE $1
8690 Gulf Blvd.	$	Florida
Saint Pete Beach, FL 33706	Dep. 30%	9am-9pm 7 days

More RSOs...

Bed & Breakfast Company   P.O. Box 262, Miami 33243   305-661-3270
Magic Bed & Breakfast   8328 Curry Ford Rd., Orlando 32822   407-277-6602
Open House B&B Registry   P.O. Box 3025, Palm Beach 33480   407-842-5190

GEORGIA

B&B Atlanta	404-875-0525	Brochure SASE
1801 Piedmont NE #208	$	Georgia
Atlanta, GA 30324	Dep. 1 night	Metro Atlantic
	Visa, MC, AmEx	9-12, 2-5 M-F
	Heb,Fr, Ger,Yid	

R.S.V.P. Savannah B&B	912-232-7787	Free brochure
417 E. Charlton St.	$$$	Georgia, SC
Savannah, GA 31401	Dep. 1 night	North Florida
	Visa, MC, AmEx	9am-6pm daily
	personal check	

Savannah Historic Inns	800-262-4667	Free brochure
& Guest Houses	912-233-7660	Georgia
147 Bull St.	$40-135	9am-5pm M-F
Savannah, GA 31401	Dep. 1 night	
	Visa, MC, AmEx	

Quail Country B&B, Ltd.	912-226-7218	Free brochure
1104 Old Monticello Rd.	912-226-6882	Thomasville, GA
Thomasville, GA 31792	$	9am-9pm Mon.-Sun.
	Dep. $25	

More RSOs...

Atlanta Hospitality   2472 Lauderdale Dr., Atlanta 30345   404-493-1930
Savannah Area Visitors   222 W. Oglethorpe Ave., Savannah 31499   912-944-0444

HAWAII

B&B Honolulu (Statewide)	808-595-7622	Free brochure
3242 Kaohinani Dr.	800-288-2666	Hawaiian Islands
Honolulu, HI 96817	$	8am-5pm Mon.-Sat.
	Dep. 3 days or 50%	
	Visa, MC	

B&B Pacific—Hawaii	808-262-6026	Brochure $3
19 Kai Nani Pl.	800-999-6026	Hawaiian Islands
Kailua, Oahu, HI 96734	$	Germany
	Dep. 20%	24 hours, 7 days

Bed & Breakfast Hawaii P.O. Box 449 Kapaa, Kauai, HI 96746	808-822-7771 800-657-7832 $ Dep. 20% Visa, MC Ger,Fr, Hun,Swiss	Free brochure Guide book $6 Hawaii all islands 8:30-4:30 Mon.-Fri.
B&B Maui Style P.O. Box 886 Kihei, Maui, HI 96753	808-878-7865 $ Dep. 20%	Free listing Hawaii 8-9am during day

IDAHO ─────

Bed & Breakfast of Idaho P.O. Box 7323 Boise, ID 83707	208-336-5174 $ Dep. $20 Visa, MC	Directory SASE Idaho 9am-5pm M-F

ILLINOIS ─────

Bed & Breakfast/Chicago P.O. Box 14088 Chicago, IL 60614	312-951-0085 $$ Dep. $25 Visa, MC, AmEx Fr, Sp, Assy,Per	Free brochure Downtown Chicago North Shore 9am-4pm Mon.-Fri.

More RSOs...
Heritage Bed & Breakfast   P.O. Box 60054, Chicago 60660   312-728-7935

B&B NW Suburban—Chicago P.O. Box 95503 Hoffman Estates, IL 60195	708-310-0488 $ Dep. $40 Visa, MC	Free brochure Illinois 7am-9pm Mon.-Fri. 10am-5pm Sat.

INDIANA ─────

More RSOs...
Indiana Amish Country B&B   1600 W. Market St., Nappanee 46550   219-773-4188

IOWA ─────

Bed & Breakfast In Iowa P.O. Box 430 Preston, IA 52069	319-689-4222 $ Dep. $20 or 1 night Ger,Fr	List $1 Iowa, USA Canada, Europe 7am-10pm Mon.-Sat.

KENTUCKY ─────

B&B Alliance of Kentucky 331 South Fourth St. Danville, KY 40422	606-236-1430 $60-120 Dep. 25% Visa, MC Free broch. SASE	Brochure SASE Kentucky 9am-7pm 24 hr. phone
Kentucky Homes B&B, Inc. 1431 St. James Court Louisville, KY 40208	502-635-7341 $& Dep. $25 Visa, MC, AmEx It,Fr, Ger,Port	Listing $1 Kentucky Southern Indiana 9am-noon and 2pm-5pm Mon.-Fri.

Bluegrass Bed & Breakfast	606-873-3208	Free Brochure
Route 1, Box 263	$	Kentucky
Versailles, KY 40383	Dep. 25% + tax	9am-9pm 7 days

LOUISIANA

Southern Comfort B&B Res.	504-346-1928	Directory $3
2856 Hundred Oaks Ave.	504-346-9815	Louisiana
Baton Rouge, LA 70808	$	MI/FL/TX
	Dep. $20 per night	8am-8pm daily
	Visa, MC, AmEx	
	Fr, Sp, It	

New Orleans B&B	504-822-5038	Free brochure
P.O. Box 8163	504-822-5046	Louisiana
New Orleans, LA 70182	$	8am-4:30pm M-F
	Dep. 20%	
	Visa, MC	
	Ger,Fr, Rus	

More RSOs...

B&B Reservation Services   P.O. Box 14797, Baton Rouge 70898   504-346-1928
Bed & Breakfast Inc.   1360 Moss St, Box 52257, New Orleans 70152   504-525-4640
Bed, Bath & Breakfast   3307 Prytania, Box 52466, New Orleans 70115   504-897-3867

MAINE

Bed & Breakfast of Maine	207-781-4528	Print listing $1
32 Colonial Village	$	Maine
Falmouth, ME 04105	Dep. 1 night	Evenings/weekends
	Visa, MC	or ans. machine
	Fr, Sp, Ger	

MARYLAND

Traveller in Maryland	301-269-6232	Maryland
P.O. Box 2277	301-261-2233	UK
Annapolis, MD 21404	$	9-5 M-Th, 9-12n F
	Dep. 1 night	
	Visa, MC, AmEx	

Amanda's B&B Reservation	301-225-0001	Brochure SASE
1428 Park Ave.	$$	Maryland
Baltimore, MD 21217	Dep. 1 night	8:30-5pm M-F
	Visa, MC, AmEx	
	Fr, Ger,It,Arab	

More RSOs...

Great Inns of America   2666 Riva Road, St. 410, Annapolis 21401

MASSACHUSETTS

B&B Agency of Boston	617-720-3540	Free brochure
47 Commercial Wharf	$$	Massachusetts
Boston, MA 02110	Dep. 30%	Cambridge, Boston
	Visa, MC	9am-9pm daily
	Fr,Sp,Ger,Arab,It	also ans. machine

B&B Associates Bay Colony Box 57166, Babson Park Boston, MA 02157	617-449-5302 $$ Dep. 30% Visa, MC, AmEx Fr,Ger,It,Nor,Sp,Gr	Brochure $3.75 Massachusetts 10am-5pm Mon.-Fri.
Host Homes of Boston Box 117, Waban Branch Boston, MA 02168	617-244-1308 $ Dep. 1 night Visa, MC, AmEx Fr,Ger,Sp,Gr,Jap,Rus	Free brochure MA, Boston, Cape Cod, Marblehead 9am-noon and 1:30pm-4:30pm M-F
Greater Boston Hospitality P.O. Box 1142 Brookline, MA 02146	617-277-5430 $$ Dep. 50% Visa, MC, AmEx Sp,Fr,Heb,Ger,It,Pol	Free brochure Massachusetts 8am-6pm Mon.-Fri. 8am-1pm Sat
B&B Cambridge & Gtr Boston P.O. Box 665 Cambridge, MA 02140	617-576-1492 617-576-2112 $$ Dep. 30% Visa, MC, AmEx	Free brochure Cambridge & Greater Boston 9a-6p M-F 2p-6p Sat
Pineapple Hospitality Inc. P.O.Box F 821 New Bedford, MA 02742	508-990-1696 $$ Dep. $15 per night Visa, MC, AmEx French, German	Brochure $5.95 CT,RI,MA,VT,NH,ME Bermuda 9am-5pm M-F
House Guests Cape Cod P.O. Box 1881 Orleans, MA 02653	800-666-HOST 617-896-7053 $$ Dep. 50% Visa, MC, AmEx	Listing $3.50 Cape Cod, Nantuck Martha's Vineyard 9am-7pm daily
Be Our Guest B&B, Ltd. P.O. Box 1333 Plymouth, MA 02360	617-837-9867 $$ Dep. $25 or 25% Visa, MC, AmEx Fr	Brochure $1 Massachusetts 10am-10pm daily
Berkshire Bed & Breakfast P.O. Box 211 Williamsburg, MA 01096	413-268-7244 $ Dep. 50% Visa, MC	Listing SASE Massachusetts 9am-6pm Mon.-Fri. 10am-1pm Sat.

More RSOs . . .

In The Country B&B   P.O. Box 457, Ashfield 01330
Folkestone Bed & Breakfast   P.O. Box 931, Boylston 01505   617-869-2687
University Bed & Breakfast   12 Churchill Street, Brookline 02146
Battina's Bed & Breakfast   P.O. Box 585, Cambridge 02238
Nantucket Accommodations   Box 426, Nantucket 02554
Nantucket Vacation Plan.   Airport-Tower Bldg., Nantucket 02554
B&B Marblehead/Northshore   P.O. Box 35, Newtonville 02160   617-964-1606
Dukes County Reserv. Serv.   P.O. Box 2370, Oak Bluffs 02557

B&B/The National Network   Box 4616, Springfield 01101
Greater Springfield B&B   25 Bellevue Avenue, Springfield 01108
Martha's Vineyard Reserv.   P.O. Box 1769, Vineyard Haven 02568

MICHIGAN

B&B in Michigan	313-561-6041	Brochure SASE
P.O. Box 1731	$	Michigan
Dearborn, MI 48121	Dep. $25 minimum	6-10pm M-F
	Visa, MC	
	Ger	

Go Native. . . Hawaii	517-349-9598	Free brochure
P.O. Box 13115	$$	Hawaiian Islands
Lansing, MI 48901	Dep 60%	U.S., Worldwide
	Directory $2	24 hr. ans. mach.
	Ger,Sp,Sw,Jap,Kor	

MISSISSIPPI

Lincoln, Ltd. B&B Reserv.	601-482-5483	List $3.50
Box 3479, 2303 23rd Ave	$	Mississippi
Meridian, MS 39303	Dep. 1 night	AL, TN, LA
	Visa, MC	9am-5pm Mon.-Fri.
	Fr, Ger	

Natchez Pilgrimage Tours	800-647-6742	13 antebellum
Box 347, Canal at State	601-446-6631	homes in Natchez
Natchez, MS 39120	$$$	
	Visa, MC, AmEx	

Natchez Pilgrimage Tours	601-446-6631	Free brochure
P.O. Box 347	800-647-6742	Mississippi only
Natchez, MS 39121	$$	Natchez
	Visa, MC, AmEx	8:30am-5:00pm

More RSOs. . .

Creative Travel B&B Center   Canal Street Depot, Natchez 39120   800-824-0355

MISSOURI

Ozark Mountain Country		
B&B	417-334-5077	SASE brochure
Box 295-IG	417-334-4720	SW Missouri
Branson, MO 65726	$	NW Ark., Nebraska
	Dep. 50%	7:30am-10:30pm
	Visa, MC	

B&B Kansas City	913-888-3636	Free list SASE
P.O. Box 14781	$	Missouri, Kansas
Lenexa, KS, MO 66215	Dep. 20% + tax	9am-11pm daily
		also ans. machine

MONTANA

More RSOs. . .

B&B Western Adventure   P.O. Box 20972, Billings 59102   406-259-7993

NEBRASKA ————————————————————————————

More RSOs...

B&B of the Great Plains   P.O. Box 2333, Lincoln 68502   402-423-3480

NEW HAMPSHIRE ————————————————————————

More RSOs...

Valley Bed & Breakfast   P.O. Box 1190, Conway 03818   207-935-3799

NEW JERSEY ————————————————————————————

B&B of New Jersey 103 Godwin, Suite 132 Midland Park, NJ 07432	201-444-7409 609-344-6166 $ Full deposit Visa, MC, AmEx Sp,Fr,It,Ge,Ar,Sw,Yi,Lux	Free brochure Directory $10 NJ, entire US International 9:30am-3pm M-F
B&B of Princeton P.O. Box 571 Princeton, NJ 08540	609-924-3189 $$ Dep. 1 night	Info. sheet SASE Princeton, NJ 24 hr. ans. machine

More RSOs...

B&B of Greater Summit Inc   P.O. Box 783, Summit 07901

NEW MEXICO ————————————————————————————

B&B of New Mexico P.O. Box 2805 Santa Fe, NM 87504	505-982-3332 800-648-0513 $ Full amount Visa, MC, AmEx	Free brochure New Mexico 9am-5pm Mon.-Fri.

NEW YORK ————————————————————————————

Bed & Breakfast USA Ltd. 129 Grand St., Box 606 Croton-on-Hudson, NY 10520	914-271-6228 800-255-7213 $ Dep 50% or 1 night Visa, MC Fr,Ger,Jap,Rom,Heb	List $4 NY, MA, PA, FL Virgin Islands 9am-3pm Mon.-Fri.
Hampton Bed & Breakfast P.O. Box 378 East Moriches, NY 11940	516-878-8197 $$$ Dep. 1 night	Brochure SASE New York 7 days-machine
Bed & Breakfast Rochester P.O. Box 444 Fairport, NY 14450	716-223-8877 $$ Dep. 1 night	Free brochure Rochester & Finger Lakes area Evenings & wkends
B&B Connections 389 Brockway Rd. Frankfort, NY 13340	315-733-0040 $ Dep. 50% 1st night Visa, MC, AmEx Fr, Sp, Ger	Directory $2 Central New York 8am-9pm daily

North Country B&B Reserv. P.O. Box 286 Lake Placid, NY 12946	518-523-9474 $ Dep. 1 night	Free brochure Adirondacks, NY 10am-10pm daily
...Aaah! B&B #1, Ltd. P.O. Box 200 New York, NY 10108	212-246-4000 800-776-4001 $ Dep. 25% AmEx	Free brochure New York City London, Paris 24 hours 7 days
Abode Bed & Breakfast,Ltd. P.O. Box 20022 New York, NY 10028	212-472-2000 $$ Dep. 25% AmEx 2 night minimum	Free brochure NY: Manhattan and Brooklyn Heights 9am-5pm M-F, 10am-2pm Sat.
B&B Network of New York 134 W. 32nd St, Ste 602 New York, NY 10001	212-645-8134 $$ Dep. 25%	Free brochure New York 8am-6pm M-F
Bed & Breakfast (& Books) 35 W. 92nd St. New York, NY 10025	212-865-8740 $$ Dep. 1 night AmEx Fr, Ger	Free list SASE Manhattan only 9am-5pm Mon.-Fri.
New World Bed & Breakfast 150 5th Ave., Suite 711 New York, NY 10011	212-675-5600 800-443-3800 $$ Dep. 25% Visa, MC, AmEx	Brochure Manhattan 9am-5pm Mon.-Fri.
Urban Ventures, Inc. P.O. Box 426 New York, NY 10024	212-594-5650 $$ Dep. 1 night Visa, MC, AmEx Discover	Free list SASE New York City Eng, Fr, Belg, It 9am-5pm Mon.-Fri. 9am-3pm Sat.
American Country Collection 984 Gloucester Pl. Schenectady, NY 12309	518-370-4948 $ Dep 50% or 1 night Visa, MC, AmEx Free brochure Fr, Sp, Ch	Directory $ New York, Vermont W. Massachusetts M-F 10-12, 1-5
Elaine's B&B & Inn Reserv. 143 Didama St. Syracuse, NY 13224	315-446-4199 $ Dep. 1 night or 50%	Brochure SASE Central New York Western Mass. 9:30am-9:30pm daily

More RSOs...

B&B of Long Island   P.O. Box 392, Old Westbury 11568   516-334-6231

OHIO ─────────────────────────────────────

Private Lodgings, Inc.   216-321-3213   Free brochure
P.O. Box 18590 $ Ohio
Cleveland, OH 44118   Full deposit   9-12n, 3-5pm M-F
                                  Ger,Fr, Yid

Private Lodgings, Inc.   216-321-3213   Free brochure
P.O. Box 18590 $ Ohio
Cleveland, OH 44118   Full deposit   9-12n, 3-5pm M-F
                                  Ger,Fr, Yid

OREGON ───────────────────────────────────

NW B&B Travel Unlimited   503-243-7616   Directory $9.50
610 SW Broadway $ Northwest, HI, CA
Portland, OR 97205   No dep. required   Canada, Europe
                                  Personal checks   9am-5pm Mon.-Fri.
                                  Free brochure
                                  Fr,Ger,It,Sp,Du,Heb,Arab

More RSOs...

Gallucci Hosts Hostels B&B   P.O. Box 1303, Lake Oswego 97035   503-636-6933
Country Host Registry   901 NW Chadwick Lane, Myrtle Creek 97457   503-863-5168

PENNSYLVANIA ─────────────────────────────

B&B Connections   215-687-3565   Free sample dir.
P.O. Box 21 $ Philadephia &
Devon, PA 19333   Dep. 1 night or 20% suburbs
                                  Visa, MC, AmEx   M-Sat. 9am-9pm
                                                       Sun. 1pm-9pm

B&B of Philadelphia   215-827-9650   Brochure $3
P.O. Box 252   800-733-4747   Southeast PA
Gradyville, PA 19039 $ Southern NJ
                                  Dep. 1 night   9am-7pm Mon.-Fri.
                                  Visa, MC, AmEx   10am-4pm Sat.

B&B of Chester County   215-444-1367   Brochure $3
P.O. Box 825 $ Pennsylvania
Kennett Square, PA 19348   Dep. 20%   Delaware
                                  Fr,Sp,Du,Ger,It   8am-8pm daily

B&B Lancaster County   717-285-7200   Print listing $2
P.O. Box 19 $$ Lancaster Cty, PA
Mountville, PA 17554   Dep. 1 night   9am-2pm, 4pm-9pm
                                  Visa, MC   daily

B&B of Valley Forge   215-783-7838   Free broch. SASE
P.O. Box 562 $ Pennsylvania
Valley Forge, PA 19481   Dep. $25 minimum   all year 9am-11pm
                                  Visa, MC, AmEx
                                  Sp,Fr,It,Dutch,Germa

Pittsburgh Bed & Breakfast   412-934-1212   Brochure SASE
785 Stonegate Dr. $ Pennsylvania
Welford, PA 15090   Dep. $20 or 20%   9am-5pm Mon.-Fri.
                                  Visa, MC   closed holidays

Guesthouses, Inc P.O. Box 2137 West Chester, PA 19380	800-950-9130 215-692-4575 $$ Dep. 1 night + tax Visa, MC, AmEx Fr	Free Brochure PA/DE/NJ/MD England, Israel Noon-4pm M-F RES. plus ans. machine

More RSOs. . .

B&B of SE Pennsylvania   146 W. Philadelphia Ave, Boyertown 19512   215-367-4688
Bed & Breakfast—The Manor   P.O. Box 656, Havertown 19083   215-642-1323
Rest & Repast B&B Service   P.O. Box 126, Pine Grove Mills 16868   814-238-1484

RHODE ISLAND

Annas Victorian Connection 5 Fowler Ave. Newport, RI 02840	401-849-2489 $$ Dep. 1 night Visa, MC, AmEx En Route	Free Brochure Rhode Island 24 hr. year-round
B&B of Rhode Island Bx 3292-PL, 38 Bellevue Newport, RI 02840	401-849-1298 $ Dep 1 night+ ½ bal Visa, MC, AmEx Free brochure Fr,Ger,It,Malay	Directory $3 Rhode Island 9-8 M-F, 10-2 Sat 9-5 M-F off-seas.
Guest House Assoc.-Newport P.O. Box 981 Newport, RI 02840	401-846-ROOM $$ Dep. 50% full amt. Visa, MC, AmEx	Brochure SASE Rhode Island 24 hours
Newport Reservation Serv. P.O. Box 518 Newport, RI 02840	401-847-8878 $$ Deposit required Visa, MC, AmEx	Rhode Island 9am-4pm M-F

SOUTH CAROLINA

Charleston Society B&B 84 Murray Blvd. Charleston, SC 29401	803-723-4948 $$ Dep. 1 night	Free brochure Charleston, SC 9am-5pm Mon.-Fri.
Historic Charleston B&B 43 Legare St. Charleston, SC 29401	803-722-6606 $$ Dep. 1 night Visa, MC, AmEx Fr, Sp	Free brochure South Carolina Savannah, Georgia 9:30am-5pm M-F
Charleston East B&B League 1031 Tall Pine Rd. Mount Pleasant, SC 29464	803-884-8208 $ Dep. 20%	Free Broch SASE South Carolina 10am-6pm, ans. mach other times

SOUTH DAKOTA

More RSOs. . .

South Dakota B&B   P.O. Box 90137, Sioux Falls 57105   605-339-0759

TENNESSEE

Bed & Breakfast in Memphis P.O. Box 41621 Memphis, TN 38174	901-726-5920 $ Full payment Visa, MC Fr, Sp	Brochure SASE Memphis the mid-South 8:30am-6pm M-F 1-5 Sat. & Sun.
B&B Hospitality Tennessee P.O. Box 110227 Nashville, TN 37222	615-331-5244 800-528-8433 $ Full amount Visa, MC, AmEx Sp, Fr, Ger	Free Broch SASE TN, KY, FL, & international 10am-5pm Mon.-Fri. also ans. machine

TEXAS

B&B Country Style Box 1100, 1160 N Hwy 19 Canton, TX 7513	214-567-2899 $ Dep. 1 night Visa, MC, AmEx	Brochure SASE Canton area, TX 9am-5pm Mon.-Sat.
B&B Texas Style 4224 W. Red Bird Lane Dallas, TX 75237	214-298-8586 $ Dep. 1 night Visa, MC Free broch. SASE Fr, Ger, Sp, It	Directory $3.50 Texas New Mexico 9am-5pm Mon.-Fri. ans. mach. wkends
B&B of Fredericksburg 102 S. Cherry St. Fredericksburg, TX 78624	512-997-4712 $$ Dep. credit card Visa, MC	Free brochure Texas 9am-7pm daily
Gasthaus Schmidt 501 W. Main Fredericksburg, TX 78624	512-997-5612 Dep. 1 night or credit card Visa, MC, AmEx	Free brochure Fredericksburg,TX 10am-5pm M-F 1pm-5pm Sat.

More RSOs...

B&B of Wimberley Texas   P.O. Box 589, Wimberley 78676   512-847-9666

VERMONT

More RSOs...

Vermont Travel Info. Serv.   Pond Village, Brookfield 05036   802-276-3120
Vermont Bed & Breakfast   P.O. Box 1, East Fairfield 05448   802-827-3827
American B&B—New England   Box 983, Saint Albans 05478

VIRGINIA

Guesthouses B&B P.O. Box 5737 Charlottesville, VA 22905	804-979-7264 $$ Dep. 25% Visa, MC, AmEx Fr, Ger	List $1 SASE Charlottesville Luray, Albemarle Noon-5pm Mon.-Fri.

B&B of Tidewater Virginia P.O. Box 3343 Norfolk, VA 23514	804-627-1983 804-627-9409 $ Dep. 20%	Free brochure VA coastal area 24 hours answering machine
Bensonhouse of Richmond 2036 Monument Ave. Richmond, VA 23220	804-648-7560 $55-105 Dep. 30% Visa, MC, AmEx	List $2 SASE Richmnd/Wllmsburg Fredericksburg 10-6 M-F wkend hrs. vary
Travel Tree P.O. Box 838 Williamsburg, VA 23187	804-253-1571 $ Dep. $20	Free Brochure Williamsburg 6-9pm Mon.-Thur.

More RSOs...

Princely B&B Ltd.   819 Prince St., Alexandria 22314   703-683-2159
Blue Ridge B&B Res. Serv.   Route 2, Box 3895, Berryville 22611   703-955-1246
Historic VA B&B Res. Serv.   2036 Monument Avenue, Richmond 23220

WASHINGTON

Pacific B&B Agency 701 N.W. 60th St. Seattle, WA 98107	206-784-0539 $ Dep. $25 Visa, MC, AmEx Free brochure Ger,Fr,Dan,Nor,Du	Sample $2 SASE Washington British Columbia 9am-5pm Mon.-Fri. Answering machine

More RSOs...

B&B Guild—Whatcom County   2610 Eldridge Ave., Bellingham 98225   206-676-4560
Seattle B&B Inn Assoc.   P.O. Box 95853, Seattle 98145   206-547-1020

WASHINGTON, D.C.

B&B League/Sweet Dreams P.O. Box 9490 Washington, D.C. 20016	202-363-7767 $ Dep. $25 Visa, MC, AmEx	Free broch. SASE Washington, DC & surrounding areas 9am-5pm Mon.-Thur. 9am-1pm Fri.
Bed & Breakfast League **Sweet Dreams & Toast, Inc.** P.O. Box 4835-0035 Washington, D.C. 20008	202-483-9191 $$ Dep $50, Visa MC Sp, Fr, Ger, Rus	Free Brochure RSO List $3 SASE Distr of Columbia 11am-5pm Mon.-Fri. also ans. machine
Bed 'n' Breakfast Ltd. P.O. Box 12011 Washington, D.C. 20005	202-328-3510 $ Dep. $40 Visa, MC, AmEx Diners Club Fr, Sp	Free brochure Washington, D.C. nearby MD & VA 10am-5pm Mon.-Fri. 10am-1pm Sat.

WISCONSIN

B&B Guest Homes	414-743-9742	Free broch SASE
Route 2, 698 Country U	$	Wisconsin
Algoma, WI 54201	Dep. 1 night	Door County
	Visa, MC	Wisconsin
	Swe,Nor,Ger,Kor	6am-9pm daily

B&B of Milwaukee, Inc.	414-242-9680	Free broch SASE
1916 W. Donges Bay Rd.	$	Wisconsin
Mequon, WI 53092	Full deposit	surrounding areas
	Visa, MC, AmEx	9am-5pm Mon-Fri
	Sp, Fr, Port	also ans. machine

ALBERTA

More RSOs...

Big Country B&B   P.O. Box 714, Rosebud T0J 2T0   403-677-2269

BRITISH COLUMBIA

Born Free B&B of B.C. Ltd.	604-298-8815	Free brochure
4390 Frances St.	$$	Greater Vancouver
Burnaby, BC V5C 2R3	Dep. 1 night	Victoria
	Visa, MC	9-5 + ans. serv.
	Dut,Ger,It,Fr	

Vancouver B&B Ltd.	604-291-6147	Free Brochure
1685 Ingleton Ave.	$$	Greater Vancouver
Burnaby, BC V5C 4L8	Dep 20% or 1 night	8:30-4:30 M-F
	Visa	ans. mach. aft. hrs.
	Fr, Sp, Jap, Pol	

Old English B&B Registry	604-986-5069	Free brochure
P.O. Box 86818	$$	Vancouver
North Vancouver, BC V7L 4L3	Dep. 1 night	11am-4pm & ans. mach.
	Visa, MC	

A B & C B&B of Vancouver	604-298-8815	Free brochure
4390 Frances St.	$$	British Columbia
Vancouver, BC V5C 2R3	Dep. 1 night	9am-5pm Mon.-Fri.
	Visa, MC	also ans. machine

Town & Country B&B in B.C.	604-731-5942	Guide $10.50
P.O. Box 46544, Stn. G	$$	British Columbia
Vancouver, BC V6R 4G6	Dep. 1-2 nights	9am-4:30pm M-F
	Free brochure	evening & wkends
	Fr, Ger,Sp	

All Season B&B Agency	604-595-2337	Free brochure
Box 5511, Stn. B	604-595-BEDS	Book $6
Victoria, BC V8R 6S4	$	British Columbia
	Dep. 20%	9am-5pm Mon.-Fri.
	Visa, MC	also ans. machine
	Fr, Du,Ger	

Garden City B&B Res. Serv.	604-479-9999	Victoria/Gulf &
660 Jones Terrace	604-479-1986	Vancouver Islands
Victoria, BC V8Z 2L7	$	7am-10pm Mon.-Sat.
	Dep. 1 night	2:30pm-10pm Sun.
	Visa, MC, AmEx	
	Fr,Ger,Sp,Wel,Dan,Ja	

More RSOs...

Alberta Bed & Breakfast   Box 15477, Main P.O., Vancouver V6B 5B2   604-682-4610
First Choice B&B Agency   658 E. 29th Ave., Vancouver V5V 2R9   604-875-8888

MANITOBA ────────────

B&B of Manitoba	204-256-6151	Brochure $1
93 Healey Crescent	$	Manitoba
Winnipeg, MB R2N 2S2	Dep. 1 night	9am-5pm
	Ger,Pol,Ukr	

ONTARIO ────────────

Serena's Place	519-471-6228	Brochure $1 SASE
720 Headley Dr.	$	Ontario
London, ON N6H 3V6		8am-6pm

Niagara Region B&B Service	416-358-8988	Free brochure
2631 Dorchester Rd.	$$	Ontario
Niagara Falls, ON L2J 2Y9	Dep. $25	Niagara Peninsula
	Visa, MC, AmEx	9am-9pm daily
	Ger,Pol,Ukr,Fr	

Ottawa Area B&B	613-563-0161	Free brochure
P.O. Box 4848 Station E	$	Ontario
Ottawa, ON K1S 5J1	Dep. 1 night	England, W. Germ.
	Fr, Sp, Ger	10am-10pm daily
		also ans. machine

Downtown Toronto Assoc.	416-977-6841	Free brochure
P.O. Box 190 Station B	416-598-4562	Downtown Toronto
Toronto, ON M5T 2W1	$	24 hours 7 days
	Dep. 50%	
	Visa	
	Sp, It, Fr	

Toronto B&B (1987) Inc.	416-961-3676	Free brochure
Box 269, 253 College St	$$	Toronto, Ontario
Toronto, ON M5T 1R5	Dep. 1 night	Niagara-on-the-Lk
	Visa, MC	9am-7pm Mon.-Fri.
	Fr,Ger,It,Pol,Uk,Jap	

QUEBEC ────────────

Bed & Breakfast Montreal	514-738-9410	Free Brochure
4912 Victoria	$	Montreal
Montreal, PQ H3W 2N1	Dep $15 per night	Quebec City
	Visa, MC, AmEx	8:30am-8pm daily
	Fr,Ger,Du,Slavic	

Downtown B&B Network	514-289-9749	Free Brochure
3458 Laval Ave.	$	Montreal, Quebec
Montreal, PQ H2X 3C8	Dep. $15	8am-8pm M-F summ.
	Visa, MC, AmEx	8am-6pm winter
	Fr,Ger,Sp,Ch,Viet,Po	

B&B Bonjour Quebec	418-527-1465	Free brochure
3765, Bd. Monaco	Dep. 1 night	9am-7pm
Quebec, PQ G1P 3J3		

More RSOs. . .

B&B Network Hospitality   3977 Ave Laval, Montreal H2W 2H9   514-287-9635
Mont—Royal Chez Soi, Inc.   5151 Cote-St.-Antoine, Montreal H4A 1P1

SASKATCHEWAN ——————————————————————

More RSOs. . .

Saskatchewan Country Vaca.   Box 89, Blaine Lake S0J 0J0   306-497-2782

YUKON ——————————————————————————

More RSOs. . .

Northern Network of B&B's   Box 302, Dawson City Y0B 1G0   403-993-5772

B&B Inns with Special Features

Antiques

Many of the inns we list are graced by antiques. These inns have put a special emphasis on antiques and period decor.

Magic Canyon Ranch
Homer, AK

Greenway House
Bisbee, AZ

Happy Landing Inn
Carmel, CA

City Hotel
Columbia, CA

Carter House
Eureka, CA

Gingerbread Mansion
Ferndale, CA

Eastlake Victorian Inn
Los Angeles, CA

Meadow Creek Ranch Inn
Mariposa, CA

Whitegate Inn
Mendocino, CA

Beazley House
Napa, CA

Maison Bleue French B&B
Pacific Grove, CA

Driver Mansion Inn
Sacramento, CA

Heritage Park B&B Inn
San Diego, CA

The Monte Cristo
San Francisco, CA

Blue Quail Inn & Cottages
Santa Barbara, CA

Old Yacht Club Inn
Santa Barbara, CA

Trojan Horse Inn
Sonoma, CA

Wick's
Yuba City, CA

Holden House—1902
Colorado Springs, CO

Queen Anne Inn
New London, CT

Manor House
Norfolk, CT

Captain Stannard House
Westbrook, CT

Pleasant Inn Lodge
Rehoboth Beach, DE

Norment-Parry Inn
Orlando, FL

De Loffre House
Columbus, GA

Stovall House
Sautee, GA

Jesse Mount House
Savannah, GA

Stillman's Country Inn
Galena, IL

The Redstone Inn
Dubuque, IA

Almeda's B&B Inn
Tonganoxie, KS

Lafitte Guest House
New Orleans, LA

Lamothe House Hotel
New Orleans, LA

Maine Stay Inn
Camden, ME

English Meadows Inn
Kennebunkport, ME

Broad Bay Inn & Gallery
Waldoboro, ME

Strawberry Inn
New Market, MD

Glenburn
Taneytown, MD

Beechwood Inn
Barnstable, MA

Cyrus Kent House Inn
Chatham, MA

Inn on Sea Street
Hyannis, MA

Wingate Crossing
North Falmouth, MA

Addison Choate Inn
Rockport, MA

Isaiah Jones Homestead
Sandwich, MA

Raymond House Inn
Port Sanilac, MI

Hamilton Place
Holly Springs, MS

Rosswood Plantation
Lorman, MS

Linden
Natchez, MS

Oak Square Plantation
Port Gibson, MS

Borgman's Bed & Breakfast
Arrow Rock, MO

Garth Woodside Mansion
Hannibal, MO

Harding House B&B
Saint Joseph, MO

Inn St. Gemme Beauvais
Sainte Genevieve, MO

Nevada City Hotel
Nevada City, MT

Steele Homestead Inn
Antrim, NH

Inn at Crystal Lake
Eaton Center, NH

Bungay Jar Bed & Breakfast
Franconia, NH

New London Inn
New London, NH

Conover's Bay Head Inn
Bay Head, NJ

The Abbey
Cape May, NJ

Mainstay Inn & Cottage
Cape May, NJ

Queen Victoria
Cape May, NJ

Ashling Cottage
Spring Lake, NJ

Brae Loch Inn
Cazenovia, NY

Rose Inn
Ithaca, NY

Belle Crest House
Shelter Island, NY

Hist. James R. Webster
Waterloo, NY

Cedar Crest Victorian Inn
Asheville, NC

Cider Mill B&B
Zoar, OH

Cobbler Shop Inn
Zoar, OH

Barley Sheaf Farm
Holicong, PA

Witmer's Tavern—1725 Inn
Lancaster, PA

Pineapple Hill
New Hope, PA

Millstone Inn
Schellsburg, PA

Hotel Manisses
Block Island, RI

Country Victorian B&B
Charleston, SC

Vendue Inn
Charleston, SC

Clardy's Guest House
Murfreesboro, TN

Annie's B&B Country Inn
Big Sandy, TX

Pine Colony Inn
Center, TX

Imperial Hotel
Park City, UT

Seven Wives Inn
Saint George, UT

Inn at Woodchuck Hill Farm
Grafton, VT

Governor's Inn
Ludlow, VT

Historic Brookside Farms
Orwell, VT

Lareau Farm Country Inn
Waitsfield, VT

Village Inn of Woodstock
Woodstock, VT

Fountain Hall B&B Inn
Culpepper, VA

Mayhurst Inn
Orange, VA

Conyers House
Sperryville, VA

Williamsburg Legacy Inn
Williamsburg, VA

Inn at Narrow Passage
Woodstock, VA

Chelsea Station B&B Inn
Seattle, WA

General Lewis Inn
Lewisburg, WV

Yesterdays Ltd. B&B
Wheeling, WV

Old Rittenhouse Inn
Bayfield, WI

Thorp House Inn
Fish Creek, WI

Savery Creek Thoroughbred
Savery, WY

Auberge Manoir de Tilly
Saint Antoine de Tilly, PQ

Comfort

Old-fashioned comfort and friendly staff are important to every lodging. These inns have these qualities in abundance.

Aztec Bed & Breakfast
Flagstaff, AZ

Hacienda del Sol Ranch
Tucson, AZ

Pelican Cove Inn
Carlsbad, CA

Glass Beach B&B Inn
Fort Bragg, CA

Dunbar House, 1880
Murphys, CA

Beazley House
Napa, CA

Grandmere's Inn
Nevada City, CA

Little Inn on the Bay
Newport Beach, CA

Valley View Citrus Ranch
Orosi, CA

The Centrella Hotel
Pacific Grove, CA

Cinnamon Bear B&B
Saint Helena, CA

Balboa Park Inn
San Diego, CA

Edgemont Inn
San Diego, CA

Bed & Breakfast Inn
San Francisco, CA

The Monte Cristo
San Francisco, CA

Bed & Breakfast San Juan
San Juan Bautista, CA

Old Yacht Club Inn
Santa Barbara, CA

Olive House
Santa Barbara, CA

Hendrick Inn
West Covina, CA

Cottenwood House
Estes Park, CO

Brewery Inn B&B
Silver Plume, CO

Alma House
Silverton, CO

Inn at Chester
Chester, CT

Under Mountain Inn
Salisbury, CT

Small Wonder B&B
Wilmington, DE

Kenwood Inn
Saint Augustine, FL

Foley House Inn
Savannah, GA

'417' Haslam-Fort House
Savannah, GA

Harrison House B&B
Naperville, IL

Davis House
Crawfordsville, IN

Checkerberry Inn
Goshen, IN

Patchwork Quilt Inn
Middlebury, IN

Hotel—The Frenchmen
New Orleans, LA

Lamothe House Hotel
New Orleans, LA

Castlemaine Inn
Bar Harbor, ME

Maine Stay Inn
Camden, ME

Windward House B&B
Camden, ME

Cape Neddick House
Cape Neddick, ME

Castine Inn
Castine, ME

1802 House B&B Inn
Kennebunkport, ME

Dock Square Inn
Kennebunkport, ME

Old Fort Inn
Kennebunkport, ME

Gosnold Arms
New Harbor, ME

Newcastle Inn
Newcastle, ME

Broad Bay Inn & Gallery
Waldoboro, ME

Jo-Mar B&B on the Ocean
York Beach, ME

Kemp House Inn
Saint Michaels, MD

The Newel Post
Uniontown, MD

Point Way Inn
Edgartown, MA

Grafton Inn
Falmouth, MA

Pistachio Cove
Lakeville, MA

Haus Andreas
Lee, MA

Amity House
Lenox, MA

Walker House
Lenox, MA

Whistler's Inn
Lenox, MA

Corner House
Nantucket, MA

Seven Sea Street Inn
Nantucket, MA

Rocky Shores Inn/Cottages
Rockport, MA

Coach House Inn
Salem, MA

Golden Goose
Tyringham, MA

The Bayberry
Vineyard Haven, MA

Honeysuckle Hill
West Barnstable, MA

Raymond House Inn
Port Sanilac, MI

Thorwood Inn
Hastings, MN

Canterbury Inn B&B
Rochester, MN

Haverhill Inn
Haverhill, NH

Forest, A Country Inn
Intervale, NH

Benjamin Prescott Inn
Jaffrey, NH

Crab Apple Inn
Plymouth, NH

Snowvillage Inn
Snowville, NH

Mountain Laurel Inn
Wentworth, NH

Conover's Bay Head Inn
Bay Head, NJ

Holly House
Cape May, NJ

Queen Victoria
Cape May, NJ

Normandy Inn
Spring Lake, NJ

Lamplight Inn
Lake Luzerne, NY

Lanza's Country Inn
Livingston Manor, NY

Genesee Country Inn
Mumford, NY

Fourth Ward B&B
Charlotte, NC

Mountain High
Glenville, NC

Baird House
Mars Hill, NC

Colonel Ludlow Inn
Winston-Salem, NC

Chanticleer Inn
Ashland, OR

Country Willows Inn
Ashland, OR

Edinburgh Lodge B&B
Ashland, OR

Romeo Inn
Ashland, OR

Country Lane B&B
Lakeside, OR

Corbett House B&B
Portland, OR

Spring House
Airville, PA

Covered Bridge Inn B&B
Ephrata, PA

Smithton Inn
Ephrata, PA

Las Tres Palmas Guesthouse
San Juan, PR

Edgeworth Inn
Monteagle, TN

Blue Mountain Mist Inn
Sevierville, TN

Old Miners' Lodge B&B
Park City, UT

Pullman B&B Inn
Provo, UT

Zion House Bed & Breakfast
Springdale, UT

Inn at Long Last
Chester, VT

Garrison Inn
East Burke, VT

1811 House
Manchester, VT

Brookside Meadows
Middlebury, VT

Stone House Inn
North Thetford, VT

Golden Kitz Lodge
Stowe, VT

Raspberry Patch
Stowe, VT

Lareau Farm Country Inn
Waitsfield, VT

Nutmeg Inn
Wilmington, VT

Juniper Hill Inn
Windsor, VT

Fountain Hall B&B Inn
Culpepper, VA

King Carter Inn
Irvington, VA

Fassifern Bed & Breakfast
Lexington, VA

Conyers House
Sperryville, VA

North Garden Inn
Bellingham, WA

Palmer's Chart House
Deer Harbor, WA

Saratoga Inn
Langley, WA

Inn at Swifts Bay
Lopez Island, WA

Chelsea Station B&B Inn
Seattle, WA

Galer Place B&B
Seattle, WA

The Swallow's Nest	**Abendruh B&B Swiss-style**	**Viroqua Heritage Inn B&B**
Vashon Island, WA	Belleville, WI	Viroqua, WI

Conference

Small conferences can be very productive when held in the inns listed below, all of which have the facilities you need and the quiet and opportunity, too, for the fellowship you require.

Power's Mansion Inn	**Trojan Horse Inn**	**Whistling Swan Inn**
Auburn, CA	Sonoma, CA	Stanhope, NJ
Fairview Manor	**Vineyard Inn**	**Troutbeck**
Ben Lomond, CA	Sonoma, CA	Amenia, NY
Bear Wallow Resort	**St. George Hotel**	**Brae Loch Inn**
Boonville, CA	Volcano, CA	Cazenovia, NY
Cobblestone Inn	**Hotel Lenado**	**Balsam House**
Carmel, CA	Aspen, CO	Chestertown, NY
Valley Lodge	**Wanek's Lodge at Estes**	**Inn at Cooperstown**
Carmel Valley, CA	Estes Park, CO	Cooperstown, NY
Murphy's Inn	**New Sheridan Hotel**	**Geneva on the Lake**
Grass Valley, CA	Telluride, CO	Geneva, NY
Old Milano Hotel	**Inn at Chapel West**	**Genesee Country Inn**
Gualala, CA	New Haven, CT	Mumford, NY
San Benito House	**Susina Plantation Inn**	**Garnet Hill Lodge**
Half Moon Bay, CA	Thomasville, GA	North River, NY
Sorensen's Resort	**Manoa Valley Inn**	**Richmond Hill Inn**
Hope Valley, CA	Honolulu, Oahu, HI	Asheville, NC
Julian Gold Rush Hotel	**Rokeby Hall**	**Lords Proprietors' Inn**
Julian, CA	Lexington, KY	Edenton, NC
Eagles Landing	**High Meadows B&B**	**Swag Country Inn**
Lake Arrowhead, CA	Eliot, ME	Waynesville, NC
Hill House Inn	**Goose Cove Lodge**	**Shelter Harbor Inn**
Mendocino, CA	Sunset, ME	Westerly, RI
Gosby House Inn	**East Wind Inn/Meeting Hse**	**The Graustein Inn**
Pacific Grove, CA	Tenants Harbor, ME	Knoxville, TN
Old St. Angela Inn	**Inn at Buckeystown**	**Bullis House Inn**
Pacific Grove, CA	Buckeystown, MD	San Antonio, TX
Briggs House	**Strawberry Inn**	**Old Miners' Lodge B&B**
Sacramento, CA	New Market, MD	Park City, UT
Archbishop's Mansion Inn	**Corner House**	**Village Inn of Bradford**
San Francisco, CA	Nantucket, MA	Bradford, VT
Edward II Inn & Suites	**Wood Farm**	**Kedron Valley Inn**
San Francisco, CA	Townsend, MA	South Woodstock, VT
Jackson Court	**Dunleith**	**Ten Acres Lodge**
San Francisco, CA	Natchez, MS	Stowe, VT
Petite Auberge	**Schwegmann House B&B Inn**	**Lareau Farm Country Inn**
San Francisco, CA	Washington, MO	Waitsfield, VT
Madison Street Inn	**Watson Manor Inn**	**Wallingford Inn**
Santa Clara, CA	North Platte, NE	Wallingford, VT
Babbling Brook Inn	**Lyme Inn**	**Hermitage Inn & Brookbound**
Santa Cruz, CA	Lyme, NH	Wilmington, VT
Darling House	**New London Inn**	**Fountain Hall B&B Inn**
Santa Cruz, CA	New London, NH	Culpepper, VA

Admiral's Hideaway Anacortes, WA	**La Conner Country Inn** La Conner, WA	**Countryside** Summit Point, WV

Decor

Distinctive decor and unusual architecture are always a pleasure. Enjoy them in these inns.

Marks House Inn Prescott, AZ	**The Gables** Santa Rosa, CA	**Greenville Inn** Greenville, ME
Graham's B&B Inn Sedona, AZ	**Casa Madrona Hotel** Sausalito, CA	**Captain Lord Mansion** Kennebunkport, ME
Williams House B&B Inn Hot Springs Nat'l Park, AR	**Trojan Horse Inn** Sonoma, CA	**The Walker Wilson House** Topsham, ME
Union Hotel Benicia, CA	**Oleander House** Yountville, CA	**White Swan Tavern** Chestertown, MD
Mount View Hotel Calistoga, CA	**Hotel Lenado** Aspen, CO	**Ashley Manor** Barnstable, MA
Carter House Eureka, CA	**Pikes Peak Paradise** Colorado Springs, CO	**Bradford Inn & Motel** Chatham, MA
Gingerbread Mansion Ferndale, CA	**The Lovelander** Loveland, CO	**The Gables Inn** Lenox, MA
Saint Orres Gualala, CA	**Sandford/Pond House** Bridgewater, CT	**Thorncroft Inn** Martha's Vineyard, MA
Blackthorne Inn Inverness, CA	**Chimney Crest Manor B&B** Bristol, CT	**Farmhouse at Nauset Beach** Orleans, MA
Beazley House Napa, CA	**Palmer Inn** Mystic, CT	**Amelia Payson Guest House** Salem, MA
Old World Inn Napa, CA	**Bailey House** Fernandina Beach, FL	**Stephen Daniels House** Salem, MA
Grandmere's Inn Nevada City, CA	**Watson House** Key West, FL	**Kemah Guest House** Saugatuck, MI
Green Gables Inn Pacific Grove, CA	**De Loffre House** Columbus, GA	**Maplewood Hotel** Saugatuck, MI
James Blair House Placerville, CA	**Wedgwood Bed & Breakfast** Hamilton, GA	**Grand View Lodge** Brainerd, MN
Morey Mansion B&B Inn Redlands, CA	**Ballastone Inn** Savannah, GA	**Chatsworth Bed & Breakfast** Saint Paul, MN
Driver Mansion Inn Sacramento, CA	**Rock House** Morgantown, IN	**The Burn** Natchez, MS
Alamo Square Inn San Francisco, CA	**The Redstone Inn** Dubuque, IA	**Dunleith** Natchez, MS
Inn on Castro San Francisco, CA	**Die Heimat Country Inn** Homestead, IA	**Anchuca** Vicksburg, MS
The Monte Cristo San Francisco, CA	**Mintmere Plantation House** New Iberia, LA	**Coachlight B&B** Saint Louis, MO
Sherman House San Francisco, CA	**Columns Hotel** New Orleans, LA	**Walnut Street B&B** Springfield, MO
Willows B&B Inn San Francisco, CA	**Hotel—The Frenchmen** New Orleans, LA	**Nevada City Hotel** Nevada City, MT
Bayberry Inn Santa Barbara, CA	**Lamothe House Hotel** New Orleans, LA	**Bel-Horst Inn** Belgrade, NE
Sovereign at Santa Monica Santa Monica, CA	**Brannon Bunker Inn** Damariscotta, ME	**Manor on Golden Pond** Holderness, NH

Mt. Adams Inn
North Woodstock, NH

The Abbey
Cape May, NJ

Bedford Inn
Cape May, NJ

Benn Conger Inn
Groton, NY

Lake Keuka Manor
Hammondsport, NY

Genesee Country Inn
Mumford, NY

H.W. Allen B&B
Troy, OH

Grandview Bed & Breakfast
Astoria, OR

Huntington Manor
Corvallis, OR

Corbett House B&B
Portland, OR

Farm Fortune
New Cumberland, PA

Two Meeting Street Inn
Charleston, SC

Villa de La Fontaine B&B
Charleston, SC

Annie's B&B Country Inn
Big Sandy, TX

Historical Hudspeth House
Canyon, TX

Pullman B&B Inn
Provo, UT

Seven Wives Inn
Saint George, UT

Brigham Street Inn
Salt Lake City, UT

South Shire Inn
Bennington, VT

Reluctant Panther Inn
Manchester, VT

Fassifern Bed & Breakfast
Lexington, VA

Mayhurst Inn
Orange, VA

Catlin-Abbott House
Richmond, VA

Old Rittenhouse Inn
Bayfield, WI

Eagle Harbor Inn/Cottages
Ephraim, WI

Franklin Victorian
Sparta, WI

Gray Goose Bed & Breakfast
Sturgeon Bay, WI

Viroqua Heritage Inn B&B
Viroqua, WI

Tucker's Bed & Breakfast
Victoria, BC

Family Fun

Be sure to check this list if you're traveling with your brood of six. The inns below are ideal for a family fun vacation.

Lynx Creek Farm B&B
Prescott, AZ

Hacienda del Sol Ranch
Tucson, AZ

Ames Lodge
Mendocino, CA

Kelsall's Ute Creek Ranch
Ignacio, CO

E.T.'s Bed & Breakfast
Paonia, CO

Shady Maples
Bar Harbor, ME

Hiram Alden Inn
Belfast, ME

Windward House B&B
Camden, ME

Gosnold Arms
New Harbor, ME

Goose Cove Lodge
Sunset, ME

B&B at Ludington
Ludington, MI

Pentwater Inn
Pentwater, MI

Down Over Inn
JArrow Rock, MO

Richardson House B&B
Jamesport, MO

Lone Mountain Ranch
Big Sky, MT

Cottonwood Ranch Retreat
Roberts, MT

Franconia Inn
Franconia, NH

Dana Place Inn
Jackson, NH

Nestlenook Inn
Jackson, NH

Lake Shore Farm
Northwood, NH

Cordova
Ocean Grove, NJ

All Breeze Guest Farm
Barryville, NY

Corner Birches B&B Guests
Lake George, NY

Carefree Cottages
Nags Head, NC

Hugging Bear Inn & Shoppe
Chester, VT

Tyler Place-Lake Champlain
Highgate Springs, VT

Johnny Seesaw's
Peru, VT

Liberty Hill Farm
Rochester, VT

Angie's Guest Cottage
Virginia Beach, VA

Teton Tree House
Jackson Hole, WY

Savery Creek Thoroughbred
Savery, WY

Tucker's Bed & Breakfast
Victoria, BC

Farm Vacations

The inns listed below are working farms. Take this opportunity to experience rural America.

Lynx Creek Farm B&B
Prescott, AZ

Inn at Shallow Creek Farm
Orland, CA

Kelsall's Ute Creek Ranch
Ignacio, CO

Litco Farms B&B
Cooperstown, NY

Meadow Spring Farm
Kennett Square, PA

New Canaan Farm
Elkhart, TX

Hill Farm Inn
Arlington, VT

Just-N-Trails B&B
Sparta, WI

Fishing

Nothing like a good catch. These inns are near the haunts of the really big ones. Fishing over, head back to the inn and tell tales to fellow enthusiasts.

Gustavus Inn
Gustavus, AK

River Beauty B&B
Talkeetna, AK

Matlick House
Bishop, CA

Chalet de France
Eureka, CA

Sorensen's Resort
Hope Valley, CA

Charlaine's Bay View B&B
Monterey, CA

Jean Pratt's Riverside B&B
Oroville, CA

River Rock Inn
Placerville, CA

Faulkner House
Red Bluff, CA

Darling House
Santa Cruz, CA

Parrish's Country Squire
Berthoud, CO

Harbour Inne & Cottage
Mystic, CT

1735 House
Amelia Island, FL

Hopp-Inn Guest House
Marathon, FL

McBride's B&B Guesthouse
Irwin, ID

Redfish Lake Lodge
Stanley, ID

Dockside Guest Quarters
York, ME

Jonah Williams Inn
Annapolis, MD

Blue Lake Lodge B&B
Mecosta, MI

Grand View Lodge
Brainerd, MN

Lone Mountain Ranch
Big Sky, MT

Izaak Walton Inn
Essex, MT

Old Pioneer Garden Inn
Imlay, NV

Inn at Crystal Lake
Eaton Center, NH

Inn at Coit Mountain
Newport, NH

Cranmore Mountain Lodge
North Conway, NH

Follansbee Inn
North Sutton, NH

Mt. Adams Inn
North Woodstock, NH

The Cable House
Rye, NH

Mountain Laurel Inn
Wentworth, NH

Chestnut Hill on Delaware
Milford, NJ

Thousand Islands Inn
Clayton, 1000 Islands, NY

Lakeside Terrace B&B
Dundee, NY

Garnet Hill Lodge
North River, NY

Langdon House B&B
Beaufort, NC

Randolph House Country Inn
Bryson City, NC

Gingerbread Inn
Chimney Rock, NC

The Tar Heel Inn
Oriental, NC

Blue Boar Lodge
Robbinsville, NC

Holmes Sea Cove B&B
Brookings, OR

The Tu Tu Tun Lodge
Gold Beach, OR

The Handmaiden's Inn
Grants Pass, OR

Inn at Turkey Hill
Bloomsburg, PA

La Anna Guest House
Cresco, PA

Fairfield-by-The-Sea B&B
Green Hill, RI

John C. Rogers House
Center, TX

Meadeau View Lodge
Cedar City, UT

Old Miners' Lodge B&B
Park City, UT

Hill Farm Inn
Arlington, VT

Churchill House Inn
Brandon, VT

Rowell's Inn
Chester, VT

Tyler Place-Lake Champlain
Highgate Springs, VT

Okemo Inn
Ludlow, VT

Inn at Manchester
Manchester, VT

Black Lantern Inn
Montgomery Village, VT

North Hero House
North Hero, VT

Lake St. Catherine Inn
Poultney, VT

Lareau Farm Country Inn
Waitsfield, VT

Highland Inn
Monterey, VA

Turtleback Farm Inn
Eastsound, WA

Tudor Inn
Port Angeles, WA

Orchard Hill Inn
White Salmon, WA

Greenbrier River Inn
Caldwell, WV

Cobblestone-on-The-Ohio
Sistersville, WV

Griffin Inn
Ellison Bay, WI

Viroqua Heritage Inn B&B
Viroqua, WI

Gingerbread House
Mayne Island, BC

Sunnymeade House Inn
Victoria, BC

Northern Wilderness Lodge
Plaster Rock, NB

Gardens

Ah, to while away an hour in a lovely garden. What could be more relaxing? These inns are renowned for their lush gardens.

Culbert House Inn
Amador City, CA

Gramma's B&B Inn
Berkeley, CA

Wayside Inn
Calistoga, CA

Holiday House
Carmel, CA

Monte Verde Inn
Carmel, CA

Sandpiper Inn-At-the-Beach
Carmel, CA

Vintage Towers Inn
Cloverdale, CA

Gingerbread Mansion
Ferndale, CA

Old Milano Hotel
Gualala, CA

Mill Rose Inn
Half Moon Bay, CA

Gate House Inn
Jackson, CA

B&B Inn at La Jolla
La Jolla, CA

Casa Laguna Inn
Laguna Beach, CA

Victorian Farmhouse
Little River, CA

Brewery Gulch Inn
Mendocino, CA

Hill House Inn
Mendocino, CA

Goose & Turrets
Montara, CA

House of a 1000 Flowers
Monte Rio, CA

The Jabberwock
Monterey, CA

Country Garden Inn
Napa, CA

Villa Royale Inn
Palm Springs, CA

Harvest Inn
Saint Helena, CA

Union Street Inn
San Francisco, CA

Babbling Brook Inn
Santa Cruz, CA

Cliff Crest B&B Inn
Santa Cruz, CA

Seal Beach Inn & Gardens
Seal Beach, CA

Victorian Garden Inn
Sonoma, CA

Barretta Gardens Inn
Sonora, CA

Sutter Creek Inn
Sutter Creek, CA

Country House Inn
Templeton, CA

Byron Randall's Victorian
Tomales, CA

Howard Creek Ranch
Westport, CA

Butternut Farm
Glastonbury, CT

Eaton Lodge
Key West, FL

Merlinn Guesthouse
Key West, FL

Wicker Guesthouse
Key West, FL

St. Francis Inn
Saint Augustine, FL

Jesse Mount House
Savannah, GA

Liberty Inn 1834
Savannah, GA

Manor House Inn
Bar Harbor, ME

Hartwell House
Ogunquit, ME

Shiverick Inn
Edgartown, MA

Seekonk Pines Inn
Great Barrington, MA

Apple Tree Inn
Lenox, MA

Corner House
Nantucket, MA

The Summer House
Siasconset, MA

Hutchinson's Garden B&B
Northport, MI

Dunleith
Natchez, MS

Hope Farm
Natchez, MS

Old Red Inn & Cottages
North Conway, NH

Martin Hill Inn
Portsmouth, NH

Woolverton Inn
Stockton, NJ

Back of the Beyond
Colden, NY

Geneva on the Lake
Geneva, NY

Swiss Hutte
Hillsdale, NY

Rose Mansion & Gardens
Rochester, NY

Bakers Bed & Breakfast
Stone Ridge, NY

Sage Cottage
Trumansburg, NY

Ray House Bed & Breakfast
Asheville, NC

Edinburgh Lodge B&B
Ashland, OR

Endicott Gardens
Gold Beach, OR

Salisbury House
Allentown, PA

Garrott's Bed & Breakfast
Cowansville, PA

Bishop's Rocking Horse Inn
Gettysburg, PA

Back Street Inn
New Hope, PA

Villa de La Fontaine B&B
Charleston, SC

Annie's B&B Country Inn
Big Sandy, TX

Inn on the Common
Craftsbury Common, VT

Brookside Meadows
Middlebury, VT

Trail's End
Wilmington, VT

Juniper Hill Inn
Windsor, VT

Conyers House
Sperryville, VA

Schnauzer Crossing B&B
Bellingham, WA

General Lewis Inn
Lewisburg, WV

Rose Garden Guest House
Vancouver, BC

Golf

Tee off, walk and relax, then head back to your cozy inn. What could be nicer?

Dry Creek Inn
Auburn, CA

Charlaine's Bay View B&B
Monterey, CA

Napa Inn
Napa, CA

Hendrick Inn
West Covina, CA

Crown Hotel
Inverness, FL

Victoria Place
Lawai, Kauai, HI

Guesthouse at Volcano
Volcano, HI

Kinter House Inn
Corydon, IN

Teetor House
Hagerstown, IN

Old Hoosier House B&B
Knightstown, IN

Fairhaven Inn
Bath, ME

Green Acres Inn
Canton, ME

Chebeague Island Inn
Chebeague Island, ME

1802 House B&B Inn
Kennebunkport, ME

Harbourside Inn
Northeast Harbor, ME

Sign of the Unicorn House
Rockport, ME

Hynson Tourist Home
Easton, MD

Snow Hill Inn
Snow Hill, MD

Ashfield Inn
Ashfield, MA

Four Winds
Jackson, NH

Jefferson Inn
Jefferson, NH

Birchwood Inn
Temple, NH

The Kenilworth
Spring Lake, NJ

Brae Loch Inn
Cazenovia, NY

Geneva on the Lake
Geneva, NY

B&B Over Yonder
Black Mountain, NC

Buttonwood Inn
Franklin, NC

Greystone Inn
Lake Toxaway, NC

Pine Ridge Inn
Mount Airy, NC

The Tar Heel Inn
Oriental, NC

Fairway Inn
Spruce Pine, NC

Hallcrest Inn
Waynesville, NC

Heath Lodge
Waynesville, NC

Palmer House
Waynesville, NC

Paradise Ranch Inn
Grants Pass, OR

Pine Knoll Inn
Aiken, SC

Main House
Texarkana, TX

Peterson's Bed & Breakfast
Monroe, UT

Old Miners' Lodge B&B
Park City, UT

Barrows House
Dorset, VT

Governor's Inn
Ludlow, VT

1811 House
Manchester, VT

Manchester Highlands Inn
Manchester, VT

Golden Stage Inn
Proctorsville, VT

1860 House
Stowe, VT

Valley Inn
Waitsfield, VT

Beaver Pond Farm Inn
Warren, VT

Vine Cottage Inn
Hot Springs, VA

Eagle Harbor Inn/Cottages
Ephraim, WI

Sunnymeade House Inn
Victoria, BC

Gourmet

An excellent meal can add a lot to your stay. The inns listed here are particularly celebrated for their fine cuisine.

Williams House B&B Inn
Hot Springs Nat'l Park, AR

Union Hotel
Benicia, CA

Mount View Hotel
Calistoga, CA

Carter House
Eureka, CA

Chalet de France
Eureka, CA

Old Milano Hotel
Gualala, CA

Madrona Manor—Country Inn
Healdsburg, CA

Pelican Inn
Muir Beach, CA

Beazley House
Napa, CA

Sherman House
San Francisco, CA

Old Yacht Club Inn
Santa Barbara, CA

Casa Madrona Hotel
Sausalito, CA

Inn at Chester
Chester, CT

Homestead Inn
Greenwich, CT

The Copper Beech Inn
Ivorytown, CT

David Finney Inn
New Castle, DE

Chalet Suzanne Country Inn
Lake Wales, FL

Smith House
Dahlonega, GA

Stovall House
Sautee, GA

The Veranda
Senoia, GA

Patchwork Quilt Inn
Middlebury, IN

Inn at Stone City
Anamosa, IA

Talbot Tavern/McLean House
Bardstown, KY

Columns Hotel
New Orleans, LA

Hotel—The Frenchmen
New Orleans, LA

Penobscot Meadows Inn
Belfast, ME

Camden Harbour Inn
Camden, ME

Le Domaine Restaurant/Inn
Hancock, ME

Crocker House Country Inn
Hancock Point, ME

Dock Square Inn
Kennebunkport, ME

The White Barn Inn
Kennebunkport, ME

Newcastle Inn
Newcastle, ME

Bramble Inn Restaurant
Brewster, MA

Old Manse Inn
Brewster, MA

Turning Point Inn
Great Barrington, MA

Haus Andreas
Lee, MA

Country Inn at Princeton
Princeton, MA

The Bayberry
Vineyard Haven, MA

Inn at Duck Creeke
Wellfleet, MA

Schumacher's New Prague
New Prague, MN

Canterbury Inn B&B
Rochester, MN

Der Klingerbau Inn
Hermann, MO

Bel-Horst Inn
Belgrade, NE

Bradford Inn
Bradford, NH

The Hitching Post B&B
Chichester, NH

Staffords in the Field
Chocorua, NH

Inn at Crystal Lake
Eaton Center, NH

New London Inn
New London, NH

Stonehurst Manor
North Conway, NH

Follansbee Inn
North Sutton, NH

Mt. Adams Inn
North Woodstock, NH

Chesterfield Inn
West Chesterfield, NH

Bay Head Sands Inn
Bay Head, NJ

El Paradero
Santa Fe, NM

Troutbeck
Amenia, NY

Crabtree's Kittle House
Chappaqua, NY

Balsam House
Chestertown, NY

Hedges House
East Hampton, NY

Benn Conger Inn
Groton, NY

Swiss Hutte
Hillsdale, NY

Rose Inn
Ithaca, NY

Interlaken Inn—Restaurant
Lake Placid, NY

Taughannock Farms Inn
Trumansburg, NY

Hist. James R. Webster
Waterloo, NY

Randolph House Country Inn
Bryson City, NC

Eli Olive's Inn
Smithfield, NC

Grandview Lodge
Waynesville, NC

Paradise Ranch Inn
Grants Pass, OR

Steamboat Inn
Steamboat, OR

Spring House
Airville, PA

Overlook Inn
Canadensis, PA

Pine Barn Inn
Danville, PA

Golden Pheasant Inn
Erwinna, PA

Academy Street B&B
Hawley, PA

Black Bass Hotel
Lumberville, PA

Longswamp Bed & Breakfast
Mertztown, PA

Centre Bridge Inn
New Hope, PA

Inn at Phillips Mill
New Hope, PA

White Cloud Sylvan Retreat
Newfoundland, PA

Wycombe Inn
Wycombe, PA

Hotel Manisses
Block Island, RI

Shelter Harbor Inn
Westerly, RI

The Willcox Inn
Aiken, SC

Phelp's House Inn
Highlands, TN

Inn on the River
Glen Rose, TX

Old Miners' Lodge B&B
Park City, UT

Arlington Inn
Arlington, VT

Hill Farm Inn
Arlington, VT

Craftsbury Inn
Craftsbury, VT

Blueberry Hill Inn
Goshen, VT

Vermont Inn
Killington, VT

Governor's Inn
Ludlow, VT

Reluctant Panther Inn
Manchester, VT

Red Clover Inn
Mendon, VT

Middletown Springs Inn
Middletown Springs, VT

Old Newfane Inn
Newfane, VT

Norwich Inn
Norwich, VT

Millbrook Inn
Waitsfield, VT

Colonial House
Weston, VT

Inn at Weston
Weston, VT

Channel Bass Inn
Chincoteague, VA

Kenmore Inn
Fredericksburg, VA

Ravenswood Inn
Mathews, VA

Guest House B&B Cottages
Greenbank, WA

Shelburne Country Inn
Seaview, WA

Gite du Mont Albert
Saint Anne des Mont, PQ

Auberge Manoir de Tilly
Saint Antoine de Tilly, PQ

Historic Sites

Inns situated in historic buildings or locales hold a special appeal for many people. The following is a sampling.

Webster House
Alameda, CA

Mine House Inn
Amador City, CA

Power's Mansion Inn
Auburn, CA

Coloma Country Inn
Coloma, CA

City Hotel
Columbia, CA

Rock Haus Inn
Del Mar, CA

Gingerbread Mansion
Ferndale, CA

The Heirloom
Ione, CA

Julian Gold Rush Hotel
Julian, CA

Victorian Farmhouse
Little River, CA

Eastlake Victorian Inn
Los Angeles, CA

Meadow Creek Ranch Inn
Mariposa, CA

Headlands Inn
Mendocino, CA

Beazley House
Napa, CA

Ink House Bed & Breakfast
Saint Helena, CA

Washington Square Inn
San Francisco, CA

Bed & Breakfast San Juan
San Juan Bautista, CA

Thistle Dew Inn
Sonoma, CA

St. George Hotel
Volcano, CA

House of Yesteryear
Ouray, CO

Teller House Hotel
Silverton, CO

New Sheridan Hotel
Telluride, CO

Killingworth Inn
Killingworth, CT

Red Brook Inn
Old Mystic, CT

French Renaissance House
Plainfield, CT

Old Riverton Inn
Riverton, CT

Spring Garden B&B
Laurel, DE

David Finney Inn
New Castle, DE

William Penn Guest House
New Castle, DE

Historic Island Hotel
Cedar Key, FL

Bailey House
Fernandina Beach, FL

Ritz-Ocala's Historic Inn
Ocala, FL

York House
Mountain City, GA

Stovall House
Sautee, GA

Bed & Breakfast Inn
Savannah, GA

Comer House
Savannah, GA

The Brick House B&B
Goodfield, IL

Teetor House
Hagerstown, IN

The Old World Inn
Spillville, IA

Almeda's B&B Inn
Tonganoxie, KS

Talbot Tavern/McLean House
Bardstown, KY

Tezcuco Plantation Village
Darrow, LA

Mintmere Plantation House
New Iberia, LA

Parkview Guest House
New Orleans, LA

Blue Hill Inn
Blue Hill, ME

The Elms
Camden, ME

Maine Stay Inn
Camden, ME

Norumbega Inn
Camden, ME

Lincoln House Country Inn
Dennysville, ME

Weston House B&B
Eastport, ME

High Meadows B&B
Eliot, ME

Bagley House
Freeport, ME

Captain Lord Mansion
Kennebunkport, ME

Clark Perry House
Machias, ME

Homeport Inn
Searsport, ME

Gibson's Lodgings
Annapolis, MD

White Swan Tavern
Chestertown, MD

Inn at Perry Cabin
Saint Michaels, MD

Piper House B&B Inn
Sharpsburg, MD

Glenburn
Taneytown, MD

Winchester Country Inn
Westminster, MD

Thomas Huckins House
Barnstable, MA

Chatham Town House Inn
Chatham, MA

Cyrus Kent House Inn
Chatham, MA

Osterville Fairways Inn
Marstons Mill, MA

Easton House
Nantucket, MA

Penny House
North Eastham, MA

Perryville Inn
Rehoboth, MA

Egremont Inn
South Egremont, MA

Merrell Tavern Inn
South Lee, MA

Lion's Head Inn
West Harwich, MA

Colonial House Inn
Yarmouth Port, MA

Old Wing Inn
Holland, MI

National House Inn
Marshall, MI

Clifford Lake Hotel
Stanton, MI

Archer House
Northfield, MN

Millsaps Buie House
Jackson, MS

Rosswood Plantation
Lorman, MS

Dunleith
Natchez, MS

Hope Farm
Natchez, MS

Linden
Natchez, MS

Oak Square Plantation
Port Gibson, MS

Anchuca
Vicksburg, MS

The Corners Mansion
Vicksburg, MS

Borgman's Bed & Breakfast
Arrow Rock, MO

Inn St. Gemme Beauvais
Sainte Genevieve, MO

The Hitching Post B&B
Chichester, NH

Six Chimneys
East Hebron, NH

Historic Tavern Inn
Gilmanton, NH

1785 Inn
North Conway, NH

Mt. Adams Inn
North Woodstock, NH

Acorn Lodge
Ossipee, NH

The Cable House
Rye, NH

Captain Mey's Inn
Cape May, NJ

Chestnut Hill on Delaware
Milford, NJ

Ashling Cottage
Spring Lake, NJ

Casita Chamisa B&B
Albuquerque, NM

Preston House
Santa Fe, NM

Genesee Country Inn
Mumford, NY

Ray House Bed & Breakfast
Asheville, NC

The Inn at Brevard
Brevard, NC

King's Arms Inn
New Bern, NC

Oakwood Inn
Raleigh, NC

Cider Mill B&B
Zoar, OH

Haven @ 4th & Park
Zoar, OH

Edinburgh Lodge B&B
Ashland, OR

McCully House Inn
Jacksonville, OR

Inn at Fordhook Farm
Doylestown, PA

Covered Bridge Inn B&B
Ephrata, PA

Osceola Mill House
Gordonville-Intercourse, PA

Ash Mill Farm
Holicong, PA

Witmer's Tavern—1725 Inn
Lancaster, PA

Pineapple Inn
Lewisburg, PA

Cameron Estate Inn
Mount Joy, PA

Wedgewood B&B Inn
New Hope, PA

Limestone Inn B&B
Strasburg, PA

Strasburg Village Inn
Strasburg, PA

Bellevue House
Newport, RI

Melville House
Newport, RI

Old Dennis House
Newport, RI

Country Victorian B&B
Charleston, SC

Kings Courtyard Inn
Charleston, SC

Maison DuPre
Charleston, SC

Palmer Home
Charleston, SC

Sword Gate Inn
Charleston, SC

Nicholls-Crook Plantation
Spartanburg, SC

Hale Springs Inn
Rogersville, TN

Gast Haus Lodge
Comfort, TX

Country Cottage Inn
Fredericksburg, TX

J Bar K Ranch B&B
Fredericksburg, TX

Old Miners' Lodge B&B
Park City, UT

Pullman B&B Inn
Provo, UT

Seven Wives Inn
Saint George, UT

Brigham Street Inn
Salt Lake City, UT

National Historic B&B
Salt Lake City, UT

Beauchamp Place
Brandon, VT

Shire Inn
Chelsea, VT

Chester House
Chester, VT

Governor's Inn
Ludlow, VT

Okemo Inn
Ludlow, VT

1811 House
Manchester, VT

Swift House Inn
Middlebury, VT

A Century Past
Newbury, VT

Old Newfane Inn
Newfane, VT

Golden Stage Inn
Proctorsville, VT

Lareau Farm Country Inn
Waitsfield, VT

West Dover Inn
West Dover, VT

Pink Fancy Hotel
Christiansted, St. Croix, VI

Edgewood Plantation
Charles City, VA

North Bend Plantation B&B
Charles City, VA

Fountain Hall B&B Inn
Culpepper, VA

La Vista Plantation
Fredericksburg, VA

Wayside Inn since 1797
Middletown, VA

Inn at Montross
Montross, VA

Pumpkin House Inn, Ltd.
Mount Crawford, VA

Mayhurst Inn
Orange, VA

High Meadows Inn
Scottsville, VA

1763 Inn
Upperville, VA

Shelburne Country Inn
Seaview, WA

Greenbrier River Inn
Caldwell, WV

Prospect Hill B&B
Gerrardstown, WV

General Lewis Inn
Lewisburg, WV

Boydville at Martinsburg
MartinsburgCARLTON PROBL, WV

Plough Inn B&B
Madison, WI

Victoria's Historic Inn
Wolfville, NS

Willow Place Inn
Hudson, PQ

Low Price

The following lodgings are particularly noted for modest pricing. It is possible to obtain a room for $30 or less.

Krafts' Korner
Mobile, AL

Inn at Castle Rock
Bisbee, AZ

Cedar Bed & Breakfast
Flagstaff, AZ

Creekside Inn & Resort
Guerneville, CA

Pelennor B&B
Mariposa, CA

Rockridge Bed & Breakfast
Oakland, CA

Jean Pratt's Riverside B&B
Oroville, CA

Casa Arguello
San Francisco, CA

Edward II Inn & Suites
San Francisco, CA

Pensione San Francisco
San Francisco, CA

Hendrick Inn
West Covina, CA

Little Red Ski Haus
Aspen, CO

Snow Queen Victorian Lodge
Aspen, CO

Purple Mountain Lodge
Crested Butte, CO

Midwest Motel / Country Inn
Limon, CO

St. Elmo Hotel
Ouray, CO

Alma House
Silverton, CO

Teller House Hotel
Silverton, CO

Colonial House
Edgewater, FL

Publick House
Metamora, IN

Die Heimat Country Inn
Homestead, IA

The Old World Inn
Spillville, IA

Almeda's B&B Inn
Tonganoxie, KS

Doe Run Inn
Brandenburg, KY

Marquette House Hostel
New Orleans, LA

Shady Maples
Bar Harbor, ME

Old Tavern Inn
Litchfield, ME

Captain's House B&B
Newcastle, ME

Farmhouse Inn
Rangeley, ME

Crab Apple Acres Inn
The Forks, ME

Kawanhee Inn
Weld, ME

Wood Farm
Townsend, MA

Governor's Inn
Lexington, MI

Blue Lake Lodge B&B
Mecosta, MI

Evelo's Bed & Breakfast
Minneapolis, MN

Mission Mountain B&B
Saint Ignatius, MT

Bel-Horst Inn
Belgrade, NE

Old Pioneer Garden Inn
Imlay, NV

The Hitching Post B&B
Chichester, NH

Ellis River House B&B
Jackson, NH

Lake Shore Farm
Northwood, NH

Casa del Rey
Los Alamos, NM

Orange Street B&B
Los Alamos, NM

All Breeze Guest Farm
Barryville, NY

Edge of Thyme B&B
Candor, NY

Sunrise Inn B&B
Hancock, NY

Corner Birches B&B Guests
Lake George, NY

Napoli Stagecoach Inn
Little Valley, NY

Tibbitt's House Inn
Rensselaer, NY

Spencertown Guests
Spencertown, NY

Country Road Lodge
Warrensburg, NY

Womble Inn
Brevard, NC

Mountain High
Glenville, NC

Brookside Lodge
Lake Junaluska, NC

Sunset Inn
Lake Junaluska, NC

Portage House
Akron, OH

Coach House Inn
Ashland, OR

Out of the Blue B&B
Independence, OR

Winding Glen Farm Home
Christiana, PA

La Anna Guest House
Cresco, PA

Villamayer
Jamestown, PA

Groff Tourist Farm Home
Kinzer, PA

Runnymede Farm Guesthouse
Quarryville, PA

Homestead Lodging
Smoketown, PA

Arcade Inn Guest House
San Juan, PR

Lakeside Farm B&B
Webster, SD

Clardy's Guest House
Murfreesboro, TN

Nolan House Inn
Waverly, TN

Bullis House Inn
San Antonio, TX

Cardinal Cliff
San Antonio, TX

Main House
Texarkana, TX

Rio Grande Bed & Breakfast
Weslaco, TX

Poplar Manor
Bethel, VT

Garrison Inn
East Burke, VT

Inn at Manchester
Manchester, VT

Valley House Inn
Orleans, VT

Fox Stand Inn
Royalton, VT

Fiddler's Green Inn
Stowe, VT

Weathervane Lodge
West Dover, VT

Palmer's Chart House
Deer Harbor, WA

Crawford's Country Corner
Lost Creek, WV

Mesa Creek Ranch Vacation
Millarville, AB

Sea Breeze Lodge
Hornby Island, BC

Silver Creek Guest House
Salmon Arm, BC

Deerbank Farm
Morris, MB

Reid's Farm Tourist Home
Centreville, NB

Cailswick Babbling Brook
Riverside, NB

Village Inn
Trinity, NF

Shining Tides
Granville Ferry, NS

Blue Heron Inn
Pugwash, NS

Glenroy Farm
Braeside, ON

Australis Guest House
Ottawa, ON

Beatrice Lyon Guest House
Ottawa, ON

Obanlea Farm Tourist Home
Cornwall, PEI

Sherwood Acres Guest Home
Kensington, PEI

Auberge Laketree
Knowlton, PQ

Chateau Beauvallon, Inc.
Mont Tremblant, PQ

Armor Inn
Montreal, PQ

Edale Place
Portneuf, PQ

Luxury

These establishments are famed for their luxurious appointments and special attention to creature comforts and style.

Dairy Hollow House
Eureka Springs, AR

Gramma's B&B Inn
Berkeley, CA

Carriage House
Laguna Beach, CA

Mountain Home Inn
Mill Valley, CA

Doryman's Inn
Newport Beach, CA

Villa St. Helena
Saint Helena, CA

Jackson Court
San Francisco, CA

Sherman House
San Francisco, CA

West Lane Inn
Ridgefield, CT

Ballastone Inn
Savannah, GA

Charlton Court
Savannah, GA

Foley House Inn
Savannah, GA

Rokeby Hall
Lexington, KY

Lamothe House Hotel
New Orleans, LA

Soniat House
New Orleans, LA

Harraseeket Inn
Freeport, ME

Captain Lord Mansion
Kennebunkport, ME

Deerfield Inn
Deerfield, MA

Country Inn at Princeton
Princeton, MA

The Burn
Natchez, MS

Linden
Natchez, MS

Oak Square Plantation
Port Gibson, MS

Stonehurst Manor
North Conway, NH

Mainstay Inn & Cottage
Cape May, NJ

Preston House
Santa Fe, NM

Brae Loch Inn
Cazenovia, NY

Geneva on the Lake
Geneva, NY

Hist. James R. Webster
Waterloo, NY

Romeo Inn
Ashland, OR

Overlook Inn
Canadensis, PA

Guesthouse at Doneckers
Ephrata, PA

Admiral Fitzroy Inn
Newport, RI

The Willcox Inn
Aiken, SC

Elliott House Inn
Charleston, SC

Kings Courtyard Inn
Charleston, SC

Vendue Inn
Charleston, SC

Brigham Street Inn
Salt Lake City, UT

Captain's Palace Inn
Victoria, BC

Northumberland Heights Inn
Cobourg, ON

Jakobstettel Guest House
Saint Jacobs, ON

Le Chateau De Pierre
Quebec City, PQ

Nature

Nature lovers, alert! Whether your fancy is ornithology or whale watching, these inns will speak to your heart.

Homer B&B/Seekins
Homer, AK

River Beauty B&B
Talkeetna, AK

Arizona Mountain Inn
Flagstaff, AZ

Graham's B&B Inn
Sedona, AZ

Bolinas Villa
Bolinas, CA

Cazanoma Lodge
Cazadero, CA

Elk Cove Inn
Elk, CA

Narrow Gauge Inn
Fish Camp, CA

Grey Whale Inn
Fort Bragg, CA

Creekside Inn & Resort
Guerneville, CA

Sorensen's Resort
Hope Valley, CA

Meadow Creek Ranch Inn
Mariposa, CA

Ames Lodge
Mendocino, CA

House of a 1000 Flowers
Monte Rio, CA

Bear Valley Inn
Olema, CA

Inn at Shallow Creek Farm
Orland, CA

River Rock Inn
Placerville, CA

Marsh Cottage
Point Reyes, CA

Horseshore Farm Cottage
Point Reyes Station, CA

Twain Harte's B&B
Twain Harte, CA

Wilbur Hot Springs
Williams, CA

Outlook Lodge
Green Mountain Falls, CO

Pelican Inn
Carrabelle, FL

Laurel Ridge
Dahlonega, GA

York House
Mountain City, GA

Little St. Simons Island
Saint Simons Island, GA

Holmes Retreat
Pocatello, ID

Stillwaters Country Inn
Galena, IL

Manor House Inn
Bar Harbor, ME

Anchor Watch B&B
Boothbay Harbor, ME

Lincoln House Country Inn
Dennysville, ME

Inn at Harbor Head
Kennebunkport, ME

Cedarholm Cottages
Lincolnville, ME

Breezemere Farm Inn
South Brooksville, ME

Goose Cove Lodge
Sunset, ME

Kawanhee Inn
Weld, ME

Bayview Inn B&B
Wells Beach, ME

Jonah Williams Inn
Annapolis, MD

Wades Point Inn On The Bay
McDaniel, MD

Inn at Duck Creeke
Wellfleet, MA

Pincushion Mountain B&B
Grand Marais, MN

Kettle Falls Hotel
Orr, MN

Lone Mountain Ranch
Big Sky, MT

Izaak Walton Inn
Essex, MT

Dana Place Inn
Jackson, NH

Province Inn
Strafford, NH

Bear Mtn. Guest Ranch
Silver City, NM

Benn Conger Inn
Groton, NY

R.M. Farm
Livingston Manor, NY

Genesee Falls Hotel
Portageville, NY

Taughannock Farms Inn
Trumansburg, NY

B&B Over Yonder
Black Mountain, NC

Randolph House Country Inn
Bryson City, NC

Trestle House Inn
Edenton, NC

Havenshire Inn
Hendersonville, NC

Berkley Center Country Inn
Ocracoke, NC

Snowbird Mountain Lodge
Robbinsville, NC

Heath Lodge
Waynesville, NC

Swag Country Inn
Waynesville, NC

Mirror Pond House
Bend, OR

Holmes Sea Cove B&B
Brookings, OR

Captain's Quarters B&B
Coos Bay, OR

Backroads Bed & Breakfast
Eugene, OR

Fair Winds Bed & Breakfast
Gold Beach, OR

Barkheimer House / Lakecliff
Hood River, OR

Mountain Shadows B&B
Welches, OR

Swiss Woods B&B
Lititz, PA

Millstone Inn
Schellsburg, PA

Woodhill Farms Inn
Washington Crossing, PA

Alford House
Chattanooga, TN

Wind Hover
Gatlinburg, TN

Bluff Bed & Breakfast
Bluff, UT

Meadeau View Lodge
Cedar City, UT

Zion House Bed & Breakfast
Springdale, UT

Three Mountain Inn
Jamaica, VT

Village Inn
Jay, VT

Inn at Long Trail
Killington, VT

Johnny Seesaw's
Peru, VT

Green Mountain Tea Room
South Wallingford, VT

Lareau Farm Country Inn
Waitsfield, VT

Estate Zootenvaal
Saint John, VI

Selene's
Saint John, VI

Vine Cottage Inn
Hot Springs, VA

Trillium House
Nellysford, VA

Burrow's Bay B&B
Anacortes, WA

Growly Bed & Breakfast
Ashford, WA

Mountain Meadows Inn
Ashford, WA

Eagles Nest Inn B&B
Langley, WA

Puget View Guesthouse B&B
Olympia, WA

Whispering Pines B&B
Spokane, WA

Orchard Hill Inn
White Salmon, WA

Spahn's Big Horn Mountain
Big Horn, WY

Teton Tree House
Jackson Hole, WY

Black Cat Guest Ranch
Hinton, AB

Yellow Point Lodge
Ladysmith, BC

Sooke Harbour House
Sooke, BC

Village Inn
Trinity, NF

Shining Tides
Granville Ferry, NS

Outstanding

The following inns are some that, due to attention to detail, amenities, and ambience, are truly oustanding.

Graham's B&B Inn
Sedona, AZ

Dairy Hollow House
Eureka Springs, AR

Williams House B&B Inn
Hot Springs Nat'l Park, AR

Union Hotel
Benicia, CA

Grey Whale Inn
Fort Bragg, CA

Pelican Inn
Muir Beach, CA

Dunbar House, 1880
Murphys, CA

Beazley House
Napa, CA

Briggs House
Sacramento, CA

Britt House
San Diego, CA

Mansion Hotel
San Francisco, CA

Seal Beach Inn & Gardens
Seal Beach, CA

Bishopsgate Inn
East Haddam, CT

St. Francis Inn
Saint Augustine, FL

Inn at Stone City
Anamosa, IA

Beaumont Inn
Harrodsburg, KY

Grenoble House Inn
New Orleans, LA

Hotel Maison de Ville
New Orleans, LA

Soniat House
New Orleans, LA

Bramble Inn Restaurant
Brewster, MA

Cambridge House B&B Inn
Cambridge, MA

Whalewalk Inn
Eastham, MA

Stephen Daniels House
Salem, MA

Schumacher's New Prague
New Prague, MN

Bel-Horst Inn
Belgrade, NE

Franconia Inn
Franconia, NH

Snowvillage Inn
Snowville, NH

The Abbey
Cape May, NJ

Barnard-Good House
Cape May, NJ

Mainstay Inn & Cottage
Cape May, NJ

Lodge at Cloudcroft
Cloudcroft, NM

Grant Corner Inn
Santa Fe, NM

Troutbeck
Amenia, NY

1770 House
East Hampton, NY

Adelphi Hotel
Saratoga Springs, NY

Hist. James R. Webster
Waterloo, NY

Woodfield Inn
Flat Rock, NC

Havenshire Inn
Hendersonville, NC

Swag Country Inn
Waynesville, NC

Coachaus
Allentown, PA

Inn at Turkey Hill
Bloomsburg, PA

Overlook Inn
Canadensis, PA

Admiral Benbow Inn
Newport, RI

Battery Carriage House
Charleston, SC

Indigo Inn
Charleston, SC

Planters Inn
Charleston, SC

Green Trails Country Inn
Brookfield, VT

Inn on the Common
Craftsbury Common, VT

Black River Inn
Ludlow, VT

Governor's Inn
Ludlow, VT

Galer Place B&B
Seattle, WA

Kalorama Guest House
Washington, DC

Romance

Ah, romance! These inns offer a hideaway, a peaceful space in which to be together and let the world go by.

Crescent Moon Townhouse
Eureka Springs, AR

Dairy Hollow House
Eureka Springs, AR

Knickerbocker Mansion
Big Bear Lake, CA

Happy Landing Inn
Carmel, CA

Elk Cove Inn
Elk, CA

Gingerbread Mansion
Ferndale, CA

The Heirloom
Ione, CA

Murphy's Jenner Inn
Jenner, CA

Cypress House
Mendocino, CA

Pelican Inn
Muir Beach, CA

Beazley House
Napa, CA

Maison Bleue French B&B
Pacific Grove, CA

Cricket Cottage
Point Reyes Station, CA

East Brother Light Station
Point Richmond, CA

Creekwood
Saint Helena, CA

Villa St. Helena
Saint Helena, CA

Grand Cottages
San Pedro, CA

Glenborough Inn B&B
Santa Barbara, CA

Simpson House Inn
Santa Barbara, CA

Babbling Brook Inn
Santa Cruz, CA

Cliff Crest B&B Inn
Santa Cruz, CA

Darling House
Santa Cruz, CA

Seal Beach Inn & Gardens
Seal Beach, CA

Jameson's
Sonora, CA

Holden House—1902
Colorado Springs, CO

Queen Anne Inn
Denver, CO

Simsbury 1820 House
Simsbury, CT

York House
Mountain City, GA

Liberty Inn 1834
Savannah, GA

The Veranda
Senoia, GA

Inn at Stone City
Anamosa, IA

Cornstalk Hotel
New Orleans, LA

Lafitte Guest House
New Orleans, LA

The Ledgelawn Inn
Bar Harbor, ME

Blue Hill Inn
Blue Hill, ME

Chebeague Island Inn
Chebeague Island, ME

Newcastle Inn
Newcastle, ME

Ashley Manor
Barnstable, MA

Beechwood Inn
Barnstable, MA

Old Sea Pines Inn
Brewster, MA

Chatham Town House Inn
Chatham, MA

Thorncroft Inn
Martha's Vineyard, MA

Country Inn at Princeton
Princeton, MA

Stephen Daniels House
Salem, MA

Wedgewood Inn
Yarmouth Port, MA

Victorian Villa Guesthouse
Union City, MI

Schumacher's New Prague
New Prague, MN

Rosswood Plantation
Lorman, MS

Oak Square Plantation
Port Gibson, MS

Augustin River Bluff Farm
New Haven, MO

Gunstock Inn
Gilford, NH

Greenfield Inn
Greenfield, NH

Barnard-Good House
Cape May, NJ

Gingerbread House
Cape May, NJ

Chestnut Hill on Delaware
Milford, NJ

Sierra Mesa Lodge
Alto, NM

La Posada de Taos
Taos, NM

Inn at Shaker Mill Farm
Canaan, NY

Rose Inn
Ithaca, NY

Lamplight Inn
Lake Luzerne, NY

Mt. Tremper Inn
Mount Tremper, NY

Oliver Loud's Inn
Pittsford, NY

Village Victorian Inn
Rhinebeck, NY

Rowan Oak House
Salisbury, NC

Livingston Mansion B&B
Jacksonville, OR

Sandlake Country Inn
Sandlake, OR

Spring House
Airville, PA

Canadensis Old Village Inn
Canadensis, PA

Clarion River Lodge
Cooksburg, PA

Brinley Victorian Inn
Newport, RI

Willows of Newport
Newport, RI

Two Meeting Street Inn
Charleston, SC

Wind Hover
Gatlinburg, TN

Durham House B&B
Houston, TX

Black River Inn
Ludlow, VT

Inn at Manchester
Manchester, VT

Manchester Highlands Inn
Manchester, VT

Reluctant Panther Inn
Manchester, VT

White House of Wilmington
Wilmington, VT

Edgewood Plantation
Charles City, VA

Silver Thatch Inn
Charlottesville, VA

Channel Bass Inn
Chincoteague, VA

Ravenswood Inn
Mathews, VA

Conyers House
Sperryville, VA

Guest House B&B Cottages
Greenbank, WA

White Lace Inn
Sturgeon Bay, WI

Captain's Palace Inn
Victoria, BC

Faye & Eric's B&B
Summerside, PEI

Skiing

These inns share a proximity to downhill or cross-country skiing. Nothing like coming back from an exhilarating day on the slopes to a warm, cozy fire.

Gold Mountain Manor Inn
Big Bear City, CA

Sorensen's Resort
Hope Valley, CA

Snow Goose B&B Inn
Mammoth Lakes, CA

Jameson's
Sonora, CA

River Ranch
Tahoe City, CA

Captain's Alpenhaus Inn
Tahoma, CA

Little Red Ski Haus
Aspen, CO

Ullr Lodge
Aspen, CO

Hardy House B&B Inn
Georgetown, CO

Kelsall's Ute Creek Ranch
Ignacio, CO

Eagle River Inn
Minturn, CO

New Sheridan Hotel
Telluride, CO

Busterback Ranch
Ketchum, ID

Noble House B&B Inn
Bridgton, ME

Maine Stay Inn
Camden, ME

Center Lovell Inn
Center Lovell, ME

Ashfield Inn
Ashfield, MA

Seekonk Pines Inn
Great Barrington, MA

Turning Point Inn
Great Barrington, MA

Birchwood Inn
Lenox, MA

Cornell Inn
Lenox, MA

Country Cottage B&B
Maple City, MI

Lone Mountain Ranch
Big Sky, MT

Izaak Walton Inn
Essex, MT

Steele Homestead Inn
Antrim, NH

Country Inn at Bartlett
Bartlett, NH

Bradford Inn
Bradford, NH

Darby Field Inn
Conway, NH

Chase House
Cornish, NH

Inn at Danbury
Danbury, NH

Franconia Inn
Franconia, NH

Trumbull House
Hanover, NH

Notchland Inn
Hart's Location, NH

Haverhill Inn
Haverhill, NH

Meeting House Inn
Henniker, NH

Dana Place Inn
Jackson, NH

Nestlenook Inn
Jackson, NH

Maple Hill Farm
New London, NH

Cranmore Mountain Lodge
North Conway, NH

Old Red Inn & Cottages
North Conway, NH

Sunny Side Inn
North Conway, NH

Follansbee Inn
North Sutton, NH

Mt. Adams Inn
North Woodstock, NH

Meadow Farm B&B
Northwood, NH

Snowvillage Inn
Snowville, NH

Haus Edelweiss B&B
Sunapee, NH

Back of the Beyond
Colden, NY

Benn Conger Inn
Groton, NY

Mt. Tremper Inn
Mount Tremper, NY

Garnet Hill Lodge
North River, NY

Inn on Bacon Hill
Saratoga Springs, NY

La Anna Guest House
Cresco, PA

Meadeau View Lodge
Cedar City, UT

505 Woodside, B&B Place
Park City, UT

Imperial Hotel
Park City, UT

Old Miners' Lodge B&B
Park City, UT

Washington School Inn
Park City, UT

Brigham Street Inn
Salt Lake City, UT

Mountain Hollow B&B Inn
Sandy, UT

Hill Farm Inn
Arlington, VT

Alpenrose Inn
Bondville, VT

Arches Country Inn
Brandon, VT

Mill Brook B&B & Gallery
Brownsville, VT

Shire Inn
Chelsea, VT

Greenleaf Inn
Chester, VT

Craftsbury Inn
Craftsbury, VT

Maple Crest Farm
Cuttingsville, VT

Little Lodge at Dorset
Dorset, VT

Garrison Inn
East Burke, VT

Blueberry Hill Inn
Goshen, VT

Village Inn
Jay, VT

Inn at Long Trail
Killington, VT

Vermont Inn
Killington, VT

Blue Gentian Lodge
Londonderry, VT

Country Hare
Londonderry, VT

Black River Inn
Ludlow, VT

Okemo Inn
Ludlow, VT

Manchester Highlands Inn
Manchester, VT

Brookside Meadows
Middlebury, VT

Black Lantern Inn
Montgomery Village, VT

Johnny Seesaw's
Peru, VT

Salt Ash Inn
Plymouth Union, VT

Liberty Hill Farm
Rochester, VT

Green Mountain Tea Room
South Wallingford, VT

1860 House
Stowe, VT

Raspberry Patch
Stowe, VT

The Siebeness
Stowe, VT

Lareau Farm Country Inn
Waitsfield, VT

Sugartree—A Country Inn
Warren, VT

Shield Inn
West Dover, VT

Snow Den Inn
West Dover, VT

Weathervane Lodge
West Dover, VT

West Dover Inn
West Dover, VT

Windham Hill Inn
West Townshend, VT

Colonial House
Weston, VT

Vine Cottage Inn
Hot Springs, VA

Tudor Inn
Port Angeles, WA

Jefferson-Day House
Hudson, WI

Amherst Shore Country Inn
Amherst, NS

Little Inn of Bayfield Ltd
Bayfield, ON

Jakobstettel Guest House
Saint Jacobs, ON

Otter Lake Haus
Huberdeau, PQ

Schweizer Lodge
Sutton, PQ

Spas

Hot mineral waters are nature's own relaxant. These inns are close to, or are, spas!

Williams House B&B Inn
Hot Springs Nat'l Park, AR

Brannan Cottage Inn
Calistoga, CA

Culver's, A Country Inn
Calistoga, CA

Foothill House
Calistoga, CA

Pine Street Inn
Calistoga, CA

Scarlett's Country Inn
Calistoga, CA

White Sulphur Springs Rnch
Clio, CA

Mill Rose Inn
Half Moon Bay, CA

Ojai Manor Hotel
Ojai, CA

Aunt Abigail's B&B Inn
Sacramento, CA

Howard Creek Ranch
Westport, CA

Wilbur Hot Springs
Williams, CA

House of Yesteryear
Ouray, CO

St. Elmo Hotel
Ouray, CO

Poor Farm Country Inn
Salida, CO

Idaho City Hotel
Idaho City, ID

Peterson's Bed & Breakfast
Monroe, UT

Vine Cottage Inn
Hot Springs, VA

Inn at Gristmill Square
Warm Springs, VA

Folkestone Bed & Breakfast
Berkeley Springs, WV

Maria's Garden & Inn
Berkeley Springs, WV

Manan Island Inn & Spa
Grand Manan, NB

Special

These inns all have an extra special, out-of-the-ordinary something that distinguishes them. We hope you'll agree.

Dairy Hollow House
Eureka Springs, AR
Antique bathtub "big enough for two."

Gingerbread Mansion
Ferndale, CA
Twin clawfoot tubs—"his & her" bubble baths.

Swan-Levine House
Grass Valley, CA
Guest may observe and participate in the fine art of printmaking.

Saint Orres
Gualala, CA
Incredibly beautiful handwrought fantasy building.

Eastlake Victorian Inn
Los Angeles, CA
Celebrate a Dickens Christmas in LA's only Victorian B&B.

B.G. Ranch & Inn
Mendocino, CA
Grow own eggs, vegetables & herbs; fluent French & Italian, trout pond.

Chichester House B&B
Placerville, CA
Gourmet breakfast served above a gold mine.

East Brother Light Station
Point Richmond, CA
On an island in the middle of San Francisco Bay!

Mansion Hotel
San Francisco, CA
Magic show and a resident "spirit."

Darling House
Santa Cruz, CA
Oceanside horse-drawn carriage rides.

Country House Inn
Templeton, CA
Near Hearst Castle.

Byron Randall's Victorian
Tomales, CA
Gallery showing Byron Randall's artwork; potato masher collection.

Home Ranch
Clark, CO
Sleigh rides and a herd of llamas.

Queen Anne Inn
New London, CT
Antique Gallery.

Jules' Undersea Lodge
Key Largo, FL
World's only undersea lodge.

Susina Plantation Inn
Thomasville, GA
Pretend you're Scarlett O'Hara.

Patchwork Quilt Inn
Middlebury, IN
Meet Amish families on Backroads Tour. Quilt collection.

Inn at Stone City
Anamosa, IA
Moonlight surrey serenade.

Myrtles Plantation
Saint Francisville, LA
On "Mystery Weekends" guests wear period costumes and solve murders.

Holbrook House
Bar Harbor, ME
Large doll collection.

Greenville Inn
Greenville, ME
Largest seaplane base on the East Coast.

The Keeper's House
Isle Au Haut, ME
Island lighthouse inn with working lighthouse.

Crab Apple Acres Inn
The Forks, ME
Guided whitewater rafting trips on the Kennebeck or Dead rivers.

Spring Bank
Frederick, MD
Wide view from observatory; china collection in use.

Old Manse Inn
Brewster, MA
During the Civil War, a link to the underground railroad.

Seekonk Pines Inn
Great Barrington, MA
Fresh vegetables for sale in the garden.

Wildwood Inn
Ware, MA
Refreshing "Norman Rockwell" brook-fed swimming hole.

Birk's Goethe St. Gasthaus
Hermann, MO
Mansion Mystery Weekends with local actors and special guests.

Lazy K Bar Ranch
Big Timber, MT
Exclusive use of a horse for your holiday on working dude ranch.

Scottish Lion Inn
North Conway, NH
Highland hospitality amid tartans. Scotish paintings and cuisine.

Mt. Adams Inn
North Woodstock, NH
Unique rock formations called "mummies" in back of inn.

Casita Chamisa B&B
Albuquerque, NM
Archaeologist innkeeper delighted to show guests Pueblo Indian ruins.

Taos Inn
Taos, NM
Original town well located in the center of the lobby.

Brae Loch Inn
Cazenovia, NY
A wee bit o' Scotland.

Gasho Inn
Central Valley, NY
In 30-acre Japanese theme area with gardens, fish pond, & tea-houses.

Golden Eagle
Garrison, NY
Film location for the movie Hello Dolly.

Barkheimer House / Lakecliff
Hood River, OR
"Windsurfing capital of the world."

Harry Packer Mansion
Jim Thorpe, PA
"Mystery Weekends" adventure packages, Victorian balls.

Pineapple Inn
Lewisburg, PA
Room decorated with furniture from summer palace (London), ca. 1880.

Wedgewood B&B Inn
New Hope, PA
Attend the Inn School and learn the "inns and outs of innkeeping."

Hugging Bear Inn & Shoppe
Chester, VT
Teddy Bear motif and shop.

Inwood Manor
East Barnet, VT
Canoeing on the Connecticut River from the inn.

Fox Stand Inn
Royalton, VT
Special herd of polled Hereford cattle.

Butternut Inn at Stowe
Stowe, VT
Texas Bar-B-Q Aniversary Party held three weekends in July.

Hermitage Inn & Brookbound
Wilmington, VT
Spring maple sugaring—3,500 trees.

Jordan Hollow Farm Inn
Stanley, VA
Restored colonial horse farm in the Shenandoah Valley—horseback rides.

Nantucket Inn
Anacortes, WA
Handmade quilts.

Maria's Garden & Inn
Berkeley Springs, WV
Miraculous painting of the Virgin Mary.

Spahn's Big Horn Mountain
Big Horn, WY
Solar power.

Beulah Land
Treherne, MB
Home-grown, home-cooked meals.

Village Inn
Trinity, NF
Cetacean contact experiences with Christine & Peter Beamish.

Shining Tides
Granville Ferry, NS
Near the Bay of Fundy. View the rise & fall of the Annapolis River.

Waterlot Inn
New Hamburg, ON
Just the place for a romantic gourmet.

Sports

Sports are an integral part of many people's vacation plans. These inns are noted for their sporting facilities or locales. Be sure to call ahead to see if they have the special facilities you require.

Murphy's Inn
Grass Valley, CA

North Coast Country Inn
Gualala, CA

Darling House
Santa Cruz, CA

Twain Harte's B&B
Twain Harte, CA

Victorian Inn
Durango, CO

Wanek's Lodge at Estes
Estes Park, CO

Harbour Inne & Cottage
Mystic, CT

Inn on Lake Waramaug
New Preston, CT

Under Mountain Inn
Salisbury, CT

1735 House
Amelia Island, FL

Center Lovell Inn
Center Lovell, ME

Bittersweet Inn
Walpole, ME

Davis House
Solomons Island, MD

Ship's Inn at Chatham
Chatham, MA

Grandmother's House
Colrain, MA

Apple Tree Inn
Lenox, MA

Raymond House Inn
Port Sanilac, MI

Gunflint Lodge
Grand Marais, MN

Winters Creek Ranch B&B
Carson City, NV

Highlands Inn
Bethlehem, NH

Sugar Hill Inn
Franconia, NH

Dana Place Inn
Jackson, NH

Ammonoosuc Inn
Lisbon, NH

Cranmore Mountain Lodge
North Conway, NH

Lake Shore Farm
Northwood, NH

Snowvillage Inn
Snowville, NH

Gregory House
Averill Park, NY

Balsam House
Chestertown, NY

Country Road Lodge
Warrensburg, NY

Randolph House Country Inn
Bryson City, NC

Greenwood Bed & Breakfast
Greensboro, NC

Ye Olde Cherokee Inn
Kill Devil Hills, NC

Snowbird Mountain Lodge
Robbinsville, NC

Mast Farm Inn
Valle Crucis, NC

Gateway Lodge & Cabins
Cooksburg, PA

La Anna Guest House
Cresco, PA

Cherry Mills Lodge
Dushore, PA

Harry Packer Mansion
Jim Thorpe, PA

Inn at Starlight Lake
Starlight, PA

Wycombe Inn
Wycombe, PA

Cherry Mills Lodge
Wyomissing, PA

Meadeau View Lodge
Cedar City, UT

Peterson's Bed & Breakfast
Monroe, UT

Old Miners' Lodge B&B
Park City, UT

Parmenter House
Belmont, VT

Black Bear Inn
Bolton Valley, VT

Churchill House Inn
Brandon, VT

Craftsbury Inn
Craftsbury, VT

Barrows House
Dorset, VT

Kincraft Inn
Hancock, VT

Vermont Inn
Killington, VT

Okemo Inn
Ludlow, VT

1811 House
Manchester, VT

Manchester Highlands Inn
Manchester, VT

Red Clover Inn
Mendon, VT

Golden Stage Inn
Proctorsville, VT

Quechee Inn-Marshland Farm
Quechee, VT

Fox Stand Inn
Royalton, VT

Londonderry Inn
South Londonderry, VT

Gables Inn
Stowe, VT

Snow Den Inn
West Dover, VT

Vine Cottage Inn
Hot Springs, VA

Palmer's Chart House
Deer Harbor, WA

Teton Tree House
Jackson Hole, WY

Quilchena Hotel
Quilchena, BC

Shadow Lawn Country Inn
Rothesay, NB

Jakobstettel Guest House
Saint Jacobs, ON

Vegetarian

Inns where vegetarian meals are prepared for guests.

Webster House
Alameda, CA

Chatsworth Bed & Breakfast
Saint Paul, MN

Corrales Inn B&B
Corrales, NM

Grandview Lodge
Waynesville, NC

Bavarian Meadows B&B
Leavenworth, WA

Rose Garden Guest House
Vancouver, BC

Schweizer Lodge
Sutton, PQ

Subscribe To
THE COMPLETE GUIDE'S GAZETTE
Newsletter for B&Bs, Inns,
Guest Houses and Small Hotels

To get all the latest on the North American inn scene, events, tips and news, send $35 for your subscription to this informative newsletter. Inns that subscribe to the Gazette have first priority to a full listing in this guide. Don't forget to include your name and address with your order. Send your order to:

The Complete Guide's Gazette
P.O. Box 20467
Oakland, CA 94620-0467

ON BECOMING AN INNKEEPER

Do you dream of being an innkeeper, meeting and making friends with interesting guests and regaling them with your own special brand of hospitality? Make no mistake, innkeeping is hard work, but it can be very rewarding.

We have prepared a packet of information on resources for prospective innkeepers which we will send you free of charge.

Many people prefer to buy an established inn. If you are interested in buying an inn you may wish to contact the editor of this guide regarding information we have on inns for sale. To receive the resource packet or information on inns for sale, please send your request and a legal size, stamped, self-addressed envelope to:

The Complete Guide to Bed & Breakfasts, Inns & Guesthouses
P.O. Box 20467
Oakland, CA 94620-0467

Your wonderful book gives us more guests than any other affiliation we have. Keep up the good work!
—Phyllis Combs, Ye Old Cherokee Inn, Kill Devil Hills, NC

We have been delighted with the response from your '89-90 edition. Your readers have written us after a stay here with various and encouraging kind words and for that, too, we thank you. We also want you to know that we use your book when traveling. It is a real help to us.
—Stuart W. Smith, Churchtown Inn B&B, Churchtown, PA

Many thanks for all the wonderful people your book has sent us over the years!
—Stephanie Templeton, The Golden Eagle, Garrison, NY

As always, we anxiously await each update. Each and every year we receive more and more reservations from your exceptionally complete guide. It continues to remain our first choice as a reference guide personally, as well as for our guests. Thank you for your continued professional representation of our inn as well as the inns around the country.
—Lisa Wild-Runnells, Shady Oaks Country Inn, St. Helena, CA

I should have written to you earlier and let you know what a smashing success our first year in your book was. We received reservation calls before we even had our copy of your book; what a pleasant surprise. Thank you again for publishing such a great profitable guidebook. Our guests use our books and also buy them, so it works out well for all.
—Bill Saunders, Red Gables Inn, Lake City, MN

We have had a wonderful response to our listing in your complete guide with guests coming here from as far away as Montreal and Louisiana. We have found your readers to be experienced travelers, excited about the B&B experience and extremely grateful for the Irish hospitality shown to them.
—Eileen & Jack Connell, Sunny Pines B&B Inn, West Harwich, MA

We have enjoyed your book through the numerous reservations that we receive weekly as well as for our own personal reference. The Guide *has become a priceless source of information for our guests when we discuss their next destination and accommodations available.*
—Betty Gladden, Garratt Mansion, Alameda, CA

VOTE

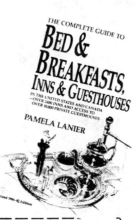

THE COMPLETE GUIDE TO

BED &
BREAKFASTS,
INNS & GUESTHOUSES
IN THE UNITED STATES AND CANADA
—OVER 2400 INNS AND ACCESS TO
OVER 10,000 PRIVATE GUESTHOUSES

PAMELA LANIER

FOR YOUR CHOICE OF
INN OF THE YEAR

To the editors of **The Complete Guide to Bed & Breakfasts, Inns and Guesthouses in the U.S. and Canada:**

I cast my vote for "Inn of the Year" for:

Name of Inn _____

Address _____

_____

Phone _____

Reasons _____

_____

_____

I would also like to (please check one):

____ Recommend a new Inn   ____ Comment

____ Critique   ____ Suggest

Name of Inn _____

Address _____

_____

Phone _____

Comment _____

_____

_____

Please send your entries to:
The Complete Guide to Bed & Breakfast Inns
P.O. Box 20467
Oakland, CA 94620 0467

Other Books from John Muir Publications

22 Days Series

These pocket-size itineraries are a refreshing departure from ordinary guidebooks. Each author has an in-depth knowledge of the region covered and offers 22 tested daily itineraries through their favorite destinations. Included are not only "must see" attractions but also little-known villages and hidden "jewels" as well as valuable general information.

22 Days Around the World by R. Rapoport and B. Willes (65-31-9)
22 Days in Alaska by Pamela Lanier (28-68-0)
22 Days in the American Southwest by R. Harris (28-88-5)
22 Days in Asia by R. Rapoport and B. Willes (65-17-3)
22 Days in Australia by John Gottberg (65-40-8)
22 Days in California by Roger Rapoport (28-93-1)
22 Days in China by Gaylon Duke and Zenia Victor (28-72-9)
22 Days in Dixie by Richard Polese (65-18-1)
22 Days in Europe by Rick Steves (65-05-X)
22 Days in Florida by Richard Harris (65-27-0)
22 Days in France by Rick Steves (65-07-6)
22 Days in Germany, Austria & Switzerland by R. Steves (65-39-4)
22 Days in Great Britain by Rick Steves (65-38-6)
22 Days in Hawaii by Arnold Schuchter (28-92-3)

22 Days in India by Anurag Mathur (28-87-7)
22 Days in Japan by David Old (28-73-7)
22 Days in Mexico by S. Rogers and T. Rosa (65-41-6)
22 Days in New England by Anne Wright (28-96-6)
22 Days in New Zealand by Arnold Schuchter (28-86-9)
22 Days in Norway, Denmark & Sweden by R. Steves (28-83-4)
22 Days in the Pacific Northwest by R. Harris (28-97-4)
22 Days in Spain & Portugal by Rick Steves (65-06-8)
22 Days in the West Indies by C. & S. Morreale (28-74-5)

All 22 Days titles are 128 to 152 pages and $7.95 each, except *22 Days Around the World* and *22 Days in Europe*, which are 192 pages and $9.95.

"Kidding Around" Travel Guides for Children

Written for kids eight years of age and older. Generously illustrated in two colors with imaginative characters and images. An adventure to read and a treasure to keep.
Kidding Around Atlanta, Anne Pedersen (65-35-1) 64 pp. $9.95
Kidding Around London, Sarah Lovett (65-24-6) 64 pp. $9.95
Kidding Around Los Angeles, Judy Cash (65-34-3) 64 pp. $9.95
Kidding Around New York City, Sarah Lovett (65-33-5) 64 pp. $9.95
Kidding Around San Francisco, Rosemary Zibart (65-23-8) 64 pp. $9.95

Kidding Around Washington, D.C., Anne Pedersen (65-25-4) 64 pp. $9.95

Asia Through the Back Door, Rick Steves and John Gottberg (28-76-1) 336 pp. $15.95

Buddhist America: Centers, Retreats, Practices, Don Morreale (28-94-X) 400 pp. $12.95

Bus Touring: Charter Vacations, U.S.A., Stuart Warren (28-95-8) 168 pp. $9.95

Catholic America: Self-Renewal Centers and Retreats, Patricia Christian-Meyer (65-20-3) 325 pp. $13.95

Preconception: A Woman's Guide to Preparing for Pregnancy and Parenthood, Brenda Aikey-Keller (65-44-0) 236 pp. $14.95

Complete Guide to Bed & Breakfasts, Inns & Guesthouses, Pamela Lanier (65-43-2) 512 pp. $15.95

Elderhostels: The Students' Choice, Mildred Hyman (65-28-9) 224 pp. $12.95

Europe 101: History & Art for the Traveler, Rick Steves and Gene Openshaw (28-78-8) 372 pp. $12.95

Europe Through the Back Door, Rick Steves (65-42-4) 432 pp. $16.95

Floating Vacations: River, Lake, and Ocean Adventures, Michael White (65-32-7) 256 pp. $17.95

Gypsying After 40: A Guide to Adventure and Self-Discovery, Bob Harris (28-71-0) 264 pp. $12.95

The Heart of Jerusalem, Arlynn Nellhaus (28-79-6) 312 pp. $12.95

Indian America: A Traveler's Companion, Eagle/Walking Turtle (65-29-7) 424 pp. $16.95

Mona Winks: Self-Guided Tours of Europe's Top Museums, Rick Steves (28-85-0) 450 pp. $14.95

The On and Off the Road Cookbook, Carl Franz (28-27-3) 272 pp. $8.50

The People's Guide to Mexico, Carl Franz (28-99-0) 608 pp. $15.95

The People's Guide to RV Camping in Mexico, Carl Franz with Steve Rogers (28-91-5) 256 pp. $13.95

Ranch Vacations: The Complete Guide to Guest and Resort, Fly-Fishing, and Cross-Country Skiing Ranches, Eugene Kilgore (65-30-0) 392 pp. $18.95

The Shopper's Guide to Mexico, Steve Rogers and Tina Rosa (28-90-7) 224 pp. $9.95

Ski Tech's Guide to Equipment, Skiwear, and Accessories, edited by Bill Tanler (65-45-9) 144 pp. $11.95

Ski Tech's Guide to Maintenance and Repair, edited by Bill Tanler (65-46-7) 144 pp. $11.95

Traveler's Guide to Asian Culture, Kevin Chambers (65-14-9) 224 pp. $13.95

Traveler's Guide to Healing Centers and Retreats in North America, Martine Rudee and Jonathan Blease (65-15-7) 240 pp. $11.95

Undiscovered Islands of the Caribbean, Burl Willes (28-80-X) 216 pp. $14.95

Automotive Repair Manuals

Each JMP automotive manual gives clear step-by-step instructions together with illustrations that show exactly how each system in the vehicle comes apart and goes back together. They tell everything a novice or experienced mechanic needs to know to perform periodic maintenance, tune-ups, troubleshooting, and repair of the brake, fuel and emission control, electrical, cooling, clutch, transmission, driveline, steering, and suspension systems and even rebuild the engine.

How to Keep Your VW Alive
(65-12-2) 424 pp. $19.95
How to Keep Your Rabbit Alive
(28-47-8) 420 pp. $19.95
How to Keep Your Subaru Alive
(65-11-4) 480 pp. $19.95
How to Keep Your Toyota Pickup Alive (28-81-3) 392 pp. $19.95
How to Keep Your Datsun/ Nissan Alive (28-65-6) 544 pp. $19.95

Other Automotive Books

The Greaseless Guide to Car Care Confidence: Take the Terror Out of Talking to Your Mechanic, Mary Jackson (65-19-X) 224 pp. $14.95
Off-Road Emergency Repair & Survival, James Ristow (65-26-2) 160 pp. $9.95
Road & Track's Used Car Classics, edited by Peter Bohr (28-69-9) 272 pp. $12.95

Ordering Information

If you cannot find our books in your local bookstore, you can order directly from us. Your books will be sent to you via UPS (for U.S. destinations), and you will receive them approximately 10 days from the time that we receive your order. Include $2.75 for the first item ordered and $.50 for each additional item to cover shipping and handling costs. UPS shipments to post office boxes take longer to arrive; if possible, please give us a street address. For airmail within the U.S., enclose $4.00 per book for shipping and handling. All foreign orders will be shipped surface rate. Please enclose $3.00 for the first item and $1.00 for each additional item. Please inquire for airmail rates.

Method of Payment

Your order may be paid by check, money order, or credit card. We cannot be responsible for cash sent through the mail. All payments must be made in U.S. dollars drawn on a U.S. bank. Canadian postal money orders in U.S. dollars are also acceptable. For VISA, MasterCard, or American Express orders, include your card number, expiration date, and your signature, or call (505)982-4078. Books ordered on American Express cards can be shipped only to the billing address of the cardholder. Sorry, no C.O.D.'s. Residents of sunny New Mexico, add 5.625% tax to the total.

Address all orders and inquiries to:
John Muir Publications
P.O. Box 613
Santa Fe, NM 87504
(505) 982-4078